2019 EDITION

Greenberg's GUIDES

LIONEL® TRAINS

POCKET PRICE GUIDE

Edited by Roger Carp

D1412447

Kalmbach Media

Kalmbach Media
21027 Crossroads Circle
Waukesha, Wisconsin 53186
www.KalmbachHobbyStore.com

Published in 2018
Thirty-ninth Edition

Manufactured in the United States of America

ISBN: 978-1-62700-530-2

Front cover photo: 2521 President McKinley Observation Car,
model courtesy Joe Algozzini

Back cover photo: 3428 U.S. Mail Operating Boxcar

Library of Congress Control Number: 2018931216

CONTENTS

INTRODUCTION

Whether you are a longtime Lionel enthusiast or a newcomer to the toy train hobby, this guide contains the information you need to identify and evaluate thousands of items made by Lionel since 1901. Most of all, you'll have at your fingertips the most up-to-date prices for locomotives, freight cars, passenger cars, stations, tunnels, signals, track sections, transformers, and other items.

What is listed

Almost every Lionel O gauge toy train produced over the years is listed in the pages that follow.

This edition of the *Lionel Pocket Price Guide* contains information about new additions to the product line as described in Lionel catalogs, press releases, and other sources. Any additions that Lionel makes to its line after this book is printed will be reported in the next edition.

In addition, the *Lionel Pocket Price Guide* provides information about items associated with Lionel yet not mentioned in its catalogs. These uncataloged or promotional items include unique models and specially decorated locomotives and cars that Lionel produces for national and regional toy train collecting and operating groups, museums, local railroad clubs, and other customers.

When to consult this guide

Many readers of the *Lionel Pocket Price Guide* use it after the fact. They already have some trains and accessories and now want to identify and evaluate those items. Maybe someone lucked upon a bridge at a garage sale and wants to know whether it's a 300 Hellgate or a 314 deck girder type. Somebody else needs to provide his or her insurance agent with a complete list of O gauge locomotives that includes their conditions and current values. This guide contains the information needed to identify that bridge as well as determining present values for that engine roster.

In addition, the *Lionel Pocket Price Guide* can help you think about what to acquire in the future. That's really when the fun begins! You just have to spend some time considering how you want to approach the hobby. Collect, operate, or both? Prewar, postwar, or modern? Particular types of locomotives or cars? Favorite railroads? Promotional items?

Once you have a general idea of how to enjoy this hobby, you can make informed decisions about which trains you want.

UNDERSTANDING VALUES

The values presented here are an averaged reflection of prices for items bought and sold across the country during the year prior to the publication of this edition. These values are offered as guidelines and should be viewed as starting points that buyers and sellers can use to begin informed and reasonable negotiations.

In a listing for a steam locomotive, the value includes a tender, even if the tender is not listed in the description. The value of steam locomotives, particularly prewar items, may be affected significantly by the type of tender included.

Values for individual items may differ from what is listed in this price guide due to a few key factors. Where collectible trains are scarce and demand outruns supply, actual values may exceed what is shown. Values may also rise where certain items are especially popular, often because of their road names. And as with all collectibles, national and local economic conditions will impact values, which tend to drop when times are tough and demand falls.

Original packaging

Items in Like New or better condition require their original packaging to maintain their high level of value. The values given for items in Good and Excellent condition are not based on the expectation that a box and other associated items are present.

Items that do have their original packaging, especially if it is complete and undamaged, command a premium among collectors of prewar and postwar trains. No hard-and-fast rules can be stated as to how much higher their value is over the same items in Excellent condition. Generally speaking, though, boxed items in Like New condition are valued about 50 percent above the same item without a box.

Using the values

The values listed are what a consumer would pay—more or less—to get a particular item in a specific condition. One collector selling that item to another would probably ask the stated value and expect to get something close to it.

However, someone selling that same item to a person or business that intends to resell it (a train dealer) is unlikely to receive the stated value. Experience shows that sellers get about half the amount. Dealers offer less so they can earn a profit when reselling an item.

When buying or selling a toy train, you should learn more about it. Start by consulting this price guide and then look for more about it in a reference guide or website on toy trains. You can also ask more experienced hobbyists for their opinion about the item's condition and value.

FINDING A PRODUCT

The *Lionel Pocket Price Guide* has been divided into seven major sections.

Section 1: Prewar 1901–1942

Section 1 of the *Lionel Pocket Price Guide* is devoted to the prewar period. The entries cover just about every train, accessory, and transformer associated with Lionel's line during its first 42 years.

The only outfits (sets) listed are those of articulated streamlined trains that consist of a powered unit and attached unpowered cars.

In an item's listing, the basic description specifies its gauge (the distance between the inside of the outermost rails). During this time, Lionel catalogued models in four sizes. It is noted in parentheses whether an item is 2⅞-inch, Standard (2⅛ inches), O (1¼ inches), or OO (¾ inches). O gauge models intended to run on tighter 27-inch-diameter track belong to Lionel's O27 gauge line and are identified as such.

Transformers, rheostats, and many accessories were not limited to a single gauge, so their descriptions do not specify a gauge.

Section 2: Postwar 1945–1969

Section 2 concentrates on the postwar period. Nearly every train and accessory (except outfits) that Lionel cataloged between 1945 and 1969 has its own listing. By this time, Lionel no longer made trains in 2⅞-inch, Standard, or OO gauge. Instead, it offered trains that ran on track that had a diameter of either 31 inches (O gauge) or 27 inches (O27 gauge). However, the entries in this section do not distinguish between O and O27 since only a handful of locomotives and cars could operate solely on the wider curves.

Section 3: Modern Era 1970–2019

Section 3 shows the trains, accessories, transformers, and other items that Lionel has cataloged since 1970. The modern era encompasses the products of three companies: Model Products Corp. (MPC, a division of General Mills), 1970–85; Lionel Trains Inc. (LTI), 1986–95; and Lionel LLC (LLC), 1996–2019.

These incarnations of Lionel are responsible for an enormous inventory of trains, rolling stock, transformers, and accessories. Cataloged and uncataloged O gauge items (ranging from the near-scale Standard O to the toy-like O27) can be found within the pages of this section.

All items in Section 3 are arranged according to their Lionel catalog number (omitting the numeral 6 used as a prefix). The descriptions of products made during the modern era may include information that relates to where in the product line a particular item belongs. Models derived from MPC designs have been described as *traditional*. Rolling stock whose dimensions and features approach scale realism may be designated as Standard O (abbreviated as std O). Locomotives equipped with TrainMaster Command Control or its successor, Legacy, are identified with the abbreviation CC.

Section 4: Lionel Corporation Tinplate

Section 4 features 800 products developed jointly by Lionel and MTH Electric Trains since 2009. These Lionel Corporation trains and accessories are reproductions of Lionel (and some American Flyer) tinplate items from the prewar era. You'll find trains here that operate as tinplate trains did prior to 1942 as well as others that have been updated with modern features and technology, such as Proto-Sound. The retail prices are listed for these products.

Section 5: Club Cars and Special Production

Section 5 gathers the various items, principally locomotives and rolling stock, that Lionel has made or sponsored for different hobby organizations, museums, and businesses since the 1970s. These uncataloged club cars and special production items are arranged according to the groups that offered them for sale. Those groups are listed alphabetically; regional divisions of national organizations follow the parent organization's listing. Within each subordinate section, items are listed in numerical (not chronological) order, with a basic description similar to that used for cataloged entries.

Section 6: Boxes

Over the past 25 years, original boxes and other forms of packaging have assumed significance for some collectors. These hobbyists insist that the trains they buy come in the boxes and have the paperwork and ancillary pieces (inserts, instruction sheets, and envelopes) that the manufacturer packed with them before offering them for sale.

Cardboard boxes, inserts, and assorted sheets of paper are more fragile than die-cast metal or plastic trains. They were also deemed to be less important to the children playing with toy trains long ago and so were not treated with the same care. Instruction sheets were lost, and boxes were discarded. As a result, fewer boxes and instruction sheets have survived than have the trains and accessories that went with them. In some cases, the box that a particular locomotive, car, or even set came in is now valued more than the item itself.

Boxes are evaluated according to standards and conditions established by the Train Collectors Association, similar to those developed for toy trains and accessories:

P-10 **Mint:** Brand new, complete, all original as manufactured, and unused. Flaps appear to never have been opened, and edges are crisp. No tears, fading, or wear marks. Contains original contents and all applicable sealing tape, wrap, and staples.

P-9 **Store New:** Complete, all original, and unused. Box may have merchant additions such as store stamps and price tags. Must have appropriate inner liners.

P-8 **Like New:** Complete and all original. There is evidence of light use and aging. Box may have notations (discrete) added since leaving the manufacturer.

P-7 **Excellent:** Complete and all original. Box shows moderate signs of being opened and closed including edge and corner wear. All flaps must be intact.

P-6 **Very Good:** Complete and all original. Box shows signs of usage such as minor abrasions, small tears, color changes, and minor soiling. Inner liners may be missing, and inner flaps may require strengthening. The box can still safely store its original contents.

P-5 **Good:** Box shows substantial wear, and edges may be damaged. Box may have extensive color fading but no evident water damage or cardboard deterioration. Exterior flaps are present, but their connection to the box may require repair. Inner liners may be missing. With care, the box can still store contents. (Any box that has been repaired cannot be graded above P-5.)

P-4 **Fair:** Box shows heavy damage and may have been repaired. Inner flaps may be missing. Box cannot store its original contents. Water damage may be present.

Values for postwar boxes in this section are shown for Good (P-5) and Excellent (P-7) conditions.

Lionel used these box types during the postwar years:

Art Deco: Original postwar box with bold orange and blue design and lettering. It was used in 1946 and 1947.

Classic: More understated design than Art Deco. It was the main component box from 1948 through 1958. Boxes can be divided into Early (1948–49), Middle (1949–55), and Late (1956–58) Classic designs, which are marked by minor lettering changes.

Orange Perforated: This was a significant change from the Classic design. The solid orange box features white lettering and a tear-out perforated front panel. It was used in 1959 and 1960.

Orange Picture: Instead of a perforated panel, this version of the Orange Perforated box features an illustration of a steam locomotive and an F3 diesel on the front. It was used from 1961 to 1964.

Hillside Orange Picture: Similar to an Orange Picture box, it is labeled with Hillside, N.J., where Lionel's plant was located. It was used in 1965.

Cellophane: Used in 1966, this box features a clear cellophane window on the front.

Hagerstown Checkerboard: It has a Lionel checkerboard pattern and Hagerstown, Maryland, printed on end flap bottoms. The box was used in 1968.

Hillside Checkerboard: This 1969 box is the same as the Hagerstown Checkerboard box, but with Hillside, New Jersey, printed on it.

Lionel also used brown corrugated and plain white boxes.

Section 7: Sets

This section lists boxed train sets catalogued by Lionel during the postwar years, 1945–1969. When collecting sets, it is important that the sets, or outfits, contain all the items, including ancillary ones, that Lionel packed with them. These items include the locomotive (and tender if a steam engine) rolling stock, any accessories, track, transformer, instructions and other paper pieces, component boxes, and the set box.

The listings include the set's catalog number, a short description, and product numbers for the locomotives, rolling stock, and any major accessories. Sets came with O27 gauge, O gauge, or Super O track. O27 and Super O track are listed in the set's description. If no track is listed, the set came with O gauge.

Set values are listed for Excellent (C-7) condition. The presence and condition of original component boxes, set boxes, inserts and other packaging materials can have a significant effect on a set's value. The values reflect the inclusion of these materials. Values of individual set and component boxes can be found in Section 6.

Due to space constraints, not every item found in a set is listed in the description. You can find more complete information on a set's contents on various websites and in *Greenberg's Guide to Lionel Trains 1945–1969 Volume III: Catalogued Sets* by Paul Ambrose. (Although the book is out of print, it is available from booksellers on the Internet.)

USING THE GUIDE

Number	Description	Condition ——— Good	Exc	Cond/$
2561	Vista Valley Observation Car, *59–61**	75	230	___
X6454	NYC Boxcar, *48*			
	(A) Brown body	15	35	___
	(B) Orange body	50	140	___
	(C) Tan body	20	60	___
6475	Libby's Crushed Pineapple Vat Car, *63 u*	35	90	___

Identifying a catalog number

A Lionel catalog number is usually stamped, printed, or painted on an item. However, some products do not contain a catalog number. In these cases, you can match the product with its catalog number using a comprehensive reference book or website, including Lionel.com, which contains past and current catalogs.

Two-, three-, and four-digit numbers predominated during the prewar (1901–42) and postwar (1945–69) periods. Four- and five-digit numbers have been most common during the modern era (1970–2019).

On the models, catalog numbers often double as road numbers, although sometimes separate road numbers were added.

Locating an item

Sections are arranged in numerical order of catalog numbers. Items having one or more zeroes as placeholders are listed before those without placeholders. For example, a 004 4-6-4 Locomotive is listed before a 4 Electric Locomotive.

In the prewar and postwar sections, some items such as transformers and track pieces, are identified by a letter. These products follow the numbered items.

Reading an entry

Every entry begins with the product's catalog number assigned by Lionel. (Club and special production cars may have numbers that were assigned by the group.)

A basic description of the model follows. It gives the type of product, lists the name of any railroad identified with it, and includes identifying characteristics, such as color or lettering. If the item has a road number that differs from its catalog number, that number is shown in quotation marks. (Most of these are seen in Section 3). Abbreviations used in the descriptions, including those of railroad names, are listed at the back of the price guide.

Next, you'll find the year or years during which that item was part of Lionel's cataloged product line. The years are shown in italics. If a year is followed by a *u*, this item is considered to be uncataloged. It was not part of the cataloged line but a promotional item that Lionel made or sponsored for an outside business or group.

Entries that show an asterisk (*) after the year have had one or more reissues of the item made.

Many entries feature variations, each indicated by a separate letter (A, B, and so forth). Variations amount to slight yet noteworthy differences in appearance that distinguish models that otherwise seem identical. These differences can relate to color, lettering, and details that were added or deleted. For items having many variations, an entry may not include every variation.

An entry concludes with an indication of the value of the item for several common conditions.

Condition

Lionel enthusiasts should be familiar with the condition and grading standards established by the Train Collectors Association, which are used as the basis for evaluating the condition of toy trains and accessories:

C-10 **Mint:** Brand new—all original, unused, and unblemished.

C-9 **Factory New:** Same condition as Mint but with evidence of factory rubs or slight signs of handling, shipping, and being test run at the factory.

C-8 **Like New:** Complete and all original with no rust or no missing parts; may show effects of being displayed or signs of age and may have been run.

C-7 **Excellent:** All original and may have minute scratches and paint nicks; no rust, no missing parts, and no distortion of component parts.

C-6 **Very Good:** Has minor scratches, paint nicks, or minor spots of surface rust; is free of dents and may have minor parts replaced.

C-5 **Good:** Shows evidence of heavy use and signs of play wear—small dents, scratches, minor paint loss, and minor surface rust.

C-4 **Fair:** Shows evidence of heavy use—scratches and dents, moderate paint loss, missing parts, and surface rust.

C-3 **Poor:** Requires major body repair and is a candidate for restoration; major rust, missing parts, and heavily scratched.

C-2 **Restoration:** Needs to be restored.

C-1 **Junk:** Parts value only.

Values are listed for prewar and postwar trains in Good (C-5) and Excellent (C-7) conditions. For modern-era trains, including special production and club cars, the values for Excellent (C-7) and Mint (C-10) are shown.

You may also see NRS listed as a value. NRS (No Reported Sales) refers to an item with limited pricing data since only a handful of these scarce items may have been reported.

Determining a model's condition

Look over a model carefully to see whether it has suffered serious damage, including warping and breaking. Then note whether any parts are missing. Feel for dents in metal and cracks in plastic. Check for areas marred by rust, mildew, or chipped paint.

The TCA condition standards will assist you in evaluating your model, such as deciding whether a prewar or postwar model falls below Good or above Excellent.

The assessment of a toy train's value is based on the expectations that it has not been modified and that all parts are present and original to it. Repainting or relettering a model seriously undermines a train's value, regardless of how beat-up and scratched it may have been before undergoing modification. Any model that has been altered should be labeled as a restoration; potential buyers deserve to be informed about how it has been modified, so they do not mistake it for an original.

A model that is missing some parts should be sold *as is* or have those parts replaced by identical originals. A tank car cataloged in 1935 that needs a brake wheel must have a part from 1935 put on it to be considered a true original. Adding a brake wheel from 1936 undermines the car's legitimacy as much as adding one from 2018 does.

The same rule applies to the ancillary items that came with various models. The value of a flatcar may depend largely on the miniature airplane or rocket packed with it; therefore, having a load that is a genuine original is essential to maintaining the value of that flatcar. Similarly, freight loaders must have whatever cargo came with them (coal, logs, trailers, and so forth). Reproductions should be identified as such.

		Good	Exc	
001	4-6-4 Locomotive (OO), *38–42*	195	360	____
1	Bild-A-Motor (O), *28–31*	60	140	____
1	Trolley (std), *06–14*			
	(A) Cream body, orange band and roof	1900	4750	____
	(B) White body, blue band and roof	1750	4750	____
	(C) Cream body, blue band and roof	1300	3150	____
	(D) Cream body, blue band and roof, Curtis Bay	2150	5550	____
	(E) Blue, cream band, blue roof	1450	3150	____
1/111	Trolley Trailer (std), *06–14*	1000	2700	____
002	4-6-4 Locomotive (OO), *39–42*	160	285	____
2	Bild-A-Motor (std), *28–31*	100	180	____
2	Trolley (std), *06–16**			
	(A) Yellow, red band	1200	3575	____
	(B) Red, yellow band	1200	2250	____
2/200	Trolley Trailer (std), *06–16*	1000	1800	____
003	4-6-4 Locomotive (OO), *39–42*			
	(A) 003W whistling Tender	190	395	____
	(B) 003T nonwhistling Tender	175	355	____
3	Trolley (std), *06–13*			
	(A) Cream, orange band	1400	3100	____
	(B) Cream, dark olive green band	1400	3100	____
	(C) Orange, dark olive green band	1400	3100	____
	(D) Dark green, cream windows	1400	3100	____
	(E) Green, cream windows, Bay Shore	1650	3700	____
3/300	Trolley Trailer (std), *06–13*	1500	3500	____
004	4-6-4 Locomotive (OO), *39–42*			
	(A) 004W whistling Tender	210	350	____
	(B) 004T nonwhistling Tender	190	310	____
4	Electric Locomotive 0-4-0 (O), *28–32**			
	(A) Orange, black frame	550	875	____
	(B) Gray, apple green stripe	580	1050	____
4	Trolley (std), *06–12*			
	(A) Cream, dark olive green band	3000	4950	____
	(B) Green or olive green, cream roof	3000	4950	____
4U	No. 4 Kit Form (O), *28–29*	1150	1600	____
5	0-4-0 Locomotive, no tender, early (std), *06–07*			
	(A) NYC & HRR	1000	1450	____
	(B) Pennsylvania	1400	2300	____
	(C) NYC & HRRR (3 Rs)	1250	2050	____
	(D) B&O RR	1500	2400	____
5	0-4-0 Locomotive, tender, early Special (std), *06–09*	980	1300	____

			Good	Exc
___ 5	0-4-0 Locomotive, no tender, later (std), *10–11*		750	1150
5 ___	0-4-0 Locomotive, tender, later Special (std), *10–11*		920	1200
___ 5/51	0-4-0 Locomotive, tender, latest (std), *12–23*		800	1100
___ 6	4-4-0 Locomotive (std), *06–23*		860	1250
___ 6	0-4-0 Locomotive Special (std), *08–09*		2050	2950
___ 7	Steam 4-4-0 Locomotive (std), *10–23**		1850	2300
8	Electric Locomotive 0-4-0 (std), *25–32*			
___	(A) Maroon or mojave, brass windows and trim		130	250
___	(B) Olive green, brass windows		155	205
___	(C) Red, brass or cream windows		195	250
___	(D) Peacock, orange windows		520	750
8	Trolley (std), *08–14**			
___	(A) Cream, orange band and roof		3000	5400
___	(B) Dark green, cream windows		3000	5400
8E	Electric Locomotive 0-4-0 (std), *26–32*			
___	(A) Mojave, brass windows and trim		175	250
___	(B) Red, brass or cream windows		150	225
___	(C) Peacock, orange windows		370	590
___	(D) Pea green, cream stripe		465	670
___ 9	Electric Locomotive 0-4-0 (std), *29**		1200	2150
___ 9	Motor Car (std), *09–12*			NRS
___ 9	Trolley (std), *09*		3000	5400
9E	Electric Locomotive (std), *28–35**			
___	(A) 0-4-0, orange		700	1250
___	(B) 2-4-2, two-tone green		880	1600
___	(C) 2-4-2, gunmetal gray		860	1100
___ 9U	Electric Locomotive 0-4-0 Kit (std), *28–29*		975	1975
10	Electric Locomotive 0-4-0 (std), *25–29**			
___	(A) Mojave, brass trim		145	215
___	(B) Gray, brass trim		125	205
___	(C) Peacock, brass inserts		145	205
___	(D) Red, cream stripe		580	880
10	Interurban (std), *10–16*			
___	(A) Maroon		3000	5750
___	(B) Dark olive green		1200	2150
___ 10E	Electric Locomotive 0-4-0 (std), *26–30*			
___	(A) Olive green, black frame			NRS
___	(B) Peacock, dark green or black frame		245	400
___	(C) State brown, dark green frame		435	630
___	(D) Gray, black frame		165	220
___	(E) Red, cream stripe		620	890
___ 011	Switches, pair (O), *33–37*		18	38
___ 11	Flatcar, early (std), *06–08*		150	360
___ 11	Flatcar, later (std), *09–15*		45	90

PREWAR 1901-1942

		Good	Exc	
11	Flatcar, latest (std), *16–18*	50	90	___
11	Flatcar, Lionel Corp. (std), *18–26*	50	80	___
012	Switches, pair (O), *27–33*	20	40	___
12	Gondola, early (std), *06–08*	150	360	___
12	Gondola, later (std), *09–15*	50	100	___
12	Gondola, latest (std), *16–18*	35	70	___
12	Gondola, Lionel Corp. (std), *18–26*	50	70	___
013	012 Switches and 439 panel board, *27–33*	120	190	___
13	Cattle Car, early (std), *06–08*	300	450	___
13	Cattle Car, later (std), *09–15*	150	225	___
13	Cattle Car, latest (std), *16–18*	65	115	___
13	Cattle Car, Lionel Corp. (std), *18–26*	65	115	___
0014	Boxcar (OO), *38–42*			
	(A) Yellow, Lionel Lines	80	155	___
	(B) Tuscan, Pennsylvania	40	75	___
14	Boxcar, early (std), *06–08*	195	435	___
14	Boxcar, later (std), *09–15*	80	105	___
14	Boxcar, latest (std), *16–18*	75	105	___
14	Boxcar, Lionel Corp. (std), *18–26*	80	105	___
0015	Tank Car (OO), *38–42*			
	(A) Silver, Sun Oil	40	90	___
	(B) Black, Shell	50	85	___
15	Oil Car, early (std), *06–08*	200	360	___
15	Oil Car, later (std), *09–15*	75	115	___
15	Oil Car, latest (std), *16–18*	75	115	___
15	Oil Car, Lionel Corp. (std), *18–26*	75	115	___
0016	Hopper Car (OO), *38–42*			
	(A) Gray	75	160	___
	(B) Black	60	115	___
16	Ballast Dump Car, early (std), *06–11*	400	700	___
16	Ballast Dump Car, later (std), *09–15*	95	175	___
16	Ballast Dump Car, latest (std), *16–18*	95	175	___
16	Ballast Dump Car, Lionel Corp. (std), *18–26*	95	175	___
0017	Caboose (OO), *38–42*	40	90	___
17	Caboose, early (std), *06–08*	220	440	___
17	Caboose, later (std), *09–15*	70	135	___
17	Caboose, latest (std), *16–18*	75	135	___
17	Caboose, Lionel Corp. (std), *18–26*	50	90	___
18	Pullman Car (std), *08*			
	(A) Dark olive green, nonremovable roof	700	2150	___
	(B) Dark olive green, removable roof	90	215	___
	(C) Yellow-orange, removable roof	315	870	___
	(D) Orange, removable roof	90	205	___
	(E) Mojave, removable roof	305	890	___
18	Pullman Car (std), *11–13*	600	900	___

		Good	Exc
_____ 18	Pullman Car (std), *13–15*	150	270
_____ 18	Pullman Car (std), *15–18*	150	270
_____ 18	Pullman Car (std), *18–22*	90	155
_____ 18	Pullman Car (std), *23–26*	270	530
19	Combine Car (std), *08*		
_____	(A) Dark olive green, nonremovable roof	1100	2600
_____	(B) Dark olive green, removable roof	80	145
_____	(C) Yellow-orange, removable roof	260	430
_____	(D) Orange, removable roof	115	205
_____	(E) Mojave, removable roof	305	890
_____ 19	Combine Car (std), *11–13*	600	900
_____ 19	Combine Car (std), *13–15*	200	270
_____ 19	Combine Car (std), *15–18*	200	270
_____ 19	Combine Car (std), *18–22*	90	155
_____ 19	Combine Car (std), *23–26*	265	520
_____ 020	90-degree Crossover (O), *15–42*	4	15
_____ 020X	45-degree Crossover (O), *17–42*	3	10
_____ 20	90-degree Crossover (std), *09–32*	4	10
_____ 20	Direct Current Reducer, *06*	95	195
_____ 20X	45-degree Crossover (std), *28–32*	5	10
_____ 021	Switches, pair (O), *15–37*	20	50
_____ 21	90-degree Crossover (std), *06*	10	20
_____ 21	Switches, pair (std), *15–25*	35	70
_____ 022	Remote Control Switches, pair (O), *38–42*	40	70
_____ 22	Manual Switches, pair (std), *06–25*	45	75
_____ 023	Bumper (O), *15–33*	15	35
_____ 23	Bumper (std), *06–23*	15	40
_____ 0024	Pennsylvania Boxcar (OO), *39–42*	45	75
_____ 24	Railway Station (std), *06*		NRS
_____ 025	Bumper (O), *28–42*	15	40
0025	Tank Car (OO), *39–42*		
_____	(A) Black, Shell	40	90
_____	(B) Silver, Sunoco	40	80
_____ 25	Open Station (std), *06*		NRS
_____ 25	Bumper (std), *27–42*	25	45
_____ 26	Passenger Bridge (std), *06*	15	40
_____ 0027	Caboose (OO), *39–42*	40	70
_____ 27	Lighting Set, *11–23*	15	40
_____ 27	Station (std), *09–12*		NRS
_____ 28	Double Station with dome, *09–12*		NRS

		Good	Exc	
29	Day Coach (std), *07–22*			
	(A) Dark olive green, 9 windows	1500	3000	____
	(B) Maroon, 10 windows	1200	1500	____
	(C) Dark green, 10 windows	3000	4500	____
	(D) Dark olive green, 10 windows	680	1000	____
	(E) Dark green, 10 windows	450	900	____
0031	2-rail 13" Curve Track (OO), *39–42*	5	10	____
31	Combine Car (std), *21–25*			
	(A) Maroon	70	90	____
	(B) Orange	125	195	____
	(C) Dark olive green	65	90	____
	(D) Brown	75	95	____
0032	2-rail 12" Straight Track (OO), *39–42*	10	15	____
32	Mail Car (std), *21–25*			
	(A) Maroon	85	125	____
	(B) Orange	120	185	____
	(C) Dark olive green	65	85	____
	(D) Brown	70	90	____
32	Miniature Figures, *09–18*	95	250	____
33	Electric Locomotive 0-6-0, early (std), *13*			
	(A) Dark olive green, NYC in oval	105	190	____
	(B) Black, NYC	320	950	____
	(C) Dark olive green, NYC	440	950	____
	(D) Pennsylvania RR	580	1250	____
33	Electric Locomotive 0-4-0, later (std), *13–24*			____
	(A) Dark olive green or black, NYC	105	170	____
	(B) Black, lettered C&O	395	720	____
	(C) Maroon, red, or peacock	340	620	____
0034	2-rail 13" Curve Track, electrical connectors (OO), *39–42*	10	15	____
34	Electric Locomotive 0-6-0, early (std), *12*	520	860	____
34	Electric Locomotive 0-4-0 (std), *13*	200	385	____
35	Pullman Car (std), *12–13*			
	(A) Dark blue	470	900	____
	(B) Dark olive green	170	235	____
35	Pullman Car (std), *14–16*			
	(A) Dark olive green, maroon windows	35	70	____
	(B) Maroon, green windows	75	105	____
	(C) Orange, maroon windows	125	195	____
35	Pullman Car (std), *15–18*	40	70	____

			Good	Exc
35		Pullman Car (std), *18–23*		
___		(A) Dark olive green, maroon windows	30	50
___		(B) Maroon, green windows	25	45
___		(C) Orange, maroon windows	120	210
___		(D) Brown, green windows	30	50
___	**35**	Boulevard Street Lamp, 6⅛" high, *40–42*	25	50
___	**35**	Pullman Car (std), *24*	40	55
___	**35**	Pullman Car (std), *25–26*	40	55
	36	Observation Car (std), *12–13*		
___		(A) Dark blue	315	810
___		(B) Dark olive green	145	205
	36	Observation Car (std), *14–16*		
___		(A) Dark olive green, maroon windows	60	95
___		(B) Maroon, green windows	50	70
___		(C) Orange, maroon windows	180	290
___		(D) Brown, green windows	50	75
___	**36**	Observation Car (std), *15–18*	60	80
	36	Observation Car (std), *18–23*		
___		(A) Dark olive green, maroon windows	40	55
___		(B) Maroon, green windows	40	55
___		(C) Orange, maroon windows	130	215
___		(D) Brown, green windows	40	55
___	**36**	Observation Car (std), *24*	40	55
___	**36**	Observation Car (std), *25–26*	40	55
	38	Electric Locomotive 0-4-0 (std), *13–24*		
___		(A) Black	100	135
___		(B) Red	475	680
___		(C) Mojave or pea green	405	540
___		(D) Dark green	270	360
___		(E) Brown	270	315
___		(F) Red, cream trim	405	540
___		(G) Maroon	170	270
___		(H) Gray	70	125
___	**41**	Accessory Contactor, *37–42*	3	7
___	**042**	Switches, pair (O), *38–42*	15	40
___	**42**	Electric Locomotive 0-4-4-0, square hood, early (std), *12**	760	1650
	42	Electric Locomotive 0-4-4-0 , round hood, later (std), *13–23*		
___		(A) Black or gray	300	510
___		(B) Maroon	1250	2050
___		(C) Dark gray	375	600
___		(D) Dark green or mojave	500	800
___		(E) Peacock	1100	1800
___		(F) Olive or dark olive green	750	1200

		Good	Exc	
043/43	Bild-A-Motor Gear Set, *29*	40	85	___
0044	Boxcar (OO), *39–42*	40	80	___
0044K	Boxcar Kit (OO), *39–42*	75	120	___
0045	Gateman, *35–36*	15	35	___
0045	Tank Car (OO), *39–42*			
	(A) Black, Shell	40	95	___
	(B) Silver, Sunoco	40	80	___
45	Gateman, *35–36*	10	25	___
0045K	Tank Car Kit (OO), *39–42*	75	120	___
45N	Automatic Gateman (std O), *37–42*	40	85	___
0046	Hopper Car (OO), *39–42*	50	90	___
0046K	Hopper Car Kit (OO), *39–42*			
	(A) Southern Pacific	75	135	___
	(B) Reading		NRS	___
46	Crossing Gate, *39–42*	75	120	___
0047	Caboose (OO), *39–42*	30	60	___
0047K	Caboose Kit (OO), *39–42*	75	135	___
47	Crossing Gate, *39–42*	70	140	___
48W	Whistle Station, *37–42*	20	65	___
50	Electric Locomotive 0-4-0 (std), *24*			
	(A) Dark green or dark gray	135	250	___
	(B) Maroon	315	600	___
	(C) Mojave	175	345	___
50	Cardboard Train, Cars, Accessory (O), *43**	200	360	___
0051	7" Curve Track (OO), *39–42*	5	15	___
51	0-4-0 Locomotive, late, 8-wheel (std), *12–23*	800	1150	___
0052	7" Straight Track (OO), *39–42*	10	15	___
52	Lamp Post, *33–41*	45	95	___
53	Electric Locomotive 0-4-4-0, early (std), *12–14*	1200	2450	___
53	Electric Locomotive 0-4-0, later (std), *15–19*			
	(A) Maroon	550	950	___
	(B) Mojave	670	1350	___
	(C) Dark olive green	560	1150	___
53	Electric Locomotive 0-4-0, latest (std), *20–21*	200	450	___
53	Electric Locomotive 0-6-6-0, early (std), *11*		NRS	___
53	Lamp Post, *31–42*	30	50	___
0054	7" Curve Track, electrical connectors (OO), *39–42*	10	15	___
54	Electric Locomotive 0-4-4-0, early (std), *12**	2500	4050	___
54	Electric Locomotive 0-4-4-0, late (std), *13–23*	1800	2700	___
54	Lamp Post, *29–35*	60	110	___

			Good	Exc
	56	Lamp Post, removable lens and cap, *24–42*		
___		(A) Mojave	85	185
___		(B) Dark gray	50	110
___		(C) 45N green	25	45
___		(D) Pea green	30	50
___		(E) Aluminum	30	45
___		(F) Copper	60	160
___		(G) Dark green	30	45
	57	Lamp Post with street names, *22–42*		
___		(A) Orange post, Main St. & Broadway	35	55
___		(B) Orange post, Fifth Ave. & 42nd St.	40	95
___		(C) Orange post, Broadway & 21st St.	45	90
___		(D) Orange post, Broadway, 42nd St., Fifth Ave. & 21st St.	70	120
___		(E) Yellow post, Main St. & Broadway	35	75
	58	Lamp Post, 7⅜" high, *22–42*		
___		(A) Cream	30	60
___		(B) Peacock	30	60
___		(C) Silver	30	60
___		(D) Maroon	35	85
___		(E) Dark green	30	50
___		(F) Orange	30	60
___	**59**	Lamp Post, 8¾" high, *20–36*	40	100
___	**060**	Telegraph Post (O), *29–42*	10	25
___	**60**	Telegraph Post (std), *20–28*	10	25
___	**60**	Electric Locomotive 0-4-0, FAO Schwartz (std), *15 u*		NRS
___	**0061**	7" Curve Track, tubular (00), *38*	3	10
___	**61**	Lamp Post, one globe, *14–36*	35	65
___	**61**	Electric Locomotive 0-4-4-0, FAO Schwartz (std), *15 u*		NRS
___	**0062**	7" Straight Track, tubular (00), *38*	5	10
___	**62**	Semaphore, *20–32*	30	50
___	**62**	Electric Locomotive 0-4-0, FAO Schwartz (std), *24–32 u*		NRS
___	**0063**	Half Curve Track, tubular (00), *38–42*	8	15
___	**63**	Semaphore, single arm, *15–21*	25	50
___	**63**	Lamp Post, two globes, *33–42*	135	265
___	**0064**	7" Curve Track, tubular, electrical connectors (00), *38*	8	15
___	**64**	Lamp Post, *40–42*	35	70
___	**64**	Semaphore, double arm, *15–21*	30	60
___	**0065**	Half Straight Track, tubular (00), *38–42*	10	15
___	**65**	Semaphore, one-arm, *15–26*	30	60
___	**65**	Whistle Controller, *35*	8	15
___	**0066**	5⅝" Straight Track (00), *38–42*	10	15

		Good	Exc	
66	Semaphore, two-arm, *15–26*	35	70	____
66	Whistle Controller, *36–39*	5	10	____
67	Lamp Post, *15–32*	85	145	____
67	Whistle Controller, *36–39*	10	30	____
068	Warning Signal (O), *25–42*	10	25	____
69N	Electric Warning Signal (std O), *36–42*	35	70	____
0070	90-degree Crossing, *38–42*	5	10	____
70	Outfit: 62 (2), 59 (1), 68 (1), *21–32*	60	130	____
071	060 Telegraph Poles, 6 pieces (std), *24–42*	70	160	____
71	60 Telegraph Post Set, 6 pieces, *21–31*	70	160	____
0072	Remote Control Switches, pair (OO), *38–42*	155	290	____
0072L	Remote Control Switch, left hand (OO), *38–42*	50	95	____
0072R	Remote Control Switch, right hand (OO)	50	95	____
0074	Boxcar (OO), *39–42*	35	85	____
0075	Tank Car (OO), *39–42*	50	145	____
076	Block Signal (O), *23–28*	35	105	____
76	Warning Bell and Shack, *39–42*	55	180	____
0077	Caboose (OO), *39–42*	30	60	____
77/077	Automatic Crossing Gate, *23–35*	25	50	____
78/078	Train Signal, *24–32*	40	100	____
79	Flashing Signal, *28–42*	85	150	____
80/080	Semaphore, *26–35*	50	120	____
81	Controlling Rheostat, *27–33*	5	10	____
82/082	Semaphore, *27–35*	40	120	____
83	Flashing Traffic Signal, *27–42*	65	195	____
084	Semaphore, *28–32*	60	100	____
84	Semaphore, *27–32*	45	85	____
85	Telegraph Pole (std), *29–42*	15	30	____
86	Telegraph Poles, 6 pieces, *29–42*	60	120	____
87	Flashing Crossing Signal, *27–42*	85	300	____
88	Rheostat, *15–27*	3	10	____
88	Direction Controller, *33–42*	4	10	____
89	Flagpole, *23–34*	40	75	____
90	Flagpole, *27–42*	40	95	____
91	Circuit Breaker, *30–42*	30	50	____
092	Signal Tower, *23–27*	85	190	____
92	Floodlight Tower, *31–42**	150	215	____
93	Water Tower, *31–42*	60	110	____
94	High Tension Tower, *32–42**	150	290	____
95	Controlling Rheostat, *34–42*	5	15	____
96	Coal Elevator, manual, *38–40*	165	220	____
097	Telegraph Set (O)	45	75	____
97	Coal Elevator, *38–42*	125	240	____
98	Coal Bunker, *38–40*	160	320	____
99N	Train Control Block Signal, *36–42*	45	180	____

		Good	Exc
____ **100**	Wooden Gondola (2⅞"), *01*		NRS
____ **100**	Bridge Approaches, 2 ramps (std), *20–31*	20	40
____ **100**	Electric Locomotive (2⅞"), *03–05**	2900	5200
100	Trolley (std), *10–16*		
____	(A) Blue, white windows	1300	2700
____	(B) Blue, cream windows	1850	3600
____	(C) Red, cream windows	1300	2700
101	Bridge, span (104) and 2 approaches (100), *20–31*		
____		65	120
____ **101**	Summer Trolley (std), *10–13*	1300	2700
102	Bridge, 2 spans (104) and 2 approaches (100), *20–31*		
____		70	175
____ **103**	Bridge (std), *13–16*	40	75
103	Bridge, 3 spans (104) and 2 approaches (100), *20–31*		
____		60	145
____ **104**	Bridge Center Span (std), *20–31*	20	45
____ **104**	Tunnel, papier mache (std), *09–14*	50	135
____ **105**	Bridge (std), *11–14*	40	70
____ **105**	Bridge Approaches, 2 ramps (O), *20–31*	50	70
106	Bridge, span (110) and 2 approaches (105), *20–31*		
____		30	65
____ **106**	Rheostat, *11–14*	3	10
____ **107**	DC Reducer, 110V, *23–32*		NRS
108	Bridge, 2 spans (110) and 2 approaches (105), *20–31*		
____		50	90
109	Bridge, 3 spans, (110) and 2 approaches (105), *20–32*		
____		50	115
____ **109**	Tunnel, papier mache (std), *13–14*	30	70
____ **110**	Bridge Center Span (O), *20–31*	10	25
____ **111**	Box of 50 Bulbs, *20–31*	55	105
____ **112**	Gondola, early (std), *10–12*	225	400
____ **112**	Gondola, later (std), *12–16*	40	65
____ **112**	Gondola, latest (std), *16–18*	40	65
____ **112**	Gondola, Lionel Corp. (std), *18–26*	40	65
____ **112**	Station, *31–35*	145	270
____ **113**	Cattle Car, later (std), *12–16*	50	70
____ **113**	Cattle Car, latest (std), *16–18*	50	70
____ **113**	Cattle Car, Lionel Corp. (std), *18–26*	30	55
____ **113**	Station with light fixtures, *31–34*	150	310
____ **114**	Boxcar, later (std), *12–16*	50	90
____ **114**	Boxcar, latest (std), *16–18*	40	70
____ **114**	Boxcar, Lionel Corp. (std), *18–26*	40	70
____ **114**	Station with light fixtures, *31–34*	530	1200
____ **115**	Station with train control, *35–42**	185	370
____ **116**	Ballast Car, early and later (std), *10–16*	85	115
____ **116**	Ballast Car, latest (std), *16–18*	65	105
____ **116**	Ballast Car, Lionel Corp. (std), *18–26*	55	95

		Good	Exc	
116	Station with train control, 35–42*	640	920	___
117	Caboose, early (std), 12	40	75	___
117	Caboose, later (std), 12–16	40	75	___
117	Caboose, latest (std), 16–18	40	75	___
117	Caboose, Lionel Corp. (std), 18–26	30	60	___
117	Station, 36–42	125	235	___
118	Tunnel, metal, 8" long (O), 20–32	23	60	___
118L	Tunnel, metal, lighted, 8" long, 27	20	55	___
119	Tunnel, metal, 12" long, 20–42	25	60	___
119L	Tunnel, metal, lighted, 12" long, 27–33	20	55	___
120	Tunnel, metal, 17" long, 22–27	30	75	___
120L	Tunnel, metal, lighted, 17" long, 27–42	75	140	___
121	Station, lighted (std), 09–16			
	(A) 14" x 10" x 9"		NRS	___
	(B) 13" x 9" x 13"	150	300	___
121	Station (std), 20–26	75	165	___
121X	Station (std), 17–19	110	255	___
122	Station (std), 20–30	80	190	___
123	Station (std), 20–23	75	210	___
123	Tunnel, paperboard base, 18½" long (O), 33–42	105	235	___
124	Lionel City Station, 20–36*			
	(A) Tan or gray base, pea green roof	90	240	___
	(B) Pea green base, red roof	200	360	___
125	Lionelville Station, 23–25	80	185	___
125	Track Template, 38	1	5	___
126	Lionelville Station, 23–36	95	205	___
127	Lionel Town Station, 23–36	80	160	___
128	115 Station and 129 Terrace, 35–42*	900	1900	___
128	124 Station and 129 Terrace, 31–34*	900	1900	___
129	Terrace, 28–42*	600	1100	___
130	Tunnel, 26" long (O), 20–36	100	415	___
130L	Tunnel, lighted, 26" long, 27–33	150	450	___
131	Corner Display, 24–28	125	295	___
132	Corner Grass Plot, 24–28	125	295	___
133	Heart-shaped Plot, 24–28	125	295	___
134	Lionel City Station with stop, 37–42	230	445	___
134	Oval-shaped Plot, 24–28	125	300	___
135	Circular Plot, 24–28	125	295	___
136	Large Elevation, 24–28		NRS	___
136	Lionelville Station with stop, 37–42	85	180	___
137	Station with stop, 37–42	80	160	___
140L	Tunnel, lighted, 37" long, 27–32	460	1050	___
150	Electric Locomotive 0-4-0, early (O), 17	95	180	___

		Good	Exc
150	Electric Locomotive 0-4-0, late (0), *18–25*		
___	(A) Brown, brown or olive windows	95	150
___	(B) Maroon, dark olive windows	90	135
152	Electric Locomotive 0-4-0 (0), *17–27*		
___	(A) Dark green	90	135
___	(B) Gray	100	160
___	(C) Mojave	340	680
___	(D) Peacock	340	680
___ **152**	Crossing Gate, *40–42*	20	40
___ **153**	Block Signal, *40–42*	25	45
153	Electric Locomotive 0-4-0 (0), *24–25*		
___	(A) Dark green	100	160
___	(B) Gray	100	160
___	(C) Mojave	100	160
___ **154**	Electric Locomotive 0-4-0 (0), *17–23*	100	180
154	Highway Signal, *40–42*		
___	(A) Black base	25	50
___	(B) Orange base	95	220
155	Freight Shed, *30–42**		
___	(A) Cream base, terra cotta floor	180	320
___	(B) Ivory base, red floor	240	400
___ **156**	Electric Locomotive 0-4-0 (0), *17–23*	400	720
___ **156**	Station Platform, *39–42*	85	115
156	Electric Locomotive 4-4-4 (0), *17–23*		
___	(A) Dark green	475	810
___	(B) Maroon	540	890
___	(C) Olive green	600	1050
___	(D) Gray	670	1200
156X	Electric Locomotive 0-4-0 (0), *23–24*		
___	(A) Maroon	330	495
___	(B) Olive green	200	400
___	(C) Gray	530	710
___	(D) Brown	420	600
___ **157**	Hand Truck, *30–32*	20	40
158	Electric Locomotive 0-4-0 (0), *19–23*		
___	(A) Gray or red windows	75	205
___	(B) Black	95	250
___ **158**	Station Set: 136 Station and 2 platforms (156), *40–42*	120	280
___ **159**	Block Actuator, *40*	10	30
___ **161**	Baggage Truck, *30–32**	40	80
___ **162**	Dump Truck, *30–32**	40	80
___ **163**	Freight Accessory Set: 2 hand trucks (157), baggage truck (161), and dump truck (162), *30–42**	220	360
___ **164**	Log Loader, *40–42*	160	225

		Good	Exc	
165	Magnetic Crane, *40–42*	175	340	____
165-22	Scrap Steel with bag, *40–42*	50	125	____
165-83	Steel Blanks with bag, *40–42*	50	110	____
166	Whistle Controller, *40–42*	3	10	____
167	Whistle Controller, *40–42*	8	25	____
167X	Whistle Controller (OO), *40–42*	5	15	____
168	Magic Electrol Controller, *40–42*	25	50	____
169	Controller, *40–42*	4	20	____
170	DC Reducer, 220V, *14–38*	5	10	____
171	DC to AC Inverter, 110V, *36–42*	5	15	____
172	DC to AC Inverter, 229V, *39–42*	3	7	____
180	Pullman Car (std), *11–13*			
	(A) Maroon body and roof	145	205	____
	(B) Brown body and roof	145	255	____
180	Pullman Car (std), *13–15*	80	160	____
180	Pullman Car (std), *15–18*	80	160	____
180	Pullman Car (std), *18–22*	80	135	____
181	Combine Car (std), *11–13*			
	(A) Maroon, dark olive doors	145	205	____
	(B) Brown, dark olive doors	145	205	____
	(C) Yellow-orange, orange doors	350	495	____
181	Combine Car (std), *13–15*	80	160	____
181	Combine Car (std), *15–18*	80	160	____
181	Combine Car (std), *18–22*	80	135	____
182	Observation Car (std), *11–13*			
	(A) Maroon, dark olive doors	145	205	____
	(B) Brown, dark olive doors	145	205	____
	(C) Yellow-orange, orange doors	300	495	____
182	Observation Car (std), *13–15*	80	160	____
182	Observation Car (std), *15–18*	80	160	____
182	Observation Car (std), *18–22*	80	135	____
184	Bungalow, illuminated, *23–32**	65	85	____
185	Bungalow, *23–24*	50	115	____
186	184 Bungalows, set of 5, *23–32*	195	610	____
186	Log Loader Outfit, *40–41*	130	340	____
187	185 Bungalows, set of 5, *23–24*	170	590	____
188	Elevator and Car Set, *38–41*	115	370	____
189	Villa, illuminated, *23–32**	133	225	____
190	Observation Car (std), *08*			
	(A) Dark olive green, nonremovable roof	1150	2600	____
	(B) Dark olive green, removable roof	115	205	____
	(C) Yellow-orange, removable roof	320	620	____
	(D) Orange, removable roof	115	205	____
	(E) Mojave, removable roof	345	870	____

		Good	Exc
____ **190**	Observation Car (std), *11–13*	600	900
____ **190**	Observation Car (std), *13–15*	200	295
____ **190**	Observation Car (std), *15–18*	200	295
____ **190**	Observation Car (std), *18–22*	80	135
____ **190**	Observation Car (std), *23–26*	230	475
____ **191**	Villa, illuminated, *23–32**	125	325
____ **192**	Illuminated Villa Set: 189, 191, 184 (2), *27–32*	400	800
____ **193**	Automatic Accessory Set (O), *27–29*	150	325
____ **194**	Automatic Accessory Set (std), *27–29*	100	325
____ **195**	Terrace, *27–30*	350	740
____ **196**	Accessory Set, *27*	200	335
____ **200**	Electric Express (2⅞"), *03–05**	4000	6300
____ **200**	Trailer, matches No. 2 Trolley (std), *11–16*	1200	2400
____ **200**	Turntable (std), *28–33**	85	190
201	0-6-0 Locomotive (O), *40–42*		
____	(A) 2201B Tender, bell	375	760
____	(B) 2201T Tender, no bell	345	690
202	Summer Trolley (std), *10–13*		
____	(A) Electric Rapid Transit	1300	2700
____	(B) Preston St.	3250	4500
____ **203**	Armored 0-4-0 (O), *17–21*	1100	1800
203	0-6-0 Locomotive (O), *40–42*		
____	(A) 2203B Tender, bell	400	495
____	(B) 2203T Tender, no bell	375	550
204	2-4-2 Locomotive (O), *40–42 u*		
____	(A) Black	55	105
____	(B) Gunmetal gray	80	165
____ **205**	Merchandise Containers, 3 pieces, *30–38**	130	320
____ **206**	Sack of Coal, *38–42*	5	20
____ **208**	Tool Set: 6 assorted tools, *34–42**	65	150
0209	Barrels, wooden, 6 pieces (O), *34–42*		
____	(A) Solid barrels	10	25
____	(B) 2-piece barrels	53	145
____ **209**	Barrels, wooden, 4 pieces (std), *34–42*	10	25
____ **210**	Switches, pair (std), *26, 34–42*	40	75
____ **211**	Flatcar (std), *26–40**	125	195
212	Gondola (std), *26–40**		
____	(A) Gray or light green	100	205
____	(B) Maroon	75	135
213	Cattle Car (std), *26–40**		
____	(A) Mojave, maroon roof	160	365
____	(B) Terra-cotta, pea green roof	130	290
____	(C) Cream, maroon roof	300	650

Good Exc

		Good	Exc	
214	Boxcar (std), *26–40**			
	(A) Terra-cotta, dark green roof	195	390	____
	(B) Cream body, orange roof	150	270	____
	(C) Yellow, brown roof	300	495	____
214R	Refrigerator Car (std), *29–40**			
	(A) Ivory or white, peacock roof	325	495	____
	(B) White, light blue roof	435	790	____
215	Tank Car (std), *26–40**			
	(A) Pea green	150	215	____
	(B) Ivory	220	360	____
	(C) Aluminum	315	720	____
216	Hopper Car (std), *26–38**			
	(A) Dark green, brass plates	195	335	____
	(B) Dark green, nickel plates	445	1100	____
217	Caboose (std), *26–40**			
	(A) Orange, maroon roof	250	510	____
	(B) Red, peacock roof	120	235	____
	(C) Red body and roof, ivory doors	150	320	____
217	Lighting Set, *14–23*		NRS	____
218	Dump Car (std), *26–38**	220	365	____
219	Crane Car (std), *26–40**			
	(A) Peacock, red boom	135	255	____
	(B) Yellow, light green or red boom	270	440	____
	(C) Ivory, light green boom	270	520	____
220	Floodlight Car (std), *31–40**			
	(A) Terra-cotta base	225	385	____
	(B) Green base	340	485	____
220	Switches, pair (std), *26**	25	90	____
222	Switches, pair (std), *26–32*	40	100	____
223	Switches, pair (std), *32–42*	35	120	____
224/224E	2-6-2 Locomotive (O), *38–42*			
	(A) Black, die-cast 2224 Tender	140	255	____
	(B) Black, plastic 2224 Tender	110	195	____
	(C) Gunmetal, die-cast 2224 Tender	385	950	____
	(D) Gunmetal, sheet-metal 2689 Tender	120	210	____
225	222 Switches and 439 Panel, *29–32*	115	260	____
225/225E	2-6-2 Locomotive (O), *38–42*			
	(A) Black, 2235 or 2245 Tender	210	370	____
	(B) Black, 2235 plastic Tender	185	320	____
	(C) Gunmetal, 2225 or 2265 Tender	210	360	____
	(D) Gunmetal, 2235 die-cast Tender	285	730	____
226/226E	2-6-4 Locomotive (O), *38–41*	275	630	____
227	0-6-0 Locomotive (O), *39–42*			
	(A) 2227B Tender, bell	600	1250	____
	(B) 2227T Tender, no bell	600	1150	____

			Good	Exc
228		0-6-0 Locomotive (0), *39–42*		
____		(A) 2228B Tender, bell	600	1250
____		(B) 2228T Tender, no bell	600	1150
	229	2-4-2 Locomotive (0), *39–42*		
____		(A) Black or gunmetal, 2689W Tender	155	240
____		(B) Black or gunmetal, 2689T Tender	120	200
____		(C) Black, 2666W whistle Tender	155	280
____		(D) Black, 2666T nonwhistling Tender	120	200
____	**230**	0-6-0 Locomotive (0), *39–42*	1100	2050
____	**231**	0-6-0 Locomotive (0), *39*	1000	1800
____	**232**	0-6-0 Locomotive (0), *40–42*	1000	1800
____	**233**	0-6-0 Locomotive (0), *40–42*	1000	1800
____	**238**	4-4-2 Locomotive (0), *39–40 u*	430	710
	238E	4-4-2 Locomotive (0), *36–38*		
____		(A) 265W or 2225W whistle Tender	280	345
____		(B) 265 or 2225T nonwhistling Tender	275	360
____	**248**	Electric Locomotive 0-4-0 (0), *27–32*	150	240
	249/249E	2-4-2 Locomotive (0), *36–39*		
____		(A) Gunmetal, 265T or 265W Tender	100	270
____		(B) Black, 265W Tender	110	210
____	**250**	Electric Locomotive 0-4-0, early (0), *26*	125	220
	250	Electric Locomotive 0-4-0, late (0), *34*		
____		(A) Yellow-orange body, terra-cotta frame	145	245
____		(B) Terra-cotta body, maroon frame	160	270
____	**250E**	4-4-2 Hiawatha Locomotive (0), *35–42**	400	1100
____	**250W**	Hiawatha Tender (0), *35–42**	125	250
	251	Electric Locomotive 0-4-0 (0), *25–32*		
____		(A) Gray body, red windows	190	340
____		(B) Red body, ivory stripe	215	410
____		(C) Red body, no ivory stripe	200	380
	251E	Electric Locomotive 0-4-0 (0), *27–32*		
____		(A) Red body, ivory stripe	225	425
____		(B) Red body, no ivory stripe	215	395
____		(C) Gray, red trim	195	350
	252	Electric Locomotive 0-4-0 (0), *26–32*		
____		(A) Peacock or olive green	85	130
____		(B) Terra-cotta or yellow-orange	115	220
	252E	Electric Locomotive 0-4-0 (0), *33–35*		
____		(A) Terra-cotta	145	250
____		(B) Yellow-orange	125	205

		Good	Exc	
253	Electric Locomotive 0-4-0 (O), *24–32*			
	(A) Maroon	180	430	____
	(B) Dark green	105	250	____
	(C) Mojave	105	235	____
	(D) Terra-cotta	180	430	____
	(E) Peacock	95	195	____
	(F) Red	210	475	____
253E	Electric Locomotive 0-4-0 (O), *31–36*			
	(A) Green	150	205	____
	(B) Terra-cotta	190	305	____
254	Electric Locomotive 0-4-0 (O), *24–32*	240	340	____
254E	Electric Locomotive 0-4-0 (O), *27–34*	180	270	____
255E	2-4-2 Locomotive (O), *35–36*	485	1000	____
256	Electric Locomotive 0-4-4-0 (O), *24–30**			
	(A) Rubber-stamped lettering	470	1175	____
	(B) no outline around Lionel	425	770	____
	(C) Lionel Lines and No. 256 on brass	450	1050	____
257	2-4-0 Locomotive (O), *30–35 u*			
	(A) Black tender	145	300	____
	(B) Black crackle-finish tender	240	435	____
258	2-4-0 Locomotive, early (O), *30–35 u*			
	(A) 4-wheel 257 Tender	85	170	____
	(B) 8-wheel 258 Tender	100	195	____
258	2-4-2 Locomotive, late (O), *41 u*			
	(A) Black	60	100	____
	(B) Gunmetal	85	135	____
259	2-4-2 Locomotive (O), *32*	70	135	____
259E	2-4-2 Locomotive (O), *33–42*	80	165	____
259T	Tender	15	30	____
260E	2-4-2 Locomotive (O), *30–35**			
	(A) Black body, green or black frame	385	475	____
	(B) Dark gunmetal body and frame	440	640	____
261	2-4-2 Locomotive (O), *31*	125	210	____
261E	2-4-2 Locomotive (O), *35*	190	285	____
262	2-4-2 Locomotive (O), *31–32*	185	320	____
262E	2-4-2 Locomotive (O), *33–36*			
	(A) Gloss black, copper and brass trim	110	210	____
	(B) Satin black, nickel trim	125	260	____
263E	2-4-2 Locomotive (O), *36–39**			
	(A) Gunmetal gray	315	610	____
	(B) 2-tone blue, from Blue Comet	415	950	____
263W	Tender, gunmetal	90	200	____

			Good	Exc
264E		2-4-2 Locomotive (O), *35–36*		
____		(A) Red, Red Comet	135	295
____		(B) Black	220	380
265E		2-4-2 Locomotive (O), *35–40*		
____		(A) Black or gunmetal	170	330
____		(B) Light blue, Blue Streak	460	800
____		(B) Tender	30	55
____	**267E/W**	Set: 616, 617 (2), 618, *35–41*	275	560
____	**270**	Bridge, 10" long (O), *31–42*	20	50
____	**270**	Lighting Set, *15–23*		NRS
____	**271**	270 Bridges, set of 2, *31–33, 35–40*	65	150
____	**271**	Lighting Set, *15–23*		NRS
____	**272**	270 Bridges, set of 3, *31–33, 35–40*	60	165
____	**280**	Bridge, 14" long (std), *31–42*	50	115
____	**281**	280 Bridges, set of 2, *31–33, 35–40*	90	205
____	**282**	280 Bridges, set of 3, *31–33, 35–40*	105	265
____	**289E**	2-4-2 Locomotive (O), *37 u*	120	305
____	**300**	Electric Trolley Car (2⅞"), *01–05*	2000	3600
	300	Hellgate Bridge (std), *28–42**		
____		(A) Cream towers, green truss	800	1350
____		(B) Ivory towers, aluminum truss	765	1600
____	**303**	Summer Trolley, *10–13*	1500	3150
____	**308**	Signs, set of 5 (O), *40–42*	30	70
____	**309**	Electric Trolley Trailer (2⅞"), *01–05*	2500	4050
	309	Pullman Car (std), *26–39*		
____		(A) Maroon body and roof, mojave windows	100	160
____		(B) Mojave body and roof, maroon windows	100	160
____		(C) Light brown body, dark brown roof	120	190
____		(D) Medium blue body, dark blue roof	170	280
____		(E) Apple green body, dark green roof	170	280
____		(F) Pale blue body, silver roof	100	185
____		(G) Maroon body, terra-cotta roof	130	195
____	**310**	Rails and Ties, complete section (2⅞"), *01–02*	5	15
	310	Baggage Car (std), *26–39*		
____		(A) Maroon body and roof, mojave windows	100	160
____		(B) Mojave body and roof, maroon windows	85	160
____		(C) Light brown body, dark brown roof	115	185
____		(D) Medium blue body, dark blue roof	170	280
____		(E) Apple green body, dark green roof	170	280
____		(F) Pale blue body, silver roof	100	175

		Good	Exc

		Good	Exc
312	Observation Car (std), *24–39*		
	(A) Maroon body and roof, mojave windows	100	160 ____
	(B) Mojave body and roof, maroon windows	85	160 ____
	(C) Light brown body, dark brown roof	120	185 ____
	(D) Medium blue body, dark blue roof	170	280 ____
	(E) Apple green body, dark green roof	170	280 ____
	(F) Pale blue body, silver roof	100	175 ____
	(G) Maroon body, terra-cotta roof	130	195 ____
313	Bascule Bridge (O), *40–42*		
	(A) Silver bridge	235	500 ____
	(B) Gray bridge	250	590 ____
314	Girder Bridge (O), *40–42*	20	40 ____
315	Illuminated Trestle Bridge (O), *40–42*	30	80 ____
316	Trestle Bridge (O), *40–42*	25	50 ____
318	Electric Locomotive 0-4-0 (std), *24–32*		
	(A) Gray, dark gray, or mojave	150	250 ____
	(B) Pea green	150	250 ____
	(C) State brown	250	395 ____
318E	Electric Locomotive 0-4-0, *26–35*		
	(A) Gray, mojave, or pea green	150	250 ____
	(B) State brown	275	440 ____
	(C) Black	550	1275 ____
319	Pullman Car (std), *24–27*	105	175 ____
320	Baggage Car (std), *25–27*	100	175 ____
320	Switch and Signal (2⅞"), *02–05*		NRS ____
322	Observation Car (std), *24–27, 29–30 u*	100	175 ____
330	90-degree Crossing (2⅞"), *02–05*		NRS ____
332	Baggage Car (std), *26–33*		
	(A) Red body and roof, cream doors	80	120 ____
	(B) Peacock body and roof, orange doors	75	115 ____
	(C) Gray body and roof, maroon doors	75	115 ____
	(D) Olive green body and roof, red doors	90	145 ____
	(E) State brown body, dark brown roof	190	430 ____
337	Pullman Car (std), *25–32*		
	(A) Red body and roof, cream doors	95	190 ____
	(B) Mojave body and roof, maroon doors	95	190 ____
	(C) Olive green body and roof, red doors	105	225 ____
	(D) Olive green body and roof, maroon doors	95	190 ____
	(E) Pea green body and roof, cream doors	210	500 ____
338	Observation Car (std), *25–32*		
	(A) Red body and roof, cream doors	95	190 ____
	(B) Mojave body and roof, maroon doors	95	190 ____
	(C) Olive green body and roof, red doors	105	225 ____
	(D) Olive green body and roof, maroon doors	95	190 ____

			Good	Exc
339		Pullman Car (std), *25–33*		
___		(A) Peacock body and roof, orange doors	55	90
___		(B) Gray body and roof, maroon doors	55	100
___		(C) State brown body, dark brown roof	135	380
___		(D) Peacock body, dark green roof	75	130
___		(E) Mojave body, maroon roof and doors	145	230
___	**340**	Suspension Bridge (2⅞"), *02–05**		NRS
	341	Observation Car (std), *25–33*		
___		(A) Peacock body and roof, orange doors	50	70
___		(B) Gray body and roof, maroon doors	50	70
___		(C) State brown body, dark brown roof	75	160
___		(D) Peacock body, dark green roof	65	95
___		(E) Mojave body, maroon roof and doors	135	165
___	**350**	Track Bumper (2⅞"), *02–05*	225	550
___	**380**	Elevated Pillars (2⅞"), *04–05**	30	70
___	**380**	Electric Locomotive 0-4-0 (std), *23–27*	310	440
	380E	Electric Locomotive 0-4-0 (std), *26–29*		
___		(A) Mojave	445	630
___		(B) Maroon	295	400
___		(C) Dark green	370	460
___	**381**	Electric Locomotive 4-4-4 (std), *28–29**	1600	2100
	381E	Electric Locomotive 4-4-4 (std), *28–36**		
___		(A) State green, apple green subframe	1500	2500
___		(B) State green, red subframe	1900	3250
___	**381U**	Electric Locomotive 4-4-4 Kit (std), *28–29*	1600	4100
___	**384**	2-4-0 Locomotive (std), *30–32**	415	730
___	**384E**	2-4-0 Locomotive (std), *30–32**	425	650
___	**385E**	2-4-2 Locomotive (std), *33–39**	370	670
___	**390**	2-4-2 Locomotive (std), *29**	460	820
	390E	2-4-2 Locomotive (std), *29–31**		
___		(A) Black, with or without orange stripe	460	690
___		(B) 2-tone blue, cream-orange stripe	650	1050
___		(C) 2-tone green, orange or green stripe	990	2050
	392E	4-4-2 Locomotive (std), *32–39**		
___		(A) Black, 384 Tender	750	1250
___		(B) Black, large 12-wheel tender	1050	1850
___		(C) Gunmetal gray	1000	1800
___	**400**	Express Trail Car (2⅞"), *03–05**	3500	5850
	400E	4-4-4 Locomotive (std), *31–39**		
___		(A) Black	1400	2150
___		(B) Blue	1550	2350
___		(C) Gunmetal or light blue	1650	2800
___		(D) Black crackle finish	1600	3500

PREWAR 1901-1942

		Good	Exc	
402	Electric Locomotive 0-4-4-0 (std), *23–27*	365	570	___
402E	Electric Locomotive 0-4-4-0 (std), *26–29*	345	550	___
404	Summer Trolley (std), *10*		NRS	___
408E	Electric Locomotive 0-4-4-0 (std), *27–36**			
	(A) Apple green or mojave, red pilots	770	980	___
	(B) State brown, brown pilots	2000	3000	___
	(C) State green, red pilots	2000	3800	___
412	California Pullman Car (std), *29–35**			
	(A) Light green body, dark green roof	590	1750	___
	(B) Light brown body, dark brown roof	620	2100	___
413	Colorado Pullman Car (std), *29–35**			
	(A) Light green body, dark green roof	590	1750	___
	(B) Light brown body, dark brown roof	620	2100	___
414	Illinois Pullman Car (std), *29–35**			
	(A) Light green body, dark green roof	590	1750	___
	(B) Light brown body, dark brown roof	620	2050	___
416	New York Observation Car (std), *29–35**			
	(A) Light green body, dark green roof	590	1750	___
	(B) Light brown body, dark brown roof	620	2100	___
418	Pullman Car (std), *23–32**	225	320	___
419	Combination (std), *23–32**	190	280	___
420	Faye Pullman Car (std), *30–40**			
	(A) Brass trim	485	900	___
	(B) Nickel trim	500	1200	___
421	Westphal Pullman Car (std), *30–40**			
	(A) Brass trim	500	900	___
	(B) Nickel trim	500	1200	___
422	Tempel Observation Car (std), *30–40**			
	(A) Brass trim	485	900	___
	(B) Nickel trim	500	1200	___
424	Liberty Bell Pullman Car (std), *31–40**			
	(A) Brass trim	350	530	___
	(B) Nickel trim	385	650	___
425	Stephen Girard Pullman Car (std), *31–40**			
	(A) Brass trim	350	530	___
	(B) Nickel trim	385	650	___
426	Coral Isle Observation Car (std), *31–40**			
	(A) Brass trim	350	530	___
	(B) Nickel trim	385	650	___
428	Pullman Car (std), *26–30**			
	(A) Dark green body and roof	250	385	___
	(B) Orange body and roof, apple green windows	390	890	___

		Good	Exc
429	Combine Car (std), *26–30**		
___	(A) Dark green body and roof	250	385
___	(B) Orange body and roof, apple green windows	390	890
430	Observation Car (std), *26–30**		
___	(A) Dark green body and roof	250	385
___	(B) Orange body and roof, apple green windows	390	890
431	Diner (std), *27–32**		
___	(A) Mojave body, screw-mounted roof	350	540
___	(B) Mojave body, hinged roof	465	720
___	(C) Dark green body, orange windows	410	720
___	(D) Orange body, apple green windows	410	720
___	(E) Apple green body, red windows	410	720
___ **435**	Power Station, *26–38**	215	400
436	Power Station, *26–37**		
___	(A) Power Station plate	135	265
___	(B) Edison Service plate	270	610
___ **437**	Switch Signal Tower, *26–37**	190	430
438	Signal Tower, *27–39**		
___	(A) Mojave base, orange house	185	325
___	(B) Black base, white house	325	640
___ **439**	Panel Board, *28–42**	85	145
___ **440/0440**	Signal Bridge, *32–35**	180	470
___ **440C**	Panel Board, *32–42*	90	145
___ **441**	Weighing Station (std), *32–36*	495	1325
___ **442**	Landscaped Diner, *38–42*	120	215
___ **444**	Roundhouse (std), *32–35**	1350	2850
___ **444-18**	Roundhouse Clip, *33*		NRS
450	Electric Locomotive 0-4-0, Macy's (O), *30 u*		
___	(A) Red, black frame	295	700
___	(B) Apple green, dark green frame	415	880
___ **450**	Set: 450, matching 605, 606 (2), *30 u*	750	1800
___ **490**	Observation Car (std), *23–32**	190	255
___ **500**	Electric Derrick Car (2⅞"), *03–04**	5000	6750
511	Flatcar (std), *27–40*		
___	(A) Dark green	65	95
___	(B) Medium green	75	165
512	Gondola (std), *27–39*		
___	(A) Peacock	35	60
___	(B) Light green	50	95
513	Cattle Car (std), *27–38*		
___	(A) Olive green, orange roof	70	165
___	(B) Orange, pea green roof	60	110
___	(C) Cream, maroon roof	90	250

		Good	Exc	
514	Boxcar (std), *29–40*			
	(A) Cream, orange roof	90	155	____
	(B) Yellow, brown roof	115	285	____
514	Refrigerator Car, ivory or white, peacock roof, (std), *27–28*	240	400	____
514R	Refrigerator Car (std), *29–40*			
	(A) Ivory, peacock roof	140	190	____
	(B) White, light blue roof	350	540	____
515	Tank Car (std), *27–40*			
	(A) Terra-cotta	90	145	____
	(B) Ivory	105	185	____
	(C) Aluminum	90	175	____
	(D) Orange, red Shell decal	340	750	____
516	Hopper Car (std), *28–40*			
	(A) Red	170	240	____
	(B) Red, rubber-stamped data	200	300	____
	(C) Light red, nickel trim	200	325	____
517	Caboose (std), *27–40*			
	(A) Pea green body, red roof	50	85	____
	(B) Red body and roof	105	155	____
	(C) Red body, black roof, orange windows	355	640	____
520	Floodlight Car (std), *31–40*			
	(A) Terra-cotta base	110	210	____
	(B) Green base	110	240	____
529	Pullman Car (O), *26–32*			
	(A) Olive green body and roof	25	45	____
	(B) Terra-cotta body and roof	25	60	____
530	Observation Car (O), *26–32*			
	(A) Olive green body and roof	25	45	____
	(B) Terra-cotta body and roof	25	60	____
550	Miniature Figures, boxed (std), *32–36**	175	455	____
551	Engineer (std), *32*	25	45	____
552	Conductor (std), *32*	20	40	____
553	Porter with stool (std), *32*	25	50	____
554	Male Passenger (std), *32*	25	45	____
555	Female Passenger (std), *32*	25	45	____
556	Red Cap with suitcase (std), *32*	25	65	____
600	Derrick Trailer (2⅞"), *03–04**	5000	8550	____
600	Pullman Car, early (O), *15–23*			
	(A) Dark green	65	170	____
	(B) Maroon or brown	45	85	____
600	Pullman Car, late (O), *33–42*			
	(A) Light red or gray, red roof	50	90	____
	(B) Light blue, aluminum roof	70	120	____

		Good	Exc
601	Observation Car, late (O), *33–42*		
___	(A) Light red body and roof	50	85
___	(B) Light gray, red roof	50	90
___	(C) Light blue body, aluminum roof	70	120
___ **601**	Pullman Car, early (O), *15–23*	50	70
602	Lionel Lines Baggage Car, late (O), *33–42*		
___	(A) Light red or gray, red roof	60	110
___	(B) Light blue, aluminum roof	90	150
___ **602**	NYC Baggage Car (O), *15–23*	30	45
___ **602**	Observation Car (O), *22 u*	30	45
___ **603**	Pullman Car, early (O), *22 u*	40	70
___ **603**	Pullman Car, later (O), *20–25*	20	45
603	Pullman Car, latest (O), *31–36*		
___	(A) Light red body and roof	45	85
___	(B) Red body, black roof	35	60
___	(C) Stephen Girard green body, dark green roof	35	60
___	(D) Maroon body and roof, Macy Special	60	125
___ **604**	Observation Car, later (O), *20–25*	35	60
604	Observation Car, latest (O), *31–36*		
___	(A) Light red body and roof	45	85
___	(B) Red body, black roof	35	60
___	(C) Yellow-orange body, terra-cotta roof	35	60
___	(D) Stephen Girard green body, dark green roof	35	60
___	(E) Maroon body and roof	70	150
605	Pullman Car (O), *25–32*		
___	(A) Gray, Lionel Lines	85	170
___	(B) Gray, Illinois Central	85	170
___	(C) Red, Lionel Lines	170	255
___	(D) Red, Illinois Central	255	340
___	(E) Orange, Lionel Lines	170	255
___	(F) Orange, Illinois Central	300	430
___	(G) Olive green, Lionel Lines	255	340
606	Observation Car (O), *25–32*		
___	(A) Gray, Lionel Lines	130	215
___	(B) Gray, Illinois Central	90	170
___	(C) Red, Lionel Lines	170	255
___	(D) Red, Illinois Central	255	340
___	(E) Orange, Lionel Lines	170	255
___	(F) Orange, Illinois Central	170	255
___	(G) Olive green, Lionel Lines	255	340
607	Pullman Car (O), *26–27*		
___	(A) Peacock, Lionel Lines	50	70
___	(B) Peacock, Illinois Central	75	115
___	(C) 2-tone green, Lionel Lines	50	75
___	(D) Red, Lionel Lines	75	110

		Good	Exc	
608	Observation Car (O), *26–37*			
	(A) Peacock, Lionel Lines	50	70	____
	(B) Peacock, Illinois Central	75	115	____
	(C) 2-tone green, Lionel Lines	50	75	____
	(D) Red, Lionel Lines	75	110	____
609	Pullman Car (O), *37*	60	85	____
610	Pullman Car, early (O), *15–25*			
	(A) Dark green body and roof	50	65	____
	(B) Maroon body and roof	60	95	____
	(C) Mojave body and roof	60	95	____
610	Pullman Car, late (O), *26–30*			
	(A) Olive green body and roof	65	80	____
	(B) Mojave body and roof	55	80	____
	(C) Terra-cotta body, maroon roof	100	155	____
	(D) Pea green body and roof	70	115	____
	(E) Light blue body, aluminum roof	130	260	____
	(F) Light red body, aluminum-painted roof	100	155	____
611	Observation Car (O), *37*	55	80	____
612	Observation Car, early (O), *15–25*			
	(A) Dark green body and roof	40	60	____
	(B) Maroon body and roof	70	90	____
	(C) Mojave body and roof	70	90	____
612	Observation Car, late (O), *26–30*			
	(A) Olive green body and roof	55	80	____
	(B) Mojave body and roof	55	80	____
	(C) Terra-cotta body, maroon roof	100	155	____
	(D) Pea green body and roof	70	115	____
	(E) Light blue body, aluminum roof	130	260	____
	(F) Light red body, aluminum-painted roof	100	155	____
613	Pullman Car (O), *31–40**			
	(A) Terra-cotta body, maroon/terra-cotta roof	85	195	____
	(B) Light red body, light red/aluminum roof	175	350	____
	(C) Blue, two-tone blue roof	115	225	____
614	Observation Car (O), *31–40**			
	(A) Terra-cotta body, maroon/terra-cotta roof	100	190	____
	(B) Light red body, light red/aluminum roof	175	350	____
	(C) Blue, two-tone blue roof	115	225	____
615	Baggage Car (O), *33–40**	150	260	____
616E/W	Diesel only (O), *35–41*	90	215	____
616E/W	Set: 616, 617 (2), 618	225	570	____
617	Coach (O), *35–41*			
	(A) Blue and white	55	85	____
	(B) Chrome, gunmetal skirts	55	85	____
	(C) Chrome, chrome skirts	55	85	____
	(D) Silver-painted	55	85	____

		Good	Exc
618	Observation Car (0), *35–41*		
___	(A) Blue and white	55	85
___	(B) Chrome, gunmetal skirts	55	85
___	(C) Chrome, chrome skirts	55	85
___	(D) Silver-painted	55	85
619	Combine Car (0), *36–38*		
___	(A) Blue, white windows band	100	205
___	(B) Chrome, chrome skirts	100	205
___ **620**	Floodlight Car (0), *37–42*	50	85
629	Pullman Car (0), *24–32*		
___	(A) Dark green body and roof	25	40
___	(B) Orange body and roof	25	40
___	(C) Red body and roof	20	35
___	(D) Light red body and roof	30	55
630	Observation Car, *24–32*		
___	(A) Dark green body and roof	25	40
___	(B) Orange body and roof	25	40
___	(C) Red body and roof	20	35
___	(D) Light red body and roof	30	55
___ **636W**	Diesel only (0), *36–39*	90	175
___ **636W**	Set: 636W, 637 (2), 638, *36–39*	375	640
___ **637**	Coach (0), *36–39*	70	105
___ **638**	Observation Car (0), *36–39*	70	105
___ **651**	Flatcar (0), *35–40*	30	65
___ **652**	Gondola (0), *35–40*	30	55
___ **653**	Hopper Car (0), *34–40*	35	65
654	Tank Car (0), *34–42*		
___	(A) Orange or aluminum	35	60
___	(B) Gray	40	75
655	Boxcar (0), *34–42*		
___	(A) Cream, maroon roof	35	60
___	(B) Cream, tuscan roof	45	75
656	Cattle Car (0), *35–40*		
___	(A) Light gray, vermilion roof	40	100
___	(B) Burnt orange, tuscan roof	70	125
657	Caboose (0), *34–42*		
___	(A) Red body and roof	20	35
___	(B) Red body, tuscan roof	25	40
___ **659**	Dump Car (0), *35–42*	40	90
___ **700**	Electric Locomotive 0-4-0 (0), *15–16*	360	690
___ **700E**	4-6-4 NYC Hudson "5344," scale (0), *37–42**	1400	2950
700K	4-6-4 Locomotive, unbuilt gray primer (0),		
___	*38–42*	4400	5950
___ **701**	0-6-0 PRR Locomotive "8976", *41*	900	2100

		Good	Exc	
701	Electric Locomotive 0-4-0 (O), *15–16*	390	660	___
702	Baggage Car (O), *17–21*	115	305	___
703	Electric Locomotive 4-4-4 (O), *15–16*	1400	2350	___
706	Electric Locomotive 0-4-0 (O), *15–16*	375	630	___
708	0-6-0 PRR Locomotive "8976" (O), *39–42**	1450	2850	___
710	Pullman Car (O), *24–34*			
	(A) Red, Lionel Lines	200	300	___
	(B) Orange, Lionel Lines	150	225	___
	(C) Orange, New York Central	175	225	___
	(D) Orange, Illinois Central	300	450	___
	(E) 2-tone blue, Lionel Lines	300	415	___
	(F) Orange, New York Central	200	260	___
711	Remote Control Switches, pair (O72), *35–42*	80	190	___
712	Observation Car (O), *24–34*			
	(A) Red, Lionel Lines	185	355	___
	(B) Orange, Lionel Lines	140	265	___
	(C) Orange, New York Central	160	310	___
	(D) Orange, Illinois Central	280	530	___
	(E) 2-tone blue, Lionel Lines	280	485	___
714	Boxcar (O), *40–42**	350	610	___
714K	Boxcar, unbuilt (O), *40–42*	220	480	___
715	Tank Car (O), *40–42**			
	(A) SEPS 8124 decal	340	610	___
	(B) SUNX 715 decal	435	880	___
715K	Tank Car, unbuilt (O), *40–42*	250	530	___
716	Hopper Car (O), *40–42**	290	400	___
716K	Hopper Car, unbuilt (O), *40–42*	350	730	___
717	Caboose (O), *40–42**	340	510	___
717K	Caboose, unbuilt (O), *40–42*	275	590	___
720	90-degree Crossing (O72), *35–42*	20	40	___
721	Manual Switches, pair (O72), *35–42*	50	105	___
730	90-degree Crossing (O72), *35–42*	20	40	___
731	Remote Control Switches, pair, T-rail (O72), *35–42*	80	135	___
751E/W	Set: 752, 753 (2), 754 (O), *34–41**	640	1050	___
752E	Diesel only (O), *34–41**			
	(A) Yellow and brown	170	355	___
	(B) Aluminum	145	340	___
753	Coach (O), *36–41*			
	(A) Yellow and brown	85	185	___
	(B) Aluminum	75	180	___
754	Observation Car (O), *36–41*			
	(A) Yellow and brown	80	185	___
	(B) Aluminum	75	180	___

			Good	Exc
____	**760**	Curved Track, 16 pieces, (072), *35–42*	40	80
____	**761**	Curved Track (072), *34–42*	1	2
____	**762**	Straight Track (072), *34–42*	1	2
____	**762S**	Insulated Straight Track (072), *34–42*	2	5
	763E	4-6-4 Locomotive (0), *37–42*		
____		(A) Gunmetal, 263 or 2263W Tender	1000	2125
____		(B) Gunmetal, 2226X or 2226WX Tender	1150	2950
____		(C) Black, 2226WX Tender	965	2650
____	**771**	Curved Track, T-rail (072), *35–42*	3	10
____	**772**	Straight Track, T-rail (072), *35–42*	5	20
____	**772S**	Insulated Straight Track, T-rail (072), *35–42*	15	30
____	**773**	Fishplate Set, 50 plates (072), *36–42*	15	30
____	**782**	Hiawatha Combine Car (0), *35–41**	230	380
____	**783**	Hiawatha Coach (0), *35–41**	140	290
____	**784**	Hiawatha Observation Car (0), *35–41**	205	445
____	**792**	Rail Chief Combine Car (0), *37–41**	215	580
____	**793**	Rail Chief Coach (0), *37–41**	290	800
____	**794**	Rail Chief Observation Car (0), *37–41**	250	800
____	**800**	Boxcar (2⅞"), *04–05**	2500	4050
	800	Boxcar (0), *15–26*		
____		(A) Light orange body, brown-maroon roof	45	70
____		(B) Orange body and roof, PRR	25	45
____	**801**	Caboose (0), *15–26*	30	50
____	**802**	Stock Car (0), *15–26*	40	60
____	**803**	Hopper Car, early (0), *23–28*	25	55
____	**803**	Hopper Car, late (0), *29–34*	30	55
____	**804**	Tank Car (0), *23–28*	20	45
	805	Boxcar (0), *27–34*		
____		(A) Pea green, terra-cotta roof	35	55
____		(B) Pea green, maroon roof	45	115
____		(C) Orange, maroon roof	45	95
	806	Stock Car (0), *27–34*		
____		(A) Pea green, terra-cotta roof	40	75
____		(B) Orange, various color roofs	35	50
	807	Caboose (0), *27–40*		
____		(A) Peacock body, dark green roof	20	35
____		(B) Red body, peacock roof	20	40
____		(C) Light red body and roof	20	40
	809	Dump Car (0), *31–41*		
____		(A) Orange bin	40	55
____		(B) Green bin	40	85
	810	Crane Car (0), *30–42*		
____		(A) Terra-cotta cab, maroon roof	170	270
____		(B) Cream cab, vermilion roof	130	205

		Good	Exc
811	Flatcar (O), *26–40*		
	(A) Maroon	40	70 ____
	(B) Aluminum	50	100 ____
812	Gondola (O), *26–42*	40	70 ____
812T	Tool Set: pick, shovel, hammer, *30–41*	40	105 ____
813	Stock Car (O), *26–42*		
	(A) Orange body, pea green roof	65	145 ____
	(B) Orange body, maroon roof	55	135 ____
	(C) Cream body, maroon roof	100	225 ____
	(D) Tuscan body and roof	800	1600 ____
814	Boxcar (O), *26–42*		
	(A) Cream, orange roof	50	145 ____
	(B) Cream, maroon roof	115	140 ____
	(C) Yellow, brown roof	110	120 ____
814R	Refrigerator Car (O), *29–42*		
	(A) Ivory, peacock roof	100	200 ____
	(B) White, light blue roof	105	230 ____
	(C) Flat white, brown roof	600	900 ____
815	Tank Car (O), *26–42*		
	(A) Pea green, maroon frame	250	510 ____
	(B) Pea green, black frame	70	155 ____
	(C) Aluminum, black frame	50	100 ____
	(D) Orange-yellow, black frame	150	255 ____
816	Hopper Car (O), *27–42*		
	(A) Olive green	85	155 ____
	(B) Red body	65	140 ____
	(C) Black body	370	680 ____
817	Caboose (O), *26–42*		
	(A) Peacock body, dark green roof	45	70 ____
	(B) Red body, peacock roof	45	80 ____
	(C) Light red body and roof	45	80 ____
820	Boxcar (O), *15–26*		
	(A) Orange, Illinois Central	40	80 ____
	(B) Orange, Union Pacific	50	105 ____
820	Floodlight Car (O), *31–42*		
	(A) Terra-cotta	100	180 ____
	(B) Green	100	175 ____
	(C) Light green	105	180 ____
821	Stock Car (O), *15–16, 25–26*	45	85 ____
822	Caboose (O), *15–26*	35	65 ____
831	Flatcar (O), *27–34*	20	45 ____
840	Industrial Power Station, *28–40**	1200	3050 ____
900	Ammunition Car (O), *17–21*	120	340 ____
900	Box Trail Car (2⅞"), *04–05**	2000	3600 ____
901	Gondola (O), *19–27*	25	50 ____

			Good	Exc
___	**902**	Gondola (0), *27–34*	25	45
___	**910**	Grove of Trees, *32–42*	70	180
___	**911**	Country Estate, *32–42*	195	440
___	**912**	Suburban Home	300	620
___	**913**	Landscaped Bungalow, *40–42*	140	285
___	**914**	Park Landscape, *32–35*	90	205
___	**915**	Tunnel, 65" or 60" long, *32–33, 35*	160	435
___	**916**	Tunnel, 29" long, *35*	95	180
___	**917**	Scenic Hillside, 34" x 15", *32–36*	90	205
___	**918**	Scenic Hillside, 30" x 10", *32–36*	90	205
___	**919**	Park Grass, cloth bag, *32–42*	10	20
___	**920**	Village, *32–33*	600	1600
___	**921**	Scenic Park, 3 pieces, *32–33*	980	2600
___	**921C**	Park Center, *32–33*	400	1050
___	**922**	Terrace, *32–36*	90	255
___	**923**	Tunnel, 40" long, *33–42*	125	225
___	**924**	Tunnel, 30" long (072), *35–42*	50	135
___	**925**	Lubricant, *35–42*	25	120
___	**927**	Flag Plot, *37–42*	70	135
___	**1000**	Passenger Car (2⅞"), *05**	4500	6750
___	**1000**	Trolley Trailer (std), *10–16*	1400	2250
___	**1010**	Electric Locomotive 0-4-0, Winner Lines (0), *31–32*	90	160
___	**1010**	Interurban Trailer (std), *10–16*	1000	1800
___	**1011**	Pullman Car, Winner Lines (0), *31–32*	45	75
___	**1012**	Station, *32*	40	70
___	**1015**	0-4-0 Locomotive (0), *31–32*	100	205
___	**1017**	Winner Station, *33*	25	70
___	**1019**	Observation Car (0), *31–32*	50	70
___	**1020**	Baggage Car (0), *31–32*	65	110
___	**1021**	90-degree Crossover (027), *32–42*	1	5
___	**1022**	Tunnel, 18" long (0), *35–42*	15	30
___	**1023**	Tunnel, 19" long, *34–42*	20	40
___	**1024**	Switches, pair (027), *37–42*	5	15
___	**1025**	Bumper (027), *40–42*	15	25
___	**1027**	Transformer Station, *34*	50	115
___	**1028**	Transformer, 40 watts, *39*	3	10
___	**1029**	Transformer, 25 watts, *36*	5	20
___	**1030**	Electric Locomotive 0-4-0 (0), *32*	75	135
___	**1030**	Transformer, 40 watts, *35–38*	6	25
___	**1035**	0-4-0 Locomotive (0), *32*	75	115
___	**1037**	Transformer, 40 watts, *40–42*	7	25
___	**1038**	Transformer, 30 watts, *40*	2	5
___	**1039**	Transformer, 35 watts, *37–40*	7	20

		Good	Exc	
1040	Transformer, 60 watts, *37–39*	10	30	____
1041	Transformer, 60 watts, *39–42*	15	30	____
1045	Watchman, *38–42*	30	65	____
1050	Passenger Car Trailer (2⅞"), *05**	5000	7200	____
1100	Summer Trolley Trailer (std), *10–13*		NRS	____
1100	Mickey Mouse Handcar, *35–37**			
	(A) Red base	405	640	____
	(B) Apple green base, orange shoes	500	880	____
	(C) Orange base	600	1225	____
1103	Peter Rabbit Handcar (O), *35–37**	330	820	____
1105	Santa Claus Handcar (O), *35–35**			
	(A) Red base	660	1050	____
	(B) Green base	720	1200	____
1107	Transformer Station, *33*	25	70	____
1107	Donald Duck Handcar (O), *36–37**			
	(A) White dog house, red roof	475	1200	____
	(B) White dog house, green roof	450	1100	____
	(C) Orange dog house, green roof	640	1850	____
1121	Switches, pair (027), *37–42*	15	35	____
1506L	0-4-0 Locomotive (O), *33–34*	95	125	____
1506M	0-4-0 Locomotive (O), *35*	250	430	____
1508	0-4-0 Commodore Vanderbilt with 1509 Mickey Mouse stoker Tender, *35*	420	690	____
1511	0-4-0 Locomotive (O), *36–37*	110	160	____
1512	Gondola (O), *31–33, 36–37*	25	50	____
1514	Boxcar (O), *31–37*	25	40	____
1515	Tank Car (O), *33–37*	25	40	____
1517	Caboose (O), *31–37*	25	40	____
1518	Mickey Mouse Circus Dining Car (O), *35*	120	260	____
1519	Mickey Mouse Band Car (O), *35*	120	260	____
1520	Mickey Mouse Circus Car (O), *35*	120	260	____
1536	Mickey Mouse Circus Set: 1508, 1509, 1518, 1519, 1520, *35*	770	1350	____
1550	Switches, for windup trains, pair, *33–37*	2	5	____
1555	90-degree Crossover, for windup trains, *33–37*	1	2	____
1560	Station, *33–37*	15	35	____
1569	Accessory Set, 8 pieces, *33–37*	35	70	____
1588	0-4-0 Locomotive (O), *36–37*	150	250	____
1630	Pullman Car (O), *38–42*			
	(A) Aluminum windows	35	70	____
	(B) Light gray windows	45	80	____
1631	Observation Car (O), *38–42*			
	(A) Aluminum windows	35	70	____
	(B) Light gray windows	45	80	____

			Good	Exc
____	**1651E**	Electric Locomotive 0-4-0 (O), *33*	130	240
____	**1661E**	2-4-0 Locomotive (O), *33*	75	160
____	**1662**	0-4-0 Locomotive (027), *40–42*	218	420
____	**1663**	0-4-0 Locomotive (027), *40–42*	200	385
	1664/E	2-4-2 Locomotive (027), *38–42*		
____		(A) Gunmetal	60	100
____		(B) Black	60	95
	1666/E	2-6-2 Locomotive (027), *38–42*		
____		(A) Gunmetal	115	170
____		(B) Black	95	145
	1668/E	2-6-2 Locomotive (027), *37–41*		
____		(A) Gunmetal	75	115
____		(B) Black	75	130
	1673	Coach (O), *36–37*		
____		(A) Aluminum windows	35	75
____		(B) Light gray windows	45	90
____	**1674**	Pullman Car (O), *36–37*	35	75
____	**1675**	Observation Car (O), *36–37*	30	70
	1677	Gondola (O), *33–35, 39–42*		
____		(A) Light blue, Ives	40	60
____		(B) Blue or red, Lionel	20	40
	1679	Boxcar (O), *33–42*		
____		(A) Cream, Ives	25	40
____		(B) Cream, Lionel	25	40
____		(C) Cream or yellow, Baby Ruth	20	40
	1680	Tank Car (O), *33–42*		
____		(A) Aluminum, Ives Tank Lines	60	95
____		(B) Aluminum, no Ives lettering	20	35
____		(C) Orange, Shell Oil	15	30
	1681	2-4-0 Locomotive (O), *34–35*		
____		(A) Black, red frame	55	120
____		(B) Red, red frame	110	145
	1681E	2-4-0 Locomotive (O), *34–35*		
____		(A) Black, red frame	65	130
____		(B) Red, red frame	130	165
	1682	Caboose (O), *33–42*		
____		(A) Vermilion, Ives	35	70
____		(B) Red or tuscan, Lionel	15	40
	1684	2-4-2 Locomotive (027), *41–42*		
____		(A) Black	45	70
____		(B) Gunmetal	45	70
	1685	Coach (O), *33–37 u*		
____		(A) Gray, maroon roof	240	495
____		(B) Red, maroon roof	170	335
____		(C) Blue, silver roof	170	315

		Good	Exc	
1686	Baggage Car (0), *33–37 u*			
	(A) Gray, maroon roof	240	495	____
	(B) Red, maroon roof	170	335	____
	(C) Blue, silver roof	170	315	____
1687	Observation Car (0), *33–37 u*			
	(A) Gray, maroon roof	170	315	____
	(B) Red, maroon roof	180	315	____
	(C) Blue, silver roof	170	315	____
1688/E	2-4-2 Locomotive (027), *36–46*	50	125	____
1689E	2-4-2 Locomotive (027), *36–37*			
	(A) Gunmetal	75	115	____
	(B) Black	60	100	____
1689T	Tender, black	15	30	____
1690	Pullman Car (0), *33–40*	35	60	____
1691	Observation Car (0), *33–40*	35	60	____
1692	Pullman Car (027), *39 u*	45	70	____
1693	Observation Car (027), *39 u*	45	70	____
1700E	Diesel, power unit only (027), *35–37*	45	70	____
1700E	Set: 1700, 1701 (2), 1702, *35–37 u*			
	(A) Aluminum and light red	140	250	____
	(B) Chrome and light red	140	250	____
	(C) Orange and gray	155	285	____
1701	Coach (027), *35–37*			
	(A) Chrome sides and roof	20	45	____
	(B) Silver sides and roof	30	55	____
	(C) Orange and gray	75	150	____
1702	Observation Car (027), *35–37*			
	(A) Chrome sides and roof	20	45	____
	(B) Silver sides and roof	30	55	____
	(C) Orange and gray	75	150	____
1703	Observation Car, hooked coupler, *35–37 u*	50	110	____
1717	Gondola (0), *33–40 u*	30	50	____
1717X	Gondola (0), *40 u*	25	50	____
1719	Boxcar (0), *33–40 u*	30	50	____
1719X	Boxcar (0), *41–42 u*	30	50	____
1722	Caboose (0), *33–42 u*	25	50	____
1722X	Caboose (0), *39–40 u*	25	40	____
1766	Pullman Car (std), *34–40**			
	(A) Terra-cotta, maroon roof, brass trim	300	650	____
	(B) Red, maroon roof, nickel trim	300	540	____
1767	Baggage Car (std), *34–40**			
	(A) Terra-cotta, maroon roof, brass trim	295	850	____
	(B) Red, maroon roof, nickel trim	295	700	____

			Good	Exc
1768		Observation Car (std), *34–40**		
____		(A) Terra-cotta, maroon roof, brass trim	300	650
____		(B) Red, maroon roof, nickel trim	300	540
____	**1811**	Pullman Car (O), *33–37*	35	70
____	**1812**	Observation Car (O), *33–37*	30	65
____	**1813**	Baggage Car (O), *33–37*	60	135
____	**1816/W**	Diesel (O), *35–37*	100	240
____	**1817**	Coach (O), *35–37*	25	50
____	**1818**	Observation Car (O), *35–37*	25	50
____	**1835E**	2-4-2 Locomotive (std), *34–39*	470	730
____	**1910**	Electric Locomotive 0-6-0, early (std), *10–11*	920	1550
____	**1910**	Electric Locomotive 0-6-0, late (std), *12*	550	1350
____	**1910**	Pullman Car (std), *09–10 u*	860	1800
____	**1911**	Electric Locomotive 0-4-0, early (std), *10–12*	860	1700
____	**1911**	Electric Locomotive 0-4-0, late (std), *13*	700	1100
____	**1911**	Electric Locomotive 0-4-4-0 Special (std), *11–12*	860	2500
	1912	Electric Locomotive 0-4-4-0 (std), *10–12**		
____		(A) New York, New Haven & Hartford	1550	3200
____		(B) New York Central Lines	1300	2700
____	**1912**	Electric Locomotive 0-4-4-0 Special (std), *11**	2500	4500
____	**2200**	Summer Trolley Trailer (std), *10–13*	1100	2250
____	**2203B**	Tender	40	80
____	**2224W**	Tender	55	115
____	**2225W**	Tender	30	60
____	**2228B**	Tender	140	280
____	**2235W**	Tender	25	50
____	**2600**	Pullman Car (O), *38–42*	80	155
____	**2601**	Observation Car (O), *38–42*	60	115
____	**2602**	Baggage Car (O), *38–42*	90	185
	2613	Pullman Car (O), *38–42**		
____		(A) Blue, 2-tone blue roof	100	300
____		(B) State green, 2-tone green roof	200	440
	2614	Observation Car (O), *38–42**		
____		(A) Blue, 2-tone blue roof	100	300
____		(B) State green, 2-tone green roof	200	440
	2615	Baggage Car (O), *38–42**		
____		(A) Blue, 2-tone blue roof	115	300
____		(B) State green, 2-tone green roof	200	420
____	**2620**	Floodlight Car (O), *38–42*	65	100
	2623	Pullman Car (O), *41–42*		
____		(A) Irvington	175	335
____		(B) Manhattan	165	310
____	**2624**	Pullman Car (O), *41–42*	750	1700
____	**2630**	Pullman Car (O), *38–42*	30	70

		Good	Exc
2631	Observation Car (O), *38–42*	30	70 ____
2640	Pullman Car, illuminated (O), *38–42*		
	(A) Light blue, aluminum roof	30	70 ____
	(B) State green, dark green roof	30	70 ____
2641	Observation Car, illuminated (O), *38–42*		
	(A) Light blue, aluminum roof	30	70 ____
	(B) State green, dark green roof	30	70 ____
2642	Pullman Car (O), *41–42*	30	70 ____
2643	Observation Car (O), *41–42*	30	65 ____
2651	Flatcar (O), *38–42*	30	50 ____
2652	Gondola (O), *38–41*	25	65 ____
2653	Hopper Car (O), *38–42*		
	(A) Stephen Girard green	35	70 ____
	(B) Black	60	130 ____
2654	Tank Car (O), *38–42*		
	(A) Aluminum, Sunoco	35	60 ____
	(B) Orange, Shell	35	60 ____
	(C) Light gray, Sunoco	40	70 ____
2655	Boxcar (O), *38–42*		
	(A) Cream, maroon roof	35	65 ____
	(B) Cream, tuscan roof	40	70 ____
2656	Stock Car (O), *38–41*		
	(A) Light gray, red roof	45	75 ____
	(B) Burnt orange, tuscan roof	75	115 ____
2657	Caboose (O), *40–41*	30	45 ____
2657X	Caboose (O), *40–41*	25	40 ____
2659	Dump Car (O), *38–41*	40	70 ____
2660	Crane Car (O), *38–42*	85	165 ____
2672	Caboose (O27), *41–42*	20	50 ____
2677	Gondola (O27), *39–41*	25	40 ____
2679	Boxcar (O27), *38–42*	15	30 ____
2680	Tank Car (O27), *38–42*		
	(A) Aluminum, Sunoco	15	40 ____
	(B) Orange, Shell	15	40 ____
2682	Caboose (O27), *38–42*	15	30 ____
2682X	Caboose (O27), *38–42*	20	35 ____
2689T	Tender	15	35 ____
2689W	Tender	35	50 ____
2717	Gondola (O), *38–42 u*	20	40 ____
2719	Boxcar (O), *38–42 u*	30	50 ____
2722	Caboose (O), *38–42 u*	25	50 ____
2755	Tank Car (O), *41–42*	70	130 ____
2757	Caboose (O), *41–42*	25	45 ____
2757X	Caboose (O), *41–42*	25	40 ____
2758	Automobile Boxcar (O), *41–42*	35	60 ____

		Good	Exc
____ 2810	Crane Car (O), *38–42*	145	210
____ 2811	Flatcar (O), *38–42*	50	95
2812	Gondola (O), *38–42*		
____	(A) Green	40	85
____	(B) Dark orange	45	95
____ 2813	Stock Car (O), *38–42*	120	225
2814	Boxcar (O), *38–42*		
____	(A) Cream, maroon roof	85	150
____	(B) Orange, brown roof, rubber-stamped lettering	200	700
2814R	Refrigerator Car (O), *38–42*		
____	(A) White, light blue roof, nickel plates	140	260
____	(B) White, brown roof, no plates	375	660
2815	Tank Car (O), *38–42*		
____	(A) Aluminum	85	165
____	(B) Orange	135	215
2816	Hopper Car (O), *35–42*		
____	(A) Red	100	190
____	(B) Black	110	220
2817	Caboose (O), *36–42*		
____	(A) Light red body and roof	78	140
____	(B) Flat red body, tuscan roof	115	180
2820	Floodlight Car (O), *38–42*		
____	(A) Stamped nickel searchlights	110	205
____	(B) Gray die-cast searchlights	120	260
____ 2954	Boxcar (O), *40–42**	145	350
2955	Sunoco Tank Car (O), *40–42**		
____	(A) Shell decal	225	500
____	(B) Sunoco decal	340	690
____ 2956	Hopper Car (O), *40–42**	160	400
____ 2957	Caboose (O), *40–42**	70	260
____ 3300	Summer Trolley Trailer (std), *10–13*	1400	2250
____ 3651	Operating Lumber Car (O), *39–42*	25	55
____ 3652	Operating Gondola (O), *39–42*	35	75
____ 3659	Operating Dump Car (O), *39–42*	20	40
____ 3811	Operating Lumber Car (O), *39–42*	35	90
____ 3814	Operating Merchandise Car (O), *39–42*	90	195
____ 3859	Operating Dump Car (O), *38–42*	45	90

Other Transformers and Motors

		Good	Exc	
A	Miniature Motor, *04*	50	95	___
A	Transformer, 40, 60 watts, *21–37*	10	25	___
B	New Departure Motor, *06–16*	75	135	___
B	Transformer, 50, 75 watts, *16–38*	7	25	___
C	New Departure Motor, *06–16*	100	180	___
D	New Departure Motor, *06–14*	100	180	___
E	New Departure Motor, *06–14*	100	180	___
F	New Departure Motor, *06–14*	100	180	___
G	Fan Motor, battery-operated, *06–14*	100	180	___
K	Transformer, 150, 200 watts, *13–38*	20	75	___
L	Transformer, 50, 75 watts, *13–16, 33–38*	10	25	___
M	Peerless Motor, battery-operated, *15–20*	30	80	___
N	Transformer, 50 watts, *41–42*	7	20	___
Q	Transformer, 50 watts, *14–15*	10	20	___
Q	Transformer, 75 watts, *38–42*	12	28	___
R	Peerless Motor, battery-operated, reversing, *15–20*	30	75	___
R	Transformer, 100 watts, *38–42*	20	45	___
S	Transformer, 50 watts, *14–17*	13	28	___
T	Transformer, 75, 100, 150 watts, *14–28*	8	30	___
U	Transformer, Aladdin, *32–33*	5	15	___
V	Transformer, 150 watts, *39–42*	40	75	___
W	Transformer, 75 watts, *32–33*	10	35	___
Y	Peerless Motor, battery-operated, 3-speed, *15–20*	40	80	___
Z	Transformer, 250 watts, *39–42*	85	140	___

Track, Lockons, and Contactors

	Good	Exc	
O Straight		1	___
O Curve		1	___
O72 Straight	1	2	___
O72 Curve	1	2	___
O27 Straight		1	___
O27 Curve		1	___
Standard Straight	1	3	___
Standard Curve	1	2	___
Standard Insulated Straight, *33–42*	2	4	___
Standard Insulated Curve, *33–42*	1	2	___
O Gauge Lockon		1	___
Standard Gauge Lockon		1	___
UTC Lockon		1	___
145C Contactor	3	10	___
153C Contactor	3	7	___
Track Clips, dozen (O), *37*	5	10	___

			Good	Exc
____ 5C		Test Set	861	1476
____ 5D		Test Set, *54*	1225	2500
____ 5E		Electronic Set Tester, *46-49*	1000	3000
____ 5F		Test Set	1100	2180
____ 011-11		Fiber Pins, dozen (O), *46-50*	1	3
____ 011-43		Insulating Pins, dozen (O), *61*	1	2
____ 020		90-degree Crossover (O), *45-61*	3	8
____ 020X		45-degree Crossover (O), *46-59*	3	8
____ 022		Remote Control Switches, pair (O), *45-69*	24	46
____ 022-500		Adapter Set (O), *57-61*	1	7
____ 022A		Remote Control Switches, pair (O), *47*	27	98
____ 022C-1		Switch Controller	5	11
____ 25		Bumper (O), *46-47*	5	15
26		Bumper, *48-50*		
____		(A) Red, *49-50*	5	14
____		(B) Gray, *48*	16	60
____ 027C-1		Track Clips, box of 12 (027), *47, 49*	4	17
____ 027C-1		Track Clips, box of 50 (027)	21	67
30		Water Tower, *47-50*		
____		(A) Single-walled	19	75
____		(B) Double-walled	20	90
____ 31		Curved Track (Super O), *57-66*	1	4
____ 31-7		Power Blade Connection, dozen (Super O), *57-60*		11
____ 31-15		Ground Rail Pin, dozen (Super O), *57-66*	1	4
____ 31-45		Power Blade Connection, dozen (Super O), *61-66*	2	11
____ 32		Straight Track (Super O), *57-66*	2	5
____ 32-10		Insulating Pin, dozen (Super O), *57-60*		12
____ 32-20		Power Blade Insulator, dozen (Super O), *57-60*	1	5
____ 32-25		Insulating Pin (Super O), *57-61*		1
____ 32-30		Ground Pin (Super O), *57-61*		1
____ 32-31		Power Pin (Super O), *57-61*		1
____ 32-32		Insulating Pin (Super O), *57-61*		1
____ 32-33		Ground Pin (Super O), *57-61*		1
____ 32-34		Power Pin (Super O), *57-61*		1
____ 32-35		Insulating Pin, dozen (Super O to 027), *57-61*		3
____ 32-45		Power Blade Insulators, dozen (Super O), *61-66*	3	8
____ 32-55		Insulating Pins, dozen (Super O), *61-66*	3	8
____ 33		Half Curved Track (Super O), *57-66*	1	3
____ 34		Half Straight Track (Super O), *57-66*	2	4
____ 35		Boulevard Lamp, *45-49*	12	40
36		Operating Car Remote Control Set (Super O), *57-66*	10	20
____ 37		Uncoupling Track Set (Super O), *57-66*	8	18

		Good	Exc
38-85	Accessory Adapter Tracks, pair (Super O), *57-61*	6	18____
38	Operating Water Tower, *46-47*	103	295____
39	Operating Set (Super O), *57*	4	8____
39-5	Operating Set (Super O), *57-58*	4	8____
39-6	Operating Set (Super O), *57-58*	4	11____
39-10	Operating Set (Super O), *58*	4	8____
39-15	Operating Set with blade (Super O), *57-58*	4	8____
39-20	Operating Set (Super O), *57-58*	4	8____
39-25	Operating Set (Super O), *61-66*	8	28____
39-35	Operating Set (Super O), *59*	8	30____
40	Hookup Wire, *50-51, 53-63*		
	(A) Single reel, orange or gray, with tape	7	39____
	(B) 8 sealed reels in dealer box	103	392____
40-25	Conductor Wire with envelope, *56-59*	9	38____
40-50	Cable Reel with envelope, *60-61*	10	71____
41	Contactor (Super O)	1	2____
41	U.S. Army Switcher, *55-57*		
	(A) Unpainted black body	50	103____
	(B) Black-painted body	225	850____
042/42	Manual Switches, pair (O), *46-59*	10	25____
42	Picatinny Arsenal Switcher, *57*	80	248____
43	Power Track (Super O), *59-66*	4	13____
44	U.S. Army Mobile Launcher, *59-62*	60	211____
44-80	Missiles, *59-60*	10	23____
45	U.S. Marines Mobile Launcher, *60-62*	80	260____
45	Automatic Gateman, *46-49*	15	43____
45N	Automatic Gateman, *45*	18	48____
48	Insulated Straight Track (Super O), *57-66*	4	9____
49	Insulated Curved Track (Super O), *57-66*	4	9____
50	Section Gang Car, *54-64*		
	(A) Gray bumpers, rotating blue man and fixed olive men, center horn, *54*	195	633____
	(B) Blue bumpers, rotating olive man and fixed blue men, center horn	31	54____
	(C) Blue bumpers, rotating olive man and fixed blue men, off-center horn	23	46____
51	Navy Yard Switcher, *56-57*	69	144____
52	Fire Car, *58-61*	64	178____
53	Rio Grande Snowplow, *57-60*		
	(A) Backwards "a" in Rio Grande	68	205____
	(B) Correctly printed "a"	149	559____
54	Ballast Tamper, *58-61, 66, 68-69*	55	167____
55	PRR Tie-Jector Car, *57-61*		
	(A) Ventilation slot behind motorman	52	147____
	(B) No slot behind motorman	45	105____
55-150	Ties, 24 pieces, *57-60*	13	33____
56	Lamp Post, *46-49*	23	45____

			Good	Exc
____56	M&StL Mine Transport, *58*		135	345
____57	AEC Switcher, *59-60*		140	504
____58	GN Snowplow, *59-61*		145	367
____58	Lamp Post, *46-50*		17	39
____59	Minuteman Switcher, *62-63*		207	464
60	Lionelville Rapid Transit Trolley, *55-58*			
____	(A) Metal motorman silhouettes		95	237
____	(B) No motorman silhouettes		37	100
____61	Ground Lockon (Super O), *57-66*		2	5
61-25	Super O Ground clips, dozen, with dealer envelope		5	17
____				
____62	Power Lockon (Super O), *57-66*		1	4
____64	Highway Lamp Post, *45-49*		15	39
65	Handcar, *62-66*			
____	(A) Light yellow		80	270
____	(B) Dark yellow		70	240
____68	Executive Inspection Car, *58-61*		61	143
____69	Maintenance Car, *60-62*		79	190
____70	Yard Light, *49-50*		11	33
____71	Lamp Post, *49-59*		8	14
____75	Goose Neck Lamps, set of 2, *61-63*		10	25
____76	Boulevard Street Lamps, set of 3, *59-66, 68-69*		15	30
____80	Controller, *60*		5	25
____88	Controller, *46-60*		9	15
____89	Flagpole, *56-58*		15	50
90	Controller, *55-66*			
____	(A) Metal clip		6	10
____	(B) No metal clip		5	8
____91	Circuit Breaker, *57-60*		10	23
____92	Circuit Breaker, *59-66, 68-69*		6	13
____93	Water Tower, *46-49*		17	42
____96C	Controller, *45-54*		4	8
____97	Coal Elevator, *46-50*		55	139
____108	Trestle Set, 12 black piers,		9	35
____109	Partial Trestle Set, *61*		5	17
____110	Graduated Trestle Set, 22 or 24 piers, *55-69*		8	16
____110-75	Graduated Trestle Set with 110-78 envelope		10	28
____111	Elevated Trestle Set, 10 A piers, *56-69*		7	13
____111-100	Elevated Trestle Piers, set of 2, *60-63*		13	35
____112	Remote Control Switches, pair (Super O), *57-66*		43	83
____114	Newsstand with horn, *57-59*		34	80
____115	Passenger Station, *46-49*		110	270
____118	Newsstand with whistle, *57-58*		38	85
____119	Landscaped Tunnel, *57-58*		200	400
____120	90-degree Crossing (Super O), *57-66*		6	13
____121	Landscaped Tunnel, *59-66*			NRS
____122	Lamp Assortment, *48-52*		33	173

		Good	Exc
123	Lamp Assortment, *55-59*	60	155____
123-60	Lamp Assortment, *60-63*	28	164____
125	Whistle Shack, *50-55*		
	(A) Gray base	13	40____
	(B) Green base	22	48____
128	Animated Newsstand, *57-60*	57	102____
130	60-degree Crossing (Super O), *57-66*	7	18____
131	Curved Tunnel, *59-66*		NRS____
132	Passenger Station, *49-55*	35	64____
133	Passenger Station, *57, 61-62, 66*	20	47____
138	Water Tower, *53-57*	23	62____
140	Automatic Banjo Signal, *54-66*	13	27____
142	Manual Switches, pair (Super O), *57-66*	28	56____
145	Automatic Gateman, *50-66*		
	(A) Red roof	11	38____
	(B) Maroon roof	10	32____
145C	Contactor, *50-60*	3	7____
147	Whistle Controller, *61-66*	2	6____
148	Dwarf Trackside Signal, *57-60*	23	47____
148-100	Controller (SPDT switch), *57-60*	6	20____
150	Telegraph Pole Set, *47-50*	30	39____
151	Automatic Semaphore, *47-69*		
	(A) Green base, yellow blade, *47*	20	55____
	(B) Black base, yellow blade, *47*	10	25____
	(C) Black base, red blade, *47*	155	373____
	(D) Green base, yellow blade with raised lenses	18	74____
152	Automatic Crossing Gate, *45-49*	8	17____
153	Automatic Block Control Signal, *45-59*	13	23____
153C	Contactor	3	6____
154	Automatic Highway Signal, *45-69*	12	21____
154C	Contactor	4	7____
155	Blinking Light Signal with bell, *55-57*	20	48____
156	Station Platform, *46-49*	29	85____
156-5	Station Platform Fence with envelope	23	57____
157	Station Platform, *52-59*		
	(A) Maroon base	15	37____
	(B) Red base	25	75____
157-23	Station Platform Fence with envelope	14	48____
160	Unloading Bin, *52-57*		
	(A) Black plastic, long	2	7____
	(B) Black metal, short	31	72____
	(C) Multicolor Bakelite, short	6	25____
	(D) Black Bakelite, short	4	9____
161	Mail Pickup Set, *61-63*	23	64____
163	Single Target Block Signal, *61-69*	15	25____
164	Log Loader, *46-50*	64	160____

			Good	Exc
___	**164-64**	Log Set, 5 pieces, *52-58*	31	68
___	**167**	Whistle Controller, *45-46*	3	10
___	**175**	Rocket Launcher, *58-60*	54	162
___	**175-50**	Extra Rocket, *59-60*	10	26
___	**182**	Magnetic Crane, *46-49*	129	250
___	**182-22**	Steel Scrap with bag, *46-49*	45	146
___	**192**	Operating Control Tower, *59-60*	107	242
	193	Industrial Water Tower, *53-55*		
___		(A) Red	43	78
___		(B) Black, *53*	83	159
	195	Floodlight Tower, *57-69*		
___	**195**	(A) Medium tan base, rubber-stamped lettering	25	70
___	**195**	(B) All other variations	23	55
___	**195-75**	Floodlight Extension, 8-bulb (with box), *58-60*	30	81
___	**196**	Smoke Pellets, *46-47*	28	111
	197	Rotating Radar Antenna, *57-59*		
___		(A) Orange platform	33	99
___		(B) Gray platform	27	70
___	**197-75**	Separate Sale Radar Head with box	48	130
___	**199**	Microwave Relay Tower, *58-59*	30	70
___	**202**	UP Alco Diesel A Unit, *57*	33	75
___	**204**	Santa Fe Alco Diesel AA Units, *57*	72	174
	205	Missouri Pacific Alco Diesel AA Units, *57-58*		
___		(A) Pilot without support	45	123
___		(B) Pilot with painted metal support	75	165
___	**206**	Artificial Coal, large bag, *46-68*	12	21
___	**207**	Artificial Coal, small bag, *46-48*	7	15
___	**208**	Santa Fe Alco Diesel AA Units, *58-59*	57	235
___	**209**	New Haven Alco Diesel AA Units, *58*	192	568
___	**209**	Wooden Barrels, set of 6, *46-50*	9	18
___	**210**	Texas Special Alco Diesel AA Units, *58*	50	130
___	**211**	Texas Special Alco Diesel AA Units, *62-66*	60	132
___	**212**	Santa Fe Alco Diesel AA Units, *64-66*	83	216
___	**212T**	Santa Fe Alco Diesel Dummy A Unit, *64-66*	27	75
___	**212**	USMC Alco Diesel A Unit, *58-59*	65	145
___	**212T**	USMC Diesel Dummy A Unit, *58 u*	315	988
___	**213**	M&StL Alco Diesel AA Units, *64*	75	205
___	**214**	Plate Girder Bridge, *53-69*	7	15
	215	Santa Fe Alco Diesel Units, *65 u*		
___		(A) AB Units	63	130
___		(B) AA Units	86	163
___	**216**	Burlington Alco Diesel A Unit, *58*	129	333
___	**216**	M&StL Alco Diesel AA Units (213T dummy A unit), *64 u*	63	190
___	**217**	B&M Alco Diesel AB Units, *59*	90	208
___	**217C**	B&M Alco Diesel B Unit, *59*	30	70

		Good	Exc	
218	Santa Fe Alco Diesel Units, *59-63*			
	(A) AA Units	76	300	
	(B) AB Units	70	145	
	(C) AA Units, solid nose decal	70	217	
218C	Santa Fe Alco B Unit, *61-63*	40	109	
219	Missouri Pacific Alco Diesel AA Units, *59 u*	75	153	
220	Santa Fe Alco Diesel Units, *60-61*			
	(A) A Unit	35	119	
	(B) AA Units	76	185	
221	2-6-4 Locomotive, 221W Tender, *46-47*			
	(A) Gray body, black drivers	60	138	
	(B) Black body, nickel-rimmed black drivers, *47*	70	170	
	(C) Gray body, cast-aluminum drivers, *46*	110	240	
221	Rio Grande Alco Diesel A Unit, *63-64*	28	60	
221	Santa Fe Alco Diesel A Unit, *63-64 u*	176	706	
221	U.S. Marine Corps Alco Diesel A Unit, *63-64 u*	180	505	
221T	Tender			
	(A) Gray	18	40	
	(B) Black	15	45	
221W	Whistle Tender	28	60	
222	Rio Grande Alco Diesel A Unit, *62*	25	60	
223	Santa Fe Alco Diesel AB Units, *63*	64	182	
224	2-6-2 Locomotive, 2466W or 2466WX Tender, *45-46*			
	(A) Blackened handrails, *45*	118	245	
	(B) Silver handrails	75	153	
224	US Navy "B" Unit	43	80	
224	U.S. Navy Alco Diesel AB Units, *60*	120	248	
225	C&O Alco Diesel A Unit, *60*	40	75	
226	B&M Alco Diesel AB Units, *60 u*	73	181	
226C	B&M Alco Diesel B Unit, *60 u*	35	83	
227	CN Alco Diesel A Unit, *60 u*	70	161	
228	CN Alco Diesel A Unit, *61 u*	70	145	
229	M&StL Alco Diesel Units, *61-62*			
	(A) A Unit, *61*	55	99	
	(B) AB Units, *62*	80	185	
229C	M&StL Alco Diesel B Unit, *61-62*	30	65	
230	C&O Alco Diesel A Unit, *61*	48	98	
231	Rock Island Alco Diesel A Unit, *61-63*			
	(A) With red stripe	50	103	
	(B) Without red stripe	150	419	
232	New Haven Alco Diesel A Unit, *62*	57	134	
233	2-4-2 Scout Locomotive, 233W Tender, *61-62*	30	68	
233W	Whistle Tender	20	43	
234T	Lionel Lines Tender	8	23	
234T	Pennsylvania Tender	13	50	

		Good	Exc
234W	Lionel Whistle Tender	23	48
234W	Pennsylvania Whistle Tender	25	100
235	2-4-2 Scout Locomotive, 1130T or 1060T Tender, *60 u*	75	224
236	2-4-2 Scout Locomotive, *61-62*		
	(A) 1050T slope-back Tender	15	43
	(B) 1130T Tender	15	45
237	2-4-2 Scout Locomotive, *63-66*		
	(A) 1060T Tender	25	65
	(B) 234W Tender	31	75
238	2-4-2 Scout Locomotive, stripe on running board, 234W Tender, *63-64*	55	150
239	2-4-2 Scout Locomotive, 234W Tender, *65-66*	40	88
240	2-4-2 Scout Locomotive, 242T Tender, *64 u*	87	267
241	2-4-2 Scout Locomotive, *65 u*		
	(A) Narrow stripe, 234W Tender	32	98
	(B) Wide stripe, 1130T Tender	25	69
242	2-4-2 Scout Locomotive, 1060T or 1062T Tender, *62-66*	18	38
243	2-4-2 Scout Locomotive, 243W Tender, *60*	32	88
243W	Whistle Tender	15	45
244	2-4-2 Scout Locomotive, 244T or 1130T Tender, *60-61*	18	44
244T	Tender	7	18
245	2-4-2 Scout Locomotive, 1130T Tender, *59 u*	25	71
246	2-4-2 Scout Locomotive, 244T or 1130T Tender, *59-61*	13	27
247	2-4-2 Scout Locomotive, 247T Tender, *59*		
	(A) Closed pilot	15	70
	(B) Open pilot	15	150
247T	B&O Tender	15	30
248	2-4-2 Scout Locomotive, 1130T Tender, *58*	25	75
249	2-4-2 Scout Locomotive, 250T Tender, *58*	20	58
250	2-4-2 Scout Locomotive, 250T Tender, *57*	20	58
250T	Tender	10	24
251	2-4-2 Scout Locomotive, *66 u*		
	(A) 1062T slope-back Tender	82	210
	(B) 250T-type Tender	78	210
252	Crossing Gate, *50-62*	9	21
253	Block Control Signal, *56-59*	14	28
256	Illuminated Freight Station, *50-53*		
	(A) Standard	23	45
	(B) Light green roof	58	114
257	Freight Station with diesel horn, *56-57*		
	(A) Maroon base	30	85
	(B) Brown base	40	105
257	(C) Maroon or brown base, light green roof	68	145

		Good	Exc
260	Bumper, *51-69*		
	(A) Die-cast	7	13____
	(B) Black plastic	15	38____
262	Highway Crossing Gate, *62-69*	15	44____
264	Operating Forklift Platform, *57-60*	85	232____
282	Portal Gantry Crane, *54-57*	80	172____
282R	Portal Gantry Crane, *56-57*	70	171____
299	Code Transmitter Beacon Set, *61-63*	43	111____
308	Railroad Sign Set, die-cast, *45-49*	23	35____
309	Yard Sign Set, plastic, *50-59*	8	22____
309-100	Yard Sign Set in Plastic Packaging, *66-69 u*		67____
310	Billboard Set, *50-68*	10	20____
313	Bascule Bridge, *46-49*	95	316____
313-82	Fiber Pins, dozen, *46-60*	1	2____
313-121	Fiber Pins, dozen, *61*	1	2____
314	Scale Model Girder Bridge, *45-50*	10	32____
315	Illuminated Trestle Bridge, *46-48*	36	109____
316	Trestle Bridge, *49*	18	37____
317	Trestle Bridge, *50-56*	17	31____
321	Trestle Bridge, *58-64*	15	38____
321-100	Trestle Bridge	23	72____
332	Arch-Under Trestle Bridge, *59-66*	20	38____
334	Operating Dispatching Board, *57-60*	80	200____
342	Culvert Loader, *56-58*	38	162____
345	Culvert Unloader, *57-59*	40	207____
346	Culvert Unloader, manual, *65 u*	55	140____
347	Cannon Firing Range Set, *64 u*	277	748____
348	Culvert Unloader, manual, *66-69*	75	160____
350	Engine Transfer Table, *57-60*	105	236____
350-50	Transfer Table Extension, *57-60*	78	154____
352	Ice Depot with 6352 Ice Car, *55-57*	55	137____
353	Trackside Control Signal, *60-61*	11	33____
356	Operating Freight Station, *52-57*		
	(A) Dark green roof, *52-57*	36	93____
	(B) Light green roof, *57*	70	169____
362	Barrel Loader, *52-57*		
	(A) Gold lettering	24	68____
	(B) Red lettering	97	355____
362-78	Wooden Barrels, 6 pieces, *52-57*		
	(A) Brown	7	18____
	(B) Red	88	274____
364	Conveyor Lumber Loader, *48-57*	25	73____
364C	On/Off Switch, *48-64*	6	11____
365	Dispatching Station, *58-59*	47	113____
375	Turntable, *62-64*	67	173____
390C	Switch, double-pole, double-throw, *60-64*	6	13____
394	Rotary Beacon, *49-53*		

		Good	Exc
____	(A) Steel tower, red platform	20	45
____	(B) Steel tower, green platform	33	77
____	(C) Aluminum tower, platform, and base	18	35
____	(D) Aluminum tower, red steel base	33	63
____	(E) Steel tower, red platform, stick-on nameplate	32	77
395	Floodlight Tower, *49-56*		
____	(A) Light green, silver, or unpainted aluminum	20	45
____	(B) Red	33	104
____	(C) Dark green	87	300
____	(D) Yellow	44	125
397	Operating Coal Loader, *48-57*		
____	(A) Yellow generator, *48*	120	313
____	(B) Blue generator, *49-57*	35	80
____**400**	B&O Passenger Rail Diesel Car, *56-58*	75	168
____**404**	B&O Baggage-Mail Rail Diesel Car, *57-58*	135	304
____**410**	Billboard Blinker, *56-58*	18	48
____**413**	Countdown Control Panel, *62*	17	58
____**415**	Diesel Fueling Station, *55-57*	48	128
____**419**	Heliport Control Tower, *62*	165	358
____**443**	Missile Launching Platform with ammo dump, *60-62*	28	63
____**445**	Switch Tower, lighted, *52-57*	23	53
____**448**	Missile Firing Range Set, *61-63*	47	152
____**450**	Operating Signal Bridge, *52-58*	22	48
____**450L**	Signal Light Head, *52-58*	13	26
____**452**	Overhead Gantry Signal, *61-63*	40	98
455	Operating Oil Derrick, *50-54*		
____	(A) Dark green tower, green top	50	119
____	(B) Dark green tower, red top	58	163
____	(C) Apple green tower, red top	88	389
456	Coal Ramp with 3456 Hopper, *50-55*		
____	(A) Light gray ramp	53	135
____	(B) Dark gray ramp	73	153
____**456C**	Coal Ramp Controller	8	33
460	Piggyback Transportation Set, *55-57*		
____	(A) Metal stick-on signs on lift truck	49	113
____	(B) Rubber-stamped lettering on lift truck	70	134
____**460P**	Piggyback Platform, *55-57*	20	65
____**460-150**	Separate Sale 2 Trailers in Box	48	219
____**461**	Platform with truck and trailer, *66*	60	175
____**462**	Derrick Platform Set, *61-62*	109	245
____**464**	Lumber Mill, *56-60*	44	110
____**465**	Sound Dispatching Station, *56-57*	37	84
470	Missile Launching Platform with target car, *59-62*	51	95
____**479-1**	Truck for 6362 Truck Car with envelope, *55-56*	25	88
____**480-25**	Conversion Magnetic Coupler, *50-60*	1	5

		Good	Exc
480-32	Conversion Magnetic Coupler, *61-69*	1	5____
494	Rotary Beacon, *54-66*		
	(A) Painted steel	23	43____
	(B) Unpainted aluminum	20	61____
497	Coaling Station, *53-58*	55	124____
520	LL Boxcab Electric Locomotive, *56-57*		
	(A) Black pantograph	33	78____
	(B) Copper-colored pantograph	40	98____
600	MKT NW2 Switcher, *55*		
	(A) Black frame, black end rails	63	117____
	(B) Gray frame, yellow or black end rails	80	201____
601	Seaboard NW2 Switcher, *56*		
	(A) Red stripes with square ends	79	173____
	(B) Red stripes with round ends	88	162____
602	Seaboard NW2 Switcher, *57-58*	77	155____
610	Erie NW2 Switcher, *55*		
	(A) Black frame	53	123____
	(B) Black frame, two-axle Magnetraction	30	150____
	(C) Yellow frame	124	402____
	(D) Replacement body with nameplates	90	261____
611	Jersey Central NW2 Switcher, *57-58*	60	152____
613	UP NW2 Switcher, *58*	77	223____
614	Alaska NW2 Switcher, *59-60*		
	(A) Plastic bell, no brake	100	190____
	(B) No bell, yellow brake	113	230____
	(C) "Built by Lionel" outlined in yellow near nose	178	341____
616	Santa Fe NW2 Switcher, *61-62*		
	(A) Open E-unit slot and bell/horn slots	98	197____
	(B) Plugged E-unit slot and open bell/horn slots	101	254____
	(C) Plugged E-unit slot and bell/horn slots	108	269____
617	Santa Fe NW2 Switcher, *63*	110	249____
621	Jersey Central NW2 Switcher, *56-57*	70	147____
622	Santa Fe NW2 Switcher, *49-50*		
	(A) Large GM decal on cab	138	270____
	(B) Small GM decal on side	103	209____
623	Santa Fe NW2 Switcher, *52-54*	75	137____
624	C&O NW2 Switcher, *52-54*	75	175____
625	LV GE 44-ton Switcher, *57-58*	42	104____
626	B&O GE 44-ton Switcher, *56-57, 59*	138	305____
627	LV GE 44-ton Switcher, *56-57*	33	75____
628	NP GE 44-ton Switcher, *56-57*	46	103____
629	Burlington GE 44-ton Switcher, *56*	146	340____
633	Santa Fe NW2 Switcher, *62*	58	130____
634	Santa Fe NW2 Switcher, *63, 65-66*		
	(A) Safety stripes	80	145____
	(B) No safety stripes	48	110____

		Good	Exc
__ **635**	UP NW2 Switcher, *65 u*	48	114
637	2-6-4 Locomotive, 2046 736W Tender, *59-63*		
__	(A) 2046W Lionel Lines Tender	55	150
__	(B) 736W Pennsylvania Tender	70	170
__ **638-2361**	Van Camp's Pork & Beans Boxcar, *62 u*	15	40
__ **645**	Union Pacific NW2 Switcher, *69*	48	132
__ **646**	4-6-4 Locomotive, 2046W Tender, *54-58*	90	244
665	4-6-4 Locomotive, 2046W, 6026W, or 736W Tender, *54-59, 66*	83	233
671	6-8-6 Steam Turbine Locomotive, smoke bulb, *46*	105	198
671	6-8-6 Steam Turbine Locomotive, *47-49*		
__	(A) 671W Tender	75	190
__	(B) 2671W Tender, backup lights	117	408
__	(C) 2671W Tender, no backup lights	101	223
__ **671-75**	Smoke Lamp, 12 volt, *46*	10	18
671R	6-8-6 Steam Turbine Locomotive, 4424W or 4671 Tender, *46-49*	165	303
671RR	6-8-6 Steam Turbine Locomotive, 2046W-50 Tender, *52*	90	195
__ **671S**	Smoke Conversion Kit	20	130
__ **671W**	Whistle Tender, *46-48*	30	63
675	2-6-2 Locomotive, 2466WX or 6466WX Tender, *47-49*		
__	(A) Aluminum smokestack, *47*	74	340
__	(B) Black smokestack, *48-49*	63	264
__ **675**	2-6-4 Locomotive, 2046W Tender, *52*	69	183
681	6-8-6 Steam Turbine Locomotive, 2046W-50 or 2671W Tender, *50-51, 53*	98	212
682	6-8-6 Steam Turbine Locomotive, 2046W-50 Tender, *54-55*	136	284
__ **685**	4-6-4 Hudson Locomotive, 6026W Tender, *53*	80	224
__ **703-10**	Smoke Lamp, 18 volt, *46*	12	22
726	2-8-4 Berkshire, *46-49*		
__	(A) 2426W Tender, smoke lamp, *46*	230	535
__	(B) 2426W Tender, *47-49*	210	487
__ **726RR**	2-8-4 Berkshire Locomotive, 2046W Tender, *52*	117	269
__ **726S**	Smoke Conversion Kit	40	115
736	2-8-4 Berkshire Locomotive, 2671WX, 2046W, or 736W Tender, *50-51*	225	325
736	2-8-4 Berkshire Locomotive, 2671WX, 2046W, or 736W Tender, *53-66*	146	291
__ **736W**	PRR Whistle Tender	22	65
746	N&W 4-8-4 Class J Northern, *57-60*		
__	(A) Tender with long stripe	493	983
__	(B) Tender with short stripe	300	770
__ **746W**	Tender, short stripe	30	115

		Good	Exc
760	Curved Track, 16 sections (O72), *54-57*	18	60____
773	4-6-4 Hudson Locomotive, 2426W Tender, *50*	673	1493____
773	4-6-4 Hudson Locomotive, *64-66*		
	(A) 773W NYC Tender	667	1103____
	(B) 736W PRR Tender	535	930____
773T	NYC Tender	70	150____
773W	NYC Whistle Tender	100	220____
902	Elevated Trestle Set, *60*	25	147____
908	Union Station, *1959*, u		899____
909	Smoke Fluid, large or small bottle, *57-66, 68-69*		
	(A) 1/2 ounce bottle	7	26____
	(B) 2 ounce bottle	9	39____
B909	Smoke Capsules, pack of three, *57-66, 68-69*	8	28____
919	Artificial Grass, *46-64*	7	17____
920	Scenic Display Set, *57-58*	34	72____
920-2	Tunnel Portals, pair, *58-59*	13	33____
920-3	Green Grass, *57*	3	12____
920-4	Yellow Grass, *57*	7	15____
920-5	Artificial Rock, *57-58*	3	13____
920-6	Dry Glue, *57-58*	3	10____
920-8	Dyed Lichen, *57-58*	3	15____
925	Lubricant, 2 ounce tube, *46-69*	3	12____
925-1	Lubricant, 1 ounce tube, *50-69*	1	5____
926	Lubricant, 1/2 ounce tube, *55*	2	3____
926-5	Instruction Booklet, *46-48*	1	5____
927	Lubricating Kit, *50-59*	11	27____
928	Maintenance and Lubricating Kit, *60-63*	31	60____
943	Ammo Dump, *59-61*	16	42____
950	U.S. Railroad Map, *58-66*	20	70____
951	Farm Set, 13 pieces, *58*	50	125____
952	Figure Set, 30 pieces, *58*	34	57____
953	Figure Set, 32 pieces, *59-62*	43	82____
954	Swimming Pool and Playground Set, 30 pieces, *59*	40	106____
955	Highway Set, 22 pieces, *58*	30	65____
956	Stockyard Set, 18 pieces, *59*	40	89____
957	Farm Building and Animal Set, 35 pieces, *58*	60	120____
958	Vehicle Set, 24 pieces, *58*	45	83____
959	Barn Set, 23 pieces, *58*	39	78____
960	Barnyard Set, 29 pieces, *59-61*	73	156____
961	School Set, 36 pieces, *59*	45	108____
962	Turnpike Set, 24 pieces, *58*	60	183____
963T	Frontier Set, 18 pieces, *59-60*	60	163____
964	Factory Site Set, 18 pieces, *59*	70	230____
965	Farm Set, 36 pieces, *59*	55	168____
966	Firehouse Set, 45 pieces, *58*	70	168____
967	Post Office Set, 25 pieces, *58*	50	111____

			Good	Exc
___	**968**	TV Transmitter Set, 28 pieces, *58*	55	120
___	**969**	Construction Set, 23 pieces, *60*	65	113
___	**970**	Ticket Booth, *58-60*	35	153
___	**971**	Lichen with box, *60-64*	33	80
___	**972**	Landscape Tree Assortment, *61-64*	25	83
___	**973**	Complete Landscaping Set, *60-64*	45	129
___	**974**	Scenery Set, *58*	70	223
___	**980**	Ranch Set, 14 pieces, *60*	50	123
___	**981**	Freight Yard Set, 10 pieces, *60*	50	178
___	**982**	Suburban Split Level Set, 18 pieces, *60*	42	187
___	**983**	Farm Set, 7 pieces, *60-61*	33	75
___	**984**	Railroad Set, 22 pieces, *61-62*	56	137
___	**985**	Freight Area Set, 32 pieces, *61*	35	165
___	**986**	Farm Set, 20 pieces, *62*	45	168
___	**987**	Town Set, 24 pieces, *62*	35	65
___	**988**	Railroad Structure Set, 16 pieces, *62*	40	93
	1001	2-4-2 Scout Locomotive, plastic body, 1001T Tender, *48*		
___		(A) Silver rubber-stamped cab number	25	75
___		(B) White heat-stamped cab number	15	38
___	**1001T**	Tender	6	16
	1002	Gondola, *48-52*		
___		(A) Black, white lettering	4	12
___		(B) Blue, white lettering	5	14
___		(C) Silver, black lettering	125	412
___		(D) Yellow, black lettering	120	388
___		(E) Red, white lettering	120	337
___	**X1004**	PRR Baby Ruth Boxcar, *48-52*	5	9
___	**1005**	Sunoco 1-D Tank Car, *48-50*	6	11
	1007	LL SP-type Caboose, *48-52*		
___		(A) Red body	3	9
___		(B) Red body, raised board on catwalk	10	35
___		(C) Tuscan body	192	925
___	**1008**	Uncoupling Unit (027), *57-62*	2	6
___	**1008-50**	Uncoupling Track Section (027), *57-62*	3	7
___	**1009**	Manumatic Track Section (027), *48-52*	5	10
___	**1010**	Transformer, 35 watts, *61-66*	6	11
___	**1011**	Transformer, 25 watts, *48-49*	4	12
___	**1012**	Transformer, 35 watts, *50-54*	5	9
___	**1013**	Curved Track (027), *45-69*		1
___	**1013-17**	Steel Pins, dozen (027), *46-60*		1
___	**1013-42**	Steel Pins, dozen (027), *61-68*		2
___	**1014**	Transformer, 40 watts, *55*	5	10
___	**1015**	Transformer, 45 watts, *56-60*	8	14
___	**1016**	Transformer, 35 watts, *59-60*	6	10
___	**1018**	Half Straight Track (027), *55-69*		1
___	**1018**	Straight Track (027), *45-69*		1

		Good	Exc
1019	Remote Control Track Set (027), *46-48*	3	11___
1020	90-degree Crossing (027), *55-69*	2	4___
1021	90-degree Crossing (027), *45-54*	2	4___
1022	Manual Switches, pair (027), *53-69*	6	14___
1023	45-degree Crossing (027), *56-69*	3	5___
1024	Manual Switches, pair (027), *46-52*	6	14___
1025	Illuminated Bumper (027), *46-47*	8	14___
1025	Transformer, 45 watts, *61-69*	5	13___
1026	Transformer, 25 watts, *61-64*	3	5___
1032	Transformer, 75 watts, *48*	12	23___
1033	Transformer, 90 watts, *48-56*	18	33___
1034	Transformer, 75 watts, *48-54*	9	23___
1035	Transformer, 60 watts, *47*	8	16___
1037	Transformer, 40 watts, *46-47*	4	9___
1041	Transformer, 60 watts, *45-46*	11	21___
1042	Transformer, 75 watts, *47-48*	13	23___
1043	Transformer, 50 watts, *53-57*	5	10___
1043-500	Transformer, 60 watts, ivory, *57-58*	81	140 ___
1044	Transformer, 90 watts, *57-69*	25	56___
1045	Operating Watchman, *46-50*	18	50___
1045C	Contactor	4	11___
1047	Operating Switchman, *59-61*	21	93___
1050	0-4-0 Scout Locomotive, 1050T Tender, *59 u*	42	142___
1050T	Tender	5	18___
1053	Transformer, 60 watts, *56-60*	9	18___
1055	Texas Special Alco Diesel A Unit, *59-60*	25	60___
1060	2-4-2 Locomotive, 1050T or 1060T Tender, *60-62*	10	30 ___
1060T	Lionel Lines Tender	9	18___
1060T-50	Southern Pacific Tender, *63-64 u*	12	33 ___
1061	0-4-0 or 2-4-2 Scout Locomotive, 1061T Tender, *64, 69*		
	(A) Slope-back Lionel Lines tender	14	32___
	(B) Paper number labels	39	174___
	(C) No number stamped on cab	30	80___
1061T	Tender	4	16___
1062	0-4-0 or 2-4-2 Scout Locomotive, *63-64*		
	(A) Streamlined Southern Pacific Tender	20	45___
	(B) Other tenders	18	33___
1063	Transformer, 75 watts, *60-64*	13	24___
1063	Transformer 75 watt, with green whistle control		206___
1065	Union Pacific Alco Diesel A Unit, *61*	28	65___
1066	Union Pacific Alco Diesel A Unit, *64 u*	33	75___
1073	Transformer, 60 watts, *61-66*	10	19___
1101	Transformer, 25 watts, *48*	3	7___

			Good	Exc
___**1101**	2-4-2 Scout Locomotive, 1001T Tender, *48 u*			
___	(A) Cab correctly marked "1101"		15	38
	(B) Cab marked "1001"		121	311
___**1110**	2-4-2 Locomotive, 1001T Tender, *49, 51-52*		13	28
___**1120**	2-4-2 Scout Locomotive, 1001T Tender, *50*		18	33
___**1121**	Remote Control Switches, pair (O27), *46-51*		11	28
___**1122**	Remote Control Switches, pair (O27), *52-53*		13	30
___**1122-34**	Remote Control Switches, pair, *52-53*		14	27
___**1122-500**	Gauge Adapter (O27), *57-66*		4	10
___**1122E**	Remote Control Switches, pair (O27), *53-69*		11	32
1130	2-4-2 Locomotive, 6066T or 1130T Tender, *53-54*			
___	(A) Plastic body		15	44
___	(B) Die-cast body		33	118
1130T	Tender			
___	(A) Black-painted shell		33	89
	(B) Black plastic shell		7	21
___**1130T-500**	Tender, pink, from Girls Set		83	192
___**1144**	Transformer, 75 watts, *61-66*		10	23
___**1232**	Transformer, 75 watts, made for export, *48*		15	40
1615	0-4-0 Locomotive, 1615T Tender, *55-57*			
___	(A) No grab irons		69	140
___	(B) Grab irons on locomotive and tender		135	268
___**1615T**	Tender		14	26
___**1625**	0-4-0 Locomotive, 1625T Tender, *58*		147	270
___**1625T**	Tender		23	46
___**1640-100**	Presidential Kit, *60*		48	168
___**1654**	2-4-2 Locomotive, 1654W Tender, *46-47*		35	78
___**1654T**	Tender		10	20
___**1654W**	Whistling Tender		15	33
___**1655**	2-4-2 Locomotive, 6654W Tender, *48-49*		39	74
1656	0-4-0 Locomotive, 6403B Tender, *48-49*			
___	(A) Large silver cab number		120	245
___	(B) Small silver cab number		125	278
___**1665**	0-4-0 Locomotive, 2403B Tender, *46*		190	362
1666	2-6-2 Locomotive, 2466W or 2466WX Tender, *46-47*			
___	(A) Number plate and two-piece bell		53	125
___	(B) Rubber-stamped number and one-piece bell		68	150
___**1666T**	Tender		10	25
1862	4-4-0 Civil War General, 1862T Tender, *59-62*			
___	(A) Gray smokestack		95	169
___	(B) Black smokestack		100	190
___**1862T**	Tender		24	39
___**1865**	Western & Atlantic Coach, *59-62*		25	45

		Good	Exc
1866	Western & Atlantic Mail-Baggage Car, *59-62*	28	47____
1872	4-4-0 Civil War General, 1872T Tender, *59-62*	130	255____
1872T	Tender	28	48____
1875	Western & Atlantic Coach, *59-62*	75	242____
1875W	Western & Atlantic Coach, whistle, *59-62*	50	138____
1876	Western & Atlantic Baggage Car, *59-62*	35	101____
1877	Flatcar with fence and horses, *59-62*	47	94____
1882	4-4-0 Civil War General, 1882T Tender, *60 u*	204	414____
1882T	Tender, *60 u*	31	141____
1885	Western & Atlantic Coach, *60 u*	115	232____
1887	Flatcar with fences and horses, *60 u*	70	165____
2001	Track Make-up Kit (O27), *63*	300	750____
2002	Track Make-up Kit (O27), *63*	495	1162____
2003	Track Make-up Kit (O27), *63*	600	1900____
2016	2-6-4 Locomotive, 6026W Tender, *55-56*	45	88____
2018	2-6-4 Locomotive, *56-59, 61*		
	(A) 6026T Tender	33	63____
	(B) 6026W Tender	50	98____
	(C) 1130T Tender	35	65____
2020	6-8-6 Steam Turbine Locomotive, 2020W or 2466WX Tender, smoke lamp, *46*	83	180 ____
2020	6-8-6 Steam Turbine Locomotive, 2020W or 6020W Tender, *47-49*	67	163 ____
2020W	Whistling Tender	33	58____
2023	Union Pacific Alco Diesel AA Units, *50-51*		
	(A) Yellow body	98	217____
	(B) Gray nose and side frames	1080	3088____
	(C) Silver body	65	199____
2024	C&O Alco Diesel A Unit, *69*	31	81____
2025	2-6-2 Locomotive, 2466WX or 6466WX Tender, *47-49*		
	(A) Black smokestack, *48-49*	73	165____
	(B) Aluminum smokestack, *47*	83	185____
2025	2-6-4 Locomotive, 6466W Tender, *52*	81	162____
2026	2-6-2 Locomotive, 6466WX Tender, *48-49*	55	90____
2026	2-6-4 Locomotive, 6466W, 6466T, or 6066T Tender, *51-53*	38	85 ____
2028	Pennsylvania GP7 Diesel, *55*		
	(A) Gold lettering	142	291____
	(B) Yellow lettering	108	230____
	(C) Tan frame	238	584____
2029	2-6-4 Locomotive, *64-69*		
	(A) 234W Lionel Lines Tender	48	112____
	(B) LL Tender with "Hagerstown" on bottom	58	128____
	(C) 234W Pennsylvania Tender	88	195____
2031	Rock Island Alco Diesel AA Units, *52-54*	67	224____

			Good	Exc
____	2032	Erie Alco Diesel AA Units, *52-54*	87	317
____	2033	Union Pacific Alco Diesel AA Units, *52-54*	72	182
____	2034	2-4-2 Scout Locomotive, 6066T Tender, *52*	27	63
____	2035	2-6-4 Locomotive, 6466W Tender, *50-51*	57	150
____	2036	2-6-4 Locomotive, 6466W Tender, *50*	48	110
	2037	2-6-4 Locomotive, *54-55*, *57-63*		
____		(A) 6026T or 1130T Tender	34	84
____		(B) 6026W, 233W, or 234W whistle Tender	65	123
____	2037-500	2-6-4 Locomotive, pink, 1130T-500 Tender, *57-58*	379	815
____	2041	Rock Island Alco Diesel AA Units, *69*	52	145
____	2046	4-6-4 Locomotive, 2046W Tender, *50-51, 53*	81	175
____	2046T	Tender, for export	70	223
____	2046W	Whistle Tender	30	61
____	2046W-50	PRR Whistle Tender	31	71
____	2055	4-6-4 Locomotive, 2046W or 6026W Tender, *53-55*	74	158
____	2056	4-6-4 Locomotive, 2046W Tender, *52*	73	203
____	2065	4-6-4 Locomotive, 2046W or 6026W Tender, *54-56*	76	170
____	2203B	Tender	58	120
____	2224W	Whistle Tender	24	75
____	2240	Wabash F3 AB Units, *56*	183	488
____	2242	New Haven F3 AB Units, *58-59*	176	802
____	2242C	New Haven F3 B Unit, *58-59*	60	205
	2243	Santa Fe F3 AB Units, *55-57*		
____		(A) Gray body mold, raised molded cab door ladder	108	277
____		(B) Typical molded cab door ladder	90	226
____	2243C	Santa Fe F3 B Unit, *55-57*	60	143
	2245	Texas Special F3 AB Units, *54-55*		
____		(A) B Unit with portholes, *54*	202	416
____		(B) B Unit without portholes, *55*	233	760
	2257	SP-type caboose, *47*		
____		(A) Red body, no smokestack	5	15
____		(B) Tuscan body and smokestack	74	301
____		(C) Red body and smokestack	110	406
	2321	Lackawanna FM Train Master Diesel, *54-56*		
____		(A) Gray roof	161	499
____		(B) Maroon roof	152	463
	2322	Virginian FM Train Master Diesel, *65-66*		
____		(A) Unpainted blue body, yellow stripes	245	487
____		(B) Blue or black body, painted blue and yellow stripes	315	630
____	2328	Burlington GP7 Diesel, *55-56*	90	215

		Good	Exc
2329	Virginian GE E-33 or EL-C Electric Locomotive, *58-59*	179	499 ___
2330	Pennsylvania GG1 Electric Locomotive, green, *50*	362	1042 ___
2331	Virginian FM Train Master Diesel, *55-58*		
	(A) Black and yellow stripes, gray mold, *55*	349	662 ___
	(B) Yellow stripes, blue mold, *56-58*	235	548 ___
	(C) Blue and yellow stripes, gray mold	525	1038 ___
2332	Pennsylvania GG1 Electric Locomotive, *47-49*		
	(A) Black	527	1228 ___
	(B) Dark green	184	520 ___
2333	NYC F3 Diesel AA Units, *48-49*		
	(A) Rubber-stamped lettering	229	593 ___
	(B) Heat-stamped lettering	173	471 ___
2333	Santa Fe F3 Diesel AA Units, *48-49*	190	395 ___
2337	Wabash GP7 Diesel, *58*	97	237 ___
2338	Milwaukee Road GP7 Diesel, *55-56*		
	(A) Orange band around shell	383	1323 ___
	(B) Interrupted orange band	73	187 ___
2339	Wabash GP7 Diesel, *57*	126	262 ___
2340	Pennsylvania GG1 Electric Locomotive, *55*		
	(A) Tuscan	442	954 ___
	(B) Dark green	322	758 ___
2341	Jersey Central FM Train Master Diesel, *56*		
	(A) High-gloss orange	980	2088 ___
	(B) Dull orange	875	1834 ___
2343	Santa Fe F3 Diesel AA Units, *50-52*	143	438 ___
2343C	Santa Fe F3 B Unit, *50-55*		
	(A) Screen roof vents	104	238 ___
	(B) Louver roof vents	73	192 ___
2344	NYC F3 Diesel AA Units, *50-52*	174	536 ___
2344C	NYC F3 B Unit, *50-55*	96	212 ___
2345	Western Pacific F3 Diesel AA Units, *52*	447	972 ___
2346	B&M GP9 Diesel, *65-66*	137	330 ___
2347	C&O GP7 Diesel, *65 u*	1440	3925 ___
2348	M&StL GP9 Diesel, *58-59*	154	253 ___
2349	Northern Pacific GP9 Diesel, *59-60*	159	359 ___
2350	New Haven EP-5 Electric Locomotive, *56-58*		
	(A) Painted nose trim, white N and orange H	232	587 ___
	(B) Decaled nose trim, white N and orange H	127	285 ___
	(C) Painted nose trim, orange N and black H	760	1887 ___
	(D) Decaled nose trim, orange N and black H	431	815 ___
	(E) Orange and white stripes go through doorjambs	345	1114 ___
2351	Milwaukee Road EP-5 Electric Locomotive, *57-58*	192	421 ___
2352	Pennsylvania EP-5 Electric Locomotive, *58-59*		
	(A) Tuscan body	159	432 ___
	(B) Chocolate brown body	186	390 ___

			Good	Exc
___	2353	Santa Fe F3 Diesel AA Units, *53-55*	167	416
___	2354	NYC F3 Diesel AA Units, *53-55*	228	443
___	2355	Western Pacific F3 Diesel AA Units, *53*	438	819
___	2356	Southern F3 Diesel AA Units, *54-56*	344	779
___	2356C	Southern F3 B Unit, *54-56*	134	249
	2357	SP-type Caboose, *47-48*		
___		(A) Red body and smokestack	137	507
___		(B) Tuscan body and smokestack	15	35
___		(C) Tile red, no smokestack, "6357" stamped on bottom	70	231
___	2358	Great Northern EP-5 Electric Locomotive, *59-60*	230	568
___	2359	Boston & Maine GP9 Diesel, *61-62*	105	315
	2360	Pennsylvania GG1 Electric Locomotive, *56-58, 61-63*		
___		(A) Tuscan, 5 gold stripes	570	1253
___		(B) Dark green, 5 gold stripes	374	823
___		(C) Tuscan, gold stripe, heat-stamped letters	387	745
___		(D) Tuscan, gold stripe, decaled lettering	430	713
	2363	Illinois Central F3 Diesel AB Units, *55-56*		
___		(A) Black lettering	344	702
___		(B) Brown lettering	372	812
___	2363C	Illinois Central "B" Unit		160
___	2365	C&O GP7 Diesel, *62-63*	101	276
___	2367	Wabash F3 Diesel AB Units, *55*	345	554
___	2367C	Wabash F3 Diesel B Unit, *55*	80	175
___	2368	B&O F3 Diesel AB Units, *56*	445	1008
___	2368P	B&O F3 Diesel A Unit		
___	2373	CP F3 Diesel AA Units, *57*	653	1355
	2378	Milwaukee Road F3 Diesel AB Units, *56*		
___		(A) Yellow roof line stripes	668	1268
___		(B) No roof line stripes	522	1038
___	2378C	Milwaukee Road F3 Diesel B Unit, yellow roof line stripe, *56*	270	532
___	2379	Rio Grande F3 Diesel AB Units, *57-58*	358	712
___	2379C	Denver & Rio Grande B Unit		179
___	2383	Santa Fe F3 Diesel AA Units, *58-66*	179	419
___	2400	Maplewood Pullman Car, green, *48-49*	45	106
___	2401	Hillside Observation Car, green, *48-49*	37	100
___	2402	Chatham Pullman Car, green, *48-49*	43	105
___	2404	Santa Fe Vista Dome Car, *64-65*	33	75
___	2405	Santa Fe Pullman Car, *64-65*	33	76
___	2406	Santa Fe Observation Car, *64-65*	32	70
___	2408	Santa Fe Vista Dome Car, *66*	48	80
___	2409	Santa Fe Pullman Car, *66*	43	73
___	2410	Santa Fe Observation Car, *66*	35	75
	2411	Lionel Lines Flatcar, *46-48*		
___		(A) With pipes, *46*	32	80

		Good	Exc
	(B) With logs, *47-48*	13	38____
2412	Santa Fe Vista Dome Car, *59-63*	35	78____
2414	Santa Fe Pullman Car, *59-63*	35	79____
2416	Santa Fe Observation Car, *59-63*	28	70____
2419	DL&W Work Caboose, *46-47*	20	48____
2420	DL&W Work Caboose with searchlight, *46-48*		
	(A) Light or dark gray, heat-stamped lettering	52	99____
	(B) Light or dark gray, rubber-stamped lettering	62	139____
2421	Maplewood Pullman Car, *50-53*		
	(A) Gray roof	30	70____
	(B) Silver roof	25	50____
2422	Chatham Pullman Car, *50-53*		
	(A) Gray roof	32	70____
	(B) Silver roof	25	51____
2423	Hillside Observation Car, *50-53*		
	(A) Gray roof	27	66____
	(B) Silver roof	22	46____
2426W	Whistle Tender, *50*	120	226____
2429	Livingston Pullman Car, *52-53*	50	99____
2430	Pullman Car, blue, *46-47*	30	95____
2431	Observation Car, blue, *46-47*	25	90____
2432	Clifton Vista Dome Car, *54-58*	34	62____
2434	Newark Pullman Car, *54-58*	35	80____
2435	Elizabeth Pullman Car, *54-58*	40	112____
2436	Mooseheart Observation Car, *57-58*	30	75____
2436	Summit Observation Car, *54-56*	28	59____
2440	Pullman Car, green, *46-47*		____
	(A) Silver lettering	40	73____
	(B) White lettering	26	68____
2441	Observation Car, green, *46-47*		____
	(A) Silver lettering	40	73____
	(B) White lettering	29	63____
2442	Clifton Vista Dome Car, *56*	45	95____
2442	Pullman Car, brown, *46-48*		
	(A) Silver lettering	43	78____
	(B) White lettering	30	65____
2443	Observation Car, brown, *46-48*		
	(A) Silver lettering	38	73____
	(B) White lettering	30	65____
2444	Newark Pullman Car, *56*	45	100____
2445	Elizabeth Pullman Car, *56*	85	225____
2446	Summit Observation Car, *56*	45	99____
2452	Pennsylvania Gondola, *45-47*		
	(A) Whirly wheels, *45*	18	40____
	(B) Regular wheels	9	20____
	(C) Early flying shoe trucks, two holes in floor, *45*	33	109____

			Good	Exc
	2452X	Pennsylvania Gondola, *46-47*	8	18
	X2454	Baby Ruth Boxcar, PRR logo, *46-47*	20	40
	X2454	Pennsylvania Boxcar, *46*		
		(A) Brown door	70	189
		(B) Orange door	126	351
	2456	Lehigh Valley Hopper, *48*		
		(A) Flat black, 2 lines of data, *48*	13	33
		(B) Flat black, 3 lines of data, *48*	93	230
	2457	PRR N5-type Caboose "477618," tintype, *45-47*		
		(A) Red, white lettering	18	38
		(B) Brown, offset white lettering	173	590
		(C) Brown, centered white lettering	30	90
	X2458	PRR Automobile Boxcar, *46-48*	28	53
	2460	Bucyrus Erie Crane Car, *12-wheel, 46-50*		
		(A) Gray cab	78	245
		(B) Black cab	35	102
	2461	Transformer Car, die-cast, *47-48*		
		(A) Red transformer	28	85
		(B) Black transformer	30	75
		(C) Red transformer, number rubber-stamped on bottom	42	157
	2465	Sunoco 2-D Tank Car, *46-48*		
		(A) "Gas, Sunoco, and Oils" in diamond, centered	188	590
		(B) "Sunoco" in diamond	7	18
		(C) "Sunoco" extends beyond diamond	8	18
	2466T	Tender	19	43
	2466WX	Whistle Tender, *45-48*	25	65
	2472	PRR N5-type Caboose, tintype, *46-47*	10	28
	2481	Plainfield Pullman Car, yellow, *50*	89	244
	2482	Westfield Pullman Car, yellow, *50*	92	251
	2483	Livingston Observation Car, yellow, *50*	77	244
	2521	President McKinley Observation Car, *62-66*	55	160
	2522	President Harrison Vista Dome Car, *62-66*	67	170
	2523	President Garfield Pullman Car, *62-66*	63	163
	2530	REA Baggage Car, *54-60*		
		(A) Large doors	173	360
		(B) Small doors	64	151
	2531	Silver Dawn Observation Car, *52-60*		
		(A) Ribbed channels, round rivets	35	121
		(B) Ribbed channels, hex rivets	44	99
		(C) Ribbed channels, hex rivets, red center taillight	59	148
		(D) Flat channels, glued nameplates	56	118
	2532	Silver Range Vista Dome Car, *52-60*	55	115

		Good	Exc	
	(A) Ribbed channels, or hex rivets	41	97	___
	(B) Flat channels, glued nameplates	38	148	___
2533	Silver Cloud Pullman Car, *52-59*			
	(A) Ribbed channels, or hex rivets	39	88	___
	(B) Flat channels, glued nameplates	42	148	___
2534	Silver Bluff Pullman Car, *52-59*			
	(A) Ribbed channels, or hex rivets	46	86	___
	(B) Flat channels, glued nameplates	33	160	___
2541	Alexander Hamilton Observation Car, *55-56**	58	160	___
2542	Betsy Ross Vista Dome Car, *55-56**	59	163	___
2543	William Penn Pullman Car, *55-56**	60	165	___
2544	Molly Pitcher Pullman Car, *55-56**	60	165	___
2550	B&O Baggage-Mail Rail Diesel Car, *57-58*	186	436	___
2551	Banff Park Observation Car, *57**	109	249	___
2552	Skyline 500 Vista Dome Car, *57**	124	258	___
2553	Blair Manor Pullman Car, *57**	171	396	___
2554	Craig Manor Pullman Car, *57**	167	396	___
2555	Sunoco 1-D Tank Car, *46-48*	21	59	___
2559	B&O Passenger Rail Diesel Car, *57-58*	110	278	___
2560	Lionel Lines Crane Car, 8-wheel, *46-47*			
	(A) Black boom	22	80	___
	(B) Brown boom	25	84	___
	(C) Green boom	31	95	___
2561	Vista Valley Observation Car, *59-61**	81	230	___
2562	Regal Pass Vista Dome Car, *59-61**	90	262	___
2563	Indian Falls Pullman Car, *59-61**	98	272	___
2625	Irvington Pullman Car, *46-50**			
	(A) No silhouettes	55	150	___
	(B) Silhouettes	85	253	___
2625	Madison Pullman Car, *46-47**	65	167	___
2625	Manhattan Pullman Car, *46-47**	65	167	___
2627	Madison Pullman Car, *48-50**			
	(A) No silhouettes	58	160	___
	(B) Silhouettes	87	247	___
2628	Manhattan Pullman Car, *48-50**			
	(A) No silhouettes	58	147	___
	(B) Silhouettes	88	249	___
2671T	PRR Tender, for export	38	103	___
2671W	Whistle Tender	40	83	___
2671W	PRR Tender with silver letters and back-up light	169	384	___
2671WX	Whistle Tender	44	82	___
2755	Sunoco 1-D Tank Car, *45*	27	73	___
X2758	PRR Automobile Boxcar, *45-46*	29	48	___
2855	Sunoco 1-D Tank Car, *46-47*			
	(A) Black	76	243	___
	(B) Black, decal without "Gas" and "Oils"	60	203	___

			Good	Exc
___		(C) Gray	45	185
___	3309	Turbo Missile Launch Car, red body, *63-64*	16	49
___	3309-50	Turbo Missile Launch Car, olive body, *63-64*	166	570
___	3330	Flatcar with submarine kit, *60-62*	60	165
___	3330-100	Operating Submarine Kit with box, *60-61*	105	376
___	3349	Turbo Missile Launch Car, red body, *62-65*	16	45
___	3356	Operating Horse Car and Corral Set, *56-60, 64-66*	43	125
	3356	Operating Horse Car only, *56-60, 64-66*		
___		(A) Built date, bar-end trucks, *56-60*	30	73
___		(B) No built date, AAR trucks, *64-66*	43	137
___	3356-100	Black Horses, 9 pieces, *56-59*	15	28
___	3356-150	Horse Car Corral, *57-60*	24	49
___	3357	Hydraulic Maintenance Car, *62-64*	20	65
___	3357-27	Trestle Components for Cop and Hobo Car, *62*	23	50
___	3359	Lionel Lines Twin-bin Coal Dump Car, *55-58*	18	42
___	3360	Operating Burro Crane, self-propelled, *56-57*	73	183
___	3361	Operating Log Dump Car, *55-58*	15	37
___	3362	Helium Tank Unloading Car, *61-63, 69*	20	45
___	3364	Operating Dump Car with 3 logs, *65-66, 68*	15	34
___	3366	Circus Car Corral Set, *59-62*	114	259
___	3366	Circus Car only, *59-62*	68	134
___	3366-100	White Horses, 9 pieces, *59-62*	32	57
	3370	W&A Sheriff and Outlaw Car, *61-64*		
___		(A) AAR trucks	18	48
___		(B) Archbar trucks	25	63
	3376	Bronx Zoo Car, *60-66, 69*		
___		(A) Blue, white lettering	21	56
___		(B) Green, yellow lettering	35	62
___		(C) Blue, yellow lettering	98	286
___	3386	Bronx Zoo Car, *60*	25	60
___	3409	Helicopter Car, *61*	33	117
	3410	Helicopter Car, *61-63*		
___		(A) 2 operating couplers, gray Navy helicopter	33	85
___		(B) Single operating coupler, yellow helicopter, *63*	58	139
___	3413	Mercury Capsule Car, *62-64*	42	155
___	3419	Helicopter Car, *59-65*	35	80
___	3424	Wabash Operating Boxcar, *56-58*	25	60
___	3424-75	Low Bridge Signal, *56-57*	80	292
___	3424-100	Low Bridge Signal Set, *56-58*	24	48
___	3428	U.S. Mail Operating Boxcar, *59-60*	40	75
___	3429	USMC Helicopter Car, *60*	170	487
	3434	Poultry Dispatch Car, *59-60, 64-66*		

		Good	Exc	
	(A) Gray man	50	100	___
	(B) Blue man	58	120	___
3435	Traveling Aquarium Car, *59-62*			
	(A) Gold lettering, tank designations, and circle around L	425	1059	___
	(B) Gold lettering, tank designations, no circle around L	260	664	___
	(C) Gold lettering, no tank designations, no circle around L	115	267	___
	(D) Yellow lettering, no tank designations, no circle around L	50	116	___
3444	Erie Operating Gondola, *57-59*	28	60	___
3451	Operating Log Dump Car, *46-48*			
	(A) Heat-stamped lettering	15	38	___
	(B) Rubber-stamped lettering	20	65	___
3454	PRR Operating Merchandise Car, *46-47*			
	(A) Red lettering	1120	4164	___
	(B) Blue lettering	35	127	___
3456	N&W Operating Hopper, *50-55*	18	55	___
3459	LL Operating Coal Dump Car, *46-48*			
	(A) Aluminum bin	87	250	___
	(B) Black bin	18	50	___
	(C) Green bin	26	76	___
3460	Flatcar with trailers, *55-57*	32	65	___
3461	LL Operating Log Car, *49-55*			
	(A) Black car, heat-stamped lettering	20	36	___
	(B) Black car, rubber-stamped lettering	132	341	___
3461-25	LL Operating Log Car, green	18	53	___
3462	Automatic Milk Car, *47-48*			
	(A) Flat white or cream, steel base mechanism	13	52	___
	(B) Flat white or cream, brass base mechanism	25	65	___
	(C) Glossy cream	64	244	___
3462-70	Magnetic Milk Cans, *52-59*	8	17	___
3462P	Milk Car Platform, *47-48*	7	16	___
X3464	ATSF Operating Boxcar, *49-52*			
	(A) Orange body	9	21	___
	(B) Tan body	400	1300	___
X3464	NYC Operating Boxcar, *49-52*	10	23	___
3469	LL Operating Coal Dump Car, *49-55*	15	45	___
3470	Target Launching Car, dark blue, *62-64*	23	65	___
3470-100	Target Launching Car, light blue, *63*	58	207	___
3472	Automatic Milk Car, *49-53*	20	53	___
3474	Western Pacific Operating Boxcar, *52-53*	25	60	___
3482	Automatic Milk Car, *54-55*			
	(A) "RT3472" on right	31	86	___
	(B) "RT3482" on right	21	62	___

		Good	Exc
____ 3484	Pennsylvania Operating Boxcar, *53*	22	55
3484-25	ATSF Operating Boxcar, *54*		
____	(A) White lettering	25	77
____	(B) Black lettering	320	1235
____ 3494-1	NYC Operating Boxcar, *55*	37	108
3494-150 ____	MP Operating Boxcar, *56*	52	139
3494-275	State of Maine Operating Boxcar, *56-58*		
____	(A) "3494275" on side	40	100
____	(B) No number on side	61	162
3494-550 ____	Monon Operating Boxcar, *57-58*	198	389
3494-625 ____	Soo Operating Boxcar, *57-58*	189	440
3509	Satellite Launching Car, *61*		
____	(A) Chrome satellite cover	30	70
____	(B) Gray satellite cover	75	246
____ 3510	Satellite Launching Car, *62*	43	107
3512	Fireman and Ladder Car, *59-61*		
____	(A) Black extension ladder	52	121
____	(B) Silver extension ladder	63	218
____ 3519	Satellite Launching Car, *61-64*	23	69
3520	Searchlight Car, *52-53*		
____	(A) Serif lettering	17	54
____	(B) Sans serif lettering	16	35
3530	GM Generator Car, *56-58*		
____	(A) Blue fuel tank	45	130
____	(B) Black fuel tank	43	115
____	(C) 3530 underscored	415	1767
____ 3530-50	Searchlight with pole and base, *56-56*	19	59
____ 3535	Security Car with searchlight, *60-61*	33	105
____ 3540	Operating Radar Car, *59-60*	33	103
____ 3545	Operating TV Monitor Car, *61-62*	49	143
3559	Operating Coal Dump Car, *46-48*		
____	(A) Black coil housing	15	44
____	(B) Brown coil housing	40	118
3562-1	ATSF Operating Barrel Car, *54*		
____	(A) Black, black unloading trough	61	201
____	(B) Black, yellow unloading trough	58	204
____	(C) Gray, red lettering	800	2970
3562-25	ATSF Operating Barrel Car, gray, *54*		
____	(A) Red lettering, no bracket tab	160	477
____	(B) Blue lettering, no bracket tab	17	50
____	(C) Blue lettering, bracket tab	17	72

		Good	Exc
3562-50	ATSF Operating Barrel Car, yellow, *55-56*		
	(A) Painted	37	96____
	(B) Unpainted	28	60____
3562-75	ATSF Operating Barrel Car, orange, *57-58*	36	83____
3619	Helicopter Reconnaissance Car, *62-64*		
	(A) Light yellow	43	128____
	(B) Dark yellow	65	194____
3620	Searchlight Car, orange generator, *54-56*		
	(A) Unpainted gray plastic searchlight	17	38____
	(B) Gray-painted gray plastic searchlight	28	45____
	(C) Unpainted orange plastic searchlight	48	125____
	(D) Gray-painted orange plastic searchlight	50	183____
3650	Extension Searchlight Car, *56-59*		
	(A) Light gray	28	78____
	(B) Dark gray	45	148____
	(C) Olive gray	103	265____
3656	Armour Operating Cattle Car, some with an open coil, *49-55*		
	(A) Black letters, Armour sticker	105	245____
	(B) White letters, Armour sticker	25	63____
	(C) Black letters, no Armour sticker	67	190____
	(D) White letters, no Armour sticker	25	56____
3656	Stockyard with cattle, *49-55*	24	58____
3656-34	Cattle, black, 9 pieces, *49-58*		
	(A) Rounded ridge on base, *49*	60	131____
	(B) Plain base	15	40____
3656-150	Corral Platform, yellow tray	215	490 ____
3662	Automatic Milk Car, *55-60, 64-66*	39	73____
3662-79	Nonmagnetic Milk Cans, 7 pieces, white envelope	19	52 ____
3662-80	Nonmagnetic Milk Cans, 7 pieces, manila envelope	17	48 ____
3665	Minuteman Operating Car, *61-64*		
	(A) Medium blue roof	60	190____
	(B) Dark blue roof	38	94____
3666	Minuteman Boxcar with cannon, *64 u*	192	428____
3672	Bosco Operating Milk Car, *59-60*		
	(A) Unpainted yellow body	85	180____
	(B) Painted yellow body	140	259____
3672-79	Bosco Can Set, 7 pieces, *59-60*	25	74____
3820	USMC Operating Submarine Car, *60-62*	96	207____
3830	Operating Submarine Car, *60-63*	38	87____
3854	Automatic Merchandise Car, *46-47*	170	513____
3927	Lionel Lines Track Cleaning Car, *56-60*	30	46____
3927-38	Track Cleaning Fluid Bottle	9	17____
3927-50	Track Wiping Cylinders, 25 pieces, *57-60*	13	30____
3927-75	Track-Clean Detergent, can, *56-69*	5	17____

			Good	Exc
	4357	SP-type Caboose, electronic, die-cast stack, *48-49*		
___		(A) Die-cast metal smokestack	60	200
___		(B) Matching plastic smokestack	115	270
___		(C) Matching plastic smokestack, raised board on catwalk	110	265
___	**4452**	PRR Gondola, electronic, *46-49*	48	122
___	**4454**	Baby Ruth PRR Boxcar, electronic, *46-49*	60	160
___	**4457**	PRR N5-type Caboose, tintype, electronic, *46-47*	43	150
___	**4671W**	Whistle Tender	80	178
___	**5102**	Railroad and Roadway Crossing	10	60
___	**5159-50**	Maintenance and Lube Kit, *66-69*	25	63
___	**5160**	Viewing Stand, *63*	40	125
___	**5459**	LL Coal Dump Car, electronic, *46-49*	49	134
___	**6001T**	Tender	8	17
___	**6002**	NYC Gondola, *50*	4	8
___	**X6004**	Baby Ruth PRR Boxcar, *50*	4	7
___	**6007**	Lionel Lines SP-type Caboose, *50*	3	7
___	**6009**	Remote Control Uncoupling Track, *53-54*	2	7
___	**6012**	Gondola, *51-56*	2	6
	6014	Bosco PRR Boxcar, *58*		
___		(A) White body	22	49
___		(B) Red body	4	9
___		(C) Orange body	4	7
___	**6014**	Chun King Boxcar, *57 u*	46	138
	6014	Frisco Boxcar, *57, 63-69*		
___		(A) White body	5	11
___		(B) Red body	5	7
___		(C) White body, coin slot	16	45
___		(D) Orange body, *57*	18	50
___		(E) Orange body, *69*	10	23
	X6014	Baby Ruth PRR Boxcar, *51-56*		
___		(A) White body	5	9
___		(B) Red body	3	8
___	**6014-100**	Airex Boxcar, *60 u*	14	40
___	**6014-150**	Wix Boxcar, *59 u*	66	195
	6015	Sunoco 1-D Tank Car, *54-55*		
___		(A) Painted tank	70	289
___		(B) Unpainted tank	4	12
	6017	Lionel Lines SP-type Caboose, *51-62*		
___		(A) Glossy tuscan-painted orange mold	23	80
___		(B) Semigloss tuscan-painted, orange mold	13	34
___		(C) Tile red-painted, blue mold	13	34
___		(D) Common red, tuscan, and brown bodies	4	9
___		(E) Bright red, black mold, *62*	63	219

		Good	Exc
6017	SP-type Caboose, maroon, "Lionel" only, *56*	10	35____
6017-50	U.S. Marine Corps SP-type Caboose, *58*	23	70____
6017-85	LL SP-type Caboose, gray, *58*	22	67____
6017-100	B&M SP-type Caboose, *59, 62, 65-66*		
	(A) Purple-blue	118	429____
	(B) Medium or light blue	15	42____
6017-185	ATSF SP-type Caboose, *59-60*	12	33 ____
6017-200	U.S. Navy SP-type Caboose, *60*	43	145 ____
6017-225	ATSF SP-type Caboose, *61-62*	15	40 ____
6017-235	ATSF SP-type Caboose, *62*	15	45 ____
6019	Remote Control Track (027), *48-66*	2	10____
6020W	Whistle Tender	34	67____
6024	Nabisco Shredded Wheat Boxcar, *57*	10	30____
6024	RCA Whirlpool Boxcar, *57 u*	20	60____
6025	Gulf 1-D Tank Car, *56-58*		
	(A) Gray body, blue lettering	5	12____
	(B) Orange body, blue lettering	6	16____
	(C) Black body, red-orange Gulf emblem	5	15____
6026T	Tender	11	28____
6026W	Whistle Tender	22	59____
6027	Alaska SP-type Caboose, *59*	23	63____
6029	Remote Control Uncoupling Track, *55-63*	3	11____
6032	Short Gondola, black (027), *52-54*	2	6____
X6034	Baby Ruth PRR Boxcar, *53-54*		
	(A) Orange, blue lettering	5	10____
	(B) Orange, black lettering	5	11____
6035	Sunoco 1-D Tank Car, *52-53*	3	8____
6037	Lionel Lines SP-type Caboose, *52-54*		
	(A) Tuscan	3	6____
	(B) Red	5	11____
6042	Short Gondola, *59-61, 62-64 u*	3	11____
6044	Airex Boxcar, orange lettering, *59-60 u*		
	(A) Medium blue	10	29____
	(B) Teal blue	31	87____
	(C) Purple-blue	103	236____
6044-1X	Nestles/McCall's Boxcar, *62-63 u*	350	1467____
6045	Lionel Lines 2-D Tank Car, *59-64*		
	(A) Gray	10	20____
	(B) Orange	15	33____
	(C) Beige	10	30____

		Good	Exc
6045	Cities Service 2-D Tank, *60 u*	15	35
6047	Lionel Lines SP-type Caboose, *62*		
	(A) Unpainted, medium red	2	5
	(B) Painted, brown	160	733
	(C) Unpainted, coral pink	15	62
6050	Lionel Savings Bank Boxcar, *61*		
	(A) Type I body, Blt by Lionel	19	48
	(B) Type I body, Built by Lionel	43	160
	(C) Type IIa body, Blt by Lionel	150	275
6050-110	Swift Boxcar, *62-63*		
	(A) Red body	8	24
	(B) Dark red body, 2 open holes in roof walk	45	127
6050-175	Libby's Tomato Juice Boxcar, *63 u*		
	(A) Green stems on tomatoes	15	40
	(B) Green stems missing	19	55
	(C) No white lines between glass and tomatoes	25	82
6057	LL SP-type Caboose, *59-62*		
	(A) Unpainted red plastic	3	7
	(B) Red-painted	32	98
	(C) Unpainted coral pink plastic	18	65
6057-50	LL SP-type Caboose, orange, *62*	20	52
6058	C&O SP-type Caboose, *61*		
	(A) Blue lettering	17	47
	(B) Black lettering	28	81
6059	M&StL SP-type Caboose, *61-69*		
	(A) Painted, red	13	38
	(B) Unpainted, red	5	11
	(C) Unpainted, maroon	6	13
6062	NYC Gondola with 3 cable reels, *59-62*		
	(A) No metal undercarriage	10	28
	(B) Metal undercarriage	19	66
	(C) No metal undercarriage, no paint on bottom	45	80
6062-50	NYC Gondola with 2 canisters, *69*	7	17
6066T	Tender	8	18
6067	SP-type Caboose, unmarked, *61-62*		
	(A) Red	3	8
	(B) Yellow	6	14
	(C) Brown	9	18
6076	ATSF Hopper, *63 u*	8	28
6076	Lehigh Valley Hopper, short, *63*		
	(A) Gray body	8	14
	(B) Black body	7	13
	(C) Red body	8	13

		Good	Exc	
	(D) Yellow body, painted	350	1294	___
6076-100	Hopper, gray, unmarked, *63*	10	24	___
6110	2-4-2 Locomotive, 6001T Tender, *50-51*	15	35	___
6111	Flatcar with logs, *55-57*			
	(A) Yellow with black lettering	10	35	___
	(B) Yellow with white lettering	106	529	___
6112	Short Gondola with 4 canisters, *56-58*			
	(A) Black body	6	18	___
	(B) Blue body	6	18	___
	(C) White body	14	44	___
6112-5	Canister, *56-58*			
	(A) Red or white	1	3	___
	(B) Red with black letters	18	55	___
6112-25	Canister Set, 4 pieces, red or white, with box, *56-58*	28	60	___
6119	DL&W Work Caboose, red, *55-56*	12	24	___
6119-25	DL&W Work Caboose, orange, *56-59*	15	37	___
6119-50	DL&W Work Caboose, brown, *56*	23	53	___
6119-75	DL&W Work Caboose, *57*			
	(A) Heat-stamped letters on frame	15	35	___
	(B) Closely spaced rubber-stamped letters on frame	55	219	___
	(C) Widely spaced rubber-stamped letters on frame	47	186	___
6119-100	DL&W Work Caboose, red cab, gray tool tray, *57-66, 69*			
	(A) Black frame, white letters	10	25	___
	(B) "Built By Lionel" builders plate, *66*	22	84	___
	(C) Black frame, red-painted cab	53	199	___
	(D) Santa Fe cab, gray tool box	10	35	___
6119-125	Rescue Caboose, olive, black frame, *64*	63	170	___
6120	Work Caboose, yellow, unmarked, *61-62*	8	14	___
6121	Flatcar with pipes, *56-57*			
	(A) Yellow, red, or gray	10	57	___
	(B) Maroon	16	84	___
6130	ATSF Work Caboose, *61, 65-69*			
	(A) Red painted, no builders plate	14	35	___
	(B) Red unpainted, builders plate	10	30	___
	(C) Red painted, builders plate	64	251	___
6139	Remote Control Uncoupling Track (027), *63*	1	4	___
6142	Short Gondola, green, blue, or black, with 2 canisters, *63-66, 69*	6	14	___
6142-175	Short Gondola, olive drab, with 2 canisters	48	160	___
6149	Remote Control Uncoupling Track (027), *64-69*	2	6	___

		Good	Exc
6151	Flatcar with patrol truck, *58*		
	(A) Yellow frame	37	85
	(B) Orange frame	25	73
	(C) Cream frame	35	85
6162	NYC Gondola with 3 white canisters, *59-68*		
	(A) Blue body	9	25
	(B) Red body	74	295
	(C) Teal body/or green body	30	65
6162-60	Alaska Gondola with 3 red canisters, *59*	39	80
6167	LL SP-type Caboose, red, *63-64*		
	(A) Unpainted	5	9
	(B) Painted	30	127
6167	SP-type Caboose, unmarked, no end rails, *63-64*		
	(A) Red body	3	9
	(B) Brown body	7	22
6167-50	SP-type Caboose, unmarked, yellow	5	27
6167-85	Union Pacific SP-type Caboose, *69*	10	35
6167-175	SP-type Caboose, unmarked, olive	109	380
6175	Flatcar with rocket, *58-61*		
	(A) Black frame	28	67
	(B) Red frame	25	67
6176	Hopper, unmarked, *63-69*		
	(A) Dark yellow	10	34
	(B) Gray	8	15
	(C) Red	10	25
	(D) Bright yellow	25	59
6176	Lehigh Valley Hopper, *64-66, 69*		
	(A) Dark yellow	5	14
	(B) Gray	6	11
	(C) Black	3	8
	(D) Red	13	29
	(E) Bright yellow	25	55
6176-100	Olive Drab Hopper, unmarked	35	111
6219	C&O Work Caboose, *60*	20	45
6220	Santa Fe NW2 Switcher, *49-50*		
	(A) Large GM decal on cab	120	264
	(B) Small GM decal on side	85	218
6250	Seaboard NW2 Switcher, *54-55*		
	(A) Seaboard decal	89	230
	(B) Widely spaced rubber-stamped letters	111	245
	(C) Closely spaced rubber-stamped letters	128	468
6257	SP-type Caboose, *48-52*		
	(A) Dark red, matching plastic smokestack	165	434
	(B) All other variations	5	14

		Good	Exc
6257-25 SP-type Caboose, circled-L logo, *53-55*			
	(A) Red painted	7	16____
	(B) Unpainted red plastic	4	11____
6257-50 SP-type Caboose, *56*		4	11____
6257-100	Lionel Lines SP-type Caboose, smokestack, *63-64*	10	25 ____
6257X	SP-type Caboose, red, 2 couplers, with box, *48*	27	51____
6262	Flatcar with wheel load, *56-57*		
	(A) Black frame, *56-57*	28	70____
	(B) Red frame, *56*	384	702____
6264	Flatcar with lumber for 264 Fork Lift Platform, *57-60*		
	(A) Bar-end trucks	27	62____
	(B) Plastic trucks	33	70____
	(C) Separate-sale box and envelope	100	254____
6311	Flatcar with 3 pipes, *55*	20	47____
6315	Gulf 1-D Chemical Tank Car, *56-59, 68-69*		
	(A) Early, painted	30	78____
	(B) Late, unpainted	22	55____
	(C) Late, unpainted, built date	50	120____
6315	Lionel Lines 1-D Tank Car, *63-66*		
	(A) Unpainted orange body	15	30____
	(B) Painted orange body	93	340____
6342	NYC Gondola with culvert channel and 7 pipes, *56-58, 64-66*	18	42 ____
6343	Barrel Ramp Car with 6 barrels, *61-62*	20	39____
6346	Alcoa Quad Hopper, *56*	28	60____
6352-1 PFE Ice Car from 352 Ice Depot, *55-57*			
	(A) 3 lines of data	66	121____
	(B) 4 lines of data	48	98____
	(C) Separate-sale box	875	3109____
6356	NYC Stock Car, 2-level, *54-55*		
	(A) Heat-stamped lettering	18	40____
	(B) Rubber-stamped lettering	25	85____
6357	SP-type Caboose, SP logo, *48-53*		
	(A) Tile red, tuscan, or maroon	10	31____
	(B) Tile red, extra board on catwalk	138	496____
6357	SP-type Caboose, no logo, *57-61*		
	(A) Number to left	9	40____
	(B) Number to right	16	64____
6357-25 SP-type Caboose, circle L logo, *53-56*			
	(A) Maroon or tuscan body, black metal smokestack	10	25 ____
	(B) Maroon body, maroon metal smokestack	103	394____
6357-50 ATSF SP-type Caboose, lighted, *60*		297	947____
6361	Timber Transport Car, *60-61, 64-69*		
	(A) White lettering	27	69____

		Good	Exc
	(B) No lettering	53	145
6362	Truck Car with 3 trucks, *55-56*		
	(A) Shiny orange	23	44
	(B) Dull orange	33	96
6376	LL Circus Stock Car, *56-57*	27	62
6401	Flatcar, no load, gray, *60*	4	10
6401-25	Gray flatcar with load, *64-67*		
	(A) Jeep and cannon	115	263
	(B) Tank	95	200
	(C) Payton automobile	25	50
	(D) Logs	11	21
6402	Flatcar with orange or gray reels, *62, 64-66*	10	25
6402	Flatcar with blue boat, *69*	28	64
6402-150	Maroon Flatcar with white trailer	13	35
6403B	Tender	35	80
6404	Black Flatcar with auto, *60 u*		
	(A) Red auto	28	65
	(B) Yellow auto	50	125
	(C) Brown auto	75	234
	(D) Green auto	90	243
6405	Flatcar with piggyback van, *61*	17	48
6406	Flatcar with auto, *61*		
	(A) Maroon frame, red auto	25	60
	(B) Maroon frame, yellow auto	55	137
	(C) Gray frame, dark brown auto	80	290
	(D) Gray frame, green auto	90	230
	(E) Gray frame, yellow auto	50	113
6407	Flatcar with rocket, *63*	186	420
6408	Flatcar with pipes, *63 u*	18	42
6408	Flatcar with 2 orange cable reels, *67 u*	15	45
6409-25	Flatcar with pipes, *63 u*	15	43
6410-25	Flatcar with 2 automobiles, *63 u*		
	(A) Yellow autos	115	505
	(B) Brown autos	150	630
6411	Flatcar with logs, *48-50*	13	39
6413	Mercury Capsule Carrying Car, *62-63*		
	(A) Medium blue frame	67	152
	(B) Aquamarine frame	98	210
	(C) Teal frame	90	258
6414	Evans Auto Loader with 4 cars, *55-66*		
	(A) Premium cars (chrome bumpers, windows, rubber wheels): red, yellow, blue-green, and white	55	107
	(B) Cheapie cars (no wheels): 2 red and 2 yellow	160	379
	(C) Red cars with gray bumpers	70	168

		Good	Exc
	(D) Yellow cars with gray bumpers	160	395____
	(E) Brown cars with gray bumpers	258	808____
	(F) Green cars with gray bumpers	457	954____
	(G) Metal trucks, number right of Lionel, premium cars with nubs on axle first run	50	123 ____
	(H) Metal trucks, number right of Lionel without nubs on axle	58	161 ____
6414-25	Set of 4 Automobiles, separate sale box, *55-58*	120	363____
6415	Sunoco 3-D Tank Car, *53-55, 64-66, 69*	13	32____
6416	Boat Transport Car, 4 boats, *61-63*	85	260____
6417	PRR N5c Porthole Caboose, *53-57*		
	(A) New York Zone	15	35____
	(B) Without New York Zone	156	239____
6417-25	Lionel Lines N5c Porthole Caboose, *54*	15	35____
6417-50	LV N5c Porthole Caboose, *54*		
	(A) Tuscan	398	1350____
	(B) Gray	60	132____
6418	Machinery Car with 2 steel girders, *55-57*		
	(A) Black girders, "Lionel" in raised letters	68	130____
	(B) Orange girders, "Lionel" in raised letters	58	105____
	(C) Pinkish orange girders, U.S. Steel	68	120____
	(D) Black girders, U.S. Steel	70	128____
6419	DL&W Work Caboose, *48-50, 52-55*	15	36____
6419-25	DL&W Work Caboose, one coupler, *54-55*	15	35____
6419-50	DL&W Work Caboose, short smokestack, *56-57*	15	39____
6419-75	DL&W Work Caboose, one coupler, *56-57*	15	38____
6419-100	N&W Work Caboose, *57-58*	45	109 ____
6420	DL&W Work Caboose with searchlight, *48-50*		
	(A) Heat-stamped serif lettering	38	75____
	(B) Rubber-stamped sans serif lettering	68	147____
6424	Twin Auto Flatcar, *56-59*		
	(A) Black frame, premium cars	21	58____
	(B) 6805 slots, no rail stops	53	123____
	(C) AAR trucks, number on right	29	74____
6424-110	Twin Auto FlatcaR, 6805 slots and rail stops, *58-59*	85	184 ____
6425	Gulf 3-D Tank Car, *56-58*	13	35____
6427	Lionel Lines N5c Porthole Caboose, *54-60*	15	33____
6427-60	Virginian N5c Porthole Caboose, *58*	233	385____
6427-500	PRR N5c Porthole Caboose, sky blue, from Girls Set, *57-58**	154	335 ____
6428	U.S. Mail Boxcar, *60-61, 65-66*	20	47____
6429	DL&W Work Caboose, AAR trucks, *63*	130	265____
6430	Flatcar with 2 trailers, *56-58*		
	(A) Gray Cooper-Jarrett trailers	25	60____
	(B) White Cooper-Jarrett trailers	27	74____
	(C) Green Fruehauf trailers	25	54____

		Good	Exc
	(D) Gray Cooper-Jarrett trailers with Fruehauf stickers	35	90
6431	Flatcar with 2 vans and Midgetoy tractor, *66*		
	(A) White vans, *66*	65	225
	(B) Yellow vans, *66*	85	350
6434	Poultry Dispatch Stock Car, *58-59*	32	70
6436-1	LV Open Quad Hopper, black, *55, 66*		
	LV Hopper uncataloged AAR trucks with roof, 1963	45	143
	(A) No spreader brace holes	15	35
6436-1	(B) Spreader brace with holes	47	110
6436-25	LV Open Quad Hopper, maroon, *55-57*		
	(A) No spreader brace holes	153	488
	(B) Spreader brace with holes	20	45
6436-110	LV Quad Hopper, red, *63-68*		
	(A) No built date	20	40
	(B) Built date "New 3-55"	36	92
6436-500	LV Open Quad Hopper, lilac, from Girls Set, *57-58**		
	(A) No spreader brace holes	117	371
	(B) Spreader brace with holes	75	253
6437	PRR N5c Porthole Caboose, *61-68*	17	37
6440	Flatcar with gray vans, *61-63*	35	80
6440	Green Pullman Car, *48-49*	35	88
6441	Green Observation Car, *48-49*	30	78
6442	Brown Pullman Car, *49*	40	83
6443	Brown Observation Car, *49*	37	73
6445	Fort Knox Gold Reserve Boxcar with coin slot, *61-63*	45	99
6446	N&W Covered Quad Hopper, black or gray, *54-55*	25	55
6446-25	N&W Covered Quad Hopper, *55-57*		
	(A) Black, white lettering	26	65
	(B) Gray, black lettering	32	73
	(C) Gray, AAR truck, spreader brace holes	64	189
6446-60	LV Covered Quad Hopper, *63*	90	244
6447	PRR N5c Porthole Caboose, *63*	104	308
6448	Exploding Target Range Boxcar, *61-64*		
	(A) Red sides, white roof and ends	16	40
	(B) White sides, red roof and ends	17	40
6452	Pennsylvania Gondola, black, *48-49*		
	(A) Numbered "6462", *48*	15	48
	(B) Numbered "6452", *49*	8	23
X6454	Baby Ruth PRR Boxcar, *48*	90	269
X6454	Santa Fe Boxcar, *48*	10	32
X6454	NYC Boxcar, *48*		
	(A) Brown body	15	34

		Good	Exc
	(B) Orange body	53	139___
	(C) Tan body	23	60___
X6454	Erie Boxcar, *49-52*	15	44___
X6454	PRR Boxcar, *49-52*	18	45___
X6454	SP Boxcar, *49-52*		
	(A) Break in herald circle between R and N, *49*	29	85___
	(B) Complete herald circle	17	44___
6456	Lehigh Valley Short Hopper, *48-55*		
	(A) Black	10	25___
	(B) Maroon	8	20___
6456-25	Lehigh Valley Short Hopper, gray, *54-55*	20	40___
6456-50	Lehigh Valley Short Hopper, enamel red, white lettering, *54*	261	696 ___
6456-75	Lehigh Valley Short Hopper, enamel red, yellow lettering, *54*	65	162 ___
6457	SP-type Caboose, *49-52*	14	25___
6460	Bucyrus Erie Crane Car, black cab, 8-wheel, *52-54*	20	45 ___
6460-25	Bucyrus Erie Crane Car, red cab, 8-wheel, *54*	38	95___
6461	Transformer Car, *49-50*	33	70___
6462	NYC Gondola, black or red, with 6 barrels, *49-54*	8	20___
6462-25	NYC Gondola, green, with 6 barrels, *54-57*		
	(A) N in second panel, 2 lines of data	11	35___
	(B) N in third panel, 3 lines of data	15	45___
6462-75	NYC Gondola, red-painted, with 6 barrels, *52-55*	11	28___
6462-125	NYC Gondola, red plastic, with 6 barrels, *55-57*	8	21 ___
6462-500	NYC Gondola, pink, from Girls Set, with 4 canisters, *57-58**	55	151 ___
6463	Rocket Fuel 2-D Tank Car, *62-63*	19	60___
6464-1	WP Boxcar, *53-54*		
	(A) Blue lettering	28	55___
	(B) Red lettering	425	1444___
6464-25	GN Boxcar, *53-54*	31	85___
6464-50	M&StL Boxcar, *53-56*	23	70___
6464-75	RI Boxcar, green, *53-54, 69*		
	(A) Built date, *53-54*	30	95___
	(B) No built date, *69*	40	85___
6464-100	Western Pacific Boxcar, *54-55*		
	(A) Silver body, yellow feather	40	125___
	(B) Orange body, blue feather	197	810___
6464-125	NYC Pacemaker Boxcar, *54-56*	43	83 ___
6464-150	MP Boxcar, *54-55, 57*	45	108 ___
6464-175	Rock Island Boxcar, *54-55*		

		Good	Exc
_____	(A) Blue lettering	40	117
_____	(B) Black lettering	375	1067
6464-200 _____	Pennsylvania Boxcar, *54-55, 69*	70	131
6464-225 _____	SP Boxcar, *54-56*	45	117
6464-250 _____	WP Boxcar, *66*	65	239
6464-275	State of Maine Boxcar, *55, 57-59*		
_____	(A) Striped doors	35	75
_____	(B) Solid doors	55	127
6464-300	Rutland Boxcar, *55-56*		
_____	(A) Rubber-stamped lettering	45	105
_____	(B) Split door with bottom painted green	230	960
_____	(C) Rubber-stamped lettering with solid shield	1413	3944
_____	(D) Heat-stamped lettering	75	160
_____	(E) Painted yellow body	300	924
6464-325 _____	B&O Sentinel Boxcar, *56*	182	391
6464-350 _____	MKT Boxcar, *56*	110	319
6464-375	Central of Georgia Boxcar, *56-57, 66*		
_____	(A) Unpainted maroon body	40	80
_____	(B) Painted red body	775	3282
6464-400	B&O Time-Saver Boxcar, *56-57, 69*		
_____	(A) BLT 5-54	43	97
_____	(B) BLT 2-56	109	265
_____	(C) No built date	45	127
_____	(D) 54 built date on one side/56 built date on other		950
6464-425 _____	New Haven Boxcar, *56-58*	29	60
6464-450 _____	Great Northern Boxcar, *56-57, 66*	63	130
6464-475	B&M Boxcar, *57-60, 65-66, 68*		
_____	(A) Medium blue-painted or unpainted plastic	38	75
_____	(B) Dark purple-painted, gray or blue mold	74	283
_____	(C) Dark blue-painted, yellow mold	127	460
6464-500	Timken Boxcar, white side band and charcoal lettering, *57-59, 69*		
_____	(A) Unpainted yellow body	45	128
_____	(B) Painted yellow body, Type IV	48	135
_____	(C) Painted yellow body, Type II	140	433
6464-510 _____	NYC Pacemaker Boxcar, *57-58*	304	528

		Good	Exc	
6464-515	MKT Boxcar, *57-58*	290	524	___
6464-525	M&StL Boxcar, *57-58, 64-66*			
	(A) Red, white lettering	27	75	___
	(B) Maroon, white lettering	115	455	___
6464-650	D&RGW Boxcar, *57-58, 66*			
	(A) Yellow body, silver roof, black stripe	65	135	___
	(B) Yellow body, silver roof, no black stripe	95	229	___
	(C) Painted yellow body and yellow roof	500	2540	___
6464-700	Santa Fe Boxcar, *61, 66*	40	145	___
6464-725	New Haven Boxcar, *62-66, 68*			
	(A) Orange body	23	50	___
	(B) Black body	63	237	___
6464-825	Alaska Boxcar, *59-60*	110	303	___
6464-900	NYC Boxcar, *60-66*	39	90	___
6464-900	NYC Boxcar with black doors	45	123	___
6465	Gulf 2-D Tank Car, *58*			
	(A) Black tank	15	53	___
	(B) Gray tank	11	35	___
6465	Sunoco 2-D Tank Car, *48-56*			
	(A) Silver tank, rubber-stamped "6465"	6	12	___
	(B) Silver tank, rubber-stamped "6455"	20	65	___
	(C) Silver tank, no number on frame	7	18	___
	(D) Glossy gray tank	10	40	___
6465-85	LL 2-D Tank Car, black, *59*	20	53	___
6465-110	Cities Service 2-D Tank, *60-62*	23	59	___
6465-160	LL 2-D Tank Car, orange with black ends, *63-64*	10	27	___
6466T	Tender, *49-53*	13	30	___
6466W	Whistle Tender, *49-53*	18	45	___
6466WX	Whistle Tender, *49-53*	20	50	___
6467	Miscellaneous Car, *56*	25	46	___
6468	B&O Auto Boxcar, blue, *53-55*	15	42	___
6468X	B&O Auto Boxcar, tuscan, *53-55*	101	222	___
6468-25	NH Auto Boxcar, *56-58*			
	(A) Black N over white H, black doors	25	75	___
	(B) White N over black H, black doors	66	267	___
	(C) Black N over white H, painted Tuscan doors	33	84	___
6469	Liquified Gas Tank Car, *63*	39	131	___
6470	Explosives Boxcar, *59-60*	12	36	___
6472	Refrigerator Car, *50-53*	11	25	___

			Good	Exc
____	**6473**	Horse Transport Car, *62-69*	13	25
____	**6475**	Libby's Crushed Pineapple Vat Car, *63 u*	35	90
____	**6475**	Pickles Vat Car, *60-62*	20	77
	6476	LV Short Hopper, *57-63*		
____		(A) Red body	6	19
____		(B) Gray body	8	20
____		(C) Black body	6	19
____	**6476-75**	LV Short Hopper, black, Type VI body, *63*	8	20
____	**6476-135**	LV Short Hopper, yellow, *64-66, 68*	6	19
____	**6476-160**	LV Short Hopper, black, *69*	6	17
____	**6476-185**	LV Short Hopper, yellow, *69*	6	19
____	**6477**	Miscellaneous Car with pipes, *57-58*	20	65
____	**6480**	Explosives Boxcar, red, *61*	17	43
____	**6482**	Refrigerator Car, *57*	14	40
	6500	Flatcar with Bonanza airplane, *62, 65*		
____		(A) Plane, red top and wings	342	662
____		(B) Plane, white top and wings	385	775
____	**6501**	Flatcar with jet boat, *62-63*	52	162
	6502	Flat Car with Girder, *62*		
____		(A) Black flatcar	19	70
____		(B) Red flatcar	35	109
____	**6502-50**	Flatcar, blue or teal, no lettering, with bridge girder, *62*	10	44
	6511	Flatcar with pipes, *53-56*		
____		(A) Die-cast truck plates, *53*	18	58
____		(B) Stamped metal truck plates	13	40
____	**6511-24**	Set of 6 pipes with box, *55-58*	51	150
____	**6512**	Cherry Picker Car, *62-63*	28	85
	6517	LL Bay Window Caboose, *55-59*		
____		(A) Built date underscored	25	75
____		(B) Built date not underscored	20	50
____		(C) Built date not underscored, lettering higher	20	53
____	**6517-75**	Erie Bay Window Caboose, *66*	147	484
____	**6518**	Transformer Car, *56-58*	23	64
	6519	Allis-Chalmers Flatcar, *58-61*		
____		(A) Dark or medium orange base	25	70
____		(B) Dull light orange base	42	130
	6520	Searchlight Car, *49-51*		
____		(A) Tan generator	625	1444
____		(B) Green generator	93	257
____		(C) Maroon generator	17	47
____		(D) Orange generator	15	41
____		(E) Green generator, black searchlight housing	88	300
	6530	Firefighting Instruction Car, *60-61*		
____		(A) Red body, white lettering	25	83

		Good	Exc
	(B) Black body, white lettering	105	415
6536	M&StL Open Quad Hopper, *58-59, 63*		
	(A) AAR trucks, *59, 63*	27	69
	(B) Bar-end trucks, *58*	45	135
6544	Missile Firing Car, 4 missiles, *60-64*		
	(A) White-lettered console	45	159
	(B) Black-lettered console	100	342
6555	Sunoco 1-D Tank Car, *49-50*	15	65
6556	MKT Stock Car, *58*	118	294
6557	SP-type Smoking Caboose, *58-59*		
	(A) Tuscan, with non-reverse lettering	83	194
	(B) Brown, with reverse lettering	463	1125
6560	Bucyrus Erie Crane Car, smokestack, *55-58, 68-69*		
	(A) Black frame, red-orange cab	36	102
	(B) Black frame, gray cab	27	72
	(C) Black frame, red cab	19	40
	(D) Dark blue frame, red cab	30	108
	(E) Black frame, red cab, rubber-stamped "6560"	86	327
	(F) Black frame, black cab	53	150
6560-25	Bucyrus Erie Crane Car, 8-wheel, *56*	33	84
6561	Cable Car, 2 reels, *53-56*		
	(A) Orange reels	23	58
	(B) Gray reels	23	93
6562	NYC Gondola with 4 red canisters, *56-58*		
	(A) Gray body, *56*	15	45
	(B) Red body, *56, 58*	10	30
	(C) Black body, *57*	9	28
6572	REA Refrigerator Car, *58-59, 63*		
	(A) Passenger trucks	99	227
	(B) Bar-end trucks	45	106
	(C) AAR trucks, *63*	25	69
6630	Missile Launching Car, *61*	22	73
6636	Alaska Open Quad Hopper, *59-60*	36	91
6640	USMC Missile Launching Car, *60*	73	220
6646	Lionel Lines Stock Car, *57*	14	43
6650	IRBM Rocket Launcher, *59-63*		
	(A) "6650" stamped on left	18	51
	(B) "6650" stamped on right	76	242
6650-80	Missile, *60*	4	10
6651	USMC Cannon Car, *64 u*	73	196
6654W	Whistle Tender	18	40
6656	Lionel Lines Stock Car, *49-55*		
	(A) Brown Armour decal	22	60
	(B) No decal	9	30
6657	Rio Grande SP-type Caboose, *57-58*		
	(A) With ladder slots	59	156

			Good	Exc
____		(B) Without ladder slots	135	430
____	6660	Boom Car, *58*	25	77
	6670	Derrick Car, *59-60*		
____		(A) "6670" stamped on left	22	75
____		(B) "6670" stamped on right	83	219
	6672	Santa Fe Refrigerator Car, *54-56*		
____		(A) Blue lettering, 2 lines of data	18	39
____		(B) Black lettering, 2 lines of data	22	63
____		(C) Blue lettering, 3 lines of data	91	289
____	6736	Detroit & Mackinac Open Quad Hopper, *60-62*	14	40
	6800	Flatcar with airplane, *57-60*		
____		(A) Plane, black top and wings	33	87
____		(B) Plane, yellow top and wings	40	112
____	6800-60	Airplane, *57-58*	46	243
____	6801	Flatcar with boat, white hull, brown deck, *57*	28	68
____	6801-50	Flatcar with boat, yellow hull, white deck, *58-60*	32	82
____	6801-60	Boat, *57-58*	20	110
____	6801-75	Flatcar with boat, blue hull, white deck, *58-60*	33	88
____	6802	Flatcar with 2 U.S. Steel girders, *58-59*	15	37
____	6803	Flatcar with USMC tank and sound truck, *58-59*	104	221
____	6804	Flatcar with USMC antiaircraft and sound trucks, *58-59*	107	208
____	6805	Atomic Energy Disposal Flatcar, *58-59*	40	200
____	6806	Flatcar with USMC radar and medical trucks, *58-59*	98	206
____	6807	Flatcar with amphibious vehicle, *58-59*	62	141
____	6808	Flatcar with USMC tank and searchlight truck, *58-59*	97	255
____	6809	Flatcar with USMC antiaircraft and medical trucks, *58-59*	97	209
____	6810	Flatcar with trailer, *58*	20	48
	6812	Track Maintenance Car, *59*		
____		(A) Dark yellow superstructure	17	70
____		(B) Black base, gray platform and crank handle	17	69
____		(C) Gray base, black platform and crank handle	17	69
____		(D) Cream superstructure	40	190
____		(E) Light yellow superstructure	20	73
____	6814	Rescue Caboose, *59-61*	43	108
	6816	Flatcar with Allis-Chalmers bulldozer, *59-60*		
____		(A) Red car	170	440
____		(B) Black car	575	1175
	6816-100	Allis-Chalmers Bulldozer, *59-60*		
____		(A) No box	70	233

		Good	Exc	
	(B) Separate-sale box	264	707	___
6817	Flatcar with Allis-Chalmers motor scraper, *59-60*			
	(A) Red car	193	435	___
	(B) Black car	520	1189	___
6817-100	Allis-Chalmers Motor Scraper, *59-60*			
	(A) No box	118	258	___
	(B) Separate-sale box	233	725	___
6818	Flatcar with transformer, *58*	10	35	___
6819	Flatcar with helicopter, *59-60*	17	61	___
6820	Aerial Missile Transport Car with helicopter, *60-61*			
	(A) Light blue frame	85	225	___
	(B) Medium blue frame	94	190	___
6821	Flatcar with crates, *59-60*	15	38	___
6822	Searchlight Car, *61-69*			
	(A) Black base, gray light	15	38	___
	(B) Gray base, black light	23	47	___
6823	Flatcar with 2 IRBM missiles, *59-60*	25	65	___
6824	USMC Work Caboose, *60*	112	262	___
6824-50	Rescue Caboose, white, *64*	37	113	___
6825	Flatcar with arch trestle bridge, *59-62*	18	38	___
6826	Flatcar with Christmas trees, *59-60*	26	95	___
6827	Flatcar with Harnischfeger power shovel, *60-63*	70	225	___
6827-100	Harnischfeger Power Shovel, *60*			
	(A) No box	55	122	___
	(B) Separate-sale box	115	253	___
6828	Flatcar with Harnischfeger crane, *60-63, 66*			
	(A) Black flatcar, light yellow crane cab	79	235	___
	(B) Black flatcar, dark yellow crane cab	75	265	___
	(C) Red flatcar, dark yellow crane cab	323	1193	___
6828-100	Harnischfeger Construction Crane, *60*			
	(A) No box	35	105	___
	(B) Separate-sale box	90	258	___
6830	Flatcar with submarine, *60-61*	48	150	___
6844	Missile Carrying Car, 6 missiles, *59-60*			
	(A) Black frame	26	85	___
	(B) Red frame	345	1075	___
Other Track, Transformers, and Assorted Items				
A	Transformer, 90 watts, *47-48*	13	43	___
CO-1	Track Clips, dozen, with envelope (O), *49*	5	12	___
CO-1	Track Clips, box of 50 (O), *49*	25	85	___
CO-1	Track Clips, box of 100 (O), *49*	33	113	___
CTC	Lockon (O and O27), *47-69*	1	2	___

		Good	Exc
CTC-14	Lockons, dozen, with envelope	13	38
ECU-1	Electronic Control Unit, *46*	30	88
KW	Transformer, 190 watts, *50-65*	33	74
LTC	Lockon (0 and 027), *50-69*	2	8
LW	Transformer, 125 watts, *55-56*	36	65
OC	Curved Track (0), *45-61*	0	1
OC1/2	Half Section Curved Track (0), *45-66*	0	1
OCS	Curved Insulated Track (0), *46-50*	8	20
OS	Straight Track (0), *45-61*	0	2
OSS	Straight Insulated Track, *46-50*	5	18
OTC	Lockon Track (0 and 027)	2	4
Q	Transformer, 75 watts, *46*	11	32
R	Transformer, 110 watts, *46-47*	13	32
RCS	Remote Control Track (0), *45-48*	4	10
RW	Transformer, 110 watts, *48-54*	11	28
RX	Transformer, 100 watts, *47-48*	13	33
S	Transformer, 80 watts, *47*	13	33
SP	Smoke Pellets, bottle, *48-69*		
	(A) Tall, light amber bottle	13	48
	(B) Tall, dark amber bottle	10	50
	(C) Short, light amber bottle	16	56
	(D) All other bottles	5	12
	(E) Bottle on blister pack, *65*	20	58
SP-12	Dealer Display Box with 12 full smoke bottles	105	318
ST-300	Nut Driver Set with holder, service station item	541	1068
ST-301	Wheel Puller, service station item	50	170
ST-302	Spring Adjusting Tool	100	179
ST-303	E Unit Spreader, service station item	40	85
ST-311	Wheel Puller, service station item	73	185
ST-320	Phillips Screwdriver, service station item	143	265
ST-321	Flathead Screwdriver, short, service station item	180	440
ST-322	Flathead Screwdriver, long, service station item	40	150
ST-325	Screwdriver Set, service station item	400	900
ST-342	Track Pliers, service station item	75	165
ST-343	O Gauge Track Pliers, service station item	278	590
ST-350	Rivet Press, service station item	424	693
ST-350-6	Rivet Press Tool Block with tools, service station item	391	587
ST-350-17	Sliding Shoe Anvil, service station item	7	18
ST-375	Wheel Cup Tool Set, service station item	292	1130
ST-378	E Unit Vice, service station item	159	285
ST-384	Track Pliers, service station item	137	230
SW	Transformer, 130 watts, *61-66*	25	70
TW	Transformer, 175 watts, *53-60*	35	90
TOC	Curved Track (0), *62-66, 68-69*		1
TOC1/2	Half Section Straight Track (0), *62-66*		1

POSTWAR 1945-1969

		Good	Exc
TOS	Straight Track (O), *62-69*		1____
UCS	Remote Control Track (O), *45-69*	5	13____
UTC	Lockon (O, 027, Standard), *45*	1	3____
V	Transformer, 150 watts, *46-47*	45	87____
VW	Transformer, 150 watts, *48-49*	37	83____
Z	Transformer, 250 watts, *45-47*	63	115____
ZW	Transformer, 250 watts, *48-49*	41	102____
ZW	Transformer, 275 watts, *50-56*	63	163____
ZW	Transformer, 275 watts, R type, *57-66*	87	181____

			Exc	Mint
____	**366**	Menards C&NW 4-4-2 Locomotive with tender, *09*	45	75
____	**400**	Menards C&NW Chicago Combine Car, *09*	25	40
____	**403**	Menards C&NW Lake Superior Observation Car, *09*	25	40
____	**410**	Menards C&NW Lake Michigan Coach, *09*	40	65
____	**0512**	Toy Fair Reefer, *81 u*	60	70
____	**550C**	31" Diameter Curved Track (O), *70*	1	2
____	**550S**	Straight Track (O), *70*	1	2
____	**665E**	Johnny Cash Blue Train 4-6-4 Locomotive, *71 u*		NRS
____	**1050**	New Englander Set, *80-81*	155	205
____	**1052**	Chesapeake Flyer Set, *80*	140	150
____	**1053**	James Gang Set, *80-82*	155	195
____	**1070**	Royal Limited Set, *80*	285	350
____	**1071**	Mid Atlantic Limited Set, *80*	225	230
____	**1072**	Cross Country Express Set, *80-81*	240	385
____	**1081**	Wabash Cannonball Set, *70-72*	105	120
____	**1082**	Yard Boss Set, *70*	120	165
____	**1083**	Pacemaker Set, *70*	105	120
____	**1084**	Grand Trunk Western Freight Set, *70*	120	140
____	**1085**	Santa Fe Express Diesel Freight Set, *70*	175	190
____	**1091**	Sears Special Steam Freight Set, *70 u*	150	165
____	**1092**	Sears GTW Steam Freight Set, *70 u*	150	165
____	**1100**	Happy Huff n' Puff, *74-75 u*	55	70
____	**1150**	L.A.S.E.R. Train Set, *81-82*	155	195
____	**1151**	Union Pacific Thunder Freight Set, *81-82*	150	175
____	**1153**	JCPenney Thunderball Freight Set, *81 u*	165	180
____	**1154**	Reading Yard King Set, *81-82*	170	190
____	**1155**	Cannonball Freight Set, *82*	75	85
____	**1157**	Lionel Leisure Wabash Cannonball Set, *81 u*		250
____	**1158**	Maple Leaf Limited Set, *81*	405	435
____	**1159**	Toys "R" Us Midnight Flyer Set, *81 u*	130	140
____	**1160**	Great Lakes Limited Set, *81*	280	330
____	**T-1171**	CN Locomotive Set, *71 u*	240	275
____	**1182**	Yardmaster Set, *71-72*	85	105
____	**T-1172**	Yardmaster Set, *71 u*		200
____	**1183**	Silver Star Set, *71-72*	65	80
____	**T-1173**	Grand Trunk Western Freight Set, *71-73 u*	175	195
____	**1184**	Allegheny Set, *71*	120	150
____	**T-1174**	Canadian National Set, *71-73 u*	265	300
____	**1186**	Cross Country Express Set, *71-72*	210	260
____	**1187**	Illinois Central Set (SSS), *71*	400	485
____	**1190**	Sears Special #1 Set, *71 u*	85	100
____	**1195**	JCPenney Special Set, *71 u*	150	165
____	**1198**	Unnamed Set, *71 u*		175
____	**1199**	Ford-Autolite Allegheny Set, *71 u*	187	207
____	**1200**	Gravel Gus, *75 u*	75	100
____	**1250**	New York Central Set (SSS), *72*	315	380
____	**1252**	Heavy Iron Set, *82-83*	90	130
____	**1253**	Quicksilver Express Set, *82-83*	265	340
____	**1254**	Black Cave Flyer Set, *82*	75	105
____	**1260**	Continental Limited Set, *82*	290	385
____	**1261**	Sears Black Cave Flyer Set, *82 u*	165	195

		Exc	Mint
1262	Toys "R" Us Heavy Iron Set, *82 u*	150	165____
1263	JCPenney Overland Freight Set, *82 u*	150	165____
1264	Nibco Express Set, *82 u*	190	195____
1265	Tappan Special Set, *82 u*	130	155____
1280	Kickapoo Valley & Northern Set, *72*	60	75____
1284	Allegheny Set, *72*	140	165____
1285	Santa Fe Twin Diesel Set, *72*	95	140____
1287	Pioneer Dockside Switcher Set, *72*	95	100____
T-1272	Yardmaster Set, *72-73 u*	150	165____
1290	Sears Steam Freight Set, *72 u*	150	165____
T-1273	Silver Star Set, *72-73 u*	90	115____
1291	Sears Steam Freight Set, *72 u*	150	165____
1300	Gravel Gus Junior, *75 u*	70	90____
1350	Canadian Pacific Set (SSS), *73*	460	620____
1351	Baltimore & Ohio Set, *83-84*	205	280____
1352	Rocky Mountain Freight Set, *83-84*	75	95____
1353	Southern Streak Set, *83-85*	75	95____
1354	Northern Freight Flyer Set, *83-85*	230	280____
1355	Commando Assault Train, *83-84*	175	248____
1359	Display Case for Set 1355, *83 u*	75	95____
1361	Gold Coast Limited Set, *83*	390	400____
1362	Lionel Leisure BN Express Set, *83 u*	200	300____
1380	U.S. Steel Industrial Switcher Set, *73-75*	60	75____
1381	Cannonball Set, *73-75*	70	75____
1382	Yardmaster Set, *73-74*	110	135____
1383	Santa Fe Freight Set, *73-75*	100	125____
1384	Southern Express Set, *73-76*	75	120____
1385	Blue Streak Freight Set, *73-74*	100	120____
1386	Rock Island Express Set, *73-74*	120	140____
1387	Milwaukee Road Special Set, *73*	185	285____
1388	Golden State Arrow Set, *73-75*	215	240____
1390	Sears 7-unit Steam Freight Set, *73 u*	170	190____
1392	Sears 8-unit Steam Freight Set, *73 u*	150	165____
1393	Sears 6-unit Diesel Freight Set, *73 u*	150	165____
1395	JCPenney Set, *73 u*	150	165____
1400	Happy Huff n' Puff Junior, *75 u*	130	140____
1402	Chessie System Set, *84-85*	125	150____
1403	Redwood Valley Express Set, *84-85*	170	205____
1450	D&RGW Set (SSS), *74*	335	415____
1451	Erie-Lackawanna Limited Set, *84*	415	465____
1460	Grand National Set, *74*	300	330____
1461	Black Diamond Set, *74 u, 75*	100	120____
1463	Coca-Cola Special Set, *74 u, 75*	220	270____
1487	Broadway Limited Set, *74-75*	160	255____
1489	Santa Fe Double Diesel Set, *74-76*	140	165____
1492	Sears 7-unit Steam Freight Set, *74 u*	150	165____
1493	Sears 7-unit Steam Freight Set, *74 u*	150	165____
1499	JCPenney Great Express Set, *74 u*	150	165____
1501	Midland Freight Set, *85-86*	75	95____
1502	Yard Chief Set, *85-86*	205	230____
1506	Sears Centennial Chessie System Set, *85 u*	165	195____
1512	JCPenney Midland Freight Set, *85 u*	90	115____
1549	Toys "R" Us Heavy Iron Set, *85-89 u*	180	215____

		Exc	Mint
_____ **1552**	Burlington Northern Limited Set, _85_	500	570
_____ **1560**	North American Express Set, _75_	275	365
_____ **1562**	Fast Freight Flyer Set, _85 u_	120	140
_____ **1577**	Liberty Special Set, _75 u_	227	235
_____ **1579**	Milwaukee Road Set (SSS), _75_	325	410
_____ **1581**	Thunderball Freight Set, _75-76_	90	100
_____ **1582**	Yard Chief Set, _75-76_	115	155
_____ **1584**	N&W "Spirit of America" Set, _75_	160	180
_____ **1585**	75th Anniversary Special Set, _75-77_	220	235
_____ **1586**	Chesapeake Flyer Set, _75-77_	160	190
_____ **1587**	Capitol Limited Set, _75_	270	300
_____ **1593**	Sears Set, _75 u_		100
_____ **1595**	Sears 6-unit Diesel Freight Set, _75 u_	150	165
_____ **1602**	Nickel Plate Special Set, _86-91_	120	125
_____ **1606**	Sears Centennial Nickel Plate Set, _86 u_	165	195
_____ **1608**	American Express General Set, _86 u_	205	320
_____ **1615**	Cannonball Express Set, _86-90_	65	75
_____ **1632**	Santa Fe Work Train (SSS), _86_	220	255
_____ **1652**	B&O Freight Set, _86_	140	185
_____ **1658**	Town House TV and Appliances Set, _86 u_	80	95
_____ **1660**	Yard Boss Set, _76_	100	115
_____ **1661**	Rock Island Line Set, _76-77_	80	100
_____ **1662**	Black River Freight Set, _76-78_	75	95
_____ **1663**	Amtrak Lake Shore Limited Set, _76-77_	215	265
_____ **1664**	Illinois Central Freight Set, _76-77_	265	355
_____ **1665**	NYC Empire State Express Set, _76_	310	435
_____ **1672**	Northern Pacific Set (SSS), _76_	215	280
_____ **1685**	True Value Freight Flyer Set, _86-87 u_	60	75
_____ **1686**	Kay Bee Toys Freight Flyer Set, _86 u_	150	165
_____ **1687**	Freight Flyer Set, _87-90_	39	47
_____ **1693**	Toys "R" Us Rock Island Line Set, _76 u_	110	130
_____ **1694**	Toys "R" Us Black River Freight Set, _76 u_	110	130
_____ **1696**	Sears Steam Freight Set, _76 u_	110	130
_____ **1698**	True Value Rock Island Line Set, _76 u_	125	145
_____ **1760**	Trains n' Truckin' Steel Hauler Set, _77-78_	105	110
_____ **1761**	Trains n' Truckin' Cargo King Set, _77-78_	95	165
_____ **1762**	Wabash Cannonball Set, _77_	135	190
_____ **1764**	Heartland Express Set, _77_	185	240
_____ **1765**	Rocky Mountain Special Set, _77_	210	315
_____ **1766**	B&O Budd Car Set (SSS), _77_	335	390
_____ **1776**	Seaboard U36B Diesel, _74-76_	74	120
_____ **1790**	Lionel Leisure Steel Hauler Set, _77 u_	150	200
_____ **1791**	Toys "R" Us Steel Hauler Set, _77 u_	130	175
_____ **1792**	True Value Rock Island Line Set, _77 u_	100	135
_____ **1793**	Toys "R" Us Black River Freight Set, _77 u_	120	155
_____ **1796**	JCPenney Cargo Master Set, _77 u_		200
_____ **1860**	"Workin' on the Railroad" Timberline Set, _78_	65	85
_____ **1862**	"Workin' on the Railroad" Logging Empire Set, _78_	85	110
_____ **1864**	Santa Fe Double Diesel Set, _78-79_	155	190
_____ **1865**	Chesapeake Flyer Set, _78-79_	155	180
_____ **1866**	Great Plains Express Set, _78-79_	195	285
_____ **1867**	Milwaukee Road Limited Set, _78_	230	275
_____ **1868**	M&StL Set (SSS), _78_	215	255

		Exc	Mint
1892	JCPenney Logging Empire Set, *78 u*	95	125____
1893	Toys "R" Us Logging Empire Set, *78 u*	175	225____
1960	Midnight Flyer Set, *79-81*	55	75____
1962	Wabash Cannonball Set, *79*	90	105____
1963	Black River Freight Set, *79-81*	75	85____
1965	Smokey Mountain Line Set, *79*	65	85____
1970	Southern Pacific Limited Set, *79 u*	340	365____
1971	Quaker City Limited Set, *79*	315	335____
1990	Mystery Glow Midnight Flyer Set, *79 u*	75	90____
1991	JCPenney Wabash Cannonball Deluxe Express Set, *79 u*	150	165____
1993	Toys "R" Us Midnight Flyer Set, *79 u*	110	130____
2110	Graduated Trestle Set, 22 pieces, *70-88*	9	13____
2111	Elevated Trestle Set, 10 pieces, *70-88*	8	11____
2113	Tunnel Portals, pair, *84-87*	11	16____
2115	Dwarf Signal, *84-87*	9	13____
2117	Block Target Signal, *84-87*	23	29____
2122	Extension Bridge, rock piers, *76-87*	24	34____
2125	Whistling Freight Shed, *71*	36	43____
2126	Whistling Freight Shed, *76-87*	18	26____
2127	Diesel Horn Shed, *76-87*	25	30____
2128	Operating Switchman, *83-86*	26	29____
2129	Illuminated Freight Station, *83-86*	30	33____
2133	Lighted Freight Station, *72-78, 80-84*	34	38____
2140	Automatic Banjo Signal, *70-84*	17	21____
2145	Automatic Gateman, *72-84*	31	47____
2151	Operating Semaphore, *78-82*	15	19____
2152	Automatic Crossing Gate, *70-84*	21	25____
2154	Automatic Highway Flasher, *70-87*	19	24____
2156	Illuminated Station Platform, *70-71*	26	34____
2162	Automatic Crossing Gate and Signal, "262," *70-87, 94, 96-98, 05*	16	27____
2163	Block Target Signal, *70-78*	14	19____
2170	Street Lamps, set of 3, *70-87*	13	19____
2171	Gooseneck Street Lamps, set of 2, *80-81, 83-84*	15	18____
2175	"Sandy Andy" Gravel Loader Kit, *76-79*	34	55____
2180	Road Signs, 16 pieces, *77-98*		6____
2181	Telephone Pole Set "150," *77-98*		5____
2195	Floodlight Tower, *70-71*	38	50____
2199	Microwave Tower, *72-75*	30	39____
2214	Girder Bridge, *70-71, 72 u, 73-87*	5	9____
2256	Station Platform, *73-81*	12	18____
2260	Illuminated Bumper, *70-71, 72 u, 73*	23	35____
2280	Nonilluminated Bumpers, set of 3, *73-84*	2	4____
2282	Die-cast Bumpers, pair, *83 u*	12	18____
2283	Die-cast Illuminated Bumpers, "260," *84-99*	10	16____
2290	Illuminated Bumpers, pair, *75 u, 76-86*	7	11____
2292	Station Platform, *85-87*	5	9____
2300	Operating Oil Drum Loader, *83-87*	80	90____
2301	Operating Sawmill, *80-84*	60	65____
2302	Union Pacific Manual Gantry Crane, *80-82*	24	31____
2303	Santa Fe Manual Gantry Crane, *80-81, 83 u*	17	21____
2305	Getty Operating Oil Derrick, *81-84*	105	115____
2306	Operating Ice Station with 6700 Ice Car, *82-83*	90	105____

		Exc	Mint
____ 2307	Lighted Billboard, *82-86*	12	13
____ 2308	Animated Newsstand, *82-83*	105	120
____ 2309	Mechanical Crossing Gate, *82-92*	4	7
____ 2310	Mechanical Crossing Gate, *73-77*	2	4
____ 2311	Mechanical Semaphore, *82-92*	4	7
____ 2312	Mechanical Semaphore, *73-77*	2	4
____ 2313	Floodlight Tower, *75-86*	22	27
____ 2314	Searchlight Tower, *75-84*	22	27
____ 2315	Operating Coaling Station, *83-84*	80	83
____ 2316	N&W Operating Gantry Crane, *83-84*	90	125
____ 2317	Operating Drawbridge, *75 u, 76-81*	100	130
____ 2318	Operating Control Tower, *83-86*	40	50
____ 2319	Illuminated Watchtower, *75-78, 80*	29	56
____ 2320	Flagpole Kit, *83-87*	10	14
____ 2321	Operating Sawmill, *84, 86-87*	115	133
____ 2323	Operating Freight Station, *84-87*	43	47
____ 2324	Operating Switch Tower, *84-87*	60	65
____ 2390	Lionel Mirror, *82 u*	95	125
____ 2494	Rotary Beacon, *72-74*	37	44
____ 2709	Rico Station Kit, *81-98*		42
____ 2710	Billboards, set of 5, *70-84*	4	10
____ 2714	Tunnel, *75 u, 76-77*	36	43
____ 2716	Short Extension Bridge, *88-98*	3	8
____ 2717	Short Extension Bridge, *77-87*	2	4
____ 2718	Barrel Platform Kit, *77-84*	3	5
____ 2719	Watchman's Shanty Kit, *77-87*	3	5
____ 2720	Lumber Shed Kit, *77-84, 87*	3	5
____ 2721	Operating Log Mill Kit, *78*	2	4
____ 2722	Barrel Loader Kit, *78*	2	4
____ 2783	Freight Station Kit, *84*	6	10
____ 2784	Freight Platform Kit, *81-90*	5	8
____ 2785	Engine House Kit, *73-77*	31	39
____ 2786	Freight Platform Kit, *73-77*	4	6
____ 2787	Freight Station Kit, *73-77, 83*	7	10
____ 2788	Coal Station Kit, *75 u, 76-77*	18	30
____ 2789	Water Tower Kit, *75-77, 80*	19	24
____ 2791	Cross Country Set, *70-71*	22	30
____ 2792	Whistle Stop Set, *70-71*	24	34
____ 2792	Layout Starter Pack, *80-84*	9	21
____ 2793	Alamo Junction Set, *70-71*	22	30
____ 2796	Grain Elevator Kit, *76 u, 77*	43	47
____ 2797	Rico Station Kit, *76-77*	23	37
____ 2900	Lockon, *70-98*		1
____ 2901	Track Clips, dozen (027), *71-98*		6
____ 2905	Lockon and Wire, *74-00*		3
____ 2909	Smoke Fluid, *70-98*		8
____ 2910	OTC Contactor, *84-86, 88*	4	7
____ 2911	Smoke Pellets, *70-73*	18	35
____ 2925	Lubricant, *70-71, 72 u, 73-75*		2
____ 2927	Maintenance Kit, *70, 78-98*		11
____ 2928	Oil, *71*		2
____ 2951	Track Layout Book, *70-86*	1	2
____ 2952	Train and Accessory Manual, *70-74*	1	2

		Exc	Mint
2953	Train and Accessory Manual, *75-86*	1	2___
2960	Lionel 75th Anniversary Book, *75 u, 76*	15	30___
2980	Magnetic Conversion Coupler, *70-71*	1	2___
2985	The Lionel Train Book, *86-98*		18___
3100	Great Northern 4-8-4 (FARR 3), *81*	335	388___
4044	Transformer, *45*-watt, *70-71*	2	7___
4045	Safety Transformer, *70-71*	2	3___
4050	Safety Transformer, *72-79*	2	3___
4060	Power Master Transformer, *80-93*		13___
4090	Power Master Transformer, *70-84*	47	65___
4125	Transformer, *25*-watt, *72*	2	3___
4150	Trainmaster Transformer, *72-73, 75-77*	6	15___
4250	Trainmaster Transformer, *74*	5	10___
4651	Trainmaster Transformer, *78-79*	1	2___
4690	MW Transformer, *86-89*	60	80___
4851	AC Transformer, red or black, *85-91, 94-96*	5	10___
5012	27" Diameter Curved Track, card of 4 (027), *70-96*		17___
5013	27" Diameter Curved Track (027), *70-78*		1___
5014	Half Curved Track (027), *70-98*		1___
5016	36" Straight Track (027), *87-88*	1	2___
5017	Straight Track, card of 4 (027), *70-96*		4___
5018	Straight Track (027), *70-78*		1___
5019	Half Straight Track (027), *70-98*		1___
5020	90-degree Crossover (027), *70-98*		7___
5021	27" Manual Switch, left hand (027), *70-98*		15___
5022	27" Manual Switch, right hand (027), *70-98*		15___
5023	45-degree Crossover (027), *70-98*		6___
5024	35" Straight Track (027), *88-98, 05*		3___
5025	Manumatic Uncoupler, *71-72*	1	2___
5027	27" Manual Switches, pair (027), *74-84*	13	21___
5030	Track Expander Set (027), *71-84*	18	26___
5031	Ford-Autolite Layout Expander Set, *71 u*	50	65___
5033	27" Diameter Curved Track (027), *79-98*		1___
5038	Straight Track (027), *79-98*		1___
5041	Insulator Pins, dozen (027), *70-98*		1___
5042	Steel Pins, dozen (027), *70-98*		1___
5045	54" Diameter Curved Track Ballast (027), *87-88*	1	2___
5046	27" Diameter Curved Track Ballast (027), *87-88*	1	2___
5047	Straight Track Ballast (027), *87-88*	1	2___
5049	42" Diameter Curved Track (027), *88-98*	1	2___
5090	27" Manual Switches, 3 pair (027), *78-84*	55	70___
5113	54" Diameter Curved Track (027), *79-98*	1	2___
5121	27" Remote Switch, left hand (027), *70-98*	18	22___
5122	27" Remote Switch, right hand (027), *70-98*	20	22___
5125	27" Remote Switches, pair (027), *71-83*	20	30___
5132	31" Remote Switch, right hand (O), *80-94*	29	30___
5133	31" Remote Switch, left hand (O), *80-94*	22	30___
5149	Remote Uncoupling Section (027), *70-98*		15___
5165	72" Remote Switch, right hand (O), *87-98*	23	65___
5166	72" Remote Switch, left hand (O), *87-98*	23	75___
5167	42" Remote Switch, right hand (027), *88-98*	25	37___
5168	42" Remote Switch, left hand (027), *88-98*	25	37___
5193	27" Remote Switches, 3 pair (027), *78-83*	80	95___

MODERN ERA 1970-2019

		Exc	Mint
5500	10" Straight Track (0), *71-98*		1
5501	31" Diameter Curved Track (0), *71-98*		1
5502	Remote Uncoupling Section (0), *71-72*	7	9
5504	Half Curved Track (0), *83-98*		1
5505	Half Straight Track (0), *83-98*		1
5520	90-degree Crossover (0), *71-72*	6	9
5522	36" Straight, *87-88*		3
5523	40" Straight Track (0), *88-98*		4
5530	Remote Uncoupling Section (0), *81-98*	10	19
5540	90-degree Crossover (0), *81-98*		10
5543	Insulator Pins, dozen (0), *70-98*		1
5545	45-degree Crossover (0), *83-98*		11
5551	Steel Pins, dozen (0), *70-98*		1
5554	54" Diameter Curved Track (0), *90-98*		2
5560	72" Diameter Curved Track Ballast (0), *87-88*	1	2
5561	31" Diameter Curved Track Ballast (0), *87-88*	1	2
5562	Straight Track Ballast (0), *87-88*	1	2
5572	72" Diameter Curved Track (0), *79-98*	2	3
5600	Curved Track (Trutrack), *73-74*	1	2
5601	Curved Track, card of 4 (Trutrack), *73-74*	6	10
5602	Curved Track Ballast, card of 4 (Trutrack), *73-74*	5	9
5605	Straight Track (Trutrack), *73-74*	1	2
5606	Straight Track, card of 4 (Trutrack), *73-74*	5	9
5607	Straight Track Ballast, card of 4 (Trutrack), *73-74*	5	9
5620	Manual Switch, left hand (Trutrack), *73-74*	4	13
5625	Remote Switch, left hand (Trutrack), *73-74*	9	17
5630	Manual Switch, right hand (Trutrack), *73-74*	4	13
5635	Remote Switch, right hand (Trutrack), *73-74*	9	17
5640	Left Switch Ballast, card of 2 (Trutrack), *73-74*	5	9
5650	Right Switch Ballast, card of 2 (Trutrack), *73-74*	5	9
5655	Lockon (Trutrack), *73-74*	1	2
5660	Terminal Track with lockon (Trutrack), *74*	1	3
5700	Oppenheimer Reefer, *81*	30	38
5701	Dairymen's League Reefer, *81*	21	23
5702	National Dairy Despatch Reefer, *81*	16	21
5703	North American Despatch Reefer, *81*	22	26
5704	Budweiser Reefer, *81-82*	64	70
5705	Ball Glass Jars Reefer, *81-82*	30	35
5706	Lindsay Brothers Reefer, *81-82*	26	27
5707	American Refrigerator Transit Reefer, *81-82*	17	20
5708	Armour Reefer, *82-83*	16	21
5709	REA Reefer, *82-83*	22	26
5710	Canadian Pacific Reefer, *82-83*	22	25
5711	Commercial Express Reefer, *82-83*	13	15
5712	Lionel Lines Reefer, *82 u*	47	75
5713	Cotton Belt Reefer, *83-84*	19	22
5714	Michigan Central Reefer, *83-84*	17	24
5715	Santa Fe Reefer, *83-84*	19	26
5716	Vermont Central Reefer, *83-84*	20	23
5717	Santa Fe Bunk Car, *83*	22	30
5719	Canadian National Reefer, *84*	10	16
5720	Great Northern Reefer, *84*	75	90
5721	Soo Line Reefer, *84*	21	23

		Exc	Mint
5722	NKP Reefer, *84*	16	18____
5724	PRR Bunk Car, *84*	15	23____
5726	Southern Bunk Car, *84 u*	22	27____
5727	USMC Bunk Car, *84-85*	25	30____
5728	Canadian Pacific Bunk Car, *86*	18	23____
5730	Strasburg Reefer, *85-86*	20	27____
5731	L&N Reefer, *85-86*	19	24____
5732	Jersey Central Reefer, *85-86*		24____
5733	Lionel Lines Bunk Car, *86 u*	18	24____
5735	NYC Bunk Car, *85-86*	33	35____
5739	B&O Tool Car, *86*	32	37____
5745	Santa Fe Bunk Car (SSS), *86*	39	45____
5760	Santa Fe Tool Car (SSS), *86*	30	35____
5900	AC/DC Converter, *79-83*	3	10____
6076	LV Hopper (O27), *70 u*	17	21____
6100	Ontario Northland Covered Quad Hopper, *81-82*	30	34____
6101	BN Covered Quad Hopper, *81-82*	17	31____
6102	GN Covered Quad Hopper (FARR 3), *81*	26	28____
6103	Canadian National Covered Quad Hopper, *81*	35	38____
6104	Southern Quad Hopper with coal (FARR 4), *83*	50	60____
6105	Reading Operating Hopper, *82*	34	39____
6106	N&W Covered Quad Hopper, *82*	30	40____
6107	Shell Covered Quad Hopper, *82*	22	26____
6109	C&O Operating Hopper, *83*	29	41____
6110	MP Covered Quad Hopper, *83-84*	17	27____
6111	L&N Covered Quad Hopper, *83-84*	13	20____
6113	Illinois Central Hopper (O27), *83-85*	15	25____
6114	C&NW Covered Quad Hopper, *83*	54	80____
6115	Southern Hopper (O27), *83-86*	15	19____
6116	Soo Line Ore Car, *84*	21	27____
6117	Erie Operating Hopper, *84*	29	39____
6118	Erie Covered Quad Hopper, *84*	31	45____
6122	Penn Central Ore Car, *84*	20	25____
6123	PRR Covered Quad Hopper (FARR 5), *84-85*	55	105____
6124	D&H Covered Quad Hopper, *84*	19	32____
6126	Canadian National Ore Car, *86*	18	24____
6127	Northern Pacific Ore Car, *86*	20	24____
6131	Illinois Terminal Covered Quad Hopper, *85-86*	15	21____
6134	BN 2-bay ACF Hopper (std O), *86 u*	95	115____
6135	C&NW 2-bay ACF Hopper (std O), *86 u*	65	80____
6137	NKP Hopper (O27), *86-91*	13	17____
6138	B&O Quad Hopper with coal, *86*	21	28____
6142	Gondola, black, *70*	20	33____
6150	Santa Fe Hopper (O27), *85-86, 92 u*	10	15____
6177	Reading Hopper (O27), *86-90*	14	19____
6200	FEC Gondola with canisters, *81-82*	13	24____
6201	Union Pacific Animated Gondola, *82-83*	19	25____
6202	WM Gondola with coal, *82*	34	36____
6203	Black Cave Gondola (O27), *82*	2	4____
6205	CP Gondola with canisters, *83*	18	26____
6206	C&IM Gondola with canisters, *83-85*	18	26____
6207	Southern Gondola with canisters (O27), *83-85*	6	8____
6208	Chessie System Gondola with canisters, *83 u*	21	24____

		Exc	Mint
____ **6209**	NYC Gondola with coal (std O), *84-85*	42	46
____ **6210**	Erie-Lackawanna Gondola with canisters, *84*	21	30
____ **6211**	C&O Gondola with canisters, *84-85*		10
____ **6214**	Lionel Lines Gondola with canisters, *84 u*	38	45
____ **6230**	Erie-Lackawanna Reefer (std O), *86 u*	95	120
____ **6231**	Railgon Gondola with coal (std O), *86 u*	66	76
____ **6232**	Illinois Central Boxcar (std O), *86 u*	65	80
____ **6233**	CP Flatcar with stakes (std O), *86 u*	47	50
____ **6234**	Burlington Northern Boxcar (std O), *85*	55	75
____ **6235**	Burlington Northern Boxcar (std O), *85*	33	43
____ **6236**	Burlington Northern Boxcar (std O), *85*	33	43
____ **6237**	Burlington Northern Boxcar (std O), *85*	32	47
____ **6238**	Burlington Northern Boxcar (std O), *85*	33	43
____ **6239**	Burlington Northern Boxcar (std O), *86 u*	37	55
____ **6251**	NYC Coal Dump Car, *85*	25	42
____ **6254**	NKP Gondola with canisters, *86-91*	6	11
____ **6258**	Santa Fe Gondola with canisters (O27), *85-86, 92 u*		3
____ **X6260**	NYC Gondola with canisters, *85-86*	13	15
____ **6272**	Santa Fe Gondola with cable reels (SSS), *86*	20	25
____ **6300**	Corn Products 3-D Tank Car, *81-82*	19	25
____ **6301**	Gulf 1-D Tank Car, *81*	20	26
____ **6302**	Quaker State 3-D Tank Car, *81*	42	46
____ **6304**	GN 1-D Tank Car (FARR 3), *81*	44	55
____ **6305**	British Columbia 1-D Tank Car, *81*	55	76
____ **6306**	Southern 1-D Tank Car (FARR 4), *83*	45	50
____ **6307**	PRR 1-D Tank Car (FARR 5), *84-85*	70	75
____ **6308**	Alaska 1-D Tank Car (O27), *82-83*	27	35
____ **6310**	Shell 2-D Tank Car (O27), *83-84*	19	24
____ **6312**	C&O 2-D Tank Car (O27), *84-85*	18	26
____ **6313**	Lionel Lines 1-D Tank Car, *84 u*	43	50
____ **6314**	B&O 3-D Tank Car, *86*	31	38
____ **6317**	Gulf 2-D Tank Car (O27), *84-85*	18	22
____ **6357**	Frisco 1-D Tank Car, *83*	42	50
____ **6401**	Virginian Bay Window Caboose, *81*	37	47
____ **6403**	Amtrak Vista Dome Car (O27), *76-77*	24	31
____ **6404**	Amtrak Passenger Coach (O27), *76-77*	24	31
____ **6405**	Amtrak Passenger Coach (O27), *76-77*	24	31
____ **6406**	Amtrak Observation Car (O27), *76-77*	22	29
____ **6410**	Amtrak Passenger Coach (O27), *77*	28	48
____ **6411**	Amtrak Passenger Coach (O27), *77*	24	35
____ **6412**	Amtrak Vista Dome Car (O27), *77*	22	33
____ **6420**	Reading Transfer Caboose, *81-82*	20	28
____ **6421**	Joshua L. Cowen Bay Window Caboose, *82*	34	40
____ **6422**	DM&IR Bay Window Caboose, *81*	32	38
____ **6425**	Erie-Lackawanna Bay Window Caboose, *83-84*	35	43
____ **6426**	Reading Transfer Caboose, *82-83*	14	24
____ **6427**	BN Transfer Caboose, *83-84*	12	21
____ **6428**	C&NW Transfer Caboose, *83-85*	22	25
____ **6430**	Santa Fe SP-type Caboose, *83-89*	4	14
____ **6431**	Southern Bay Window Caboose (FARR 4), *83*	42	55
____ **6432**	Union Pacific SP-type Caboose, *81-82*	6	10
____ **6433**	Canadian Pacific Bay Window Caboose, *81*	60	70
____ **6435**	U.S. Marines Transfer Caboose, *83-84*	9	17

		Exc	Mint
6438	GN Bay Window Caboose (FARR 3), *81*	48	65 ___
6439	Reading Bay Window Caboose, *84-85*	22	30 ___
6441	Alaska Bay Window Caboose, *82-83*	45	50 ___
6446-25	N&W Covered Quad Hopper, *70 u*	203	290 ___
6449	Wendy's N5c Caboose, *81-82*	64	74 ___
6464-500	Timken BoxCar, orange, *70 u*	208	324 ___
6464-500	Timken BoxCar, yellow, *70 u*	210	350 ___
6476-135	LV Hopper "25000," (027), *70-71 u*	6	11 ___
6478	Black Cave SP-type Caboose, *82*	5	9 ___
6482	Nibco Express SP-type Caboose, *82 u*	26	34 ___
6485	Chessie System SP-type Caboose, *84-85*	6	10 ___
6486	Southern SP-type Caboose, *83-85*	5	7 ___
6490	NKP N5c Caboose, *84 u*		NRS ___
6491	Erie-Lackawanna Transfer Caboose, *85-86*	9	17 ___
6493	L&C Bay Window Caboose, *86-87*	21	36 ___
6494	Santa Fe Bobber Caboose, *85-86*	7	9 ___
6496	Santa Fe Work Caboose (SSS), *86*	21	29 ___
6504	L.A.S.E.R. Flatcar with helicopter (027), *81-82*	18	26 ___
6505	L.A.S.E.R. Radar Car, *81-82*	17	25 ___
6506	L.A.S.E.R. Security Car, *81-82*	18	26 ___
6507	L.A.S.E.R. Flatcar with cruise missile, *81-82*	21	30 ___
6508	Canadian Pacific Crane Car, *81*	50	70 ___
6509	Depressed Center Flatcar with girders, *81*	60	85 ___
6510	Union Pacific Crane Car, *82*	55	60 ___
6515	Union Pacific Flatcar (027), *83-84, 86*	5	9 ___
6521	NYC Flatcar with stakes (std 0), *84-85*	29	35 ___
6522	C&NW Searchlight Car, *83-85*	27	30 ___
6524	Erie Crane Car, *84*	55	60 ___
6526	Searchlight Car, *84-85*	23	25 ___
6529	NYC Searchlight Car, *85-86*	21	27 ___
6531	Express Mail Flatcar with trailers, *85-86*	23	32 ___
6560	Bucyrus Erie Crane Car, *71*	100	130 ___
6561	Flatcar with cruise missile (027), *83-84*	13	26 ___
6562	Flatcar with fences (027), *83-84*	13	21 ___
6564	U.S. Marines Flatcar with 2 tanks (027), *83-84*	13	21 ___
6573	Redwood Valley Express Log Dump Car (027), *84-85*	8	13 ___
6574	Redwood Valley Express Crane Car (027), *84-85*	7	13 ___
6575	Redwood Valley Express Flatcar with fences (027), *84-85*	7	13 ___
6576	Santa Fe Crane Car (027), *85-86, 92 u*	7	10 ___
6579	NYC Crane Car, *85-86*	36	44 ___
6585	PRR Flatcar with fences (027), *86-90*	5	9 ___
6587	W&ARR Flatcar with horses, *86 u*	18	26 ___
6593	Santa Fe Crane Car (SSS), *86*	41	48 ___
6700	PFE Ice Car, *82-83*		70 ___
6900	N&W Extended Vision Caboose, *82*	60	65 ___
6901	Ontario Northland Extended Vision Caboose, *82 u*	44	55 ___
6903	Santa Fe Extended Vision Caboose, *83*	80	95 ___
6904	Union Pacific Extended Vision Caboose, *83*	115	135 ___
6905	NKP Extended Vision Caboose, *83 u*	50	65 ___

			Exc	Mint
____	6906	Erie-Lack. Extended Vision Caboose, *84*	75	90
____	6907	NYC Wood-sided Caboose (std O), *86 u*	90	92
____	6908	PRR N5c Caboose (FARR 5), *84-85*	43	47
____	6910	NYC Extended Vision Caboose, *84 u*	55	60
____	6912	Redwood Valley Express SP-type Caboose, *84-85*	9	16
____	6913	Burlington Northern Extended Vision Caboose, *85*	70	90
____	6916	NYC Work Caboose, *85-86*	16	22
____	6917	Jersey Central Extended Vision Caboose, *86*	36	50
____	6918	B&O SP-type Caboose, *86*	10	15
____	6919	Nickel Plate Road SP-type Caboose, *86-91*	5	9
____	6920	B&A Wood-sided Caboose (std O), *86 u*	65	80
____	6921	PRR SP-type Caboose, *86-90*	5	9
____	7200	Quicksilver Passenger Coach (O27), *82-83*	26	34
____	7201	Quicksilver Passenger Coach (O27), *82-83*	26	34
____	7202	Quicksilver Observation Car (O27), *82-83*	26	34
____	7203	N&W Diner "491," *82 u*	130	180
____	7204	Southern Pacific Diner, *82 u*	190	235
____	7207	NYC Diner, *83 u*	70	140
____	7208	PRR Diner, *83 u*	80	90
____	7210	Union Pacific Diner, *84*	85	110
____	7211	Southern Pacific Vista Dome Car, *83 u*	145	185
____	7215	B&O Passenger Coach, *83-84*	43	50
____	7216	B&O Passenger Coach, *83-84*	43	50
____	7217	B&O Baggage Car, *83-84*	43	50
____	7220	Illinois Central Baggage Car, *85, 87*	105	135
____	7221	Illinois Central Combination Car, *85, 87*	85	105
____	7222	Illinois Central Passenger Coach, *85, 87*	85	105
____	7223	Illinois Central Passenger Coach, *85, 87*	85	105
____	7224	Illinois Central Diner, *85, 87*	75	90
____	7225	Illinois Central Observation Car, *85, 87*	95	115
____	7227	Wabash Diner (FF 1), *86-87*	115	130
____	7228	Wabash Baggage Car (FF 1), *86-87*	90	100
____	7229	Wabash Combination Car (FF 1), *86-87*	90	100
____	7230	Wabash Passenger Coach (FF 1), *86-87*	90	100
____	7231	Wabash Passenger Coach (FF 1), *86-87*	90	100
____	7232	Wabash Observation Car (FF 1), *86-87*	85	95
____	7241	W&ARR Passenger Coach, *86 u*	43	50
____	7242	W&ARR Baggage Car, *86 u*	43	50
____	7301	Norfolk & Western Stock Car, *82*	34	45
____	7302	Texas & Pacific Stock Car (O27), *83-84*	11	14
____	7303	Erie Stock Car, *84*	41	50
____	7304	Southern Stock Car (FARR 4), *83 u*	41	45
____	7309	Southern Stock Car (O27), *85-86*	12	16
____	7312	W&ARR Stock Car (O27), *86 u*	25	30
____	7401	Chessie System Stock Car (O27), *84-85*	13	17
____	7404	Jersey Central BoxCar, *86*	26	40
____	7500	Lionel 75th Anniversary U36B Diesel, *75-77*	130	150
____	7501	Lionel 75th Anniversary BoxCar, *75-77*	28	38
____	7502	Lionel 75th Anniversary Reefer, *75-77*	30	40
____	7503	Lionel 75th Anniversary Reefer, *75-77*	41	47
____	7504	Lionel 75th Anniversary Covered Quad Hopper, *75-77*	28	40
____	7505	Lionel 75th Anniversary BoxCar, *75-77*	41	50
____	7506	Lionel 75th Anniversary BoxCar, *75-77*	20	25

		Exc	Mint
7507	Lionel 75th Anniversary Reefer, *75-77*	27	39____
7508	Lionel 75th Anniversary N5c Caboose, *75-77*	24	29____
7509	Kentucky Fried Chicken Reefer, *81-82*	75	85____
7510	Red Lobster Reefer, *81-82*	70	75____
7511	Pizza Hut Reefer, *81-82*	65	75____
7512	Arthur Treacher's Reefer, *82*	65	75____
7513	Bonanza Reefer, *82*	65	75____
7514	Taco Bell Reefer, *82*	66	85____
7515	Denver Mint Car, *81*	64	81____
7517	Philadelphia Mint Car, *82*	38	39____
7518	Carson City Mint Car, *83*	34	43____
7519	Toy Fair Reefer, *82 u*	35	42____
7520	Nibco Express BoxCar, *82 u*	265	440____
7521	Toy Fair Reefer, *83 u*	50	65____
7522	New Orleans Mint Car, *84 u*	33	38____
7523	Toy Fair Reefer *84 u*	44	49____
7524	Toy Fair Reefer, *85 u*	55	60____
7525	Toy Fair BoxCar, *86 u*	65	80____
7530	Dahlonega Mint Car, *86 u*	37	48____
7600	Frisco, "Spirit of '76," N5c Caboose, *74-76*	33	39____
7601	Delaware BoxCar, *74-76*	14	19____
7602	Pennsylvania BoxCar, *74-76*	17	27____
7603	New Jersey BoxCar, *74-76*	15	24____
7604	Georgia BoxCar, *74 u, 75-76*	22	26____
7605	Connecticut BoxCar, *74 u, 75-76*	17	32____
7606	Massachusetts BoxCar, *74 u, 75-76*	25	29____
7607	Maryland BoxCar, *74 u, 75-76*	17	34____
7608	South Carolina BoxCar, *75 u, 76*	38	50____
7609	New Hampshire BoxCar, *75 u, 76*	38	46____
7610	Virginia BoxCar, *75 u, 76*	155	200____
7611	New York BoxCar, *75 u, 76*	50	65____
7612	North Carolina BoxCar, *75 u, 76*	35	60____
7613	Rhode Island BoxCar, *75 u, 76*	36	50____
7700	Uncle Sam BoxCar, *75 u*	44	51____
7701	Camel BoxCar, *76-77*	60	70____
7702	Prince Albert BoxCar, *76-77*	62	78____
7703	Beechnut BoxCar, *76-77*	33	51____
7704	Toy Fair BoxCar, *76 u*	110	120____
7705	Canadian Toy Fair BoxCar, *76 u*	130	145____
7706	Sir Walter Raleigh BoxCar, *77-78*	65	75____
7707	White Owl BoxCar, *77-78*	65	75____
7708	Winston BoxCar, *77-78*	65	80____
7709	Salem BoxCar, *78*	62	71____
7710	Mail Pouch BoxCar, *78*	65	75____
7711	El Producto BoxCar, *78*	65	75____
7712	Santa Fe Boxcar (FARR 1), *79*	30	50____
7800	Pepsi BoxCar, *76 u, 77*	79	88____
7801	A&W BoxCar, *76 u, 77*	52	65____
7802	Canada Dry BoxCar, *76 u, 77*	44	57____
7803	Trains n' Truckin' BoxCar, *77 u*	20	26____
7806	Season's Greetings BoxCar, *76 u*	70	95____
7807	Toy Fair BoxCar, *77 u*	70	95____
7808	Northern Pacific Stock Car, *77*	37	44____

		Exc	Mint
____7809	Vernors BoxCar, *77 u, 78*	50	65
____7810	Orange Crush BoxCar, *77 u, 78*	45	60
____7811	Dr Pepper BoxCar, *77 u, 78*	48	63
____7813	"Season's Greetings" BoxCar, *77 u*	65	90
____7814	"Season's Greetings" BoxCar, *78 u*	70	95
____7815	Toy Fair BoxCar, *78 u*	65	85
____7816	Toy Fair BoxCar, *79 u*	65	85
____7817	Toy Fair BoxCar, *80 u*	95	105
____7900	D&RGW Operating Cowboy Car (O27), *82-83*	22	26
____7901	LL Cop and Hobo Car (O27), *82-83*	24	27
____7902	Santa Fe Boxcar (O27), *82-85*	5	9
____7903	Rock Island Boxcar (O27), *83*	8	13
____7904	San Diego Zoo Giraffe Car (O27), *83-84*	44	55
____7905	Black Cave Boxcar (O27), *82*	6	9
____7908	Tappan Boxcar (O27), *82 u*	39	55
____7909	L&N Boxcar (O27), *83-84*	40	49
____7910	Chessie System Boxcar (O27), *84-85*	18	23
____7912	Toys "R" Us Giraffe Car (O27), *82-84 u*	70	80
____7913	Turtleback Zoo Giraffe Car (O27), *85-86*	50	60
____7914	Toys "R" Us Giraffe Car (O27), *85-89 u*	70	90
____7920	Sears Centennial Boxcar (O27), *85-86 u*	39	44
____7925	Erie-Lackawanna Boxcar (O27), *86-90*	10	18
____7926	NKP Boxcar (O27), *86-91*	8	10
____7930	True Value Boxcar (O27), *86-87 u*	34	50
____7931	Town House TV and Appliances Boxcar (O27), *86 u*	31	39
____7932	Kay Bee Toys Boxcar (O27), *86-87 u*	40	49
____8001	NKP 2-6-4 Locomotive, *80 u*	55	65
____8002	Union Pacific 2-8-4 Locomotive (FARR 2), *80*	310	345
____8003	Chessie System 2-8-4 Locomotive, *80*	360	540
____8004	Rock Island 4-4-0 Locomotive, *80-82*	190	220
____8005	Santa Fe 4-4-0 Locomotive, *80-82*	65	75
____8006	ACL 4-6-4 Locomotive, *80 u*	245	340
____8007	NYNH&H 2-6-4 Locomotive, *80-81*	65	75
____8008	Chessie System 4-4-2 Locomotive, *80*	65	75
____8010	Santa Fe NW2 Switcher, *70, 71 u*	48	79
____8020	Santa Fe Alco Diesel A Unit, dummy, *70*	45	60
____8020	Santa Fe Alco Diesel A Unit, *70-72, 74-76*	65	85
____8021	Santa Fe Alco Diesel B Unit, *71-72, 74-76*	47	63
____8022	Santa Fe Alco Diesel A Unit, *71 u*	80	105
____8025	CN Alco Diesel A Unit, *71-73 u*	85	105
____8025	CN Alco Diesel A Unit, dummy, *71-73 u*	45	65
____8030	Illinois Central GP9 Diesel, *70-72*	103	140
____8031	Canadian National GP7 Diesel, *71-73 u*	80	150
____8031	Illinois Central GP9 Diesel Dummy Unit, *70*		NRS
____8040	Canadian National 2-4-2 Locomotive, *71 u*	43	85
____8040	NKP 2-4-2 Locomotive, *70-72*	26	34
____8041	NYC 2-4-2 Locomotive, *70*	55	65
____8041	PRR 2-4-2 Locomotive, *71 u*	55	65
____8042	GTW 2-4-2 Locomotive, *70, 71-73 u*	26	34
____8043	NKP 2-4-2 Locomotive, *70 u*	45	65
____8050	D&H U36C Diesel, *80*	105	220
____8051	D&H U36C Diesel Dummy Unit, *80*	95	115
____8054/55	Burlington F3 Diesel AA Set, *80*	360	385

		Exc	Mint	
8056	C&NW FM Train Master Diesel, 80	175	225	___
8057	Burlington NW2 Switcher, 80	100	115	___
8059	Pennsylvania F3 Diesel B Unit, 80 u	190	290	___
8060	Pennsylvania F3 Diesel B Unit, 80 u	335	420	___
8061	Chessie System U36C Diesel, 80	110	140	___
8062	Burlington F3 Diesel B Unit, 80 u	205	255	___
8063	Seaboard SD9 Diesel, 80	80	100	___
8064	Florida East Coast GP9 Diesel, 80	150	200	___
8065	Florida East Coast GP9 Diesel Dummy Unit, 80	95	120	___
8066	TP&W GP20 Diesel, 80-81, 83 u	65	80	___
8071	Virginian SD18 Diesel, 80 u	135	155	___
8072	Virginian SD18 Diesel Dummy Unit, 80 u	75	110	___
8100	Norfolk & Western 4-8-4,"611," 81	360	402	___
8101	Chicago & Alton 4-6-4 Locomotive "659," 81	275	445	___
8102	Union Pacific 4-4-2 Locomotive, 81-82	49	65	___
8104	Union Pacific 4-4-0 Locomotive,"3," 81 u	180	235	___
8111	DT&I NW2 Switcher, 71-74	55	65	___
8140	Southern 2-4-0 Locomotive, 71 u	22	30	___
8141	PRR 2-4-2 Locomotive, 71-72	41	43	___
8142	C&O 4-4-2 Locomotive, 71-72		55	___
8150	PRR GG1 Electric Locomotive "4935," 81	330	395	___
8151	Burlington SD28 Diesel, 81	120	145	___
8152	Canadian Pacific SD24 Diesel, 81	170	180	___
8153	Reading NW2 Switcher, 81-82	100	155	___
8154	Alaska NW2 Switcher, 81-82	120	160	___
8155	Monon U36B Diesel, 81-82	110	135	___
8156	Monon U36B Diesel Dummy Unit, 81-82		65	___
8157	Santa Fe FM Train Master, 81	280	325	___
8158	DM&IR GP35 Diesel, 81-82	90	150	___
8159	DM&IR GP35 Diesel Dummy Unit, 81-82	55	75	___
8160	Burger King GP20 Diesel, 81-82	106	128	___
8161	L.A.S.E.R. Switcher, 81-82	23	55	___
8162	Ontario Northland SD18 Diesel, 81 u	150	210	___
8163	Ontario Northland SD18 Diesel Dummy Unit, 81 u	95	140	___
8164	Pennsylvania F3 Diesel B Unit, 81 u	340	370	___
8182	Nibco Express NW2 Switcher, 82 u	90	130	___
8190	Diesel Horn Kit, 81 u		30	___
8200	Kickapoo Dockside 0-4-0T, 72	28	39	___
8203	PRR 2-4-2 Locomotive, 72, 74 u, 75	26	34	___
8204	C&O 4-4-2 Locomotive, 72	55	60	___
8206	NYC 4-6-4 Locomotive, 72-75	140	155	___
8209	Pioneer Dockside 0-4-0T with tender, 72	45	65	___
8209	Pioneer Dockside 0-4-0T, no tender, 73-76	42	55	___
8210	Joshua L. Cowen 4-6-4 Locomotive, 82	245	350	___
8212	Black Cave 0-4-0 Locomotive, 82	30	49	___
8213	D&RGW 2-4-2 Locomotive, 82-83, 84-91 u	65	70	___
8214	Pennsylvania 2-4-2 Locomotive, 82-83	55	65	___
8215	Nickel Plate Road 2-8-4 Locomotive "779," 82 u	245	285	___
8250	Santa Fe GP9 Diesel, 72, 74-75	120	145	___
8251-50	Horn/Whistle Controller, 72-74	1	2	___
8252	D&H Alco Diesel A Unit, 72	85	125	___
8253	D&H Alco Diesel B Unit, 72	50	70	___
8254	Illinois Central GP9 Diesel Dummy Unit, 72	60	65	___

			Exc	Mint
____	8255	Santa Fe GP9 Diesel Dummy Unit, *72*	60	65
____	8258	Canadian National GP7 Diesel Dummy Unit, *72-73 u*	65	85
____	8260/62	Southern Pacific F3 Diesel AA Set, *82*	490	520
____	8261	Southern Pacific F3 Diesel B Unit, *82 u*	435	445
____	8263	Santa Fe GP7 Diesel, *82*	65	80
____	8264	CP Vulcan Switcher Snowplow, *82*	80	100
____	8265	Santa Fe SD40 Diesel, *82*	205	225
____	8266	Norfolk & Western SD24 Diesel, *82*	150	225
____	8268	Quicksilver Alco Diesel A Unit, *82-83*	85	105
____	8269	Quicksilver Alco Diesel A Unit, dummy, *82-83*	55	65
____	8272	Pennsylvania EP-5 Electric Locomotive, *82 u*	205	265
____	8300	Santa Fe 2-4-0 Locomotive, *73-74*	22	25
____	8302	Southern 2-4-0 Locomotive, *73-76*	29	30
____	8303	Jersey Central 2-4-2 Locomotive, *73-74*	55	59
____	8304	B&O 4-4-2 Locomotive, *75*	75	105
____	8304	Rock Island 4-4-2 Locomotive, *73-75*	85	105
____	8304	Pennsylvania 4-4-2 Locomotive, *74-75*	75	105
____	8304	C&O 4-4-2 Locomotive, *75-77*	75	105
____	8305	Milwaukee Road 4-4-2 Locomotive, *73*	95	120
____	8307	Southern Pacific 4-8-4 Locomotive "4449," *83*	490	560
____	8308	Jersey Central 2-4-2 Locomotive, *73-74 u*	36	43
____	8309	Southern 2-8-2 Locomotive "4501" (FARR 4), *83*	385	495
____	8310	Nickel Plate Road 2-4-0 Locomotive, *73 u*	26	50
____	8310	Santa Fe 2-4-0 Locomotive, *74-75 u*	26	34
____	8310	Jersey Central 2-4-0 Locomotive, *74-75 u*	26	50
____	8311	Southern 0-4-0 Locomotive, *73 u*	26	34
____	8313	Santa Fe 0-4-0 Locomotive, *83-84*	13	17
____	8314	Southern 2-4-0 Locomotive, *83-85*	17	21
____	8315	B&O 4-4-0 Locomotive, *83-84*	85	120
____	8341	ACL SP-type Caboose, *86 u, 87-90*	6	8
____	8350	U.S. Steel Switcher, *73-75*	18	26
____	8351	Santa Fe Alco Diesel A Unit, *73-75*	60	65
____	8352	Santa Fe GP20 Diesel, *73-75*	65	105
____	8353	Grand Trunk Western GP7 Diesel, *73-75*	90	120
____	8354	Erie NW2 Switcher, *73, 75*	80	105
____	8355	Santa Fe GP20 Diesel Dummy Unit, *73-74*	65	90
____	8356	Grand Trunk Western GP7 Diesel Dummy Unit, *73-75*	65	75
____	8357	PRR GP9 Diesel, *73-75*	100	120
____	8358	PRR GP9 Diesel Dummy Unit, *73-75*	55	100
____	8359	Chessie System GP7 Diesel "GM50," *73*	95	120
____	8360	Long Island GP20 Diesel, *73-74*	70	105
____	8361	Western Pacific Alco Diesel A Unit, *73-75*	50	70
____	8362	Western Pacific Alco Diesel B Unit, *73-75*	45	65
____	8363	B&O F3 Diesel A Unit, *73-75*	280	310
____	8364	B&O F3 Diesel A Unit, dummy, *73-75*	120	160
____	8365/66	CP F3 Diesel AA Set (SSS), *73*	355	405
____	8367	Long Island GP20 Diesel Dummy Unit, *73-75*	80	100
____	8368	Alaska Vulcan Switcher, *83*	120	129
____	8369	Erie-Lackawanna GP20 Diesel, *83-85*	125	140
____	8370/72	NYC F3 Diesel AA Set, *83*	330	435
____	8371	NYC F3 Diesel B Unit, *83*	105	150
____	8374	Burlington Northern NW2 Switcher, *83-85*	105	110
____	8375	C&NW GP7 Diesel, *83-85*	135	165

		Exc	Mint
8376	Union Pacific SD40 Diesel, *83*	175	200____
8377	U.S. Marines Switcher, *83-84*	55	65____
8378	Wabash FM Train Master Diesel "550," *83 u*	500	690____
8379	PRR Fire Car, *83 u*	80	100____
8380	Lionel Lines SD28 Diesel, *83 u*	235	315____
8402	Reading 4-4-2 Locomotive, *84-85*	47	55____
8403	Chessie System 4-4-2 Locomotive, *84-85*	55	65____
8404	PRR 6-8-6 "6200" (FARR 5), *84-85*	360	460____
8406	NYC 4-6-4 Locomotive "783," *84*	445	571____
8410	Redwood Valley Express 4-4-0 Locomotive, *84-85*	34	50____
8452	Erie Alco Diesel A Unit, *74-75*	75	95____
8453	Erie Alco Diesel B Unit, *74-75*	55	75____
8454	D&RGW GP7 Diesel, *74-75*	80	110____
8455	D&RGW GP7 Diesel Dummy Unit, *74-75*	50	85____
8458	Erie-Lackawanna SD40 Diesel, *84*	160	190____
8459	D&RGW Vulcan Rotary Snowplow, *84*	125	146____
8460	MKT NW2 Switcher, *74-75*	45	65____
8463	Chessie System GP20 Diesel, *74 u*	130	190____
8466	Amtrak F3 Diesel A Unit, *74-76*	225	250____
8464/65	D&RGW F3 Diesel AA Set (SSS), *74*	220	325____
8467	Amtrak F3 Diesel A Unit, dummy, *74-76*	80	90____
8468	B&O F3 Diesel B Unit, *74-75*	95	100____
8469	CP F3 Diesel B Unit (SSS), *74*	85	110____
8470	Chessie System U36B Diesel, *74*	80	110____
8471	Pennsylvania NW2 Switcher, *74-76*	170	195____
8473	Coca-Cola NW2 Switcher, *74 u, 75*	120	130____
8474	D&RGW F3 Diesel B Unit (SSS), *74*	110	125____
8475	Amtrak F3 Diesel B Unit, *74*	85	105____
8477	NYC GP9 Diesel, *84 u*	150	205____
8480/82	Union Pacific F3 Diesel AA Set, *84*	280	365____
8481	Union Pacific F3 Diesel B Unit, *84*	150	155____
8485	USMC NW2 Switcher, *84-85*	105	135____
8500	Pennsylvania 2-4-0 Locomotive, *75-76*	17	21____
8502	Santa Fe 2-4-0 Locomotive, *75*	17	21____
8506	PRR 0-4-0 Locomotive, *75-77*	75	90____
8507	Santa Fe 2-4-0 Locomotive, *75 u*	25	30____
8512	Santa Fe 0-4-0T Locomotive, *85-86*	22	30____
8516	NYC 0-4-0 Locomotive, *85-86*	115	140____
8550	Jersey Central GP9 Diesel, *75-76*	120	155____
8551	Pennsylvania EP-5 Electric Locomotive, *75-76*	115	120____
8552/53/54	SP Alco Diesel ABA Set, *75-76*	200	245____
8555/57	Milwaukee Road F3 Diesel AA Set (SSS), *75*	240	315____
8556	Chessie System NW2 Switcher, *75-76*	160	200____
8558	Milwaukee Road EP-5 Electric Locomotive, *76-77*	160	195____
8559	N&W GP9 Diesel "1776," *75*	115	145____
8560	Chessie System U36B Diesel Dummy Unit, *75*	85	130____
8561	Jersey Central GP9 Diesel Dummy Unit, *75-76*	70	95____
8562	Missouri Pacific GP20 Diesel, *75-76*	130	145____
8563	Rock Island Alco Diesel A Unit, *75-76 u*	65	90____
8564	Union Pacific U36B Diesel, *75*	110	155____
8565	Missouri Pacific GP20 Diesel Dummy Unit, *75-76*	55	70____
8566	Southern F3 Diesel A Unit, *75-77*	220	370____
8567	Southern F3 Diesel A Unit, dummy, *75-77*	105	135____

		Exc	Mint
____ 8568	Preamble Express F3 Diesel A Unit, *75 u*	90	115
____ 8569	Soo Line NW2 Switcher, *75-77*	60	65
____ 8570	Liberty Special Alco Diesel A Unit, *75 u*	75	90
____ 8571	Frisco U36B Diesel, *75-76*	75	95
____ 8572	Frisco U36B Diesel Dummy Unit, *75-76*		55
____ 8573	Union Pacific U36B Diesel Dummy Unit, *75 u*	145	190
____ 8575	Milwaukee Road F3 Diesel B Unit (SSS), *75*	105	160
____ 8576	Penn Central GP7 Diesel, *75 u, 76-77*	90	120
____ 8578	NYC Ballast Tamper, *85, 87*	85	90
____ 8580/82	Illinois Central F3 Diesel AA Set, *85, 87*	420	485
____ 8581	Illinois Central F3 Diesel B Unit, *85, 87*	130	155
____ 8585	Burlington Northern SD40 Diesel, *85*	355	385
____ 8587	Wabash GP9 Diesel "484," *85 u*	250	280
____ 8600	NYC 4-6-4 Locomotive, *76*	175	195
____ 8601	Rock Island 0-4-0 Locomotive, *76-77*	17	21
____ 8602	D&RGW 2-4-0 Locomotive, *76-78*	22	26
____ 8603	C&O 4-6-4 Locomotive, *76-77*	135	190
____ 8604	Jersey Central 2-4-2 Locomotive, *76 u*	39	44
____ 8606	B&A 4-6-4 Locomotive "784," *86 u*	720	760
____ 8610	Wabash 4-6-2 "672" (FF 1), *86-87*	435	610
____ 8615	L&N 2-8-4 Locomotive "1970," *86 u*	540	630
____ 8616	Santa Fe 4-4-2 Locomotive, *86*	60	65
____ 8617	Nickel Plate Road 4-4-2 Locomotive, *86-91*	60	65
____ 8625	Pennsylvania 2-4-0 Locomotive, *86-90*	21	34
____ 8630	W&ARR 4-4-0 Locomotive "3," *86 u*	125	150
____ 8635	Santa Fe 0-4-0 (SSS), *86*	80	100
____ 8650	Burlington Northern U36B Diesel, *76-77*	120	170
____ 8651	Burlington Northern U36B Diesel Dummy Unit, *76-77*	70	90
____ 8652	Santa Fe F3 Diesel A Unit, *76-77*	260	510
____ 8653	Santa Fe F3 Diesel A Unit, dummy, *76-77*	135	160
____ 8654	Boston & Maine GP9 Diesel, *76-77*	155	195
____ 8655	Boston & Maine GP9 Diesel Dummy Unit, *76-77*	90	110
____ 8656	Canadian National Alco Diesel A Unit, *76*	150	195
____ 8657	Canadian National Alco Diesel B Unit, *76*	60	75
____ 8658	CN Alco Diesel A Unit, dummy, *76*	85	170
____ 8659	Virginian Electric Locomotive, *76-77*	125	137
____ 8660	CP Rail NW2 Switcher, *76-77*	100	135
____ 8661	Southern F3 Diesel B Unit, *76*	165	170
____ 8662	B&O GP7 Diesel, *86*	120	130
____ 8664	Amtrak Alco Diesel A Unit, *76-77*	85	120
____ 8665	BAR Jeremiah O'Brien GP9 Diesel, "1776," *76 u*	100	170
____ 8666	Northern Pacific GP9 Diesel (SSS), *76*	125	175
____ 8667	Amtrak Alco Diesel B Unit, *76-77*	60	80
____ 8668	Northern Pacific GP9 Diesel Dummy Unit (SSS), *76*	100	130
____ 8669	Illinois Central Gulf U36B Diesel, *76-77*	125	165
____ 8670	Chessie System Switcher, *76*	30	55
____ 8679	Northern Pacific GP20 Diesel, *86*	90	105
____ 8687	Jersey Central FM Train Master Diesel, *86*	198	276
____ 8690	Lionel Lines Trolley, *86*	105	115
____ 8701	W&ARR 4-4-0 Locomotive "3," *77-79*	157	210
____ 8702	Southern 4-6-4 Locomotive, *77-78*	280	398
____ 8703	Wabash 2-4-2 Locomotive, *77*	22	30
____ 8750	Rock Island GP7 Diesel, *77-78*	110	125

		Exc	Mint	
8751	Rock Island GP7 Diesel Dummy Unit, *77-78*	50	70	___
8753	Pennsylvania GG1 Electric Locomotive, *77 u*	290	315	___
8754	New Haven Electric Locomotive, *77-78*	100	115	___
8755	Santa Fe U36B Diesel, *77-78*	130	150	___
8756	Santa Fe U36B Diesel Dummy Unit, *77-78*	75	95	___
8757	Conrail GP9 Diesel, *76 u, 77-78*	110	140	___
8758	Southern GP7 Diesel Dummy Unit, *77 u, 78*	75	95	___
8759	Erie-Lackawanna GP9 Diesel, *77-79*	115	175	___
8760	Erie-Lackawanna GP9 Diesel Dummy Unit, *77-79*	95	115	___
8761	GTW NW2 Switcher, *77-78*	95	130	___
8762	Great Northern EP-5 Electric Locomotive, *77-78*	130	140	___
8763	Norfolk & Western GP9 Diesel, *76 u, 77-78*	110	120	___
8764	B&O Budd RDC Passenger (SSS), *77*	110	135	___
8765	B&O Budd RDC Baggage Dummy Unit (SSS), *77*	80	100	___
8766	B&O Budd RDC Baggage (SSS), *77*		310	___
8767	B&O Budd RDC Passenger Dummy Unit (SSS), *77*	85	105	___
8768	B&O Budd RDC Passenger Dummy Unit (SSS), *77*	85	105	___
8769	Republic Steel Switcher, *77-78*	22	39	___
8770	NW2 Switcher, *77-78*		65	___
8771	Great Northern U36B Diesel, *77*	110	140	___
8772	GM&O GP20 Diesel, *77*	85	95	___
8773	Mickey Mouse U36B Diesel, *77-78*	493	645	___
8774	Southern GP7 Diesel, *77 u, 78*	110	135	___
8775	Lehigh Valley GP9 Diesel, *77 u, 78*	85	105	___
8776	C&NW GP20 Diesel, *77 u, 78*	87	129	___
8777	Santa Fe F3 Diesel B Unit (SSS), *77*	160	175	___
8778	Lehigh Valley GP9 Diesel Dummy Unit, *77 u, 78*	90	110	___
8779	C&NW GP20 Diesel Dummy Unit, *77 u, 78*	73	109	___
8800	Lionel Lines 4-4-2 Locomotive, *78-81*	75	105	___
8801	Blue Comet 4-6-4 Locomotive, *78-80*	380	500	___
8803	Santa Fe 0-4-0 Locomotive, *78*	14	24	___
8850	Penn Central GG1 Electric Locomotive, *78 u, 79*	250	305	___
8851/52	New Haven F3 Diesel AA Set, *78 u, 79*	320	430	___
8854	CP Rail GP9 Diesel, *78-79*	100	120	___
8855	Milwaukee Road SD18 Diesel, *78*		115	___
8857	Northern Pacific U36B Diesel, *78-80*	140	180	___
8858	Northern Pacific U36B Diesel Dummy Unit, *78-80*	55	85	___
8859	Conrail Electric Locomotive, *78-82*	105	150	___
8860	Rock Island NW2 Switcher, *78-79*	85	100	___
8861	Santa Fe Alco Diesel A Unit, *78-79*	65	85	___
8862	Santa Fe Alco Diesel B Unit, *78-79*	36	43	___
8864	New Haven F3 Diesel B Unit, *78*	85	105	___
8866	M&StL GP9 Diesel (SSS), *78*	85	120	___
8867	M&StL GP9 Diesel Dummy Unit (SSS), *78*	65	95	___
8868	Amtrak Budd RDC Baggage, *78, 80*	195	235	___
8869	Amtrak Budd RDC Passenger Dummy Unit, *78, 80*	75	95	___
8870	Amtrak Budd RDC Passenger Dummy Unit, *78, 80*	85	115	___
8871	Amtrak Budd RDC Baggage Dummy Unit, *78, 80*	85	105	___
8872	Santa Fe SD18 Diesel, *78 u*	125	155	___
8873	Santa Fe SD18 Diesel Dummy Unit, *78 u*	60	85	___
8900	Santa Fe 4-6-4 Locomotive (FARR 1), *79*	270	310	___
8902	ACL 2-4-0 Locomotive, *79-82, 86 u, 87-90*	13	17	___
8903	D&RGW 2-4-2 Locomotive, *79-81*	17	21	___

		Exc	Mint
___ **8904**	Wabash 2-4-2 Locomotive, *79, 81 u*	30	34
___ **8905**	Smokey Mountain Dockside 0-4-0T Locomotive, *79*	9	17
___ **8950**	Virginian FM Train Master Diesel, *79*	230	285
___ **8952/53**	PRR F3 Diesel AA Set, *79*	350	500
___ **8951**	Southern Pacific FM Train Master Diesel, *79*	237	335
___ **8955**	Southern U36B Diesel, *79*	120	195
___ **8956**	Southern U36B Diesel Dummy Unit, *79*	80	125
___ **8957**	Burlington Northern GP20 Diesel, *79*	120	150
___ **8958**	Burlington Northern GP20 Diesel Dummy Unit, *79*	85	90
___ **8960**	Southern Pacific U36C Diesel, *79 u*	130	180
___ **8961**	Southern Pacific U36C Diesel Dummy Unit, *79 u*	70	80
___ **8962**	Reading U36B Diesel, *79*	115	130
___ **8970/71**	PRR F3 Diesel AA Set, *79 u, 80*	330	425
___ **9001**	Conrail Boxcar (027), *86-87 u, 88-90*	5	10
___ **9010**	GN Hopper (027), *70-71*	6	8
___ **9011**	GN Hopper (027), *70 u, 75-76, 78-83*	8	10
___ **9012**	TA&G Hopper (027), *71-72*	7	8
___ **9013**	Canadian National Hopper (027), *72-76*	5	8
___ **9015**	Reading Hopper (027), *73-75*	17	21
___ **9016**	Chessie System Hopper (027), *75-79, 87-88, 89 u*	4	6
___ **9017**	Wabash Gondola with canisters (027), *78-82*	3	5
___ **9018**	DT&I Hopper (027), *78-79, 81-82*	6	7
___ **9019**	Flatcar (027), *78*	2	3
___ **9020**	Union Pacific Flatcar (027), *70-78*	3	5
___ **9021**	Santa Fe Work Caboose, *70-71, 73-75*	9	13
___ **9022**	Santa Fe Bulkhead Flatcar (027), *70-72, 75-79*	7	13
___ **9023**	MKT Bulkhead Flatcar (027), *73-74*	7	10
___ **9024**	C&O Flatcar (027), *73-75*	3	6
___ **9025**	DT&I Work Caboose, *71-74, 77-78*	8	10
___ **9026**	Republic Steel Flatcar (027), *75-82*	5	7
___ **9027**	Soo Line Work Caboose, *75-76*	7	9
___ **9030**	Kickapoo Gondola (027), *72, 79*	5	9
___ **9031**	NKP Gondola with canisters (027), *73-75, 82-83, 84-91 u*	4	8
___ **9032**	SP Gondola with canisters (027), *75-78*		3
___ **9033**	PC Gondola with canisters (027), *76-78, 82, 86 u, 87-90, 92 u*		3
___ **9034**	Lionel Leisure Hopper (027), *77 u*	30	34
___ **9035**	Conrail Boxcar (027), *78-82*	5	12
___ **9036**	Mobilgas 1-D Tank Car (027), *78-82*	7	19
___ **9037**	Conrail Boxcar (027), *78 u, 80*	7	10
___ **9038**	Chessie System Hopper (027), *78 u, 80*	15	19
___ **9039**	Mobilgas 1-D Tank Car (027), *78 u, 80*	10	15
___ **9040**	General Mills Wheaties Boxcar (027), *70-72*	9	13
___ **9041**	Hershey's Boxcar (027), *70-71, 73-76*	16	25
___ **9042**	Ford-Autolite Boxcar (027), *71 u, 72, 74-76*	13	21
___ **9043**	Erie-Lackawanna Boxcar (027), *73-75*	13	20
___ **9044**	D&RGW Boxcar (027), *75-76*	5	8
___ **9045**	Toys "R" Us Boxcar (027), *75 u*	35	42
___ **9046**	True Value Boxcar (027), *76 u*	26	34
___ **9047**	Toys "R" Us Boxcar (027), *76 u*	40	43
___ **9048**	Toys "R" Us Boxcar (027), *76 u*	33	41
___ **9049**	Toys "R" Us Boxcar (027), *78 u*		NRS
___ **9050**	Sunoco 1-D Tank Car (027), *70-71*	17	23

		Exc	Mint
9051	Firestone 1-D Tank Car (027), *74-75, 78*	15	19____
9052	Toys "R" Us Boxcar (027), *77 u*	26	34____
9053	True Value Boxcar (027), *77 u*	28	40____
9054	JCPenney Boxcar (027), *77 u*	14	19____
9055	Republic Steel Gondola with canisters, *78 u*	9	10____
9057	CP Rail SP-type Caboose, *78-79*	10	15____
9058	Lionel Lines SP-type Caboose, *78-79, 83*	5	7____
9059	Lionel Lines SP-type Caboose, *79 u, 81 u*	7	9____
9060	Nickel Plate Road SP-type Caboose, *70-72*	5	7____
9061	Santa Fe SP-type Caboose, *70-76*	5	8____
9062	Penn Central SP-type Caboose, *70-72, 74-76*	7	9____
9063	GTW SP-type Caboose, *70, 71-73 u*	15	19____
9064	C&O SP-type Caboose, *71-72, 75-77*	7	10____
9065	Canadian National SP-type Caboose, *71-73 u*	19	24____
9066	Southern SP-type Caboose, *73-76*	7	9____
9067	Kickapoo Valley Bobber Caboose, *72*	6	9____
9068	Reading Bobber Caboose, *73-76*	5	7____
9069	Jersey Central SP-type Caboose, *73-74, 75-76 u*	5	8____
9070	Rock Island SP-type Caboose, *73-74*	13	17____
9071	Santa Fe Bobber Caboose, *74 u, 77-78*	7	9____
9073	Coca-Cola SP-type Caboose, *74 u, 75*	30	35____
9075	Rock Island SP-type Caboose, *75-76 u*	13	17____
9076	"We The People" SP-type Caboose, *75 u*	19	28____
9077	D&RGW SP-type Caboose, *76-83, 84-91 u*	7	8____
9078	Rock Island Bobber Caboose, *76-77*	5	7____
9079	GTW Hopper (027), *77*	28	32____
9080	Wabash SP-type Caboose, *77*	9	10____
9085	Santa Fe Work Caboose, *79-82*	4	5____
9090	General Mills Mini-Max Car, *71*	27	32____
9106	Miller Vat Car, *84-85*	33	52____
9107	Dr Pepper Vat Car, *86-87*	30	36____
9110	B&O Quad Hopper, *71*	25	30____
9111	N&W Quad Hopper, *72-75*	15	20____
9112	D&RGW Covered Quad Hopper, *73-75*	20	23____
9113	Norfolk & Western Quad Hopper (SSS), *73*	27	32____
9114	Morton Salt Covered Quad Hopper, *74-76*	18	27____
9115	Planter's Covered Quad Hopper, *74-76*	21	33____
9116	Domino Sugar Covered Quad Hopper, *74-76*	22	29____
9117	Alaska Covered Quad Hopper (SSS), *74-76*	29	33____
9119	Detroit & Mackinac Covered Hopper, *75 u*		20____
9120	Northern Pacific Flatcar with trailers, *70-71*	33	38____
9121	L&N Flatcar with bulldozer and scraper, *71-79*	47	54____
9122	Northern Pacific Flatcar with trailers, *72-75*	19	32____
9123	C&O Auto Carrier, 3-tier, *72 u, 73-74*	18	27____
9124	P&LE Flatcar with logs, *73-74*	18	25____
9125	Norfolk & Western Auto Carrier, 2-tier, *73-77*	23	28____
9126	C&O Auto Carrier, 3-tier, *73-75*	23	34____
9128	Heinz Vat Car, *74-76*	25	34____
9129	N&W Auto Carrier, 3-tier, *75-76*	17	19____
9130	B&O Quad Hopper, *70*	23	24____
9131	D&RGW Gondola with canisters, *73-77*	5	8____
9132	Libby's Vat Car (SSS), *75-77*	16	23____
9133	BN Flatcar with trailers, *76-77, 80*	20	28____

			Exc	Mint
_____	**9134**	Virginian Covered Quad Hopper, *76-77*		32
_____	**9135**	N&W Covered Quad Hopper, *70 u, 71, 75*	17	26
_____	**9136**	Republic Steel Gondola with canisters, *72-76, 79*	9	11
_____	**9138**	Sunoco 3-D Tank Car (SSS), *78*	33	37
_____	**9139**	PC Auto Carrier, 3-tier, *76-77*	21	29
_____	**9140**	Burlington Gondola with canisters, *70, 73-82, 87-89*	7	9
_____	**9141**	BN Gondola with canisters, *70-72*	8	10
_____	**9143**	CN Gondola with canisters, *71-73 u*	30	34
_____	**9144**	D&RGW Gondola with canisters (SSS), *74-76*	9	13
_____	**9145**	ICG Auto Carrier, 3-tier, *77-80*	21	29
_____	**9146**	Mogen David Vat Car, *77-81*	21	26
_____	**9147**	Texaco 1-D Tank Car, *77-78*	46	63
_____	**9148**	Du Pont 3-D Tank Car, *77-81*	25	28
_____	**9149**	CP Rail Flatcar with trailers, *77-78*	22	35
_____	**9150**	Gulf 1-D Tank Car, *70 u, 71*	22	28
_____	**9151**	Shell 1-D Tank Car, *72*	27	31
_____	**9152**	Shell 1-D Tank Car, *73-76*	25	34
_____	**9153**	Chevron 1-D Tank Car, *74-76*	28	35
_____	**9154**	Borden 1-D Tank Car, *75-76*	33	47
_____	**9156**	Mobilgas 1-D Tank Car, *76-77*	30	40
_____	**9157**	C&O Crane Car, *76-78, 81-82*	35	44
_____	**9158**	PC Flatcar with shovel, *76-77, 80*	40	55
_____	**9159**	Sunoco 1-D Tank Car, *76*	35	50
_____	**9160**	Illinois Central N5c Caboose, *70-72*	17	23
_____	**9161**	CN N5c Caboose, *72-74*	14	25
_____	**9162**	PRR N5c Caboose, *72-76*	25	30
_____	**9163**	Santa Fe N5c Caboose, *73-76*	17	24
_____	**9165**	Canadian Pacific N5c Caboose (SSS), *73*	21	30
_____	**9166**	D&RGW SP-type Caboose (SSS), *74-75*	20	25
_____	**9167**	Chessie System N5c Caboose, *74-76*	24	31
_____	**9168**	Union Pacific N5c Caboose, *75-77*	17	19
_____	**9169**	Milwaukee Road SP-type Caboose (SSS), *75*	16	19
_____	**9170**	N&W N5c Caboose "1776," *75*	27	30
_____	**9171**	MP SP-type Caboose, *75 u, 76-77*	19	20
_____	**9172**	Penn Central SP-type Caboose, *75 u, 76-77*	23	31
_____	**9173**	Jersey Central SP-type Caboose, *75 u, 76-77*	22	33
_____	**9174**	NYC (P&E) Bay Window Caboose, *76*	65	70
_____	**9175**	Virginian N5c Caboose, *76-77*	24	26
_____	**9176**	BAR N5c Caboose, *76 u*	17	30
_____	**9177**	Northern Pacific Bay Window Caboose (SSS), *76*	25	35
_____	**9178**	ICG SP-type Caboose, *76-77*	19	24
_____	**9179**	Chessie System Bobber Caboose, *76*	7	11
_____	**9180**	Rock Island N5c Caboose, *77-78*	12	23
_____	**9181**	B&M N5c Caboose, *76 u, 77*	39	49
_____	**9182**	N&W N5c Caboose, *76 u, 77-80*	20	26
_____	**9183**	Mickey Mouse N5c Caboose, *77-78*	32	50
_____	**9184**	Erie Bay Window Caboose, *77-78*	24	30
_____	**9185**	GTW N5c Caboose, *77*	21	28
_____	**9186**	Conrail N5c Caboose, *76 u, 77-78*	27	29
_____	**9187**	Gulf, Mobile & Ohio SP-type Caboose, *77*	10	16
_____	**9188**	GN Bay Window Caboose, *77*	22	27
_____	**9189**	Gulf 1-D Tank Car, *77*	40	60
_____	**9193**	Budweiser Vat Car, *83-84*	92	121

MODERN ERA 1970-2019

		Exc	Mint
9200	Illinois Central BoxCar, *70-71*	19	25____
9201	Penn Central BoxCar, *70*	17	25____
9202	Santa Fe BoxCar, *70*	20	24____
9203	Union Pacific BoxCar, *70*		21____
9204	Northern Pacific BoxCar, *70*		21____
9205	Norfolk & Western BoxCar, *70*	22	25____
9206	Great Northern BoxCar, *70-71*		20____
9207	Soo Line BoxCar, *71*	11	18____
9208	CP Rail BoxCar, *71*	21	23____
9209	Burlington Northern BoxCar, *71-72*	16	21____
9210	B&O DD BoxCar, *71*	16	20____
9211	Penn Central BoxCar, *71*	17	28____
9213	M&StL Covered Quad Hopper (SSS), *78*	20	29____
9214	Northern Pacific BoxCar, *71-72*	16	21____
9215	Norfolk & Western BoxCar, *71*	19	24____
9216	Great Northern Auto Carrier, 3-tier, *78*	25	39____
9217	Soo Line Operating BoxCar, *82-84*	29	36____
9218	Monon Operating BoxCar, *81*	25	30____
9219	Missouri Pacific Operating BoxCar, *83*	27	33____
9220	Borden Operating Milk Car, *83-86*	95	113____
9221	Poultry Dispatch Operating Chicken Car, *83-85*	45	50____
9222	L&N Flatcar with trailers, *83-84*	38	60____
9223	Reading Operating BoxCar, *84*	33	40____
9224	Churchill Downs Operating Horse Car, *84-86*	85	110____
9225	Conrail Operating Barrel Car, *84*	42	55____
9226	Delaware & Hudson Flatcar with trailers, *84-85*	31	34____
9228	Canadian Pacific Operating BoxCar, *86*	24	37____
9229	Express Mail Operating BoxCar, *85-86*	21	27____
9230	Monon Boxcar (SSS), *71, 72 u*	17	24____
9231	Reading Bay Window Caboose, *79*	24	32____
9232	Allis-Chalmers Condenser Car, *80-81, 83 u*	42	50____
9233	Depressed Center Flatcar with transformer, *80*	55	65____
9234	Radioactive Waste Car, *80*	53	78____
9235	Union Pacific Derrick Car, *83-84*	16	22____
9236	C&NW Derrick Car, *83-85*	22	30____
9238	Northern Pacific Log Dump Car, *84*	16	24____
9239	Lionel Lines N5c Caboose, *83 u*	50	60____
9240	NYC Operating Hopper, *86*	32	39____
9240	NYC Hopper (O27), *87 u*	20	29____
9241	PRR Log Dump Car, *85-86*	21	27____
9250	WaterPoxy 3-D Tank Car, *70-71*	23	34____
9260	Reynolds Aluminum Covered Quad Hopper, *75-77*	19	22____
9261	Sun-Maid Raisins Covered Quad Hopper, *75 u, 76*	22	29____
9262	Ralston Purina Covered Quad Hopper, *75 u, 76*	36	58____
9263	PRR Covered Quad Hopper, *75 u, 76-77*	23	30____
9264	Illinois Central Covered Quad Hopper, *75 u, 76-77*	28	39____
9265	Chessie System Covered Quad Hopper, *75 u, 76-77*	21	27____
9266	Southern "Big John" Covered Quad Hopper, *76*	46	65____
9267	Alcoa Covered Quad Hopper (SSS), *76*	20	25____
9268	Northern Pacific Bay Window Caboose, *77 u*	33	40____
9269	Milwaukee Road Bay Window Caboose, *78*	34	47____
9270	Northern Pacific N5c Caboose, *78*	14	27____
9271	M&StL Bay Window Caboose (SSS), *78-79*	18	30____

		Exc	Mint
____ 9272	New Haven Bay Window Caboose, *78-80*	20	34
____ 9273	Southern Bay Window Caboose, *78 u*	36	45
____ 9274	Santa Fe Bay Window Caboose, *78 u*	40	47
____ 9276	Peabody Quad Hopper, *78*	19	28
____ 9277	Cities Service 1-D Tank Car, *78*	41	45
____ 9278	Life Savers 1-D Tank Car, *78-79*	112	152
____ 9279	Magnolia 3-D Tank Car, *78, 79 u*	13	19
____ 9280	Santa Fe Operating Stock Car (027), *77-81*	20	24
____ 9281	Santa Fe Auto Carrier, 3-tier, *78-80*	21	27
____ 9282	GN Flatcar with trailers, *78-79, 81-82*	22	28
____ 9283	Union Pacific Gondola with canisters, *77*	15	21
____ 9284	Santa Fe Gondola with canisters, *77*	16	27
____ 9285	ICG Flatcar with trailers, *77*	47	48
____ 9286	B&LE Covered Quad Hopper, *77*	14	26
____ 9287	Southern N5c Caboose, *77 u, 78*	18	30
____ 9288	Lehigh Valley N5c Caboose, *77 u, 78, 80*	25	31
____ 9289	C&NW N5c Caboose, *77 u, 78, 80*	25	36
____ 9290	Union Pacific Operating Barrel Car, *83*	65	75
____ 9300	PC Log Dump Car, *70-75, 77*	18	24
____ 9301	U.S. Mail Operating BoxCar, *73-84*	32	42
____ 9302	L&N Searchlight Car, *72 u, 73-78*	21	24
____ 9303	Union Pacific Log Dump Car, *74-78, 80*	17	22
____ 9304	C&O Coal Dump Car, *74-78*	11	23
____ 9305	Santa Fe Operating Cowboy Car (027), *80-82*	16	23
____ 9306	Santa Fe Flatcar with horses, *80-82*	18	26
____ 9307	Erie Animated Gondola, *80-84*	55	70
____ 9308	Aquarium Car, *81-84*	125	129
____ 9309	TP&W Bay Window Caboose, *80-81, 83 u*	19	25
____ 9310	Santa Fe Log Dump Car, *78 u, 79-83*	13	24
____ 9311	Union Pacific Coal Dump Car, *78 u, 79-82*	13	24
____ 9312	Conrail Searchlight Car, *78 u, 79-83*	18	27
____ 9313	Gulf 3-D Tank Car, *79 u*	43	50
____ 9315	Southern Pacific Gondola with canisters, *79 u*	16	23
____ 9316	Southern Pacific Bay Window Caboose, *79 u*	47	50
____ 9317	Santa Fe Bay Window Caboose, *79*	21	36
____ 9320	Fort Knox Mint Car, *79 u*	110	135
____ 9321	Santa Fe 1-D Tank Car (FARR 1), *79*	25	31
____ 9322	Santa Fe Covered Quad Hopper (FARR 1), *79*	30	38
____ 9323	Santa Fe Bay Window Caboose (FARR 1), *79*	39	49
____ 9324	Tootsie Roll 1-D Tank Car, *79-81*	67	96
____ 9325	Norfolk & Western Flatcar with fences, *79-81 u*	6	10
____ 9326	Burlington Northern Bay Window Caboose, *79-80*	34	44
____ 9327	Bakelite 3-D Tank Car, *80*	19	29
____ 9328	Chessie System Bay Window Caboose, *80*	33	42
____ 9329	Chessie System Crane Car, *80*	40	47
____ 9330	Kickapoo Dump Car, *72, 79*	3	7
____ 9331	Union 76 1-D Tank Car, *79*	39	44
____ 9332	Reading Crane Car, *79*	37	50
____ 9333	Southern Pacific Flatcar with trailers, *79-80*	33	47
____ 9334	Humble 1-D Tank Car, *79*	21	26
____ 9335	B&O Log Dump Car, *86*	16	22
____ 9336	CP Rail Gondola with canisters, *79*	20	29
____ 9338	Pennsylvania Power & Light Quad Hopper, *79*	60	75

MODERN ERA 1970-2019

		Exc	Mint
9339	GN Boxcar (027), *79-83, 85 u, 86*	7	10 ___
9340	Illinois Central Gondola with canisters (027), *79-81, 82 u, 83*	5	9 ___
9341	ACL SP-type Caboose, *79-82, 86 u 87-90*	6	8 ___
9344	Citgo 3-D Tank Car, *80*	23	38 ___
9345	Reading Searchlight Car, *84-85*	20	25 ___
9346	Wabash SP-type Caboose, *79*	6	10 ___
9348	Santa Fe Crane Car (FARR 1), *79 u*	60	70 ___
9349	San Francisco Mint Car, *80*	55	70 ___
9351	PRR Auto Carrier, 3-tier, *80*	23	40 ___
9352	Trailer Train Flatcar with C&NW trailers, *80*	29	55 ___
9353	Crystal Line 3-D Tank Car, *80*	18	26 ___
9354	Pennzoil 1-D Tank Car, *80, 81 u*	60	85 ___
9355	Delaware & Hudson Bay Window Caboose, *80*	37	45 ___
9357	Smokey Mountain Bobber Caboose, *79*	8	10 ___
9359	National Basketball Association Boxcar (027), *79-80 u*	19	24 ___
9360	National Hockey League Boxcar (027), *79-80 u*	21	26 ___
9361	C&NW Bay Window Caboose, *80*	47	50 ___
9362	Major League Baseball Boxcar (027), *79-80 u*	17	21 ___
9363	N&W Log Dump Car "9325," (027), *79*	4	7 ___
9364	N&W Crane Car "9325," (027), *79*	7	9 ___
9365	Toys "R" Us Boxcar (027), *79 u*	30	37 ___
9366	UP Covered Quad Hopper (FARR 2), *80*	19	23 ___
9367	Union Pacific 1-D Tank Car (FARR 2), *80*	21	30 ___
9368	Union Pacific Bay Window Caboose (FARR 2), *80*	30	36 ___
9369	Sinclair 1-D Tank Car, *80*	60	85 ___
9370	Seaboard Gondola with canisters, *80*	19	21 ___
9371	Atlantic Sugar Covered Quad Hopper, *80*	19	22 ___
9372	Seaboard Bay Window Caboose, *80*	30	41 ___
9373	Getty 1-D Tank Car, *80-81, 83 u*	31	42 ___
9374	Reading Covered Quad Hopper, *80-81, 83 u*	39	40 ___
9376	Soo Line Boxcar (027), *81 u*	40	50 ___
9378	Derrick Car, *80-82*	18	22 ___
9379	Santa Fe Gondola with canisters, *80-81, 83 u*	22	30 ___
9380	NYNH&H SP-type Caboose, *80-81*	7	10 ___
9381	Chessie System SP-type Caboose, *80*	7	9 ___
9382	Florida East Coast Bay Window Caboose, *80*	34	48 ___
9383	UP Flatcar with trailers (FARR 2), *80 u*	27	34 ___
9384	Great Northern Operating Hopper, *81*	50	55 ___
9385	Alaska Gondola with canisters, *81*	27	34 ___
9386	Pure Oil 1-D Tank Car, *81*	38	50 ___
9387	Burlington Bay Window Caboose, *81*	46	52 ___
9388	Toys "R" Us Boxcar (027), *81 u*	38	45 ___
9389	Radioactive Waste Car, *81-82*	65	80 ___
9398	PRR Coal Dump Car, *83-84*	28	38 ___
9399	C&NW Coal Dump Car, *83-85*	17	22 ___
9400	Conrail BoxCar, *78*	14	20 ___
9401	Great Northern BoxCar, *78*	18	23 ___
9402	Susquehanna BoxCar, *78*	30	33 ___
9403	Seaboard Coast Line BoxCar, *78*	12	17 ___
9404	NKP BoxCar, *78*	19	21 ___
9405	Chattahoochee BoxCar, *78*	14	19 ___
9406	D&RGW BoxCar, *78-79*	17	21 ___

		Exc	Mint
____ 9407	Union Pacific Stock Car, *78*	18	25
____ 9408	Lionel Lines Circus Stock Car (SSS), *78*	31	40
____ 9411	Lackawanna Phoebe Snow BoxCar, *78*	35	43
____ 9412	RF&P BoxCar, *79*	21	27
____ 9413	Napierville Junction BoxCar, *79*	18	24
____ 9414	Cotton Belt BoxCar, *79*	19	23
____ 9415	Providence & Worcester BoxCar, *79*	17	25
____ 9416	MD&W BoxCar, *79, 81*	13	19
____ 9417	CP Rail BoxCar, *79*	45	50
____ 9418	FARR BoxCar, *79 u*	50	60
____ 9419	Union Pacific Boxcar (FARR 2), *80*	10	17
____ 9420	B&O Sentinel BoxCar, *80*	21	26
____ 9421	Maine Central BoxCar, *80*	10	17
____ 9422	EJ&E BoxCar, *80*	12	20
____ 9423	NYNH&H BoxCar, *80*	14	22
____ 9424	TP&W BoxCar, *80*	17	21
____ 9425	British Columbia DD BoxCar, *80*	27	35
____ 9426	Chesapeake & Ohio BoxCar, *80*	19	30
____ 9427	Bay Line BoxCar, *80-81*	12	17
____ 9428	TP&W BoxCar, *80-81, 83 u*		23
____ 9429	"The Early Years" BoxCar, *80*	20	27
____ 9430	"The Standard Gauge Years" BoxCar, *80*	22	25
____ 9431	"The Prewar Years" BoxCar, *80*	20	25
____ 9432	"The Postwar Years" BoxCar, *80*	50	55
____ 9433	"The Golden Years" BoxCar, *80*	33	43
____ 9434	Joshua Lionel Cowen "The Man" BoxCar, *80 u*	29	37
____ 9436	Burlington BoxCar, *81*	25	30
____ 9437	Northern Pacific Stock Car, *81*	22	36
____ 9438	Ontario Northland BoxCar, *81*	25	31
____ 9439	Ashley Drew & Northern BoxCar, *81*	11	19
____ 9440	Reading BoxCar, *81*	50	65
____ 9441	Pennsylvania BoxCar, *81*	32	42
____ 9442	Canadian Pacific BoxCar, *81*	13	21
____ 9443	Florida East Coast BoxCar, *81*	19	24
____ 9444	Louisiana Midland BoxCar, *81*	14	18
____ 9445	Vermont Northern BoxCar, *81*	14	17
____ 9446	Sabine River & Northern BoxCar, *81*	15	21
____ 9447	Pullman Standard BoxCar, *81*	16	21
____ 9448	Santa Fe Stock Car, *81-82*	34	40
____ 9449	Great Northern Boxcar (FARR 3), *81*	27	31
____ 9450	Great Northern Stock Car (FARR 3), *81 u*	50	60
____ 9451	Southern Boxcar (FARR 4), *83*	26	32
____ 9452	Western Pacific BoxCar, *82-83*	12	16
____ 9453	MPA BoxCar, *82-83*	14	19
____ 9454	New Hope & Ivyland BoxCar, *82-83*	21	27
____ 9455	Milwaukee Road BoxCar, *82-83*	15	19
____ 9456	PRR DD Boxcar (FARR 5), *84-85*	24	30
____ 9461	Norfolk & Southern BoxCar, *82*	25	43
____ 9462	Southern Pacific BoxCar, *83-84*	18	23
____ 9463	Texas & Pacific BoxCar, *83-84*	15	19
____ 9464	NC&StL BoxCar, *83-84*	16	22
____ 9465	Santa Fe BoxCar, *83-84*	12	19
____ 9466	Wanamaker BoxCar, *82 u*	60	70

		Exc	Mint
9467	Tennessee World's Fair BoxCar, *82 u*	26	31____
9468	Union Pacific DD BoxCar, *83*	31	34____
9469	NYC Pacemaker Boxcar (std O), *84-85*	37	53____
9470	Chicago Beltline BoxCar, *84*	15	20____
9471	Atlantic Coast Line BoxCar, *84*	13	20____
9472	Detroit & Mackinac BoxCar, *84*	22	26____
9473	Lehigh Valley BoxCar, *84*	24	28____
9474	Erie-Lackawanna BoxCar, *84*	31	35____
9475	D&H "I Love NY" BoxCar, *84 u*	28	37____
9476	PRR Boxcar (FARR 5), *84-85*	27	36____
9480	MN&S BoxCar, *85-86*	15	18____
9481	Seaboard System BoxCar, *85-86*	15	18____
9482	Norfolk & Southern BoxCar, *85-86*	13	17____
9483	Manufacturers Railway BoxCar, *85-86*	14	19____
9484	Lionel 85th Anniversary BoxCar, *85*	22	26____
9486	GTW "I Love Michigan" BoxCar, *86*	23	34____
9490	Christmas Boxcar for Lionel Employees, *85 u*		1800____
9491	Christmas BoxCar, *86 u*	26	37____
9492	Lionel Lines BoxCar, *86*	23	29____
9500	Milwaukee Road Passenger Coach, *73*	28	75____
9501	Milwaukee Road Passenger Coach, *73 u, 74-76*	33	37____
9502	Milwaukee Road Observation Car, *73*	30	48____
9503	Milwaukee Road Passenger Coach, *73*	33	48____
9504	Milwaukee Road Passenger Coach, *73 u, 74-76*	33	37____
9505	Milwaukee Road Passenger Coach, *73 u, 74-76*	35	38____
9506	Milwaukee Road Combination Car, *74 u, 75-76*	32	37____
9507	PRR Passenger Coach, *74-75*	34	55____
9508	PRR Passenger Coach, *74-75*	32	50____
9509	PRR Observation Car, *74-75*	41	60____
9510	PRR Combination Car, *74 u, 75-76*	30	47____
9511	Milwaukee Road Passenger Coach, *74 u*	33	48____
9513	PRR Passenger Coach, *75-76*	25	44____
9514	PRR Passenger Coach, *75-76*	23	36____
9515	PRR Passenger Coach, *75-76*	22	34____
9516	B&O Passenger Coach, *76*	27	42____
9517	B&O Passenger Coach, *75*	45	65____
9518	B&O Observation Car, *75*	45	65____
9519	B&O Combination Car, *75*	55	85____
9521	PRR Baggage Car, *75 u, 76*	65	95____
9522	Milwaukee Road Baggage Car, *75 u, 76*	65	80____
9523	B&O Baggage Car, *75 u, 76*	60	70____
9524	B&O Passenger Coach, *76*	27	37____
9525	B&O Passenger Coach, *76*	30	43____
9527	Milwaukee Road Campaign Observation Car, *76 u*	38	60____
9528	PRR Campaign Observation Car, *76 u*	48	75____
9529	B&O Campaign Observation Car, *76 u*	35	59____
9530	Southern Baggage Car, *77-78*	45	65____
9531	Southern Combination Car, *77-78*	29	37____
9532	Southern Passenger Coach, *77-78*	33	47____
9533	Southern Passenger Coach, *77-78*	27	38____
9534	Southern Observation Car, *77-78*	31	47____
9536	Blue Comet Baggage Car, *78-80*	39	55____
9537	Blue Comet Combination Car, *78-80*	35	50____

		Exc	Mint
9538	Blue Comet Passenger Coach, *78-80*	35	47
9539	Blue Comet Passenger Coach, *78-80*	35	48
9540	Blue Comet Observation Car, *78-80*	27	40
9541	Santa Fe Baggage Car, *80-82*	21	30
9545	Union Pacific Baggage Car, *84*	135	200
9546	Union Pacific Combination Car, *84*	85	105
9547	Union Pacific Observation Car, *84*	85	105
9548	UP Placid Bay Passenger Coach, *84*	90	110
9549	UP Ocean Sunset Passenger Coach, *84*	85	105
9551	W&ARR Baggage Car, *77 u, 78-80*	36	48
9552	W&ARR Passenger Coach, *77 u, 78-80*	46	60
9553	W&ARR Flatcar with horses, *77 u, 78-80*	32	50
9554	Chicago & Alton Baggage Car, *81*	55	85
9555	Chicago & Alton Combination Car, *81*	50	75
9556	Chicago & Alton Wilson Passenger Coach, *81*	50	75
9557	Chicago & Alton Webster Groves Passenger Coach, *81*	45	65
9558	Chicago & Alton Observation Car, *81*	50	75
9559	Rock Island Baggage Car, *81-82*	42	65
9560	Rock Island Passenger Coach, *81-82*	43	65
9561	Rock Island Passenger Coach, *81-82*	42	65
9562	N&W Baggage Car "577," *81*	80	110
9563	N&W Combination Car "578," *81*	80	105
9564	N&W Passenger Coach "579," *81*	90	100
9565	N&W Passenger Coach "580," *81*	85	100
9566	N&W Observation Car "581," *81*	90	95
9567	N&W Vista Dome Car "582," *81 u*	160	255
9569	PRR Combination Car, *81 u*	115	160
9570	PRR Baggage Car, *79*	85	115
9571	PRR Passenger Coach, *79*	125	145
9572	PRR Passenger Coach, *79*	110	125
9573	PRR Vista Dome Car, *79*	95	120
9574	PRR Observation Car, *79*	75	100
9575	PRR Passenger Coach, *79-80 u*	100	135
9576	Burlington Baggage Car, *80*	145	175
9577	Burlington Passenger Coach, *80*	95	105
9578	Burlington Passenger Coach, *80*	105	110
9579	Burlington Vista Dome Car, *80*	95	110
9580	Burlington Observation Car, *80*	95	110
9581	Chessie System Baggage Car, *80*	55	62
9582	Chessie System Combination Car, *80*	47	55
9583	Chessie System Passenger Coach, *80*	40	47
9584	Chessie System Passenger Coach, *80*	31	37
9585	Chessie System Observation Car, *80*	55	65
9586	Chessie System Diner, *86 u*	85	90
9588	Burlington Vista Dome Car, *80 u*	110	120
9589	Southern Pacific Baggage Car, *82-83*	110	135
9590	Southern Pacific Combination Car, *82-83*	90	105
9591	Southern Pacific Pullman Passenger Coach, *82-83*	85	105
9592	Southern Pacific Pullman Passenger Coach, *82-83*	85	105
9593	Southern Pacific Observation Car, *82-83*	100	130
9594	NYC Baggage Car, *83-84*	105	130
9595	NYC Combination Car, *83-84*	75	85
9596	NYC Wayne County Passenger Coach, *83-84*	80	95

		Exc	Mint
9597	NYC Hudson River Passenger Coach, *83-84*	70	85
9598	NYC Observation Car, *83-84*	75	85
9599	Chicago & Alton Diner, *86 u*	80	90
9600	Chessie System Hi-Cube BoxCar, *75 u, 76-77*	19	25
9601	ICG Hi-Cube BoxCar, *75 u, 76-77*	20	21
9602	Santa Fe Hi-Cube BoxCar, *75 u, 76-77*	17	20
9603	Penn Central Hi-Cube BoxCar, *76-77*	12	18
9604	Norfolk & Western Hi-Cube BoxCar, *76-77*	23	26
9605	NH Hi-Cube BoxCar, *76-77*	17	21
9606	Union Pacific Hi-Cube BoxCar, *76 u, 77*	10	17
9607	Southern Pacific Hi-Cube BoxCar, *76 u, 77*	12	15
9608	Burlington Northern Hi-Cube BoxCar, *76 u, 77*	21	23
9610	Frisco Hi-Cube BoxCar, *77*	25	34
9620	NHL Wales BoxCar, *80*	27	35
9621	NHL Campbell BoxCar, *80*	27	34
9622	NBA Western BoxCar, *80*	24	30
9623	NBA Eastern BoxCar, *80*	26	34
9624	National League Baseball BoxCar, *80*	27	34
9625	American League Baseball BoxCar, *80*	27	35
9626	Santa Fe Hi-Cube BoxCar, *82-84*	10	14
9627	Union Pacific Hi-Cube BoxCar, *82-83*	15	21
9628	Burlington Northern Hi-Cube BoxCar, *82-84*	14	19
9629	Chessie System Hi-Cube BoxCar, *83-84*	24	36
9660	Mickey Mouse Hi-Cube BoxCar, *77-78*	34	46
9661	Goofy Hi-Cube BoxCar, *77-78*	53	61
9662	Donald Duck Hi-Cube BoxCar, *77-78*	38	49
9663	Dumbo Hi-Cube BoxCar, *77 u, 78*	43	58
9664	Cinderella Hi-Cube BoxCar, *77 u, 78*	56	86
9665	Peter Pan Hi-Cube BoxCar, *77 u, 78*	49	77
9666	Pinocchio Hi-Cube BoxCar, *78*	113	161
9667	Snow White Hi-Cube BoxCar, *78*	354	466
9668	Pluto Hi-Cube BoxCar, *78*	149	193
9669	Bambi Hi-Cube BoxCar, *78 u*	67	105
9670	Alice In Wonderland Hi-Cube BoxCar, *78 u*	61	91
9671	Fantasia Hi-Cube BoxCar, *78 u*	56	91
9672	Mickey Mouse 50th Anniversary Hi-Cube BoxCar, *78 u*	368	468
9700	Southern BoxCar, *72-73*	22	30
9701	B&O DD BoxCar, *72*	14	19
9702	Soo Line BoxCar, *72-73*	15	21
9703	CP Rail BoxCar, *72*	34	44
9704	Norfolk & Western BoxCar, *72*	10	17
9705	D&RGW BoxCar, *72*	13	20
9706	C&O BoxCar, *72*	17	19
9707	MKT Stock Car, *72-75*	14	22
9708	U.S. Mail Toy Fair BoxCar, *73 u*	85	95
9708	U.S. Mail BoxCar, *72-75*	18	23
9709	BAR State of Maine Boxcar (SSS), *72-74*	29	32
9710	Rutland Boxcar (SSS), *72-74*	24	28
9711	Southern BoxCar, *74-75*	19	25
9712	B&O DD BoxCar, *73-74*	31	34
9713	CP Rail "Season's Greetings" BoxCar, *74 u*	95	120
9713	CP Rail BoxCar, *73-74*	24	30
9714	D&RGW BoxCar, *73-74*	16	20

		Exc	Mint
____ **9715**	C&O BoxCar, *73-74*	17	22
____ **9716**	Penn Central BoxCar, *73-74*	15	20
____ **9717**	Union Pacific BoxCar, *73-74*	21	25
____ **9718**	Canadian National BoxCar, *73-74*	23	31
____ **9719**	New Haven DD BoxCar, *73 u*	23	32
____ **9723**	Western Pacific Toy Fair BoxCar, *74 u*	20	60
____ **9723**	Western Pacific Boxcar (SSS), *73-74*	27	29
____ **9724**	Missouri Pacific Boxcar (SSS), *73-74*	21	24
____ **9725**	MKT Stock Car (SSS), *73-75*	15	18
____ **9726**	Erie-Lackawanna Boxcar (SSS), *78*	25	30
____ **9729**	CP Rail BoxCar, *78*		34
____ **9730**	CP Rail BoxCar, *74-75*	23	27
____ **9731**	Milwaukee Road BoxCar, *74-75*	16	21
____ **9732**	Southern Pacific BoxCar, *79*	24	31
____ **9734**	Bangor & Aroostook BoxCar, *79*	30	38
____ **9735**	Grand Trunk Western BoxCar, *74-75*	15	21
____ **9737**	Vermont Central BoxCar, *74-76*	27	34
____ **9738**	Illinois Terminal BoxCar, *82*	33	45
____ **9739**	D&RGW Boxcar (SSS), *74-76*	17	25
____ **9740**	Chessie System BoxCar, *74-75*	15	19
____ **9742**	M&StL BoxCar, *73 u*	12	19
____ **9742**	M&StL "Season's Greetings" BoxCar, *73 u*	85	105
____ **9743**	Sprite BoxCar, *74 u, 75*	19	27
____ **9744**	Tab BoxCar, *74 u, 75*	17	24
____ **9745**	Fanta BoxCar, *74 u, 75*	19	29
____ **9747**	Chessie System DD BoxCar, *75-76*	24	28
____ **9748**	CP Rail BoxCar, *75-76*	16	20
____ **9749**	Penn Central BoxCar, *75-76*	16	21
____ **9750**	DT&I BoxCar, *75-76*	13	20
____ **9751**	Frisco BoxCar, *75-76*	21	23
____ **9752**	L&N BoxCar, *75-76*	20	23
____ **9753**	Maine Central BoxCar, *75-76*	16	22
____ **9754**	NYC Pacemaker Boxcar (SSS), *75-77*	20	30
____ **9755**	Union Pacific BoxCar, *75-76*	20	24
____ **9757**	Central of Georgia BoxCar, *74 u*	16	17
____ **9758**	Alaska Boxcar (SSS), *75-77*	24	31
____ **9759**	Paul Revere BoxCar, *75 u*	36	43
____ **9760**	Liberty Bell BoxCar, *75 u*	30	40
____ **9761**	George Washington BoxCar, *75 u*	36	43
____ **9762**	Toy Fair BoxCar, *75 u*	125	170
____ **9763**	D&RGW Stock Car, *76-77*	15	20
____ **9764**	GTW DD BoxCar, *76-77*	40	63
____ **9767**	Railbox BoxCar, *76-77*	15	20
____ **9768**	B&M BoxCar, *76-77*	18	27
____ **9769**	B&LE BoxCar, *76-77*	15	21
____ **9770**	Northern Pacific BoxCar, *76-77*	14	18
____ **9771**	Norfolk & Western BoxCar, *76-77*	16	24
____ **9772**	Great Northern BoxCar, *76*	60	85
____ **9773**	NYC Stock Car, *76*	32	39
____ **9775**	M&StL Boxcar (SSS), *76*	19	23
____ **9776**	SP Overnight Boxcar (SSS), *76*	32	34
____ **9777**	Virginian BoxCar, *76-77*	22	25
____ **9778**	"Season's Greetings" BoxCar, *75 u*	165	185

		Exc	Mint
9780	Johnny Cash BoxCar, *76 u*	50	61____
9781	Delaware & Hudson BoxCar, *77-78*	19	23____
9782	Rock Island BoxCar, *77-78*	14	17____
9783	B&O Time-Saver BoxCar, *77-78*	18	27____
9784	Santa Fe BoxCar, *77-78*	13	17____
9785	Conrail BoxCar, *77-78*	20	23____
9786	C&NW BoxCar, *77-79*	18	27____
9787	Jersey Central BoxCar, *77-79*	12	19____
9788	Lehigh Valley BoxCar, *77-79*	17	21____
9789	Pickens BoxCar, *77*	25	33____
9801	B&O Sentinel Boxcar (std O), *73-75*	18	26____
9802	Miller High Life Reefer (std O), *73-75*	32	36____
9803	Johnson Wax Boxcar (std O), *73-75*	27	33____
9805	Grand Trunk Western Reefer (std O), *73-75*	20	31____
9806	Rock Island Boxcar (std O), *74-75*	38	46____
9807	Stroh's Beer Reefer (std O), *74-76*	70	82____
9808	Union Pacific Boxcar (std O), *75-76*	36	50____
9809	Clark Reefer (std O), *75-76*	33	41____
9811	Pacific Fruit Express Reefer (FARR 2), *80*	26	33____
9812	Arm & Hammer Reefer, *80*	24	30____
9813	Ruffles Reefer, *80*	20	28____
9814	Perrier Reefer, *80*	21	30____
9815	NYC "Early Bird" Reefer (std O), *84-85*	34	40____
9816	Brach's Candy Reefer, *80*	21	26____
9817	Bazooka Bubble Gum Reefer, *80*	24	31____
9818	Western Maryland Reefer, *80*	18	23____
9819	Western Fruit Express Reefer (FARR 3), *81*	22	29____
9820	Wabash Gondola with coal (std O), *73-74*	24	38____
9821	SP Gondola with coal (std O), *73-75*	28	32____
9822	GTW Gondola with coal (std O), *74-75*	24	29____
9823	Santa Fe Flatcar with crates (std O), *75-76*	34	44____
9824	NYC Gondola with coal (std O), *75-76*	41	56____
9825	Schaefer Reefer (std O), *76-77*	45	60____
9826	P&LE Boxcar (std O), *76-77*	34	39____
9827	Cutty Sark Reefer, *84*	36	46____
9828	J&B Reefer, *84*	34	48____
9829	Dewar's White Label Reefer, *84*	41	48____
9830	Johnnie Walker Red Label Reefer, *84*	32	49____
9831	Pepsi Cola Reefer, *82*	82	95____
9832	Cheerios Reefer, *82*	165	190____
9833	Vlasic Pickles Reefer, *82*	23	29____
9834	Southern Comfort Reefer, *83-84*	34	47____
9835	Jim Beam Reefer, *83-84*	45	62____
9836	Old Grand-Dad Reefer, *83-84*	42	52____
9837	Wild Turkey Reefer, *83-84*	66	100____
9840	Fleischmann's Gin Reefer, *85*	38	43____
9841	Calvert Gin Reefer, *85*	42	48____
9842	Seagram's Gin Reefer, *85*	42	47____
9843	Tanqueray Gin Reefer, *85*	42	46____
9844	Sambuca Reefer, *86*	37	49____
9845	Baileys Irish Cream Reefer, *86*	65	92____
9846	Seagram's Vodka Reefer, *86*	42	48____
9847	Wolfschmidt Vodka Reefer, *86*	36	41____

		Exc	Mint
____ **9849**	Lionel Lines Reefer, *83 u*	20	32
____ **9850**	Budweiser Reefer, *72 u, 73-75*	56	67
____ **9851**	Schlitz Reefer, *72 u, 73-75*	29	35
____ **9852**	Miller Reefer, *72 u, 73-77*	32	38
____ **9853**	Cracker Jack Reefer, *72 u, 73-75*		
____	(A) Caramel-colored body	29	34
____	(B) White body, black logo border	23	28
____ **9854**	Baby Ruth Reefer, *72 u, 73-76*	22	26
____ **9855**	Swift Reefer, *72 u, 73-77*	23	28
____ **9856**	Old Milwaukee Reefer, *75-76*	33	40
____ **9858**	Butterfinger Reefer, *73 u, 74-76*	22	28
____ **9859**	Pabst Reefer, *73 u, 74-75*	41	48
____ **9860**	Gold Medal Reefer, *73 u, 74-76*	12	21
____ **9861**	Tropicana Reefer, *75-77*	23	35
____ **9862**	Hamm's Reefer, *75-76*	35	42
____ **9863**	REA Reefer (SSS), *74-76*	24	28
____ **9866**	Coors Reefer, *76-77*	42	58
____ **9867**	Hershey's Reefer, *76-77*	73	85
____ **9869**	Santa Fe Reefer (SSS), *76*	32	37
____ **9870**	Old Dutch Cleanser Reefer, *77-78, 80*	15	21
____ **9871**	Carling Black Label Reefer, *77-78, 80*	33	45
____ **9872**	Pacific Fruit Express Reefer, *77-79*	24	28
____ **9873**	Ralston Purina Reefer, *78*	25	38
____ **9874**	Miller Lite Beer Reefer, *78-79*	55	62
____ **9875**	A&P Reefer, *78-79*	23	31
____ **9876**	Vermont Central Reefer, *78*	26	31
____ **9877**	Gerber Reefer, *79-80*	68	78
____ **9878**	Good and Plenty Reefer, *79*	24	31
____ **9879**	Hills Bros. Reefer, *79-80*	23	29
____ **9880**	Santa Fe Reefer (FARR 1), *79*	27	31
____ **9881**	Rath Packing Reefer, *79 u*	23	31
____ **9882**	NYC "Early Bird" Reefer, *79*	25	29
____ **9883**	Nabisco Oreo Reefer, *79*	90	98
____ **9884**	Fritos Reefer, *81-82*	26	34
____ **9885**	Lipton Tea Reefer, *81-82*	30	38
____ **9886**	Mounds Reefer, *81-82*	24	30
____ **9887**	Fruit Growers Express Reefer (FARR 4), *83*	29	38
____ **9888**	Green Bay & Western Reefer, *83*	42	49
____ **11000**	Holiday Express Freight Set, *08*		280
____ **11004**	NASCAR Diesel Freight Set, *06-07*		300
____ **11005**	Dale Earnhardt Jr. Diesel Freight Set, *06-07*		240
____ **11006**	Lionel Lion Set, *03 u*		230
____ **11006**	Kasey Kahne Expansion Pack, *06-07*		130
____ **11007**	Dale Earnhardt Sr. Expansion Pack, *06-07*		130
____ **11008**	Dale Earnhardt Jr. Expansion Pack, *06-07*		130
____ **11009**	Tony Stewart Expansion Pack, *06-07*		130
____ **11010**	Jimmie Johnson Expansion Pack, *06-07*		130
____ **11011**	Jeff Gordon Expansion Pack, *06-07*		130
____ **11020**	Harry Potter Hogwarts Express Steam Passenger Set, *08-13*		330
____ **11025**	Jimmie Johnson 2006 Champion BoxCar, *07*		45
____ **11038**	Snow-covered Straight Track 4-pack, *08*		14
____ **11041**	Holiday Calliope Car, *08*		45
____ **11067**	Lionel Bear, *08*		25

		Exc	Mint
11077	Harry Potter Figures, *08*		27____
11096	Engineer Hat, *08*		18____
11098	Holiday Toy Soldier Car, *08*		50____
11100	PRR 2-8-2 Mikado Locomotive "9631," CC, *07*		370____
11101	LL 2-8-4 Berkshire Locomotive "737," CC, *06*		350____
11103	Southern PS-4 4-6-2 Pacific Locomotive "1403," CC, *06*	1000	____
11104	UP Big Boy Locomotive "4014," CC, *06*		1800____
11105	NYC L-2A 4-8-2 Mohawk Locomotive "2770," CC, *06*	1100	____
11107	LionMaster SP Cab Forward Locomotive "4276," RailSounds, *06-07*	850	____
11108	C&O F-19 4-6-2 Pacific Locomotive "494," CC, *06-07*	1160	____
11109	C&O 0-8-0 Locomotive "79," TrainSounds, *06*		420____
11110	NYC 0-8-0 Locomotive "7805," TrainSounds, *06*		420____
11116	UP 4-8-4 FEF-3 Locomotive "844," gray, CC, *08-09*		1160____
11117	Santa Fe E6 4-4-2 Atlantic Locomotive "1484," CC, *07-09*	600	____
11119	Southern 0-8-0 Locomotive "6535," TrainSounds, *07*		420____
11122	UP Big Boy Locomotive "4024," CC, *06*		1700____
11123	UP Big Boy Locomotive "4023," CC, *06*		1700____
11126	UP Big Boy Locomotive "4012," CC, *06*		1700____
11127	SP GS-4 4-8-4 Northern Locomotive "4436," CC, *07-09*	1200	____
11128	C&O F-19 4-6-2 Pacific Locomotive "490," CC, *07*	1160	____
11131	UP 4-8-4 FEF-3 Locomotive "844," black, CC, *08-09*	1160	____
11132	Reading 2-8-0 Consolidation Locomotive "1914," RailSounds, *08*	450	____
11133	NYC 2-8-0 Consolidation Locomotive "1149," RailSounds, *08*	450	____
11134	WM 2-8-0 Consolidation Locomotive "729," RailSounds, *08*	450	____
11135	B&O 2-8-0 Consolidation Locomotive "2784," RailSounds, *08*	450	____
11136	WP 2-8-2 Mikado Locomotive "322," CC, *08*		800____
11137	UP 2-8-2 Mikado Locomotive "1925," CC, *08*		800____
11138	ATSF 2-8-2 Mikado Locomotive "3156," CC, *08*		800____
11139	MILW 2-8-2 Mikado Locomotive "462," CC, *08*		800____
11140	Cass Scenic Shay Locomotive "7," CC, *07*		800____
11141	Birch Valley Lumber Shay Locomotive "5," CC, *07*		800____
11142	Hogwarts Express Add-on 2-pack, *09-10*		120____
11143	SP AC-4 Cab Forward Locomotive "4100," CC, *08*	1670	____
11146	Pere Marquette 2-8-4 Berkshire Locomotive "1225," CC, *08*	1290	____
11147	PRR 4-8-2 Mib Locomotive "6750," CC, *08*		1290____
11148	NYC Dreyfuss J-3a 4-6-4 Hudson Locomotive "5448," CC, *08*	1130	____
11149	LionMaster UP Big Boy 4-8-8-4 Locomotive "4006," CC, *08*	860	____
11150	NYC F-12e 4-6-0 10-wheel Locomotive "827," CC, *08*	700	____
11151	Polar Express Tender, RailSounds, *08-10*		440____
11152	D&RGW LionMaster 4-6-6-4 Challenger Locomotive "3805," CC, *09*	900	____
11153	Stourbridge Lion Steam Locomotive, *09-10*		430____

Exc Mint

		Exc	Mint
11154	PRR CC2s 0-8-8-0 Mallet Locomotive "8183," CC, *09-10*		2000
11155	ATSF 2-10-10-2 Mallet Locomotive "3000," CC, *09-10*		2500
11156	C&O 4-6-0 Ten-Wheeler Locomotive, CC, *10*		740
11157	WM Shay Locomotive "6," CC, *10*		800
11162	Lone Ranger Add-on 3-pack, *10*		165
11164	Dewitt Clinton Passenger Set, *10*		630
11165	Dewitt Clinton Add-on Coach, *10*		70
11166	CSX Merger Freight 2-pack #1, *10-11*		130
11167	CSX Merger Freight 2-pack #2, *10-11*		105
11168	CSX Merger Freight 2-pack #3, *10-11*		130
11169	Strasburg Freight Add-on 2-pack, *10*		100
11170	Three Rivers Fast Freight Set, *10-12*		400
11172	Santa Fe 4-4-2 Steam Freight Set, *13*		200
11173	Texan Freight Add-on 2-pack, *10-11*		130
11174	Maple Leaf Freight Add-on 2-pack, *10-11*		110
11175	Operation Eagle Justice Add-on 2-pack, *10-11*		125
11180	Motor City Express Diesel Freight Train Set, CC, *12-13*		1150
11181	CN GP9 Diesel Piggyback Train Set, CC, *12*		850
11182	Dixie Special FT Diesel Freight Set, *11*		700
11183	Lincoln Funeral Train, *13*		1140
11194	Texas Special Diesel Passenger Set, CC, *13-14*		1110
11195	PRR Diesel Passenger Set, CC, *13-14*		1110
11199	UP NW2 Diesel Switcher Work Train Set, CC, *12*		600
11200	UP LionMaster Challenger Locomotive "3985," CC, *10*		900
11201	WM LionMaster Challenger Locomotive "1204," CC, *10*		900
11202	CP 4-6-0 Ten-Wheeler Locomotive "914," CC, *10*		740
11203	Pere Marquette Berkshire Locomotive "1225," CC, *09*		980
11204	Pere Marquette Tender, RailSounds, *09*		440
11207	PRR LionMaster T1 Duplex Locomotive "5511," CC, *10*		800
11208	UP LionMaster Big Boy Locomotive "4011," CC, *10*		900
11209	Vision NYC Hudson Locomotive "5344," CC, *10*		1600
11210	UP Challenger Locomotive "3967," CC, *10*		1825
11211	UP 4-6-6-4 Challenger Locomotive "3976," CC, *10*		1825
11212	NKP Berkshire Locomotive "765," CC, *10*		1400
11215	LV 4-6-0 Camelback Locomotive "1598," CC, *10*		550
11216	Jersey Central 4-6-0 Camelback Locomotive, CC, *10*		550
11217	PRR 4-6-0 Camelback Locomotive "822," CC, *10*		550
11218	Vision NYC Hudson Locomotive "5331," CC, *10*		1600
11219	Clinchfield Challenger Locomotive "672," CC, *10*		1825
11220	UP Challenger Locomotive "3989," CC, *10*		1825
11221	UP Challenger Locomotive "3983," CC, *10*		1825
11224	PRR Atlantic Locomotive "460," CC, *10-11*		700
11225	B&O Atlantic Locomotive "1440," CC		700
11226	UP Water Tender, black, CC, *11*		300
11227	UP Water Tender, gray, CC, *11*		300
11228	Clinchfield Water Tender, CC, *11*		300
11229	MILW 4-8-4 Northern Locomotive "261," CC, *11*		995
11230	MILW 4-8-4 Northern Locomotive "267," CC, *11*		995

	Exc	Mint
11232 Reading Atlantic Locomotive "351," CC, *11*	700	___
11233 Pennsylvania Power & Light 2-Truck Shay Locomotive, CC, *11*	900	___
11234 Pennsylvania Power & Light 2-Truck Shay Locomotive, *11*	750	___
11235 West Side Lumber 2-Truck Shay Steam Locomotive, CC, *11*	900	___
11236 West Side Lumber 2-Truck Shay Steam Locomotive, *11*	750	___
11237 Sugar Pine Lumber Shay Locomotive "4," CC, *11*	900	___
11238 Sugar Pine Lumber Shay Locomotive "5," *11*	750	___
11239 Merrill & Ring Lumber 2-Truck Shay Steam Locomotive, CC, *11*	900	___
11240 Merrill & Ring Lumber 2-Truck Shay Steam Locomotive, *11*	750	___
11247 Erie USRA 0-8-0 Steam Switcher "121," CC, *11-12*	700	___
11248 Erie USRA 0-8-0 Steam Switcher "127," *11-12*	550	___
11249 L&N USRA 0-8-0 Steam Switcher "2119," CC, *11-12*	700	___
11250 L&N USRA 0-8-0 Steam Switcher "2121," *11-12*	550	___
11251 Pere Marquette USRA 0-8-0 Steam Switcher "1300," CC, *11-12*	700	___
11252 Pere Marquette USRA 0-8-0 Steam Switcher "1307," *11-12*	550	___
11253 NH 0-8-0 Steam Switcher "3603," CC, *11-13*	700	___
11254 NH 0-8-0 Steam Switcher "3606," *11-13*	550	___
11255 C&O 2-8-2 Mikado Steam Locomotive "1062," CC, *12*	900	___
11256 NH 2-8-2 Mikado Steam Locomotive "3021," CC, *12*	900	___
11257 PRR 2-8-2 Mikado Steam Locomotive "8631," CC, *12*	900	___
11258 Southern 2-8-2 Mikado Steam Locomotive "4501," CC, *12*	900	___
11259 UP 2-8-2 Mikado Steam Locomotive "2840," CC, *12*	900	___
11260 Rio Grande 2-8-2 Mikado Steam Locomotive "1207," CC, *12*	900	___
11261 DM&I 2-8-2 Mikado Steam Locomotive "1305," CC, *12*	900	___
11262 Erie 2-8-2 Mikado Steam Locomotive "3007," CC, *12*	900	___
11264 PRR K4 4-6-2 Pacific Steam Locomotive "1361," CC, *11*	900	___
11265 PRR K4 4-6-2 Pacific Steam Locomotive "1330," CC, *11*	900	___
11266 PRR K4 4-6-2 Pacific Steam Locomotive "1361," *11*	750	___
11268 Strasburg 2-6-0 Mogul Steam Locomotive "89," *11*	550	___
11269 RI 2-6-0 Mogul Steam Locomotive "750," *11-13*	550	___
11270 GN 2-6-0 Mogul Steam Locomotive "453," *11*	550	___
11271 C&O 2-6-0 Mogul Steam Locomotive "49," *11-12*	550	___
11272 ATSF 2-6-0 Mogul Steam Locomotive "573," *11*	550	___
11273 Central Pacific 2-6-0 Mogul Steam Locomotive "1470," *11-13*	550	___
11274 MKT USRA 0-8-0 Steam Switcher "46," CC, *11-12*	700	___
11275 MKT 0-8-0 Steam Switcher "51," CC, *11*	550	___
11276 Lionelville & Western 0-8-0 Steam Switcher "1," CC, *11-13*	700	___
11277 Lionelville & Western 0-8-0 Steam Switcher "2," *11-13*	550	___

		Exc	Mint
___	**11278** WP 2-8-2 Mikado Steam Locomotive "322," CC, *11*		900
___	**11279** WP 2-8-2 Mikado Steam Locomotive "327," *11*		750
___	**11280** B&O 2-8-2 Mikado Steam Locomotive "4507," CC, *11*		900
___	**11281** B&O 2-8-2 Mikado Steam Locomotive "451," *11*		750
___	**11282** GN 2-8-2 Mikado Steam Locomotive "3125," CC, *11*		900
___	**11284** MP 2-8-2 Mikado Steam Locomotive "1310," CC, *11*		900
___	**11286** RI 2-8-2 Mikado Steam Locomotive "2302," CC, *11*		900
___	**11287** RI 2-8-2 Mikado Steam Locomotive "2305," *11*		750
___	**11288** T&P 2-8-2 Mikado Steam Locomotive "552," CC, *11*		900
___	**11289** T&P 2-8-2 Mikado Steam Locomotive "557," *11*		750
___	**11290** Bethlehem Steel 2-6-0 Mogul Steam Locomotive "28," *11*		550
___	**11291** Weyerhaeuser 2-6-0 Mogul Locomotive "288," *11-13*		550
___	**11295** Elk River Lumber 2-Truck Shay Locomotive "1," CC, *11*		900
___	**11296** Elk River Lumber 2-Truck Shay Locomotive "2," *11*		750
___	**11297** P. Bunyan Lumber 2-Truck Shay Locomotive "18," CC, *11*		900
___	**11298** P. Bunyan Lumber 2-Truck Shay Locomotive "23," *11*		750
___	**11299** C&O 2-6-6-2 Mallet Steam Locomotive "875," CC, *12*		1300
___	**11300** PRR 2-10-4 Texas Steam Locomotive "6479," CC, *11*		1300
___	**11301** PRR 2-10-4 Texas Steam Locomotive "6498," CC, *11*		1300
___	**11303** C&O 2-10-4 Texas Steam Locomotive "3011," CC, *11*		1300
___	**11304** C&O 2-10-4 Texas Steam Locomotive "3025," CC, *11*		1300
___	**11306** NKP 2-10-4 Texas Steam Locomotive "801," CC, *11*		1300
___	**11308** Erie 2-10-4 Texas Steam Locomotive "3405," CC, *11*		1300
___	**11310** Pere Marquette 2-10-4 Texas Locomotive "1241," CC, *11*		1300
___	**11312** MILW S3 4-8-4 Northern Steam Locomotive "265," CC, *11*		995
___	**11315** Pennsylvania-Reading Seashore Atlantic Locomotive, *11*		550
___	**11316** PRR 4-4-2 Atlantic Steam Locomotive "272," *11*		550
___	**11317** Southern 4-4-2 Atlantic Steam Locomotive "1910," *11*		550
___	**11318** CN 4-4-2 Atlantic Steam Locomotive "1630," *11*		550
___	**11319** PRR K4 4-6-2 Pacific Locomotive "5409," *13*		900
___	**11320** PRR K4 4-6-2 Pacific Locomotive "5436," *13*		750
___	**11321** C&O 2-6-6-2 Mallet Steam Locomotive "1525," CC, *12*		1300
___	**11322** NKP 2-6-6-2 Mallet Steam Locomotive "943," CC, *12*		1300
___	**11323** W&LE 2-6-6-2 Mallet Steam Locomotive "8002," CC, *12*		1300
___	**11327** PRR Prewar K4 4-6-2 Pacific Locomotive "3667," CC, *11*		900
___	**11328** PRR Prewar K4 4-6-2 Pacific Locomotive "3672," CC, *11*		900
___	**11329** PRR Prewar K4 4-6-2 Pacific Locomotive "3678," *11*		750
___	**11330** Polar K4 4-6-2 Pacific Locomotive, CC, *11-14*		900

		Exc	Mint
11331	Polar K4 4-6-2 Pacific Locomotive, *11*	750	____
11332	ATSF 4-8-4 Northern Steam Locomotive "3751," CC, *12*	1300	____
11333	ATSF 4-8-4 Northern Steam Locomotive "3759," CC, *12*	1300	____
11334	Southern Crescent Limited 4-6-2 Pacific Locomotive, CC, *12*	1100	____
11335	Blue Comet 4-6-2 Pacific Steam Locomotive "832," CC, *12*	1100	____
11337	B&O 2-8-8-4 Steam Locomotive "7621," CC, *12*	1300	____
11338	Alton Limited 4-6-2 Pacific Steam Locomotive "657," CC, *12*	1100	____
11339	N&W 2-6-6-2 Mallet Steam Locomotive "1409," CC, *12*	1300	____
11340	B&O 2-8-8-4 Steam Locomotive "659," CC, *12*	1300	____
11341	Pilot 4-12-2 Locomotive, CC, *13*	1300	____
11342	UP 4-12-2 Steam Locomotive "9004," CC, *12-13*	1300	____
11343	UP 4-12-2 Steam Locomotive, black, "9000," CC, *12-13*	1300	____
11344	UP 4-12-2 Steam Locomotive, greyhound, "9000," CC, *12*	1300	____
11363	Cass Scenic RR 2-Truck Shay Steam Locomotive "3," CC, *12*	900	____
11364	Meadow River 2-Truck Shay Steam Locomotive "1," CC, *12-13*	900	____
11365	Weyerhaeuser 2-Truck Shay Steam Locomotive "3," CC, *12-13*	900	____
11366	Pickering Lumber 2-Truck Shay Locomotive "3," CC, *12-13*	900	____
11367	CP 2-Truck Shay Steam Locomotive "111," CC, *12-13*	900	____
11368	WM 2-Truck Shay Steam Locomotive "2," CC, *12*	900	____
11369	Bethlehem Steel 2-Truck Shay Steam Locomotive "5," CC, *12-13*	900	____
11374	DM&I 2-8-8-4 Steam Locomotive "223," CC, *12*	1300	____
11375	WP 2-8-8-4 Steam Locomotive "258," CC, *12*	1300	____
11376	NP 2-8-8-4 Steam Locomotive "5000," CC, *12*	1300	____
11377	GN 2-8-8-4 Steam Locomotive "2060," CC, *12*	1300	____
11379	PRR 0-4-0 Shifter Steam Locomotive "112," *12*	450	____
11380	PRR 0-4-0 Shifter Steam Locomotive "94," *12*	450	____
11381	North Pole Central 0-4-0 Switcher (std O), *12*	450	____
11382	Transylvania 0-4-0 Shifter Steam Locomotive "13," *12*	450	____
11383	Bethlehem Steel 0-4-0 Shifter Steam Locomotive "134," *12*	450	____
11384	ATSF 0-4-0 Shifter Steam Locomotive "2301," *13*	450	____
11385	UP 0-4-0 Shifter Steam Locomotive "206," *13*	450	____
11386	B&M 2-8-4 Berkshire Steam Locomotive "4018," CC, *12-13*	1250	____
11387	ATSF 2-8-4 Berkshire Steam Locomotive "4199," CC, *12-13*	1250	____
11388	SP 2-8-4 Berkshire Steam Locomotive "3505," CC, *12-13*	1250	____
11389	B&A 2-8-4 Berkshire Steam Locomotive "1404," CC, *12-13*	1250	____
11390	Lima Demonstrator 2-8-4 Berkshire Locomotive "1," CC, *12-13*	1250	____

		Exc Mint
11391	IC 2-8-4 Berkshire Steam Locomotive "7020," CC, *12-13*	1250
11392	Michigan Central 2-8-4 Berkshire Locomotive "1420," CC, *12-13*	1250
11399	UP H7 Class 2-8-8-2 Steam Locomotive "3595," CC, *13-14*	1350
11400	C&O H7 Class 2-8-8-2 Steam Locomotive "1578," CC, *13-14*	1350
11401	Pilot H7 Class 2-8-8-2 Locomotive, CC, *14-15*	1350
11402	Virginian USRA Y3 2-8-8-2 Locomotive, CC, *13-14*	1350
11403	Pilot USRA 2-8-8-2 Locomotive, CC, *13-15*	1350
11404	ATSF USRA Y3 2-8-8-2 Locomotive, CC, *13-14*	1350
11405	N&W USRA Y3 2-8-8-2 Locomotive, CC, *13-14*	1350
11410	Pilot 4-8-2 Mohawk Locomotive, CC, *13-15*	1300
11411	NYC 4-8-2 Mohawk Locomotive "2854," CC, *12-13*	1300
11412	NYC 4-8-2 Mohawk Locomotive "2867," CC, *12-13*	1300
11413	Pilot 4-8-4 J-Class Locomotive, CC, *13-15*	1300
11414	N&W 4-8-4 Steam Locomotive "612," CC, *12-13*	1300
11415	Pilot S2 6-8-6 Turbine Locomotive, CC, *14-15*	1300
11416	PRR S2 6-8-6 Steam Turbine Locomotive "6200," CC, *12-14*	1300
11417	PRR S2 6-8-6 Steam Turbine Locomotive "6200," CC, *12-13*	1300
11418	Pilot GS-6 Locomotive, CC, *13-14*	1300
11419	SP 4-8-4 GS-2 Locomotive, black, CC, *12-13*	1300
11420	SP 4-8-4 GS-2 Locomotive, Daylight, CC, *12*	1300
11421	SP 4-8-4 GS-6 Locomotive, black, CC, *12*	1300
11422	WP 4-8-4 GS-64 Locomotive "482," CC, *12*	1300
11423	CNJ Blue Comet Locomotive "833," CC, *12-13*	1100
11425	Alaska 0-4-0 Locomotive, RailSounds, *12-13*	1100
11426	Rio Grande 0-4-0 Locomotive, RailSounds, *12-13*	450
11427	SP 0-4-0 Locomotive "14," RailSounds, *12-13*	450
11428	MILW 0-4-0 Locomotive, RailSounds, *12-13*	450
11429	Southern 0-4-0 Locomotive, RailSounds, *12-13*	450
11430	GN 0-4-0 Locomotive "1066," RailSounds, *12-13*	450
11431	N&W 4-8-4 Locomotive "611," CC, *12*	1300
11432	LL S2 6-8-6 Steam Turbine Locomotive, CC, *13-14*	1300
11433	PRR S2 6-8-6 Steam Turbine Locomotive CC, *13-14*	1300
11434	UP Big Boy Locomotive "4006," CC, *14*	2700
11435	UP Big Boy Locomotive "4018," CC, *14*	2700
11436	UP Big Boy Locomotive "4005," CC, *14*	2700
11437	UP Big Boy Locomotive "4014," CC, *14*	2700
11438	UP Big Boy Locomotive "4017," CC, *14*	2700
11446	UP USRA Y3 2-8-8-2 Locomotive "3671," CC, *13-14*	1350
11447	PRR USRA Y3 2-8-8-2 Locomotive "376," CC, *13-14*	1350
11448	UP Big Boy Locomotive "4012," CC, *14*	2700
11449	UP Big Boy Locomotive "4004," CC, *14*	2700
11450	Polar Express Berkshire Scale Locomotive, gold, CC, *14*	1500
11451	Polar Express Berkshire Scale Locomotive, black, CC, *14*	1500
11452	C&O 2-8-4 Berkshire Locomotive "2687," CC, *14*	1500
11453	Erie 2-8-4 Berkshire Locomotive "3321," CC, *14*	1500
11454	NKP 2-8-4 Berkshire Locomotive "765," CC, *14*	1500

		Exc	Mint
11455	Pere Marquette 2-8-4 Berkshire Locomotive "1225," CC, *14*		1500
11456	Pere Marquette 2-8-4 Berkshire Locomotive "1227," CC, *14*		1500
11462	SP AC-12 Cab-Forward Locomotive "4291," CC, *14*		1700
11463	SP AC-12 Cab-Forward Locomotive "4286," CC, *14*		1700
11464	SP AC-12 Cab-Forward Locomotive "4294," CC, *14*		1700
11465	SP AC-12 Cab-Forward Locomotive "4275," CC, *14*		1700
11469	Pilot AC-12 Cab-Forward Locomotive, CC, *14-15*		1700
11528	Frosty the Snowman Figure Pack, *14, 16*		30
11650	Alderney Dairy General American Milk Car 2-pack (std O), *07*		130
11651	Freeport General American Milk Car 2-pack (std O), *07*		130
11652	BNSF Mechanical Reefer 2-pack (std O), *07-09*		140
11653	SPFE Mechanical Reefer 2-pack (std O), *07*		140
11654	UPFE Mechanical Reefer 2-pack (std O), *07*		140
11655	GN WFE Mechanical Reefer 2-pack (std O), *07*		140
11657	PFE Wood-sided Reefer 3-pack (std O), *06*		190
11658	John Bull Add-on Coach, *08*		80
11700	Conrail Limited Set, *87*	320	370
11701	Rail Blazer Set, *87-88*		60
11702	Black Diamond Set, *87*	195	265
11703	Iron Horse Freight Set, *88-91*	100	105
11704	Southern Freight Runner Set (SSS), *87*	210	285
11705	Chessie System Unit Train, *88*	360	450
11706	Dry Gulch Line Set (SSS), *88*	190	260
11707	Silver Spike Set, *88-89*	175	245
11708	Midnight Shift Set, *88 u, 89*	60	75
11710	CP Rail Freight Set, *89*	375	447
11711	Santa Fe F3 Diesel ABA Set, *91*	480	590
11712	Great Lakes Express Set (SSS), *90*	260	280
11713	Santa Fe Dash 8-40B Set, *90*	395	480
11714	Badlands Express Set, *90-91*	49	60
11715	Lionel 90th Anniversary Set, *90*	300	375
11716	Lionelville Circus Special Set, *90-91*	155	190
11717	CSX Freight Set, *90*	230	240
11718	Norfolk Southern Dash 8-40C Unit Train, *92*	445	481
11719	Coastal Freight Set (SSS), *91*	165	215
11720	Santa Fe Special Set, *91*	49	60
11721	Mickey's World Tour Train Set, *91, 92 u*	118	158
11722	Girls Train Set, *91*	560	825
11723	Amtrak Maintenance Train, *91, 92 u*	210	245
11724	GN F3 Diesel ABA Set, *92*	730	840
11726	Erie-Lackawanna Freight Set, *91 u*	225	275
11727	Coastal Limited Set, *92*	90	110
11728	High Plains Runner Set, *92*	120	130
11733	Feather River Set (SSS), *92*	285	330
11734	Erie Alco Diesel ABA Set (FF 7), *93*	250	305
11735	NYC Flyer Freight Set "1735WS," *93-99*	125	160
11736	Union Pacific Express Set, *93-95*	110	130
11738	Soo Line Set (SSS), *93*	250	280
11739	Super Chief Set, *93-94*	135	155
11740	Conrail Consolidated Set, *93*	200	240

		Exc	Mint
____	**11741** Northwest Express Set, *93*	130	155
____	**11742** Coastal Limited Set, *93 u*	90	115
____	**11743** Chesapeake & Ohio Freight Set, *94*	240	280
____	**11744** NYC Passenger/Freight Set (SSS), *94*	295	335
____	**11745** U.S. Navy Set, *94-95*	260	305
____	**11746** Seaboard Freight Set, *94, 95 u*	90	115
____	**11747** Lionel Lines Steam Set, *95*	310	340
____	**11748** Amtrak Alco Diesel Passenger Set, *95-96*	130	185
____	**11749** Western Maryland Set (SSS), *95*	275	300
____	**11750** McDonald's Nickel Plate Special Set, *87 u*	143	153
____	**11751** Sears PRR Passenger Set, *87 u*	120	155
____	**11752** JCPenney Timber Master Set, *87 u*	75	115
____	**11753** Kay Bee Toys Rail Blazer Set, *87 u*	80	100
____	**11754** Key America Set, *87 u*	150	165
____	**11755** Timber Master Set, *87 u*	150	165
____	**11756** Hawthorne Freight Flyer Set, *87-88 u*	65	85
____	**11757** Chrysler Mopar Express Set, *88 u*	330	390
____	**11758** Desert King Set (SSS), *89*	195	250
____	**11759** JCPenney Silver Spike Set, *88 u*	175	250
____	**11761** JCPenney Iron Horse Freight Set, *88 u*	120	125
____	**11762** True Value Cannonball Express Set, *89 u*	95	145
____	**11763** United Model Freight Hauler Set, *88 u*	135	145
____	**11764** Sears Iron Horse Freight Set, *88 u*	155	190
____	**11765** Spiegel Silver Spike Set, *88 u*	175	250
____	**11767** Shoprite Freight Flyer Set, *88 u*	80	125
____	**11769** JCPenney Midnight Shift Set, *89 u*	100	175
____	**11770** Sears Circus Set, *89 u*	185	220
____	**11771** K-Mart Microracers Set, *89 u*	80	110
____	**11772** Macy's Freight Flyer Set, *89 u*	170	220
____	**11773** Sears NYC Passenger Set, *89 u*	175	200
____	**11774** Ace Hardware Cannonball Express Set, *89.u*	145	175
____	**11775** Anheuser-Busch Set, *89-92 u*	260	350
____	**11776** Pace Iron Horse Freight Set, *89 u*	115	135
____	**11777** Sears Lionelville Circus Set, *90 u*	175	190
____	**11778** Sears Badlands Express Set, *90 u*	49	60
____	**11779** Sears CSX Freight Set, *90 u*	190	230
____	**11780** Sears NP Passenger Set, *90 u*	155	190
____	**11781** True Value Cannonball Express Set, *90 u*	75	115
____	**11783** Toys "R" Us Heavy Iron Set, *90-91 u*	135	160
____	**11784** Pace Iron Horse Freight Set, *90 u*	115	135
____	**11785** Costco Union Pacific Express Set, *90 u*	200	230
____	**11789** Sears Illinois Central Passenger Set, *91 u*	170	200
____	**11793** Santa Fe Set, *91 u*	49	60
____	**11794** Mickey's World Tour Set, *91 u*	80	100
____	**11796** Union Pacific Express Set, *91 u*	150	160
____	**11797** Sears Coastal Limited Set, *92 u*	80	100
____	**11800** Toys"R" Us Heavy Iron Thunder Limited Set, *92-93 u*	235	295
____	**11803** Nickel Plate Special Set, *92 u*	135	145
____	**11804** K-Mart Coastal Limited Set, *92 u*	80	100
____	**11809** Village Trolley Set, *95-97*	55	85
____	**11810** Budweiser Modern Era Set, *93-94 u*	220	235
____	**11811** United Auto Workers Set, *93 u*	189	447
____	**11812** Coastal Limited Special Set, *93 u*	95	115

		Exc	Mint
11813	Crayola Activity Train Set, *94 u, 95*	115	139____
11814	Ford Limited Edition Set, *94 u*	214	259____
11818	Chrysler Mopar Set, *94 u*	210	250____
11819	Georgia Power Set, *95 u*	550	575____
11820	Red Wing Shoes NYC Flyer Set, *95 u*	270	325____
11821	Sears Zenith Set, *95 u*		780____
11822	Chevrolet Set, *96 u*	280	335____
11825	Bloomingdale's Set, *96 u*		322____
11826	Sears Freight Set, *95-96 u*		769____
11827	Zenith Employees Set, *96 u*		850____
11828	NJ Transit Passenger Set, *96 u*		180____
11833	NJ Transit GP38 Diesel Passenger Set, *97*	275	300____
11837	Union Pacific GP9 Diesel Set, *97*		520____
11838	ATSF Warhorse Hudson Freight Set, *97*		810____
11839	SP&S 4-6-2 Steam Freight Set, *97*		280____
11841	Bloomingdale's Set, *97 u*		325____
11843	Boston & Maine GP9 Diesel ABA Set, *98*		510____
11844	Union Pacific Die-cast Ore Cars 4-pack, *98*		225____
11846	Kal Kan Pet Care Train Set, *97 u*		850____
11849	Lionel Centennial Series Reefer 4-pack, *98*		120____
11850	Rice A Roni Trolley Set, *02 u*		265____
11851	PFE Reefer 6-pack (std O), *02*	225	255____
11852	Clinchfield PS-2 2-bay Hopper, *04*		70____
11853	B&M PS-2 2-bay Hopper 2-pack, *05*		128____
11854	N&W PS-2 Covered Hopper 2-pack, *04*		70____
11855	GN Offset Hopper with coal, 2-pack, *05*		120____
11856	Green Bay & Western Offset Hopper 2-pack, *05*		120____
11857	Baltimore & Ohio Offset Hopper 2-pack, *05*		120____
11858	PRR PS-4 Flatcar with trailers, 2-pack (std O), *05*		160____
11859	GN PS-4 Flatcar with trailers (std O), *05*		160____
11860	SP PS-4 Flatcar with trailers (std O), *05*		160____
11861	C&O PS-4 Flatcar with trailers (std O), *05*		160____
11863	Southern Pacific GP9 Diesel "2383," *98*		225____
11864	New York Central GP9 Diesel "2383," *98*		275____
11865	Alaska GP7 Diesel "1802," *98-99*		90____
11866	Govt. of Canada Cylindrical Hopper 2-pack (std O), *05*		120 ____
11867	CN Cylindrical Hopper 2-pack (std O), *05*		120____
11868	BN Husky Stack Car 2-pack (std O), *05*		160____
11869	SP Husky Stack Car 2-pack (std O), *05*		160____
11870	CSX Husky Stack Car 2-pack (std O), *05*		220____
11871	TTX Trailer Train Stack Car 2-pack (std O), *05*		160____
11872	PFE Orange Steel-sided Reefer 3-pack (std O), *05*		130____
11873	C&O Offset Hopper 3-pack (std O), *05*		130____
11874	PFE Orange Steel-sided Reefer 3-pack (std O), *05*		130____
11875	NP Steel-sided Reefer 3-pack (std O), *05*		130____
11876	PFE Silver Steel-sided Reefer 3-pack (std O), *05*		130____
11877	C&NW Steel-sided Reefer 3-pack (std O), *05*		130____
11878	Santa Fe PS-2 2-bay Covered Hopper 3-pack (std O), *06*		125 ____
11879	MKT PS-2 2-bay Covered Hopper 3-pack (std O), *06*		125____
11880	Boraxo PS-2 2-bay Covered Hopper 3-pack (std O), *06*		125 ____
11881	PRR PS-2 2-bay Covered Hopper 3-pack (std O), *06*		125____

		Exc	Mint
____	**11882** RI Offset Hopper with gravel, 3-pack (std O), *06*		125
____	**11883** CNJ Offset Hopper 3-pack (std O), *06*		145
____	**11884** Maine Central Offset Hopper 3-pack (std O), *06*		145
____	**11891** Pennsylvania 3-bay Hopper 3-pack (std O), *06*		155
____	**11892** Conrail ACF 3-bay Hopper 3-pack (std O), *06*		155
____	**11893** N&W 3-bay Hopper 3-pack (std O), *06*		155
____	**11894** UP 3-bay Hopper 3-pack (std O), *06*		155
____	**11895** GN Steel-sided Reefer 3-pack (std O), *06*		145
____	**11896** Santa Fe Steel-sided Reefer 3-pack (std O), *06*		145
____	**11897** Pepper Packing Steel-sided Reefer 3-pack (std O), *06*		145
____	**11900** SF Steam Freight Set, *96-01*		130
____	**11903** ACL F3 Diesel ABA Set, *96*		716
____	**11905** U.S. Coast Guard Set, *96*	160	180
____	**11906** Factory Selection Special Set, *95 u*		85
____	**11909** N&W J 4-8-4 Warhorse Set, *96*	560	720
____	**11910** Lionel Lines Set (O27), *96*	140	160
____	**11912** "57" Switcher Service Exclusive, *96*		310
____	**11913** SP GP9 Diesel Freight Set, *97*		440
____	**11914** NYC GP9 Diesel Freight Set, *97*		370
____	**11918** Conrail SD20 Service Exclusive "X1144" (SSS), *97*		255
____	**11919** Docksider Set, *97*		70
____	**11920** Port of Lionel City Dive Team Set, *97*		185
____	**11921** Lionel Lines Freight Set, *97*		130
____	**11929** ATSF Warbonnet Passenger Set, *97-99*		132
____	**11930** ATSF Warbonnet Passenger Car 2-pack, *97-99*		80
____	**11931** Chessie Flyer Freight Set, "1931S," *97-99*		165
____	**11933** Dodge Motorsports Freight Set, *96 u*		315
____	**11934** Virginian Electric Locomotive Freight Set, *97-99*		260
____	**11935** NYC Flyer Freight Set, *97*		155
____	**11936** Little League Baseball Steam Set, *97*	235	305
____	**11939** SP&S 4-6-2 Steam Freight Set, *97*		220
____	**11940** Southern Pacific SD40 Warhorse Coal Set, *98*		600
____	**11944** Lionel Lines 4-4-2 Steam Freight Set, *98*		175
____	**11956** UP GP9 Diesel Set, *97*	330	380
____	**11957** Mobil Oil Steam Special Set, *97*		429
____	**11971** D&H 4-4-2 Steam Freight Set, *98*	125	155
____	**11972** Alaska GP7 Diesel Set, *98-99*	180	215
____	**11974** Station Accessory Set, *98*		22
____	**11975** Freight Accessory Pack, *98*		23
____	**11977** NP Freight Cars 4-pack, *98*		170
____	**11979** N&W 4-4-2 Steam Freight Set, *98*		75
____	**11981** 1998 Holiday Trolley Set, *98*		75
____	**11982** New Jersey Transit Ore Car Set, *98*		250
____	**11983** Farmrail Agricultural Set, *99*		480
____	**11984** Corvette GP7 Diesel Set, *99*		455
____	**11988** NYC FireCar "18444" and Instruction Car "19853," *99*		210
____	**12000** NY Yankees Berkshire Passenger Set, *13*		380
____	**12004** Philadelphia Phillies Berkshire Passenger Set, *13*		380
____	**12008** Boston Red Sox Berkshire Passenger Set, *13*		380
____	**12012** Chicago Cubs Berkshire Passenger Set, *13*		380
____	**12013** NY Mets and Yankees Subway Series Set, *13*		400
____	**12014** 10" Straight Track (FasTrack), *03-18*		6

		Exc	Mint
12015	036 Curved Track (FasTrack), *03-18*	6	___
12016	10" Terminal Track (FasTrack), *03-14, 16, 18*	6	___
12017	036 Manual Switch, left hand (FasTrack), *03-18*	50	___
12018	036 Manual Switch, right hand (FasTrack), *03-18*	50	___
12019	90-degree Crossover (FasTrack), *03-18*	26	___
12020	5" Uncoupling Track (FasTrack), *03-18*	42	___
12022	036 Half Curved Track (FasTrack), *03-14, 16, 18*	5	___
12023	036 Quarter Curved Track (FasTrack), *03-14, 16, 18*	5	___
12024	5" Straight Track (FasTrack), *03-17, 18*	5	___
12025	4" Straight Track (FasTrack), *03-14, 16, 18*	5	___
12026	1" Straight Track (FasTrack), *03-14, 16, 18*	5	___
12027	10" Insulated Track (FasTrack), *03-14, 16, 18*	5	___
12028	Inner Passing Loop Track Pack (FasTrack), *03-16, 18*	115	___
12029	Accessory Activator Pack (FasTrack), *03-18*	21	___
12030	Figure 8 Track Pack (FasTrack), *03-16, 18*	75	___
12031	Outer Passing Loop Track Pack (FasTrack), *03-16, 18*	145	___
12032	10" Straight Track 4-pack (FasTrack), *03-18*	22	___
12033	036 Curved Track, card of 4 (FasTrack), *03-18*	22	___
12035	FasTrack Lighted Bumper 2-pack, *05-18*	33	___
12036	Grade Crossing 2-pack (FasTrack), *05-16, 18*	17	___
12037	Graduated Trestle Set (FasTrack), *05-16, 18*	85	___
12038	Elevated Trestle Set (FasTrack), *05-16, 18*	45	___
12039	Railer (FasTrack), *04-16, 18*	10	___
12040	0 Gauge Transition Piece (FasTrack), *04-14, 16, 18*	9	___
12041	072 Curved Track (FasTrack), *04-14, 16, 18*	7	___
12042	30" Straight Track (FasTrack), *04-14, 16, 18*	15	___
12043	048 Curved Track (FasTrack), *04-14, 16, 18*	5	___
12044	Siding Track Add-on Track Pack (FasTrack), *04-16, 18*	120	___
12045	036 Remote Switch, left hand (FasTrack), *04-17*	95	___
12046	036 Remote Switch, right hand (FasTrack), *04-17*	95	___
12047	072 Wye Remote Switch (FasTrack), *04-14*	97	___
12048	072 Remote Switch, left hand (FasTrack), *04-14*	104	___
12049	072 Remote Switch, right hand (FasTrack), *04-14*	104	___
12050	22 1/2-degree Crossover (FasTrack), *04-14, 16, 18*	46	___
12051	45-degree Crossover (FasTrack), *04-14, 16, 18*	24	___
12052	Grade Crossing with flashers (FasTrack), *05-16, 18*	100	___
12053	Accessory Power Wire (FasTrack), *04-18*	5	___
12054	Operating Track with half straight (FasTrack), *05-18*	45	___
12055	072 Half Curved Track (FasTrack), *04-14, 16, 18*	6	___
12056	060 Curved Track (FasTrack), *05-14, 16, 18*	7	___
12057	060 Remote Switch, left hand, *05-14*	104	___
12058	060 Remote Switch, right hand (FasTrack), *05-14*	104	___
12059	Earthen Bumper (FasTrack), *04-16, 18*	11	___
12060	Block Section (FasTrack), *05-14, 16, 18*	9	___
12061	084 Curved Track (FasTrack), *05-14, 16, 18*	7	___
12062	Grade Crossing with gates and flashers (FasTrack), *06-14, 18*	165	___
12065	048 Remote Switch, left hand (FasTrack), *07-14*	104	___
12066	048 Remote Switch, right hand (FasTrack), *07-14*	104	___
12073	1 3/8" Track Section (FasTrack), *07-14, 16, 18*	5	___
12074	1 3/8" Track Section, no roadbed (FasTrack), *07-14, 16, 18*	5	___
12080	42" Path Remote Switch, right hand, *07-12*	80	___

MODERN ERA 1970-2019

		Exc	Mint
____ **12081** 42" Path Remote Switch, left hand, *07-12*			80
____ **12700** Erie Magnetic Gantry Crane, *87*		125	150
____ **12701** Operating Fueling Station, *87*		60	74
____ **12702** Control Tower, *87*		60	75
____ **12703** Icing Station, *88-89*		60	65
____ **12704** Dwarf Signal, *88-93*		9	11
____ **12705** Lumber Shed Kit, *88-99*			9
____ **12706** Barrel Loader Building Kit, *87-99*			10
____ **12707** Billboards, set of 3, *87-99*			5
____ **12708** Street Lamps, set of 3, *88-93*		6	9
____ **12709** Banjo Signal, *87-91, 95-00*			29
____ **12710** Engine House Kit, *87-91*		21	25
____ **12711** Water Tower Kit, *87-99*			13
____ **12712** Automatic Ore Loader, *87-88*		17	21
____ **12713** Automatic Gateman, *87-88, 94-00*		30	40
____ **12714** Crossing Gate, *87-91, 93-18*			50
____ **12715** Illuminated Bumpers, set of 2, *87-15*			13
____ **12716** Searchlight Tower, *87-89, 91-92*		15	22
____ **12717** Nonilluminated Bumpers, set of 3, *87-17*			7
____ **12718** Barrel Shed Kit, *87-99*			10
____ **12719** Animated Refreshment Stand, *88-89*		65	70
____ **12720** Rotary Beacon, *88-89*		40	45
____ **12721** Illuminated Extension Bridge, rock piers, *89*		26	38
____ **12722** Roadside Diner, smoke, *88-89*		27	38
____ **12723** Microwave Tower, *88-91, 94-95*		14	19
____ **12724** Double Signal Bridge, *88-90*		39	50
____ **12725** Lionel Tractor and Trailer, *88-89*		10	18
____ **12726** Grain Elevator Kit, *88-91, 94-99*			36
____ **12727** Operating Semaphore, *89-99*			26
____ **12728** Illuminated Freight Station, *89*		29	38
____ **12729** Mail Pickup Set, *88-91, 95*		12	16
____ **12730** Lionel Girder Bridge, *88-03, 08-18*			21
____ **12731** Station Platform, *88-00*			8
____ **12732** Coal Bag, *88-18*			7
____ **12733** Watchman Shanty Kit, *88-99*			5
____ **12734** Passenger/Freight Station, *89-99*			18
____ **12735** Diesel Horn Shed, *88-91*		19	24
____ **12736** Coaling Station Kit, *88-91*		21	31
____ **12737** Whistling Freight Shed, *88-99*			28
____ **12739** Lionel Gas Company Tractor and Tanker, *89*		20	25
____ **12740** Genuine Wood Logs, set of 3, *88-92, 94-95, 97-99*			5
____ **12741** Union Pacific Intermodal Crane, *89*		165	185
____ **12742** Gooseneck Lamps, set of 2, *89-00*			21
____ **12743** Track Clips, dozen (O), *89-16*			12
____ **12744** Rock Piers, set of 2, *89-92, 94-05, 08, 11-15, 18*			15
____ **12745** Barrel Pack, set of 6, *89-18*			8
____ **12746** Operating/Uncoupling Track (027), *89-16*			10
____ **12748** Illuminated Passenger Platform, *89-99*			18
____ **12749** Rotary Radar Antenna, *89-92, 95*		28	38
____ **12750** Crane Kit, *89-91*		8	10
____ **12751** Shovel Kit, *89-91*		8	10
____ **12752** History of Lionel Trains Video, *89-92, 94*		19	21
____ **12753** Ore Load, set of 2, *89-91, 95*		1	2

	Exc	Mint
12754 Graduated Trestle Set, 22 pieces, *89-15*		27____
12755 Elevated Trestle Set, 10 pieces, *89-15*		27____
12756 The Making of the Scale Hudson Video, *91-94*	20	22____
12759 Floodlight Tower, *90-00*		25____
12760 Automatic Highway Flasher, *90-91*	23	27____
12761 Animated Billboard, *90-91, 93, 95*	12	23____
12763 Single Signal Bridge, *90-91, 93*	31	35____
12767 Steam Clean and Wheel Grind Shop, *92-93, 95*	240	290____
12768 Burning Switch Tower, *90, 93*	85	90____
12770 Arch-Under Bridge, *90-03, 08-18*		30____
12771 Mom's Roadside Diner, smoke, *90-91*	34	50____
12772 Truss Bridge, flasher and piers, *90-16, 18*		70____
12773 Freight Platform Kit, *90-98*		32____
12774 Lumber Loader Kit, *90-99*		19____
12777 Chevron Tractor and Tanker, *90-91*	9	15____
12778 Conrail Tractor and Trailer, *90*	9	16____
12779 Lionelville Grain Company Tractor and Trailer, *90*	11	19____
12780 RS-1 50-watt Transformer, *90-93*	95	130____
12781 N&W Intermodal Crane, *90-91*	145	160____
12782 Lift Bridge, *91-92*	428	518____
12783 Monon Tractor and Trailer, *91*	11	19____
12784 Intermodal Containers, set of 3, *91*	12	17____
12785 Lionel Gravel Company Tractor and Trailer, *91*	9	15____
12786 Lionel Steel Company Tractor and Trailer, *91*	10	16____
12791 Animated Passenger Station, *91*	45	60____
12794 Lionel Tractor, *91*	7	13____
12795 Cable Reels, pair, *91-98*	3	5____
12798 Forklift Loader Station, *92-95*	33	44____
12800 Scale Hudson Replacement Pilot Truck, *91 u*	13	17____
12802 Chat & Chew Roadside Diner, smoke and lights, *92-95*	41	50____
12804 Highway Lights, set of 4, *92-99, 02-04, 13-18*	9	27____
12805 Intermodal Containers, set of 3, *92*	10	14____
12806 Lionel Lumber Company Tractor and Trailer, *92*	10	15____
12807 Little Caesars Tractor and Trailer, *92*	9	14____
12808 Mobil Tractor and Tanker, *92*	8	13____
12809 Animated Billboard, *92-93*	12	22____
12810 American Flyer Tractor and Trailer, *94*	12	18____
12811 Alka Seltzer Tractor and Trailer, *92*	11	19____
12812 Illuminated Freight Station, *93-00*		27____
12818 Animated Freight Station, *92, 94-95*	50	60____
12819 Inland Steel Tractor and Trailer, *92*	9	16____
12821 Lionel Catalog Video, *92*	13	17____
12826 Intermodal Containers, set of 3, *93*	10	16____
12831 Rotary Beacon, *93-95*	22	32____
12832 Block Target Signal, *93-98*		25____
12833 RoadRailer Tractor and Trailer, *93*	9	15____
12834 Pennsylvania Magnetic Gantry Crane, *93*	130	170____
12835 Operating Fueling Station, *93*	55	60____
12836 Santa Fe Quantum Tractor and Trailer, *93*	8	14____
12837 Humble Oil Tractor and Tanker, *93*	9	16____
12838 Crate Load, set of 2, *93-97*		3____
12839 Grade Crossings, set of 2, *93-16*		7____
12840 Insulated Straight Track (O), *93-16*		8____

		Exc	Mint
12841	Insulated Straight Track (O27), *93-16*		5
12842	Dunkin' Donuts Tractor and Trailer, *92 u*	13	25
12843	Die-cast Sprung Trucks, pair, *93-99*		10
12844	Coil Covers, pair (O), *93-98*		3
12847	Animated Ice Depot, *94-99*		65
12848	Lionel Oil Company Derrick, *94*	55	75
12849	Lionel Controller with wall pack, *94, 95 u*		NRS
12852	Die-cast Intermodal Trailer Frame, *94-01*		6
12853	Coil Covers, pair (std O), *94-98*		7
12854	U.S. Navy Tractor and Tanker, *94-95*		33
12855	Intermodal Containers, set of 3, *94-95*	9	13
12860	Lionel Visitor's Center Tractor and Trailer, *94 u*	10	14
12861	Lionel Leasing Company Tractor, *94*	8	13
12862	Oil Drum Loader, *94-95*	75	85
12864	Little Caesars Tractor and Trailer, *94*	8	14
12865	Wisk Tractor and Trailer, *94*	12	55
12866	TMCC 135-watt PowerHouse Power Supply, *94 u, 95-03*		46
12867	TMCC 135 PowerMaster Power Distribution Center, *94 u, 95-04*		49
12868	TMCC CAB-1 Remote Controller, *94 u, 95-09*		115
12869	Marathon Oil Tractor and Tanker, *94*	15	22
12873	Operating Sawmill, *95-97*		70
12874	Classic Street Lamps, set of 3, *94-00*		13
12877	Operating Fueling Station, *95*	75	85
12878	Control Tower, *95*	49	60
12881	Chrysler Mopar Tractor and Trailer, *94 u*	41	52
12882	Lighted Billboard, *95*	9	14
12883	Dwarf Signal, *95-18*		27
12884	Truck Loading Dock Kit, *95-98*		16
12885	40-watt Control System, *94 u, 95-05*		35
12886	Floodlight Tower, *95-98*		31
12888	Railroad Crossing Flasher, *95-18*		56
12889	Operating Windmill, *95-98*		34
12890	Big Red Control Button, *94 u, 95-00*		43
12891	Lionel Refrigerator Lines Tractor and Trailer, *95*	12	16
12892	Automatic Flagman, *92-98*		25
12893	TMCC PowerMaster Power Adapter Cable, *94 u, 95-13, 17-18*		20
12894	Signal Bridge, *95-01*		22
12895	Double-track Signal Bridge, *95-00*		44
12896	Tunnel Portals, pair, *95-18*		20
12897	Engine House Kit, *96-98*		29
12898	Flagpole, *95-97*		9
12899	Searchlight Tower, *95-98*	10	25
12900	Crane Kit, *95-98*		8
12901	Shovel Kit, *95-98*		7
12902	Marathon Oil Derrick, *94 u, 95*	109	161
12903	Diesel Horn Shed, *95-98*		29
12904	Coaling Station Kit, *95-98*		19
12905	Factory Kit, *95-98*		20
12906	Maintenance Shed Kit, *95-98*		20
12907	Intermodal Containers, set of 3, *95*	9	14
12911	TMCC Command Base, *95-09*		80

		Exc	Mint
12912	Oil Pumping Station, *95-98*	38	65___
12914	SC-1 Switch and Accessory Controller, *95-98*		35___
12915	Log Loader, *96*		115___
12916	Water Tower, *96-97*		56___
12917	Animated Switch Tower, *96-98*		29___
12922	NYC Operating Gantry Crane, coil covers, *96*	75	90___
12923	Red Wing Shoes Tractor and Trailer, *95 u*	34	38___
12925	42" Diameter Curved Track Section (O), *96-16*		4___
12926	Globe Street Lamps, set of 3, *96-03, 08-09, 16-18*		25___
12927	Yard Light, set of 3, *96-18*		27___
12929	Rail-truck Loading Dock, *96*		44___
12930	Lionelville Oil Company Derrick, *95 u, 96*	55	75___
12931	Electrical Substation, *96*		22___
12932	Laimbeer Packaging Tractor and Trailer Set, *96*		14___
12933	GM Parts Tractor and Trailer, *95*		NRS___
12935	Zenith Tractor and Trailer, *96*		24___
12936	SP Intermodal Crane, *97*		195___
12937	NS Intermodal Crane, *97*		200___
12938	PowerStation Controller and PowerHouse 135-watt Power Supply, *97-00*		150 ___
12943	Illuminated Station Platform, *97-00*		24___
12944	Sunoco Oil Derrick, *97*		85___
12945	Sunoco Pumping Oil Station, *97*		80___
12948	Bascule Bridge, *97*	75	315___
12949	Billboards, set of 3, *97-00*		7___
12951	Airplane Hangar Kit, *97-98*		29___
12952	Big L Diner Kit, *97*		24___
12953	Linex Gas Tall Oil Tank, *97*		9___
12954	Linex Gas Wide Oil Tank, *97*		10___
12955	Road Runner and Wile E. Coyote Ambush Shack, *97*		100___
12958	Industrial Water Tower, *97-98*		50___
12960	Rotary Radar Antenna, *97*		26___
12961	Newsstand with diesel horn, *97*		30___
12962	LL Passenger Service Train Whistle, *97-99*		30___
12964	Donald Duck Radar Antenna, *97*		72___
12965	Goofy Rotary Beacon, *97*		58___
12966	Rotary Aircraft Beacon, *97-00*		35___
12968	Girder Bridge Building Kit, *97*		22___
12969	TMCC Command Set, *97-09*		148___
12974	Blinking Light Billboard, *97-00*		15___
12975	Steiner Victorian Building Kit, *97-98*		33___
12976	Dobson Victorian Building Kit, *97-98*		24___
12977	Kindler Victorian Building Kit, *97-98*		35___
12982	Culvert Loader, conventional, *98-00*		190___
12983	Culvert Unloader, conventional, *99*		185___
12987	Intermodal Containers, set of 3, *98*		15___
12989	Lionel Tractor and Trailer, *98*		16___
12991	Linex Gas Tractor-Tanker, *98*		16___
14000	Operating Forklift Platform, *00*		160___
14001	Operating Belt Lumber Loader, *00*		95___
14002	ZW Amp/Volt Meter, *00-04*		80___
14003	80-watt Transformer/Controller, *00-03*		70___
14004	Operating Coal Loader, *00*		135___
14005	Operating Coal Ramp, *00*		130___

		Exc	Mint
14018	ElectroCoupler Kit for Command Upgradeable GP9s, *00*		20
14062	31" Path Remote Switch, left hand, *01-14*		55
14063	31" Path Remote Switch, right hand, *01-14*		75
14065	Nuclear Reactor, *00*		233
14071	Yard Light 3-pack, *00-18*		35
14072	Haunted House, *01*		181
14073	History of Lionel, The First 90 Years Video, *00*		15
14075	A Century of Lionel, 1900-1969 Video, *00*		15
14076	A Century of Lionel, 1970-2000 Video, *00*		15
14077	ZW Amp/Volt Meter, *00-03*		70
14078	Die-cast Sprung Trucks, *00-05, 07-18*		24
14079	Operating North Pole Pylon, *01*		70
14080	Hobo Hotel, *01*	30	65
14081	Shell Oil Derrick, *01*		100
14082	Pedestrian Walkover, speed sensor, *01-03*		50
14083	Pedestrian Walkover, *01-03, 08, 12-16*		55
14084	Lionel Heliport, *01*		85
14085	Newsstand, *01*		75
14086	Water Tower, *00*		105
14087	Lighthouse, *01*		95
14090	Banjo Signal, *01-18*		60
14091	Automatic Gateman, *01-03, 07-09*		38
14092	Floodlight Tower, *01-05, 08-16*		48
14093	Single Signal Bridge, *01-04, 08*		22
14094	Double Signal Bridge, *01-04, 08*		30
14095	Illuminated Station Platform, *01-04*		20
14096	Station Platform, *01-04*		10
14097	Rotary Aircraft Beacon, *01-04, 07-10*		40
14098	Auto Crossing Gate, *01-18*		100
14099	Block Target Signal, *01-04, 07-08*		22
14100	Blinking Light Billboard, *01-03*		23
14101	Red Baron Pylon, *01*		85
14102	Rocket Launcher, *01*		250
14104	Burning Switch Tower, *00*		70
14105	Aquarium, *01*		175
14106	Operating Freight Station, *00*		70
14107	Coaling Station, *01-03*		95
14109	Carousel, *01*		230
14110	Operating Ferris Wheel, *01-02, 04*		170
14111	1531R Controller, *00-17*		46
14112	Lighted Lockon, *01-10, 13-16*		6
14113	Engine Transfer Table, *01*		210
14114	Engine Transfer Table Extension, *01*		75
14116	PRR Die-cast Girder Bridge, *01*		20
14117	NYC Die-cast Girder Bridge, *01*		20
14119	Gooseneck Lamps, set of 2, *01-04, 07*		22
14121	Classic Billboards, set of 3, *01-03*		10
14124	ZW Controller with 2 transformers, *01*		300
14125	Christmas Tree with 400E Train, *00*		65
14126	Exploding Ammo Dump		55
14133	Madison Hobby Shop, *01*		290
14134	Triple Action Magnetic Crane, *01*		230
14135	NS Black Die-cast Girder Bridge, *02*		15

		Exc	Mint
14137	Die-cast Girder Bridge, *01-07*		25___
14138	Snap-On Tool Animated Billboard, *01 u*		NRS___
14142	Industrial Smokestack, *02-04*		50___
14143	Industrial Tank, *02-04*		40___
14145	Operating Lumberjacks, *02-03*		65___
14147	Die-cast Old Style Clock Tower, *02-04, 08-18*		47___
14148	Operating Billboard Signmen, *02-03*		60___
14149	Scale-sized Banjo Signal, *02-05*		40___
14151	Mainline Dwarf Signal, *02-08*		43___
14152	Passenger Station, *02-04*		37___
14153	Lion Oil Derrick, *02-03*		50___
14154	Water Tower, *01-02*		65___
14155	Floodlight Tower, *02-03*		55___
14156	Lion Oil Diesel Fueling Station, *02-03*		70___
14157	Coal Loader, *01-03*		120___
14158	Icing Station, *01-02*		75___
14159	Animated Billboard, *02-04*		20___
14160	Frank's Hotdog Stand, *03-04*		55___
14161	Smoking Hobo Shack, *02*		60___
14162	Missile Launching Platform, *02-03*		48___
14163	Industrial Power Station, *02-03*		550___
14164	Lionelville Bandstand, *02*		140___
14166	Train Orders Building, *04-05*		49___
14167	Operating Lift Bridge, *02*		380___
14168	Operating Harry's Barber Shop, *02-04*		100___
14170	Amusement Park Swing Ride, *03-04*		150___
14171	Pirate Ship Ride, *02-04*		130___
14172	NYC Railroad Tugboat, *02*		180___
14173	Drawbridge, *02-04*		70___
14175	Santa Fe Die-cast Girder Bridge, *01-03*		17___
14176	Norfolk Southern Die-cast Girder Bridge, *02-03*		18___
14178	TMCC Direct Lockon, *02-03*		25___
14179	TMCC Track Power Controller, *02-13*		230___
14180	B&O Railroad Tugboat, *02-03*		155___
14181	TMCC Action Recorder Controller, *02-13*		115___
14182	TMCC Accessory Switch Controller, *02-13*		115___
14183	TMCC Accessory Motor Controller, *02-13*		115___
14184	TMCC Block Power Controller, *02-12*		90___
14185	TMCC Operating Track Controller, *02-13*		100___
14186	TMCC Accessory Voltage Controller, *02-13*		160___
14187	TMCC How-to Video, *02-04*		11___
14189	TMCC Track Power Controller, *02-13*		175___
14190	The Lionel Train Book, *04-14*		30___
14191	TMCC Command Base Cable, 6 feet, *02-13*		14___
14192	TMCC 3-wire Command Base Cable, *02-13*		15___
14193	TMCC Controller to Controller Cable, 1 foot, *02-13*		6___
14194	TMCC TPC Cable Set, *02-13*		16___
14195	TMCC Command Base Cable, 20 feet, *02-07*		12___
14196	TMCC Controller to Controller Cable, 6 feet, *02-13*		9___
14197	TMCC Controller to Controller Cable, 20 feet, *02-07*		9___
14198	CW-80 80-watt Transformer, *03-18*	65	150___
14199	Playground Swings, *03-04, 08-09*		50___
14201	Burning Switch Tower, *05*		70___

		Exc	Mint
____	**14202** Water Tower, *05*		140
____	**14203** Amusement Park Swing Ride, *06-07*		230
____	**14209** U.S. Steel Gantry Crane, *05*		180
____	**14210** Pony Ride, *06-07*		70
____	**14211** Road Crew, *07-08*		90
____	**14214** Lionelville Mini Golf, *06*		80
____	**14215** Tug-of-War, *06-08*		60
____	**14217** Helicopter Pylon, *06-09*		140
____	**14218** Downtown People Pack, *06-18*		27
____	**14219** Ice Rink, *06-08*		80
____	**14220** Lionelville Water Tower, *06-08*		21
____	**14221** Witches Cauldron, *06-08*		70
____	**14222** Die-cast Girder Bridge, *06-09*		30
____	**14225** Sunoco Industrial Tank, *06-09*		70
____	**14227** Yard Tower, *06-08*		45
____	**14229** Crossing Shanty, *06-09*		20
____	**14230** Milk Bottle Toss Midway Game, *06*		20
____	**14231** Cotton Candy Midway Booth, *06*		20
____	**14236** Operating Freight Station, *06-07*		105
____	**14237** Rocket Launcher, *06-07*		320
____	**14240** Ice Block Pack, *06-18*		6
____	**14241** Work Crew People Pack, *06-18*		27
____	**14242** Hard Rock Cafe, *06*		50
____	**14243** U.S. Army Water Tower, *06-08*		95
____	**14244** Ammo Loader, *06-07*		105
____	**14251** Die-cast Sprung Trucks, rotating bearing caps, *07-18*		25
____	**14255** Sand Tower, *06-18*		35
____	**14257** Passenger Station, *06-13*		60
____	**14258** North Pole Passenger Station, *06-10*		53
____	**14259** Christmas People Pack, *06-12*		23
____	**14260** Christmas Tractor and Trailer, *06-08*		25
____	**14261** Christmas Tree Lot, *06*		70
____	**14262** Elevated Tank, *07*		70
____	**14265** Sawmill with sound, *08*		130
____	**14267** Sir Topham Hatt Gateman, *07-12*		80
____	**14273** Polar Express Add-on Figures, *06-07, 12-14, 16-18*		30
____	**14289** Operating Santa Gateman, *08*		80
____	**14290** UPS Store, *06*		30
____	**14291** Operating Milk Loading Depot, K-Line, *08*		100
____	**14294** 993 Legacy Expansion Set, *07-16, 18*		320
____	**14295** 990 Legacy Command Set, *07-16, 18*		400
____	**14297** Halloween Witch Pylon, *07-08*		140
____	**14500** KCS F3 Diesel AA Set, Railsounds, CC, *01*	380	660
____	**14512** F3 Diesel ABA Demonstrator "291," CC, *01*	360	425
____	**14517** Santa Fe F3 Diesel B Unit "2343C," powered, *01*		280
____	**14518** CP F3 Diesel B Unit "2373C," RailSounds, CC, *01*		345
____	**14520** Texas Special F3 Diesel B Unit, RailSounds, *01*		360
____	**14521** Rock Island E6 Diesel AA Set, *01*		530
____	**14524** Atlantic Coast Line E6 Diesel AA Set, *01*		630
____	**14536** Santa Fe F3 Diesel AA Set, RailSounds, CC, *03-04*		800
____	**14539** Santa Fe F3 Diesel B Unit, *03*		300
____	**14540** D&RGW F3 Diesel B Unit, RailSounds, CC, *01*		315
____	**14541** C&O F3 Diesel B Unit, RailSounds, CC, *01*		300

Exc Mint

		Exc	Mint
14542 KCS F3 Diesel B Unit "2388C," RailSounds, CC, *01*			375____
14543 SP F3 Diesel B Unit, RailSounds, CC, *01*			282____
14544 Southern E6 AA Diesel Set, CC, *02*			560____
14547 Burlington E5 AA Diesel Set, CC, *02*			570____
14552 NYC F3 Diesel AA Set, RailSounds, CC, *03-04*			740____
14555 NYC F3 Diesel B Unit, *03*			200____
14557 WP F3 Diesel B Unit, nonpowered, *03-04*			190____
14558 B&O F3 Diesel B Unit, nonpowered, *03-04*			155____
14559 D&RGW F3 Diesel AA Set, *01*			620____
14560 NP F3 Diesel A Unit "2390B," freight, *02*			175____
14561 NP F3 Diesel A Unit "2390B," passenger, *02*			190____
14562 Milwaukee Road F3 Diesel A Unit "75C," *02*			190____
14563 Erie-Lackawanna F3 Diesel A Unit "7094," *02*			175____
14564 CP F3 Diesel B Unit "237C," CC, *02*			350____
14565 B&O F3 Diesel AA Set, *03-04*			650____
14568 WP F3 Diesel AA Set, *03-04*			780____
14571 Santa Fe PA Diesel AA Set, CC, *03*			660____
14574 D&H PA Diesel AA Set, CC, *03*			580____
14584 Wabash F3 Diesel A Unit, nonpowered, *03*			180____
14586 D&H PB Unit, *03*			125____
14587 Santa Fe PB Unit, *03*			125____
14588 Santa Fe F3 Diesel ABA Set, CC, *04-05*			980____
14592 PRR F3 Diesel ABA Set, CC, *04-05*			750____
14596 NH Alco PA Diesel AA Set, *04-05*			700____
14599 NH Alco PB Diesel B Unit "0767-B," *04*-05			150____
15000 D&RGW Waffle-sided BoxCar, *95*		12	18____
15001 Seaboard Waffle-sided BoxCar, *95*		14	19____
15002 Chesapeake & Ohio Waffle-sided BoxCar, *96*		16	20____
15003 Green Bay & Western Waffle-sided BoxCar, *96*		16	20____
15004 Bloomingdale's BoxCar, *97 u*			40____
15005 "I Love NY" BoxCar, *97 u*			65____
15008 CP Rail Boxcar			30____
15013 L&N Waffle-sided Boxcar "102402," *00*			29____
15014 Seaboard Waffle-sided Boxcar "125925," *00*			25____
15015 C&NW Waffle-sided Boxcar "161013," *03*			18____
15016 IC Waffle-sided Boxcar "12981," *04*			20____
15017 CSX Waffle-sided BoxCar, *05*			27____
15018 D&H Waffle-sided Boxcar "24052," *06*			30____
15020 NH Waffle-sided BoxCar, *07*			30____
15021 MKT Waffle-sided BoxCar, *08*			35____
15024 UP Waffle Boxcar "960860," *09-11*			40____
15028 Southern Waffle-sided Boxcar "539889," *10*			40____
15029 Western & Atlantic Wood-sided Reefer, *10*			53____
15033 MTK Stock Car, *10*			65____
15038 CSX Hi-Cube BoxCar, *11-12*			40____
15039 NS Waffle-sided Boxcar, *11-12*			40____
15041 BNSF Hi-Cube BoxCar, *10*			50____
15042 CSX Waffle-sided BoxCar, *11*			40____
15051 Lionel Lines BoxCar, *11-12*			40____
15052 Amtrak Hi-Cube BoxCar, *11-12*			40____
15053 REA Waffle-sided BoxCar, *11-12*			40____
15054 C&NW Wood-sided Reefer, *11-12*			40____
15060 K-Line BoxCar, *06*			40____

		Exc	Mint
____	**15063** U.S.A.F. Minuteman BoxCar, *11*		55
____	**15069** Coke Wood-sided Reefer #1, *09-16*		65
____	**15071** Coca-Cola Christmas BoxCar, *12*		70
____	**15072** Halloween BoxCar, *09-11*		55
____	**15074** Mr. Goodbar Wood-sided Reefer, *09-11*		55
____	**15075** Boy Scouts of America Eagle Scout BoxCar, *11-14*		60
____	**15077** ATSF Stock Car, *11*		55
____	**15078** Pabst Wood-sided Reefeer, *11*		65
____	**15079** Schlitz Wood-sided Reefer, *11*		58
____	**15080** C&O 40' BoxCar, *11*		55
____	**15083** CP Rail Waffle-sided BoxCar, *13*		43
____	**15084** GN Hi-Cube BoxCar, *13-14*		43
____	**15086** Alaska Wood-Sided Reefer, *12*		40
____	**15091** Angela Trotta Thomas "High Hopes" Hi-Cube BoxCar, *12*		55
____	**15094** Sleepy Hollow Halloween Reefer, *14-15*		60
____	**15095** 1953 Lionel Catalog Art Reefer, *13*		55
____	**15096** Hershey's Kisses Christmas BoxCar, *12*		70
____	**15097** Peanuts Christmas BoxCar, *12-13*		70
____	**15098** Lone Ranger BoxCar, *12-14*		60
____	**15100** Amtrak Passenger Coach, *95-97*		35
____	**15101** Reading Baggage Car (027), *96*		34
____	**15102** Reading Combination Car (027), *96*		23
____	**15103** Reading Passenger Coach (027), *96*		23
____	**15104** Reading Vista Dome Car (027), *96*		26
____	**15105** Reading Full Vista Dome Car (027), *96*		26
____	**15106** Reading Observation Car (027), *96*		23
____	**15107** Amtrak Vista Dome Car, *96*		38
____	**15108** Northern Pacific Vista Dome Car, *96*		34
____	**15109** ATSF Combine Car "2407," *97*		35
____	**15110** ATSF Vista Dome Car 2404," *97*		35
____	**15111** ATSF Observation Car "2406," *97*		35
____	**15112** ATSF Albuquerque Coach "2405," *97*		34
____	**15113** ATSF Culebra Vista Dome Car "2404," *97*		34
____	**15114** NJ Transit Coach "5610," *96 u*		45
____	**15115** NJ Transit Coach "5611," *96 u*		45
____	**15116** NJ Transit Coach "5612," *96 u*		45
____	**15117** Annie Passenger Coach, *97*		26
____	**15118** Clarabel Passenger Coach, *97*		26
____	**15122** NJ Transit Passenger Coach "5613," *97 u*		45
____	**15123** NJ Transit Passenger Coach "5614," *97 u*		45
____	**15124** NJ Transit Passenger Coach "5615," *97 u*		45
____	**15125** Amtrak Observation Car, *97 u*		50
____	**15126** Stars & Stripes Abraham Lincoln General Coach, *99*		60
____	**15127** Stars & Stripes Ulysses S. Grant General Coach, *99*		60
____	**15128** Pride of Richmond Robert E. Lee General Coach, *99*		60
____	**15129** Pride of Richmond Jefferson Davis General Coach, *99*		60
____	**15136** Custom Series Short Observation Car, blue, *99*		40
____	**15137** Custom Series Short Observation Car, red, *99*		34
____	**15138** Pratt's Hollow Baggage Car, *98*		100
____	**15139** Pratt's Hollow Vista Dome Car, *98*		100
____	**15140** Pratt's Hollow Coach, *98*		100
____	**15141** Pratt's Hollow Observation, *98*		100

		Exc	Mint
15142	U.S. Army Baby Heavyweight Coach, *00*	50	___
15143	U.S. Army Baby Heavyweight Coach, *00*	50	___
15153	Pullman Baby Madison Set 4-pack, *01*	190	___
15163	T&P Baby Heavyweight Coach, *01*	30	___
15166	Union Pacific Whistling Baggage Car, *04*	41	___
15169	C&O Streamliner Car 4-pack, *03*	140	___
15170	L&N Streamliner Car 4-pack, *03*	140	___
15180	NYC Streamliner Car 4-pack, *04*	340	___
15185	UP Streamliner Car 4-pack, *04*	340	___
15300	NYC Superliner Aluminum Passenger Car 4-pack, *02*	360	___
15301	NYC Manhattan Superliner Passenger Coach, *02*	90	___
15302	NYC Queens Superliner Passenger Coach, *02*	90	___
15304	NYC Staten Island Superliner Passenger Coach, *02*	90	___
15305	NYC Brooklyn Superliner Passenger Coach, *02*	90	___
15311	CB&Q California Zephyr Aluminum Passenger Car 4-pack, *03*	350	___
15312	Santa Fe Super Chief Aluminum Passenger Car 4-pack, *03*	275	___
15313	D&H Aluminum Passenger Car 4-pack, *03*	415	___
15314	Amtrak Superliner 2-pack, *03*	220	___
15315	Santa Fe Superliner 2-pack, *03*	200	___
15316	NYC Superliner 2-pack, *03*	195	___
15317	Southern Aluminum Passenger Car 4-pack, *03*	350	___
15318	Lionel Lines Aluminum Passenger Car 2-pack, *03*	125	___
15319	Santa Fe Superliner Aluminum Passenger Car 2-pack, *03*	145	___
15326	NYC 20th Century Limited Aluminum Passenger Car 6-pack, *02*	485	___
15333	N&W Powhatan Arrow Aluminum Passenger Car 6-pack, *02*	435	___
15340	PRR South Wind Aluminum Passenger Car 6-pack, *02*	435	___
15379	Lionel Lines Silver Valley Aluminum Combination Car, *03*	100	___
15380	Lionel Lines Silver Spoon Aluminum Diner, *03*	100	___
15381	Santa Fe Aluminum Baggage Car "2571," *03*	100	___
15382	Santa Fe Regal Dome Aluminum Vista Dome Car, *03*	100	___
15383	NYC 20th Century Limited Diner, StationSounds, *03*	195	___
15384	N&W Powhatan Arrow Diner, StationSounds, *03*	190	___
15385	Pennsylvania South Wind Diner, StationSounds, *03*	190	___
15394	Amtrak Streamliner Car 4-pack, *03-04*	450	___
15395	Alaska Streamliner Car 4-pack, *03-04*	355	___
15396	Amtrak Superliner Diner, StationSounds, *03*	220	___
15397	Santa Fe Superliner Diner, StationSounds, *03*	200	___
15398	NYC Superliner Diner, StationSounds, *03*	200	___
15405	50th Anniversary Hillside Heavyweight Diner, StationSounds, *02*	195	___
15406	Blue Comet Giacobini Heavyweight Diner, StationSounds, *02*	300	___
15504	Alton Limited Diner, StationSounds, *03*	230	___
15507	Phantom III Passenger Car 4-pack (15508 Baggage, 15509 Vista Dome, 15510 Coach, 15511 Observation), *02*	245	___
15512	Phantom II Passenger Car 4-pack, *02*	250	___

		Exc	Mint
15517	Southern Crescent Limited Heavyweight Passenger Car 2-pack, *03-04*		205
15520	Southern Crescent Limited Heavyweight Diner, StationSounds, *03-04*		220
15521	NYC 20th Century Limited Heavyweight Passenger Car 4-pack, *04*		345
15526	Santa Fe Chief Heavyweight Passenger Car 4-pack, *04*		370
15538	NYC 20th Century Limited Heavyweight Passenger Car 2-pack, *04*		200
15541	NYC 20th Century Limited Heavyweight Diner, StationSounds, *04*		200
15542	Santa Fe Chief Heavyweight Passenger Car 2-pack, *04*		195
15545	Santa Fe Chief Heavyweight Diner, StationSounds, *04*		200
15546	Napa Valley Wine Train Heavyweight 2-pack, *05*		250
15549	Napa Valley Wine Train Diner, StationSounds, *05*		280
15554	Pennsylvania Heavyweight Car 3-pack (std O), *05*		375
15558	Pennsylvania Heavyweight Add-on Coach (std O), *05*		140
15559	PRR Reading Seashore Heavyweight Car 3-pack (std O), *05*		370
15563	PRR Reading Seashore Heavyweight Add-on Coach, *05*		130
15564	LIRR Heavyweight Car 3-pack (std O), *05*		370
15568	LIRR Heavyweight Add-on Coach (std O), *05*		130
15570	LIRR Heavyweight Car 3-pack (std O), *06*		230
15574	LIRR Heavyweight Car Add-on (std O), *06*		140
15575	C&O Heavyweight Diner, StationSounds (std O), *06-07*		295
15576	C&O Heavyweight Passenger Car 2-pack (std O), *06-07*		265
15577	NYC Heavyweight 3-pack (std O), *05-06*		370
15581	NYC Heavyweight Add-on Coach (std O), *05-06*		130
15584	Amtrak Acela Passenger Car 3-pack (std O), *06*		580
15588	Southern Heavyweight Passenger Car 4-pack, *06*		495
15593	Southern Heavyweight Passenger Car 2-pack, *06*		265
15596	Southern Heavyweight Diner, StationSounds, *06*		295
15597	C&O Heavyweight Passenger Car 4-pack (std O), *06-07*		495
15906	RailSounds Trigger Button, *90-95*		12
16000	PRR Vista Dome Car (O27), *87-88*	37	55
16001	PRR Passenger Coach (O27), *87-88*	33	41
16002	PRR Passenger Coach (O27), *87-88*	24	29
16003	PRR Observation Car (O27), *87-88*	24	29
16009	PRR Combination Car (O27), *88*	36	38
16010	Virginia & Truckee Passenger Coach (SSS), *88*	36	47
16010	Railbox Modern Boxcar 6-pack, LionScale, *16*		360
16011	Virginia & Truckee Passenger Coach (SSS), *88*	36	47
16012	Virginia & Truckee Baggage Car (SSS), *88*	36	47
16013	Amtrak Combination Car (O27), *88-89*	21	34
16014	Amtrak Vista Dome Car (O27), *88-89*	21	34
16015	Amtrak Observation Car (O27), *88-89*	21	34
16016	NYC Baggage Car (O27), *89*	36	55
16017	NYC Combination Car (O27), *89*	21	29
16018	NYC Passenger Coach (O27), *89*	21	29

	Exc	Mint
16019 NYC Vista Dome Car (027), *89*	21	29___
16020 NYC Passenger Coach (027), *89*	23	33___
16020 BNSF Modern Boxcar 6-pack, LionScale, *16*		360___
16021 NYC Observation Car (027), *89*	20	28___
16022 Pennsylvania Baggage Car (027), *89*	27	38___
16023 Amtrak Passenger Coach (027), *89*	21	30___
16024 Northern Pacific Diner (027), *92*	39	44___
16027 LL Combination Car (027, SSS), *90*	39	48___
16028 LL Passenger Coach (SSS, 027), *90*	35	42___
16029 LL Passenger Coach (SSS, 027), *90*	35	42___
16030 LL Observation Car (SSS, 027), *90*	35	42___
16030 CSX Modern Boxcar 6-pack, LionScale, *16*		360___
16031 Pennsylvania Diner (027), *90*	35	39___
16033 Amtrak Baggage Car (027), *90*	28	38___
16034 NP Baggage Car (027), *90-91*	30	45___
16035 NP Combination Car (027), *90-91*	18	26___
16036 NP Passenger Coach (027), *90-91*	21	30___
16037 NP Vista Dome Car (027), *90-91*	18	26___
16038 NP Passenger Coach (027), *90-91*	17	25___
16039 NP Observation Car (027), *90-91*	21	30___
16040 Southern Pacific Baggage Car, *90-91*	22	30___
16040 NS Modern Boxcar 6-pack, LionScale, *16*		360___
16041 NYC Diner (027), *91*	37	47___
16042 Illinois Central Baggage Car (027), *91*	24	34___
16043 Illinois Central Combination Car (027), *91*	22	30___
16044 Illinois Central Passenger Coach (027), *91*	24	34___
16045 Illinois Central Vista Dome Car (027), *91*	22	30___
16046 Illinois Central Passenger Coach (027), *91*	24	34___
16047 Illinois Central Observation Car (027), *91*	24	34___
16048 Amtrak Diner (027), *91-92*	33	40___
16049 Illinois Central Diner (027), *92*	27	38___
16050 C&NW Baggage Car "6620," *93*	44	55___
16050 AT&SF 3-bay Offset Hopper 6-pack, LionScale, *16*		330___
16051 C&NW Combination Car "6630," *93*	40	50___
16052 C&NW Passenger Coach "6616," *93*	34	42___
16053 C&NW Passenger Coach "6602," *93*	37	46___
16054 C&NW Observation Car "6603," *93*	38	47___
16055 Santa Fe Passenger Coach (027), *93-94*	29	38___
16056 Santa Fe Vista Dome Car (027), *93-94*	25	32___
16057 Santa Fe Passenger Coach (027), *93-94*	30	40___
16058 Santa Fe Combination Car (027), *93-94*	27	35___
16059 Santa Fe Vista Dome Car (027), *93-94*	26	34___
16060 Santa Fe Observation Car (027), *93-94*	25	31___
16060 B&O 3-bay Offset Hopper 6-pack, LionScale, *16*		330___
16061 N&W Baggage Car "6061," *94*	60	85___
16062 N&W Combination Car "6062," *94*	38	50___
16063 N&W Passenger Coach "6063," *94*	43	55___
16064 N&W Passenger Coach "6064," *94*	43	55___
16065 N&W Observation Car "6065," *94*	36	48___
16066 NYC Combination Car "6066" (SSS), *94*	55	70___
16067 NYC Passenger Coach "6067" (SSS), *94*	38	47___
16068 UP Baggage Car "6068," (027), *94*	50	65___
16069 UP Combination Car "6069," (027), *94*	36	43___

		Exc	Mint
___	**16070** UP Passenger Coach "6070," (027), *94*	36	43
___	**16070** B&M 3-bay Offset Hopper 6-pack, LionScale, *16*		330
___	**16071** UP Diner "6071" (027), *94*	36	46
___	**16072** UP Vista Dome Car "6072" (027), *94*	36	43
___	**16073** UP Passenger Coach "6073" (027), *94*	36	42
___	**16074** UP Observation Car "6074" (027), *94*	36	43
___	**16075** Missouri Pacific Baggage Car "6620," *95*	44	55
___	**16076** Missouri Pacific Combination Car "6630," *95*	34	41
___	**16077** Missouri Pacific Passenger Coach "6616," *95*	34	41
___	**16078** Missouri Pacific Passenger Coach "7805," *95*	34	39
___	**16079** Missouri Pacific Observation Car "6609," *95*	34	41
___	**16080** New Haven Baggage Car "6080" (027), *95*	35	44
___	**16080** C&O 3-bay Offset Hopper 6-pack #1, LionScale, *16*		330
___	**16081** New Haven Combination Car "6081" (027), *95*	28	37
___	**16082** New Haven Passenger Coach "6082" (027), *95*	28	37
___	**16083** New Haven Vista Dome Car "6083" (027), *95*	30	39
___	**16084** New Haven Full Vista Dome Car "6084" (027), *95*	33	39
___	**16086** New Haven Observation Car "6086" (027), *95*	31	40
___	**16087** NYC Baggage Car "6087" (SSS), *95*	48	65
___	**16088** NYC Passenger Coach "6088" (SSS), *95*	36	43
___	**16089** NYC Diner "6089" (SSS), *95*	36	43
___	**16090** NYC Observation Car "6090" (SSS), *95*	38	46
___	**16090** C&O 3-bay Offset Hopper 6-pack #2, LionScale, *16*		330
___	**16091** NYC Passenger Cars, set of 4 (SSS), *95*	140	165
___	**16092** Santa Fe Full Vista Dome Car (027), *95*	30	38
___	**16093** Illinois Central Full Vista Dome Car (027), *95*	29	38
___	**16094** Pennsylvania Full Vista Dome Car (027), *95*	30	39
___	**16095** Amtrak Combination Car (027), *95*	19	23
___	**16096** Amtrak Vista Dome Car (027), *95*	19	23
___	**16097** Amtrak Observation Car (027), *95*	19	23
___	**16098** Amtrak Passenger Coach, *95-97*	20	33
___	**16099** Amtrak Vista Dome Car, *95-97*	20	33
___	**16100** Alaska RR 3-bay 9-panel Hopper 6-pack, LionScale, *16*		330
___	**16102** Southern 3-D Tank Car (SSS), *87*	23	30
___	**16103** Lehigh Valley 2-D Tank Car (027), *88*	19	25
___	**16104** Santa Fe 2-D Tank Car (027), *89*	19	23
___	**16105** D&RGW 3-D Tank Car (SSS), *89*	48	65
___	**16106** Mopar Express 3-D Tank Car, *88 u*	100	151
___	**16107** Sunoco 2-D Tank Car (027), *90*	16	20
___	**16108** Racing Fuel 1-D Tank Car "6108" (027), *89 u, 92 u*	9	13
___	**16109** B&O 1-D Tank Car (SSS), *91*	29	34
___	**16110** Circus Animals Operating Stock Car "1989" (027), *89 u*	24	34
___	**16110** Chessie 3-bay 9-panel Hopper 6-pack, LionScale, *16*		330
___	**16111** Alaska 1-D Tank Car (027), *90-91*	22	27
___	**16112** Dow Chemical 3-D Tank Car, *90*	20	26
___	**16113** Diamond Shamrock 2-D Tank Car (027), *91*	20	25
___	**16114** Hooker Chemicals 1-D Tank Car (027), *91*	13	17
___	**16115** MKT 3-D Tank Car, *92*	13	16
___	**16116** U.S. Army 1-D Tank Car, *91 u*	36	42
___	**16119** MKT 2-D Tank Car (027), *92, 93 u*	14	19
___	**16120** Southern 3-bay 9-panel Hopper 6-pack, LionScale, *16*		330

Exc Mint

		Exc	Mint
16121	C&NW Stock Car (SSS), *92*	33	43___
16123	Union Pacific 3-D Tank Car, *93-95*	16	22___
16124	Penn Salt 3-D Tank Car, *93*	21	26___
16125	Virginian Stock Car, *93*	19	24___
16126	Jefferson Lake 3-D Tank Car, *93*	22	26___
16127	Mobil 1-D Tank Car, *93*	28	33___
16128	Alaska 1-D Tank Car, *94*	24	29___
16129	Alaska 1-D Tank Car (O27), *93 u, 94*	21	28___
16130	SP Stock Car (O27), *93 u, 94*	10	13___
16130	WM 3-bay 9-panel Hopper 6-pack, LionScale, *16*		330___
16131	T&P Reefer, *94*	19	24___
16132	Deep Rock 3-D Tank Car, *94*	25	30___
16133	Santa Fe Reefer, *94*	22	28___
16134	Reading Reefer, *94*	17	21___
16135	C&O Stock Car, *94*	23	27___
16136	B&O 1-D Tank Car, *94*	28	32___
16137	Ford 1-D Tank Car "12," *94 u*	34	39___
16138	Goodyear 1-D Tank Car, *95*	28	34___
16140	Domino Sugar 1-D Tank Car, *95*	24	29___
16140	Klemme Coop PS-2CD Covered Hopper 6-pack, LionScale, *16*		360___
16141	Erie Stock Car, *95*	22	30___
16142	Santa Fe 1-D Tank Car, *95*	26	30___
16143	Reading Reefer, *95*	18	23___
16144	San Angelo 3-D Tank Car, *95*	22	25___
16146	Dairy Despatch Reefer, *95*	15	20___
16147	Clearly Canadian 1-D Tank Car (O27), *94 u*	25	40___
16149	Zep Chemical 1-D Tank Car (O27), *95 u*	65	82___
16150	Sunoco 1-D Tank Car "6315," *97*	35	38___
16150	D&RGW PS-2CD Covered Hopper 6-pack, LionScale, *16*		360___
16152	Sunoco 3-D Tank Car "6415," *97*		26___
16153	AEC Reactor Fluid 1-D Tank Car "6515-1," *97*		92___
16154	AEC Reactor Fluid 1-D Tank Car "6515-2," *97*		103___
16155	AEC Reactor Fluid 1-D Tank Car "6515-3," *97*		103___
16157	Gatorade Little League Baseball 1-D Tank Car "6315," *97 u*		58___
16160	AEC Tank Car "6515" with reactor fluid, *98*		80___
16160	MILW PS-2CD Covered Hopper 6-pack, LionScale, *16*		360___
16162	Hooker 1-D Tank Car "6315-1," *97*		50___
16163	Hooker 1-D Tank Car "6315-2," *97*		50___
16164	Hooker 1-D Tank Car "6315-3," *97*		50___
16165	Mobilfuel 3-D Tank Car "6415," *97 u*		50___
16170	RFMX PS-2CD Covered Hopper 6-pack, LionScale, *16*		360___
16170	RFMX PS-2CD Covered Hopper 6-pack, LionScale, *16*		360___
16171	Alaska 1-D Tank Car "6171," *98-99*		33___
16173	Harold the Helicopter FlatCar, *98*	45	60___
16175	NJ Transit Port Morris Ore Car "9125," *98*		45___
16176	NJ Transit Raritan Yard Ore Car "9126," *98 u*		45___
16177	NJ Transit Gladstone Yard Ore Car "9127," *98 u*		45___
16178	NJ Transit Bay Head Yard Ore Car "9128," *98 u*		45___
16179	NJ Transit Dover Yard Ore Car "9129," *98 u*		45___

		Exc	Mint
_____ **16180**	Tabasco 1-D Tank Car, *98*	63	79
_____ **16181**	Biohazard Tank Car with Lights, *98*		84
_____ **16182**	Gatorade 1-D Tank Car "6315," *98 u*		64
_____ **16187**	Linex 3-D Tank Car "6425," *99*		30
_____ **16188**	Kodak 1-D Tank Car "6515," *99*	74	91
_____ **16199**	UP 1-D Tank Car "6035," *99-00*		25
_____ **16200**	Rock Island Boxcar (027), *87-88*	7	10
_____ **16201**	Wabash Boxcar (027), *88-91*	7	10
_____ **16203**	Key America Boxcar (027), *87 u*	45	65
_____ **16204**	Hawthorne Boxcar (027), *87 u*	50	85
_____ **16205**	Mopar Express Boxcar "1987" (027), *87-88 u*	50	60
_____ **16206**	D&RGW Boxcar (SSS), *89*	37	42
_____ **16207**	True Value Boxcar (027), *88 u*	32	115
_____ **16208**	PRR Auto Carrier, 3-tier, *89*	24	37
_____ **16209**	Disney Magic Boxcar (027), *88 u*	90	110
_____ **16211**	Hawthorne Boxcar (027), *88 u*	45	65
_____ **16213**	Shoprite Boxcar (027), *88 u*	55	80
_____ **16214**	D&RGW Auto Carrier, *90*	24	32
_____ **16215**	Conrail Auto Carrier, *90*	27	38
_____ **16217**	Burlington Northern Auto Carrier, *92*	24	36
_____ **16219**	True Value Boxcar (027), *89 u*	55	75
_____ **16220**	Ace Hardware Boxcar (027), *89 u*	55	80
_____ **16221**	Macy's Boxcar (027), *89 u*	55	80
_____ **16222**	Great Northern Boxcar (027), *90-91*	8	15
_____ **16223**	Budweiser Reefer, *89-92 u*	61	84
_____ **16224**	True Value "Lawn Chief" Boxcar (027), *90 u*	45	60
_____ **16225**	Budweiser Vat Car, *90-91 u*	123	161
_____ **16226**	Union Pacific Boxcar "6226" (027), *90-91 u*	15	19
_____ **16227**	Santa Fe Boxcar (027), *91*	13	17
_____ **16228**	Union Pacific Auto Carrier, *92*	26	33
_____ **16229**	Erie-Lackawanna Auto Carrier, *91 u*	45	55
_____ **16232**	Chessie System BoxCar, *92, 93 u, 94, 95 u*	25	30
_____ **16233**	MKT DD BoxCar, *92*	20	29
_____ **16234**	ACY Boxcar (SSS), *92*	34	41
_____ **16235**	Railway Express Agency Reefer, *92*	19	23
_____ **16236**	NYC Pacemaker BoxCar, *92 u*	18	24
_____ **16237**	Railway Express Agency BoxCar, *92 u*	21	23
_____ **16238**	NYNH&H BoxCar, *93-95*		3
_____ **16239**	Union Pacific BoxCar, *93-95*	15	20
_____ **16241**	Toys "R" Us BoxCar, *92-93 u*	35	45
_____ **16242**	Grand Trunk Western Auto Carrier, *93*	35	40
_____ **16243**	Conrail BoxCar, *93*	26	34
_____ **16244**	Duluth, South Shore & Atlantic BoxCar, *93*	20	24
_____ **16245**	Contadina BoxCar, *93*	16	20
_____ **16247**	ACL BoxCar, *94*	15	19
_____ **16248**	Budweiser BoxCar, *93-94 u*	46	63
_____ **16249**	United Auto Workers BoxCar, *93 u*		55
_____ **16250**	Santa Fe Boxcar (027), *93 u, 94*	8	10
_____ **16251**	Columbus & Greenville BoxCar, *94*	8	15
_____ **16252**	U.S. Navy Boxcar "6106888," *94-95*		30
_____ **16253**	Santa Fe Auto Carrier, *94*	32	38
_____ **16255**	Wabash DD BoxCar, *95*	20	26
_____ **16256**	Ford DD BoxCar, *94 u*	30	34

		Exc	Mint
16257	Crayola BoxCar, *94 u, 95*	17	23____
16258	Lehigh Valley BoxCar, *95*	17	22____
16259	Chrysler Mopar BoxCar, *97 u*	33	43____
16260	Chrysler Mopar Auto Carrier, *96 u*	54	64____
16261	Union Pacific DD BoxCar, *95*	26	29____
16263	ATSF BoxCar, *96-99*		25____
16264	Red Wing Shoes BoxCar, *95*	26	32____
16265	Georgia Power "Atlanta '96" BoxCar, *95 u*	200	236____
16266	Crayola BoxCar, *95*	17	23____
16267	Sears Zenith BoxCar, *95-96 u*		55____
16268	GM/AC Delco BoxCar, *95 u*		51____
16269	Lionel Lines BoxCar, *96*		10____
16272	Christmas BoxCar, *97*		36____
16273	Lionel Employee Christmas BoxCar, *97*		55____
16274	Marvin the Martian BoxCar, *97*		60____
16279	Dodge Motorsports BoxCar, *96 u*	142	185____
16284	Galveston Wharves BoxCar, *98*		28____
16285	Savannah State Docks BoxCar, *98*		26____
16291	Christmas BoxCar, *98*		34____
16292	Lionel Employee Christmas BoxCar, *98*	309	369____
16293	JCPenney BoxCar, *97*		100____
16294	Pedigree BoxCar, *97*	145	165____
16295	Kal Kan BoxCar, *97*	145	166____
16296	Whiskas BoxCar, *97*	137	162____
16297	Sheba BoxCar, *97*	136	160____
16298	Mobil BoxCar, *97*		50____
16300	Rock Island Flatcar with fences (027), *87-88*	8	10____
16301	Lionel Barrel Ramp Car, *87*	14	19____
16303	PRR Flatcar with trailers, *87*	26	33____
16304	RI Gondola with cable reels (027), *87-88*	5	9____
16305	Lehigh Valley Ore Car, *87*	80	130____
16306	Santa Fe Barrel Ramp Car, *88*	12	16____
16307	NKP Flatcar with trailers, *88*	30	40____
16308	Burlington Northern Flatcar with trailer, *88-89*	20	25____
16309	Wabash Gondola with canisters, *88-91*	9	13____
16310	Mopar Express Gondola with canisters, *87-88 u*	35	39____
16311	Mopar Express Flatcar with trailers, *87-88 u*	116	160____
16313	PRR Gondola with cable reels (027), *88 u, 89*	5	10____
16314	Wabash Flatcar with trailers, *89*	26	30____
16315	PRR Flatcar with fences (027), *88 u, 89*	7	9____
16317	PRR Barrel Ramp Car, *89*	18	22____
16318	LL Depressed Center Flatcar with cable reels, *89*	22	26____
16320	Great Northern Barrel Ramp Car, *90*	13	19____
16321/22	Sealand TTUX Flatcar Set with trailers, *90*	65	73____
16323	Lionel Lines Flatcar with trailers, *90*	21	25____
16324	PRR Depressed Center Flatcar with cable reels, *90*	16	20____
16325	Microracers Exhibition Ramp Car, *89 u*	21	28____
16326	Santa Fe Depressed Center Flatcar with cable reels, *91*	16	21 ____
16327	"The Big Top" Circus Gondola with canisters, *89 u*	19	24____
16328	NKP Gondola with cable reels, *90-91*	17	23____
16329	SP Flatcar with horses (027), *90-91*	19	24____
16330	MKT Flatcar with trailers, *91*	25	30____
16332	LL Depressed Center Flatcar with transformer, *91*	28	33____

		Exc	Mint
_____ **16333**	Frisco Bulkhead Flatcar with lumber, _91_	17	22
_____ **16334**	C&NW Flatcar Set ("16337, 16338") with trailers, _91_	55	60
_____ **16335**	NYC Pacemaker Flatcar with trailer (SSS), _91_	46	65
_____ **16336**	UP Gondola "6336" with canisters, _90-91 u_	17	21
_____ **16339**	Mickey's World Tour Gondola with canisters (O27), _91, 92 u_	17	21
_____ **16341**	NYC Depressed Center Flatcar with transformer, _92_	29	32
_____ **16342**	CSX Gondola with coil covers, _92_	18	23
_____ **16343**	Burlington Gondola with coil covers, _92_	20	23
_____ **16345/46**	SP TTUX Flatcar Set with trailers, _92_	55	65
_____ **16347**	Ontario Northland Bulkhead Flatcar with pulp load, _92_	22	26
_____ **16348**	Erie Liquefied Petroleum Car, _92_	23	25
_____ **16349**	Allis Chalmers Condenser Car, _92_	28	35
_____ **16350**	CP Rail Bulkhead Flatcar with lumber, _91 u_	20	29
_____ **16351**	Flatcar with U.S. Navy submarine, _92_	27	33
_____ **16352**	U.S. Military Flatcar with cruise missile, _92_	33	43
_____ **16353**	B&M Gondola with coil covers, _91 u_	33	39
_____ **16355**	Burlington Gondola, _92, 93 u, 94-95_	11	17
_____ **16356**	MKT Depressed Center Flatcar with cable reels, _92_	17	21
_____ **16357**	L&N Flatcar with trailer, _92_	24	31
_____ **16358**	L&N Gondola with coil covers, _92_	17	21
_____ **16359**	Pacific Coast Gondola with coil covers (SSS), _92_	33	38
_____ **16360**	N&W Maxi-Stack Flatcar Set ("16361, 16362") with containers, _93_	44	55
_____ **16363**	Southern TTUX Flatcar Set ("16364, 16365") with trailers, _93_	38	49
_____ **16367**	Clinchfield Gondola with coil covers, _93_	18	21
_____ **16368**	MKT Liquid Oxygen Car, _93_	21	22
_____ **16369**	Amtrak Flatcar with wheel load, _92 u_	19	28
_____ **16370**	Amtrak Flatcar with rail load, _92 u_	19	28
_____ **16371**	BN I-Beam Flatcar with load, _92 u_	24	29
_____ **16372**	Southern I-Beam Flatcar with load, _92 u_	24	34
_____ **16373**	Erie-Lackawanna Flatcar with stakes, _93_	19	23
_____ **16374**	D&RGW Flatcar with trailer, _93_	25	28
_____ **16375**	NYC Bulkhead FlatCar, _93-95_	21	25
_____ **16376**	UP Flatcar with trailer, _93-95_	31	37
_____ **16378**	Toys "R" Us Flatcar with trailer, _92-93 u_	60	95
_____ **16379**	NP Bulkhead Flatcar with pulp load, _93_	16	23
_____ **16380**	UP I-Beam Flatcar with load, _93_	20	26
_____ **16381**	CSX I-Beam Flatcar with load, _93_	20	25
_____ **16382**	Kansas City Southern Bulkhead FlatCar, _93_	14	18
_____ **16383**	Conrail Flatcar with trailer, _93_	50	58
_____ **16384**	Soo Line Gondola with cable reels, _93_	14	19
_____ **16385**	Soo Line Ore Car, _93_	65	75
_____ **16386**	SP Flatcar with lumber, _94_	15	19
_____ **16387**	KCS Gondola with coil covers, _94_	13	16
_____ **16388**	LV Gondola with canisters, _94_	16	20
_____ **16389**	PRR Flatcar with wheel load, _94_	27	32
_____ **16390**	Flatcar with water tank, _94_	24	27
_____ **16391**	Lionel Lines Gondola, _93 u_		15
_____ **16392**	Wabash Gondola with canisters (O27), _93 u, 94_	7	9
_____ **16393**	Wisconsin Central Bulkhead FlatCar, _94_	13	19
_____ **16394**	Vermont Central Bulkhead FlatCar, _94_	20	30

	Exc	Mint
16395 CP Flatcar with rail load, *94*	18	23___
16396 Alaska Bulkhead FlatCar, *94*	17	22___
16397 Milwaukee Road I-Beam Flatcar with load, *94*	30	34___
16398 C&O Flatcar with trailer, *94*	80	85___
16399 Western Pacific I-Beam Flatcar with load, *94*	31	35___
16400 PRR Hopper (027), *88 u, 89*	15	18___
16402 Southern Quad Hopper with coal (SSS), *87*	30	42___
16406 CSX Quad Hopper with coal, *90*	29	34___
16407 B&M Covered Quad Hopper (SSS), *91*	28	37___
16408 UP Hopper "6408" (027), *90-91 u*	17	21___
16410 MKT Hopper (027), *92, 93 u*	19	24___
16411 L&N Quad Hopper with coal, *92*	28	32___
16412 C&NW Covered Quad Hopper, *94*	16	21___
16413 Clinchfield Quad Hopper with coal, *94*	16	22___
16414 CCC&StL Hopper (027), *94*	18	25___
16416 D&RGW Covered Quad Hopper, *95*	16	20___
16417 Wabash Quad Hopper with coal, *95*	19	21___
16418 C&NW Hopper with coal (027), *95*	15	21___
16419 Tennessee Central Hopper, *96*		17___
16420 WM Quad Hopper with coal (SSS), *95*	30	34___
16421 WM Quad Hopper with coal (SSS), *95*	30	33___
16422 WM Quad Hopper with coal (SSS), *95*		33___
16423 WM Quad Hopper with coal (SSS), *95*		30___
16424 WM Covered Quad Hopper (SSS), *95*	34	39___
16425 WM Covered Quad Hopper (SSS), *95*	25	29___
16426 WM Covered Quad Hopper (SSS), *95*	24	27___
16427 WM Covered Quad Hopper (SSS), *95*	27	30___
16429 WM Quad Hopper with coal, set of 2		70___
16430 Georgia Power Quad Hopper "82947" with coal, *95 u*		109___
16431 Lionel Corporation 2-bay Hopper "6456-1," *96*		30___
16432 Lionel Corporation 2-bay Hopper "6456-2," *96*		64___
16433 Lionel Corporation 2-bay Hopper "6456-3," *96*		18___
16434 LV 2-bay Hopper "6456", "TLDX," *97*		25___
16435 Virginian 2-bay Hopper "6456-1," *97*		30___
16436 N&W 2-bay Hopper "6456-2," *97*		33___
16437 C&O 2-bay Hopper "6456-3," *97*		33___
16438 Frisco 4-bay Covered Hopper "87538," *98*		34___
16439 Southern 4-bay Covered Hopper "77836," *98*		34___
16440 Alaska 2-bay Hopper "7100," *98-99*		35___
16441 New York Central 4-bay Hopper, *99*		26___
16442 Bethlehem Gondola "6462," (SSS), *99*		40___
16443 GN 2-bay Hopper "172364," *99-00*		20___
16444 CNJ 2-bay Hopper "643," *00*		20___
16445 Frisco 2-bay Hopper "93108," *00*		20___
16446 Burlington 2-bay Hopper, *00*		20___
16447 PRR Tuscan 2-bay Hopper, *00 u*		30___
16448 PRR Gray 2-bay Hopper, *00 u*		30___
16449 PRR Black 2-bay Hopper, *00 u*		30___
16450 PRR Green 2-bay Hopper, *00 u*		30___
16451 Lionel Mines 2-bay Hopper, *00 u*		50___
16453 SP 2-bay Hopper "460604," *01*		15___
16454 Bethlehem Steel Hopper "41025," *01*		37___
16455 Pioneer Seed 2-bay Hopper, *00 u*		50___

		Exc	Mint
____	**16456** B&O 2-bay Hopper, *01*		20
____	**16459** LV 2-bay Hopper "51102," *01*		23
____	**16460** Reading 2-bay Hopper "79636," *02*		25
____	**16463** Rio Grande Icebreaker Tunnel Car "18936," *02*		32
____	**16464** NYC Icebreaker Tunnel Car "X3200," *02*		32
____	**16465** WP 2-bay Hopper "100340," *03*		19
____	**16466** Pennsylvania Icebreaker Tunnel Car, *03*		33
____	**16467** "Naughty and Nice" Hopper 2-pack, *02*		60
____	**16469** B&O Hopper "435351," *02*		22
____	**16470** "Naughty and Nice" Ore Car 2-pack, *03*		43
____	**16473** Rock Island Ore Car "99122," *03*		18
____	**16474** Alaska Ore Car "16474," *04*		21
____	**16475** Santa Fe Hopper "16475," *04*		18
____	**16480** Lionelville Snow Transport Quad Hopper, *04*		45
____	**16482** Norfolk Southern Hopper, traditional, *05*		27
____	**16487** Alaska 2-bay Hopper, *05*		35
____	**16489** BNSF Ore Car, traditional, *05*		15
____	**16490** Sodor Mining Hopper, *05, 13*		35
____	**16491** CNJ Hopper "60714," *06*		30
____	**16492** C&NW Ore Car "114023," *06*		30
____	**16493** Christmas Ice Breaker Car, *06*		55
____	**16500** Rock Island Bobber Caboose, *87-88*	9	13
____	**16501** Lehigh Valley SP-type Caboose, *87*	19	24
____	**16503** NYC Transfer Caboose, *87*	16	22
____	**16504** Southern N5c Caboose (SSS), *87*	17	30
____	**16505** Wabash SP-type Caboose, *88-91*	10	15
____	**16506** Santa Fe Bay Window Caboose, *88*	18	28
____	**16507** Mopar Express SP-type Caboose, *87-88 u*	42	54
____	**16508** Lionel Lines SP-type Caboose "6508," *89 u*	13	17
____	**16509** D&RGW SP-type Caboose (SSS), *89*	19	24
____	**16510** New Haven Bay Window Caboose, *89*	25	30
____	**16511** PRR Bobber Caboose, *88 u, 89*	9	13
____	**16513** Union Pacific SP-type Caboose, *89*	14	21
____	**16515** Lionel Lines SP-type Caboose, RailScope, *89*	20	23
____	**16516** Lehigh Valley SP-type Caboose, *90*	15	26
____	**16517** Atlantic Coast Line Bay Window Caboose, *90*	22	26
____	**16518** Chessie System Bay Window Caboose, *90*	41	50
____	**16519** Rock Island Transfer Caboose, *90*	13	17
____	**16520** "Welcome to the Show" Circus SP-type Caboose, *89 u*	13	21
____	**16521** PRR SP-type Caboose, *90-91*	8	11
____	**16522** "Chills & Thrills" Circus N5c Caboose, *90-91*	10	15
____	**16523** Alaska SP-type Caboose, *91*	24	31
____	**16524** Anheuser-Busch SP-type Caboose, *89-92 u*	34	45
____	**16525** D&H Bay Window Caboose (SSS), *91*	30	39
____	**16526** Kansas City Southern SP-type Caboose, *91*	17	21
____	**16528** UP SP-type Caboose "6528," *90-91 u*	17	21
____	**16529** Santa Fe SP-type Caboose "16829," *91*	9	13
____	**16530** Mickey's World Tour SP-type Caboose "16830," *91, 92 u*	13	17
____	**16531** Texas & Pacific SP-type Caboose, *92*	18	23
____	**16533** C&NW Bay Window Caboose, *92*	22	30
____	**16534** Delaware & Hudson SP-type Caboose, *92*	14	19
____	**16535** Erie-Lackawanna Bay Window Caboose, *91 u*	42	50

	Exc	Mint
16536 Chessie System SP-type Caboose, *92, 93 u, 94, 95 u*		23____
16537 MKT SP-type Caboose, *92, 93 u*	17	21____
16538 L&N Bay Window Caboose "1041," *92 u*	29	33____
16539 WP Steelside Caboose "539," smoke, SSS (std O), *92*	50	55 ____
16541 Montana Rail Link Extended Vision Caboose "10131" with smoke, *93*	55	65 ____
16543 NYC SP-type Caboose, *93-95*		20____
16544 Union Pacific SP-type Caboose, *93-95*	22	26____
16546 Clinchfield SP-type Caboose, *93*	22	26____
16547 "Happy Holidays" SP-type Caboose, *93-95*	46	55____
16548 Conrail SP-type Caboose, *93*	15	20____
16549 Soo Line Work Caboose, *93*	18	26____
16550 U.S. Navy Searchlight Caboose, *94-95*	16	21____
16551 Budweiser SP-type Caboose, *93-94 u*	30	33____
16552 Frisco Searchlight Caboose, *94*	23	26____
16553 United Auto Workers SP-type Caboose, *93 u*		40____
16554 GT Extended Vision Caboose "79052," smoke, *94*	40	47____
16555 C&O SP-type Caboose, *94*	22	26____
16557 Ford SP-type Caboose, *94 u*	19	24____
16558 Crayola SP-type Caboose, *94 u, 95*	17	21____
16559 Seaboard Center Cupola Caboose "5658," *95*	23	24____
16560 Chrysler Mopar Caboose, *94 u*	24	26____
16561 UP Center Cupola Caboose "25766," *95*	27	31____
16562 Reading Center Cupola Caboose, *95*	25	29____
16563 Lionel Lines SP-type Caboose, *95*	22	26____
16564 Western Maryland Center Cupola Caboose (SSS), *95*	30	34____
16565 Milwaukee Road Bay Window Caboose, *95*	50	60____
16566 U.S. Army SP-type Caboose "907," *95*		28____
16568 ATSF SP-type Caboose, *96-99*		23____
16571 Georgia Power SP-type Caboose "52789," *95 u*		68____
16575 Sears Zenith SP-type Caboose, *95*		38____
16577 U.S. Coast Guard Work Caboose, *96*		26____
16578 Lionel Lines SP-type Caboose, *95 u*		20____
16579 GM/AC Delco, SP-type Caboose, *95*		35____
16580 SP-type Caboose, *96-99*		11____
16581 UP Illuminated Caboose, *96*		30____
16586 SP Illuminated Caboose "6357," *97*		42____
16590 Dodge Motorsports SP-type Caboose "6950," *96*		56____
16591 Little League Baseball SP-type Caboose "6397," *97*		40____
16593 Lionel Belt Line Caboose "6257," *98*		32____
16594 Caboose "6357," *98*		29____
16600 Illinois Central Coal Dump Car, *88*	14	23____
16601 Canadian National Searchlight Car, *88*	19	24____
16602 Erie-Lackawanna Coal Dump Car, *87*	16	26____
16603 Detroit Zoo Giraffe Car (O27), *87*	40	49____
16604 NYC Log Dump Car, *87*	15	27____
16605 Bronx Zoo Giraffe Car (O27), *88*	39	44____
16606 Southern Searchlight Car, *87*	13	21____
16607 Southern Coal Dump Car "16707" (SSS), *87*	18	26____
16608 Lehigh Valley Searchlight Car, *87*	22	30____
16609 Lehigh Valley Derrick Car, *87*	22	30____
16610 Track Maintenance Car, *87-88*	15	25____
16611 Santa Fe Log Dump Car, *88*	15	23____

		Exc	Mint
____ **16612**	Soo Line Log Dump Car, *89*	14	24
____ **16613**	MKT Coal Dump Car, *89*	17	26
____ **16614**	Reading Cop and Hobo Car (O27), *89*	24	25
____ **16615**	Lionel Lines Extension Searchlight Car, *89*	20	28
____ **16616**	D&RGW Searchlight Car (SSS), *89*	22	30
____ **16617**	C&NW Boxcar with ETD, *89*	23	34
____ **16618**	Santa Fe Track Maintenance Car, *89*	11	19
____ **16619**	Wabash Coal Dump Car, *90*	14	25
____ **16620**	C&O Track Maintenance Car, *90-91*	16	19
____ **16621**	Alaska Log Dump Car, *90*	24	31
____ **16622**	CSX Boxcar with ETD, *90-91*	20	28
____ **16623**	MKT DD Boxcar with ETD, *91*	16	23
____ **16624**	NH Cop and Hobo Car (O27), *90-91*	23	31
____ **16625**	NYC Extension Searchlight Car, *90*	22	30
____ **16626**	CSX Searchlight Car, *90*	18	26
____ **16627**	CSX Log Dump Car, *90*	19	23
____ **16628**	Cop and Hobo Circus Gondola, *90-91*	36	43
____ **16629**	Operating Circus Elephant Car (O27), *90-91*	38	50
____ **16630**	SP Operating Cowboy Car (O27), *90-91*	22	26
____ **16631**	RI BoxCar, steam RailSounds, *90*	110	130
____ **16632**	BN BoxCar, diesel RailSounds, *90*	90	100
____ **16634**	WM Coal Dump Car, *91*	26	32
____ **16636**	D&RGW Log Dump Car, *91*	19	25
____ **16637**	WP Extension Searchlight Car, *91*	27	30
____ **16638**	Operating Circus Animal Car (O27), *91*	50	55
____ **16639**	B&O BoxCar, steam RailSounds, *91*	100	120
____ **16640**	Rutland BoxCar, diesel RailSounds, *91*	100	120
____ **16641**	Toys "R" Us Giraffe Car (O27), *90-91 u*	45	65
____ **16642**	Mickey's World Tour Goofy Car (O27), *91, 92 u*	33	41
____ **16644**	Amtrak Crane Car, *91, 92 u*	36	42
____ **16645**	Amtrak Searchlight Caboose, *91*	27	30
____ **16649**	Railway Express Agency BoxCar, steam RailSounds, *92*	110	140
____ **16650**	NYC Pacemaker BoxCar, diesel RailSounds, *92*	100	135
____ **16651**	Operating Circus Clown Car (O27), *92*	24	30
____ **16652**	Radar Car, *92*	25	29
____ **16653**	Western Pacific Crane Car (SSS), *92*	44	60
____ **16655**	Steam Tender "1993," RailSounds, *93*	115	140
____ **16656**	Burlington Log Dump Car, *92 u*	18	25
____ **16657**	Lehigh Valley Coal Dump Car, *92 u*	22	29
____ **16658**	Erie-Lackawanna Crane Car, *93*	47	65
____ **16659**	Union Pacific Searchlight Car, *93-95*	15	18
____ **16660**	Fire Car with ladders, *93-94*	28	33
____ **16661**	Flatcar with boat, *93*	20	22
____ **16662**	Bugs Bunny and Yosemite Sam Outlaw Car (O27), *93-94*	28	30
____ **16663**	Missouri Pacific Searchlight Car, *93*	16	19
____ **16664**	L&N Coal Dump Car, *93*	22	25
____ **16665**	Maine Central Log Dump Car, *93*	23	27
____ **16666**	Toxic Waste Car, *93-94*	25	32
____ **16667**	Conrail Searchlight Car, *93*	27	30
____ **16668**	Ontario Northland Log Dump Car, *93*	20	24
____ **16669**	Soo Line Searchlight Car, *93*	17	21
____ **16670**	TV Car, *93-94*	12	22

	Exc	Mint
16673 Lionel Lines Tender, whistle, *94-97*	33	42____
16674 Pinkerton Animated Gondola, *94*	28	32____
16675 Great Northern Log Dump Car, *94*	21	25____
16676 Burlington Coal Dump Car, *94*	23	28____
16677 NATO Flatcar with Royal Navy submarine, *94*	34	44____
16678 Rock Island Searchlight Car, *94*	12	23____
16679 U.S. Mail Operating BoxCar, *94*	45	50____
16680 Cherry Picker Car, *94*	25	28____
16681 Aquarium Car, *95*	35	44____
16682 Lionelville Farms Operating Stock Car (027), *94*	23	27____
16683 Los Angeles Zoo Elephant Car (027), *94*	22	26____
16684 U.S. Navy Crane Car, *94-95*	35	40____
16685 Erie Extension Searchlight Car, *95*	30	34____
16686 Mickey Mouse Animated BoxCar, *95*	28	35____
16687 U.S. Mail Operating BoxCar, *94*	29	37____
16688 Fire Car with ladders, *94*	35	43____
16689 Toxic Waste Car, *94*	29	32____
16690 Bugs Bunny and Yosemite Sam Outlaw Car (027), *94*	30	34____
16701 Southern Tool Car (SSS), *87*	43	55____
16702 Amtrak Bunk Car, *91, 92 u*	25	27____
16703 NYC Tool Car, *92*	24	31____
16704 TV Car, *94*	27	29____
16705 Chesapeake & Ohio Cop and Hobo Car, *95*	28	34____
16706 Animal Transport Service Giraffe Car, *95*	27	30____
16708 C&NW Track Maintenance Car, *95*	24	31____
16709 New York Central Derrick Car, *95*	22	28____
16710 U.S. Army Operating Missile Car, *95*	40	42____
16711 Pennsylvania Searchlight Car, *95*	27	31____
16712 Pinkerton Animated Gondola, *95*	34	39____
16715 ATSF Log Dump Car, *96-99*		24____
16717 Jersey Central Crane Car, *96*		41____
16718 USMC Missile Launching FlatCar, *96*	26	31____
16719 Exploding BoxCar, *96*		38____
16720 Lionel Lines Searchlight Car "3650," *96-97*		50____
16724 Mickey and Friends Submarine Car, *96*		39____
16725 Rhino Transport Car, *97*		31____
16726 U.S. Army Fire Ladder Car, *96*		43____
16734 U.S. Coast Guard Searchlight Car, *96*		30____
16735 U.S. Coast Guard Flatcar with radar, *96*	28	35____
16736 U.S. Coast Guard Derrick Car, *96*		34____
16737 Road Runner and Wile E. Coyote Gondola "3444," *96*		68____
16738 Pepe LePew Boxcar "3370," *96*		40____
16739 Foghorn Leghorn Poultry Car "6434," *96*		44____
16740 Lionel Corporation Mail Car "3428," *96*		37____
16741 Union Pacific Illuminated Bunk Car, *97*		25____
16742 Trout Ranch Aquarium Car "3435," *96*		32____
16744 Port of Lionel City Searchlight Car, *97*		30____
16745 Port of Lionel City Flatcar with radar, *97*		30____
16746 Port of Lionel City Derrick Car, *97*		30____
16747 Breyer Animated Horse Car "6473," *97*		34____
16748 U.S. Forest Service Log-Dump Car "3361," *97*		30____
16749 Midget Mines Ore-Dump Car "3479," *97*		36____
16750 Lionel City Aquarium Car "3436," *97*		32____

		Exc	Mint
____ **16751**	AIREX Sports Channel TV Car "3545," *97*		25
16752	Marvin the Martian Missile Launching FlatCar "6655," *97* ____	135	145
____ **16754**	Porky Pig and Instant Martians FlatCar "6805," *97*	135	185
____ **16755**	Daffy Duck Animated Balloon Car "3470," *97*	135	175
____ **16760**	Pluto and Cats Animated Gondola "3444," *97*		55
____ **16765**	Bureau of Land Management Log Car "3351," *98*		30
____ **16766**	Bureau of Land Management Ore Car "3479," *98*		31
____ **16767**	New York Central Ice Docks Ice Car "6352," *98*		47
____ **16776**	Holiday BoxCar, RailSounds, *98*		68
____ **16777**	Animated Cola Car and Platform, *98*		100
____ **16782**	Bethlehem Ore Dump Car "3479," *99*		95
____ **16783**	Westside Lumber Log Dump Car "3351," *99*		32
____ **16784**	Pratt's Hollow Seed Dump Car "3479," *99*		36
____ **16785**	"Happy Holidays" Music Reefer "5700," *99*		100
____ **16789**	Easter Operating BoxCar, *99*		39
____ **16790**	UP Stock Car "3356," Crowsounds, *99*		90
____ **16791**	New York City Lights BoxCar, *99*		44
____ **16792**	Constellation Boxcar "9600," *99*		37
____ **16793**	Animated Glow-in-the-Dark Alien BoxCar, *99*		44
____ **16794**	Wicked Witch Halloween BoxCar, *99*		46
____ **16795**	Elf Chasing Rudolph Gondola "6462," *99*		55
____ **16796**	Snowman Loading Ice Car "6352," *99*		55
____ **16805**	Budweiser Malt Nutrine Reefer "3285," *91-92 u*	76	102
____ **16806**	Toys "R" Us BoxCar, *92 u*	21	26
____ **16807**	H.J. Heinz Reefer "301," *93*	23	27
____ **16808**	Toys "R" Us BoxCar, *93 u*	28	30
____ **16817**	Ambassador 1-D Tank Car, *00 u*		175
____ **16818**	Engineer Award Tank Car, *00 u*		715
____ **16819**	JLC Award Tank Car, *00 u*		760
____ **16820**	Ambassador BoxCar, *00 u*	309	505
____ **16822**	CSX Water Tower, *08*		23
16824	O36 Command Control Switch, left hand (FasTrack), *09-14* ____		110
16825	O36 Command Control Switch, right hand (FasTrack), *09-14* ____		110
16826	O72 Command Control Switch, left hand (FasTrack), *09-14* ____		120
16827	O72 Command Control Switch, right hand (FasTrack), *09-14* ____		120
16828	O60 Command Control Switch, left hand (FasTrack), *09-14* ____		120
16829	O60 Command Control Switch, right hand (FasTrack), *09-14* ____		120
16830	O48 Command Control Switch, left hand (FasTrack), *09-14* ____		120
16831	O48 Command Control Switch, right hand (FasTrack), *09-14* ____		120
16832	O72 Command Control Wye Switch (FasTrack), *09-14* ____		115
____ **16834**	O48 Half-Curved Track (FasTrack), *09-14, 16, 18*		6
____ **16835**	O48 Quarter-Curved Track (FasTrack), *09-14, 16, 18*		5
____ **16836**	Christmas Girder Bridge, *09*		21
____ **16837**	Christmas Operating Billboard, *09*		45
____ **16841**	Halloween Gateman, *09*		80

		Exc	Mint
16842	Big Moe Crane, *10*		70____
16843	City and Western Diorama, *10-11*		15____
16845	Bookstore, *09-10*		60____
16846	Burning Hobo Depot, *09*		90____
16847	Legacy Hotel, *10-11*		70____
16848	Creature Comforts Pet Store, sound, *09-10*		80____
16849	Rotary Dumper with coal conveyor, CC, *10*		600____
16850	Operating Wind Turbine, 3-pack, *09-11*		225____
16851	Sunoco Cylindrical Oil Tank, gray, *10-11*		100____
16852	Sunoco Cylindrical Oil Tank, yellow, *10-11*		90____
16853	Polar Express Diorama, *09-11, 13*		18____
16854	MTA LIRR Blinking Billboard, *09*		30____
16855	MTA LIRR Illuminated Station Platform, *09*		37____
16856	MTA LIRR Passenger Station, *09*		60____
16857	Thomas & Friends Diorama, *10-16*		18____
16859	Grand Central Terminal, *09*		1500____
16861	50,000-gallon Water Tank, *09-11*		150____
16863	Santa's Christmas Wish Station, *09-11*		125____
16868	Straight O Gauge Tunnel, *09-17*		55____
16871	Winter Wonderland Diorama, *09-11*		15____
16872	Illuminated Christmas Station Platform, *09*		35____
16873	Bathtub Gondola Coal Load 3-pack, *10-18*		20____
16874	Coaling Station, *10-11*		80____
16880	Freight Platform, *10-12*		30____
16881	Barrel Shed, *10-11*		30____
16882	12" Covered Bridge, *10-18*		60____
16883	Neil's Guitar Shop, *10-11*		60____
16889	Coal Tipple Pack, *11-18*		15____
16891	Tank Car Accident, *10-11*		130____
16896	Flagpole with lights, *10-16*		28____
16897	75th Anniversary Gateman, *10*		80____
16903	CP Bulkhead Flatcar with pulp load (SSS), *94*	22	25____
16904	NYC Pacemaker Flatcar Set with trailers, *94*	55	60____
16907	Flatcar with farm tractors, *94*	27	33____
16908	U.S. Navy FlatCar "04039" with submarine, *94-95*	39	46____
16909	U.S. Navy Gondola "16556" with canisters, *94-95*	16	22____
16910	Missouri Pacific Flatcar with trailer, *94*	22	27____
16911	B&M Flatcar with trailer, *94*	28	34____
16912	CN Maxi-Stack Flatcar Set with containers, *94*	70	75____
16915	Lionel Lines Gondola (O27), *93-94 u*	7	10____
16916	Ford Flatcar with trailer, *94 u*	38	45____
16917	Crayola Gondola with crayons, *94 u, 95*	8	9____
16919	Chrysler Mopar Gondola with coil covers, *94-96*	33	36____
16922	Chesapeake & Ohio Flatcar with trailer, *95*	25	31____
16923	Intermodal Service Flatcar with wheel chocks, *95*	15	22____
16924	Lionel Corporation FlatCar "6424" with trailer, *96*		24____
16925	New York Central Flatcar with trailer, *95*	65	85____
16926	Frisco Flatcar with trailers, *95*	24	31____
16927	New York Central Flatcar with gondola, *95*	17	22____
16928	Soo Line Flatcar with dump bin (O27), *95*	12	15____
16929	BC Rail Gondola with cable reels, *95*	21	25____
16930	Santa Fe Flatcar with wheel load, *95*	20	25____
16932	Erie Flatcar with rail load, *95*	17	22____

		Exc	Mint
____ **16933**	Lionel Lines Flatcar with autos, *95*	23	25
____ **16934**	Pennsylvania Flatcar with Ertl road grader, *95*	28	39
____ **16935**	UP Depressed Center Flatcar with Ertl bulldozer, *95*	22	35
____ **16936**	Sealand Maxi-Stack Flatcar Set with containers, *95*	70	85
____ **16939**	U.S. Navy FlatCar "04040" with boat, *95*	25	30
____ **16940**	ATSF Flatcar with trailer, *96-99*		40
____ **16941**	ATSF Flatcar with autos, *96-99*		25
____ **16943**	Jersey Central Gondola, *96*		18
16944	Georgia Power Depressed Center FlatCar "31438" with transformer, *95 u*		50
____			
16945	Georgia Power Depressed Center FlatCar "31950" with cable reels, *95 u*		53
____			
____ **16946**	C&O F9 Well Car "3840," *96*		31
____ **16951**	Southern I-Beam FlatCar "9823" with load, *97*		25
____ **16952**	U.S. Navy Flatcar with Ertl helicopter, *96*		25
____ **16953**	NYC Flatcar with Red Wing Shoes trailer, *95 u*	39	45
____ **16954**	NYC FlatCar "6424" with Ertl scraper, *96*		30
____ **16955**	ATSF Flatcar with Ertl Challenger, *96*		30
____ **16956**	Zenith Flatcar with trailer, *95 u*		136
16957	Depressed Center FlatCar "6461" with Ertl Case tractor, *96*		29
____			
____ **16958**	Flatcar with Ertl New Holland loader, *96*		26
____ **16960**	U.S. Coast Guard Flatcar with boat, *96*		40
____ **16961**	GM/AC Delco Flatcar with trailer, *95*		73
____ **16963**	Lionel Corporation FlatCar "6411," *96-97*		34
____ **16964**	Lionel Corporation Gondola "6462," *97*		22
____ **16965**	Scout FlatCar "6424" with stakes, *96-97*		20
16967	Depressed Center FlatCar "6461" with transformer, *96*		21
____			
16968	Depressed Center FlatCar "6461" with Ertl Helicopter, *96.*		35
____			
____ **16969**	FlatCar "6411" with Beechcraft Bonanza, *96*		33
16970	LA County FlatCar "6424" with motorized powerboat, *96*		20
____			
____ **16971**	Port of Lionel City Flatcar with boat, *97*		35
____ **16972**	P&LE Gondola "6462," *97*		22
____ **16975**	Well Car Doublestack Set, *97*		75
____ **16978**	MILW FlatCar "6424" with P&H shovel, *97*		43
____ **16980**	Speedy Gonzales Missile FlatCar "6823," *97*		46
____ **16982**	BC Rail Bulkhead FlatCar "9823" with lumber, *97*		28
____ **16983**	PRR F9 Well Car "6983" with cable reels, *97*		39
____ **16986**	Sears Zenith Bulkhead FlatCar, *96 u*		45
____ **16987**	Musco Lighting Bulkhead FlatCar, *97 u*		35
____ **16997**	Lionel Lines Recovery Crane Car, *99*		50
____ **17002**	Conrail 2-bay ACF Hopper (std O), *87*	42	47
____ **17003**	Du Pont 2-bay ACF Hopper (std O), *90*	39	45
____ **17004**	MKT 2-bay ACF Hopper (std O), *91*	23	27
____ **17005**	Cargill 2-bay ACF Hopper (std O), *92*	29	37
____ **17006**	Soo Line 2-bay ACF Hopper (std O, SSS), *93*	31	36
____ **17007**	GN 2-bay ACF Hopper "173872" (std O), *94*	26	31
____ **17008**	D&RGW 2-bay ACF Hopper "10009" (std O), *95*		31
____ **17009**	New York Central 2-bay ACF Hopper, *96*		35
17010	Govt. of Canada ACF 2-bay Covered Hopper "7000," *98*		32
____			
____ **17010**	NP PS-1 Boxcar 6-pack, LionScale, *17*		360

Exc Mint

		Exc	Mint
17011	NP ACF 2-bay Covered Hopper "75052," *98*		44____
17012	Govt. of Canada ACF 2-bay Covered Hopper "7001," *98*		30 ____
17013	NYC Graffiti 2-bay Covered Hopper "7000," *99*		55____
17014	Graffiti 2-bay Covered Hopper "7000" (std O), *99*		45____
17015	Corning 2-bay Hopper "90409" (std O), *01*		40____
17016	C&NW 2-bay Hopper "96644" (std O), *01*		46____
17017	Chessie System 2-bay Hopper "605527" (std O), *02*		32____
17018	Nickel Plate Road Offset Hopper "33074," *02*		43____
17019	Santa Fe Offset Hopper "78299," *02*		43____
17020	Frisco Offset Hopper "92092," *02*		43____
17020	UP PS-1 Boxcar 6-pack, LionScale, *17*		360____
17021	NYC Offset Hopper "867999," *02*		43____
17022	Burlington 2-bay ACF Hopper "183925" (std O), *03*		30____
17023	BNSF 2-bay Hopper "409038" (std O), *04*		30____
17024	Reading Offset Hopper "81089" (std O), *03-04*		43____
17025	C&O Offset Hopper "300027" (std O), *03-04*		43____
17026	D&H Offset Hopper "7215" (std O), *03-04*		41____
17027	IC Offset Hopper "92142" (std O), *03-04*		49____
17028	GE PS-2 2-bay Covered Hopper "326" (std O), *03-04*		35____
17029	CNJ PS-2 2-bay Covered Hopper "803" (std O), *03-04*		35 ____
17030	MILW PS-2 2-bay Covered Hopper "99708" (std O), *03-04*		35 ____
17030	Reading PS-1 Boxcar 6-pack, LionScale, *17*		360____
17031	SP PS-2 2-bay Covered Hopper "401306" (std O), *03-04*		38 ____
17038	Clinchfield PS-2 Covered Hopper, *05*		70____
17039	Boston & Maine PS-2 2-bay Covered Hopper, *05*		55____
17040	Norfolk & Western PS-2 2-bay Covered Hopper, *05*		55____
17040	NYC PS-1 Boxcar 6-pack, LionScale, *17*		360____
17041	Great Northern Offset Hopper, *05*		60____
17042	Green Bay & Western Offset Hopper, *05*		60____
17043	Baltimore & Ohio Offset Hopper, *05*		60____
17050	NYC 14-panel Hopper 6-pack, LionScale, *17*		330____
17060	D&RGW 14-panel Hopper 6-pack, LionScale, *17*		330____
17063	Santa Fe PS-2 2-bay Covered Hopper "82297" (std O), *06*		55 ____
17064	MKT PS-2 2-bay Covered Hopper "1311" (std O), *06*		55____
17065	Boraxo PS-2 2-bay Covered Hopper "31062" (std O), *06*		55 ____
17066	PRR PS-2 2-bay Covered Hopper "256177" (std O), *06*		55 ____
17067	Rock Island Offset Hopper "89500" with gravel (std O), *06*		65 ____
17068	CNJ Offset Hopper "61261" (std O), *06*		65____
17069	Maine Central Offset Hopper "3785" (std O), *06*		65____
17070	P&LE Offset Hopper "4990" (std O), *06*		65____
17070	Conrail 14-panel Hopper 6-pack, LionScale, *17*		330____
17080	EL 14-panel Hopper 6-pack, LionScale, *17*		330____
17083	C&O Offset Hopper "47386" (std O), *05*		40____
17090	Trailer Train 50' Flatcar 6-pack, *17*		330____
17100	Chessie System 3-bay ACF Hopper	49	85____
17100	BN 50' Flatcar 6-pack, *17*		330____
17101	Chessie System 3-bay ACF Hopper (std O), *88*	37	45____

		Exc	Mint
____ **17102** Chessie System 3-bay ACF Hopper (std O), *88*		35	41
____ **17103** Chessie System 3-bay ACF Hopper (std O), *88*		31	34
____ **17104** Chessie System 3-bay ACF Hopper (std O), *88*		38	46
____ **17105** Chessie System 3-bay ACF Hopper (std O), *88*		39	46
____ **17107** Sinclair 3-bay ACF Hopper (std O), *89*		40	48
____ **17108** Santa Fe 3-bay ACF Hopper (std O), *90*		42	48
____ **17109** N&W 3-bay ACF Hopper (std O), *91*		24	31
____ **17110** UP Hopper with coal (std O), *91*		24	30
____ **17110** AT&SF 50' Flatcar 6-pack, *17*			330
____ **17111** Reading Hopper with coal (std O), *91*		23	28
____ **17112** Erie-Lack. 3-bay ACF Hopper (std O), *92*		24	34
____ **17113** LV Hopper with coal (std O), *92-93*		25	32
____ **17114** Peabody Hopper with coal (std O), *92-93*		26	30
____ **17118** Archer Daniels Midland 3-bay ACF Hopper "60029" (std O), *93*		28	35
____ **17120** CSX Hopper "295110" with coal (std O), *94*		28	30
____ **17120** PRR 50' Flatcar 6-pack, *17*			330
____ **17121** ICG Hopper "72867" with coal (std O), *94*		26	33
____ **17122** RI 3-bay ACF Hopper "800200" (std O), *94*		32	39
____ **17123** Cargill Covered Grain Hopper "844304" (std O), *95*		25	34
____ **17124** Archer Daniels Midland 3-bay ACF Hopper "50224" (std O), *95*		24	30
____ **17127** Delaware & Hudson 3-bay Hopper, *96*			34
____ **17128** Chesapeake & Ohio 3-bay Hopper, *96*			30
____ **17129** WM 3-bay Hopper "9300" with coal (std O), *97*			34
____ **17130** ACFX ACF 4-bay Covered Hopper 6-pack, LionScale, *17*			360
____ **17132** PRR 3-bay ACF Hopper "260815," *98*			40
____ **17133** BNSF ACF 3-bay Covered Hopper "403698," *98*			38
____ **17134** BNSF 3-bay Covered Hopper "403698" (std O), *01*			38
____ **17135** BNSF ACF 3-bay Covered Hopper with ETD, *98*			39
____ **17137** Cargill 3-bay Covered Hopper "1219" (std O), *99*			45
____ **17138** Farmers Elevator 3-bay Covered Hopper (std O), *99*			45
____ **17139** "Grain Train" 3-bay Hopper "BLMR 1025," *99-00*			39
____ **17140** Virginian 3-bay Hopper 6-pack, "5260-5265," *99*			230
____ **17140** GN ACF 4-bay Covered Hopper 6-pack, LionScale, *17*			360
____ **17147** C&O 3-bay Hopper 6-pack, "156330-156335," *99*			230
____ **17150** AT&SF ACF 4-bay Covered Hopper 6-pack, LionScale, *17*			360
____ **17154** Alberta Cylindrical Hopper "628373" (std O), *01*			40
____ **17155** Shell Cylindrical Hopper "3527" (std O), *01*			40
____ **17156** ACF Pressureaide 3-bay Hopper "59267" (std O), *01*			27
____ **17157** Wonder Bread "56670" 3-bay Hopper (std O), *01*			45
____ **17158** Conrail Coal Hopper "487739" (std O), *01*			42
____ **17159** N&W Coal Hopper "1776" (std O), *01*			45
____ **17160** C&NW (UP) B145ACF 4-bay Covered Hopper 6-pack, LionScale, *17*			360
____ **17163** C&O 3-bay Hopper (std O), *01*			30
____ **17170** General Mills 3-bay Covered Hopper (std O), *00 u*			60
____ **17170** PFE 57' Mechanical Reefer, *17*			390
____ **17171** Lionel Lion Cylindrical Hopper (std O), *01*			45
____ **17172** CP Rail Cylindrical Hopper "385206" (std O), *02*			37
____ **17173** Govt. of Canada Cylindrical Hopper "111031" (std O), *02*			33

Exc Mint

Cat #	Description	Exc	Mint
17174	GN 3-bay Hopper "171250" (std O), *02*		29___
17175	IC PS-2CD 4427 Covered Hopper "57031" (std O), *02*		40 ___
17176	Cargill PS-2CD 4427 Covered Hopper "2514" (std O), *02*		46 ___
17177	PS-2CD 4427 Covered Hopper "2500" (std O), *02*		40___
17178	Santa Fe PS-2CD 4427 Covered Hopper "304774" (std O), *02*		40 ___
17179	Indianapolis Power & Light Coal Hopper "10074" (std O), *02*		40 ___
17180	Rock Island Coal Hopper "700665" (std O), *02*		40___
17180	SPFE 57' Mechanical Reefer 6-pack, LionScale, *17*		390___
17181	NYC 4-bay ACF Centerflow Hopper "892138" (std O), *03*		45 ___
17182	Sigco Hybrids 4-bay ACF Centerflow Hopper "1100" (std O), *03*		46 ___
17183	C&O Hopper "156341" (std O), *01*		30___
17184	Virginian Hopper "5271" (std O), *01*		30___
17185	LLCX Bathtub Gondola "877900" (std O), *01*		36___
17186	Cannonaide 4-bay ACF Centerflow Hopper "96169" (std O), *03*		40 ___
17187	Rio Grande 4-bay ACF Centerflow Hopper "15521" (std O), *03*		40 ___
17188	Govt. of Canada 3-bay Cylindrical Hopper (std O), *03*		48 ___
17189	Saskatchewan Grain 3-bay Cylindrical Hopper (std O), *03*		48 ___
17190	Soo/CP 3-bay ACF Hopper "119303" (std O), *03*		37___
17190	UPFE 57' Mechanical Reefer 6-pack, LionScale, *17*		390___
17191	BN PS-2CD 4427 Hopper "450669" (std O), *03-04*		45___
17192	Lehigh Valley PS-2CD 4427 Hopper "51118" (std O), *03-04*		40 ___
17193	Chessie System/WM PS-2CD 4427 Hopper "4673" (std O), *03-04*		30 ___
17194	MKT PS-2CD 4427 Hopper "1122" (std O), *03-04*		40 ___
17195	L&N 3-bay Hopper "240850" (std O), *04*		40 ___
17196	Firestone 4-bay Hopper "53240" (std O), *04*		40 ___
17197	Diamond Chemicals 4-bay Hopper "53286" (std O), *04*		40 ___
17198	Hercules 4-bay Hopper "50503" (std O), *04*		40___
17199	Conrail 4-bay Hopper "888367" (std O), *04*		46___
17200	Canadian Pacific Boxcar (std O), *89*	26	32___
17200	BNFE 57' Mechanical Reefer 6-pack, LionScale, *17*		390___
17201	Conrail Boxcar (std O), *87*	33	38___
17202	Santa Fe Boxcar (std O), diesel RailSounds, *90*	80	85___
17203	Cotton Belt DD Boxcar (std O), *91*	33	38___
17204	Missouri Pacific DD Boxcar (std O), *91*	27	30___
17207	C&IM DD Boxcar (std O), *92*	36	42___
17208	Union Pacific DD Boxcar (std O), *92*	35	40___
17209	B&O DD Boxcar "296000" (std O), *93*	37	43___
17210	Chicago & Illinois Midland Boxcar "16021" (std O), *92 u*	30	39 ___
17210	BN 100-Ton, 4-Bay Hopper 6-pack, *17*		330___
17211	Chicago & Illinois Midland Boxcar "16022" (std O), *92 u*	30	39 ___
17212	Chicago & Illinois Midland Boxcar "16023" (std O), *92 u*	24	31 ___

		Exc	Mint
____	**17213** Susquehanna Boxcar "501" (std O), *93*	28	31
____	**17214** Railbox Boxcar (std O), diesel RailSounds, *93*	75	85
____	**17216** PRR DD Boxcar "60155" (std O), *94*	34	38
____	**17217** New Haven State of Maine Boxcar "45003" (std O), *95*	28	35
____	**17218** BAR State of Maine Boxcar "2184" (std O), *95*	23	36
____	**17219** Tazmanian Devil 40th Birthday Boxcar (std O), *95*	40	50
____	**17220** Pennsylvania Boxcar (std O), *96*		23
____	**17220** CSX 100-Ton, 4-Bay Hopper 6-pack, *17*		330
____	**17221** NYC Boxcar (std O), *96*		34
____	**17222** Western Pacific Boxcar (std O), *96*	28	34
____	**17223** Milwaukee Road DD Boxcar (std O), *96*		34
____	**17224** Central of Georgia Boxcar "9464-197" (std O), *97*	15	29
____	**17225** Penn Central Boxcar "9464-297" (std O), *97*	13	26
____	**17226** Milwaukee Road Boxcar "9464-397" (std O), *97*		23
____	**17227** UP DD Boxcar "9200" (std O), *97*		35
____	**17230** NS 100-Ton, 4-Bay Hopper 6-pack, *17*		330
____	**17231** Wisconsin Central DD Boxcar "9200" with auto frames, *98*		40
____	**17232** SP/UP Merger DD Boxcar "9200," *98*		33
____	**17233** Western Pacific Boxcar "9464-198," *98*		27
____	**17234** Port Huron & Detroit Boxcar "9464-298," *98*		33
____	**17235** Boston & Maine Boxcar "9464-398," *98*		41
____	**17239** ATSF "Texas Chief" Boxcar "9464-1," *97*		50
____	**17240** ATSF "Super Chief" Boxcar "9464-2," *97*		50
____	**17240** UP 100-Ton, 4-Bay Hopper 6-pack, *17*		330
____	**17241** ATSF "El Capitan" Boxcar "9464-3," *97*		50
____	**17242** ATSF "Grand Canyon" Boxcar "9464-4," *97*		60
____	**17243** NP Boxcar "8722," *98*		48
____	**17244** Santa Fe "Chief" BoxCar, *98*		37
____	**17245** C&O Boxcar with Chessie kitten, *98*		44
____	**17246** NYC Pacemaker Rolling Stock 4-pack, *98*		200
____	**17247** NYC 9464 Boxcar "174940," *98*		135
____	**17248** NYC 9464 Boxcar "174945," *98*		115
____	**17249** NYC 9464 Boxcar "174949," *98*		60
____	**17250** UP Boxcar "507406" (std O), *99*		45
____	**17250** AT&SF Stockcar 6-pack, *17*		360
____	**17251** BNSF Boxcar "103277," *99*		41
____	**17252** NS Boxcar "564824" (std O), *99*		41
____	**17253** CSX Boxcar "141756" (std O), *99*		35
____	**17254** UP Boxcar "551967" (std O), *99*		42
____	**17255** Chevy DD Boxcar "9200" (std O), *99*		38
____	**17257** Atlantic Coast Line Boxcar "28809" (std O), *99*		36
____	**17258** D&H 9464 Boxcar "29055," std O, *99*		41
____	**17259** MKT 9464 Boxcar "1422" (std O), *99*		34
____	**17260** CP Rail 9464 Boxcar "286138" (std O), silver, *00*		45
____	**17260** PRR Stockcar 6-pack, *17*		360
____	**17261** CP Rail 9464 Boxcar "85154," green, *00*		44
____	**17262** CP Rail 9464 Boxcar "56776," red (std O), *00*		48
____	**17263** NYC Boxcar "45725" (std O), *00*		46
____	**17264** C&O Boxcar "6054" (std O), *00*		44
____	**17265** U.S. Army Boxcar (std O), *00*		35
____	**17266** Monon Boxcar "911" (std O), *00*		45
____	**17268** C&O 9464 Boxcar "12700" (std O), *01*		44

Exc Mint

	Exc	Mint
17269 Western Maryland 9464 Boxcar "29140" (std O), *01*		44 ___
17270 B&O Time-Saver 9464 Boxcar "467439" (std O), *01*		42 ___
17270 Nickel Plate Road Stockcar 6-pack, *17*		360 ___
17271 "The Rock" Boxcar "300324" (std O), *01*		37 ___
17272 Railbox Boxcar "15150" (std O), *01*		27 ___
17273 DT&I DD Boxcar "26852" (std O), *01*		44 ___
17274 Soo Line DD Boxcar "177587" (std O), *01*		42 ___
17275 NYC PS-1 Boxcar "175008" (std O), *02*		43 ___
17276 Cotton Belt PS-1 Boxcar "75000" (std O), *02*		44 ___
17277 Rio Grande PS-1 Boxcar "69676" (std O), *02*		40 ___
17278 WP PS-1 Boxcar "1953" (std O), *02*		44 ___
17279 Ontario Northland Boxcar "7428" (std O), *02*		40 ___
17280 Santa Fe Boxcar "600194" with auto frames (std O), *02*		45 ___
17280 UP Stockcar 6-pack, *17*		360 ___
17281 PRR DD Boxcar "83158" (std O), *04*		42 ___
17282 UP DD Boxcar "160300" (std O), *04*		42 ___
17283 GM&O DD Boxcar "9077" (std O), *04*		41 ___
17284 Erie DD Boxcar "66000" (std O), *04*		41 ___
17285 CSX Big Blue Boxcar "151296" (std O), *03*		36 ___
17287 BAR Boxcar "5976" (std O), *03*		35 ___
17288 NYC PS-1 Boxcar "175012" (std O), *03-04*		38 ___
17289 GN PS-1 Boxcar "18485" (std O), *03*		40 ___
17290 Seaboard PS-1 Boxcar "24452" (std O), *03-04*		42 ___
17290 Portland Terminal Wood-chip Hopper 6-pack, *17*		360 ___
17291 RI PS-1 Boxcar "21110" (std O), *03-04*		42 ___
17292 B&M PS-1 Boxcar "76182" (std O), *04*		34 ___
17293 IC PS-1 Boxcar "400666" (std O), *04*		40 ___
17294 TP&W PS-1 Boxcar "5036" (std O), *04*		36 ___
17295 Santa Fe PS-1 Boxcar "276749" (std O), *04*		40 ___
17297 UP PS-1 BoxCar, *03*		100 ___
17300 Canadian Pacific Reefer (std O), *89*	28	33 ___
17300 Chessie System Wood-chip Hopper 6-pack, *17*		360 ___
17301 Conrail Reefer (std O), *87*	35	42 ___
17302 Santa Fe Reefer with ETD (std O), *90*	35	41 ___
17303 C&O Reefer "7890" (std O), *93*	23	30 ___
17304 Wabash Reefer "26269" (std O), *94*	29	37 ___
17305 Pacific Fruit Express Reefer "459400" (std O), *94*	27	40 ___
17306 Pacific Fruit Express Reefer "459401" (std O), *94*	19	27 ___
17307 Tropicana Reefer "300" (std O), *95*	44	65 ___
17308 Tropicana Reefer "301" (std O), *95*	22	35 ___
17309 Tropicana Reefer "302" (std O), *95*	21	29 ___
17310 Tropicana Reefer "303" (std O), *95*	20	27 ___
17310 GM&O Wood-chip Hopper 6-pack, *17*		360 ___
17311 REA Reefer (std O), *96*	28	30 ___
17314 PFE Reefer "9800-198," *98*		42 ___
17315 PFE Reefer "9800-298," *98*		39 ___
17316 NP Reefer "98583," *98*		50 ___
17317 PRR Reefer FGE,"91904," *98*		36 ___
17318 UP Reefer "170650" (std O), *99*		47 ___
17319 PFE Reefer 6-pack (std O), *01*		300 ___
17320 WM Wood-chip Hopper 6-pack, *17*		360 ___
17331 Hood's General American Milk Car "802" (std O), *02*		100 ___

		Exc	Mint
17332	Pfaudler General American Milk Car "501" (std O), *02*		70
17334	REA General American Milk Car "1741" (std O), *02*		100
17335	New Haven General American Milk Car "102" (std O), *02*		75
17336	PFE Steel-sided Reefer "17760" (std O), *03*		45
17337	CN Steel-sided Reefer "209712" (std O), *03*		38
17338	Merchants Dispatch Transit Steel-sided Reefer "12322" (std O), *03*		39
17339	Burlington Steel-sided Reefer "74825" (std O), *03*		45
17340	White Bros. General American Milk Car "891" (std O), *03*		44
17341	Dairymen's League General American Milk Car "779" (std O), *03*		43
17342	Miller Beer Steel-sided Reefer (std O), *03 u*		58
17343	Miller Beer Steel-sided Reefer (std O), *03 u*		64
17349	NYC General American Milk Car "6581" (std O), *03 u*		42
17350	Hood's General American Milk Car "503" (std O), *03 u*		45
17351	Santa Fe Steel-sided Reefer "3526" (std O), *04*		43
17352	PFE Steel-sided Reefer "20043" (std O), *04*		41
17353	Needham Packing Steel-sided Reefer "60507" (std O), *04*		44
17354	Swift Steel-sided Reefer "15392" (std O), *04*		42
17355	Hood's Steel-sided Reefer "550" (std O), *04*		40
17356	Nestle Nesquik Steel-sided Reefer (std O), *04*		44
17357	Borden's Steel-sided Reefer "522" (std O), *04*		47
17358	Fairfield Farms Steel-sided Reefer (std O), *04*		44
17360	Hood's General American Milk Car "810" (std O), *03*		46
17361	Hood's General American Milk Car "811" (std O), *03*		43
17362	Pfaudler General American Milk Car "502" (std O), *03*		47
17363	Pfaudler General American Milk Car "503" (std O), *03*		40
17364	REA General American Milk Car "1742" (std O), *03*		38
17365	REA General American Milk Car "1743" (std O), *03*		44
17366	NH General American Milk Car "103" (std O), *03*		43
17367	NH General American Milk Car "104" (std O), *03*		47
17368	White Brothers General American Milk Car "892" (std O), *03*		43
17369	White Brothers General American Milk Car "893" (std O), *03*		47
17370	Dairymen's League General American Milk Car "780" (std O), *03*		47
17371	Dairymen's League Milk Car "781" (std O), *03*		47
17372	NYC General American Milk Car "6582" (std O), *03*		47
17373	NYC General American Milk Car "6583" (std O), *03*		40
17374	Hood's General American Milk Car "504" (std O), *03*		43
17375	Hood's General American Milk Car "505" (std O), *03*		47
17377	Railway Express Operating Milk Car "302" (std O), *05*		172
17378	Supplee General American Milk Car (std O), *05*		63
17379	NP Steel-sided Reefer "91353" (std O), *05*		60
17380	PFE Silver Steel-sided Reefer "45698" (std O), *05*		60
17381	North Western Steel-sided Reefer "751" (std O), *05*		40
17397	PFE Steel-sided Reefer "47767" (std O), *05*		45

Exc Mint

		Exc	Mint
17398	A&P General American Milk Car "737" (std O), *06*		65
17399	Bowman Dairy General American Milk Car "117" (std O), *06*		65
17400	CP Rail Gondola with coal (std O), *89*	30	34
17401	Conrail Gondola with coal (std O), *87*	24	26
17402	Santa Fe Gondola with coal (std O), *90*	19	25
17403	Chessie System Gondola "371629" with coil covers (std O), *93*	18	25
17404	ICG Gondola "245998" with coil covers (std O), *93*	26	32
17405	Reading Gondola "24876" with coil covers (std O), *94*	27	31
17406	PRR Gondola "385405" with coil covers (std O), *95*	37	42
17407	NKP Gondola with scrap load, *96*		24
17408	Cotton Belt Gondola "9820" with scrap load (std O), *97*		32
17410	UP Gondola "903004" with scrap load (std O), *99*		30
17412	Gondola, blue, online store, *98*		20
17413	Service Center Gondola with parts load (SSS), *00*		24
17414	Nickel Plate PS-5 Gondola "44801" (std O), *01-02*		40
17415	Frisco PS-5 Gondola "61878" (std O), *01-02*		35
17416	D&H Gondola "14011" with scrap load (std O), *01*		33
17417	BN Rotary Bathtub Gondola 3-pack, *01*		140
17421	CSX Rotary Bathtub Gondola 3-pack, *01*		135
17425	Western Maryland PS-5 Gondola "354903" (std O), *01-02*		36
17426	Maine Central PS-5 Gondola "1116" (std O), *01-02*		40
17427	CSX Rotary Bathtub Gondola Add-on Unit (std O), *02*		47
17428	BN Rotary Bathtub Gondola Add-on Unit (std O), *02*		42
17429	Conrail Rotary Bathtub Gondola 3-pack (std O), *02-03*		115
17433	BNSF Rotary Bathtub Gondola 3-pack (std O), *02-03*		145
17439	UP PS-5 Gondola "229606" (std O), *03*		35
17440	Algoma Central PS-5 Gondola "801" (std O), *03*		32
17441	Conrail Rotary Bathtub Gondola "507673" (std O), *03*		39
17442	BNSF Rotary Bathtub Gondola "668330" (std O), *03*		46
17443	NS Rotary Bathtub Gondola 3-pack (std O), *03*		90
17447	UP Rotary Bathtub Gondola 3-pack (std O), *03*		100
17457	GN PS-5 Gondola "72839" (std O), *03*		35
17458	Reading PS-5 Gondola "33267" (std O), *03*		35
17459	CP Rail PS-5 Gondola "338966" (std O), *04*		35
17460	NYC PS-5 Gondola "749592" (std O), *04*		40
17461	Pennsylvania PS-5 Gondola "374256" (std O), *04*		36
17462	Santa Fe PS-5 Gondola "167340" (std O), *04*		35
17463	NS Bathtub Gondola "10303" (std O), *04*		40
17464	UP Bathtub Gondola "28100" (std O), *04*		35
17465	CP Rail Bathtub Gondola 3-pack (std O), *04*		105
17470	CP Rail Bathtub Gondola, *05*		50
17471	Burlington PS-5 Gondola with covers (std O), *05*		44
17472	New Haven PS-5 Gondola with covers (std O), *05*		53
17473	NYC PS-5 Gondola "502351" (std O), *06-07*		65
17474	D&H PS-5 Gondola "13816" (std O), *06-07*		65
17475	Koppers PS-5 Gondola "213" (std O), *06-07*		65
17477	L&N PS-5 Gondola "170012" (std O), *06-07*		46
17478	N&W PS-5 Gondola "275005" with containers (std O), *08*		70

		Exc	Mint
_____	**17479** LV PS-5 Gondola "33455" with containers (std O), *08*		70
_____	**17480** RI PS-5 Gondola with coke containers (std O), *08-09*		70
_____	**17488** UP Bathtub Gondola 3-pack (std O), *09*		190
_____	**17500** CP Flatcar with logs (std O), *89*	17	29
_____	**17501** Conrail Flatcar with stakes (std O), *87*	37	45
_____	**17502** Santa Fe Flatcar with trailer (std O), *90*	70	75
_____	**17503** NS Flatcar with trailer (std O), *92*	55	65
_____	**17504** NS Flatcar with trailer (std O), *92*	55	65
_____	**17505** NS Flatcar with trailer (std O), *92*	50	55
_____	**17506** NS Flatcar with trailer (std O), *92*	46	55
_____	**17507** NS Flatcar with trailer (std O), *92*	50	55
_____	**17510** NP FlatCar "61200" with logs (std O), *94*	31	36
_____	**17511** WM Flatcar with logs, set of 3 (std O), *95*		145
_____	**17512** WM Flatcar with logs (std O), *95*	35	41
_____	**17513** WM Flatcar with logs (std O), *95*	43	50
_____	**17514** WM Flatcar with logs (std O), *95*	39	45
_____	**17515** Norfolk Southern Flatcar with tractors (std O), *95*	24	42
_____	**17516** T&P FlatCar "9823" with 2 Beechcraft Bonanzas (std O), *97*		50
_____	**17517** WP FlatCar "9823" with Ertl Caterpillar frontloader (std O), *97*		39
_____	**17518** PRR FlatCar "9823" with 2 Corgi Mack trucks (std O), *97*	29	50
_____	**17522** Flatcar with Plymouth Prowler, *98*		41
_____	**17527** Flatcar with 2 Dodge Vipers, *98*		38
_____	**17529** ATSF FlatCar "90010" with Ford milk truck, *99*		55
_____	**17533** MTTX Ford Flatcar with auto frames, *99*		38
_____	**17534** Diamond T Flatcar with Mack trucks "9823," *99*		55
_____	**17536** Route 66 FlatCar "9823-3" with 2 luxury coupes, *99*		37
_____	**17537** Route 66 FlatCar "9823-4" with 2 touring coupes, *99*		32
_____	**17538** NYC Flatcar with Ford tow truck, *99*		43
_____	**17539** FlatCar "9823" with 2 Corvettes (std O), *99*		70
_____	**17540** FlatCar "9823" with 2 Corvettes (std O), *99*		70
_____	**17546** LL Recovery FlatCar "6424" with rail load, *99*		50
_____	**17547** Lionel Lines Recovery FlatCar "6429" with machinery, *99*		50
_____	**17548** Route 66 FlatCar "9823-6" with 2 luxury coupes, *99*		42
_____	**17549** Route 66 FlatCar "9823-5" with station wagon and trailer, *99*		42
_____	**17550** BN Center Beam FlatCar "6216" with lumber (std O), *99*		39
_____	**17551** NYC Flatcar with NYC pickups "499," *99*		49
_____	**17553** Trailer Train FlatCar "98102" with combine (std O), *99*		125
_____	**17554** GN FlatCar "61042" with logs, *00*		32
_____	**17555** Ford Mustang Flatcar with 2 cars (std O), *01*		NRS
_____	**17556** Ford Mustang Flatcar with 2 cars (std O), *01*		NRS
_____	**17557** Route 66 FlatCar "9823-7" with black sedans, *99-00*		39
_____	**17558** Route 66 FlatCar "9823-8" with brown sedans, *99*		39
_____	**17559** Route 66 FlatCar "9823-9" with 2 wagons (std O), *01*		40
_____	**17560** Route 66 FlatCar "9823-10" with 2 sedans (std O), *01*		40

		Exc	Mint
17563	Santa Fe FlatCar "90011" with pickup trucks (std O), *01*		49 ____
17564	West Side Lumber Shay Log Car 3-pack #2 (std O), *01*		95 ____
17568	PRR FlatCar "470333" with pickup trucks (std O), *02*		50 ____
17571	UP FlatCar "909231" with pickup trucks (std O), *03*		50 ____
17572	Pioneer Seed Flatcar with pedal cars, *02 u*		220 ____
17573	WM PS-4 FlatCar "2631" (std O), *03*		35 ____
17574	Santa Fe PS-4 FlatCar "90081" (std O), *03*		35 ____
17575	NYC PS-4 FlatCar "506098" (std O), *03*		40 ____
17576	Ontario Northland PS-4 FlatCar "2020" (std O), *03*		35 ____
17577	B&O PS-4 FlatCar "8651" (std O), *04*		35 ____
17578	B&M PS-4 FlatCar "34007" (std O), *04*		35 ____
17579	Milwaukee Road PS-4 FlatCar "64073" (std O), *04*		35 ____
17580	UP PS-4 FlatCar "54603" (std O), *04*		35 ____
17581	GN FlatCar "X4168" with pickup trucks (std O), *04*		42 ____
17582	PRR FlatCar "469617" with trailers (std O), *05*		110 ____
17583	GN PS-4 Flatcar with trailers, *05*		80 ____
17584	SP PS-4 Flatcar with trailers, *05*		80 ____
17585	C&O PS-4 FlatCar "81000" with trailers (std O), *05*		80 ____
17586	BN Husky Stack Car "63322" (std O), *05*		80 ____
17587	SP Husky Stack Car "513915" (std O), *05*		80 ____
17588	CSX Husky Stack Car "620350" (std O), *05*		80 ____
17589	TTX Trailer Train Husky Stack Car "456249" (std O), *05*		65 ____
17600	NYC Wood-sided Caboose (std O), *87 u*	35	45 ____
17601	Southern Wood-sided Caboose (std O), *88*	35	44 ____
17602	Conrail Wood-sided Caboose (std O), *87*	65	75 ____
17603	RI Wood-sided Caboose (std O), *88*	19	34 ____
17604	Lackawanna Wood-sided Caboose (std O), *88*	42	53 ____
17605	Reading Wood-sided Caboose (std O), *89*	34	37 ____
17606	NYC Steel-sided Caboose, smoke (std O), *90*	49	65 ____
17607	Reading Steel-sided Caboose, smoke (std O), *90*	55	65 ____
17608	C&O Steel-sided Caboose, smoke (std O), *91*	46	55 ____
17610	Wabash Steel-sided Caboose, smoke (std O), *91*	39	55 ____
17611	NYC Wood-sided Caboose "6003" (std O), *90 u*	40	55 ____
17612	NKP Steel-sided Caboose, smoke (FF 6), *92*	60	65 ____
17613	Southern Steel-sided Caboose "7613," smoke (std O), *92*	60	65 ____
17615	NP Wood-sided Caboose, smoke (std O), *92*	65	70 ____
17617	D&RGW Steel-sided Caboose (std O), *95*	50	55 ____
17618	Frisco Wood-sided Caboose (std O), *95*	65	75 ____
17620	NP Wood-sided Caboose "1746," *98*		70 ____
17623	Farmrail Extended Vision Caboose, *99*		74 ____
17624	Conrail Extended Vision Caboose "6900," *99*		43 ____
17625	Burlington Northern Steel-sided Caboose "7606," *99*		65 ____
17626	Service Center Extended Vision Caboose (SSS), *00*		29 ____
17627	C&O Extended Vision Caboose, *01*		65 ____
17628	BNSF Extended Vision Caboose, *01*		65 ____
17629	Santa Fe Extended Vision Caboose, *01*		80 ____
17630	UP Extended Vision Caboose, *01*		85 ____
17631	Virginian Bay Window Caboose, *01*		85 ____
17632	CSX Bay Window Caboose, *01*		75 ____
17633	NYC Bay Window Caboose, *01*		90 ____

		Exc	Mint
____	**17634** Delaware & Hudson Bay Window Caboose, *01*		75
____	**17635** 100th Anniversary Die-cast Gold Caboose, *00*		345
____	**17636** NYC Die-cast Caboose "18096," *00-01*		100
____	**17637** NYC "Quicker via Peoria" Die-cast Caboose, *00*		135
____	**17638** RI Extended Vision Caboose "17011" (std O), *02*		55
____	**17639** Chessie Extended Vision Caboose "3322" (std O), *02*		55
____	**17640** CP Extended Vision Caboose "434604" (std O), *02*		57
____	**17641** Soo Line Extended Vision Caboose "2" (std O), *02*		55
____	**17642** Conrail Bay Window Caboose "21023" (std O), *02*		65
____	**17643** NKP Bay Window Caboose "480" (std O), *02*		60
____	**17644** Erie Bay Window Caboose "C307" (std O), *02*		55
____	**17645** N&W Bay Window Caboose "C-6" (std O), *02*		55
____	**17646** UP Bay Window Caboose "24555" (std O), *02*		65
____	**17647** B&O Caboose "C-2820" (std O), *03-04*		65
____	**17648** Chessie System Caboose "C-2800" (std O), *03-04*		75
____	**17649** Lionel Lines Caboose "7649" (std O), *03-04*		65
____	**17650** Rio Grande Extended Vision Caboose "01500" (std O), *03*		65
____	**17651** BN Extended Vision Caboose "10531" (std O), *03-05*		80
____	**17652** NYC Bay Window Caboose "20200" (std O), *03*		75
____	**17653** SP Bay Window Caboose "1337" (std O), *03*		65
____	**17654** Alaska Extended Vision Caboose "989" (std O), *03*		75
____	**17655** WP Bay Window Caboose "448" (std O), *03-04*		75
____	**17657** Norman Rockwell Holiday Caboose, *03*		30
____	**17658** Burlington Extended Vision Caboose "13611" (std O), *04*		70
____	**17659** CN Extended Vision Caboose "79646" (std O), *04*		70
____	**17660** Seaboard Extended Vision Caboose "5700" (std O), *04*		65
____	**17661** C&NW Bay Window Caboose "10871" (std O), *04*		65
____	**17662** PC Bay Window Caboose "21001" (std O), *04*		65
____	**17663** Southern Bay Window Caboose "X546" (std O), *04*		65
____	**17664** B&O Caboose "C-2824" (std O), *03-04*		65
____	**17665** Chessie System Caboose "C-2802" (std O), *03-04*		75
____	**17669** NYC Bay Window Caboose, smoke, *05*		85
____	**17670** CP Rail Bay Window Caboose, smoke, *05*		85
____	**17671** BN Extended Vision Caboose, *05*		85
____	**17672** GN Extended Vision Caboose "X-106" (std O), *05*		85
____	**17673** Santa Fe Extended Vision Caboose, *05*		85
____	**17674** Reading Extended Vision Caboose "94119" (std O), *05*		75
____	**17675** Rio Grande Extended Vision Caboose "01507" (std O), *06*		90
____	**17676** NYC Bay Window Caboose "20300," *07*		60
____	**17677** Erie-Lack. Bay Window Caboose "C359" (std O), *06*		90
____	**17678** B&O I-12 Caboose "C2421" (std O), *06*		90
____	**17679** Long Island Bay Window Caboose "C-62" (std O), *06*		90
____	**17682** Reading Northeastern Caboose "92841" (std O), *06-07*		85
____	**17683** Chessie System Northeastern Caboose "1893" (std O), *07*		85
____	**17684** Conrail Northeastern Caboose "18873" (std O), *07*		85
____	**17685** Jersey Central Northeastern Caboose "91533" (std O), *07*		85
____	**17690** UP CA-4 Caboose "3826" (std O), *06*		90

		Exc	Mint
17691	UP CA-4 Caboose "25103" (std O), *06*	90	____
17692	LL CA-4 B22 Caboose "7629" (std O), *06*	90	____
17693	Chessie Extended Vision Caboose "3285" (std O), *06*	90	____
17694	NS Extended Vision Caboose "555582" (std O), *06*	90	____
17695	Alaska I-12 Caboose "1001" (std O), *06*	90	____
17696	CP Bay Window Caboose "437266" (std O), *06*	90	____
17697	CN Extended Vision Caboose "78128" (std O), *06*	90	____
17699	UP Ca-4 Caboose "25193" (std O), *07*	90	____
17700	UP ACF 40-ton Stock Car "47456" (std O), *01-02*	85	____
17701	Rio Grande ACF 40-ton Stock Car "39269" (std O), *01-02*	60	____
17702	CP ACF 40-ton Stock Car "277083" (std O), *01-02*	75	____
17703	NYC ACF 40-ton Stock Car "23334" (std O), *01-02*	85	____
17703	Crayola 2-bay Hopper, LionScale, *17-18*	70	____
17704	B&O ACF 40-ton Stock Car "110234" (std O), *02*	40	____
17705	CB&Q ACF 40-ton Stock Car "52886" (std O), *02*	40	____
17707	PRR ARF 40-ton Stock Car "128994" (std O), *03*	35	____
17708	CP Rail ACF 40-ton Stock Car "277313" (std O), *03*	38	____
17709	UP Stock Car "48154" (std O), *04*	45	____
17710	Great Northern Stock Car "56385" (std O), *04*	40	____
17711	C&O ACF 40-ton Stock Car "95237" (std O), *06*	60	____
17712	N&W ACF 40-ton Stock Car "33000" (std O), *06*	60	____
17713	MKT ACF 40-ton Stock Car "47150" (std O), *06*	60	____
17714	CN 40-ton Stock Car "172755" (std O), *06*	60	____
17715	MP 40-ton Stock Car "52428" (std O), *06*	60	____
17716	CGW 40-ton Stock Car "838," *08*	60	____
17717	UP 40-ton Stock Car "48217," *08*	60	____
17718	NS Heritage 3-bay Hopper 2-pack (std O), *12*	160	____
17719	C&BQ ACF Stock Car "52925" (std O), *09*	70	____
17720	UP ACF Stock Car (std O), *10*	70	____
17721	Postwar Scale Stock Car 2-pack, *10-11*	140	____
17724	CN Scale Steel-sided Reefer "210552" (std O), *11*	80	____
17725	NP Scale Steel-sided Reefer "98528" (std O), *11*	80	____
17726	IC Scale Steel-sided Reefer "16644" (std O), *11*	80	____
17727	Mopac/Wabash Scale Steel-sided Reefer "30790" (std O), *11*	80	____
17729	C&O Scale PS-1 Boxcar "2992" (std O), *12*	70	____
17730	Seaboard Scale Round-roof Boxcar "19293" (std O), *11*	70	____
17731	Pere Marquette Scale Boxcar "81805" (std O), *12*	70	____
17732	L&N Scale PS-1 Boxcar "4798" (std O), *12*	70	____
17733	PRR Scale Round-roof Boxcar "78948" (std O), *11*	70	____
17734	PRR Scale Round-roof Boxcar "76644" (std O), *11*	70	____
17735	PRR Round-roof DD Boxcar "77851" (std O), *12*	70	____
17736	PRR Round-roof DD Boxcar "60156" (std O), *12*	70	____
17737	N&W Scale Round-roof Boxcar "46494" (std O), *11*	70	____
17738	NP Round-roof DD Boxcar "39300" (std O), *12*	70	____
17739	DT&I Round-roof DD Boxcar "12250" (std O), *12*	70	____
17740	Alaska Scale Round-roof Boxcar "27781" (std O), *11*	70	____
17741	Santa Fe Scale Slogan Reefer 5-car Set (std O), *12*	320	____
17747	Santa Fe Scale Boxcar "39009" (std O), *12*	70	____
17748	Grave's Mortuary Supply Scale PS-1 Boxcar (std O), *12-13*	70	____
17749	Erie Scale PS-1 Boxcar "90300" (std O), *12*	70	____

		Exc	Mint
___ **17750** NYC Round-roof DD Boxcar "77147" (std 0), *12*			70
___ **17751** NKP Scale PS-1 Boxcar "6605" (std 0), *12*			70
17752 Polar Round-roof Boxcar "1202" (std 0), *12-13, 16-17*			70
___			
___ **17753** LV Scale PS-1 Boxcar "65124" (std 0), *12*			70
___ **17754** EL DD Boxcar "65000" (std 0), *12*			75
___ **17755** D&H DD Boxcar "25025" (std 0), *12*			75
___ **17756** CP Rail DD Boxcar "42630" (std 0), *12*			75
___ **17757** Milwaukee Road DD Boxcar "13441" (std 0), *12*			75
___ **17758** ATSF Map and Slogan Reefer 3-pack, *12*			190
___ **17762** BN 57' Mechanical Reefer "9618" (std 0), *12*			85
___ **17763** NYC 57' Mechanical Reefer "6762" (std 0), *12*			85
___ **17764** ATSF 57' Mechanical Reefer "56244" (std 0), *12*			85
17765 Virginian Round-roof DD Boxcar "3131" (std 0), *13-14*			80
___			
___ **17766** NH Round-roof Boxcar "39303" (std 0), *13*			70
___ **17767** SP Round-roof DD Boxcar "166052" (std 0), *13-14*			80
17768 Grave's Mortuary Supply Round-roof Boxcar (std 0), *13*			70
___			
___ **17769** D&RGW PS-1 Boxcar "60046" (std 0), *13*			70
___ **17770** MILW PS-1 Boxcar "8777" (std 0), *13*			70
___ **17771** CNJ PS-1 Boxcar "23522" (std 0), *13-14*			80
___ **17772** Central of Georgia PS-1 Boxcar (std 0), *13*			70
___ **17773** D&M Round-roof Boxcar "3148" (std 0), *13-14*			80
___ **17774** D&M PS-1 Boxcar "2833" (std 0), *13*			70
___ **17775** NS Heritage 3-bay Hopper 3-pack (std 0), *13-15*			240
___ **17779** NS Heritage 3-bay Hopper 3-pack (std 0), *13-15*			240
___ **17783** NS Heritage 3-bay Hopper 3-pack (std 0), *13-15*			240
___ **17787** NS Heritage 3-bay Hopper 3-pack (std 0), *13*			240
___ **17791** NS Heritage 3-bay Hopper 3-pack (std 0), *13*			240
___ **17795** NS Heritage 3-bay Hopper 3-pack (std 0), *13*			240
___ **17800** Ontario Northland Ore Car "6126," *00*			30
___ **17801** CN Ore Car "345165," *00*			37
___ **17802** CP Ore Car "377249," *00*			28
___ **17803** DMIR Ore Car "31456," *00*			30
___ **17804** UP Ore Car "8023," *01*			29
___ **17805** CP Rail Ore Car "377238," *01*			29
___ **17806** UP Ore Car "27250," *03*			30
___ **17807** BN Ore Car "95887," *02*			28
___ **17900** Santa Fe Unibody Tank Car (std 0), *90*		37	46
___ **17901** Chevron Unibody Tank Car (std 0), *90*		26	32
___ **17902** NJ Zinc Unibody Tank Car (std 0), *91*		26	34
___ **17903** Conoco Unibody Tank Car (std 0), *91*		24	29
___ **17904** Texaco Unibody Tank Car (std 0), *92*		34	43
___ **17905** Archer Daniels Midland Unibody Tank Car (std 0), *92*		24	33
___ **17906** SCM Unibody Tank Car "78286" (std 0), *93*		47	55
___ **17908** Marathon Oil Unibody Tank Car (std 0), *95*		51	56
___ **17909** Hooker Chemicals Unibody Tank Car (std 0), *96*			55
___ **17910** Sunoco Unibody Tank Car "7900," *97*			37
___ **17913** J.M. Huber Tank Car, *98*			29
___ **17914** Englehard Tank Car, *98*			36
___ **17915** Gulf Unibody Tank Car "8438," *00*			43
___ **17916** Burlington Unibody Tank Car "130000," *00*		24	38
___ **17918** Southern Unibody Tank Car, *01*			32

		Exc	Mint
17919 Koppers Unibody Tank Car, *01*			39____
17924 Safety Kleen Unibody Tank Car "77603" (std O), *02*			40____
17925 Beefmaster Unibody Tank Car "120021" (std O), *02*			38____
17926 Cargill Unibody 1-D Tank Car "5836" (std O), *03*			40____
17927 Union Starch Unibody 1-D Tank Car "59137" (std O), *03*			35____
17928 Merck 1-D Tank Car "25421" (std O), *03*			35____
17929 Wyandotte Chemicals 1-D Tank Car "1325" (std O), *03*			34____
17930 CSX Unibody Tank Car "993369" (std O), *04*			35____
17931 UP Unibody Tank Car "6" (std O), *04*			35____
17932 CIBRO TankTrain Intermediate Car "26263" (std O), *04*			35____
17933 GATX TankTrain Intermediate Car 3-pack (std O), *04*			100____
17946 Candy Cane Unibody Tank Car, *04*			60____
17948 Philadelphia Quartz 1-D Tank Car "806" (std O), *06*			55____
17949 Skelly Oil 1-D Tank Car "2293" (std O), *06*			55____
17950 ADM Unibody Tank Car "19020" (std O), *06*			60____
17951 Cerestar Unibody Tank Car "190177" (std O), *06*			60____
17959 Dow 1-D Tank Car "310101" (std O), *07*			55____
17960 Amaizo 1-D Tank Car "15440" (std O), *07*			55____
17962 Domino Sugar 1-D Tank Car "3008" (std O), *07*			60____
17966 Procor 1-D Tank Car "82607" (std O), *07*			60____
17972 Union Starch 1-D Tank Car "724" (std O), *08*			60____
17973 UP 1-D Tank Car "907838" (std O), *08*			60____
17975 Cargill Foods Unibody Tank Car 3-pack (std O), *08-09*			195____
17976 Huber Unibody Tank Car 3-pack (std O), *08-09*			195____
17983 GATX TankTrain Intermediate Car 3-pack, *08*			195____
18000 PRR 0-6-0 Locomotive "8977," *89, 91*		258	405____
18001 Rock Island 4-8-4 Locomotive "5100," *87*		305	315____
18002 NYC 4-6-4 Locomotive "785," *87 u*		510	576____
18003 DL&W 4-8-4 Locomotive "1501," *88*		235	294____
18004 Reading 4-6-2 Locomotive "8004," *89*		185	205____
18005 NYC 4-6-4 Locomotive "5340," display case, *90*		705	799____
18006 Reading 4-8-4 Locomotive "2100," *89 u*		490	528____
18007 Southern Pacific 4-8-4 Locomotive "4410," *91*		374	392____
18008 Disneyland 35th Anniversary 4-4-0 Locomotive, display case, *90*		260	310____
18009 NYC 4-8-2 Locomotive "3000," *90 u, 91*		370	561____
18010 PRR 6-8-6 Steam Turbine Locomotive "6200," *91-92*		900	1041____
18010 L&NE AC-2 Covered Hopper 6-pack, *18*			360____
18011 Chessie System 4-8-4 Locomotive "2101," *91*		440	536____
18012 NYC 4-6-4 Locomotive "5340," *90*		710	900____
18013 Disneyland 35th Anniversary 4-4-0 Locomotive, *90*		250	290____
18014 Lionel Lines 2-6-4 Locomotive "8014," *91*		145	190____
18016 Northern Pacific 4-8-4 Locomotive "2626," *92*		385	440____
18018 Southern 2-8-2 Locomotive "4501," *92*		640	650____
18020 N&W AC-2 Covered Hopper 6-pack, *18*			360____
18022 Pere Marquette 2-8-4 Locomotive "1201," *93*		550	650____
18023 Western Maryland Shay Locomotive "6," *92*		1050	1350____
18024 Sears T&P 4-8-2 Locomotive "907," display case, *92 u*		750	790____
18025 T&P 4-8-2 Locomotive "907," *92 u*			640____

		Exc	Mint
____	**18026** NYC 4-6-4 Dreyfuss Hudson Locomotive, 2-rail, *92 u*		2350
____	**18027** NYC 4-6-4 Dreyfuss Hudson Locomotive, 3-rail, *93 u*		1450
____	**18028** Smithsonian PRR 4-6-2 Locomotive "3768," 2-rail, *93 u*		2150
____	**18029** NYC 4-6-4 Dreyfuss Hudson Locomotive, 3-rail, *93 u*	1900	2150
____	**18030** Frisco 2-8-2 Locomotive "4100," *93 u*	530	625
____	**18030** Pere Marquette AC-2 Covered Hopper 6-pack, *18*		360
	18031 2-10-0 Bundesbahn BR-50 Locomotive, 2-rail, *93 u*		NRS
____	**18034** Santa Fe 2-8-2 Locomotive "3158," *94*	540	620
	18035 2-10-0 Reichsbahn BR-50 Locomotive, 2-rail, *93 u*		NRS
	18036 2-10-0 French BR-50 Locomotive, 2-rail, *93 u*		NRS
____	**18040** N&W 4-8-4 Locomotive "612," *95*	640	710
____	**18040** WM AC-2 Covered Hopper 6-pack, *18*		360
____	**18042** Boston & Albany 4-6-4 Locomotive "618," *95*		250
____	**18043** Chesapeake & Ohio 4-6-4 Locomotive "490," *95*	680	750
____	**18044** Southern 4-6-2 Locomotive "1390," *96*		255
____	**18045** Commodore Vanderbilt Locomotive "777," *96*		678
____	**18046** Wabash 4-6-4 Locomotive "700," *96*	190	375
____	**18049** N&W Warhorse 4-8-4 Locomotive "600," *96*		490
____	**18050** JCPenney 4-6-2 Locomotive "2055," *96*	235	245
____	**18050** Continental Grain ACF 3-Bay Covered Hopper 6-pack, *18*		360
____	**18052** Pennsylvania Torpedo Locomotive "238E," *97*		455
____	**18054** NYC 0-4-0 Switcher "1665," black, *97*		145
____	**18056** NYC J1-e Hudson Locomotive "763E," Vanderbilt tender, *97*		603
____	**18060** PRR ACF 3-Bay Covered Hopper 6-pack, *18*		360
____	**18062** ATSF 4-6-4 Hudson Locomotive "3447," *97*		680
____	**18063** NYC 4-6-4 Commodore Vanderbilt Locomotive, *99*		952
____	**18064** NYC 4-8-2 Mohawk L-3A Locomotive "3005," tender, *98*	275	450
____	**18067** NYC Weathered Commodore Vanderbilt Scale Hudson Locomotive, *97*		840
____	**18070** Tenneco ACF 3-Bay Covered Hopper 6-pack, *18*		360
____	**18071** SP Daylight Locomotive "4449," *98*		680
____	**18072** Lionel Lines Torpedo Locomotive, tender, *98*		360
____	**18079** NYC 2-8-2 Mikado Locomotive "1967," *99*		710
____	**18080** D&RGW 2-8-2 Mikado Locomotive "1210," *99*		720
____	**18080** BN ACF 3-Bay Covered Hopper 6-pack, *18*		360
____	**18082** NYC 4-6-4 Hudson Locomotive "5404," *99*		230
____	**18083** C&O 4-6-4 Hudson Locomotive "305," *99*		205
____	**18084** Santa Fe 4-6-4 Hudson Locomotive "305," *99*		225
____	**18085** NH 4-6-2 Pacific Locomotive "1334," *99*		275
____	**18086** NYC 4-6-2 Pacific Locomotive "4929," *99*		235
____	**18087** Santa Fe 4-6-2 Pacific Locomotive "3448," *99*		265
____	**18088** SP 4-6-2 Pacific Locomotive "1407," *99*		350
____	**18089** CNJ 4-6-0 Camelback Locomotive "771," *99*		405
____	**18090** Vesuvius Crucible PS-1 Boxcar 6-pack, *18*		360
____	**18091** PRR 4-6-0 Camelback Locomotive "821," *99*		405
____	**18092** SP 4-6-0 Camelback Locomotive "2283," *99*		395
____	**18093** C&NW 4-6-0 Camelback Locomotive "3006," *99*		285
____	**18094** B&O 4-4-2 E6 Atlantic Locomotive, CC, *99-00*		345
____	**18095** PRR 4-4-2 E6 Atlantic Locomotive, CC, *99-00*	275	455
____	**18096** ATSF 4-4-2 E6 Atlantic Locomotive, CC, *99-00*		370

		Exc	Mint
18097	CNJ 4-6-0 Camelback Locomotive "770," *99*		330___
18098	PRR 4-6-0 Camelback Locomotive "820," *99*		355___
18099	SP 4-6-0 Camelback Locomotive "2282," *99*		360___
18100	Santa Fe F3 Diesel A Unit "8100," (see 11711)		NRS___
18100	EJ&E PS-1 Boxcar 6-pack, *18*		360___
18100	Monon PS-1 Boxcar 6-pack, *18*		360___
18101	Santa Fe F3 Diesel B Unit "8101," (see 11711)		NRS___
18102	Santa Fe F3 Diesel A Unit "8102," dummy (see 11711)		NRS___
18103	Santa Fe F3 Diesel B Unit "8103," dummy, *91 u*	180	190___
18104	GN F3 Diesel A Unit "366A," dummy (see 11724)		500___
18105	GN F3 Diesel B Unit "370B," dummy (see 11724)		NRS___
18106	GN F3 Diesel A Unit "351C," dummy (see 11724)		NRS___
18107	D&RGW Alco PA1 Diesel ABA Set, *92*	640	740___
18108	Great Northern F3 Diesel B Unit "371B," *93*	85	105___
18109	Erie Alco Diesel A Unit "725A," (see 11734)		NRS___
18110	Erie Alco Diesel B Unit "725B," (see 11734)		160___
18111	Erie Alco Diesel A Unit "736A," dummy, (see 11734)		NRS___
18115	Santa Fe F3 Diesel B Unit, *93*	90	115___
18116	Erie-Lackawanna Alco PA1 Diesel AA Set, *93*	450	490___
18117/18	Santa Fe F3 Diesel AA Set, "200," *93*	330	410___
18119/20	UP Alco Diesel AA Set, *94*	200	235___
18120	Rutland PS-1 Boxcar 6-pack, *18*		360___
18121	Santa Fe F3 Diesel B Unit "200A," *94*	75	95___
18122	Santa Fe F3 Diesel B Unit "200B," *95*	140	150___
18123	ACL F3 Diesel A Unit "342," (see 11903)		NRS___
18124	ACL F3 Diesel B Unit "342B," (see 11903)		NRS___
18125	ACL F3 Diesel A Unit "343," dummy (see 11903)		NRS___
18128	Santa Fe F3 Diesel A Unit "2343," *96*		435___
18129	Santa Fe F3 Diesel B Unit "2343C," *96*		245___
18130	Santa Fe F3 Diesel AB Set, *96*		580___
18130	NYC AAR 3-Bay Hopper 6-pack, *18*		360___
18131	NP F3 Diesel AB Set, "2390A, 2390C," *97*	295	360___
18132	NP F3 Diesel A Unit, powered		300___
18133	NP F3 Diesel B Unit, dummy		150___
18134	Santa Fe F3 Diesel A Unit "2343," dummy, *97*		195___
18136	Santa Fe F3 Diesel B Unit "2343C," *97*	135	240___
18138	Milwaukee Road F3 Diesel A Unit "75A," *98*		400___
18139	Milwaukee Road F3 Diesel B Unit "2378B," *98*		250___
18140	Milwaukee Road F3 Diesel AB Set, *98*	390	600___
18140	Nickel Plate Road AAR 3-Bay Hopper 6-pack, *18*		360___
18145	NP F3 Diesel A Unit "2390A," *97*	300	360___
18146	NP F3 Diesel B Unit "2390C," *97*		170___
18147	NP F3 Diesel AB Set, *97*	450	580___
18149	UP Veranda Gas Turbine Locomotive "61," *98*	860	900___
18150	LG Everist AAR 3-Bay Hopper 6-pack, *18*		360___
18154	Deluxe Santa Fe FT Diesel AA Set, *98-00*		375___
18155	Deluxe Santa Fe FT Diesel A Unit, powered (see 18154)		NRS___
18156	Deluxe Santa Fe FT Diesel A Unit, dummy (see 18154)		NRS___
18157	Santa Fe FT Diesel AA Set, *98-00*		240___
18158	Santa Fe FT Diesel A Unit, powered (see 18157)		NRS___
18159	Santa Fe FT Diesel A Unit, dummy (see 18157)		NRS___

		Exc	Mint
___	**18160** NYC Deluxe FT Diesel AA Set, "1602, 1603," *98-00*		500
___	**18160** UP AAR 3-Bay Hopper 6-pack, *18*		360
___	**18163** NYC FT Diesel AA Set, "1600, 2400," *98-00*		300
___	**18166** B&O FT Diesel AA Set, CC, *99-00*		340
___	**18169** B&O FT Diesel AA Set, traditional, *99-00*		240
___	**18189** Army of Potomac Operating Stock Car, *99*		45
___	**18190** McNeil's Rangers Operating Stock Car "2," *99*		45
___	**18191** WP F3 Diesel AA Set, *98*	153	570
___	**18192** WP F3 Diesel A Unit, powered, *98*		485
___	**18193** WP F3 Diesel A Unit, dummy, *98*		495
___	**18197** WP F3 Diesel B Unit "2355C," *99*	88	255
___	**18198** WP F3 Diesel B Unit "2345C," CC, *99*		360
___	**18200** Conrail SD40 Diesel "8200," *87*	180	200
___	**18201** Chessie System SD40 Diesel "8201," *88*	245	340
___	**18202** Erie-Lack. SD40 Diesel Unit "8459," dummy, *89 u*	90	140
___	**18203** CP Rail SD40 Diesel "8203," *89*	195	250
___	**18204** Chessie SD40 Diesel Unit "8204," dummy, *90 u*	135	190
___	**18205** Union Pacific Dash 8-40C Diesel "9100," *89*	275	335
___	**18206** Santa Fe Dash 8-40B Diesel "8206," *90*	195	235
___	**18207** Norfolk Southern Dash 8-40C Diesel "8689," *92*	230	270
___	**18208** BN SD40 Diesel Dummy Unit "8586," *91 u*	115	165
___	**18209** CP Rail SD40 Diesel Dummy Unit "8209," *92 u*	135	165
___	**18210** Illinois Central SD40 "6006," *93*	220	250
___	**18210** Northwestern Refrigerated Wood-sided Refrigerator Car 6-pack, *18*		360
___	**18211** Susquehanna Dash 8-40B Diesel "4002," *93*	145	165
___	**18212** Santa Fe Dash 8-40B Diesel Dummy Unit "8212," *93*	155	180
___	**18213** Norfolk Southern Dash 8-40C Diesel "8688," *94*	225	240
___	**18214** CSX Dash 8-40C Diesel "7500," *94*	235	255
___	**18215** CSX Dash 8-40C Diesel "7643," *94*	240	260
___	**18216** Conrail SD-60M Diesel "5500," *94*	355	380
___	**18217** Illinois Central SD40 Diesel "6007," *94*	170	175
___	**18218** Susquehanna Dash 8-40B Diesel "4004," *94*	205	225
___	**18219** C&NW Dash 8-40C Diesel "8501," *95*	325	330
___	**18220** C&NW Dash 8-40C Diesel "8502," *95*	215	315
___	**18220** PFE Wood-sided Refrigerator Car 6-pac, *18*		360
___	**18221** D&RGW SD50 Diesel "5512," *95*	455	520
___	**18222** D&RGW SD50 Diesel "5517," *95*	280	325
___	**18223** Milwaukee Road SD40 Diesel "154," *95*	375	380
___	**18224** Milwaukee Road SD40 Diesel "155," *95*	240	265
___	**18226** GE Dash 9 Diesel, *97*		295
___	**18228** SP Dash 9 Diesel "8228," gray with red nose, *97*		340
___	**18229** SP SD40 Diesel "7333," *98*	300	425
___	**18230** Swift Wood-sided Refrigerator Car 6-pac, *18*		360
___	**18231** BNSF Dash 9 Diesel "739," *98*		435
___	**18232** Soo Line SD60 Diesel "5500," *97*		350
___	**18233** BNSF Dash 9 Diesel "745," *98*		330
___	**18234** BNSF Dash 9 Diesel "740," CC, *98-99*		405
___	**18235** BNSF Dash 9 Diesel 2-pack, "739, 740," *98*		710
___	**18238** Conrail SD70 Diesel "4145," *99-00*		300
___	**18240** Conrail Dash 8-40B Diesel "5065," CC, *98*		260
___	**18240** Rath Wood-sided Refrigerator Car 6-pac, *18*		360
___	**18241** BN SD70 Diesel "9413," *99-00*		345
___	**18245** PRR Alco PA1 Diesel AA Set, *99*		495

	Exc	Mint
18248 PRR Alco PB-1 Diesel "5750B," *99*		215____
18249 Erie Alco PB-1 Diesel "850B," *00*		250____
18250 BNSF SD70 Diesel "9870," *99-00*		365____
18251 CSX SD60 Diesel "8701," *99-00*		300____
18252 Amtrak Dash 9 Diesel, CC, *99*		285____
18253 BNSF Dash 9 Diesel, CC, *99*		305____
18254 ATSF Dash 9 Diesel, CC, *99*		340____
18255 NS Dash 9 Diesel, CC, *99*		315____
18256 Amtrak Dash 9 Diesel, traditional, *99*		200____
18257 BNSF Dash 9 Diesel, traditional, *99*		190____
18258 ATSF Dash 9 Diesel, traditional, *99*		205____
18259 NS Dash 9 Diesel, traditional, *99*		215____
18260 Conrail SD70 Diesel "4144," *99-00*		280____
18261 BN SD60 Diesel "9412," *99-00*		255____
18262 BNSF SD70 Diesel "9869," *99-00*		250____
18263 CSX SD60 Diesel "8700," *99-00*		255____
18264 Southern Pacific SD70M Diesel "8238," *99-00*		245____
18265 Southern Pacific SD70M Diesel "9803," *99-00*		340____
18266 Norfolk Southern SD60 Diesel "6552," CC, *01-02*		400____
18268 Lionel Centennial SD90MAC Diesel, CC, *00*		420____
18269 UP SD90MAC Diesel "8006," CC, *00*		405____
18271 CP SD90MAC Diesel "9129," CC, *00*		440____
18273 UP SD40 Diesel "8071," *99-00*		330____
18274 Burlington U30C Diesel "891," CC, *01*		370____
18276 Seaboard U30C Diesel "7274," CC, *01*		325____
18278 UP U30C Diesel "2938," CC, *01*		330____
18280 Maersk SD70 Diesel, CC, *00*		345____
18281 BNSF Dash 9-44CW Diesel "788," CC, *00*		340____
18282 BNSF Dash 9-44CW Diesel "789," traditional, *00*		225____
18283 CSX Dash 9-44CW Diesel "9019," CC, *00*		340____
18284 CSX Dash 9-44CW Diesel "9020," traditional, *00*		300____
18285 UP Dash 9-44C Diesel "9659," CC, *01*		325____
18286 UP Dash 9-44CW Diesel "9717," CC, *01*		355____
18287 CN Dash 9-44C Diesel "2529," CC, *01*		460____
18288 Odyssey System SD70 Diesel, CC, *00 u*		400____
18290 Amtrak Dash 8-32BWH Diesel "509," CC, *01*		325____
18291 BNSF Dash 8-32BWH Diesel "580," CC, *02*		340____
18292 Chessie GE U30C Diesel "3312," CC, *02*		340____
18293 Santa Fe U30C Diesel, CC, *03*		395____
18294 Alaska SD70MAC Diesel "4005," CC, *01-02*		435____
18295 Conrail SD80MAC Diesel "7200," CC, *02-03*		365____
18296 CSX SD80MAC Diesel "801," CC, *02-03*		405____
18297 NYC SD80MAC Diesel "9914," CC, *02-03*		405____
18298 UP "Desert Victory" SD40-2 Diesel "3593," CC, *02-03*		380____
18299 CP Rail SD40-2 Diesel "5420," CC, *02-03*		375____
18300 PRR GG1 Electric Locomotive "8300," *87*	285	335____
18301 Southern FM Train Master Diesel "8301," *88*	150	204____
18302 GN EP-5 Electric Locomotive "8302" (FF 3), *88*	190	250____
18303 Amtrak GG1 Electric Locomotive "8303," *89*	275	338____
18304 Lackawanna MU Commuter Car Set, *91*	380	435____
18305 Lackawanna MU Commuter Car Dummy Set, *92*	230	255____
18306 PRR MU Commuter Car Set, *92*	260	330____
18307 PRR FM Train Master Diesel "8699," *94*	170	202____

		Exc	Mint
____ **18308**	PRR GG1 Electric Locomotive "4866," *92*	193	278
____ **18309**	Reading FM Train Master Diesel "863," *93*	173	212
____ **18310**	PRR MU Commuter Car Dummy Set, *93*	265	345
____ **18311**	Disney EP-5 Electric Locomotive "8311," *94*	296	397
____ **18313**	Pennsylvania GG1 Electric Locomotive "4907," *96*	75	297
____ **18314**	PRR GG1 Electric Locomotive "2332," 5 gold stripes, *97*	300	507
____ **18315**	Virginian E33 Electric Locomotive "2329," *97*		240
____ **18319**	New Haven EP-5 Electric Locomotive, *99*	200	365
____ **18321**	CNJ Train Master Diesel "2341," *99*		405
____ **18322**	Lackawanna Train Master Diesel "2321," *99*		465
____ **18326**	PRR Congressional GG1 Electric Locomotive, *00*		600
____ **18327**	Virginian FM Train Master Diesel "2331," *99-00*		410
____ **18328**	NH MU Commuter Car Set, CC, *00*		385
____ **18331**	Reading MU Commuter Car Set, CC, *00*		460
____ **18334**	NH MU Commuter Car Dummy Set, CC, *01*		180
____ **18337**	Reading MU Commuter Car Dummy Set, CC, *01*		200
____ **18343**	PRR GG1 Electric Locomotive "2332," CC, *01*		610
____ **18344**	LIRR MU Commuter Car Set, powered, CC, *01*		470
____ **18347**	IC MU Commuter Car Set, powered, CC, *01*		470
____ **18351**	NYC S1 Electric Locomotive, *03*		400
____ **18352**	JCPenney SP MU Commuter Car, display case, *02*		140
____ **18353**	Pennsylvania E33 Electric Locomotive "4403," CC, *02*		280
____ **18354**	PRR GG1 Electric Locomotive "4918," tuscan, CC, *04*		790
____ **18355**	PRR GG1 Electric Locomotive "4876," green, CC, *04*		900
18356	Penn Central GG1 Electric Locomotive "4901," CC, *04*		1050
____ **18364**	PRR BB1 Electric Locomotive "3900," CC, *05-07*		530
____ **18367**	LIRR BB3 Electric Locomotive "328 A," CC, *05*		530
____ **18371**	PRR GG1 Electric Locomotive "4912," tuscan, 5 stripes, CC, *05-07*		780
18372	PRR GG1 Electric Locomotive "4925," green, 1 stripe, CC, *05-07*		780
____ **18373**	NYC S2 Electric Locomotive "125," CC, *05-07*		410
18374	PRR GG1 Electric Locomotive "4866," silver, CC, *06-08*		900
____ **18375**	Lackawanna FM Train Master Diesel "850," CC, *06*		400
18376	Lackawanna FM Train Master Diesel "851," nonpowered (std O), *06*		130
____ **18378**	New York City R27 Subway Car 2-pack, *07*		360
____ **18384**	MILW EP-2 Electric Locomotive, CC, *07-08*		950
____ **18385**	NYC H-16-44 Diesel "7001," *07-09*		202
18386	NYC H-16-44 Diesel "7002," nonpowered (std O), *07-09*		123
____ **18389**	MILW EP-2 Electric Locomotive "E-1," CC, *07-08*		950
____ **18399**	NH EF-4 Rectifier Locomotive "306," CC, *09*		360
____ **18400**	Santa Fe Vulcan Rotary Snowplow, "8400," *87*	135	170
____ **18401**	Workmen HandCar, *87-88*	30	37
____ **18402**	Lionel Lines Burro Crane, *88*	65	80
____ **18403**	Santa Claus HandCar, *88*	26	29
____ **18404**	San Francisco Trolley, "8404," *88*	55	85
____ **18405**	Santa Fe Burro Crane, *89*	70	83
____ **18406**	Track Maintenance Car, *89, 91*	34	49
____ **18407**	Snoopy and Woodstock HandCar, *90-91*	89	103

	Exc	Mint
18408 Santa Claus HandCar, *89*	26	35____
18410 PRR Burro Crane, *90*	100	115____
18411 Canadian Pacific Fire Car, *90*	70	98____
18413 Charlie Brown and Lucy HandCar, *91*	40	68____
18416 Bugs Bunny and Daffy Duck HandCar, *92-93*	120	170____
18417 Section Gang Car, *93*	65	80____
18419 Lionelville Electric Trolley "8419," *94*	75	90____
18421 Sylvester and Tweety HandCar, *94*	44	50____
18422 Santa and Snowman HandCar, *94*	32	37____
18423 On-track Step Van, *95*	23	28____
18424 On-track Pickup Truck, *95*	20	25____
18425 Goofy and Pluto HandCar, *95*	40	55____
18426 Santa and Snowman HandCar, *95*	25	30____
18427 Tie-Jector Car "55," *97*		60____
18429 Workmen HandCar, *96*	28	34____
18430 Crew Car, *96*		28____
18431 Trolley Car, *96-97*		46____
18433 Mickey and Minnie HandCar, *96-97*	43	82____
18434 Porky and Petunia HandCar, *96*		35____
18436 Dodge Ram Track Inspection Vehicle, *97*		39____
18438 PRR High-rail Inspection Vehicle, *98*		50____
18439 Union Pacific High-rail Inspection Vehicle, *98*		42____
18440 NJ Transit High-rail Inspection Vehicle, *98*		50____
18444 Lionelville Fire Car (SSS), *98*		150____
18445 NYC Fire Car, *98*		90____
18446 Postwar "58," GN Rotary Snowplow, *99*		181____
18447 Executive Inspection Vehicle, *99*		125____
18452 Boston Trolley "3321," *99-00*		65____
18454 Executive Inspection Vehicle, blue, *00*		105____
18455 NYC Tie-Jector Car "X-2," *00-01*		74____
18456 Postwar "59" Minuteman Motorized Unit, *01-02*		290____
18457 Postwar "65" HandCar, *00-01*		45____
18458 Postwar "53" D&RGW Snowplow, *00*		160____
18459 Christmas HandCar, *01*		35____
18461 Track Cleaning Car, *02-03*		90____
18463 Hot Rod Inspection Vehicle, *01-02*		100____
18464 Postwar "54" Track Ballast Tamper, *02-03*		170____
18465 Postwar "50" Gang Car, *03*		78____
18466 UP Rotary Snow Plow, *01-02*		150____
18467 Train Robbery HandCar, *02*		45____
18468 CN Railroad Speeder, *03-04*		49____
18469 Chessie System Railroad Speeder, *03-04*		49____
18470 Postwar "52" Fire Car, *02*		105____
18471 UP GP20 Diesel "1977," *03*		105____
18473 Lehigh Valley GP38 Diesel "310," *03*		160____
18474 Postwar "41" U.S. Army Switcher, *03-04*		145____
18475 Toy Story HandCar, *03*		55____
18476 Mickey and Minnie Mouse HandCar, *03-04*		55____
18480 Hobo Motorized HandCar, *03-04*		35____
18481 Christmas Yuletide Trolley, *03*		50____
18482 New Haven Rail Bonder "16," *04*		35____
18483 C&O Ballast Tamper "48," *04*		55____
18484 NS Dodge Inspection Vehicle, *04-05*		55____

Exc Mint

		Exc	Mint
___ **18485** NYC Gang Car, *04-05*			100
___ **18486** Donald and Daisy Duck HandCar, *04-05*			63
___ **18487** Postwar "5" M&StL Mine Transport Car, *04-05*			230
___ **18489** Great Northern Rail Bonder "HR-73," *04*			35
___ **18490** UP Ballast Tamper, *04-05*			150
___ **18491** MOW Ballast Tamper "325," *04*			44
___ **18492** MOW Rail Bonder "58," *04*			35
___ **18493** Santa's Speeder, *05*			60
___ **18497** N&W Speeder "541005," traditional, *05*			65
___ **18498** New York Central Rotary Snowplow, *05*			210
___ **18500** Milwaukee Road GP9 Diesel "8500," (FF 2), *87*		175	230
___ **18501** WM NW2 Switcher "8501," (FF 4), *89*		185	215
___ **18502** LL 90th Anniversary GP9 Diesel "1900," *90*		148	173
___ **18503** Southern Pacific NW2 Switcher "8503," *90*		250	280
___ **18504** Frisco GP7 Diesel "504," (FF 5), *91*		155	240
___ **18505** NKP GP7 Diesel Set "400, 401," (FF 6)		295	365
___ **18506** CN Budd RDC Set, "D202, D203,"		210	261
___ **18507** CN Budd RDC Baggage Car "D202," powered, *92*		50	75
___ **18508** CN Budd RDC Passenger Dummy Unit "D203," *92*		125	150
___ **18510** CN Budd RDC Passenger Dummy Unit "D200"		50	75
___ **18511** CN Budd RDC Passenger Dummy Unit "D250"		50	75
___ **18512** CN Budd RDC Dummy Set, "D200, D250," *93*		125	195
___ **18513** NYC GP7 Diesel "7420," *94*		90	125
___ **18514** Missouri Pacific GP7 Diesel "4124," *95*		245	310
___ **18515** Lionel Steel Vulcan Diesel "57," (SSS), *96*			190
___ **18516** Phantom III Locomotive, CC, *02*			345
___ **18550** JCPenney MILW GP9 Diesel "8500," display case, *87 u*		180	245
___ **18551** JCPenney Susquehanna RS3 Diesel "8809," display case, *89 u*		180	195
___ **18552** JCPenney DM&IR SD18 Diesel "8813," display case, *90 u*		170	195
___ **18553** Sears UP GP9 Diesel "150," display case, *91 u*		100	150
___ **18554** JCPenney GM&O RS3 "721," display case, *92-93 u*		160	180
___ **18555** Sears C&IM SD9 Diesel "52," *92 u*		165	190
___ **18556** Sears Chicago & Illinois Midland Freight Car Set, *92 u*		110	120
___ **18557** Chessie System 4-8-4 Locomotive "2101," display case, export, *92 u*			NRS
___ **18558** JCPenney MKT GP9 Diesel "91," display case, *94 u*		160	180
___ **18562** SP GP9 Diesel "2380," *96*			195
___ **18563** NYC GP9 Diesel "2380," *96*			230
___ **18564** CP GP9 Diesel "2380," *97*			265
___ **18565** Milwaukee Road GP9 Diesel "2338," *97*			220
___ **18566** CR SD20 Diesel "8495," (SSS), *97*			150
___ **18567** PRR GP9 Diesel "2028," *97*			225
___ **18569** CB&Q GP9 Diesel "2380," *98*			190
___ **18573** Santa Fe GP9 Diesel "2380," *98*			155
___ **18574** Milwaukee Road GP20 Diesel "975," *98*			250
___ **18575** Custom Series I GP9 Diesel "2398," *98*			350
___ **18576** SP GP9 Diesel B Unit "2385," nonpowered, *98*			135
___ **18577** NYC GP9 Diesel B Unit "2385," nonpowered, *98*			145
___ **18579** MILW GP9 Diesel "2384," nonpowered, *99*			135
___ **18580** Pennsylvania GP9 Diesel B Unit "2027," *98*			165

		Exc	Mint
18582	Seaboard NW2 Switcher, *98*	250	455____
18583	AEC Switcher "57," *98*		211____
18585	Centennial SD40 Diesel, *99*		450____
18587	NKP Alco C420 Switcher "577," CC, *99-01*	215	255____
18588	D&H Alco C420 Switcher "412," CC, *99-01*	250	275____
18589	LV Alco C420 Switcher "409," CC, *99-01*	255	300____
18590	NKP Alco C420 Switcher "578," traditional, *99-01*		170____
18591	D&H Alco C420 Switche "411," traditional, *99-01*		215____
18592	LV Alco C420 Switcher "410," traditional, *99-01*		175____
18596	D&H Alco RS-11 Switcher "5001," CC, *99-01*		370____
18598	NYC Alco RS-11 Switcher "8010," CC, *99-01*		380____
18599	C&O GP38 Diesel "3855," *99-00*		145____
18600	ACL 4-4-2 Locomotive "8600," *87 u*	65	75____
18601	Great Northern 4-4-2 Locomotive "8601," *88*	80	95____
18602	PRR 4-4-2 Locomotive "8602," *87*	75	85____
18604	Wabash 4-4-2 Locomotive, "8604," *88-91*	65	75____
18605	Mopar Express 4-4-2 Locomotive "1987," *87-88 u*	75	120____
18606	NYC 2-6-4 Locomotive "8606," *89*	170	190____
18607	Union Pacific 2-6-4 Locomotive "8607," *89*	130	155____
18608	D&RGW 2-6-4 Locomotive "8608," (SSS), *89*	90	105____
18609	Northern Pacific 2-6-4 Locomotive "8609," *90*	170	195____
18610	Rock Island 0-4-0 Locomotive "8610," *90*	105	115____
18611	Lionel Lines 2-6-4 Locomotive (SSS), *90*	125	140____
18612	C&NW 4-4-2 Locomotive "8612," *89*	75	100____
18613	NYC 4-4-2 Locomotive "8613," *89 u*	75	95____
18614	Circus Train 4-4-2 Locomotive "1989," *89 u*	95	125____
18615	GTW 4-4-2 Locomotive "8615," *90*	70	85____
18616	Northern Pacific 4-4-2 Locomotive "8616," *90 u*	85	110____
18617	Adolphus III 4-4-2 Locomotive, *89-92 u*	100	125____
18620	Illinois Central 2-6-2 Locomotive "8620," *91*	165	190____
18622	Union Pacific 4-4-2 Locomotive "8622," *90-91 u*	65	80____
18623	Texas & Pacific 4-4-2 Locomotive "8623," *92*	80	110____
18625	Illinois Central 4-4-2 Locomotive "8625," *91 u*	70	95____
18626	Delaware & Hudson 2-6-2 Locomotive "8626," *92*	105	115____
18627	C&O 4-4-2 Locomotive "8627" or "8633," *92, 93 u, 94, 95 u*	75	95 ____
18628	MKT 4-4-2 Locomotive "8628," *92, 93 u*	70	85____
18630	C&NW 4-6-2 Locomotive "2903," *93*	325	370____
18632	NYC 4-4-2 Locomotive "8632," *93-95*	75	95____
18632	C&O Columbia 4-4-2 Locomotive "8632," *97-99*	75	95____
18633	C&O 4-4-2 Locomotive "8633," *94-95*	65	85____
18633	UP 4-4-2 Locomotive "8633," *93-95*	65	85____
18635	Santa Fe 2-6-4 Locomotive "8625," *93*	135	155____
18636	B&O 4-6-2 Locomotive "5300," *94*	295	315____
18637	United Auto Workers 4-4-2 Locomotive "8633," *93 u*		90____
18638	Norfolk & Western 2-6-4 Locomotive "638," *94*	170	220____
18639	Reading 4-6-2 Locomotive "639," *95*	145	170____
18640	Union Pacific 4-6-2 Locomotive "8640," *95*	110	130____
18641	Ford 4-4-2 Locomotive "8641," *94 u*	65	85____
18642	Lionel Lines 4-6-2 Locomotive, *95*	110	130____
18644	ATSF 4-4-2 Columbia Locomotive "8644," *96-99*	75	90____
18648	Sears Zenith 4-4-2 Locomotive "8632," *96 u*		140____
18649	Chevrolet 4-4-2 Locomotive "USA-1," *96 u*		150____
18650	LL 4-4-2 Columbia Locomotive "X-1110," *96-99*	95	120____

		Exc	Mint
____	**18653** B&A 4-6-2 Pacific Locomotive "2044," *97*		140
____	**18654** SP 4-6-2 Pacific Locomotive "2044," *97*		140
____	**18656** Bloomingdale's 4-4-2 Columbia Locomotive "8632," *96*		112
____	**18657** Sears Zenith 4-4-2 Columbia Locomotive "8632," *96*		120
____	**18658** LL Little League 4-4-2 Columbia Locomotive "X-1110," *97*		90
____	**18660** CN 4-6-2 Locomotive "2044," tender, *98*		175
____	**18661** N&W 4-6-2 Locomotive "2044," tender, *98*		160
____	**18662** Pennsylvania 0-4-0 Switcher, *98*	165	230
____	**18666** SP&S 4-6-2 Pacific Locomotive "2044," *97*		200
____	**18668** Bloomingdale's 4-4-2 Columbia Locomotive "8632," *97*		130
____	**18669** JCPenney IC 4-6-2 Pacific Locomotive "2099," *98*		205
____	**18670** D&H Columbia 4-4-2 Locomotive "1400," *98*		80
____	**18671** N&W Columbia 4-4-2 Locomotive "1201," *98*		70
____	**18678** Quaker Oats Columbia 4-4-2 Locomotive "8632," *98*		162
____	**18679** JCPenney T&P 4-6-2 Locomotive "2000," traditional, *99, 00 u*		250
____	**18681** PRR 4-4-2 Locomotive "460," *99*		75
____	**18682** Santa Fe 4-4-2 Columbia Locomotive "524," traditional, *00-01*		70
____	**18696** ACL 4-6-4 Locomotive "1800," *01*		120
____	**18697** Santa Fe 4-6-4 Locomotive "3465," *01*		100
____	**18699** Alaska 4-4-2 Locomotive "64," *01*		105
____	**18700** Rock Island 0-4-0T Locomotive "8700," *87-88*	36	43
____	**18701** Polar Express LionScale 3-Bay Covered Hopper, *18*		65
____	**18702** V&TRR 4-4-0 Locomotive "8702," (SSS), *88*	160	195
____	**18703** Merry Christmas LionScale 3-Bay Covered Hopper, *18*		60
____	**18704** Lionel Lines 2-4-0 Locomotive, *89 u*	36	43
____	**18704** Halloween ELX 3-Bay Hopper, LionScale, *18*		65
____	**18705** Neptune 0-4-0T Locomotive "8705," *90-91*	35	42
____	**18706** Santa Fe 2-4-0 Locomotive "8706," *91*	36	43
____	**18707** Mickey's World Tour 2-4-0 Locomotive "8707," *91, 92 u*	58	68
____	**18709** Lionel Employee Learning Center 0-4-0T Locomotive, *92 u*		140
____	**18710** SP 2-4-0 Locomotive "2000," *93*	30	38
____	**18711** Southern 2-4-0 Locomotive "2000," *93*	30	38
____	**18712** Jersey Central 2-4-0 Locomotive "2000," *93*	30	38
____	**18713** Chessie System 2-4-0 Locomotive "1993," *94-95*	30	38
____	**18716** Lionelville Circus 4-4-0 Locomotive, *90-91*	90	110
____	**18718** LL 0-4-0 Dockside Switcher "8200," *97-98*		40
____	**18719** Thomas the Tank Engine "1," *97*		158
____	**18720** Union 4-4-0 General Locomotive "1865," *99*		175
____	**18721** Confederate 4-4-0 General Locomotive "1861," *99*		175
____	**18722** Percy the Tank Engine "6," *99*		170
____	**18723** Union Pacific 4-4-0 General Locomotive, *05*		100
____	**18730** Transylvania RR 4-4-0 Locomotive "13," traditional, *05*		105
____	**18732** North Pole Central 4-4-0 Locomotive "25," *06*		110
____	**18733** Percy the Tank Engine "6," *05-12*		120
____	**18734** James the Tank Engine "5," *06-12*		120
____	**18741** Thomas the Tank Engine, *08-13*		120

Exc Mint

		Exc	Mint
18745 Hallow's Eve 4-6-0 Steam Locomotive, *11-12*			190____
18753 Route of the Reindeer RS3 Diesel, *11*			190____
18754 Polar Express 2-8-4 Berkshire Steam Locomotive, *11, 13*			300 ____
18755 C&O Berkshire Steam Locomotive "2751," TrainSounds, *11*			290 ____
18771 Percy, remote system, *13-16*			140____
18774 James, remote system, *13-16*			140____
18775 Diesel, remote system, *13-16*			140____
18799 Bethlehem Steel Switcher "44," *99*			100____
18800 Lehigh Valley GP9 Diesel "8800," *87*		80	95____
18801 Santa Fe U36B Diesel "8801," *87*		100	120____
18802 Southern GP9 Diesel "8802," (SSS), *87*		100	115____
18803 Santa Fe RS3 Diesel "8803," *88*		90	105____
18804 Soo Line RS3 Diesel "8804," *88*		95	115____
18805 Union Pacific RS3 Diesel "8805," *89*		100	125____
18806 New Haven SD18 Diesel "8806," *89*		100	115____
18807 Lehigh Valley RS3 Diesel "8807," *90*		90	120____
18808 ACL SD18 Diesel "8808," *90*		85	105____
18809 Susquehanna RS3 Diesel "8809," *89 u*			130____
18810 CSX SD18 Diesel "8810," *90*		95	130____
18811 Alaska SD9 Diesel "8811," *91*		95	135____
18812 Kansas City Southern GP38 Diesel "4000," *91*		120	140____
18813 DM&IR SD18 Diesel "8813," *90 u*		90	145____
18814 D&H RS3 Diesel "8814," (SSS), *91*		90	120____
18815 Amtrak RS3 Diesel "1815," *91, 92 u*		100	130____
18816 C&NW GP38-2 Diesel "4600," *92*		105	130____
18817 UP GP9 Diesel "150," (see 18553), *91 u*			135____
18819 L&N GP38-2 Diesel "4136," *92*		115	145____
18820 WP GP9 Diesel "8820," (SSS), *92*		120	140____
18821 Clinchfield GP38-2 Diesel "6005," *93*		125	150____
18822 Gulf, Mobile & Ohio RS3 Diesel "721," *92-93 u*			NRS____
18823 Chicago & Illinois Midland SD9 Diesel "52," *92 u*			235____
18824 Montana Rail Link SD9 Diesel "600," *93*		185	230____
18825 Soo Line GP38-2 Diesel "4000," (SSS), *93*		120	145____
18826 Conrail GP7 Diesel "5808," *93*		100	120____
18827 "Happy Holidays" RS3 Diesel "8827," *93*		165	220____
18830 Budweiser GP9 Diesel "1947," *93-94 u*		120	160____
18831 SP GP20 Diesel "4060," *94*		105	120____
18832 PRR RSD-4 Diesel "8446," *95*		110	135____
18833 Milwaukee Road RS3 Diesel "2487," *94*		100	110____
18834 C&O SD28 Diesel "8834," *94*		110	140____
18835 NYC RS3 Diesel "8223," (SSS), *94*		135	195____
18836 CN (Grand Trunk) GP38-2 Diesel "5800," *94*		135	160____
18837 "Happy Holidays" RS3 Diesel "8837," *94-95*		150	190____
18838 Seaboard RSC-3 Diesel "1538," *95*		110	140____
18840 U.S. Army GP7 Diesel "1821," *95*		85	124____
18841 Western Maryland GP20 Diesel "27," (SSS), *95*		120	150____
18842 JCPenney B&LE SD38 Diesel "868," *95 u*			265____
18843 Great Northern RS3 Diesel "197," *96*			145____
18845 D&RGW RS3 Diesel "5204," *97*			100____
18846 Lionel Centennial Series GP9 Diesel, *98*			415____
18847 Santa Fe H-12-44 Switcher "602," *99*			385____
18848 PRR H-12-44 Switcher "9087," *99*			420____

		Exc	Mint
____ **18853** JCPenney Santa Fe GP9 Diesel "2370," *97 u*			150
____ **18854** UP GP9 Diesel Dummy Set, "2380, 2387," *97*			450
____ **18856** NJ Transit GP38-2 Diesel "4303," *99*			315
____ **18857** Union Pacific GP9 Diesel "2397," *97*			240
____ **18858** Lionel Centennial GP20 Diesel, *98*			450
____ **18859** Phantom II, *99*			360
____ **18860** Pratt's Hollow Collection I: Phantom, *98*			400
____ **18864** Southern Pacific GP9 Diesel B Unit, *98*			140
____ **18865** New York Central GP9 Diesel B Unit, *98*			170
____ **18934/35** Reading Alco Diesel AA Set, *95*		75	95
____ **18866** Milwaukee Road GP7 Diesel "2383," *98*			205
____ **18868** NJ Transit GP38-2 Diesel "4300," *98 u*			140
____ **18870** Pennsylvania GP9 Diesel "2029," *98*			180
____ **18872** Wabash GP7 Diesel Set, "453, 454, 455," *99*			560
____ **18876** C&NW H-12-44 Switcher "1053," *99*		125	319
____ **18877** Union Pacific GP9 Diesel "2399," nonpowered, *99*			175
____ **18878** Alaska GP7 Diesel "1803," *99*			115
____ **18879** B&O GP9 Diesel "5616," *99*			260
____ **18881** Custom GP9 Diesel "5616," *99*			350
____ **18892** Burlington GP9 Diesel "2328," *99*			205
____ **18897** Christmas GP7 Diesel "1999," *99*			200
____ **18900** PRR Switcher "8900," *88 u, 89*		26	34
____ **18901/02** PRR Alco Diesel AA Set, *88*		110	130
____ **18903** Amtrak, "Mopar Express," *99*			500
____ **18903/04** Amtrak Alco Diesel AA Set, *88-89*		90	130
____ **18905** PRR 44-ton Switcher "9312," *92*		80	116
____ **18906** Erie-Lackawanna RS3 Diesel "8906," *91 u*		70	90
____ **18907** Rock Island 44-ton Switcher "371," *93*		95	110
____ **18908/09** NYC Alco Diesel AA Set, *93*		105	115
____ **18910** CSX Switcher "8910," *93*		40	46
____ **18911** UP Switcher "8911," *93*		33	37
____ **18912** Amtrak Switcher "8912," *93*		37	43
____ **18913** Santa Fe Alco Diesel A Unit "8913," *93-94*		55	65
____ **18915** WM Alco Diesel A Unit "8915," *93*		65	80
____ **18916** WM Alco Diesel A Unit "8916," dummy, *93*		38	42
____ **18917** Soo Line NW2 Switcher, *93*		65	75
____ **18918** B&M NW2 Switcher "8918," *93*		75	90
____ **18919** Santa Fe Alco Diesel A Unit "8919," dummy, *93-94*		36	55
____ **18920** Frisco NW2 Switcher "254," *94*		70	75
____ **18921** C&NW NW2 Switcher "1017," *94*		60	80
____ **18922** New Haven Alco Diesel A Unit "8922," *94*		75	105
____ **18923** New Haven Alco Diesel A Unit "8923," dummy, *94*		50	55
____ **18924** IC Switcher "8924," *94-95*		37	44
____ **18925** D&RGW Switcher "8925," *94-95*		32	37
____ **18926** Reading Switcher "8926," *94-95*		31	39
____ **18927** U.S. Navy NW2 Switcher "65-00637," *94-95*		65	85
____ **18928** C&NW NW2 Switcher Calf Unit, *95*		50	55
____ **18929** B&M NW2 Switcher Calf Unit, *95*		44	49
____ **18930** Crayola Switcher, *94 u, 95*		27	30
____ **18931** Chrysler Mopar NW2 Switcher "1818," *94 u*		76	88
____ **18932** Jersey Central NW2 Switcher "8932," *96*			65
____ **18933** Jersey Central NW2 Switcher Calf Unit "8933," *96*			55
____ **18936** Amtrak Alco Diesel A Unit "8936," *95*			65

		Exc	Mint
18937	Amtrak FA2 Alco Diesel, nonpowered, *95-97*		50____
18938	U.S. Navy NW2 Switcher Calf Unit, *95*	55	65____
18939	Union Pacific NW2 Switcher Set, *96*		145____
18943	Georgia Power NW2 Switcher "1960," *95 u*		170____
18946	U.S. Coast Guard NW2 Switcher "8946," *96*		80____
18947	Port of Lionel City Alco FA2 Diesel "2030," *97*		70____
18948	Port of Lionel City Alco FB2 Diesel "2030B," *97*		45____
18952	ATSF Alco PA1 Diesel "2000," *97*		345____
18953	NYC Alco PA1 Diesel "2000," *97*		260____
18954	ATSF Alco FA2 Diesel "212," powered, *97-99*		80____
18955	NJ Transit NW2 Switcher "500," *96 u*		110____
18956	Dodge Motorsports NW2 Switcher "8956," *96 u*		172____
18959	New York Central NW2 Switcher "622," *97*		475____
18961	Erie Alco PA1 Diesel "850," *98*		315____
18965	Santa Fe Alco PB1 Diesel, *98*		255____
18966	New York Central Alco BP1 Diesel "2008," *98*		250____
18971	Alco Diesel A Unit, nonpowered, *98*		60____
18973	RI Alco FA2 Diesel "2031," powered, *98-99*		NRS____
18974	RI Alco FA2 Diesel Dummy Unit, *98-99*		NRS____
18975	Southern 44-ton Switcher "1955," *99*		190____
18978	C&O NW2 Switcher "624," *99-00*		410____
18981	Pennsylvania Railroad Speeder "16," *04*		45____
18982	Santa Fe Railroad Speeder "122," *04-05*		65____
18988	MP15 Diesel, K-Line, *06*		140____
18989	Bethlehem Steel Plymouth Switcher, traditional, K-Line, *06*		100 ____
18992	SP S2 Diesel Switcher "1440," CC, *08*		410____
18993	C&NW S2 Diesel Switcher "1031," CC, *08*		410____
18994	Lionel Lines FA Diesel, traditional, *08-09*		90____
19000	Blue Comet Diner, *87 u*	60	75____
19001	Southern Diner, *87 u*	55	65____
19002	Pennsylvania Diner, *88 u*	29	41____
19003	Milwaukee Road Diner, *88 u*	29	44____
19010	B&O Diner, *89 u*	36	55____
19011	Lionel Lines Baggage Car, *93*	184	299____
19015	Lionel Lines Passenger Coach, *91*	125	180____
19016	Lionel Lines Passenger Coach, *91*	100	135____
19017	Lionel Lines Passenger Coach, *91*	85	110____
19018	Lionel Lines Observation Car, *91*	95	120____
19019	SP Baggage Car "9019," *93*	120	153____
19023	SP Passenger Coach "9023," *92*	125	160____
19024	SP Passenger Coach "9024," *92*	85	100____
19025	SP Passenger Coach "9025," *92*	100	115____
19026	SP Observation Car "9026," *92*	85	100____
19038	Adolphus Busch Observation Car, *92-93 u*		85____
19039	Pere Marquette Baggage Car, *93*		75____
19040	Pere Marquette Passenger Coach "1115," *93*		75____
19041	Pere Marquette Passenger Coach "1116," *93*		75____
19042	Pere Marquette Observation Car "36," *93*		75____
19047	Baltimore & Ohio Combination Car "9047," *96*		55____
19048	Baltimore & Ohio Passenger Coach "9048," *96*		50____
19049	Baltimore & Ohio Diner "9049," *96*		42____
19050	Baltimore & Ohio Observation Car "9050," *96*		42____
19056	NYC Heavyweight Baggage Car, *96*		105____

		Exc	Mint
___	**19057** NYC Willow Run Heavyweight Coach, *96*		95
___	**19058** NYC Willow Trail Heavyweight Coach, *96*		90
___	**19059** NYC Seneca Valley Heavyweight Observation Car, *96*		100
	19060 Pullman Heavyweight Set, *96*		473
	19061 Wabash Passenger Set, *97*		235
	19062 Wabash City of Columbia Coach "2361," *97*		90
	19063 Wabash City of Danville Coach "2362," *97*		75
	19064 Wabash REA Baggage Car "2360," *97*		47
	19065 Wabash Windy City Observation Car "2363," *97*		90
___	**19066** Commodore Vanderbilt Pullman Heavyweight 2-pack, *97*		190
___	**19067** Commodore Vanderbilt Willow River Pullman,"2543," *97*		115
___	**19068** Commodore Vanderbilt Willow Valley Pullman,"2544," *97*		100
___	**19069** Pullman Baby Madison Set "9500-02," *97*		155
___	**19070** Baby Madison Combination Car "9501," *97*		40
___	**19071** Laurel Gap Baby Madison Coach "9500," *97*		34
___	**19072** Laurel Summit Baby Madison Coach "9500," *97*		40
___	**19073** Catskill Valley Baby Madison Observation Car "9502," *97*		34
___	**19074** Legends of Lionel Madison Set, *97*		385
___	**19075** Mazzone Lionel Legends Coach "2621," *97*		105
___	**19076** Caruso Lionel Legends Coach "2624," *97*		90
___	**19077** Raphael Lionel Legends Coach "2652," *97*		90
___	**19078** Cowen Lionel Legends Observation Car "2600," *97*		95
___	**19079** NYC Heavyweight Passenger Car Set, *97*		275
___	**19080** NYC Heavyweight REA Baggage Car "2564," *97*		100
___	**19081** NYC Park Place Heavyweight Coach "2565," *97*		100
___	**19082** NYC Star Beam Heavyweight Coach "2566," *97*		100
___	**19083** NYC Hudson Valley Heavyweight Observation Car "2567," *97*		100
___	**19087** C&O Heavyweight Passenger Car 4-pack, "2571-74," *97*		290
___	**19088** C&O Heavyweight Baggage Car "2571," *97*		100
___	**19089** C&O Heavyweight Sleeper Car "2572," *97*		100
___	**19090** C&O Heavyweight Diner "2573," *97*		110
___	**19091** C&O Heavyweight Observation Car "2574," *97*		100
___	**19093** Commodore Vanderbilt Heavyweight Sleeper Car 2-pack, *98*		170
___	**19094** Commodore Vanderbilt Niagara Falls Sleeper, *98*		75
___	**19095** Commodore Vanderbilt Highland Falls Sleeper, *98*		75
___	**19096** Legends of Lionel Madison Car 2-pack, *98*		130
___	**19097** Bonnano Lionel Legends Coach "2653," *98*		80
___	**19098** Pagano Lionel Legends Coach "2654," *98*		105
___	**19099** PRR Liberty Gap Baggage Car "2623," *99*		80
___	**19100** Amtrak Baggage Car "9100," *89*	125	165
___	**19101** Amtrak Combination Car "9101," *89*	75	85
___	**19102** Amtrak Passenger Coach "9102," *89*	75	85
___	**19103** Amtrak Vista Dome Car "9103," *89*	70	90
___	**19104** Amtrak Diner "9104," *89*	65	80
___	**19105** Amtrak Full Vista Dome Car "9105," *89 u*	70	90
___	**19106** Amtrak Observation Car "9106," *89*	75	90
___	**19107** SP Full Vista Dome Car, *90 u*	70	88
___	**19108** N&W Full Vista Dome Car "576," *91 u*	75	85

No.	Description	Exc	Mint
19109	Santa Fe Baggage Car "3400," *91*	225	300____
19110	Santa Fe Combination Car "3500," *91*	80	110____
19111	Santa Fe Diner "601," *91*	100	135____
19112	Santa Fe Passenger Coach, *91*	125	175____
19113	Santa Fe Vista Dome Car, *91*	100	135____
19116	Great Northern Baggage Car "1200," *92*	135	165____
19117	Great Northern Combination Car "1240," *92*	65	80____
19118	Great Northern Passenger Coach "1212," *92*	75	95____
19119	Great Northern Vista Dome Car "1322," *92*	75	95____
19120	Great Northern Observation Car "1192," *92*	75	95____
19121	Union Pacific Vista Dome Car "9121," *92 u*	90	100____
19122	D&RGW California Zephyr Baggage Car, *93*	170	210____
19123	D&RGW California Zephyr Silver Bronco Vista Dome Car, *93*	95	115 ____
19124	D&RGW California Zephyr Silver Colt Vista Dome Car, *93*	95	115 ____
19125	D&RGW California Zephyr Silver Mustang Vista Dome Car, *93*	100	125 ____
19126	D&RGW California Zephyr Silver Pony Vista Dome Car, *93*	95	115 ____
19127	D&RGW California Zephyr Vista Dome Car, *93*	85	100____
19128	Santa Fe Full Vista Dome Car "507," *92 u*	175	185____
19129	IC Full Vista Dome Car "9129," *93*	75	85____
19130	Lackawanna Passenger Cars, set of 4, *94*	280	350____
19131	Lackawanna Baggage Car "2000," (see 19130)		150____
19132	Lackawanna Diner "469," (see 19130)		100____
19133	Lackawanna Passenger Coach "260," (see 19130)		100____
19134	Lackawanna Observation Car "789," (see 19130)		85____
19135	Lackawanna Combination Car "425," *94*	85	100____
19136	Lackawanna Passenger Coach "211," *94*	65	75____
19137	New York Central Roomette Car, *95*	90	105____
19138	Santa Fe Roomette Car, *95*	75	95____
19139	N&W Baggage Car "577," *95*	150	200____
19140	N&W Combination Car "494," *95*	60	80____
19141	N&W Diner "495," *95*	105	135____
19142	N&W Passenger Coach "538," *95*	75	95____
19143	N&W Passenger Coach "537," *95*	75	95____
19144	N&W Observation Car "582," *95*	80	95____
19145	C&O Combination Car "1403," *96*		65____
19146	C&O Passenger Coach "1623," *96*		60____
19147	C&O Passenger Coach "1803," *96*		55____
19148	C&O Chessie Club Coach "1903," *96*		55____
19149	C&O Coach/Diner "1950," *96*		50____
19150	C&O Observation Car "2504," *96*		55____
19151	Norfolk & Western Duplex Roomette Car, *96*		108____
19152	Union Pacific Duplex Roomette Car, *96*		75____
19153	C&O Passenger Cars, set of 4, *96*		340____
19154	Atlantic Coast Line Passenger Car Set, *96*		340____
19155	ACL Combination Car "101," *96*		90____
19156	ACL Talladega Diner, *96*		90____
19157	ACL Moultrie Coach, *96*		95____
19158	ACL Observation Car "256," *96*		90____
19159	N&W Passenger Cars, set of 4, *95 u*	300	385____
19160	LL REA Baggage Car, *96*		90____

		Exc	Mint
____	**19161** LL Silver Mesa Coach, *96*		80
____	**19162** LL Silver Sky Vista Dome Car, *96*		75
____	**19163** LL Silver Rail Observation Car, *96*		75
____	**19164** Chesapeake & Ohio Passenger Cars, *96*		160
____	**19165** ATSF Super Chief Set, *96*		305
____	**19166** NP Vista Dome Car Set, *97*		305
____	**19167** NP Pullman Coach "2571," *97*		105
____	**19168** NP Pullman Coach "2571," *97*		105
____	**19169** NP Pullman Coach "2570," *97*		95
____	**19170** NP Pullman Coach "2571," *97*		100
____	**19171** NYC Streamliner Car 4-pack, *97*		285
____	**19172** NYC Aluminum Passenger/Baggage Car "2570," *97*		95
____	**19173** NYC Manhattan Island Aluminum Passenger Diner, *97*		100
____	**19174** NYC Queensboro Bridge Aluminum Passenger Coach, *97*		100
____	**19175** NYC Windgate Brook Aluminum Observation Car, *97*		90
____	**19176** ATSF Indian Arrow Diner "2572," *97*		90
____	**19177** ATSF Grass Valley Coach "2573," *97*		90
____	**19178** ATSF Citrus Valley Coach "2574," *97*		90
____	**19179** ATSF Vista Heights Coach "2575," *97*		90
____	**19180** ATSF Surfliner Passenger Car 4-pack, *97*		250
____	**19181** GN Empire Builder Prairie View Full Vista Dome Car, *98*		75
____	**19182** GN Empire Builder River View Full Vista Dome Car, *98*		75
____	**19183** GN Empire Builder Vista Dome Car 2-pack, *98*		125
____	**19184** Milwaukee Road Passenger Car 4-pack, *99*		390
____	**19185** MILW Red River Valley Aluminum Passenger Coach "194," *99*		125
____	**19186** MILW Aluminum Coach/Diner "170," *99*		110
____	**19187** MILW Cedar Rapids Aluminum Observation Car "186," *99*		120
____	**19188** MILW Aluminum REA Passenger/Baggage Car "1336," *99*		95
____	**19194** KCS Aluminum Passenger Car 4-pack, *00*		380
____	**19200** Tidewater Southern BoxCar, *87*	14	21
____	**19201** Lancaster & Chester BoxCar, *87*	23	37
____	**19202** PRR BoxCar, *87*	22	30
____	**19203** D&TS BoxCar, *87*	11	18
____	**19204** Milwaukee Road Boxcar (FF 2), *87*	29	41
____	**19205** Great Northern DD Boxcar (FF 3), *88*	20	24
____	**19206** Seaboard System BoxCar, *88*	18	23
____	**19207** CP Rail DD BoxCar, *88*	17	22
____	**19208** Southern DD BoxCar, *88*	11	13
____	**19209** Florida East Coast BoxCar, *88*	15	19
____	**19210** Soo Line BoxCar, *89*	19	23
____	**19211** Vermont Railway BoxCar, *89*	18	21
____	**19212** PRR BoxCar, *89*	21	25
____	**19213** SP&S DD BoxCar, *89*	16	19
____	**19214** Western Maryland Boxcar (FF 4), *89*	23	27
____	**19215** Union Pacific DD BoxCar, *90*	17	21
____	**19216** Santa Fe BoxCar, *90*	17	22
____	**19217** Burlington BoxCar, *90*	16	21
____	**19218** New Haven BoxCar, *90*	16	20

		Exc	Mint
19219	Lionel Lines 1900-1906 BoxCar, diesel RailSounds, *90*	120	145 ___
19220	Lionel Lines 1926-1934 BoxCar, *90*	27	30 ___
19221	Lionel Lines 1935-1937 BoxCar, *90*	27	30 ___
19222	Lionel Lines 1948-1950 BoxCar, *90*	27	30 ___
19223	Lionel Lines 1979-1989 BoxCar, *90*	18	25 ___
19228	Cotton Belt BoxCar, *91*	16	22 ___
19229	Frisco BoxCar, diesel RailSounds (FF 5), *91*	75	90 ___
19230	Frisco DD Boxcar (FF 5), *91*	21	26 ___
19231	TA&G DD BoxCar, *91*	13	16 ___
19232	Rock Island DD BoxCar, *91*	17	20 ___
19233	Southern Pacific BoxCar, *91*	15	19 ___
19234	NYC BoxCar, *91*	60	65 ___
19235	MKT BoxCar, *91*	55	65 ___
19236	NKP DD Boxcar (FF 6), *92*	22	30 ___
19237	C&IM BoxCar, *92*	17	24 ___
19238	Kansas City Southern BoxCar, *92*	18	23 ___
19239	Toronto, Hamilton & Buffalo DD BoxCar, *92*	15	20 ___
19240	Great Northern DD BoxCar, *92*	15	20 ___
19241	Mickey Mouse 60th Anniversary Hi-Cube BoxCar, *91 u*	135	180 ___
19242	Donald Duck 50th Anniversary Hi-Cube BoxCar, *91 u*	135	145 ___
19243	Clinchfield Boxcar "9790," *91 u*	35	41 ___
19244	L&N World Tour Hi-Cube BoxCar "9791," *92*	35	38 ___
19245	Mickey's World Tour Hi-Cube BoxCar, *92 u*	35	40 ___
19246	Disney World 20th Anniversary Hi-Cube BoxCar, *92 u*	33	40 ___
19247	Postwar "6464," Series Boxcar Set I, 3 cars, *93*	445	610 ___
19248	Western Pacific Boxcar "6464," *93*	75	95 ___
19249	Great Northern Boxcar "6464," *93*	75	95 ___
19250	M&StL Boxcar "6464," *93*	80	105 ___
19251	Montana Rail Link DD Boxcar "10001," *93*	21	27 ___
19254	Erie Boxcar (FF 7), *93*	21	25 ___
19255	Erie DD Boxcar (FF 7), *93*	22	26 ___
19256	Goofy Hi-Cube BoxCar, *93*	23	26 ___
19257	Postwar "6464" Series Boxcar Set II, 3 cars, *94*	80	97 ___
19258	Rock Island Boxcar "6464," *94*	25	34 ___
19259	Western Pacific Boxcar "6464100," *94*	33	46 ___
19260	Western Pacific Boxcar "6464100," *94*	35	49 ___
19261	Perils of Mickey Hi-Cube Boxcar #1, *93*	20	30 ___
19262	Perils of Mickey Hi-Cube Boxcar #2, *93*	20	28 ___
19263	NYC DD Boxcar (SSS), *94*	36	42 ___
19264	Perils of Mickey Hi-Cube Boxcar #3, *94*	28	31 ___
19265	Mickey Mouse 65th Anniversary Hi-Cube BoxCar, *94*	22	44 ___
19266	Postwar "6464" Series Boxcar Set III, 3 cars, *95*	75	90 ___
19267	NYC Pacemaker Boxcar "6464125," *95*	37	42 ___
19268	Missouri Pacific Boxcar "6464150," *95*	25	29 ___
19269	Rock Island Boxcar "6464," *95*	25	26 ___
19270	Donald Duck 60th Anniversary Hi-Cube BoxCar, *95*	30	34 ___
19271	Minnie Mouse Hi-Cube BoxCar, *95*	21	43 ___
19272	Postwar "6464" Series Boxcar Set IV, 3 cars, *96*	70	85 ___
19273	BAR State of Maine Boxcar "6464275," *96*		35 ___
19274	SP Overnight Boxcar "6464225," *96*		28 ___
19275	Pennsylvania Boxcar "6464," *96*		44 ___
19276	Postwar "6464" Series Boxcar Set V, 3 cars, *96*	65	85 ___

		Exc	Mint
____ **19277**	Rutland Boxcar "6464-300," *96*		26
____ **19278**	B&O Boxcar "6464-325," *96*		30
____ **19279**	Central of Georgia Boxcar "6464-375," *96*		29
____ **19280**	Mickey's Wheat Hi-Cube BoxCar, *96*		32
____ **19281**	Mickey's Carrots Hi-Cube BoxCar, *96*		40
____ **19282**	Santa Fe "Super Chief" BoxCar "6464-196," *96*		24
____ **19283**	Erie Boxcar "6464-296," *96*		22
____ **19284**	Northern Pacific Boxcar "6464-396," *96*		29
____ **19285**	B&A State of Maine Boxcar "6464-275," *96*		27
____ **19286**	Tweety and Sylvester BoxCar, *96*		46
____ **19287**	NYC/PC Merger Boxcar "6464-125X," (SSS), *97*	50	75
____ **19288**	PRR/CR Merger Boxcar "6464-200X," (SSS), *97*	43	56
____ **19289**	Monon "Hoosier Line" Boxcar "6464," *97*		27
____ **19290**	Seaboard "Silver Meteor" Boxcar "6464," *97*		24
____ **19291**	GN Boxcar "6464-397," *97*		26
____ **19292**	Postwar "6464" Series Boxcar Set VI, 3 cars, *97*		90
____ **19293**	MKT Boxcar "6464-350," *97*	28	32
____ **19294**	B&O Boxcar "6464-400," *97*	27	34
____ **19295**	NH Boxcar "6464-425," *97*	25	34
____ **19300**	PRR Ore Car, *87*	15	23
____ **19301**	Milwaukee Road Ore Car, *87*	20	25
____ **19302**	Milwaukee Road Quad Hopper with coal (FF 2), *87*	24	35
____ **19303**	Lionel Lines Quad Hopper with coal, *87 u*	20	31
____ **19304**	GN Covered Quad Hopper (FF 3), *88*	18	25
____ **19305**	Chessie System Ore Car, *88*	18	23
____ **19307**	B&LE Ore Car with load, *89*	19	25
____ **19308**	GN Ore Car with load, *89*	18	23
____ **19309**	Seaboard Covered Quad Hopper, *89*	16	19
____ **19310**	L&C Quad Hopper with coal, *89*	16	30
____ **19311**	SP Covered Quad Hopper, *90*	13	19
____ **19312**	Reading Quad Hopper with coal, *90*	21	36
____ **19313**	B&O Ore Car with load, *90-91*	20	25
____ **19315**	Amtrak Ore Car with load, *91*	22	30
____ **19316**	Wabash Covered Quad Hopper, *91*	18	23
____ **19317**	Lehigh Valley Quad Hopper with coal, *91*	47	55
____ **19318**	NKP Quad Hopper with coal (FF 6), *92*	30	34
____ **19319**	Union Pacific Covered Quad Hopper, *92*	19	23
____ **19320**	PRR Ore Car with load, *92*	21	30
____ **19321**	B&LE Ore Car with load, *92*	21	30
____ **19322**	C&NW Ore Car with load, *93*	27	34
____ **19323**	Detroit & Mackinac Ore Car with load, *93*	20	29
____ **19324**	Erie Quad Hopper with coal (FF 7), *93*	25	33
____ **19325**	N&W 4-bay Hopper "6446-1" with coal, *97*		65
____ **19326**	N&W 4-bay Hopper "6446-2" with coal, *96*		60
____ **19327**	N&W 4-bay Hopper "6446-3" with coal, *96*		60
____ **19328**	N&W 4-bay Hopper "6446-4" with coal, *96*		60
____ **19329**	N&W 4-bay Hopper "6436" with coal, *97*		55
____ **19330**	Cotton Belt 4-bay Hopper "64661" with coal, *98*		45
____ **19331**	Cotton Belt 4-bay Hopper "64662" with coal, *98*		45
____ **19332**	Cotton Belt 4-bay Hopper "64663" with coal, *98*		45
____ **19333**	Cotton Belt 4-bay Hopper "64664" with coal, *98*		45
____ **19338**	Cotton Belt 4-bay Hopper 2-pack, *99*		120
____ **19339**	Cotton Belt 4-bay Hopper "64469," *99*		NRS

		Exc	Mint
19340	Cotton Belt 4-bay Hopper "64470," *99*		NRS____
19341	LV 2-bay Hopper "6456," *99*		30____
19344	D&RGW 3-bay Cylindrical Hopper "15990," *99-00*		42____
19345	CN 3-bay Cylindrical Hopper "370708," *99-00*		95____
19346	PRR 4-bay Hopper with coal "744433," *01*		40____
19347	LV 2-bay Hopper "643657," *01*		40____
19348	Duluth, Missabe & Iron Range Ore Car "28000," *03*		25____
19349	U.S. Steel Ore Car "19349," *03*		29____
19350	Postwar "6636" Alaska Quad Hopper, *03*		34____
19357	N&W Hopper "6446-25," Archive Collection, *07*		50____
19361	Twizzlers Quad Hopper, *10*		55____
19362	Coursers Christmas Hopper with gifts, *10*		60____
19364	Milk Duds Covered Hopper, *11*		55____
19365	Coca-Cola Quad Hopper, *10*		60____
19366	Santa's Little Hopper, *10-11*		55____
19367	ATSF Quad Hopper, *11*		60____
19368	Southern Offset Hopper "106723" (std O), *11*		70____
19369	Alaska Quad Hopper "20756," *12*		60____
19371	Burlington Northern I-Beam Car, *04*		60____
19374	NS Bathtub Gondola 2-pack (std O), *15*		140____
19377	DETX Bathtub Gondola 2-pack (std O), *15*		140____
19380	CSX Bathtub Gondola 2-pack (std O), *15*		140____
19383	UP PS-4 Flatcar "57125" (std O), *13*		70____
19384	ATSF PS-4 Flatcar "90088" (std O), *13*		70____
19385	CNJ PS-4 Flatcar "339" (std O), *13*		70____
19386	BN PS-4 Flatcar "613200" (std O), *13*		70____
19388	BN 89' Auto Carrier (std O), *13-14*		110____
19389	SP 89' Auto Carrier (std O), *13-14*		110____
19390	CP 89' Auto Carrier (std O), *13-14, 16*		110____
19391	Soo Line 89' Auto Carrier (std O), *13-14, 16*		110____
19393	BNSF Auto Carrier 2-pack (std O), *12*		220____
19394	UP Auto Carrier 2-pack (std O), *12*		220____
19395	Grand Trunk Auto Carrier 2-pack (std O), *12*		220____
19396	CSX Auto Carrier 2-pack (std O), *12*		220____
19397	CN Auto Carrier 2-pack (std O), *12*		220____
19398	Conrail Auto Carrier 2-pack (std O), *12*		220____
19400	Milwaukee Road Gondola with cable reels (FF 2), *87*	23	31____
19401	GN Gondola with coal (FF 3), *88*	14	16____
19402	GN Crane Car (FF 3), *88*	47	65____
19403	WM Gondola with coal (FF 4), *89*	20	25____
19404	Trailer Train Flatcar with WM trailers (FF 4), *89*	29	33____
19405	Southern Crane Car, *91*	42	65____
19406	West Point Mint Car, *91 u*	38	50____
19408	Frisco Gondola with coil covers (FF 5), *91*	26	31____
19409	Southern Flatcar with stakes, *91*	18	22____
19410	NYC Gondola with canisters, *91*	47	55____
19411	NKP Flatcar with Sears trailer (FF 6), *92*	50	59____
19412	Frisco Crane Car, *92*	49	65____
19413	Frisco Flatcar with stakes, *92*	16	21____
19414	Union Pacific Flatcar with stakes (SSS), *92*	19	26____
19415	Erie Flatcar with trailer "7200" (FF 7), *93*	28	39____
19416	ICG TTUX Flatcar Set with trailers (SSS), *93*	70	75____
19419	Charlotte Mint Car, *93*	25	32____

		Exc	Mint
____ **19420**	Lionel Lines Vat Car, *94*	18	22
____ **19421**	Hirsch Brothers Vat Car, *95*	16	21
____ **19423**	Circle L Racing FlatCar "6424" with stock cars, *96*		27
19424	Edison Electric Depressed Center FlatCar "6461" with transformer, *97*		31
____ **19427**	Evans Auto Loader,"6414," *99*		55
____ **19428**	Evans Boat Loader,"6414," *99*		70
____ **19429**	Culvert Gondola "6342," *98-99*		48
____ **19430**	ATSF FlatCar "6411" with Beechcraft Bonanza, *98*		47
____ **19438**	Christmas Gondola (std O), *98*		42
____ **19439**	Flatcar with safes, *98*		35
____ **19440**	Flatcar with FedEx trailer, *98*		34
____ **19441**	Lobster Vat Car, *98*		35
____ **19442**	Water Supply Flatcar with tank (SSS), *98*		31
____ **19444**	Flatcar with VW Bug, *98*		38
____ **19445**	Borden Milk Tank Car "520," *99*		38
____ **19446**	Pittsburgh Paint Vat Car, *99*		43
____ **19447**	Mama's Baked Beans Vat Car, *99*		35
____ **19448**	Easter Gondola "6462" with candy, *99*		27
____ **19449**	Liquified Gas Tank Car "6469," *99*		31
____ **19450**	Barrel Ramp Car "6343," *99*		31
____ **19451**	Wheel Car "6262," *99*		32
____ **19454**	PRR FlatCar "6424" with gondola, *99*		25
19455	Lionel Lines FlatCar "6430" with Cooper-Jarrett trailers, *99*		60
____ **19457**	Lionel Lines Extension Searchlight Car, *99*		40
____ **19459**	Valentine Gondola "6462" with candy, *99*		50
____ **19471**	Mobil Flatcar with 2 trailers, *00 u*		96
____ **19472**	Mobil Bulkhead Flatcar with tank, *00 u*		68
____ **19474**	L&N FlatCar "6424" with trailer frames, *99*		26
____ **19476**	Zoo Gondola "6462" with animals, *99-00*		43
____ **19477**	Monday Night Football Flatcar with trailer, *01*		30
____ **19478**	Culvert Gondola "6342," *99*		45
____ **19479**	Borden Milk Car "521," *00*		38
____ **19480**	Valentine's Vat Car "6475," *99-00*		30
____ **19481**	Easter Vat Car, *99-00*		38
____ **19482**	NYC Flat with trailer,"6424," *00*		50
____ **19483**	VW Beetle FlatCar, *00*		48
____ **19484**	FlatCar "6264" with timber, *00*		34
____ **19485**	PRR Culvert Gondola "347004," *01*		41
____ **19486**	NYC Lumber FlatCar, *01*		34
____ **19487**	FlatCar "6800" with airplane, *00*		41
____ **19489**	Evans Auto Loader,"500085," *00*		50
____ **19490**	Postwar "6475" Libby's Vat Car, *01-02*		36
____ **19491**	Christmas Vat Car, *01*		30
____ **19492**	WM Skeleton Log Car 3-pack, *01*		95
____ **19496**	Westside Lumber Skeleton Log Car 3-pack, *01*		112
____ **19500**	Milwaukee Road Reefer (FF 2), *87*	30	39
____ **19502**	C&NW Reefer, *87*	30	33
____ **19503**	Bangor & Aroostook Reefer, *87*	22	25
____ **19504**	Northern Pacific Reefer, *87*	16	22
____ **19505**	Great Northern Reefer (FF 3), *88*	29	35
____ **19506**	Thomas Newcomen Reefer, *88*	18	23
____ **19507**	Thomas Edison Reefer, *88*	21	27

		Exc	Mint
19508	Leonardo da Vinci Reefer, *89*	19	27____
19509	Alexander Graham Bell Reefer, *89*	17	20____
19510	PRR Stock Car (FARR 5), *89 u*	18	26____
19511	WM Reefer (FF 4), *89*	22	28____
19512	Wright Brothers Reefer, *90*	17	21____
19513	Ben Franklin Reefer, *90*	17	20____
19515	Milwaukee Road Stock Car (FF 2), *90 u*	33	41____
19516	George Washington Reefer, *89 u, 91*	14	19____
19517	Civil War Reefer, *89 u, 91*	14	19____
19518	Man on the Moon Reefer, *89 u, 91*	13	17____
19519	Frisco Stock Car (FF 5), *91*	26	31____
19520	CSX Reefer, *91*	18	23____
19522	Guglielmo Marconi Reefer, *91*	19	23____
19523	Dr. Robert Goddard Reefer, *91*	19	23____
19524	Delaware & Hudson Reefer (SSS), *91*	29	32____
19525	Speedy Alka Seltzer Reefer, *91 u*	31	32____
19526	Jolly Green Giant Reefer, *91 u*	21	33____
19527	Nickel Plate Road Reefer (FF 6), *92*	20	29____
19528	Joshua L. Cowen Reefer, *92*	23	28____
19529	A.C. Gilbert Reefer, *92*	18	23____
19530	Rock Island Stock Car, *92 u*	34	38____
19531	Rice Krispies Reefer, *92 u*	23	33____
19532	Hormel Reefer "901," *92 u*	18	24____
19535	Erie Reefer (FF 7), *93*	23	26____
19536	Soo Line REA Reefer (SSS), *93*	25	30____
19538	Hormel Reefer "102," *94*	22	25____
19539	Heinz Reefer, *94*	38	47____
19540	Broken Arrow Ranch Stock Car "3356," *97*		28____
19552	Rutland Reefer "395" (std O), *00*		32____
19553	ATSF Stock Car "23003," *00*		37____
19554	Postwar Celebration Milk Car "36621," *00*		125____
19555	Swift Reefer "5839," red, *01*		33____
19556	Swift Reefer "1020," silver, *01*		31____
19557	Circus Stock Car "6376," *00*		32____
19558	Postwar "6556" MKT Stock Car, *02*		27____
19559	MKT Stock Car, girls set add-on, *02*		95____
19560	NP 2-door Stock Car "6356," Archive Collection, *02*		33____
19561	Norman Rockwell Holiday Reefer, *03*		25____
19562	Norman Rockwell Holiday Reefer, *03*		25____
19563	Norman Rockwell Holiday Reefer, *03*		25____
19564	Postwar "6672" Santa Fe Reefer, *03*		35____
19565	Burlington Reefer "6672," Archive Collection, *03*		35____
19567	Postwar "6572" Railway Express Agency Reefer, *05*		45____
19568	GN Reefer, Archive Collection, *05*		45____
19569	Pillsbury Reefer, traditional, *05*		53____
19570	Nestle Nesquik Reefer, traditional, *05*		53____
19572	NYC Reefer "6672," Archive Collection, *06*		45____
19573	Postwar "6356" NYC Stock Car, *06-07*		50____
19574	GN Stock Car, *08*		50____
19575	REA Reefer "6721," *08-09*		50____
19576	Alaska Reefer, *08*		50____
19577	Krey's Reefer, *10-11*		60____
19578	Granny Smith Apples Wood-sided Reefer, *10-11*		53____

		Exc	Mint
19585	NS Transparent Instruction Car, *10-11*		75
19586	Alaska Husky Transport Car, *10-11*		75
19587	Hershey's Chocolate Wood-sided Reefer, *10*		75
19588	Santa's Wish Transparent Gift Car, *10*		75
19589	Blood Transfusion Bunk Car, *10-11*		60
19590	Wood-sided Reefer 2-pack, *10*		110
19593	Hershey's Kisses Wood-sided Reefer, *11-15*		60
19594	York Peppermint Patty Wood-sided Reefer, *10-11*		55
19599	Old Glory Reefers, set of 3, *89 u, 91*	37	43
19600	Milwaukee Road 1-D Tank Car (FF 2), *87*	33	40
19601	North American 1-D Tank Car (FF 4), *89*	17	29
19602	Johnson 1-D Tank Car (FF 5), *91*	24	30
19603	GATX 1-D Tank Car (FF 6), *92*	32	41
19604	Goodyear 1-D Tank Car (SSS), *93*	33	36
19605	Hudson's Bay 1-D Tank Car (SSS), *94*	25	29
19607	Sunoco 1-D Tank Car "6315," *96*		23
19608	Sunoco Aviation Services 1-D Tank Car "6315," (SSS), *97*		38
19611	Gulf Oil 1-D Tank Car "6315," *98*		33
19612	Gulf Oil 3-D Tank Car "6425," *98*		30
19614	BASF 1-D Tank Car "UTLX 78252," *99-00*		25
19615	Vulcan Chemicals 1-D Tank Car, *99-00*		25
19621	Centennial 1-D Tank Car "6015-1," *99*		55
19622	Centennial 1-D Tank Car "6015-2," *99*		62
19623	Centennial 1-D Tank Car "6015-3," *99*		62
19624	Centennial 1-D Tank Car "6015-4," *99*		58
19625	Ethyl Tank Car "6236," *01*		31
19626	Diamond Chemical Tank Car "19419," *01*		29
19627	Shell 1-D Tank Car "1227," *01*		37
19628	Lion Oil 1-D Tank Car "2256," *01*		35
19634	General American 1-D Tank Car, *01*		30
19635	U.S. Army 1-D Tank Car "10936," *01*		31
19636	Hooker Chemicals 1-D Tank Car "6180," *01*		36
19637	GATX TankTrain Intermediate Car "44589" (std O), *02*		55
19638	CN TankTrain Intermediate Car "75571" (std O), *02*		65
19639	GATX TankTrain Intermediate Car 3-pack (std O), *02*		140
19644	Union Texas 1-D Tank Car "9922," *02*		33
19645	Penn Salt 1-D Tank Car "4730," *02*		33
19646	CN TankTrain Intermediate Car "75571" (std O), *03*		45
19647	GATX TankTrain Intermediate Car "44589" (std O), *03*		45
19649	Scrooge McDuck Mint Car, *05*		195
19651	Santa Fe Tool Car, *87*	30	35
19652	Jersey Central Bunk Car, *88*	25	33
19653	Jersey Central Tool Car, *88*	26	28
19654	Amtrak Bunk Car, *89*	22	25
19655	Amtrak Tool Car, *90-91*	23	30
19656	Milwaukee Road Bunk Car, smoke, *90*	40	50
19657	Wabash Bunk Car, smoke, *91-92*	36	42
19658	Norfolk & Western Tool Car, *91*	24	29
19660	Mint Car, *98*		40
19663	Pratt's Hollow Bunk Car "5717," *99*		40
19664	Ambassador Award Bunk Car, bronze, *99 u*		440
19665	Ambassador Engineer Bunk Car, silver, *99 u*		610
19666	Ambassador Cowen Bunk Car, gold, *99 u*		440

Exc Mint

		Exc	Mint
19667 Wellspring Gold Bullion Car, *99*			56____
19669 King Tut Museum Car "9660," *99*			70____
19670 NY Federal Reserve Bullion Car "6445," *00*			44____
19671 Lionel Model Shop Display Car "6445-01," *99-00*			50____
19672 Lionel Mines Mint Car, *00 u*			250____
19673 Wellspring Capital Management Mint Car, *99 u*			215____
19674 Lionel Lines Platinum Car, *00*			43____
19675 Lionel Model Shop Display, "6445-2," *01*			42____
19676 Philadelphia Mint Car, *01*			40____
19677 Fort Knox Mint Car "6445," *00*			50____
19678 U.S. Army Bunk Car, *02*			45____
19679 St. Louis Federal Reserve Mint Car, *02*			38____
19681 Area 51 Alien Suspension Car, *02*			47____
19682 Alaska Klondike Mining Mint Car, *02*			40____
19683 Pony Express Mint Car, *02*			50____
19686 Chicago Federal Reserve Mint Car "6445," *03-04*			45____
19687 UP Bunk Car "3887," smoke, *03*			40____
19688 Postwar "6445" Fort Knox Mint Car, *02-03*			39____
19689 CIBRO TankTrain Intermediate Car 3-pack (std O), *03*			100____
19694 Pony Express Mint Car, *03*			50____
19696 U.S. Savings Bond Mint Car, *00*			150____
19697 U.S. Bureau of Engraving and Printing Mint Car "19697," *04*			40____
19698 San Francisco Federal Reserve Mint Car, *04*			40____
19700 Chessie System Extended Vision Caboose, *88*		43	50____
19701 Milwaukee Road N5c Caboose (FF 2), *88*		50	65____
19702 PRR N5c Caboose, *87*		44	55____
19703 GN Extended Vision Caboose (FF 3), *88*		42	49____
19704 WM Extended Vision Caboose, smoke (FF 4), *89*		42	49____
19705 CP Rail Extended Vision Caboose, smoke, *89*		43	47____
19706 UP Extended Vision Caboose "9706," smoke, *89*		40	56____
19707 SP Work Caboose with searchlight, smoke, *90*		55	60____
19708 Lionel Lines Bay Window Caboose, *90*		43	46____
19709 PRR Work Caboose, smoke, *89, 91*		49	70____
19710 Frisco Extended Vision Caboose, smoke (FF 5), *91*		43	47____
19711 NS Extended Vision Caboose, smoke, *92*		47	65____
19712 PRR N5c Caboose, *91*		44	47____
19714 NYC Work Caboose with searchlight, smoke, *92*		100	130____
19715 DM&IR Extended Vision Caboose "C-217," *92 u*		50	60____
19716 IC Extended Vision Caboose "9405," smoke, *93*		105	135____
19717 Susquehanna Bay Window Caboose "0121," *93*		44	55____
19718 C&IM Extended Vision Caboose "74," *92 u*		38	45____
19719 Erie Bay Window Caboose "C-300" (FF 7), *93*		47	55____
19720 Soo Line Extended Vision Caboose (SSS), *93*		32	41____
19721 GM&O Extended Vision Caboose "2956," *93 u*		47	50____
19723 Disney Extended Vision Caboose, *94*		36	45____
19724 JCPenney MKT Extended Vision Caboose "125," *94 u*		38	43____
19726 NYC Bay Window Caboose (SSS), *95*		50	60____
19727 Pennsylvania N5c Caboose "477938," *96*			30____
19728 N&W Bay Window Caboose, *96*			70____
19732 ATSF Bay Window Caboose "6517," *96*			43____
19733 New York Central Caboose "6357," *96*			30____
19734 Southern Pacific Caboose "6357," *96*			26____
19736 PRR N5c Caboose "6417," *97*			27____

		Exc	Mint
____	**19737** Lackawanna Searchlight Caboose "2420," *97*		75
____	**19738** Conrail N5c Caboose "6417" (SSS), *97*		55
____	**19739** NYC Wood-sided Caboose "6907," *97*		60
____	**19740** Virginian N5c Caboose "6427," *97 u*		65
____	**19741** Pennsylvania N5c Caboose "6417," *98*		50
____	**19742** Erie Bay Window Caboose "C301," Caboose Talk, *98*		95
____	**19748** SP&S Bay Window Caboose "6517," *97 u*		50
____	**19749** SP Bay Window Caboose "6517," *98*		100
____	**19750** Holiday Music Bay Window Caboose, *98*		160
____	**19751** PRR N5c Caboose "492418," *98*		30
____	**19752** NP Bay Window Caboose "407," *98*		50
____	**19753** UP Extended Vision Caboose "25641," *98*		55
____	**19754** NYC Caboose "20112," *98*		55
____	**19755** Centennial Porthole Caboose, *99*		68
____	**19756** Lionel Lines Bay Window Caboose, *99*		50
____	**19758** DL&W Work Caboose "6419," *99*		55
____	**19759** Corvette N5c Caboose, *99*		60
____	**19772** Lionel Visitor's Center Vat Car, *99 u*		40
____	**19773** Lionel Kids Club Barrel Ramp Car "6343," *96 u*		48
____	**19778** Case Cutlery Wood-sided Caboose "1889" (std O), *99 u*		NRS
____	**19779** SP Bay Window Caboose "1908," *99*		65
____	**19780** LV Porthole Caboose "641751," *99-00*		43
____	**19781** Vapor Records Holiday Porthole Caboose "6417," *99-00*		62
____	**19782** NYC Bay Window Caboose "21719," *00*		65
____	**19783** Ford Mustang Extended Vision Caboose, *01*		50
____	**19785** SP Bay Window Caboose "6517," *00*		55
____	**19786** PRR Extended Vision Caboose, *00 u*		40
____	**19787** PRR Extended Vision Caboose "477927," *01*		40
____	**19790** Postwar "6417" Lehigh Valley Caboose, *02*		41
____	**19792** Postwar "C301" Erie Bay Window Caboose, *03*		45
____	**19796** C&O Bay Window Caboose, *03*		50
____	**19800** Circle L Ranch Operating Cattle Car, *88*	75	95
____	**19801** Poultry Dispatch Chicken Car, *87*	20	27
____	**19802** Carnation Milk Car, *87*	87	102
____	**19803** Reading Ice Car, *87*	38	44
____	**19804** Wabash Operating Hopper, *87*	25	34
____	**19805** Santa Fe Operating BoxCar, *87*	28	36
____	**19806** PRR Operating Hopper, *88*	28	32
____	**19807** PRR Extended Vision Caboose, smoke, *88*	39	47
____	**19808** NYC Ice Car, *88*	38	49
____	**19809** Erie-Lackawanna Operating BoxCar, *88*	27	35
____	**19810** Bosco Milk Car, *88*	80	89
____	**19811** Monon Brakeman Car, *90*	50	55
____	**19813** Northern Pacific Ice Car, *89 u*	41	46
____	**19815** Delaware & Hudson Brakeman Car, *92*	49	60
____	**19816** Madison Hardware Operating Boxcar "190991," *91 u*	90	105
____	**19817** Virginian Ice Car, *94*	31	35
____	**19818** Dairymen's League Milk Car "788," *94*	65	80
____	**19819** Poultry Dispatch Car (SSS), *94*	36	43
____	**19820** Die-cast Tender, RailSounds II, *95-96*		175
____	**19821** UP Operating BoxCar, *95*	31	36
____	**19822** Pork Dispatch Car, *95*	29	39

	Exc	Mint
19823 Burlington Ice Car, *94 u, 95*	39	49____
19824 U.S. Army Target Launcher, *96*		32____
19825 Generator Car, *96*		48____
19827 NYC Operating BoxCar, *97*		37____
19828 C&NW Animated Stock Car "3356" and Stockyard, *96-97*	100	____
19830 U.S. Mail Operating Boxcar "3428," *97*		39____
19831 GM Generator Car "3530," power pole and wire, *97*		44____
19832 Cola Ice Car "6352," *97*		47____
19833 Tender,"2426RS," RailSounds II, *97*		240____
19834 LL 6-wheel Crane Car "2460," *97*		60____
19835 FedEx Animated Boxcar "3464X," *97*		38____
19837 Bucyrus 6-wheel Crane Car "2460," *99*		49____
19845 Aquarium Car "3435," CC, *98*		151____
19846 Animated Giraffe Car "3376C," *98*		105____
19850 Stock Car "33760," RailSounds, *00*		130____
19853 Firefighting Instruction Generator Car (SSS), *98*		60____
19854 Lionelville Fire Car (SSS), *98*		55____
19855 Christmas Aquarium Car, *98*		60____
19856 Mermaid Transport, *98*		65____
19857 NYC Firefighting Instruction Car "19853," *98-99*		175____
19858 Lionelville Operating Searchlight Car "19854," *99*		65____
19859 REA Boxcar "6267," steam RailSounds, *99*		170____
19860 Conrail Boxcar "169671," diesel RailSounds, *99*		140____
19864 Animated Ostrich BoxCar, *99*		37____
19867 Operating Poultry Dispatch Car "3434," *99*		48____
19868 Shark Aquarium Car "3435," *99*		190____
19869 Alien Aquarium Car "3435," *99*		49____
19877 ATSF Operating Barrel Car, *99*		55____
19878 Operating Helium Tank FlatCar "3362," *99*		40____
19880 Lionel Lines Extension Searchlight Car, *00*		50____
19882 Sanderson Farms Poultry Car "3434," *99*		41____
19883 LL Bucyrus Erie Crane Car "64608," *99*		45____
19884 Atlantis Travel Aquarium Car, *00 u*		95____
19885 N&W Operating Hopper Car, *00*		31____
19886 Seaboard Boxcar "16126," steam RailSounds, *00*		140____
19887 SP Boxcar "651663," diesel RailSounds, *00*		140____
19888 Christmas Music BoxCar, *01*		65____
19889 PRR Bay Window Caboose "477719," Crewtalk, *00*		140____
19890 Santa Fe Bay Window Caboose "999211," Crewtalk, *00*	100	____
19894 Hood's Operating Milk Car with platform, *03-04*		95____
19895 3356 Santa Fe Horse Car with corral, *04*		120____
19896 USMC Missile Launch Sound Car "45," *03-04*		165____
19897 NYC Crane Car, TMCC, *04*		255____
19898 Nestle Nesquik Operating Milk Car with platform, *04*		95____
19899 Pennsylvania Crane Car "19899," CC, *03-05*		260____
19900 Toy Fair BoxCar, *87 u*	65	80____
19901 "I Love Virginia" BoxCar, *87*	25	35____
19902 Toy Fair BoxCar, *88 u*	55	80____
19903 Christmas BoxCar, *87 u*	22	34____
19904 Christmas BoxCar, *88 u*	32	43____
19905 "I Love California" BoxCar, *88*	20	24____
19906 "I Love Pennsylvania" BoxCar, *89*	26	32____

MODERN ERA 1970-2019

		Exc	Mint
	19907 Toy Fair BoxCar, *89 u*	38	55
	19908 Christmas BoxCar, *89 u*	30	39
	19909 "I Love New Jersey" BoxCar, *90*	19	25
	19910 Christmas BoxCar, *90 u*	35	38
	19911 Toy Fair BoxCar, *90 u*	75	95
	19912 "I Love Ohio" BoxCar, *91*	21	28
	19913 Christmas BoxCar, *91*	34	52
	19913 Lionel Employee Christmas BoxCar, *91 u*	150	200
	19914 Toy Fair BoxCar, *91 u*	38	50
	19915 "I Love Texas" BoxCar, *92*	35	60
	19916 Lionel Employee Christmas BoxCar, *92 u*	190	220
	19917 Toy Fair BoxCar, *92 u*	45	53
	19918 Christmas BoxCar, *92 u*	49	70
	19919 "I Love Minnesota" BoxCar, *93*	40	60
	19920 Lionel Visitor's Center BoxCar, *92 u*	16	28
	19921 Lionel Employee Christmas BoxCar, *93 u*	140	185
	19922 Christmas BoxCar, *93*	33	41
	19923 Toy Fair BoxCar, *93 u*	65	95
	19925 Lionel Employee Learning Center BoxCar, *93 u*	55	63
	19926 "I Love Nevada" BoxCar, *94*	21	26
	19927 Lionel Visitor's Center BoxCar, *93 u*	26	33
	19928 Lionel Employee Christmas BoxCar, *94 u*	205	230
	19929 Christmas BoxCar, *94*	30	40
	19931 Toy Fair BoxCar, *94 u*	49	65
	19932 Lionel Visitor's Center BoxCar, *94 u*	26	33
	19933 "I Love Illinois" BoxCar, *95*	21	27
	19934 Lionel Visitor's Center BoxCar, *95 u*	18	22
	19937 Toy Fair BoxCar, *95 u*	55	75
	19938 Christmas BoxCar, *95*	26	34
	19939 Lionel Employee Christmas BoxCar, *95 u*	100	128
	19941 "I Love Colorado" BoxCar, *95*	23	30
	19942 "I Love Florida" BoxCar, *96*	19	27
	19943 "I Love Arizona" BoxCar, *96*	20	25
	19944 Lionel Visitor's Center Tank Car, *96 u*		35
	19945 Holiday BoxCar, *96*		29
	19946 Lionel Employee Christmas BoxCar, *96 u*		195
	19947 Lionel Toy Fair BoxCar, *96 u*		200
	19948 Visitor's Center Flatcar with trailer, *96 u*		34
	19949 "I Love NY" BoxCar, *97*		50
	19950 "I Love Montana" BoxCar, *97*		30
	19951 "I Love Massachusetts" BoxCar, *98*		26
	19952 "I Love Indiana" BoxCar, *98*		31
	19955 Lionel Visitor's Center Gondola with coil covers, *98 u*		20
	19956 Toy Fair Boxcar "777," *98 u*		65
	19957 Ambassador Caboose, *97 u*		486
	19958 Ambassador Caboose, silver (std O), *98 u*		555
	19959 Ambassador Caboose, gold (std O), *98 u*		744
	19964 U.S. JCI Senate BoxCar, *92 u*	55	63
	19968 "I Love Maine" BoxCar, *99*		40
	19969 "I Love Vermont" BoxCar, *99*		40
	19970 "I Love New Hampshire" BoxCar, *99*		34
	19971 "I Love Rhode Island" BoxCar, *99*		34
	19976 Lionel Employee Holiday BoxCar, *99 u*		150

		Exc	Mint
19977 Toy Fair BoxCar, *99 u*			50____
19981 Lionel Centennial BoxCar, *99*			36____
19982 Lionel Centennial BoxCar, *99*			36____
19983 Lionel Centennial BoxCar, *99*			36____
19984 Lionel Centennial BoxCar, *99*			36____
19985 "I Love Georgia" BoxCar, *99-00*			45____
19986 "I Love North Carolina" BoxCar, *99-00*			40____
19987 "I Love South Carolina" BoxCar, *99-00*			40____
19988 "I Love Tennessee" BoxCar, *99-00*			55____
19989 Toy Fair BoxCar, *00 u*			55____
19996 Toy Fair BoxCar, *01 u*			50____
19997 Lionel Employee BoxCar, *01 u*			125____
19998 Christmas BoxCar, *01*			33____
19999 Lionel Visitor's Center 4-bay Hopper, *02 u*			153____
20000 PRR Senator Coach 4-pack (std O), *13, 15*			640____
20005 SP Sunset Limited Coach 4-pack (std O), *13, 15*			640____
20010 UP City of Los Angeles Coach 4-pack (std O), *13, 15*			640____
20015 B&O Capitol Limited Coach 4-pack (std O), *13*			640____
20020 FEC City of Miami Coach 4-pack (std O), *13*			640____
20025 KCS Southern Belle Coach 4-pack (std O), *13*			640____
20030 MILW Olympian Coach 4-pack (std O), *13, 15*			640____
21029 World of Little Choo Choo Set, *94u, 95*		36	43____
21141 North Dakota State Quarter Gondola Bank, *07*			60____
21142 South Dakota State Quarter Hopper Bank, *07*			60____
21163 SuperStreets FasTrack Grade Crossing, *08-10*			20____
21164 SuperStreets 10" Transition to FasTrack, *08-10*			9____
21165 SuperStreets Transition to FasTrack, 2 pieces, *08-10*			17____
21168 City Traction Trolley Add-on, *08*			75____
21169 City Traction Speeder Add-on, *08*			75____
21170 NYC 15" Heavyweight Passenger Car 4-pack, *07*			250____
21175 NYC 15" Heavyweight Passenger Car 2-pack, *07*			125____
21198 ATSF Alco Diesel AA Set, horn, *08*			200____
21199 ATSF Midnight Chief Streamliner Car 4-pack, *08*			200____
21204 ATSF Midnight Chief Streamliner Car 2-pack, *08*			100____
21207 SP Diesel Work Train, *07*			175____
21212 NH Diesel Freight Set, *07*			250____
21217 Southern Diesel Executive Inspection Train, *07*			175____
21229 Ringling Bros. S2 Diesel Switcher, horn, *07*			80____
21230 Ringling Bros. Porter Locomotive, *07*			105____
21231 Ringling Bros. Streamliner Car 4-pack, *07*			210____
21234 Ringling Bros. Streamliner Car 2-pack, *07*			105____
21237 Ringling Bros. Flatcar with 3 wagons, *07*			50____
21238 Ringling Bros. Flatcar with 3 wagons, *07*			50____
21239 Ringling Bros. Flatcar with crates, *07*			45____
21240 Ringling Bros. Flatcar with front end loader and poles, *07*			45____
21252 Boy Flying Kite, *08*			60____
21253 Operating Bunk Car Yard Office, *07*			80____
21261 SuperStreets 2.5" Straight-to-Curve Connector, 4 pieces, *08-10*			9____
21265 Operating Voltmeter Car, *07*			75____
21266 SuperStreets Intersection, 4 pieces, *08-10*			40____
21267 PRR Boxcab Electric Locomotive, horn, *07*			77____
21271 WP Operating Coal Dump Car with vehicle, *07*			33____

		Exc	Mint
____ **21276**	Congressional Diner, smoke, *07*		110
____ **21277**	Operating Flagman's Shanty, *08*		70
____ **21279**	Roach Wranglers Pest Control Van, *08*		30
____ **21281**	SuperStreets D21 Curve, *08-10*		3
21282	SuperStreets 2.5" Curve-to-Curve Connector, 4 pieces, *08-10*		9
____			
____ **21283**	SuperStreets Tubular Track Grade Crossing, *08-10*		18
____ **21284**	SuperStreets 10" Tubular Transition, *08-10*		8
____ **21285**	SuperStreets 10" Tubular Transition, 2 pieces, *08-10*		14
____ **21286**	SuperStreets Intersection, *08-10*		10
____ **21287**	SuperStreets Y Roadway, *08-10*		12
____ **21288**	SuperStreets O Gauge Conversion Pins, *08-10*		2
____ **21289**	SuperStreets Connector Pins, *08-10*		2
____ **21290**	SuperStreets Hookup Wires, 2 pieces, *08-10*		3
____ **21291**	Dogbone Expander pack, *08-10*		25
____ **21296**	City Traction Classic Truck, *07*		30
____ **21298**	NYC 4-6-4 Hudson Locomotive "5279," CC, *07*		500
____ **21316**	PE RS3 Diesel "2815," CC, *07*		350
____ **21324**	Acrobats and Clowns Figures, 10 pieces, *08-10*		12
21325	Ringmaster Circus Figures, 5, with accessories, *08-10*		12
____			
____ **21326**	PRR 15" Interurban Car 2-pack, *07*		200
____ **21354**	Fresh Never Frozen Fish Transport Car, *07*		80
____ **21355**	Dump Bin, *08-10*		20
____ **21358**	Special Addition BoxCar, Girl, *08-10*		25
____ **21359**	Special Addition BoxCar, Boy, *08-10*		25
____ **21368**	Passenger Coach Figures, 9 pieces, *08-10*		11
____ **21369**	Walking Figures, 8 pieces, *08-10*		11
____ **21370**	Sitting Figures, 6, with benches, *08-10*		11
____ **21371**	Standing Figures, 8 pieces, *08-10*		11
____ **21372**	Railroad Station Figures, 6, with accessories, *08-10*		11
____ **21373**	School Figures, 7, with accessories, *08-10*		11
____ **21374**	Service Station Figures, 5, with accessories, *08-10*		11
____ **21375**	Police Figures, *10*, with dog, *08*		20
____ **21376**	Seated Passenger Figures, 40 pieces, *08*		27
____ **21377**	Mounted Police, 3, with horses, *08-10*		11
____ **21378**	Factory, *08-10*		18
____ **21379**	Police Station, *08-10*		16
____ **21380**	Colonial House, *08-10*		16
____ **21381**	Suburban Station, *08-10*		16
____ **21382**	School, *08-10*		17
____ **21383**	Suburban Ranch House, *08-10*		15
____ **21384**	Service Station with gas pumps, *08-10*		17
____ **21385**	Barn and Chicken Coop, *08-10*		20
____ **21386**	Firehouse, *08-10*		17
____ **21387**	Church, *08-10*		15
____ **21388**	Country L-shaped Ranch House, *08-10*		16
____ **21389**	Supermarket, *08-10*		12
____ **21390**	Diner, *08-10*		15
____ **21394**	Rotating Beacon, *08-09*		31
____ **21396**	Single Tunnel Portals, pair, *08-10*		15
____ **21397**	SuperSnap 31" Remote Switch, left hand, *08-09*		55
____ **21398**	SuperSnap 31" Remote Switch, right hand, *08-09*		55
____ **21399**	SuperSnap 72" Remote Switch, left hand, *08-09*		70

		Exc	Mint
21400	SuperSnap 72" Remote Switch, right hand, *08-09*	70	___
21412	NYC Plymouth Switcher Freight Set, *07*	155	___
21430	SuperStreets D16 Curve, *08-10*	2	___
21431	SuperStreets 10" Straight Track, *08-10*	2	___
21432	SuperStreets D16 Curved Track, 8 pieces, *08-10*	18	___
21433	SuperStreets 5" Straight Track, 4 pieces, *08-10*	14	___
21434	SuperStreets 10" Straight Track, 8 pieces, *08-10*	19	___
21435	World War II Seated Soldiers, 9, with benches, *08-09*	20	___
21436	Rings and Things Circus Accessories, *08-09*	10	___
21438	Remote Controller, *07-10*	35	___
21442	City Figures, 7, with scooter, *08-10*	11	___
21443	Factory Figures, 6, with accessories, *08-10*	11	___
21444	Church Figures, 5, with accessories, *08-10*	11	___
21445	Firefighting Figures, 11, with accessories, *08-10*	20	___
21449	Operating Loading Platform with flatCar, *07-08*	80	___
21450	Unloading Station with dump bins, *07*	100	___
21451	Girder Bridge with stone piers, *07*	40	___
21452	Graduated Trestle Set, 26 pieces, *07*	50	___
21453	Elevated Trestle Set, 10 pieces, *07*	40	___
21454	Double Tunnel Portals, 2 pieces, *08-10*	20	___
21456	UPS Step Van, *07*	30	___
21466	Ringling Bros. 15" Aluminum Advertising Car, *07*	110	___
21469	Ringling Bros. FlatCar, white, with container, *07*	45	___
21470	Ringling Bros. FlatCar, blue, with container, *07*	45	___
21471	Ringling Bros. Flatcar with 2 trailers, *08-10*	60	___
21472	Ringling Bros. Flatcar with 2 trailers, *08-10*	60	___
21476	Strasburg Plymouth Diesel Switcher, *07*	100	___
21494	WM RS3 Diesel "189," CC, *07*	350	___
21529	Montana State Quarter Boxcar Bank, *08*	45	___
21542	Washington State Quarter Tank Car Bank, *08*	45	___
21543	Boyd Bros. Ford Classic Truck, *08*	33	___
21549	Ringling Bros. Crew Bus, *08*	33	___
21552	S.W.A.T. Team Step Van, *08*	30	___
21560	Reading Flatcar with rail load, *07*	25	___
21567	School Bus SuperStreets Set, *08*	110	___
21568	Dirty Dogz Van SuperStreets Set, *08*	100	___
21569	Angelo's Pizza Delivery Van, *08*	30	___
21570	Flying Colors Painting Van, *08*	30	___
21571	SuperStreets 10" Insulated Roadway, 2 pieces, *08-10*	8	___
21572	SuperStreets 5" Straight School, 2 pieces, *08-10*	8	___
21573	SuperStreets 5" Straight Stop Ahead, 2 pieces, *08-10*	8	___
21574	SuperStreets 5" Straight Crosswalk, 2 pieces, *08-10*	8	___
21575	SuperStreets 10" Crossing, 2 pieces, *08-10*	10	___
21576	SuperStreets Skid Mark Roadway Pack, *08-10*	13	___
21577	Snack-On Step Van, *08*	30	___
21582	Keystone Coal Porter Locomotive, *08*	100	___
21583	Keystone Coal Freight Car 4-pack, *08*	100	___
21590	ATSF "Midnight Chief" 2-bay Hopper "162277," *08*	25	___
21591	ATSF "Midnight Chief" Flatcar "94468" with trailer, *08*	43	___
21592	ATSF "Midnight Chief" Caboose, *08*	25	___
21593	ATSF "Midnight Chief" Boxcar "621593," *08*	35	___

		Exc	Mint
21594	NYC Empire State Express 15" Aluminum Car 4-pack, *08-09*		420
21599	SP flatcar with wheel load, *07*		35
21600	B&M RS3 Diesel "1538," CC, *08-09*		350
21607	Jack Frost Hopper "327" with sugar load, *08*		25
21609	Elephants and Giraffes, 2 pair, *08-10*		13
21610	Lions and Tigers, 2 pair, *08-10*		13
21611	Horses, 4 pieces, *08*		13
21621	ATSF Operating Boxcar "22658," *08-09*		90
21623	Rutland Operating Milk Car with platform, *08-10*		150
21626	Rath Wood-sided Reefer "622," *09*		45
21627	Greenlee Packing Wood-sided Reefer "3862," *10*		45
21628	CNJ Reefer "1438," *08-09*		35
21629	C&O Reefer "7783," *08-09*		35
21630	UP Stock Car "42005," *09*		45
21631	Reading Boxcar "107984," *08-09*		35
21632	GN Boxcar "34285," *08-09*		35
21633	RI "Route of the Rockets" Boxcar "21110," *09-10*		40
21634	Tidewater Flying A 1-D Tank Car "1367," *09*		40
21635	Southern Depressed Center FlatCar, 2 transformers, *09*		43
21636	NS Flatcar with bulkheads and stakes, *08-09*		35
21637	Ontario Northland Ribbed Hopper with coal, *09*		40
21639	Pan Am Boxcar "32126," *08-09*		55
21640	UP Modern Steel-sided Reefer "499030," *08-09*		55
21641	Ringling Bros. Merchandise FlatCar, *08*		50
21643	PRR Die-cast Gondola with covers, *09*		73
21644	PRR 16-wheel Flatcar with transformer, *08-09*		80
21646	DT&I Work Crane and Boom Car, *09*		85
21649	City Traction Trolley with Ringling Bros. banner, *08-09*		80
21651	Moo-Town Creamery Step Van, *08-09*		38
21656	Quikrete Step Van, *08-09*		42
21658	Ringling Bros. Vintage Truck, *08-09*		42
21659	DT&I Flatcar "90059" with Ford trailer, *08-09*		60
21662	Moo-Town Creamery Vending Machine, *08-09*		13
21663	Moo-Town Creamery Bunk Car Ice Cream Shop, *08-09*		115
21664	RI Operating Coal Dump Car with vehicle, *08-09*		40
21665	Alaska Operating Log Dump Car with vehicle, *09*		40
21667	Red River Lumber Boxcab Diesel with horn, *08-09*		100
21668	CP Operating Hopper "9628," *08-09*		45
21675	Mountain View Creamery Loading Depot, *08-10*		130
21676	Beaver Creek Logging Die-cast Porter Locomotive, *08-09*		120
21677	Ford Factory, *09*		22
21679	Assured Comfort HVAC Van, *08-09*		38
21680	Division of Prisons Bus SuperStreets Set, *08-09*		150
21688	Ringling Bros. Heavyweight Coach 2-pack, *08-11*		240
21691	Ringling Bros. Flatcar with 2 trailers, *08-10*		60
21692	C&NW MP15 Diesel with Ringling Bros. banner, *08-09*		140
21693	Southern MP15 Diesel Pair, powered and dummy, *10*		200
21696	Ford Flatcar with 2 trucks, *08-09*		53

		Exc	Mint
21698	Lionel Van SuperStreets Set, *08-10*		130____
21701	Star Spangled GG1 Electric Locomotive "4837," *08-10*		260 ____
21702	Milwaukee Road Girder Bridge, *08-09*		15____
21703	ATSF Black Mesa Aluminum Business Car, *09-10*		160____
21704	C&O Double Searchlight Car with vehicle, *08-09*		50____
21706	Chatham Police Van, *08-09*		38____
21707	NYC Aluminum Business Car, *09*		160____
21708	CN Operating Log Dump Car, *10*		120____
21709	PRR Girder Bridge, *08-09*		15____
21715	Ringling Bros. Stock Car, *08-09*		60____
21717	Pullman-Standard 1-D Tank Car, *08-09*		35____
21719	NYC Bay Window Caboose, *99*		70____
21720	Ringling Bros. Billboard Set #2, *08-09*		10____
21721	Warning Sign Pack, 12 pieces, *08-10*		25____
21730	Regulatory Sign Pack, 12 pieces, *08-10*		25____
21738	Railroad Crossing Sign Pack, 6 pieces, *08-10*		21____
21750	NKP Rolling Stock 4-pack, *98*		160____
21751	PRR Rolling Stock 4-pack, *98*		145____
21752	Conrail Unit Trailer Train, *98*		285____
21753	Service Station Fire Rescue Train, *98*	500	585____
21754	BNSF 3-bay Covered Hopper 2-pack (std O), *98*		65____
21755	4-bay Covered Hoppers 2-pack, *98*		65____
21756	6464-style Overstamped Boxcars 2-pack, *98*		65____
21757	UP Freight Car Set, *98*		188____
21758	Bethlehem Steel "44" (SSS), *99*		375____
21759	Canadian Pacific F3 Diesel Passenger Set, *99*		930____
21761	B&M Boxcar Set, 4-pack, *99*		180____
21763	New Haven Freight Set, *99*		265____
21766	ACL Passenger Car 2-pack, *99*		385____
21769	Centennial 1-D Tank Car Set, 4-pack, *99*		230____
21770	NYC Reefer Set, 4-pack, *99*		225____
21771	D&RGW Stock Car Set, 4-pack, *99*		230____
21774	Custom Series Consist I, 3-pack, *99*		150____
21775	Train Wreck Recovery Set, *99*		190____
21778	ATSF Train Master Diesel Freight Set, *99*		NRS____
21779	Seaboard Freight Car Set, *99*		280____
21780	NYC Aluminum Passenger Car 2-pack, *99*		160____
21781	Case Cutlery Freight Set, *99 u*		1015____
21782	PRR Congressional Set, *00*		930____
21783	Monday Night Football 2-pack, *01-02*		50____
21784	QVC PRR Coal Freight Steam Set, *00 u*		360____
21785	QVC Gold Mine Freight Steam Set, *00 u*		300____
21786	Santa Fe F3 Diesel ABBA Passenger Set, *00*		1500____
21787	Blue Comet Steam Passenger Set, *01-02*		1050____
21788	Postwar Missile Launch Freight Set, *02-03*		350____
21789	Norfolk Southern Piggyback Set, CC (SSS), *01*		370____
21790	CN TankTrain Dash 9 Diesel Freight Set, *02*		630____
21791	Freedom Train Diesel Passenger Set, RailSounds, *03*		540____
21792	C&O Coal Hopper 6-pack #2 (std O), *01*		145____
21793	Virginian Coal Hopper 6-pack #2 (std O), *01*		160____
21794	Pioneer Seed GP7 Diesel Freight Set, *01 u*		900____
21795	Case Farmall Freight Set, *01 u*		990____
21796	NJ Medical Steam Freight Set, *01 u*		483____

		Mint
_____	**21797** SP Daylight Passenger Set, *01*	670
_____	**21852** MILW PS-2CD Hopper 3-pack (std 0), *06*	155
_____	**21853** BNSF PS-2CD Hopper 3-pack (std 0), *06*	155
_____	**21854** N&W PS-2CD Hopper 3-pack (std 0), *06*	155
_____	**21855** A&P Milk Car 3-pack, *06*	150
_____	**21856** Bowman Dairy Milk Car 3-pack (std 0), *06*	150
_____	**21857** Western Dairy Milk Car 3-pack (std 0), *06*	150
_____	**21858** NP PS-4 Flatcar with trailers, 2-pack (std 0), *06*	170
_____	**21859** C&NW PS-4 Flatcar with trailers, 2-pack (std 0), *06*	170
_____	**21860** UP PS-4 Flatcar with trailers, 2-pack (std 0), *06*	170
_____	**21861** PRR PS-4 Flatcar with trailers (std 0), *06*	170
_____	**21863** ADM Unibody Tank Car 3-pack (std 0), *06*	135
_____	**21864** Cerestar Unibody Tank Car 3-pack (std 0), *06*	135
_____	**21865** Coe Rail Husky Stack Car 2-pack (std 0), *06*	170
_____	**21866** Santa Fe Husky Stack Car 2-pack (std 0), *06*	170
_____	**21872** C&O Offset Hopper 3-pack (std 0), *05*	130
_____	**21873** P&LE Offset Hopper 3-pack (std 0), *06*	145
_____	**21874** TTX Trailer Train 2-pack (std 0), *06*	170
_____	**21875** CSX Husky Stack Car 2-pack (std 0), *06*	170
_____	**21876** Disney Villain Hi-Cube Boxcar 3-pack, *05-06*	135
_____	**21877** Domino Sugar 1-D Tank Car 3-pack (std 0), *07*	135
_____	**21878** Procor 1-D Tank Car 3-pack (std 0), *07*	135
_____	**21879** C&EI Offset Hopper 3-pack (std 0), *07*	145
_____	**21880** Erie Offset Hopper 3-pack (std 0), *07*	145
_____	**21881** Frisco Offset Hopper 3-pack (std 0), *07-08*	200
_____	**21882** Chessie System Offset Hopper 3-pack (std 0), *07*	145
_____	**21883** C&O 3-bay Hopper 2-pack (std 0), *07-08*	140
_____	**21884** Pennsylvania Power & Light 3-bay Hopper 2-pack (std 0), *07*	140
_____	**21885** Santa Fe 3-bay Hopper 2-pack (std 0), *07*	140
_____	**21886** C&NW 3-bay Hopper 2-pack (std 0), *07-08*	140
_____	**21888** IMC Canada Cylindrical Hopper 2-pack, *06*	130
_____	**21893** Greenbrier Husky Stack Car 2-pack (std 0), *07*	170
_____	**21894** CSX Husky Stack Car 2-pack (std 0), *07*	170
_____	**21895** BN Husky Stack Car 2-pack (std 0), *07*	170
_____	**21896** Arizona & California Husky Stack Car 2-pack (std 0), *07*	170
_____	**21897** REA PS-4 Flatcar with trailers, 2-pack (std 0), *07-08*	170
_____	**21898** NYC PS-4 Flatcar with trailers, 2-pack (std 0), *07-08*	170
_____	**21899** Lackawanna PS-4 Flatcar with trailers (std 0), *07*	170
_____	**21900** Civil War Union Train Set, *99*	375
_____	**21901** Civil War Confederate Train Set, *99*	375
_____	**21902** MILW PS-4 Flatcar with trailers, 2-pack (std 0), *07-08*	170
_____	**21902** Construction Zone Set, *99 u*	87
_____	**21904** UP PS-2 Covered Hopper 2-pack (std 0), *07*	120
_____	**21904** Safari Adventure Set, *99 u*	90
_____	**21905** NYC Flyer Set, *99 u*	100
_____	**21909** AGFA Film Steam Freight Set, *98 u*	1400
_____	**21914** Lionel Lines Freight Set, *99*	120
_____	**21916** Lionel Village Trolley, *99*	75
_____	**21917** N&W Freight Set, *99*	70
_____	**21918** PC PS-2 Covered Hopper 2-pack (std 0), *07*	120

	Exc	Mint
21918 Thomas Circus Play Set, *00*		100____
21921 Imco PS-2 Covered Hopper 2-pack (std O), *07-08*		120____
21924 Holiday Trolley Set, *99*		65____
21925 Thomas the Tank Engine Island of Sodor Train Set, *99-00*		150____
21930 NYC PS-2 Covered Hopper 2-pack (std O), *07*		120____
21932 JCPenney NYC Freight Flyer Steam Set, *00 u*		170____
21934 Custom Series Consist II, 3-pack, *99*		140____
21936 Looney Tunes Train Set, *00 u*		400____
21937 NYC Steel-sided Reefer 2-pack (std O), *07*		130____
21939 Dubuque Steel-sided Reefer 2-pack (std O), *07-08*		130____
21940 ADM Steel-sided Reefer 2-pack (std O), *07*		130____
21941 National Car Steel-sided Reefer 2-pack (std O), *07*		130____
21944 "Celebrate a Lionel Christmas" Steam Set, *00-01*		165____
21945 Christmas Trolley Set, *00*		100____
21948 NYC Freight Flyer Set, air whistle, *00*		240____
21950 Maersk SD70 Diesel Maxi-Stack Set, *00*	560	700____
21951 World War II Troop Train, *00*		410____
21952 Lionel Lines Service Station Special Set, *00*		294____
21953 Ford Mustang GP7 Diesel Set, CC, *01*		345____
21955 D&RGW F3 Diesel AA Passenger Set, CC, *01*		740____
21956 New York Central Freight Set, *99-00*		355____
21969 Lionel Village Trolley Set, *00*		85____
21970 SP RS3 Diesel Freight Set, horn, *00-01*		110____
21971 Pennsylvania Flyer Steam Set, *00*		150____
21972 Frisco GP7 Diesel Freight Set, horn, *00*		150____
21973 ATSF Passenger Set, RailSounds, *00-01*		375____
21974 ATSF Passenger Set, SignalSounds, *00-01*		240____
21975 Burlington Steam Freight Set, SignalSounds, *00*		275____
21976 Centennial Steam Freight Starter Set, *00*		650____
21977 NYC Train Master Steam Freight Set, *99-00*		620____
21978 ATSF Train Master Diesel Freight Set, *99-00*		500____
21981 JCPenney NYC Flyer Set, *00 u*		150____
21988 NYC Freight Set, RailSounds, *00*		325____
21989 Burlington Steam Freight Set, RailSounds, *00*		300____
21990 NYC Flyer Freight Set, RailSounds, *00*		175____
21999 Whirlpool Steam Freight Set, *00 u*		710____
22103 PRR A5 Scale Switcher "411," CC, *08-09*		330____
22104 PRR Freight Car 3-pack, *08*		135____
22105 NYC Empire State Express 4-6-4 Hudson Locomotive "5429," CC, *08-09*		420____
22113 NYC Empire State Express 15" Aluminum Car 2-pack, *08-10*		210____
22116 Ringling Bros. Diesel Freight Set, *08-10*		245____
22121 Ringling Bros. Freight Set, *08-10*		390____
22126 Ringling Bros. Expansion Pack, *08-10*		135____
22131 NH Streamliner Car 3-pack, *07*		150____
22135 CB&Q S2 Diesel Switcher "9305," horn, *07*		80____
22136 Erie S2 Diesel Switcher "522," horn, *07*		80____
22137 Alaska MP15 Diesel "1552," horn, *07*		100____
22138 Astoria Heat & Power Porter Locomotive "4," *07*		100____
22139 LIRR Speeder, *08*		50____
22140 CNJ Boxcab Diesel "1000," horn, *08*		90____
22141 Lackawanna 15" Interurban Car 2-pack, *07*		200____

		Mint
22142	FEC Operating Dump Car, *07*	70
22143	B&A Operating Log Dump Car, *08-09*	70
22144	Alaska Operating Coal Dump Car with vehicle, *08*	33
22145	WM Operating Log Dump Car with vehicle, *08*	33
22146	PFE Operating BoxCar, *08*	80
22147	B&O Operating Hopper with coal, *08*	35
22148	GN Operating Hopper with coal, *08*	35
22149	Dairymen's League Operating Milk Car, green, with platform, *08*	140
22150	D&RGW Bunk Car, smoke, *08*	65
22151	Alaska Searchlight Car with vehicle, *08*	45
22152	NKP 2-bay Outside-braced Hopper "31299," *08*	50
22153	L&N 2-bay Offset Hopper "78660," *08*	50
22154	D&H 2-bay Rib Side Hopper "5737," *07*	50
22155	Erie-Lack. 2-bay Aluminum Hopper "21353," *08*	60
22156	ACF Demonstrator 2-bay Aluminum Hopper "44586," *07*	60
22157	GN Aluminum Tank Car "74787," *08*	60
22158	MILW Bulkhead Flatcar "967116" with wood, *08-09*	43
22159	BNSF Flatcar "585011" with trailer, *08*	43
22160	UP Flatcar "58059" with container, *08*	43
22161	Conrail Flatcar "705910" with NS container, *08*	43
22162	Foppiano Wine 3-D Tank Car "1112," *08*	45
22163	PRR Weed Control Car "6321226," *07*	45
22166	PRR Reefer "19492," *08*	25
22167	Seaboard Reefer "16622," *08*	25
22168	N&W Boxcar "645772," *08*	25
22169	ATSF Reefer "11744," *07*	25
22170	P&LE Reefer "22300," *07*	25
22171	B&O DD Boxcar "495289," *08*	25
22172	CB&Q Stock Car "52731," *08*	25
22174	Erie-Lack. Transfer Caboose, *07*	25
22176	PRR Caboose "478884," *07*	25
22177	L&N Caboose "100," *07*	25
22179	NYC Depressed Center Flatcar "66256" with 2 girders, *08*	25
22180	IC Depressed Center Flatcar with 2 transformers, *07*	25
22182	RI Gondola "180043" with coils, *08*	25
22184	B&O Covered Hopper "604321," *08*	25
22185	UP Covered Hopper "53186," *08*	25
22186	P&LE (NYC) Gondola "17243," *08-09*	35
22187	PRR 2-D Tank Car "6351815," *07*	25
22188	Deep Rock 3-D Tank Car "2152," *08*	25
22189	NP Java Diner, smoke, *08*	110
22190	C&O Operating Billboard, *08*	65
22191	Operating Passenger Station, *08-09*	105
22192	Hot Box Operating BBQ Shack, *07*	80
22193	Cold Drinks Vending Machine, *08*	12
22194	Water Tower with light, *08-09*	20
22199	City Traction Trolley Barn, *08-09*	65
22202	Loading Ramp, *08-10*	20
22203	Dairymen's League Operating Milk Car, white, with platform, *07*	140
22204	Snacks Vending Machine, *08*	12

Exc Mint

		Exc	Mint
22205	Soup and Sandwich Vending Machine, *08*	12	___
22206	PRR Crew Bus, *08*	30	___
22222	Ringling Bros. Speeder Chase Set, *08-10*	92	___
22225	Ringling Bros. Jomar Heavyweight Private Car, *08-11*	120	___
22226	Ringling Bros. 18" Caledonia Heavyweight Private Car, *08*	100	___
22227	Ringling Bros. 18" Advertising Car, *08*	100	___
22228	Ringling Bros. Flatcar with 3 wagons, *08*	50	___
22231	Ringling Bros. Flatcar with 3 wagons, *08*	50	___
22235	Ringling Bros. Flatcar with pole wagon and truck, *08*	75	___
22238	Ringling Bros. Work Caboose with calliope wagon, *08*	40	___
22240	Ringling Bros. Flatcar/Stock Car with wagon, *08*	50	___
22243	Ringling Bros. Human Cannonball Car, *08*	45	___
22244	Ringling Bros. Operating Searchlight Car with 3 spotlights, *08*	60	___
22247	Ringling Bros. Stock Car "54," *08*	50	___
22248	Ringling Bros. Stock Car "47," *08*	50	___
22249	Ringling Bros. Dining Dept. Billboard Reefer, *08*	80	___
22250	Ringling Bros. Dining Dept. Wood-sided Reefer, *08-09*	90	___
22251	Ringling Bros. Dormitory Bunk Car "22," *08*	75	___
22252	Ringling Bros. Operating Billboard, *08-09*	75	___
22253	Ringling Bros. Vintage Billboard Set #1, *08*	9	___
22255	Ringling Bros. Aluminum Coach "40010," *08-10*	165	___
22257	Ringling Bros. Aluminum Shop Car "63002," *08-10*	165	___
22258	Ringling Bros. 18" Aluminum Large Animal Car, *08-10*	165	___
22259	Ringling Bros. Flatcar with trailer, *08*	53	___
22260	Ringling Bros. Tractor Trailer, *08*	30	___
22261	Idaho State Quarter Hopper Bank, *08*	65	___
22262	Wyoming State Quarter Tank Car Bank, *08*	50	___
22263	Utah State Quarter Boxcar Bank, *08*	45	___
22264	SuperStreets Figure-8 Expander Pack, *08-10*	35	___
22267	Mulligan Spring Water Step Van, *08*	30	___
22270	Quikrete Classic Truck with 2 pallets, *08*	33	___
22271	MILW EP-5 Electric Locomotive "E20," CC, *08-09*	460	___
22272	MILW Olympian Hiawatha 18" Aluminum Car 4-pack, *08*	480	___
22277	MILW Olympian Hiawatha 18" Aluminum Car 2-pack, *08*	250	___
22280	Erie-Lack. RS3 Diesel "933," CC, *08-09*	350	___
22281	Southern Train Master Diesel "6300," CC, *08-09*	420	___
22282	Southern Bay Window Caboose "X270," *08-09*	70	___
22283	UP S2 Diesel Switcher "1103" and Caboose "25384," *08*	130	___
22286	GN Boxcab Electric Locomotive "5008-A," horn, *08*	90	___
22287	North Shore Line 15" Interurban Car 2-pack, *08*	230	___
22288	Commuter Train Station, 6 road name stickers, *09*	25	___
22289	Ringling Bros. 18" Aluminum Passenger Car 2-pack, *08*	270	___
22290	Erie Boxcar "86448" with graffiti, *08*	46	___
22291	C&NW Stock Car "14303," *08*	46	___
22292	Land o' Lakes Butter Billboard Reefer, *08*	75	___

		Exc	Mint
____	**22293** PRR 4-bay Hopper "253776," *08*		65
____	**22294** Montana Rail Link 3-bay Aluminum Hopper "50049," *08*		70
____	**22295** Canada Wheat 4-bay Aluminum Hopper "606418," *08*		73
____	**22296** Eaglebrook Aluminum Tank Car "19039," *08*		70
____	**22297** Petri Wine 3-D Tank Car "904," *08-09*		45
____	**22298** Cotton Belt Offset Cupola Wood-sided Caboose "2230," *08*		80
____	**22299** MILW Bay Window Caboose "980502," *08-09*		70
____	**22300** Detroit, Toledo & Ironton Coil Car "1352," *08*		60
____	**22301** NYC Flatcar "506090" with freight kit, *08*		35
____	**22302** C&O Flatcar "80951" with freight kit, *08*		35
____	**22303** Extruded Aluminum I-Beam, 3 pieces, *08-09*		6
____	**22304** Rails, 12 pieces, *08-09*		6
____	**22305** Small Transformer Load, pair, *08-09*		15
____	**22306** Large Transformer Load, *08*		19
____	**22307** Forklifts, 3, with pallets, *08-09*		27
____	**22308** Loaders with crates, pair, *08-09*		13
____	**22309** Loaders with logs, pair, *08-09*		13
____	**22310** KBL Logistics Container 2-pack, *08*		40
____	**22312** Commemorative Quarter Extended Vision Caboose, *09*		80
____	**22313** ATSF Boxcar "137460," *08*		25
____	**22314** Coastal King Seafood Wood-sided Reefer, *08*		25
____	**22315** Wisconsin & Southern "God Bless America" BoxCar, *09*		43
____	**22316** NP Depressed Center Flatcar "66130" with water tank, *08*		25
____	**22317** U.S. Air Force Hopper "55175" with ballast load, *08*		25
____	**22318** DM&IR Ore Car "29991," *08*		25
____	**22319** Celanese Chemicals 1-D Tank Car "12730," *08*		25
____	**22320** Baldwin Locomotives Works 1-D Tank Car "6809," *08*		25
____	**22321** B&O Operating BoxCar, *08*		45
____	**22322** PRR Operating Ballast Dump Car, *08*		75
____	**22323** FEMA Voltmeter Car, *08*		75
____	**22324** C&NW Cop and Robber Chase Gondola, *08-09*		55
____	**22325** White Milk Cans, 10 pieces, *08-10*		8
____	**22326** Twin Searchlight Tower, *08-10*		33
____	**22327** Tommy's Bunk Car Grill, *08-09*		100
____	**22328** Santa Fe Operating Freight Transfer Platform, *08-09*		130
____	**22329** Dual Track Signal Bridge, *08-10*		45
____	**22330** Stella's Heavyweight Diner, smoke, *08-09*		140
____	**22331** Coffee Vending Machine, *08*		12
____	**22332** Spring Water Vending Machine, *08*		12
____	**22333** Candy Vending Machine, *08*		12
____	**22334** Ford Plymouth Diesel Switcher and Ore Car 6-pack, *08*		200
____	**22335** NS Operating Paint Shop with BoxCar, *08-09*		140
____	**22344** KBL Logistics ISO Tank, *08*		19
____	**22346** Tableau Circus Wagons, *08*		13
____	**22349** Forklift with 6 pallets, *08-09*		23
____	**22350** Twin Lamp Posts, 3 pieces, *08-09*		22
____	**22352** Lamp Posts, 4 pieces, *08-09*		20

		Exc	Mint
22354	Portable Spotlights, 3 pieces, *08-09*	15	___
22356	High Tension Poles, 4 pieces, *08-09*	8	___
22358	Rail Yard Signs, 12 pieces, *08-09*	10	___
22360	Telephone Poles, 6 pieces, *08-09*	7	___
22362	Girder Bridge, *08-09*	8	___
22363	Stone Bridge Piers, pair, *08-10*	27	___
22365	Heavyweight Passenger Coach 6-wheel Scale Trucks, pair, *08-09*	25	___
22366	Aluminum Passenger Coach 4-wheel Scale Trucks, pair, *08-09*	25	___
22367	Timkin Scale Sprung Trucks, pair, *08-09*	19	___
22368	Bettendorf Scale Sprung Trucks, pair, *08-09*	19	___
22369	Scale Couplers, pair, *08-09*	6	___
22379	SuperStreets Barricade, 2 pieces, *08-10*	11	___
22387	Kiosk with 3 vending machines, *08-09*	40	___
22391	Ford MP15 Diesel "10021," horn, *08*	115	___
22392	Ford Farming Boxcar "1681," *08*	30	___
22393	Ford Stampings DD Boxcar "101," *08*	35	___
22394	Ford 2-bay Covered Hopper "1667," *08*	30	___
22395	Ford Speeder "14," *08*	65	___
22396	Ford Water Tower, *08*	25	___
22397	Ford Rotating Sign Tower, *08*	55	___
22398	Boyd Bros. and Ford Barn and Chicken Coop, *08*	25	___
22399	Ford ISO Tank, *08-09*	21	___
22402	PRR Streamlined K4 4-6-2 Pacific Locomotive, tender, *09-10*	500	___
22408	Ringling Bros. Tractor Trailer #1, *08-09*	35	___
22411	Tableau Wagon Set #2, *08-10*	18	___
22412	PRR Operating Flagman's Shanty, *08-09*	90	___
22414	Linde Union Carbide Boxcar with aluminum tank, *08-09*	70	___
22415	Ringling Bros. Flatcar with circus wagon, *08*	50	___
22417	Ringling Bros. Flatcar with container, *09*	55	___
22420	PRR Broadway Limited Aluminum Passenger Car 2-pack, *09-10*	300	___
22423	GN Aluminum Passenger Car 2-pack, *09-10*	360	___
22426	Ford Gondola "13447" with coils, *08-09*	43	___
22427	Ford Operating Billboard, *08-09*	75	___
22428	Ford Tin Sign Replica 4-pack, *08-09*	17	___
22433	PRR Broadway Limited Aluminum Passenger Car 4-pack, *09-10*	600	___
22438	Mail Crane, *08-10*	30	___
22439	Milwaukee Road Aluminum Passenger Car 2-pack, *09-11*	360	___
22447	Wabash Die-cast 2-bay Ribbed Hopper "37751," *08-09*	60	___
22449	UP Crew Bus, *08-09*	38	___
22450	Seaboard Die-cast Hopper with gravel, *10*	80	___
22454	Oklahoma State Quarter Die-cast Hopper Bank, *08-09*	75	___
22455	New Mexico State Quarter Die-cast Gondola Bank, *08-09*	74	___
22456	Arizona State Quarter Tank Car Bank, *08-09*	55	___
22457	Alaska State Quarter Boxcar Bank, *09*	55	___
22458	Hawaii State Quarter Die-cast Hopper Bank, *09*	75	___

		Exc	Mint
____	**22459** Southern Aluminum Passenger Car 2-pack #1, *09*		300
____	**22460** Southern Aluminum Passenger Car 2-pack #2, *09*		300
____	**22461** Scale Skeleton Log Car 4-pack, *08-09*		160
____	**22467** Railroad Water Tower, *08-09*		23
____	**22468** Fast Eddie's Used Car Lot with 2 die-cast vehicles, *08-09*		50
____	**22469** Cola Illuminated Vending Machine, *08-09*		13
____	**22470** SuperStreets Guard Rails, *08-10*		20
____	**22472** Ringling Bros. Tin Sign Replica 4-pack, *08-09*		17
____	**22477** Lionel Tin Sign Replica 4-pack, *08-09*		15
____	**22482** Vintage Tin Sign Replica 4-pack, *08-09*		15
____	**22487** Scooter Gang with scooters, *09-10*		13
____	**22492** Airport Revolving Searchlight, *10*		40
____	**22493** Ringling Bros. Lighted Clown Wood-sided Reefer, *09*		75
____	**22494** Ford Flatcar with 2 Thunderbird convertibles, *09*		53
____	**22496** Vita O Flavored Water Vending Machine, *09*		13
____	**22497** Top Pop Soda Illuminated Vending Machine, *09*		13
____	**22498** Ringling Bros. Flatcar with 3 circus wagons, *09-10*		55
____	**22500** Defense Dept. Flatcar with 2 jeeps and soldier, *09*		50
____	**22501** C&NW Railroad Van, CC, *09-10*		100
____	**22502** Ringling Bros. Flatcar with 3 circus wagons, *09-10*		55
____	**22504** Ford Water Tower with vintage Ford logo, *09-10*		25
____	**22505** Sparkling Springs Beverage Truck, *09*		45
____	**22506** SuperStreets Fishtail Roadway, *09*		25
____	**22507** Ringling Bros. Flatcar with boxcar and ticket wagon, *09*		60
____	**22509** Pallet Pack with banded loads, *09*		20
____	**22510** Lionel Step Van, CC, *09-10*		100
____	**22511** BNSF Flatcar with helicopter, *09*		50
____	**22513** Ringling Bros. Heavyweight Advertising Car, *09*		120
____	**22514** NYC Girder Bridge, *09-10*		15
____	**22515** Milwaukee Road/REA Scale Boxcar "6436," *09*		55
____	**22516** BNSF MP15 Diesel "3704" with horn, *09*		120
____	**22517** Quick Lane Ford Motorcraft Auto Parts Van, *09-10*		42
____	**22518** Lionel Tank Container Leasing ISO Tank, *09-10*		23
____	**22519** Roma Wine Wood-sided Billboard Reefer, *09-10*		70
____	**22520** WWII Soldiers in Action, 10 pieces, *09-10*		20
____	**22521** 1959 Ford Billboard Set, *09*		10
____	**22523** American Flyer Vintage Truck, *09*		38
____	**22524** Ford Coil Car "749772," *09*		73
____	**22525** Vermont Railway Operating Boxcar "177," *09*		50
____	**22526** Crabby Matt's Smoking Heavyweight Diner, *09*		150
____	**22527** Toledo, Peoria & Western Boxcar "5067," *09-10*		55
____	**22528** GN Stock Car "55973," *09-10*		55
____	**22529** U.S. Army 1-D Tank Car "11278," *09*		35
____	**22530** Milwaukee Road Aluminum Coach "627," *09-11*		180
____	**22531** Southern Girder Bridge, *09*		15
____	**22532** Montana Rail Link 1-D Tank Car "100017," *09*		35
____	**22533** GN Aluminum Coach "1377," *09-10*		180
____	**22534** SuperStreets D16 Curve Guard Rails, *09-10*		20
____	**22536** SuperStreets D21 Curve Guard Rails, *09-10*		22
____	**22538** Ford Modern Aluminum Tank Car "30166," *09*		90
____	**22539** BNSF Flatcar "922267" with Ford trailer, *09-10*		60
____	**22542** PRR Flatcar "480227" with freight kit, *09*		40

Exc Mint

	Exc	Mint
22543 Biodiesel 2-D Tank Car "1544," *09*	40	___
22544 Ringling Bros. Wood-sided Gondola with equipment, *09*	63	___
22548 Kiosk #2 with 3 illuminated vending machines, *09*	40	___
22553 Convenience Mart, *09-10*	25	___
22554 Auto Parts Store, *09-10*	20	___
22555 Ringling Bros. Tractor with Gold Tour container, *09-10*	55	___
22558 PRR Flatcar "469301" with milk containers, *09*	50	___
22559 UP Gondola "229794" with freight kit, *09-10*	80	___
22560 CB&Q Wood-sided Gondola "85150" with spools, *09-10*	60	___
22561 Gondola Scrap Load, *09*	9	___
22562 Operation Lifesaver Boxcar with flashing LEDs, *09*	65	___
22563 Ringling Bros. Handcar and Trailer Set, *10-11*	70	___
22566 SuperStreets 2.5" Straight Roadway, 4 pieces, *10*	12	___
22568 Generators, 2 pieces, *09*	9	___
22570 Large transformer, *09*	22	___
22571 Cage Wagon Set, *09-10*	18	___
22573 Display Base, *09*	20	___
22574 Ringling Bros. Flatcar "39" with trailer, *09*	60	___
22577 Biodiesel Storage Tank with 2 figures, *09-10*	40	___
22578 Ringling Bros. Heavyweight Coach "70," *09*	120	___
22579 Circus Horses, 4 pieces, *09-10*	15	___
22580 Bollards and Chains, *09-10*	20	___
22582 Pipe Stack Load, *09*	30	___
22583 KBL Operating Wind Turbine, *09-10*	75	___
22584 KBL Die-cast 16-wheel Flatcar "34807," *09*	85	___
22587 Old Reading Flatcar Foot Bridge with stone piers, *09-10*	50	___
22590 Roadside Fender Bender, *09-10*	75	___
22592 SuperStreets D16 Turn Roadways, left and right, *10*	35	___
22595 SuperStreets D21 Turn Roadways, left and right, *10*	39	___
22598 SuperStreets Adjustable Straight Kit, *09-10*	20	___
22600 Wire Spool Load, 6 pieces, *09*	20	___
22610 Napa Valley Wine Train Alco FA Diesel AA Set, *10*	230	___
22613 Napa Valley Wine Train 15" Passenger Car 4-pack, *10*	450	___
22618 Signal Oil Co. 1-D Tank Car, *10*	40	___
22619 PRR Paoli MU Commuter Train 2-pack, *10*	290	___
22622 RR Paoli Motorized Combine, *10*	200	___
22623 PRR Commuter Train Station, *10*	35	___
22624 NH Die-cast Plymouth Switcher with snowplow, *10*	160	___
22625 Ringling Bros. 18" Aluminum Generator Car, *10-11*	180	___
22627 Ringling Bros. Lighted Clown Wood-sided Reefer, *10-11*	90	___
22628 Ringling Bros. 18" Aluminum Advertising Car, *10-11*	180	___
22629 Ringling Bros. Stock Car, *10-11*	60	___
22630 Ringling Bros. Tractor and Trailer, *10-11*	35	___
22633 Ringling Bros. 18" Aluminum Coach, *10-11*	180	___
22634 Ringling Bros. 18" Heavyweight Advertising Car, *10-11*	146	___
22635 Ringling Bros. Operating Dual Searchlight Car, *10-11*	60	___
22637 Quikrete Step Van, *10*	48	___
22638 PRR Crew Bus, *10*	45	___

		Exc	Mint
____	22639 B&O Boxcab Diesel "195," *10*		100
____	22640 Central of Georgia Boxcar "5823," *10*		45
____	22641 New Haven Boxcar "36438," *10*		45
____	22642 Ringling Bros. Operating Large Animal Feed Car, *10-11*		150
____	22643 Ford MP15 Diesel "10022," *10-11*		135
____	22644 Ford Motorcraft 48' Aluminum Tank Car, *10-11*		95
____	22645 Ringling Bros. Operating Tent Pole Dump Car, *10-11*		130
____	22646 Ford Speeder, *10-11*		75
____	22647 Rock Island Gondola "180044," *10*		35
____	22648 PRR Gondola "353381," *10*		35
____	22651 Central Vermont Operating Milk Car with platform, *10*		175
____	22653 Starlite Diner with parking lot, *10*		200
____	22654 Ringling Bros. Flatcar with 3 circus wagons, *10-11*		60
____	22656 Ringling Bros. Flatcar with 3 circus wagons, *10-11*		60
____	22658 Operating Flagman's Shanty, *10*		100
____	22659 Union 76 1-D Tank Car "6322," *10*		40
____	22660 Moose Pond Creamery Operating Loading Depot, *10*		140
____	22661 WM 2-Bay Covered Hopper "5051," *10*		35
____	22662 PRR Reefer "19494," *10*		45
____	22663 New Haven Illuminated Caboose, *10*		40
____	22667 Acme Scrap Platform Crane, *10*		60
____	22670 ATSF Operating BoxCar, *10*		140
____	22671 Smoking Southern Bay Window Caboose, *10*		90
____	22672 Ringling Bros. 18" Sarasota Observation Car, *10-11*		146
____	22673 Ford Water Tower with light, *10*		27
____	22674 MILW 21" Aluminum Passenger Car 2-pack, *10-11*		400
____	22679 Ringling Bros. Operating Billboard, *10-11*		100
____	22902 Quonset Hut, *98-99*		22
____	22907 Die-cast Girder Bridge, *98-01*		10
____	22910 Gilbert Tractor Trailer, *98*		20
____	22914 PowerHouse Lockon, *98-01*		24
____	22915 Municipal Building, *98-99*		28
____	22916 190-watt Power Accessory System, *98*		425
____	22918 Locomotive Backshop, *98*	300	460
____	22919 ElectroCouplers Kit for GP9 Diesel, *98-00*		20
____	22922 Intermodal Crane, *98*		195
____	22931 Die-cast Cantilever Signal Bridge, *98-06*		35
____	22934 Walkout Cantilever Signal, *98-03*		42
____	22936 Coaling Tower, 3 pieces, *98*		85
____	22940 Mast Signal, *98-00*		37
____	22942 Accessories Box, *98-01*		20
____	22944 Automatic Operating Semaphore, *98-03, 08*		35
____	22945 Block Target Signal, *98-00*		39
____	22946 Automatic Crossing Gate and Signal, *98-99*		45
____	22947 Auto Crossing Gate, *98-00*		36
____	22948 Gooseneck Street Lamps, set of 2, *98-00*		30
____	22949 Highway Lights, set of 4, *98-99*		20
____	22950 Classic Street Lamps, set of 3, *98-02*		20
____	22951 Dwarf Signal, *98-00*		24
____	22952 Classic Billboards, set of 3, *98-00*		15
____	22953 Linex Gasoline Tall Oil Tank, *98-99*		6
____	22954 Linex Gasoline Wide Oil Tank, *98-99*		6

		Exc	Mint
22955	ElectroCouplers Kit for J Class and B&A tenders, *98-00*		20
22956	ElectroCouplers Kit for NW2 Switcher, *98*		20____
22957	ElectroCouplers Kit for F3 Diesel, *98-01*		20____
22958	ElectroCouplers Kit for Dash 9 Diesel, *98-01*		20____
22959	ElectroCoupler Conversion Kit for Atlantic Locomotive, *98-01*		13
22960	Trainmaster Command Basic Upgrade Kit, *98-01*		34____
22961	Standard GP9 Diesel B Unit Upgrade Kit, *98-01*		30____
22962	Deluxe GP9 Diesel B Unit Upgrade Kit, black trucks, *98-01*		44
22963	RailSounds Upgrade Kit, steam RailSounds, *98-01*		55____
22964	RailSounds Upgrade Kit, diesel RailSounds, *98-01*		55____
22965	Culvert Loader, CC, *98-01*		255____
22966	Figure-8 Add-on Track Pack (O27), *98-16*		17____
22967	Double Loop Add-on Track Pack (O27), *98-16*		62____
22968	Double Loop Track Pack (O27), *98-03*		65____
22969	Deluxe Complete Track Pack (O), *98-16*		120____
22972	Bascule Bridge, *98-99*		337____
22973	Lionel Corporation Tractor and Trailer, *98*		15____
22975	Culvert Unloader, CC, *99-00*		225____
22979	GP9 Diesel B-Unit Deluxe Upgrade Kit, silver trucks, *98-01*		34
22980	TMCC SC-2 Switch Controller, *99-16*		130____
22982	Postwar ZW Controller and Transformer Set, *98*		265____
22983	180-watt PowerHouse Power Supply, *99-16, 18*		125____
22990	Flatcar with Route 66 autos, 4-pack, *99*		37____
22991	Christmas Tree and Blue Comet Train, *99-00*		60____
22993	Route 66 Sinclair Dino Cafe, *99-00*		210____
22997	Oil Drum Loader, *99-00*		100____
22998	Triple Action Magnetic Crane, *99*		220____
22999	Sound Dispatching Station, *99-00*		90____
23000	NYC Dreyfuss Hudson Operating Base, 2-rail, *92 u*		190____
23001	NYC Dreyfuss Hudson Operating Base, 3-rail, *93 u*		190____
23002	NYC Hudson Operating Base, *92 u, 93-94*		190____
23003	PRR B-6 Switcher Operating Base, *92 u, 93-94*		190____
23004	NP 4-8-4 Operating Base, *92 u, 93-94*		190____
23005	Reading T-1 Operating Base, *92 u, 93-94*		190____
23006	Chessie System T-1 Operating Base, *92 u, 93-94*		190____
23007	SP Daylight Operating Base, *92 u, 93-94*		190____
23008	NYC L-3 Mohawk Operating Base, *92 u, 93-94*		190____
23009	PRR S2 Turbine Locomotive Operating Base, *92 u, 93-94*		190
23010	31" Remote Switch, left hand (O), *95-99*	30	37____
23011	31" Remote Switch, right hand (O), *95-99*	20	30____
23012	F3 Diesel ABA Operating Base, *92 u, 93-94*		190____
24018	PRR BoxCar, *05*		25____
24101	Mainline Color Position Signal, *04-08*		25____
24102	Industrial Water Tower, *03*		55____
24103	Double Floodlight Tower, *03, 05-09*		42____
24104	Hobo Tower, *03-05*		70____
24105	Track Gang, *03-06*		70____
24106	Exploding Ammunition Dump, *02*		25____
24107	Missile Firing Range Set, *02*		60____

		Exc	Mint
_____	**24108** World War II Pylon, *03*		80
_____	**24109** Santa Fe Railroad Tugboat, *03*		125
_____	**24110** Pennsylvania Railroad Tugboat, *03*		118
_____	**24111** Swing Bridge, *03*		215
_____	**24112** Oil Field with bubble tubes, *03*		44
_____	**24113** Lionelville Ford Auto Dealership, *03*		225
_____	**24114** AMC/ARC Gantry Crane, CC, *03*		195
_____	**24115** AMC/ARC Log Loader, CC, *03, 06-07*		140
_____	**24117** Illuminated Covered Bridge, *02-16, 18*		70
_____	**24119** Big Bay Lighthouse, *04-05*		170
_____	**24122** Lionelville People Pack, *03, 08-09, 15-17*		27
_____	**24123** Passenger Station People Pack, *03, 08-09, 15-18*		27
_____	**24124** Carnival People Pack, *03, 08-11, 13-16, 18*	5	27
_____	**24130** TMCC 135/180 PowerMaster, *04-12*		79
_____	**24131** Dumbo Pylon, *03*		70
_____	**24134** Bethlehem Steel Gantry Crane, *02*		200
_____	**24135** Lionel Lighthouse, *02-03*		100
_____	**24137** Mr. Spiff and Puddles, *03, 08*		34
_____	**24138** Playtime Playground, *03, 08*		50
_____	**24139** Duck Shooting Gallery, *03*		110
_____	**24140** Charles Bowdish Homestead, *03*		60
_____	**24147** Lionel Sawmill, *03*		90
_____	**24148** Coal Tipple Coal Pack, *602, 08-10, 13-18*		15
_____	**24149** NYC Hobo Hotel, *02*		42
_____	**24151** Hobo Campfire, *03*		25
_____	**24152** Conveyor Lumber Loader, *03*		65
_____	**24153** Railroad Control Tower, *03, 08-10*		40
_____	**24154** Maiden Rescue, *03*		35
_____	**24155** Blinking Light Billboard, *04-10*		21
_____	**24156** Lionelville Street Lamps, set of 4, *04-05, 07-18*		30
_____	**24159** Illuminated Station Platform, *04-08*		32
_____	**24160** Rub-a-Dub-Dub, *04*		42
_____	**24161** Test O' Strength, *04-06*		70
_____	**24164** Summer Vacation, *04-05*		80
_____	**24168** Tire Swing, *04-05*		70
_____	**24170** Rover's Revenge, *04-05*		70
_____	**24171** Campbell's Soup Water Tower, *04*		45
_____	**24172** Balancing Man, *04-05*		70
_____	**24173** Derrick Platform, *03-05*		60
_____	**24174** Icing Station, *04-06*		100
_____	**24176** Irene's Diner, *06-07*		65
_____	**24177** Hot Air Balloon Ride, *04, 06*		95
_____	**24179** Scrambler Amusement Ride, *04-07*		165
_____	**24180** Choo Choo Barn Lionelville Zoo, *04-05*		105
_____	**24182** Lionelville Firehouse, *04*		100
_____	**24183** Lionelville Gas Station, *04, 06-09*		115
_____	**24187** Classic Billboard Set: 3 stands and 5 inserts, *04-08*		10
_____	**24190** Station Platform, *05-09*		17
_____	**24191** Park People Pack, *04-18*		27
_____	**24192** Park Benches People Pack, *04-09*		23
_____	**24193** Railroad Yard People Pack, *04-08, 14-18*		27
_____	**24194** Civil Servants People Pack, *04-18*		27
_____	**24196** Farm People Pack, *04-09*		23

		Exc	Mint
24197	City Accessory Pack, *04-17*		27___
24200	Lionel FasTrack Book, *07-10, 13-15*		35___
24201	UPS Centennial Operating Billboard Signmen, *07*		100___
24203	Polar Express Original Figures, 4 pieces, *08-14, 16*		30___
24204	Christmas Tractor Trailer with trees, *08*		25___
24205	Classic Billboard Set, *08-10*		20___
24206	MOW Gantry Crane, *08*		280___
24212	Lionel Art Blinking Billboard, *08-09*		23___
24213	Universal Lockon, *12-16*		4___
24214	Postwar "395" Floodlight Tower, *08*		75___
24215	MTA Metro-North Passenger Station, *07*		53___
24218	Sunoco Elevated Tank, *08-09*		75___
24219	PRR Plastic Girder Bridge, *08*		18___
24220	ATSF Girder Bridge, *08-09*		18___
24221	UP Die-cast Girder Bridge, *08*		30___
24222	UPS Die-cast Girder Bridge, *08*		30___
24223	Santa's Sleigh Pylon, *08*		150___
24224	Postwar "38" Water Tower, *08-09*		150___
24226	Christmas Toy Store, *08*		52___
24227	Halloween Animated Billboard, *08-09*		54___
24228	Christmas Operating Billboard, *08*		38___
24229	Pennsylvania Water Tower, *08-09*		23___
24230	Maiden Rescue, *08*		60___
24232	Burning Switch Tower, *08*		80___
24233	Exploding Ammunition Dump, *08*		36___
24234	Missile Firing Range, *08*		43___
24235	UPS Water Tower, *08*		80___
24236	Wimpy's All-Star Burger Stand, *08*		97___
24238	Sunoco Oil Derrick, *08*		90___
24240	MTA Metro-North Blinking Billboard, *07*		21___
24242	Postwar "352" Icing Station, *08*		100___
24243	Rosie's Roadside Diner, *08*		85___
24244	Commuter People, *08, 13-18*		27___
24245	MTA Metro-North Illuminated Station Platform, *07*		32___
24248	Manual Crossing Gate, *08-18*		20___
24250	Mainline Gooseneck Lamps, pair, *08-09*		32___
24251	Polar Express Caribou, *08-14, 16-18*		27___
24252	Polar Express Wolves and Rabbits, *08-14, 16-18*		27___
24264	Halloween People, *08-12*		23___
24265	Trick or Treat People, *08-13*		23___
24270	Operating Forklift Platform, *08-09*		280___
24272	Train Orders Building, *08*		80___
24273	Christmas Water Tower, *08-10*		23___
24274	Christmas Girder Bridge, *08*		18___
24279	PowerMaster Bridge, *08-13*		55___
24283	NYC Girder Bridge, *09-10*		21___
24284	Halloween Girder Bridge, *09-11*		21___
24285	CP Rail Girder Bridge, *08-09*		30___
24286	Polar Express Girder Bridge, *09-14*		21___
24287	ATSF Blinking Light Water Tower, *09*		30___
24288	NYC Blinking Light Water Tower, *09*		30___
24293	Legacy Module Garage, *08-09*		50___
24294	AEC Nuclear Reactor, *09-10*		325___

		Exc	Mint
____	**24295** Cowen's Corner Hobby Shop, *09*		420
____	**24296** Engine House, *09-12, 14*		70
____	**24299** Main Street Ice Cream Parlor, *08*		37
____	**24500** D&RGW Alco PA Diesel AA Set, *04*		530
____	**24503** D&RGW Alco PB Diesel, *04*		150
____	**24504** Santa Fe E6 Diesel AA Set, CC, *03*		530
____	**24507** Milwaukee Road E6 Diesel AA Set, CC, *03*		530
____	**24511** Burlington FT Diesel AA Set, RailSounds, *03*		225
____	**24516** Santa Fe F3 Diesel B Unit, *03*		235
____	**24517** NYC F3 Diesel B Unit "2404," powered, CC, *03*		250
____	**24518** WP F3 Diesel B Unit, *03*		275
____	**24519** B&O F3 Diesel B Unit, *03*		270
____	**24520** Alaska F3 Diesel AA Set, *03*		650
____	**24521** Alaska F3 Diesel B Unit, nonpowered, *03*		200
____	**24522** Alaska F3 Diesel B Unit "1519," powered, CC, *03*		300
____	**24528** Postwar "2379T" Rio Grande F3 Diesel A Unit, nonpowered, *04*		175
____	**24529** Santa Fe F3 Diesel AA Set, CC, *04*		690
____	**24532** Santa Fe F3 Diesel B Unit "18A," nonpowered, *04*		150
____	**24533** Santa Fe F3 Diesel B Unit "18B," *04*		200
____	**24534** Erie-Lack. F3 Diesel ABA Set, CC, *05*		900
____	**24538** Erie-Lack. F3 Diesel B Unit "8042," powered, CC, *05*		225
____	**24544** NYC FA2 Diesel AA Set, CC, *05*		600
____	**24547** NYC FB2 Diesel B Unit "3330" (std O), *05*		150
____	**24548** CN FPA-4 Diesel AA Set, CC, *05*		600
____	**24551** CN FPB-4 Diesel B Unit "6865" (std O), *05*		150
____	**24552** UP F3 Diesel ABA Set, CC, *05*		680
____	**24556** UP F3 Diesel B Unit "900C," powered, CC, *05*		285
____	**24562** Santa Fe F3 Diesel B Unit, powered, *04-05*		300
____	**24563** PRR F3 Diesel B Unit, powered, *04-05*		195
____	**24570** Santa Fe FT Diesel B Unit, nonpowered, *05*		85
____	**24573** Postwar "2383C" Santa Fe F3 Diesel B Unit, nonpowered, *05*		180
____	**24574** UP E7 Diesel AA Set, CC, *06*		700
____	**24577** UP E7 Diesel B Unit "990," nonpowered (std O), *06*		150
____	**24578** UP E7 Diesel B Unit "988," powered, *06*		300
____	**24579** NYC E7 Diesel AA Set, CC, *06*		700
____	**24582** NYC E7 Diesel B Unit "4105," nonpowered (std O), *06*		150
____	**24583** NYC E7 Diesel B Unit "4104," powered, *06*		300
____	**24584** Pennsylvania F7 Diesel ABA Set, CC, *06*		900
____	**24588** Pennsylvania F7 Diesel B Unit "9643B," powered, *06-07*		300
____	**24589** Santa Fe F7 Diesel ABA Set, CC, *06-07*		900
____	**24593** Santa Fe F7 Diesel B Unit "332B," powered, *06-07*		300
____	**24594** PRR F7 Diesel Breakdown B Unit, RailSounds, *06-07*		160
____	**24595** Santa Fe F7 Diesel Breakdown B Unit, RailSounds, *06-07*		270
____	**24596** UP E7 Diesel Breakdown B Unit, RailSounds, *06*		270
____	**24597** NYC E7 Diesel Breakdown B Unit, RailSounds, *06*		270
____	**24928** Franklin Mutual Bank, *08*		60
____	**25003** WP BoxCar, orange with silver feather, *05*		30
____	**25008** Holiday BoxCar, *06*		50
____	**25009** Santa Fe Hi-Cube Boxcar "14064," *06*		30

	Exc	Mint
25010 NP Boxcar "48189," *06*		30____
25011 Angela Trotta Thomas "Santa's Break" BoxCar, *06*		50____
25014 PRR BoxCar, silver, *10*		30____
25016 ATSF BoxCar, *10*		35____
25022 NYC BoxCar, *06*		35____
25025 Reading Boxcar "106502," *07-08*		35____
25026 RI Hi-Cube BoxCar, *07-08*		35____
25030 Billboard Boxcar with catalog art, *06*		20____
25033 Holiday BoxCar, *07*		50____
25034 Angela Trotta Thomas "Santa's Workshop" BoxCar, *07*		50____
25035 Disney Holiday BoxCar, *06*		50____
25041 UPS Centennial Boxcar #1, *06*		60____
25042 UPS Centennial Boxcar #2, *07*		60____
25043 Macy's Parade BoxCar, *06*		40____
25050 British Columbia Hi-Cube Boxcar "8008," *08*		35____
25051 Seaboard BoxCar, *08*		35____
25052 Disney Holiday BoxCar, *07*		75____
25053 NYC DD Boxcar "75500," *08*		55____
25054 Angela Trotta Thomas "Christmas Memories" BoxCar, *08*		55____
25057 PRR Boxcar "19751," *08*		20____
25058 Santa Fe BoxCar, *10*		30____
25059 Democrat 2008 Election BoxCar, *08*		50____
25060 Republican 2008 Election BoxCar, *08*		50____
25061 Holiday BoxCar, *08*		55____
25063 Conrail Boxcar "25063," *09*		40____
25064 CP Rail Hi-Cube BoxCar, *09-10*		40____
25065 Disney Holiday BoxCar, *08*		40____
25066 Holiday BoxCar, *09*		65____
25067 Angela Trotta Thomas "General Delivery" BoxCar, *09*		65____
25068 D&H BoxCar, *08 u*		60____
25077 Milwaukee Road Boxcar "8484," *09-10*		40____
25087 Wabash Boxcar "6439," *10-11*		40____
25093 Seaboard BoxCar, *10*		30____
25095 Texas Special BoxCar, *10*		100____
25096 CN BoxCar, *10*		45____
25103 Chessie "Steam Special" Madison Car 2-pack, *05*		100____
25106 Pennsylvania Madison Car 4-pack, *05*		210____
25111 Pennsylvania Madison Car 2-pack, *05*		120____
25114 Lionel Lines Passenger Car 3-pack, *05*		120____
25118 Lionel Lines Passenger Car 2-pack, *05*		80____
25121 Southern Streamliner Car 4-pack, *05*		210____
25126 Southern Streamliner Car 2-pack, *05-06*		120____
25134 Polar Express Add-on Diner, *05-14, 16-17*		70____
25135 Polar Express Add-on Baggage Car, *05-14,16-17*		70____
25148 B&O Madison Car 4-pack, *06-07*		220____
25153 B&O Madison Car 2-pack, *06-07*		125____
25156 California Zephyr Streamliner Car 4-pack (std O), *06-07*		220____
25161 California Zephyr Streamliner Car 2-pack, *06-07*		125____
25164 UP Madison Car 4-pack, *06-07*		220____
25169 UP Madison Car 2-pack, *06-07*		125____
25176 B&O Baggage Car, TrainSounds, *06-07*		160____

		Exc	Mint
____	**25177** UP Baggage Car, TrainSounds, *06-07*		160
	25178 California Zephyr Streamliner Baggage Car, TrainSounds, *06-07*		160
____			
	25186 Polar Express Hot Chocolate Car Add-on, *06-14, 16-17*		70
____			
____	**25187** GN Streamliner Car 4-pack, *07*		220
____	**25188** GN Streamliner Car 2-pack, *07*		125
____	**25189** GN Streamliner Baggage Car, TrainSounds, *07*		160
____	**25196** North Pole Central Vista Dome Car, *07-08*		45
____	**25197** North Pole Central Baggage Car, *07-10*		45
____	**25198** PRR Vista Dome Car "4058," *07-08*		45
____	**25199** PRR Baggage Car "9359," *07-09*		45
	25404 FEC Champion Aluminum Passenger Car 2-pack, *04-05*		290
____			
	25407 FEC Champion Aluminum Diner, StationSounds, *04-05*		290
____			
	25408 Santa Fe El Capitan Aluminum Passenger Car 2-pack, *05*		290
____			
	25411 Santa Fe El Capitan Aluminum Diner, StationSounds, *05*		290
____			
____	**25412** B&O Columbian Aluminum Passenger Car 2-pack, *05*		275
____	**25415** B&O Columbian Aluminum Diner, StationSounds, *05*		290
____	**25416** SP Daylight Aluminum Passenger Car 2-pack, *04-05*		290
____	**25419** SP Daylight Aluminum Diner, StationSounds, *04-05*		290
	25420 PRR Trail Blazer Aluminum Passenger Car 2-pack, *04-05*		290
____			
	25423 PRR Trail Blazer Aluminum Diner, StationSounds, *04-05*		290
____			
	25433 UP City of Denver Aluminum Passenger Car 4-pack (std O), *05*		1000
____			
____	**25438** Union Pacific Aluminum Passenger Car 2-pack, *05*		250
	25441 UP City of Denver 18" Aluminum Diner, StationSounds, *05*		290
____			
____	**25446** Santa Fe Super Chief Streamliner Car 2-pack, *05*		150
	25450 PRR Congressional Aluminum Passenger Car 4-pack (std O), *06-07*		580
____			
	25455 PRR Congressional Aluminum Passenger Car 2-pack (std O), *06-07*		300
____			
	25458 PRR Congressional Diner, StationSounds (std O), *06-07*		300
____			
	25473 NYC Commodore Vanderbilt Aluminum Passenger Car 2-pack (std O), *06*		300
____			
	25476 NYC Commodore Vanderbilt Diner, StationSounds (std O), *06*		300
____			
	25496 Texas Special 21" Streamliner Diner, StationSounds (std O), *07*		300
____			
	25503 Santa Fe Heavyweight Passenger Car 4-pack (std O), *07-09*		495
____			
	25504 Santa Fe Heavyweight Passenger Car 2-pack (std O), *07-09*		265
____			
	25505 Santa Fe Heavyweight Diner, StationSounds (std O), *07-09*		295
____			
____	**25506** SP Heavyweight Passenger Car 4-pack (std O), *07*		495
	25507 SP Heavyweight Passenger Car 2-pack (std O), *07-08*		265
____			
____	**25508** SP Heavyweight Diner, StationSounds (std O), *07-08*		295
____	**25512** Texas Special Streamliner Car 2-pack (std O), *07*		300

		Exc	Mint
25514	Best Friend of Charleston Coach, *08*	125	___
25515	MILW Heavyweight Passenger Car 4-pack (std O), *07*	495	___
25516	MILW Heavyweight Passenger Car 2-pack (std O), *07*	265	___
25517	MILW Heavyweight Diner, StationSounds (std O), *07-08*	295	___
25518	PRR Heavyweight Passenger Car 4-pack (std O), *07*	495	___
25519	PRR Heavyweight Passenger Car 2-pack (std O), *07*	265	___
25520	PRR Heavyweight Diner, StationSounds (std O), *07-08*	295	___
25521	B&O Heavyweight Passenger Car 4-pack (std O), *07*	495	___
25522	B&O Heavyweight Passenger Car 2-pack (std O), *07*	265	___
25523	B&O Heavyweight Diner, StationSounds (std O), *07-08*	295	___
25559	Phantom IV Passenger Car 4-pack, *08*	380	___
25574	UP Streamlined Diner, StationSounds (std O), *08*	325	___
25575	Polar Express Heavyweight Car 2-pack, *09*	400	___
25576	Polar Express Scale Observation Car, *14, 16*	210	___
25578	Polar Express Heavyweight Add-on Coach, *09*	200	___
25582	New York City Transit R30 Subway 2-pack, *10*	400	___
25586	Polar Express Heavyweight Baggage Car, *10, 12-14*	210	___
25587	Polar Express Abandoned Toy Car, *10, 13*	200	___
25595	New York City Transit R16 Subway 2-pack, *10*	400	___
25598	Polar Express Heavyweight Combination Car, *12-14*	210	___
25600	Postwar Scale CP 18" Aluminum Passenger Car 4-pack, *11*	640	___
25605	Postwar Scale CP 18" Aluminum Passenger Car 2-pack, *11*	320	___
25608	ATSF Super Chief 18" Aluminum Passenger Cars 4-pack, *11*	640	___
25613	ATSF Super Chief 18" Aluminum Passenger Cars 2-pack, *11*	320	___
25616	UP 18" Passenger Car 2-pack (std O), *11*	320	___
25619	PRR "Lindbergh Special" Passenger Car 2-pack, *11*	280	___
25622	Milwaukee Road 18" Passenger Car 4-pack, *11*	640	___
25623	Milwaukee Road 18" Passenger Car 2-pack, *11*	320	___
25630	Polar Express Scale Heavyweight Diner, *12-14, 16*	210	___
25631	Lionel Funeral Set Add-on 2-pack (std O), *13*	300	___
25635	PRR Red Arrow Heavyweight Coach 3-pack (std O), *13*	430	___
25639	PRR Red Arrow Heavyweight Diner (std O), *13*	150	___
25646	ATSF Scout Heavyweight Coach 4-pack (std O), *12-14*	550	___
25651	ATSF Scout Heavyweight Coach 2-pack (std O), *12-14*	280	___
25654	Southern Crescent Limited Heavyweight Passenger Car 2-pack, *12*	550	___
25655	Blue Comet Heavyweight Passenger Car 2-pack, *12-13*	550	___
25656	Alton Limited Heavyweight Passenger Car 2-pack, *12-14*	550	___
25665	Amtrak Acela Passenger Car 2-pack, *12*	500	___
25713	NYC 20th Century Limited Heavyweight Passenger Car 4-pack (std O), *12-14*	550	___
25714	NYC 20th Century Limited Van Twiller Combo Car (std O), *12*	140	___

		Mint
25715	NYC 20th Century Limited Schuyler Mansion Sleeper Car (std O), *12*	140
25716	NYC 20th Century Limited Macomb House Sleeper Car (std O), *12*	140
25717	NYC 20th Century Limited Catskill Valley Observation Car (std O), *12*	140
25718	NYC 20th Century Limited Heavyweight Passenger Car 2-pack, *12-14*	280
25719	NYC 20th Century Limited Baggage Car "4857" (std O), *12*	140
25720	NYC 20th Century Limited Poplar Highlands Sleeper Car (std O), *12*	140
25721	NYC 20th Century Limited Heavyweight Diner "655" (std O), *12*	280
25722	D&RGW California Zephyr 18" Aluminum Passenger Car 4-pack, *12*	640
25727	WP California Zephyr 18" Aluminum Passenger Car 2-pack, *12*	320
25731	CB&Q California Zephyr 18" Aluminum Passenger Car 2-pack, *12*	320
25757	Texas Special Passenger Car 2-pack, *13-14*	400
25760	PRR Passenger Car 2-pack, *13-14*	400
25773	SAL Round-roof Boxcar "19297" (std O), *14*	80
25790	NYC 20th Century Limited Heavyweight Diner (std O), *12*	140
25795	Polar Express 10th Anniversary Scale Coach, *14*	215
25795	Polar Express Gold Coach, *17*	200
25796	Polar Express 10th Anniversary Scale Observation Car, *14, 16*	215
25930	John Adams BoxCar, *13, 15-16*	70
25931	Andrew Johnson BoxCar, *13, 15-16*	70
25932	Calvin Coolidge BoxCar, *13, 15-16*	70
25933	Harry S. Truman BoxCar, *13, 15-16*	70
25934	Santa Fe Reefer 3-pack, *14-17*	145
25938	PRR Freight Expansion 3-pack, *13*	155
25942	Western Freight Expansion 3-pack, *13-16*	155
25946	SP Hi-Cube Boxcar "128132," *13, 15*	50
25947	North Pole Express Jack Frost Reefer, *13*	43
25958	Gingerbread Dough Vat Car, *13-14*	60
25959	Gingerbread 3-D Tank Car, *13*	55
25960	Christmas Tree Transparent BoxCar, *13-14*	75
25961	Thanksgiving on Parade BoxCar, *13*	60
25962	Thanksgiving Poultry Car, *13*	70
25963	A Christmas Story 30th Anniversary BoxCar, *13-14*	65
25964	Silver Bell Casting Co. Ore Car, *13*	55
25965	Polar Express 10th Anniversary BoxCar, *13*	65
25972	MILW Scale Round-roof BoxCar, (std O), *15*	50
25973	Seaboard Round-roof Boxcar "19297" (std O), *14*	80
25977	A Christmas Story Leg Lamp Mint Car, *13*	80
26000	C&O Flatcar with pipes, *01*	20
26001	BP FlatCar "6424" with trailers, *01 u*	150
26002	Monopoly Flatcar with airplane, *00 u*	NRS
26003	Lackawanna Flatcar with NH trailer, *01*	60
26004	Conrail FlatCar "71693" with trailer, *01*	50
26005	Nickel Plate Flatcar with trailer, *01*	55

	Exc	Mint
26006 Southern FlatCar "50126" with trailer, *01*	50	
26007 NW FlatCar "203029" with trailer, *01*	50	
26008 Farmall FlatCar, *01 u*	NRS	
26011 B&M Bulkhead FlatCar, *01 u*	NRS	
26013 CN Flatcar with Zamboni ice resurfacing machine, *01*	48	
26014 JCPenney FlatCar, *01 u*	145	
26016 Soo Line Flatcar with trucks, *01 u*	NRS	
26017 Soo Line Flatcar with trailer, *01 u*	NRS	
26018 Soo Line Flatcar with trailer, *01 u*	NRS	
26019 Alaska Gondola "13801," *02*	30	
26020 Postwar "3830" Flatcar with submarine, *02*	46	
26021 CN Flatcar with trailer, *02*	44	
26022 PFE Flatcar with trailer, *02*	32	
26023 Postwar "6816" Flatcar with bulldozer, *02*	65	
26024 Postwar "6817" Flatcar with scraper, *02*	65	
26025 Postwar "6407" Flatcar with rocket, *02*	42	
26026 Postwar "6413" Flatcar with Mercury capsules, *02*	95	
26027 FlatCar "6425" with U.S. Army boat, *02*	30	
26028 Conrail Well Car "768121," *02*	40	
26030 NYC FlatCar "601172" with stakes and bulkheads, *02*	22	
26033 NYC Gondola "6462," *01*	30	
26035 LL Flatcar with traffic helicopter, *01*	50	
26039 Lions Flatcar with 2 Zamboni ice resurfacing machines, *02*	39	
26042 B&O Gondola "601272" with canisters, *03*	19	
26043 Seaboard FlatCar "48109" with trailer, *03*	30	
26044 NYC FlatCar "506089" with trailers, *03*	35	
26045 Postwar "2411" Flatcar with pipes, *03*	40	
26046 Postwar "6561" Flatcar with cable reels, *03*	30	
26047 Postwar "2461" Flatcar with transformer, *03*	25	
26048 Postwar "6801" Flatcar with boat, *02*	29	
26049 Speedboat Willie Flatcar with boat, *03*	29	
26053 PRR Gondola with canisters, *04 05*	20	
26056 Southern Bulkhead FlatCar "50125," *02*	19	
26057 SP FlatCar "599365" with tractors, *02*	37	
26058 SP FlatCar "599366" with trailer frames, *02*	35	
26061 Lionelville Tree Transport Gondola, *03*	40	
26062 NYC Gondola "26062" with cable reels, *03*	19	
26063 Pennsylvania Bulkhead FlatCar "26063," *03*	19	
26064 Rock Island FlatCar "90088" with trailer, *04*	34	
26065 REA Flatcar with trailers "TLCX2," *04*	35	
26066 Great Northern Bulkhead FlatCar "26066," *04*	20	
26067 Southern Gondola "60141" with cable reels, *04*	20	
26070 Nestle Nesquik FlatCar "26070" with trailer, *03*	70	
26077 LL FlatCar "6424" with autos, girls set add-on, *03*	44	
26078 LL FlatCar "6801" with boat, boys set add-on, *03*	40	
26080 NJ Medical School Flatcar with handCar, *03*	80	
26082 Frisco Auto Carrier, 2-tier, *04*	20	
26085 New York Auto Carrier, 2-tier, *05*	27	
26086 Alaska Flatcar with bulkheads, *05*	25	
26087 Rock Island Gondola with canisters, traditional, *05*	27	
26091 Elvis Flatcar with tractor and trailer, traditional, *05*	60	

		Exc Mint
__ **26096**	BNSF Screened Auto Carrier, *04*	55
__ **26099**	PRR Auto Carrier "500423," 3-tier, *07*	30
__ **26100**	PRR 1-D Tank Car, *00*	27
__ **26101**	Lenoil 1-D Tank Car "6015," *00*	34
__ **26102**	AEC Glow-in-Dark 1-D Tank Car, *00*	55
__ **26103**	GATX Tank Train 1-D Tank Car "44588," *00*	34
__ **26107**	BP Petroleum 3-D Tank Car, *00 u*	99
__ **26108**	Lionel Visitor's Center Reefer "206482," *00 u*	38
__ **26109**	NYC (P&LE) 1-D Tank Car, *00*	42
__ **26110**	SP 3-D Tank Car "6415," *00-01*	15
__ **26111**	Frisco Tank Car, *00*	29
__ **26112**	Gulf Oil Tank Car, *00*	40
__ **26113**	U.S. Army 1-D Tank Car, *00*	35
__ **26114**	Service Station 1-D Tank Car (SSS), *00*	32
__ **26115**	Lionel Centennial Tank Car, *00 u*	90
__ **26116**	Pepe LePew 1-D Tank Car, *00 u*	85
__ **26118**	NYC Tank Car "101900," *01*	23
__ **26119**	Protex 3-D Tank Car "1054," *00*	29
__ **26120**	KCS Tank Car "1229," *00*	32
__ **26122**	Pioneer Seed Tank Car, *00 u*	NRS
__ **26123**	Santa Fe Stock Car "23002," *01*	35
__ **26124**	C&O 1-D Tank Car "X1019," *01*	30
__ **26125**	Winter Wonderland Clear Tank Car with confetti, *00*	50
__ **26126**	Cheerios BoxCar, *98*	70
__ **26127**	Wellspring Capital Management Tank Car with confetti, *00 u*	220
__ **26131**	Santa Fe 1-D Tank Car "335268," *02*	22
__ **26132**	UP 1-D Tank Car "69015, *02*	40
__ **26133**	Tootsie Roll 1-D Tank Car "26133," *02*	40
__ **26135**	Whirlpool Tank Car, *01*	NRS
__ **26136**	Southern 1-D Tank Car "8790011," *03*	20
__ **26137**	Jack Frost 1-D Tank Car "106," *03*	32
__ **26138**	Nestle Nesquik 1-D Tank Car "26138," *03*	40
__ **26139**	Lionel Lines Stock Car "26139" with horses, *03*	39
__ **26141**	Whirlpool 1-D Tank Car, *03 u*	94
__ **26144**	Chessie System 1-D Tank Car "2233," *02*	22
__ **26145**	Do It Best 1-D Tank Car, *03 u*	80
__ **26146**	Do It Best 1-D Tank Car, *03 u*	95
__ **26147**	Diamond Chemicals 1-D Tank Car "6315," Archive Collection, *02*	33
__ **26149**	Egg Nog 1-D Tank Car, *03*	43
__ **26150**	Alaska 3-D Tank Car "26150," *03*	23
__ **26151**	NP Wood-sided Reefer "26151," *03*	19
__ **26152**	Morton Salt 1-D Tank Car "26152," *04*	40
__ **26153**	Pillsbury 1-D Tank Car "26153," *04*	40
__ **26154**	NYC 3-D Tank Car "26154," *04*	25
__ **26155**	Pennsylvania 1-D Tank Car "26155," *04*	20
__ **26156**	North Western Wood-sided Reefer "15356," *04*	20
__ **26157**	Ballyhoo Brothers Circus Stock Car "26157," *04*	35
__ **26158**	Campbell's Soup 1-D Tank Car, *04*	35
__ **26164**	LL 1-D Tank Car "6315," girls set add-on, *03*	43
__ **26167**	New Haven 1-D Tank Car, traditional, *05*	27
__ **26168**	Conrail 3-D Tank Car, traditional, *05*	27
__ **26169**	Santa Fe Wood-sided Reefer, traditional, *05*	27

MODERN ERA 1970-2019

Exc Mint

		Exc	Mint
26171	Alaska 1-D Tank Car, *05*		30___
26176	Tidmouth Milk 1-D Tank Car, *05*		35___
26179	GN 3-D Tank Car, *06*		30___
26180	DM&IR 1-D Tank Car "S15," *06*		30___
26181	NYC Wood-sided Reefer, *06*		30___
26193	UP 1-D Tank Car, *07*		15___
26196	Candy Cane 1-D Tank Car, *06*		60___
26197	D&H 1-D Tank Car "55," *07*-08		35___
26198	D&RGW 3-D Tank Car, *07*		30___
26199	WP PFE Wood-sided Reefer "55327," *07*		30___
26200	NKP Boxcar "18211," *98*		35___
26201	Operation Lifesaver BoxCar, *98*		29___
26203	D&H Boxcar "1829," *98*		25___
26204	Alaska Boxcar "10806," *98-99*		35___
26205	Rocky & Bullwinkle BoxCar, *99*		36___
26206	Curious George BoxCar, *99*		40___
26208	Vapor Records Boxcar #2, *98*		60___
26214	Celebrate the Century Stamp BoxCar, *98 u*		97___
26215	AEC Glow-in-the-Dark BoxCar, *98*		100___
26216	Cheerios BoxCar, *98 u*		80___
26218	Quaker Oats BoxCar, *98 u*		460___
26219	Ace Hardware BoxCar, *98 u*		NRS___
26220	Smuckers BoxCar, *98 u*		89___
26222	Penn Central Boxcar "125962," *99*		31___
26223	FEC Boxcar "5027," *99*		31___
26224	D&H BoxCar, *99*		24___
26228	Vapor Records Holiday BoxCar, *99 u*		130___
26230	AEC Glow-in-the-Dark Boxcar #2, *99*		55___
26232	Martin Guitar Lumber Boxcar "9823," *99*		50___
26234	NYC BoxCar, *99*		29___
26235	Valentine BoxCar, *99*		40___
26236	Aircraft BoxCar, *99*		28___
26237	Boy Scout BoxCar, *99*		85___
26238	Detroit Historical Museum BoxCar, *99*		29___
26239	M.A.D.D. BoxCar, *99*		19___
26240	RailBox BoxCar, *99-00*		24___
26241	Norfolk & Western BoxCar, *99-00*		17___
26242	D.A.R.E. BoxCar, *99*		30___
26243	Christmas BoxCar, *99*		35___
26244	Woody Woodpecker BoxCar, *99*		43___
26247	Lionel Lines BoxCar, *99*		38___
26253	Acme Explosives BoxCar, *99 u*		NRS___
26254	Keebler BoxCar, *99 u*		NRS___
26255	NYC Boxcar "200495," *99 u*		30___
26256	Salvation Army Charity BoxCar, *99*		29___
26257	Wheaties BoxCar, *99*		82___
26264	Lionel Station BoxCar, *99*		44___
26265	NYC Pacemaker BoxCar, *00*		30___
26271	AEC Glow-in-the-Dark BoxCar, *99*		62___
26272	Christmas BoxCar, *00*		42___
26275	Boy Scout BoxCar, *00*		55___
26276	C&O Boxcar "23296," *99-00*		23___
26277	UP Boxcar "491050," *00*		20___

		Exc	Mint
____	26278 Cap'n Crunch Christmas BoxCar, *99*		68C
____	26280 Tinsel Town Express BoxCar, music, *00*		5C
____	26284 Toy Fair Preview BoxCar, *99 u*		725
____	26285 NYC Pacemaker BoxCar, *00*		4C
____	26288 AEC Glow-in-Dark BoxCar, *99*		5C
____	26290 SP BoxCar, *00*		2C
____	26291 Pennsylvania Boxcar "47158," *00*		2C
____	26292 Frisco Boxcar "22015," *00*		2C
____	26293 Burlington BoxCar, *00*		3C
____	26294 Centennial Express BoxCar, *00*		NRS
____	26295 Trainmaster BoxCar, *99 u*		55
____	26296 Service Station Boxcar Set (SSS), *00*		105
____	26298 Taz Bobbing BoxCar, *00*		7C
____	26300 UPS Flatcar with trailers, *04*		5C
____	26301 UPS Flatcar with airplane, traditional, *05*		53
____	26302 Troublesome Truck #1, *05*		35
____	26303 Troublesome Truck #2, *05*		35
____	26305 SP Auto Carrier, 2-tier, *06*		3C
____	26306 D&RGW Gondola "56135" with canisters, *06*		3C
____	26307 Chessie System Bulkhead FlatCar, *06*		3C
____	26308 Hard Rock Cafe Flatcar with billboards, *06*		55
____	26309 Alaska Depressed Center Flatcar with cable reels, *06*		5C
____	26310 CGW FlatCar "3707" with trailer, *06*		55
____	26311 Santa Fe Flatcar with pickups, *06*		6C
____	26317 AEC Gondola with toxic waste containers		3C
____	26318 AEC Gondola with toxic waste containers		3C
____	26330 Gondola with trees and presents, *06*		6C
____	26331 Lionel Lines Bulkhead FlatCar, *07*		3C
____	26332 CP Rail Gondola "337061" with canisters, *07*		3C
____	26335 Domino Sugar Flatcar with trailer, *07-08*		6C
____	26357 CSX FlatCar "600514" with pipes, *07-08*		5C
____	26366 REA Flatcar with trailers, *07*		6C
____	26367 Santa's Egg Nog Flatcar with container, *07*		6C
____	26368 Gondola with trees and presents, *07*		6C
____	26378 Conrail Auto Carrier "786414," 2-tier, *08*		35
____	26379 PRR Gondola with cable reels, *08-09*		35
____	26380 NYC Bulkhead FlatCar, *08*		35
____	26389 ATSF Flatcar "108477" with 2 pickups, *08*		6C
____	26390 ATSF Flatcar with bulkheads, *09-10*		4C
____	26391 NYC Gondola "263910" with containers, *09*		4C
____	26392 BNSF Auto Carrier, *09*		4C
____	26400 C&NW Hopper, *07-08*		35
____	26401 NP Ore Car "78540," *08*		35
____	26410 Chessie System Hopper "47806," *08*		35
____	26411 Lionel Lines Ore Car "2026," *08-09*		35
____	26412 Chessie System 4-bay Hopper "60573," *08*		35
____	26418 B&M Hopper, *09*		4C
____	26421 PRR Ore Car, *11*		4C
____	26422 White Pass Ice Breaker Car, *09*		5C
____	26423 Soo Line Ore Car, *10*		4C
____	26424 LV Hopper, *11*		3C
____	26425 UP Hopper, *11*		4C
____	26429 PRR Hopper, *11*		4C

Exc Mint

Cat.	Description	Exc	Mint
26435	B&M Ice Breaker Hopper, *11*		50____
26437	CSX Hopper, *11*		40____
26439	Central of Georgia Hopper, *11-12*		40____
26443	M&StL Ore Car "6700," *11*		40____
26445	Polar Hopper with presents, *11-14*		60____
26446	Thomas & Friends Troublesome Trucks Christmas 2-pack, *11-15*		70____
26448	U.S. Army Gondola with reels, *11*		40____
26449	CN Hi-Cube Boxcar "799346," *13*		55____
26451	DM&IR Ore Car "28003," *13*		43____
26452	PRR Hopper "153935," *13*		43____
26457	PRR Ore Car, *12*		40____
26473	Lackawanna NS Heritage 2-bay Hopper, *13*		55____
26474	NYC NS Heritage Quad Hopper, *13*		55____
26477	Monopoly Electric Company Hopper, *13*		65____
26481	Boy Scouts of America Christmas Gondola, *13*		65____
26488	Hershey's Ice Breakers Hopper, *13*		63____
26489	Hershey's Chistmas Bells BoxCar, *13*		65____
26491	Pennsylvania Power & Light Gondola with canisters, *13*		43____
26492	Area 51 3-D Tank Car, *13*		43____
26493	Monopoly Water Works 3-D Tank Car, *13*		65____
26494	PRR Truss Rod Gondola with vats, *13*		60____
26495	C&NW Poultry Car, *13*		60____
26496	Lionelville Aquarium Co. Fish Food Vat Car, *13-16*		65____
26497	Bethlehem Steel Depressed Flatcar with reels, *13*		43____
26499	CN Hi-Cube Boxcar "799346," *14*		55____
26502	UP Bay Window Caboose "6517," *97*		47____
26503	ATSF High-Cupola Caboose "7606R," *97*		85____
26504	Mobil Oil Square Window Caboose "6257," *97 u*		37____
26505	Rescue Unit Caboose, *98*		50____
26506	N&W Square Window Caboose "562748," *98*		15____
26507	D&H Square Window Caboose "35707," *98*		20____
26508	Alaska Square Window Caboose "1081," *98*		28____
26511	Quaker Oats Square Window Caboose, *98 u*		52____
26513	NYC Emergency Caboose "26505," *99*		47____
26515	Lionel Lines Bobber Caboose, *99*		10____
26516	Safari Bobber Caboose, *99 u*		10____
26519	Christmas Work Caboose "6496," *99*		41____
26520	Bethlehem Steel Work Caboose "6130," (SSS), *99*		55____
26523	Keebler Cheezit Square Window Caboose, *99 u*		NRS____
26524	NYC Square Window Caboose "295," *99 u*		20____
26526	Santa Fe Square Window Caboose "999471," *01*		30____
26527	Christmas Work Caboose with presents, *02*		27____
26528	PRR Square Window Caboose "6257," *99*		21____
26530	LL Square Window Caboose "6257," *99*		22____
26532	NYC Square Window Caboose "296," *00*		20____
26533	SP Square Window Caboose, *00*		20____
26534	PRR Square Window Caboose "6257," *00*		20____
26535	Frisco Square Window Caboose "1700," *00*		20____
26536	Centennial Express Square Window Caboose, *00*		NRS____
26537	Lionel Mines Square Window Caboose, *00 u*		45____
26539	Whirlpool Square Window Caboose, *00 u*		NRS____
26542	ACL Square Window Caboose "069," *01*		31____

		Exc	Mint
26543	GN Square Window Caboose "X66," *00-01*		28
26544	Alaska Square Window Caboose "1084," *01*		25
26545	Snap-On Square Window Caboose, *00 u*		NRS
26548	Pioneer Seed Square Window Caboose, *00 u*		NRS
26549	PRR Square Window Caboose "4977947," *01*		20
26550	NYC Square Window Caboose "19293," *01*		20
26551	Chessie System Center Cupola Caboose, *01*		25
26552	Santa Fe Square Window Caboose "999472," *01*		25
26553	C&O Center Cupola Caboose "A918," *01*		30
26554	Monopoly Short Line Square Window Caboose, *00 u*		NRS
26556	NH Center Cupola Caboose, *01*		35
26557	Farmall Square Window Caboose, *01 u*		NRS
26559	N&W Center Cupola Caboose "518408," *01*		20
26560	B&M Square Window Caboose, *01 u*		20
26564	Soo Line Center Cupola Caboose, *01 u*		20
26565	Lionel Employee Square Window Caboose, *01 u*		160
26566	WP Square Window Caboose "731," *02*		25
26568	NKP Square Window Caboose "1155," *02*		25
26569	Southern Square Window Caboose "252," *02*		25
26570	B&O Square Window Caboose "295," *02*		25
26572	Lionel 20th Century Square Window Caboose, *00 u*		25
26580	Wabash Square Window Caboose "2805," *03*		22
26581	C&O Square Window Caboose "C-1831," *03*		20
26582	L&N Square Window Caboose "318," *03*		20
26583	PRR Square Window Caboose "477814," *03*		25
26594	Ontario Northland Work Caboose "26594," *03*		25
26595	UP Caboose "26595," *03*		18
26596	NYC Caboose "17716," *04*		25
26597	Great Northern Caboose "X295," *04*		25
26598	UP Caboose "26598," *04*		25
26599	DM&IR Work Caboose "26599," *04*		25
26600	American Fire and Rescue Water Tank Car, *09-11*		55
26603	LV Depressed Flatcar with reels, *09*		40
26604	Halloween Spooky Grave Gondola, *09*		58
26609	NYC Gondola with Pacemaker canisters		40
26612	Christmas Gifts Gondola, *09*		60
26614	Tupelo Dairy Farms Milk Car, *10-11*		60
26616	UP Bulkhead Flatcar with pipes, *10*		40
26617	B&O Depressed Center Flatcar with generator, *10*		40
26629	PRR Flatcar with generators		35
26638	Pennsylvania Power & Light Flatcar with reels, *11*		40
26639	Cities Service 3-Tier Auto Carrier, *11-12*		40
26640	CN Maple Syrup Barrel Ramp Car, *11-12*		40
26641	Coca-Cola Flatcar with trailer, *11*		75
26642	CN Jet Snowblower, *11-12*		65
26643	D&RGW Jet Snowblower, *11-13*		65
26644	BNSF Flatcar with generator, *11*		40
26645	BNSF Flatcar with trailer, *11*		40
26646	Pennsylvania Power & Light Flatcar with transformer, *11-12*		40
26647	IC Bulkhead Flatcar with pipes, *11*		40
26649	Erie-Lack. Gondola with canisters, *11*		40
26650	M&StL Flatcar with pipes, *11*		40

		Exc	Mint
26651	ATSF Scout Heavyweight Passenger Car 2-pack (std O), *12*	280	____
26652	NYC Gondola with canisters, *11*	40	____
26653	PC Flatcar with generator, *11*	35	____
26654	Boy Scouts Flatcar with Pinewood Derby Kit, *11-13*	75	____
26660	Coca-Cola Vat Car, *11-16*	75	____
26661	Reindeer Feed Barrel Ramp Car, *09*	60	____
26665	Hershey's Special Dark Flatcar with trailer, *11*	60	____
26666	Boy Scouts Flatcar with trailer, *11*	70	____
26667	Flatcar with Santa's sleigh, *12*	70	____
26668	Strasburg Flatcar with wheels, *11*	55	____
26669	U.S. Navy Flatcar with Shark submarine, *12-13*	60	____
26673	B&M Flatcar with Milk Tank, *12*	60	____
26675	Monopoly Auto Loader, *12*	80	____
26676	Heinz Baked Beans Vat Car, *12*	60	____
26677	LIRR Gondola with canisters, *12*	40	____
26679	ATSF Gondola with reels, *12-13*	55	____
26683	Christmas Track Maintenance Car, *12-13*	67	____
26685	Flatcar with Santa's plane, *12*	55	____
26686	Hershey's Cocoa Vat Car, *12-13*	63	____
26687	Lone Ranger Gondola with gunpowder vats, *12-14*	65	____
26693	Hershey's Krackel Piggyback Flatcar with trailer, *12-13*	75	____
26694	Carnegie Science Center Flatcar with submarine, *13*	70	____
26696	NJ Transit Gondola with wood ties, *12*	75	____
26699	PRR Flatcar with wheel load, *12-14*	55	____
26706	Lighted Christmas BoxCar, *00*	47	____
26707	Lionel Steel Operating Welding FlatCar "1108," *00*	90	____
26709	FlatCar "6511" with psychedelic submarine, *99*	32	____
26710	Southern Stock Car, Carsounds, *99*	95	____
26712	Churchill Downs Horse Car "6473," *99-00*	38	____
26713	Shay Log Car 3-pack, *99*	105	____
26714	Westside Lumber Flatcar with logs (std O), *99*	45	____
26715	Westside Lumber Flatcar with logs (std O), *99*	45	____
26716	Westside Lumber Flatcar with logs (std O), *99*	45	____
26717	Orion Star Boxcar 9600, *00*	30	____
26718	Christmas BoxCar, RailSounds, *00*	160	____
26719	Bobbing Ghost Halloween BoxCar, *00*	46	____
26721	Lionel Lines Coal Dump Car "3379," *00*	31	____
26722	Lionel Lines Log Dump Car "3351," *00*	31	____
26723	Lion Chasing Trainer Gondola "3444," *00*	49	____
26724	Veterans Day BoxCar, *00*	70	____
26725	NYC Jumping Hobo Boxcar "88160," *00*	38	____
26726	T. Rex Bobbing BoxCar, *00*	41	____
26727	San Francisco City Lights BoxCar, *00*	50	____
26736	Lionel Birthday BoxCar, *02 u*	40	____
26737	Operating Santa Gondola "6462," *00 u*	65	____
26738	Lionel Mines Gondola, *00 u*	NRS	____
26739	Santa and Snowman BoxCar, *00*	46	____
26740	Reindeer Car, *00*	43	____
26741	Operating Santa BoxCar, *00*	50	____
26743	Christmas Reindeer Car, *01*	55	____
26745	Traveling Aquarium Car "506," *01*	70	____
26746	Bobbing Vampire BoxCar, *01*	46	____

		Exc	Mint
____ **26747**	Halloween Bats Aquarium Car, *01*		75
____ **26748**	T&P Operating Hopper Car "9699," *01*		38
____ **26749**	Alaska Log Dump Car, *01*		29
____ **26751**	Chessie Coal Dump Car, *01*		27
____ **26752**	Christmas Aquarium Car, *01*		55
____ **26753**	Christmas Operating Dump Car, *01*		43
____ **26757**	Operating Barrel Car "35621," *00*		55
____ **26758**	AEC Nuclear Gondola "719766," *01*		90
____ **26759**	Postwar "3459" Coal Dump Car, *02*		60
____ **26760**	Postwar "3461" Log Dump Car, *02*		60
____ **26761**	AEC Security Caboose 3535, *01*		63
____ **26762**	Postwar "3665" Minuteman Car, *01*		55
____ **26763**	Postwar "6448" Exploding BoxCar, *01*		40
____ **26764**	Bethlehem Steel Operating Welding Car, *01*		75
____ **26765**	Postwar "3370" Sheriff and Outlaw Car, *01-02*	40	49
____ **26766**	Priority Mail Operating BoxCar, *01-02*		32
____ **26768**	Postwar "6520" Searchlight Car, *02*		49
____ **26769**	Santa Fe Crane Car "199793," CC, *03*		255
____ **26770**	Wabash Brakeman Car "3424," *01*		70
____ **26773**	Chessie Searchlight Car, *01*		20
____ **26774**	Santa Fe Log Dump Car, *01*		25
____ **26775**	U.S. Army Searchlight Car, *00*		50
____ **26776**	U.S. Army Operating Boxcar "26413," *00*		55
____ **26777**	U.S. Flag BoxCar, *01 u*		250
____ **26779**	Burlington Operating Hopper "189312," *02*		40
____ **26780**	Postwar "3376" Bronx Zoo Giraffe Car, *02*	35	36
____ **26781**	Postwar "3540" Operating Radar Car, *02*		35
____ **26782**	Lenny the Lion Bobbing Head Car, *02*		38
____ **26784**	Stingray Express Aquarium Car, *02*		35
____ **26785**	Flatcar with powerboat, *02*		31
____ **26786**	Lionelville Operating Parade Car, *02*		40
____ **26787**	Erie Jumping Hobo BoxCar, *01-02*		43
____ **26788**	Christmas Music BoxCar, *02*		46
____ **26789**	Kiss Kringle Chase Gondola, *02*		35
____ **26790**	Lighted Christmas BoxCar, *02*		34
____ **26791**	UP Animated Gondola, *02*	40	50
____ **26792**	REA Operating Boxcar "6299," *03*		39
____ **26793**	Alaska Extension Searchlight Car, *01*		44
____ **26794**	Postwar "6352" PFE Ice Car, *01-02*		85
____ **26795**	NYC Stock Car "3121," Cattle Sounds, *02*		50
____ **26796**	Lionel Farms Poultry Dispatch Car, *01*		55
____ **26797**	GN Log Dump Car "60011," *02*		48
____ **26798**	Bethlehem Steel Coal Dump Car "26798," *02*		70
____ **26801**	Jumping Bart Simpson BoxCar, *04*		44
____ **26802**	Simpsons Animated Gondola, *04*		46
____ **26803**	Santa Fe Derrick Car "26803," *04*		25
____ **26804**	NYC Coal Dump Car "26804," *04*		22
____ **26805**	Pennsylvania Log Dump Car "26805," *04*		24
____ **26806**	Pillsbury Operating Boxcar "3428," Archive Collection, *04*		40
____ **26807**	Blue Chip Line Motorized Animated Gondola, *04*		40
____ **26808**	Egg Nog Barrel Car, *04*		55
____ **26809**	Santa's Extension Searchlight Car, *04*		42
____ **26810**	NYC Operating Searchlight Car, *05*		33

		Exc	Mint
26811	Pennsylvania Coal Dump Car, *05*		33____
26812	Santa Fe Log Dump Car, *05*		33____
26813	Lionel Lines Derrick Car, *05*		33____
26814	NYC Walking Brakeman Car "174226," *05*		40____
26815	PRR "Workin' on the Railroad" BoxCar "24255," *05*		42____
26816	REA BoxCar, steam TrainSounds, *05*		105____
26817	Alaska BoxCar, diesel TrainSounds, *05*		145____
26818	Christmas Music BoxCar, *05*		63____
26819	Holiday Animated Gondola, *05*		55____
26820	Penguin Transport Aquarium Car, *05*		60____
26821	NP Moe & Joe Lumber FlatCar, *05*		75____
26826	Alaska Searchlight Car, *05*		40____
26827	UPS Operating Boxcar "9237," Archive Collection, *05*		63____
26828	Tornado Chaser Radar Tracking Car, *05*		63____
26829	UPS Holiday Operating BoxCar, *05*		59____
26832	Lionel Lines Tender, TrainSounds, *07-08*		105____
26833	Wellspring Radar Car, *04*		70____
26834	PFE Ice Car "20042" (std O), *05-06*		63____
26835	MOW Track Cleaning Car, *05*		140____
26836	Halloween BoxCar, SpookySounds, *05*		105____
26841	PRR Log Dump Car, *05*		27____
26842	NYC Coal Dump Car, *05*		27____
26845	Southern Derrick Car, *06*		35____
26846	GN Coal Dump Car, *06*		38____
26847	C&O Coal Dump Car, *06-07*		80____
26848	Lionel Lines Moe & Joe FlatCar, *06*		80____
26849	SP Log Dump Car, *06-07*		80____
26850	D&RGW Searchlight Car, *06*		75____
26851	WM Log Dump Car, *06*		35____
26852	Postwar "3562-25" Santa Fe Barrel Car, *06*		75____
26853	SeaWorld Aquarium Car, *06*		75____
26854	UP Walking Brakeman Car, *06-07*		75____
26855	Halloween Animated Gondola, *06*		65____
26856	Christmas Chase Gondola, *06*		65____
26857	Alien Radar Tracking Car, *06*		65____
26858	Christmas Music BoxCar, *06*		65____
26859	Christmas Parade BoxCar, *06*		75____
26860	B&O Boxcar "466035," steam TrainSounds (std O), *06-07*		75____
26861	Santa Fe BoxCar, diesel TrainSounds (std O), *06-07*		110____
26862	Hard Rock Cafe BoxCar, *06*		35____
26863	Railway Express Operating Milk Car with platform, *06*		140____
26864	Domino Sugar Operating BoxCar, *06-07*		40____
26865	CP Animated Caboose, *06-07*		80____
26867	BoxCar, AlienSounds, *06-07*		110____
26868	U.S. Steel Operating Welding Car, *06*		75____
26869	REA Jumping Hobo BoxCar, *06-07*		70____
26870	Christmas Dump Car with presents, *06*		80____
26871	PRR Tender, steam TrainSounds (std O), *06*		105____
26872	U.S. Army Security Car, *06*		75____
26876	Missile Firing Trail Car, *06*		75____
26877	U.S. Army Missile Launch Car, *06-07*		190____
26888	Weyerhaeuser Timber Co. Log Car		40____

		Mint
____	**26889** Weyerhaeuser Timber Co. Log Car	40
____	**26891** PRR Coal Dump Car, *05*	30
____	**26897** Great Western Flatcar with handCar, *07*	65
____	**26898** NYC Log Dump Car, *05*	25
____	**26905** Bethlehem Steel Gondola "6462" with canisters, *98*	29
____	**26906** SP FlatCar "9823" with Corgi '57 Chevy, *98*	40
____	**26908** TTUX FlatCar "6300" with Apple trailers, *98*	70
____	**26913** East St. Louis Gondola "9820," *98*	29
____	**26920** Union Pacific Die-cast Ore Car "64861," *97*	70
____	**26921** Union Pacific Die-cast Ore Car "64862," *97*	55
____	**26922** Union Pacific Die-cast Ore Car "64863," *97*	65
____	**26923** Union Pacific Die-cast Ore Car "64864," *97*	55
____	**26924** Union Pacific Die-cast Ore Car "64865," *97*	55
____	**26925** Union Pacific Die-cast Ore Car "64866," *97*	60
____	**26926** Union Pacific Die-cast Ore Car, *98*	55
____	**26927** Union Pacific Die-cast Ore Car, *98*	55
____	**26928** Union Pacific Die-cast Ore Car, *98*	55
____	**26929** Union Pacific Die-cast Ore Car, *98*	40
____	**26936** Die-cast Tank Car 4-pack, *98*	335
____	**26937** Die-cast Hopper 4-pack, *98*	325
____	**26938** NYC Reefer, *99*	80
____	**26940** Rio Grande Stock Car "37710," *99*	80
____	**26946** D&H Semi-Scale Hopper "9642"	85
____	**26947** Gulf Die-cast Tank Car, *98*	120
____	**26948** P&LE Die-cast Hopper, *98*	65
____	**26949** NP Flatcar with trailer "6424-2017," *98*	47
____	**26950** NP Flatcar with trailer "6424-2016," *98*	47
____	**26951** TTX FlatCar "475185" with PRR trailer, *98*	55
____	**26952** J.B. Hunt Flatcar with trailer, *98*	40
____	**26953** J.B. Hunt Flatcar with trailer, *98*	40
____	**26954** J.B. Hunt Flatcar with trailer, *98*	40
____	**26955** J.B. Hunt Flatcar with trailer, *98*	40
____	**26956** C&O Gondola (027), *98-99*	15
____	**26957** Delaware & Hudson Flatcar with stakes, *98*	20
____	**26971** Lionel Steel 16-wheel Depressed Center FlatCar, *98*	135
____	**26972** Pony Express Animated Gondola, *98*	36
____	**26973** Getty Die-cast Tank Car 3-pack, *98*	270
____	**26974** Getty Die-cast 1-D Tank Car "4003," *98*	80
____	**26975** Getty Die-cast 1-D Tank Car "4004," *98*	90
____	**26976** Getty Die-cast 1-D Tank Car "4005," *98*	80
____	**26977** Sinclair Die-cast Tank Car 3-pack, *98*	275
____	**26978** Sinclair Tank Car UTLX "64026," *98*	105
____	**26979** Sinclair Tank Car UTLX "64027," *98*	85
____	**26980** Sinclair Tank UTLX "64028," *98*	90
____	**26981** Gulf Die-cast Tank Car 2-pack, *99*	165
____	**26985** B&O Die-cast Hopper 2-pack, *99*	160
____	**26987** Chessie System (B&O) Die-cast 4-bay Hopper "235154," *99*	90
____	**26991** Lionelville Ladder Fire Car, *99*	47
____	**26992** NYC Reefer, *99*	75
____	**26993** NYC Reefer, *99*	85
____	**26994** NYC Reefer, *99*	135
____	**26995** Rio Grande Stock Car "37714," *99*	80
____	**26996** Rio Grande Stock Car "37715," *99*	80

	Exc	Mint
26997 Rio Grande Stock Car "37716," *99*	80	___
27000 C&EI Offset Hopper "97393" (std O), *07*	65	___
27001 Erie Offset Hopper "28001" (std O), *07*	65	___
27002 Frisco Offset Hopper "92399" (std O), *07*	65	___
27003 Chessie System Offset Hopper "234355" (std O), *07*	65	___
27016 UP PS-2 Covered Hopper "1312" (std O), *07-08*	60	___
27019 Imco PS-2 Covered Hopper "41001" (std O), *07-08*	60	___
27022 PC PS-2 Covered Hopper "74217" (std O), *07*	60	___
27025 NYC PS-2 Covered Hopper "883180" (std O), *07*	60	___
27029 ATSF Offset Hopper 3-pack (std O), *08-09*	200	___
27030 Monon Offset Hopper 3-pack (std O), *08-09*	200	___
27031 MoPac Offset Hopper 3-pack (std O), *08-09*	200	___
27032 NYC Offset Hopper 3-pack (std O), *08-09*	200	___
27033 Chessie System PS-2 Hopper 3-pack (std O), *08-09*	180	___
27034 Nickel Plate Road PS-2 Hopper 3-pack (std O), *08-09*	180	___
27053 CB&Q ACF 2-bay Covered Hopper "183925" (std O), *08-09*	55	___
27059 Bakelite Plastics PS-2 Hopper "61445" (std O), *10-11*	70	___
27061 Clinchfield Freight Car 2-pack (std O), *10*	150	___
27064 PRR Flatcar with PRR piggyback trailers (std O), *12*	98	___
27065 SP Flatcar with SP piggyback trailers (std O), *12*	98	___
27066 IC Flatcar with IC piggyback trailers (std O), *12*	98	___
27067 C&O Flatcar with REA piggyback trailers (std O), *12*	98	___
27068 ATSF Flatcar with Santa Fe piggyback trailers (std O), *12*	98	___
27069 Conrail PS-2 Hopper "878330" (std O), *12-13*	70	___
27070 N&W Scale Offset Hopper "279850" (std O), *12*	70	___
27071 CSX 4-Bay Covered Hopper "256300" (std O), *12*	90	___
27072 C&NW Scale PS-1 Boxcar "7" (std O), *12-13*	70	___
27073 PRR Scale Offset Hopper 3-pack (std O), *12*	200	___
27077 L&N Scale Offset Hopper "88494" (std O), *12-13*	70	___
27078 Frisco Scale 3-Bay Open Hopper "88299" (std O), *12-14*	75	___
27079 NYC BoxCar, *09*	30	___
27080 Lionel Vision BoxCar, *14-15*	60	___
27081 BN PS-2 Hopper "424796" (std O), *12-13*	70	___
27082 Grand Trunk 4-Bay Covered Hopper "38111" (std O), *12*	90	___
27083 RI PS-2 Hopper "500751" (std O), *12-13*	70	___
27084 Seaboard 8000-gallon 1-D Tank Car "27084" (std O), *12*	70	___
27085 Wabash PS-2 Hopper "30425" (std O), *12-13*	70	___
27086 Grand Trunk 60' Boxcar "383575" (std O), *12, 14*	85	___
27087 CN 60' Boxcar "799424" (std O), *12, 14*	85	___
27088 MKT PS-5 Gondola "12447" (std O), *12-13*	65	___
27089 LIRR PS-5 Gondola "6053" (std O), *12*	65	___
27090 NP 8000-gallon 1-D Tank Car "27090" (std O), *12*	70	___
27091 WM Scale 3-Bay Open Hopper "85125" (std O), *12*	80	___
27092 CSX Heritage 60' Boxcar "176740" (std O), *12*	85	___
27093 Boy Scouts PS-2 Hopper "2013" (std O), *13*	70	___
27094 BNSF PS-2 Hopper 2-pack (std O), *13-14*	130	___
27095 KCS PS-2 Hopper 2-pack (std O), *13*	130	___
27096 C&NW PS-2 Hopper 2-pack (std O), *13*	130	___

		Mint
___	**27099** North Pole Central PS-1 Boxcar "125025" (std O), *13*	70
___	**27100** C&NW PS-2CD 4427 Hopper "450669" (std O), *04*	40
___	**27101** Morton Salt PS-2CD 4427 Hopper "504" (std O), *04*	43
___	**27102** Pillsbury PS-2CD 4427 Hopper "3980" (std O), *04*	42
___	**27103** Soo Line PS-2CD 4427 Hopper "70207" (std O), *04*	49
___	**27104** Wabash Cylindrical Hopper "33007" (std O), *03*	43
___	**27105** PC Cylindrical Hopper "884312" (std O), *03*	42
___	**27113** Govt. of Canada Cylindrical Hopper, *04-05*	60
___	**27114** Canadian National Cylindrical Hopper, *04-05*	60
___	**27115** D&H 3-bay ACF Hopper "3454" (std O), *05-06*	65
___	**27116** NYC 3-bay ACF Hopper "886270" (std O), *05-06*	65
___	**27117** DM&IR 3-bay ACF Hopper "5017" (std O), *05*	65
___	**27118** WP 3-bay ACF Hopper "11774" (std O), *05-06*	65
___	**27129** N&W 3-bay ACF Hopper "10717" (std O), *06*	70
___	**27130** PRR 3-bay ACF Hopper "180658" (std O), *06*	70
___	**27131** Conrail 3-bay ACF Hopper "473877" (std O), *06*	70
___	**27132** UP 3-bay ACF Hopper "18137" (std O), *06*	70
___	**27133** MILW PS-2CD Hopper "98606" (std O), *06*	70
___	**27134** BNSF PS-2CD Hopper "414367" (std O), *06*	70
___	**27135** N&W PS-2CD Hopper "71573" (std O), *06*	70
___	**27142** CP Rail 3-bay Hopper, *06*	48
___	**27146** CP Soo 3-bay Hopper, *06*	48
___	**27165** C&O 3-bay Hopper "86912" (std O), *07*	70
___	**27166** Pennsylvania Power & Light 3-bay Hopper "347" (std O), *07*	70
___	**27167** Santa Fe 3-bay Hopper "178558" (std O), *07-08*	70
___	**27168** C&NW 3-bay Hopper "135000" (std O), *07*	70
___	**27169** CN Cylindrical Hopper "370708" (std O), *06*	65
___	**27172** IMC Canada Cylindrical Hopper "45726" (std O), *06*	65
___	**27177** Union Starch Cylindrical Hopper 3-pack (std O), *08*	210
___	**27186** PRR Cylindrical Hopper 3-pack (std O), *08*	210
___	**27187** TH&B Cylindrical Hopper 3-pack (std O), *08*	210
___	**27188** KCS 3-bay Covered Hopper 3-pack, *08*	225
___	**27189** BNSF 3-bay Aluminum Covered Hopper 3-pack, *08*	225
___	**27190** C&NW PS-2CD Covered Hopper 3-pack (std O), *08*	225
___	**27191** RI PS-2CD Covered Hopper 3-pack, *08*	225
___	**27192** NP PS-2CD Covered Hopper 3-pack (std O), *08*	225
___	**27203** NYC DD Boxcar "75509" (std O), *05*	63
___	**27204** Grand Trunk Western DD Boxcar "596377" (std O), *05*	63
___	**27205** D&RGW DD Boxcar "63798" (std O), *05*	40
___	**27206** UP PS 60' Boxcar "960342" (std O), *08*	75
___	**27207** IC PS 60' Boxcar "44295" (std O), *08*	75
___	**27208** ATSF PS 60' Boxcar "37287" (std O), *08*	75
___	**27209** D&RGW PS 60' Boxcar "63835" (std O), *08*	75
___	**27210** PRR PS-1 Boxcar "47009" (std O), *05*	60
___	**27211** MKT PS-1 Boxcar "948" (std O), *05*	60
___	**27212** Rutland PS-1 Boxcar "358" (std O), *05*	60
___	**27213** N&W DD BoxCar, *05*	35
___	**27214** Chessie System PS-1 Boxcar "23770" (std O), *06*	60
___	**27215** Rock Island PS-1 Boxcar "57607" (std O), *06*	60
___	**27216** Erie-Lack. PS-1 Boxcar "84433" (std O), *06*	60
___	**27217** Frisco PS-1 Boxcar "17826" (std O), *06*	19
___	**27218** Santa Fe DD Boxcar "9870" (std O), *06-07*	70

	Exc	Mint
27219 GN DD Boxcar "35449" (std O), *06-07*		70___
27220 L&N DD Boxcar "41237" (std O), *06-07*		70___
27221 CB&Q DD Boxcar "48500" (std O), *06-07*		70___
27224 CGW PS-1 Boxcar "5180" (std O), *06*		60___
27225 WP PS-1 Boxcar "19528" (std O), *06*		60___
27226 NH PS-1 Boxcar "32196" (std O), *06*		60___
27227 UP PS-1 Boxcar "100306" (std O), *06*		60___
27228 UP DD Boxcar "454400" (std O), *07*		70___
27229 Nickel Plate Road DD Boxcar "87100" (std O), *08*		70___
27230 LV DD Boxcar "8505" (std O), *08*		70___
27231 GN USRA Double-sheathed Boxcar (std O), *07*		65___
27232 UP USRA Double-sheathed Boxcar (std O), *07*		65___
27233 Cotton Belt USRA Double-sheathed Boxcar (std O), *07*		65___
27234 C&NW USRA Double-sheathed Boxcar (std O), *07*		65___
27235 Railbox Boxcar "10011" (std O), *07*		55___
27239 SP DD Boxcar "232852" with auto rack (std O), *08*		75___
27240 Pere Marquette DD Boxcar with auto rack (std O), *08*		75___
27241 C&O PS-1 Boxcar "18719," *08*		60___
27242 LV PS-1 Boxcar "62080," *08*		60___
27243 SP PS-1 Boxcar "128131," *08*		60___
27244 GN PS-1 Boxcar "39404," *08*		60___
27246 SP Double-sheathed Boxcar "133" (std O), *08*		70___
27247 MP Double-sheathed Boxcar "45111" (std O), *08*		70___
27249 GN Express Boxcar "2500" (std O), *08*		65___
27250 CN Express Boxcar "11061" (std O), *08-09*		65___
27251 WP Express Boxcar "220116," *08-09*		65___
27254 Western Pacific UP Heritage Boxcar (std O), *09-11, 13*		85___
27259 PRR ACF Stock Car "128988" (std O), *10*		70___
27260 ATSF Tool Car "190021" (std O), *09-10*		80___
27261 D&RGW Double-sheathed Boxcar "3282," *09*		80___
27263 Polar Railroad PS-1 BoxCar, *09*		70___
27264 C&O Double-sheathed Boxcar "3502," *10*		80___
27265 Virginian PS-1 Boxcar "63300" (std O), *10*		70___
27266 PRR Express Boxcar "504141" (std O), *10*		70___
27267 SP UP Heritage 60' Boxcar "6991" (std O), *10*		85___
27270 B&O PS-1 Boxcar 2-pack (std O), *10-11*		140___
27273 Ann Arbor PS-1 Boxcar "1314" (std O), *11*		70___
27274 Polar Railroad Double-sheathed Boxcar "1201," *10*		70___
27275 SP Overnight PS-1 Boxcar "97938" (std O), *10*		70___
27276 NKP Double-sheathed Boxcar "10580" (std O), *10-11*		70___
27277 WP Scale PS-1 Boxcar "1925" (std O), *11*		70___
27278 Cryo-Trans Trans-Mechanical Reefer (std O), *10*		95___
27282 UP DD Boxcar "163100" (std O), *10*		70___
27283 Postwar Scale Boxcar 2-pack, *10*		140___
27286 Postwar Scale 6464 Boxcar 2-pack #2, *11-13*		140___
27287 LV Boxcar and Caboose Set (std O), *10-11*		160___
27289 Jersey Central Boxcar and Caboose Set (std O), *10-11*		160___
27291 PRR Double-sheathed Boxcar "539335" (std O), *10-11*		70___
27294 ATSF 57' Mechanical Reefer "3006" (std O), *10*		85___

		Exc	Mint
____	**27296** Cryo-Trans 57' Mechanical Reefer (std O), *11*		85
____	**27299** WM Steel-sided Reefer (std O), *11*		80
____	**27300** Western Dairy General American Milk Car (std O), *06*		65
____	**27305** GN Steel-sided Reefer "70290" (std O), *06*		65
____	**27306** Santa Fe Steel-sided Reefer "3494" (std O), *06*		42
____	**27307** Pepper Packing Steel-sided Reefer "2330" (std O), *06*		65
____	**27327** BNSF Mechanical Reefer "798870" (std O), *07*		70
____	**27328** SP Fruit Express Reefer "456465" (std O), *07-09*		70
____	**27329** UP Fruit Express Reefer "55962" (std O), *07*		70
____	**27330** Great Northern WFE Reefer "8873" (std O), *07-08*		70
____	**27331** Alderney Dairy General American Milk Car (std O), *07*		65
____	**27332** Freeport General American Milk Car (std O), *07*		65
____	**27345** Milwaukee Road 40' Steel-sided Reefer "5317" (std O), *12*		80
____	**27349** ADM Steel-sided Reefer "7019" (std O), *07*		65
____	**27350** National Car Steel-sided Reefer "2430" (std O), *07*		48
____	**27355** NYC Steel-sided Reefer "2570" (std O), *07-08*		65
____	**27358** Dubuque Steel-sided Reefer "63648" (std O), *07*		65
____	**27361** PFE Wood-sided Reefer "97680" (std O), *06*		65
____	**27364** Erie URTX Steel-sided Reefer (std O), *11*		80
____	**27365** Sheffield Farms Milk Car 2-pack (std O), *08*		140
____	**27368** CNJ 40' Steel-sided Reefer "1443" (std O), *12*		80
____	**27369** Borden's Milk Car 2-pack (std O), *08*		140
____	**27372** PFE Steel-sided Reefer 3-pack (std O), *08*		210
____	**27373** MILW Reefer 3-pack (std O), *08-09*		225
____	**27374** Alaska Reefer 3-pack (std O), *08-09*		225
____	**27375** NP Reefer 3-pack (std O), *08-09*		225
____	**27394** Detroit, Toledo & Ironton Steel-sided Reefer (std O), *09-10*		80
____	**27395** Amtrak ExpressTrak Baggage Car, *10*		75
____	**27396** C&NW UP Heritage Mechanical Reefer (std O), *10*		85
____	**27409** ATSF Water Tank Car "100844" (std O), *09-10*		70
____	**27410** 30,000-gallon Ethanol Tank Car 3-pack, sound, *09*		270
____	**27411** 30,000-gallon Ethanol Tank Car 3-pack, *09*		210
____	**27412** GATX TankTrain Car "53782" (std O), *10*		70
____	**27418** PRR NS Heritage Unibody Tank Car (std O), *10*		70
____	**27419** Pennsylvania Power & Light 3-bay Open Hopper, *08*		80
____	**27421** MoPac UP Heritage Cylindrical Hopper (std O), *09-11*		80
____	**27422** N&W 3-bay Open Hopper "1776" (std O), *09*		80
____	**27424** Penn Central PS-2 Hopper "440774" (std O), *10-11*		80
____	**27425** Saskatchewan Cylindrical Hopper "397015" (std O), *09*		80
____	**27426** Stourbridge Lion Anthracite Coal Car 2-pack, *09-10*		130
____	**27429** MKT UP Heritage PS2-CD Hopper (std O), *09*		80
____	**27431** CSX B&O Quad Hopper, *11*		50
____	**27432** UP 3-bay Open Hopper "78123" (std O), *10*		80
____	**27433** Conrail NS Heritage Cylindrical Hopper (std O), *10-11*		80
____	**27434** D&RGW UP Heritage PS2-CD Hopper (std O), *10*		80
____	**27435** Polar Railroad Tank Car, *09*		70
____	**27436** Alberta Cylindrical Hopper "396363" (std O), *10*		80
____	**27438** Virginian NS Heritage 3-bay Open Hopper (std O), *10*		80
____	**27439** NS Heritage Unibody Tank Car "14098" (std O), *10*		70
____	**27440** BN Cylindrical Hopper "458456" (std O), *10*		80

		Exc	Mint
27441	D&M PS-2 Hopper "6133" (std O), *11*	70	___
27445	N&W NS Heritage PS-2CD Hopper (std O), *10*	80	___
27446	Southern NS Heritage Cylindrical Hopper (std O), *10*	80	___
27448	PRR NS Heritage 3-Bay Open Hopper (std O), *11*	80	___
27449	UP Boy Scouts 100th Anniversary Cylindrical Hopper (std O), *11*	80	___
27450	NW NS Heritage 3-Bay Open Hopper (std O), *11*	80	___
27451	Conrail NS Heritage Unibody 1-D Tank Car (std O), *11*	70	___
27452	PRR NS Heritage PS-1 Boxcar "45540" (std O), *11*	70	___
27453	NS Heritage PS-1 Boxcar "67850" (std O), *11*	70	___
27454	CP Cylindrical Hopper (std O), *11*	80	___
27455	Amtrak 57' Mechanical Reefer (std O), *11*	85	___
27456	Soo Line PS2 Covered Hopper "70702" (std O), *11*	70	___
27457	NS 3-Bay Open Hopper "148028" (std O), *11*	80	___
27458	UP Mechanical Reefer "457244" (std O), *11*	85	___
27459	WP DD Boxcar "19404" (std O), *11*	70	___
27460	M&StL Double-sheathed Boxcar "26002" (std O), *11*	70	___
27461	UP ACF 4-Bay Covered Hopper "91341" (std O), *11*	85	___
27462	Chessie ACF 4-Bay Covered Hopper "601878" (std O), *11*	85	___
27463	PRR ACF 3-Bay Covered Hopper "259900" (std O), *11-12*	80	___
27464	BNSF ACF 3-Bay Covered Hopper "453403" (std O), *11*	80	___
27465	CSX 89' Auto Rack Car "604540" (std O), *12-13*	150	___
27466	UP 89' Auto Rack Car (std O), *12-13*	150	___
27467	ATSF 89' Auto Rack Car (std O), *12-13*	150	___
27468	Grand Truck 89' Auto Rack Car (std O), *12-13*	150	___
27469	Frisco Cylindrical Hopper "81021" (std O), *11*	80	___
27470	MKT Scale 1-D Tank Car (std O), *11*	70	___
27471	DT&I 3-Bay Hopper "2070" (std O), *11*	80	___
27472	CP Scale 1-D Tank Car "9943" (std O), *11*	70	___
27473	Conrail 89' Auto Rack Car "456249" (std O), *12*	150	___
27474	SP Cylindrical Hopper "491020" (std O), *11*	80	___
27475	Lionelville & Western Scale 1-D Tank Car "2747" (std O), *11*	80	___
27476	U.S. Army Scale 1-D Tank Car (std O), *11*	70	___
27477	D&RGW 3-Bay Hopper "14901" (std O), *11*	80	___
27478	NYC 3-Bay Hopper "922158" (std O), *11*	80	___
27479	BN Scale 3-Bay Open Hopper "516400" (std O), *12*	80	___
27480	NKP Scale Offset Hopper "33060" (std O), *12*	70	___
27481	W&LE Scale Offset Hopper "62240" (std O), *12*	70	___
27482	CP Scale Offset Hopper "354000" (std O), *12*	70	___
27483	SP Unibody 1-D Tank Car "67200" (std O), *12*	70	___
27484	D&H Unibody 1-D Tank Car "59" (std O), *12*	70	___
27485	KCS Unibody 1-D Tank Car "996" (std O), *12*	70	___
27488	Clinchfield CSX Heritage 3-Bay Open Hopper (std O), *12*	80	___
27489	Chessie System CSX Heritage 3-Bay Open Hopper (std O), *12*	80	___
27490	ATSF 3-Bay Covered Hopper "314000" (std O), *12-13*	85	___
27491	GN 3-Bay Covered Hopper "171400" (std O), *12*	85	___
27492	CN 89' Auto Rack Car "710833" (std O), *12*	150	___

		Exc	Mint
____	**27493** CN PS-4 Flatcar with piggyback trailers (std O), *12*		98
____	**27494** CN PS-4 Flatcar with piggyback trailers (std O), *12*		98
____	**27495** CN PS-4 Flatcar with piggyback trailers (std O), *12*		98
____	**27496** Polar PS-2 Covered Hopper "1245" (std O), *12, 14*		70
____	**27497** UP Offset Hopper "74556" (std O), *12*		80
____	**27498** DM&I 8000-gallon 1-D Tank Car "S19" (std O), *12*		70
____	**27499** Monon Scale PS-1 Boxcar "916" (std O), *12*		70
____	**27510** WP PS-4 FlatCar "2001" (std O), *05-06*		53
____	**27511** P&LE PS-4 FlatCar "1154" (std O), *05-06*		35
____	**27512** Reading PS-4 FlatCar "9314" (std O), *05*		53
____	**27513** UP 40' FlatCar "51219" (std O), *06*		55
____	**27514** CP 40' FlatCar "307401" (std O), *06*		55
____	**27515** Pennsylvania 40' FlatCar "473567" (std O), *06*		55
____	**27516** N&W 40' FlatCar "32900" (std O), *06*		55
____	**27517** NP PS-4 FlatCar "62829" with trailers (std O), *06*		85
____	**27518** C&NW PS-4 FlatCar "44503" with trailers (std O), *06*		85
____	**27519** UP PS-4 FlatCar "53007" with trailers (std O), *06*		85
____	**27520** Coe Rail Husky Stack Car "5540" (std O), *06*		85
____	**27521** Santa Fe Husky Stack Car "254220" (std O), *06*		85
____	**27535** UP PS-4 FlatCar "53008" with trailers (std O), *07*		65
____	**27536** UP PS-4 FlatCar "53009" with trailers (std O), *08*		65
____	**27537** UP Flatcar with wood load, *06*		39
____	**27541** NYC 40' FlatCar "496299" with load (std O), *07*		63
____	**27542** NH 40' FlatCar "17808" with load (std O), *07-08*		70
____	**27543** ATSF 40' FlatCar "191549" with load (std O), *07-08*		70
____	**27544** GT 40' FlatCar "64301" with load (std O), *07-08*		70
____	**27545** REA PS-4 FlatCar "81003" with trailers (std O), *07-08*		85
____	**27546** Greenbrier Husky Stack Car "1993" (std O), *07*		85
____	**27552** Arizona & California Husky Stack Car (std O), *07*		85
____	**27562** NYC PS-4 FlatCar "506075" with trailers (std O), *07-08*		85
____	**27563** Lackawanna PS-4 FlatCar "16540" with trailers (std O), *07*		85
____	**27564** Milwaukee Road PS-4 Flatcar with trailers "64074" (std O), *07-08*		85
____	**27583** UP 40' Flatcar "59292" with load (std O), *08*		70
____	**27584** Reading Flatcar with covered load (std O), *08-09*		70
____	**27585** B&M 40' Flatcar "33773" with stakes (std O), *08-09*		65
____	**27586** Cass Scenic Skeleton Log Car 3-pack, *07*		170
____	**27587** Birch Valley Lumber Skeleton Log Car 3-pack, *07*		170
____	**27594** Wabash PS-4 Flatcar with stakes (std O), *08-09*		65
____	**27600** RI Bay Window Caboose "17070" (std O), *07*		90
____	**27601** MILW Extended Vision Caboose "992300" (std O), *07*		90
____	**27603** MP UP Heritage Ca-4 Caboose "2891" (std O), *08*		95
____	**27604** UP Caboose "3881" (std O), *08*		90
____	**27605** Pere Marquette Northeastern Caboose "A986" (std O), *08*		90
____	**27606** LL Northeastern Caboose "4679" (std O), *08*		90
____	**27607** Monongahela NS Heritage Caboose (std O), *12*		95
____	**27608** WM Caboose "1863" (std O), *08*		85
____	**27609** B&O Caboose "C-2445" (std O), *07*		90
____	**27612** WP Bay Window Caboose "446" (std O), *08*		90
____	**27615** NYC Bay Window Caboose "20383" (std O), *07*		90

		Exc	Mint
27617	D&H Bay Window Caboose "35725" (std O), *08*	90	___
27618	MKT UP Heritage Ca-4 Caboose "8891" (std O), *08*	95	___
27619	WP UP Heritage Ca-4 Caboose "3891" (std O), *08*	95	___
27623	N&W Northeastern Caboose "500837" (std O), *09*	90	___
27624	D&RGW UP Heritage CA-4 Caboose (std O), *09*	95	___
27625	C&NW UP Heritage CA-4 Caboose (std O), *09*	95	___
27626	SP UP Heritage CA-4 Caboose (std O), *09*	95	___
27628	Wabash Northeastern Caboose "02222" (std O), *09-10*	90	___
27629	C&O Northeastern Caboose (std O), *10*	90	___
27630	Virginian NS Heritage CA-4 Caboose (std O), *10*	95	___
27631	NS Heritage CA-4 Caboose (std O), *10*	95	___
27633	UP CA-3 Caboose (std O), *10*	95	___
27634	ATSF Extended Vision Caboose (std O), *10*	85	___
27635	B&O I-12 Caboose (std O), *10*	85	___
27636	NKP Northeastern Caboose (std O), *10-11*	85	___
27638	Southern NS Heritage CA-4 Caboose (std O), *10-11*	95	___
27639	N&W NS Heritage CA-4 Caboose (std O), *10*	95	___
27640	Clinchfield Northeastern CA-3 Caboose, *10-11*	90	___
27642	Virginian Scale Caboose with smoke, *10-13*	90	___
27645	UP Boy Scouts 100th Anniversary Ca-3 Caboose (std O), *11*	95	___
27648	PRR NS Heritage Ca-3 Caboose (std O), *11*	95	___
27649	Baldwin Locomotive Works I-12 Caboose "6000" (std O), *12-13*	85	___
27650	CSX Heritage Scale Bay Window Caboose "2510" (std O), *12*	90	___
27651	B&O CSX Heritage I-12 Caboose (std O), *11*	90	___
27652	CSX Heritage Chessie System Scale Caboose (std O), *12*	90	___
27653	Family Lines CSX Heritage Ca-4 Caboose (std O), *11*	90	___
27654	CSX/Clinchfield Scale Bay-Window Caboose (std O), *12*	90	___
27655	WM CSX Heritage Extended Vision Caboose (std O), *11*	90	___
27658	Pennsylvania Power & Light Work Caboose (std O), *11*	80	___
27659	Bethlehem Steel Work Caboose (std O), *11*	80	___
27660	UP George Bush Extended Vision Caboose (std O), *11*	90	___
27661	KCS Extended Vision Caboose (std O), *11*	90	___
27662	GTW Northeastern Caboose (std O), *11*	90	___
27663	IC Extended Vision Caboose (std O), *11*	90	___
27664	Lionel & Western Northeastern Caboose (std O), *11-12*	90	___
27665	BN Bicentennial Extended Vision Caboose (std O), *11*	90	___
27666	NH Scale Northeastern Caboose "C-666" (std O), *12*	90	___
27667	UP Scale Ca-4 Caboose "3857" (std O), *12-13*	95	___
27668	UP Scale Ca-3 Caboose "3779" (std O), *12-13*	95	___
27669	PC Scale Northeastern Caboose "18420" with smoke (std O), *12-13*	90	___
27670	CP Scale Northeastern Caboose "400501" (std O), *12-13*	90	___
27671	West Side Lumber Scale Work Caboose "8" (std O), *12*	80	___
27672	Weyerhaeuser Timber Scale Work Caboose "12" (std O), *12-13*	80	___

		Exc	Mint
____	**27673** NYC Scale Northeastern Caboose "20090" (std O), *12*		90
____	**27674** Elk River Lumber Work Caboose "6" (std O), *12, 14*		80
____	**27676** CN Wood-Sided Caboose (std O), *12*		90
____	**27677** UP Work Caboose "907306" (std O), *12*		80
____	**27678** ATSF Wood-Sided Caboose "1790" (std O), *12*		85
____	**27679** NP Wood-Sided Caboose "1282" (std O), *12*		85
____	**27680** GN Wood-Sided Caboose "X499" (std O), *12*		85
____	**27681** Southern NS Heritage Caboose (std O), *12*		95
____	**27682** Conrail NS Heritage Caboose (std O), *12*		95
____	**27683** Erie NS Heritage Caboose (std O), *12, 14-15*		95
____	**27684** Illinois Terminal NS Heritage Caboose (std O), *12, 14-15*		95
____	**27685** Central of Georgia NS Heritage Caboose (std O), *12*		95
____	**27686** LV NS Heritage Caboose (std O), *12*		95
____	**27687** Reading NS Heritage Caboose (std O), *13-15*		95
____	**27688** NYC NS Heritage Caboose (std O), *13*		95
____	**27689** Wabash NS Heritage Caboose (std O), *13-15*		95
____	**27690** Virginian NS Heritage Caboose (std O), *13*		95
____	**27691** PRR NS Heritage Caboose (std O), *12*		95
____	**27692** N&W NS Heritage Caboose (std O), *12*		95
____	**27693** CNJ NS Heritage Caboose (std O), *13-14*		95
____	**27694** NS Heritage Caboose (std O), *12*		95
____	**27695** DL&W NS Heritage Caboose (std O), *13-15*		95
____	**27696** Savannah & Atlanta NS Heritage Caboose (std O), *13-15*		95
____	**27697** Nickel Plate Road NS Heritage Caboose (std O), *12*		95
____	**27698** Interstate NS Heritage Caboose (std O), *12*		95
____	**27699** PC NS Heritage Caboose (std O), *13*		95
____	**27702** Maersk Husky Stack Car 2-pack (std O), *09*		225
____	**27705** ATSF Wedge Plow Flatcar "191369" (std O), *09*		90
____	**27706** ATSF Idler Flatcar "191852" with load (std O), *09*		75
____	**27707** UP Husky Stack Car 2-pack (std O), *09-10*		225
____	**27710** No. 6464 Variation Boxcar 2-pack #2, *09*		110
____	**27767** Santa Fe Passenger 4-pack, *11-12*		240
____	**27771** Postwar "6572" REA Reefer, *11-13*		60
____	**27772** Santa Fe Baggage Car and Diner 2-pack, *11-12*		120
____	**27775** Postwar "2414" Santa Fe Blue-stripe Coach, *11-13*		60
____	**27776** No. 6464 Variation Boxcar 2-pack #3, *11*		105
____	**27779** Postwar Archive UP Caboose "8561," *11-12*		48
____	**27791** Archive 6464-50 M&StL BoxCar, *12*		55
____	**27792** Archive Pastel Freight Car 3-pack, *12*		170
____	**27800** B&M Gondola with coke containers, *09-11*		80
____	**27816** D&RGW Flatcar "22177" with pipes, *09-10*		80
____	**27820** Wabash PS-4 Flatcar with piggyback trailers (std O), *09-10*		98
____	**27824** MILW 40' Flatcar with metal pipes (std O), *10*		80
____	**27825** West Side Lumber Skeleton Log Car, *11*		70
____	**27826** CP Skeleton Log Car 2-pack (std O), *10*		133
____	**27827** UP Bathtub Gondola "28081" (std O), *10*		65
____	**27828** CN Bathtub Gondola "193140" (std O), *10*		65
____	**27829** WM Skeleton Log Car 2-pack, *10*		133
____	**27834** Pere Marquette PS-5 Gondola "18400," *11*		70
____	**27835** P. Bunyan Lumber Skeleton Log Car, *11-12*		70

Exc Mint

		Exc	Mint
27836	Elk River Lumber Skeleton Log Car "11203" (std O), *11*	70	___
27837	B&M PS-4 Flatcar with bulkheads (std O), *10-11*	80	___
27838	PRR PS-4 Flatcar with bulkheads (std O), *10*	80	___
27840	Polar Railroad PS-4 Flatcar with trailers, *10*	98	___
27841	CSX Bathtub Gondola 2-pack (std O), *11*	130	___
27842	UP Scale Flatcar with bulkheads "15775" (std O), *11*	70	___
27843	WP Scale PS-5 Gondola "6774" (std O), *11*	70	___
27844	BNSF Bathtub Gondola 3-pack (std O), *10*	200	___
27848	Virginian NS Heritage 60' Boxcar (std O), *11*	85	___
27849	Southern NS Heritage 60' Boxcar (std O), *11*	85	___
27850	CSX 60' Boxcar "196911" (std O), *11*	85	___
27851	BNSF Bathtub Gondola 2-pack, *11*	130	___
27854	B&O Double-sheathed Boxcar "196500" (std O), *11*	70	___
27855	NYC 60' DD Boxcar "53423" (std O), *11*	85	___
27856	KCS PS-1 Boxcar "18741" (std O), *11*	70	___
27857	PRR DD Boxcar "81919" (std O), *11, 14*	75	___
27858	MP DD Boxcar "90103" (std O), *11*	70	___
27860	Sugar Creek Lumber Skeleton Log Car "1749" (std O), *11*	70	___
27863	Merrill & Ring Lumber Skeleton Log Car, *11-12*	70	___
27868	NS Bathtub Gondola 2-pack (std O), *11*	130	___
27871	NS 60' Boxcar "499646" (std O), *11*	85	___
27872	Polar Hot Cocoa Milk Car, *11, 13*	70	___
27873	Polar Reindeer Stock Car, *11, 13*	70	___
27874	Grove's Mortuary Double-sheathed Boxcar (std O), *11*	70	___
27875	NYC DD Boxcar "45395" (std O), *11*	70	___
27876	State of Maine PS-1 Boxcar "5141" (std O), *11*	70	___
27877	NH DD Boxcar "40510" (std O), *11*	70	___
27882	Southern ACF 40-ton Stock Car "45655" (std O), *11*	70	___
27883	T&P ACF 40-ton Stock Car "24042" (std O), *11*	70	___
27884	RI ACF 40-ton Stock Car "77601" (std O), *11*	70	___
27885	ATSF ACF 40-ton Stock Car "60390" (std O), *11*	70	___
27886	GN PS-1 Boxcar "11310" (std O), *11*	70	___
27887	D&RGW PS-5 Gondola "56316" with covers (std O), *11*	65	___
27888	LIRR 40' Flatcar with wheels (std O), *11*	70	___
27889	Erie 40' Flatcar "6361" with wheels (std O), *11*	70	___
27890	L&N 40' Flatcar "22269" with wheels (std O), *11*	70	___
27891	NKP Heritage PS-4 Flatcar with trailers (std O), *11*	98	___
27892	Conrail PS-5 Gondola "612690" with covers (std O), *11*	65	___
27893	GTW PS-1 Boxcar "516650" (std O), *11*	70	___
27894	C&O PS-5 Gondola "362600" with covers (std O), *11*	65	___
27895	ATSF PS-4 Bulkhead Flatcar "90085" (std O), *11*	80	___
27896	CP 40' Flatcar with pipe load (std O), *11*	80	___
27899	UP Scale PS-1 Boxcar "196889" (std O), *12*	70	___
27903	Sager Place Observation Car, *09*	65	___
27912	Postwar "2445" Elizabeth Coach, *08*	60	___
27917	Postwar "2550" Baggage-Mail Rail Diesel Car, nonpowered, *13-14*	70	___
27928	UP Boy Scouts 100th Anniversary PS-1 Boxcar (std O), *11*	70	___

		Exc Mint
27929	Postwar Nos. 2484/2485 UP Passenger Car 2-pack, *12-13*	120
27935	Postwar "6820" Aerial Missile Transport Car, *13*	60
27941	Postwar "3854" Merchandise Car, *12*	75
27946	Postwar "6050-25" Christmas Savings BoxCar, *13-14*	55
27947	Postwar "6473-25" Reindeer Transport Car, *13*	60
27948	Postwar "6464-25" Great Northern Christmas BoxCar, *13*	60
27949	Postwar "3854-25" PRR Christmas Merchandise Car, *13-14*	75
27953	Reading PS-2 Hopper 2-pack (std O), *13-14*	140
27962	L&N PS-2 Hopper 2-pack (std O), *13-14*	140
27965	P&WV Offset Hopper 3-pack (std O), *13-15*	210
27969	N&W Offset Hopper 3-pack (std O), *13-15*	210
27973	C&O Offset Hopper 3-pack (std O), *13-15*	210
27977	GN Offset Hopper 3-pack (std O), *13-15*	210
27981	PRR USRA Double-sheathed Boxcar (std O), *13*	70
27982	SP USRA Double-sheathed Boxcar (std O), *13-14*	80
27983	UP USRA Double-sheathed Boxcar (std O), *13-14*	70
27984	Procor 30,000-gallon 1-D Tank Car 3-pack (std O), *13*	240
27988	UTLX 30,000-gallon 1-D Tank Car 3-pack (std O), *13*	240
27992	ADM 30,000-gallon 1-D Tank Car 3-pack (std O), *13*	240
27996	ACFX 30,000-gallon 1-D Tank Car 3-pack (std O), *13*	240
28000	C&NW 4-6-4 Hudson Locomotive "3005," *99*	205
28004	B&O 4-4-2 E6 Atlantic Locomotive, traditional, *99-00*	410
28005	PRR 4-4-2 E6 Atlantic Locomotive, traditional, *99-00*	345
28006	ATSF 4-4-2 E6 Atlantic Locomotive, traditional, *99-00*	285
28007	NYC 4-6-4 Hudson Locomotive "5406," *99*	380
28008	C&O 4-6-4 Hudson Locomotive "306," *99*	345
28009	Santa Fe 4-6-4 Hudson Locomotive "3463," *99*	330
28011	C&O 2-6-6-6 Allegheny Locomotive "1601," *99*	1800
28012	4-6-4 Commodore Vanderbilt Locomotive, red, *00 u*	1700
28013	NH 4-6-2 Pacific Locomotive "1335," *99*	325
28014	NYC 4-6-2 Pacific Locomotive "4930," *99*	305
28015	Santa Fe Pacific 4-6-2 Pacific Locomotive "3449," *99*	340
28016	Southern 4-6-2 Pacific Locomotive "1407," *99*	345
28017	Case Cutlery 4-6-2 Pacific Locomotive, *99 u*	313
28018	Reading 4-6-0 Camelback Locomotive "571," CC, *01*	495
28020	Lionel Lines 4-6-2 Pacific Locomotive "3344," *99*	250
28022	West Side Lumber Shay Locomotive "800," *99*	810
28023	PRR K4 4-6-2 Pacific Locomotive "3755," CC, *99*	375
28024	4-6-4 Commodore Vanderbilt Locomotive, blue, *00 u*	1663
28025	PRR K4 4-6-2 Pacific Locomotive, traditional, *99*	330
28026	LL 4-6-2 Pacific Locomotive, CC, *99*	325
28027	NYC 4-6-4 Hudson Locomotive "5413," *00*	590
28028	Virginian 2-6-6-6 Allegheny Locomotive "1601," *99*	1318
28029	UP 4-8-8-4 Big Boy Locomotive "4006," *99-00*	1500
28030	NYC 4-6-4 Hudson Locomotive "5450," gray, CC, *00*	315
28032	B&O 4-6-2 Pacific Locomotive, CC, *00*	315
28033	B&O 4-6-2 Pacific Locomotive, traditional, *00*	195
28034	UP 4-6-2 Pacific Locomotive, CC, *00*	310

	Exc	Mint
28035 UP 4-6-2 Pacific Locomotive, traditional, *00*	210	___
28036 SP 2-8-0 Consolidation Locomotive "2685," CC, *00-01*	270	___
28037 SP 2-8-0 Consolidation Locomotive "2686," traditional, *00-01*	295	___
28038 UP 2-8-0 Consolidation Locomotive "324," CC, *00-01*	315	___
28039 UP 2-8-0 Consolidation Locomotive "326," traditional, *00-01*	240	___
28044 NYC 4-6-4 Hudson Locomotive, *04*	250	___
28051 B&O 2-8-8-4 EM-1 Articulated Locomotive "7617," *00*	970	___
28052 N&W 2-6-6-4 Class A Locomotive "1218," *00*	870	___
28055 GN 4-6-4 Hudson Locomotive "1725," traditional, *00-01*	170	___
28057 Southern 4-8-2 Mountain Locomotive "1491," CC, *00*	690	___
28058 NH 4-8-2 Mountain Locomotive "3310," CC, *00*	670	___
28059 WP 4-8-2 Mountain Locomotive "179," CC, *00*	630	___
28062 LL Gold-plated 700E J-1E 4-6-4 Hudson Locomotive, display case, *00*	1050	___
28063 PRR T-1 4-4-4-4 Duplex Locomotive "5511," CC, *00*	910	___
28064 UP Challenger Coal Tender, "3985," CC, *00 u*	1350	1800 ___
28065 NYC Hudson 4-6-4 Locomotive "5412," RailSounds, *00*	290	___
28066 B&O President Polk 4-6-2 Locomotive, CC, *01*	750	___
28067 Erie 4-6-2 Locomotive "2934," CC, *01*	570	___
28068 D&RGW 4-6-4 Hudson Locomotive, traditional, *01 u*	300	___
28070 SP Daylight 4-4-2 Atlantic Locomotive "3000," CC, *01*	425	___
28071 NP 4-4-2 Atlantic Locomotive "604," CC, *01*	415	___
28072 NYC 4-6-4 Hudson J3a Locomotive "5444," CC, *01*	790	___
28074 NP 2-8-4 Berkshire Locomotive "759," CC, *01*	640	___
28075 C&O 2-6-6-2 Locomotive "1521," CC, *01*	930	___
28076 NKP 2-6-6-2 Locomotive "921," CC, *01*	960	___
28077 UP 4-6-6-4 Challenger Locomotive "3983," CC, *01*	680	___
28078 PRR 2-10-4 J1a Locomotive "6496," CC, *01*	880	___
28079 C&O 2-10-4 Class T Locomotive "3004," CC, *01*	882	___
28080 NYC 0-8-0 Locomotive "7745," CC, *01-02*	540	___
28081 C&O 0-8-0 Locomotive "75," CC, *01-02*	520	___
28084 NYC Dreyfuss Hudson 4-6-4 Locomotive "5452," CC, *01-02*	790	___
28085 N&W 2-8-8-2 Y6b Class Locomotive "2200," CC, *03*	1207	___
28086 PRR H9 Consolidation Locomotive "1111," CC, *01*	480	___
28087 UP Auxiliary Tender, yellow, CC, *01*	210	___
28088 N&W Auxiliary Water Tender, CC, *01-02*	200	___
28089 PRR 4-4-4-4 T-1 Duplex Locomotive "5511," 2-rail, *00*	1150	___
28090 UP Challenger Oil Tender "3977," 2-rail, *00 u*	1800	___
28098 NYC 4-6-0 10-wheel Locomotive "1916," CC, *01-02*	520	___
28099 UP Challenger Oil Tender "3977," CC, *00 u*	1700	___
28200 D&H U30C Diesel "702," CC (SSS), *02*	375	___
28201 UP SD90MAC Diesel "8049," *03*	345	___
28202 Conrail SD80MAC Diesel "7203," *03*	325	___
28203 CSX SD80MAC Diesel "803," *03*	325	___

		Exc	Mint
_____	**28204** NS SD80MAC Diesel "7201," *03*		345
_____	**28205** Chessie System SD9 Diesel "1833," CC, *03*		230
_____	**28207** Erie-Lackawanna U33C Diesel "3304," CC, *02*		355
_____	**28208** BN U33C Diesel "5734," CC, *02*		355
_____	**28211** CP SD90MAC Diesel "9107," *03*		300
_____	**28213** Amtrak GE Dash 8 Diesel "516," CC, *02*		300
_____	**28214** BNSF GE Dash 8 Diesel "582," CC, *02*		325
_____	**28215** B&O GP30 Diesel "6939," CC, *02*		315
_____	**28216** Reading GP30 Diesel "5518," CC, *02*		315
_____	**28217** Rio Grande GP30 Diesel "3013," CC, *02*		315
_____	**28218** Lehigh Valley Alco C420 Switcher "407," CC, *04*		325
_____	**28219** Seaboard Alco C420 Switcher "136," CC, *04*		300
_____	**28222** Santa Fe Dash 9 Diesel "605," CC, *05*		250
_____	**28223** BNSF SD70MAC Diesel "9433," CC, *05*		250
_____	**28224** Jersey Central SD40-2 Diesel "3067," CC, *04*		350
_____	**28225** SPSF SD40T-2 Diesel "8521," CC, *04-05*		430
_____	**28226** NS SD80MAC Diesel "7204," CC, *04-05*		430
_____	**28227** UP SD70MAC Diesel "4979," CC, *04*		375
_____	**28228** C&NW Dash 9-44CW Diesel "8669," CC, *03*		350
_____	**28229** SP Dash 9-44CW Diesel "8132," CC, *03*		350
_____	**28230** Amtrak Dash 8 Diesel "505," CC, *04*		295
_____	**28235** Great Northern U33C Diesel "2543," CC, *05*		455
_____	**28237** Reading U30C Diesel "6301," CC, *05*		455
_____	**28239** Union Pacific SD70 Diesel, TMCC, *04*		360
_____	**28241** C&NW U30C Diesel "935," CC, *06*		455
_____	**28242** SP U33C Diesel "8773," CC, *06*		475
_____	**28243** LIRR Alco C420 Hi-nose Switcher "206," CC, *06*		420
_____	**28244** N&W Alco C420 Hi-nose Switcher "417," CC, *06-07*		420
_____	**28245** Chessie System SD40T-2 Diesel "7617," RailSounds, *06*		265
_____	**28246** Chessie System SD40T-2 Diesel "7618," nonpowered (std O), *06*		160
_____	**28247** Rio Grande SD40T-2 Diesel "5348," RailSounds, *06*		265
_____	**28248** Rio Grande SD40T-2 Diesel "5349," nonpowered (std O), *06*		160
_____	**28250** N&W Alco C420 Hi-nose Switcher "416," nonpowered (std O), *06-07*		160
_____	**28251** LIRR Alco C420 Hi-nose Switcher "206," nonpowered (std O), *06*		160
_____	**28252** SP U33C Diesel "8774," nonpowered (std O), *06*		160
_____	**28253** C&NW U30C Diesel "936," nonpowered (std O), *06*		160
_____	**28255** UP SD40T-2 Diesel "4551," traditional, CC, *07-08*		265
_____	**28256** UP SD40T-2 Diesel "4596," nonpowered (std O), *07*		170
_____	**28257** NS SD40-2 Diesel "3340," CC, *06*		430
_____	**28258** NS SD40-2 Diesel "3341," nonpowered (std O), *06*		170
_____	**28259** CN SD40-2 Diesel "5383," CC, *06*		430
_____	**28260** CN SD40-2 Diesel "5384," nonpowered (std O), *06*		170
_____	**28261** UP (MP) SD70ACe Diesel "1982," CC, *07*		450
_____	**28262** UP (WP) SD70ACe Diesel "1983," CC, *07*		450
_____	**28263** UP (MKT) SD70ACe Diesel "1988," CC, *07*		450
_____	**28264** UP "Building America" SD70ACe Diesel "8348," CC, *07*		450
_____	**28265** MILW U30C Diesel "5657," CC, *07*		455
_____	**28266** MILW U30C Diesel "5657," nonpowered (std O), *07-08*		170

Exc Mint

		Exc	Mint
28267	Conrail U30C Diesel "6837," CC, 07	455	
28268	Conrail U30C Diesel "6838," nonpowered (std O), 07-08	170	
28269	ATSF Dash 8-40BW Diesel "562," CC, 08	500	
28270	ATSF Dash 8-40CW Diesel "563," nonpowered, 08	220	
28272	"I Love USA" SD60 Diesel "1776," traditional, 06	250	
28279	UP SD70ACe Diesel "1989," CC, 07	450	
28280	UP (C&NW) SD70ACe Diesel "1995," CC, 07	450	
28281	UP (SP) SD70ACe Diesel "1996," CC, 07	450	
28283	UP "Building America" SD70AC3 Diesel, nonpowered (std O), 07	170	
28284	Ferromex SD70ACe Diesel "4011," CC, 08	495	
28287	KCS SD70ACe Diesel "4050," CC, 08	495	
28292	Chessie System U30C Diesel "3312," CC, 02	300	
28293	Santa Fe U28CG Diesel "354," CC, 02	375	
28295	Conrail LionMaster SD80MAC Diesel, nonpowered, 08	200	
28296	UP AC6000 Diesel "7526," CC, 08	660	
28297	SP GP9 Diesel "446," CC, 10	390	
28298	CSX AC6000 Diesel "608," CC, 08	660	
28299	CSX AC6000 Diesel "609," nonpowered, 08	220	
28300	NS Dash 9 Diesel "9607," nonpowered, 08	220	
28302	BNSF SD70ACe Diesel "9380," CC, 08	495	
28305	CSX AC6000 Diesel "610," nonpowered, RailSounds, 08	430	
28306	GE ES44AC Evolution Hybrid Diesel "2010," CC, 09-10	1000	
28307	Wabash Train Master Diesel "550," CC, 09-10	495	
28311	UP DD35A Diesel, CC, 11	600	
28312	BN SD60 Diesel "8301," CC, 09	800	
28314	UP 3GS21B Genset Switcher "2701," CC, 10	675	
28316	PRR NS Heritage SD70ACe Diesel "1854," CC, 10	500	
28318	Conrail NS Heritage SD70ACe Diesel "1209," CC, 10	500	
28320	CP Evolution Hybrid Diesel, 10	875	
28323	NS Genset Switcher, CC, 11	800	
28327	UP AC6000 Diesel "7050," CC, 10	700	
28328	UPAC6000 Diesel "7055," nonpowered, CC, 10	350	
28330	UP SD70ACe Diesel "8444," CC, 10	500	
28331	CSX AC6000 Diesel "618," CC, 10	700	
28333	Virginian NS Heritage SD70ACe Diesel, CC, 10	500	
28334	NS Heritage SD70ACe Diesel "1982," CC, 10	500	
28338	PRR NS Heritage SD70ACe Diesel, CC, 11	500	
28339	ATSF AC6000 Diesel "9876," CC, 10	550	
28340	WP GP7 Diesel "705," CC, 10	450	
28343	Amtrak Dash 9 Diesel "519," CC, 10	500	
28344	Southern NS Heritage SD70ACe Diesel, CC, 10	500	
28345	N&W NS Heritage SD70ACe Diesel "247," CC, 10	500	
28347	UP Boy Scouts 100th Anniversary ES44AC Diesel, CC, 11	875	
28350	BNSF ES44AC Diesel, CC, 11	850	
28351	KCS ES44AC Diesel "4655," CC, 11	850	
28353	Erie GP7 Diesel, CC, 11	450	
28354	CSX Genset Switcher "1303," CC, 11	800	
28355	BNSF Genset Switcher "1249," CC, 11	800	

		Exc	Mint
____	**28356** CSX SD60 Diesel, CC, *11*		500
____	**28357** CSX SD60 Diesel, CC, *11*		500
____	**28358** Soo Line SD60 Diesel, CC, *11*		500
____	**28359** Soo Line SD60 Diesel, CC, *11*		500
____	**28360** WP GP7 Diesel "707," CC, *11*		450
____	**28361** WM GP7 Diesel "21," CC, *11*		450
____	**28362** WM GP7 Diesel "23," CC, *11*		450
____	**28363** BN SD60 Diesel "8302," CC, *11*		500
____	**28364** BNSF Dash-9 Diesel "4081," CC, *11*		500
____	**28365** BNSF Dash-9 Diesel "5121," CC, *11*		500
____	**28366** CN Dash-9 Diesel "2643," CC, *11*		500
____	**28367** CN Dash-9 Diesel "2692," CC, *11*		500
____	**28368** Amtrak Dash-9 Diesel, CC, *11*		500
____	**28369** NYC DD35A Diesel "9950," CC, *11*		600
____	**28370** UP DD35 Diesel "84," CC, *12*		600
____	**28371** UP DD35A Diesel "72," CC, *11*		600
____	**28372** NYC DD35A Diesel "9955," CC, *11*		600
____	**28373** C&NW UP Heritage SD70ACe Diesel, CC, *11*		500
____	**28374** SP UP Heritage SD70ACe Diesel, CC, *11*		500
____	**28375** Katy UP Heritage SD70ACe Diesel, CC, *11*		500
____	**28376** MoPac UP Heritage SD70ACe Diesel, CC, *11*		500
____	**28377** Rio Grande UP Heritage SD70ACe Diesel, CC, *11*		500
____	**28378** WP UP Heritage SD70ACe Diesel, CC, *11*		500
____	**28380** NYC DD35A Diesel, nonpowered, *11*		440
____	**28381** ATSF GP30 Diesel, CC, *11*		500
____	**28382** U.S. Army Genset Switcher, CC, *11*		800
____	**28383** Conrail Genset Switcher, CC, *11*		800
____	**28384** CN Genset Switcher "7990," CC, *11-12*		800
____	**28385** ATSF GP30 Diesel "1214," CC, *11*		500
____	**28386** ATSF GP30 Diesel "2710," *11*		380
____	**28387** ATSF GP30 Diesel "2715," nonpowered, *11*		240
____	**28388** ICG GP30 Diesel "2268," CC, *11*		500
____	**28389** ICG GP30 Diesel "2271," CC, *11*		500
____	**28390** UP DD35 Diesel "79," nonpowered, *12*		440
____	**28394** ICG GP30 Diesel "2277," *11*		380
____	**28395** ICG GP30 Diesel "2279," nonpowered, *11*		240
____	**28396** UP ES44AC Diesel "7454," CC, *11*		850
____	**28397** UP ES44AC Diesel "7459," CC, *11*		850
____	**28398** BNSF ES44AC Diesel "6436," CC, *11*		850
____	**28399** KCS ES44AC Diesel "4682," CC, *11*		850
____	**28400** Amtrak Rail Bonder, *05*		65
____	**28403** Pennsylvania Ballast Tamper, traditional, *05-06*		105
____	**28404** Maintenance Car, *05*		105
____	**28405** Picatinny Arsenal Switcher, CC, *05*		290
____	**28406** CSX Rail Bonder "92794," traditional, *05*		65
____	**28407** UP Speeder, *05*		65
____	**28408** CNJ Speeder "MW840," traditional, *06*		70
____	**28409** Conrail Rail Bonder "X409," traditional, *06*		70
____	**28411** U.S. Army Missile Launcher Locomotive, *06-07*		300
____	**28412** Santa's Speeder, *06*		70
____	**28413** Milwaukee Road Snowplow "X903," traditional, *06*		210
____	**28414** Lionel Lines Burro Crane, traditional, *06*		160
____	**28415** Third Avenue Trolley "1651," traditional, *06*		70

Exc Mint

		Exc	Mint
28416	Hobo HandCar, traditional, *06*	70	____
28417	Christmas Rotary Snowplow, *06*	180	____
28418	Christmas Trolley, *06*	70	____
28419	Lionel Lines Speeder, *07-08*	70	____
28420	D&RGW HandCar, *07-08*	70	____
28421	Fort Collins Trolley, *07*	73	____
28422	PRR Burro Crane, *07-08*	160	____
28423	Alaska Rotary Snowplow, *06-07*	220	____
28424	Postwar "51" Navy Switcher, *07*	210	____
28425	Polar Express Elf HandCar, *06-18*	100	____
28427	Christmas Snowplow, *08-10*	210	____
28428	Halloween HandCar, *07*	70	____
28430	Wellspring Capital Management Trolley, *06*	85	____
28432	Bethlehem Steel Switcher, traditional, *07*	210	____
28434	Christmas Trolley, *07*	70	____
28438	Portland Birney Trolley, *08-09*	65	____
28440	PRR Inspection Vehicle, *08-09*	170	____
28441	Transylvania Trolley, *08*	75	____
28442	Postwar "50" Gang Car, *08*	120	____
28444	NH HandCar, *08-09*	75	____
28445	AEC Burro Crane Car	100	____
28446	Silver Bell Trolley, *09*	90	____
28447	4850TM Factory Trackmobile, CC, *10*	300	____
28448	CSX 4850TM Trackmobile, CC, *10*	300	____
28449	UP 4850TM Trackmobile, CC, *10*	300	____
28450	CP Rail Trackmobile, CC, *11*	300	____
28451	Christmas Track Cleaning Car, *10-13*	150	____
28452	MOW Early Era Inspection Vehicle, *10*	130	____
28453	PRR Early Era Inspection Vehicle, *10*	130	____
28454	CP Early Era Inspection Vehicle, *10*	130	____
28455	NYC Trackmobile, CC, *11-13*	300	____
28456	Coca-Cola Trolley, *10*	90	____
28457	B&M Rotary Snowplow "8457," *11*	250	____
28466	U.S. Army Trackmobile, CC, *11*	300	____
28467	PRR Trackmobile, CC, *11*	300	____
28468	Amtrak Trackmobile, CC, *11*	300	____
28469	BNSF Trackmobile, CC, *11*	300	____
28470	NYC Early Era Inspection Vehicle, *11*	130	____
28471	ATSF Early Era Inspection Vehicle, CC, *11*	130	____
28472	Southern Early Era Inspection Vehicle, *11*	130	____
28473	GN Early Era Inspection Vehicle, CC, *11*	130	____
28474	North Pole Central Elf HandCar, *11*	80	____
28475	UP Early Era Insprection Vehicle, *11*	130	____
28476	IC Early Era Inspection Vehicle, *11*	130	____
28478	Frisco Early Era Inspection Vehicle, CC, *11*	130	____
28479	Christmas Early Era Inspection Vehicle, *11*	130	____
28480	Grand Trunk Early Era Inspection Vehicle, CC, *11*	130	____
28500	Mopac GP20 Diesel "2274," *99-00*	205	____
28501	ATSF GP9 Diesel "2924," traditional, *99*	200	____
28502	ATSF GP9 Diesel "2925," CC, *99-00*	255	____
28503	ACL GP7 Diesel, CC, *00*	245	____
28504	ACL GP7 Diesel, traditional, *00*	170	____
28505	Monon Alco C420 Switcher "505," CC, *00-01*	230	____

		Exc	Mint
____	**28506** Monon Alco C420 Switcher "506," traditional, *00-01*		170
____	**28507** NH Alco C420 Switcher "2556," CC, *00-01*		275
____	**28508** NH Alco C420 Switcher "2557," traditional, *00-01*		290
____	**28509** FEC GP7 Diesel Set, *99*		560
____	**28514** B&O GP9 Diesel "6590," *00*		85
____	**28515** Lionel Service Station Alco C420 Switcher, CC, *00*		205
____	**28516** Lehigh & Hudson River Alco C420 Diesel, *00*		160
____	**28517** C&NW GP7 Diesel "1518," CC, *00-01*		275
____	**28518** PRR EP-5 Electric Locomotive "2352," CC, *00*		410
____	**28519** NP GP9 Diesel "2349," CC, *01*		290
____	**28521** SP Alco RS-11 Switcher "5725," CC, *01-02*		280
____	**28522** MP Alco RS-11 Switcher "4611," CC, *01-02*		305
____	**28523** Soo SD40-2 Diesel "6622," CC, *01*		375
____	**28524** Chessie SD40-2 Diesel "7616," CC, *01*		355
____	**28527** AEC GP9 Diesel "2001," CC, *01*		390
____	**28529** Norfolk Southern GP9 Diesel, CC, *02*		200
____	**28530** NP Alco S4 Diesel "722," CC, *02*		285
____	**28531** Santa Fe Alco S2 Switcher "2337," CC, *02*		285
____	**28532** LV Alco S2 Switcher "150," CC, *02*		280
____	**28533** Seaboard Air Line Alco S4 Diesel "1489," CC, *02*		290
____	**28536** Rock Island GP7 Diesel "1274," CC, *02-03*		230
____	**28538** WP Alco S2 Switcher "553," CC, *03*		340
____	**28539** B&O Alco S2 Switcher "9045," CC, *03*		320
____	**28540** UP SD40T-2 Diesel "4455," CC, *03*		390
____	**28541** SP SD40T-2 Diesel "8239," CC, *03*		400
____	**28542** Rio Grande SD40T-2 Diesel "5350," CC, *03*		400
____	**28543** Ontario Northland RS3 Diesel "1308," *03*		80
____	**28544** Pennsylvania Alco RS-11 Switcher "8618," CC, *04*		350
____	**28545** NP Alco RS-11 Switcher "900," CC, *03*		325
____	**28548** Chessie System S4 Diesel "9009," CC, *05*		400
____	**28553** PRR Alco RS-11 Switcher "8620," traditional, *07-08*		285
____	**28554** Pennsylvania Alco RS-11 Switcher "8618," nonpowered, CC, *07*		170
____	**28554** PRR RS-11 Diesel "8621," nonpowered, *08*		170
____	**28555** Alaska GP38-2 Diesel "2001," CC, *06*		400
____	**28556** Alaska GP38-2 Diesel "2002," nonpowered (std O), *06*		160
____	**28557** CP GP30 Diesel "5000," CC, *06-07*		400
____	**28558** CP GP30 Diesel "5001," nonpowered (std O), *06-07*		150
____	**28559** Chessie System GP30 Diesel "3044," CC, *06-07*		400
____	**28560** Chessie System GP30 Diesel "3045," nonpowered (std O), *06-07*		150
____	**28561** NYC GP7 Diesel "5628," CC, *07-08*		340
____	**28562** NYC GP7 Diesel "5629," nonpowered (std O), *07*		170
____	**28563** GN GP7 Diesel "626," CC, *07*		400
____	**28564** GN GP7 Diesel "627," nonpowered (std O), *07*		170
____	**28565** RI GP7 Diesel "1265," CC, *07*		400
____	**28566** RI GP7 Diesel "1266," nonpowered (std O), *07*		170
____	**28567** UP GP7 Diesel "105," CC, *07*		400
____	**28568** UP GP7 Diesel "106," nonpowered (std O), *07*		170
____	**28570** D&RGW GP7 Diesel "5101," CC, *08*		440
____	**28573** PRR GP7 Diesel "8512," CC, *08*		440
____	**28578** D&H GP38-2 Diesel "7307," CC, *08*		440
____	**28587** PRR GP7 Diesel "8510," CC, *10*		450

		Exc	Mint
28592	N&W GP7 Diesel "2446," CC, *09*		500____
28594	White Pass & Yukon NW2 Diesel Switcher, traditional, *09-10*		300 ____
28595	ATSF SD40 Diesel "5004," CC, *09*		380____
28596	Erie GP7 Diesel "1210," CC, *11*		450____
28598	ATSF GP7 Diesel "2791," CC, *10*		450____
28599	Erie GP9 Diesel "1261," CC, *10*		390____
28612	WP 4-4-2 Atlantic Locomotive, traditional, *02*		80____
28613	Reading 0-6-0 Dockside Switcher "1251," traditional, *04*		100 ____
28615	B&O 4-6-4 Hudson Locomotive, traditional, *02*		225____
28616	Nickel Plate 2-8-4 Berkshire Locomotive, traditional, *02*		190 ____
28617	Southern 2-8-4 Berkshire Locomotive, traditional, *02*		235____
28624	Santa Fe 0-6-0 Dockside Switcher "2174," traditional, *04*		175 ____
28625	Wabash 4-4-2 Atlantic Locomotive "8625," traditional, *03*		85 ____
28626	PRR 4-6-4 Hudson Locomotive "626," traditional, *03*		175____
28627	C&O 2-8-4 Berkshire Locomotive "2755," traditional, *03*		200 ____
28628	L&N 2-8-4 Berkshire Locomotive "1970," traditional, *03*	150	200 ____
28633	JCPenney B&O 2-8-4 Berkshire Locomotive, *07*		135____
28636	D&RGW 4-4-2 Atlantic Locomotive "8636," traditional, *04*		95 ____
28637	UP 4-6-4 Hudson Locomotive "673," traditional, *04*		160____
28638	GN 2-8-4 Berkshire Locomotive "3414," traditional, *04*		200 ____
28639	NYC 2-8-4 Berkshire Locomotive "9401," traditional, *04*		200 ____
28646	North Pole Central 2-8-4 Berkshire,"1900," traditional, *04*		230 ____
28649	Polar Express 2-8-4 Berkshire Locomotive, *03 10*		120____
28650	NYC 0-6-0 Dockside Switcher "X-8688," traditional, *05*		80 ____
28651	Bethlehem Steel 0-6-0 Dockside Switcher "72," traditional, *05*		80 ____
28652	LL 4-4-2 Locomotive "8652," traditional, *05*		105____
28655	Erie 2-8-4 Berkshire Locomotive "3338," traditional, *05*		240 ____
28656	PRR 2-8-4 Berkshire Locomotive "56," traditional, *05*		240 ____
28660	North Pole Central 0-6-0 Dockside Switcher "25," traditional, *05*		105 ____
28661	Santa Fe 0-4-0 Locomotive "2300," traditional, *05*		160____
28662	C&O 0-4-0 Locomotive "39," traditional, *05*		160____
28674	C&O 0-6-0 Dockside Switcher "67," traditional, *06-07*		110 ____
28675	SP 0-6-0 Dockside Switcher "675," traditional, *06-07*		110 ____
28676	U.S. Steel 0-6-0 Dockside Switcher "76," traditional, *06-07*		110 ____
28677	WM 4-4-2 Atlantic Locomotive "103," traditional, *06*		110____
28678	Rio Grande 0-4-0 Locomotive "55," traditional, *06-07*		170 ____

		Exc	Mint
___	**28679** U.S. Army Transportation Corps 0-4-0 Locomotive "40," traditional, *06*		170
___	**28680** Reading 0-4-0 Locomotive "1152," traditional, *06*		170
___	**28681** Virginian 2-8-4 Berkshire Locomotive "509," traditional, *06*		260
___	**28683** B&O 2-8-2 Mikado Locomotive "1520," TrainSounds, *06-07*		260
___	**28684** UP 2-8-2 Mikado Locomotive "2498," TrainSounds, *06-07*		260
___	**28693** B&O 4-4-2 Locomotive "28," traditional, *05*		105
___	**28694** NYC 4-4-2 Atlantic Locomotive "8637," traditional, *06*		100
___	**28695** Halloween 0-6-0 Dockside Switcher "X-131," traditional, *06-07*		85
___	**28699** Holiday 2-8-2 Mikado Locomotive "25," red, RailSounds, *08*		260
___	**28700** CB&Q 0-8-0 Locomotive "543," RailSounds, *05*		650
___	**28701** NP 0-8-0 Locomotive "1178," RailSounds, *05*		650
___	**28702** Boston & Albany 0-8-0 Locomotive "53," RailSounds, *05*		650
___	**28704** PRR 4-4-2 Atlantic Locomotive "68," CC, *05*		550
___	**28706** PRR Reading Seashore 4-4-2 Atlantic Locomotive "6064," CC, *05*		550
___	**28742** B&O 4-6-0 Camelback Locomotive "1630," CC, *03*		335
___	**28743** B&O 4-6-0 Camelback Locomotive "1632," traditional, *03*		300
___	**28744** D&H 4-6-0 Camelback Locomotive "548," CC, *03*		325
___	**28745** D&H 4-6-0 Camelback Locomotive "555," traditional, *03*		300
___	**28746** Erie 4-6-0 Camelback Locomotive "860," CC, *03*		375
___	**28747** Erie 4-6-0 Camelback Locomotive "878," traditional, *03*		300
___	**28748** Jersey Central 4-6-0 Camelback Locomotive "772," CC, *03*		300
___	**28749** Jersey Central 4-6-0 Camelback Locomotive "773," traditional, *03*		300
___	**28750** Lackawanna 4-6-0 Camelback Locomotive "690," CC, *03*		375
___	**28751** Lackawanna 4-6-0 Camelback Locomotive "1031," traditional, *03*		300
___	**28752** LIRR 4-6-0 Camelback Locomotive "126," CC, *03*		300
___	**28753** LIRR 4-6-0 Camelback Locomotive "127," traditional, *03*		300
___	**28754** NYO&W 4-6-0 Camelback Locomotive "249," CC, *03*		300
___	**28755** NYO&W 4-6-0 Camelback, "253," Locomotive, traditional, *03*		300
___	**28756** PRR Reading Seashore 4-6-0 Camelback Locomotive "6000," CC, *03*		325
___	**28757** PRR Reading Seashore 4-6-0 Camelback Locomotive "6001," traditional, *03*		300
___	**28758** Susquehanna 4-6-0 Camelback Locomotive "30," CC, *03*		305
___	**28759** Susquehanna 4-6-0 Camelback Locomotive "36," traditional, *03*		300
___	**28800** N&W GP7 Diesel "507," *99-00*		80
___	**28801** Lionel Lines 44-ton Switcher, *99*		135
___	**28806** Jersey Central FM H16-44 Diesel "1516," CC, *01*		335

Exc Mint

28811	Santa Fe FM H16-44 Diesel "3003," CC, *01*	290	
28813	Milwaukee Road FM H16-44 Diesel "406," CC, *01*	280	
28815	B&O GP30 Diesel "6935," CC, *02*	295	
28817	Reading GP30 Diesel "5513," CC, *02*	310	
28819	Rio Grande GP30 Diesel "3013," CC, *02*	310	
28821	GT GP7 Diesel "4438," *01*	100	
28822	Southern RS3 Diesel "2127," *01*	70	
28823	Virginian Electric Locomotive "234," *01*	122	
28826	Pioneer Seed GP7 Diesel "2001," traditional, *00 u*	NRS	
28827	Chessie GP38 Diesel, traditional, *01*	100	
28830	Soo Line GP9 Diesel, traditional, *01 u*	NRS	
28831	Conrail U36B Diesel "2971," traditional, *02*	100	
28832	Santa Fe RS3 Diesel "2099," traditional, *02*	70	
28836	NYC FM H-16-44 Diesel "7000," CC, *02*	330	
28837	NH FM H-16-44 Diesel "591," CC, *02*	325	
28838	UP FM H-16-44 Diesel "1340," CC, *02*	325	
28839	Alaska GP 30 Diesel "2000," CC, *04*	315	
28840	Burlington GP30 Diesel "945," CC, *03*	325	
28841	Seaboard GP30 Diesel "1315," CC, *03*	220	
28842	C&O GP9 Diesel, horn, *04*	160	
28843	Southern GP38 Diesel, horn, *04*	140	
28845	Amtrak RS3 Diesel "106," *03*	70	
28846	Western Pacific U36B Diesel "3067," traditional, *04*	100	
28847	DM & IR GP38 Diesel "203," traditional, *04*	170	
28848	JCPenney Santa Fe GP38 Diesel, *04*	125	
28849	Western Maryland GP7 Diesel, horn, *04*	185	
28850	NYC GP30 Diesel "6115," CC, *04*	360	
28851	Pennsylvania RS3 Diesel, *04*	75	
28852	CSX U36B Diesel "1976," traditional, *05*	140	
28853	Santa Fe GP38 Diesel "2371," traditional, *05*	210	
28857	Alaska GP9 Diesel, *05*	125	
28859	Pennsylvania GP30 Diesel "2206," nonpowered, *06*	160	
28860	UP GP30 Diesel "844," CC, *06*	360	
28861	UP GP30 Diesel "845," nonpowered (std O), *06*	150	
28862	CSX GP30 Diesel "4249," CC, *06*	400	
28863	CSX GP30 Diesel "4250," nonpowered (std O), *06*	150	
28864	UP RS3 Diesel "1195," traditional, *06*	85	
28865	GN GP9 Diesel "688," traditional, *06*	160	
28866	NYC GP20 Diesel "6110," traditional, *06*	140	
28868	ATSF GP38 Diesel	140	
28873	NYC RS3 Diesel "8226," traditional, *06*	85	
28874	UP GP9 Diesel "178," traditional, *06-07*	210	
28875	Santa Fe GP20 Diesel "1107," traditional, *06*	140	
28876	GN FT Diesel "418," traditional, *07-08*	245	
28879	UPS Centennial GP38 Diesel, traditional, *06*	210	
28881	Conrail GP20 Diesel "2107," traditional, *07*	140	
28882	Alaska RS3 Diesel "1079," traditional, *07*	85	
28883	Diesel, *07-13*	120	
28884	PRR GP38 Diesel "2389," traditional, *08-09*	210	
28886	RI RS3 Diesel "492," traditional, *08*	95	
28887	Southern RS3 Diesel "2028," traditional, *08*	95	
28890	CN GP9 Diesel "4573," traditional, *08*	210	
28897	Seaboard U36B Diesel "1762," traditional, *08*	140	

		Exc	Mint
28900	Iron 'Arry and Iron Bert 2-pack, *08-09*		240
28905	ATSF FT Diesel "160," nonpowered, *09-10*		120
29000	PRR Caleb Strong Madison Coach "2622," *99*		80
29001	PRR Villa Royal Madison Coach "2621," *99*		80
29002	PRR Philadelphia Madison Coach "2624," *99*	30	80
29003	PRR Madison Car 4-pack, *98*		220
29004	NYC Heavyweight Passenger Car 2-pack, *99*		170
29007	NYC Pullman Passenger Car 2-pack, *98 u*		95
29008	NYC Heavyweight Diner "383," *98*		95
29009	NYC Van Twiller Heavyweight Combination Car, *98*		95
29010	C&O Heavyweight Passenger Car 2-pack, *99*		150
29039	Lionel Lines Recovery Combination Car "9501," *99*		NRS
29041	Alaska Streamliner Car 4-pack, *99-00*		230
29042	Alaska Streamliner Baggage Car "6310," *99-00*		50
29043	Alaska Streamliner Coach "5408," *99-00*		65
29044	Alaska Streamliner Vista Dome Car "7014," *99-00*		65
29046	B&O Streamliner Car 4-pack, *99-00*		165
29047	B&O Streamliner Baggage Car, *99-00*		35
29048	B&O Streamliner Coach, *99-00*		50
29049	B&O Streamliner Vista Dome Car, *99-00*		50
29050	B&O Streamliner Observation Car, *99-00*		40
29051	ATSF Streamliner Car 4-pack, *99-00*		200
29052	ATSF Streamliner Baggage Car, *99-00*		40
29053	ATSF Streamliner Coach, *99-00*		60
29054	ATSF Streamliner Vista Dome Car, *99-00*		60
29055	ATSF Streamliner Observation Car, *99-00*		40
29056	NYC Streamliner Car 4-pack, *99-00*		180
29057	NYC Streamliner Baggage Car, *99-00*		40
29058	NYC Streamliner Coach, *99-00*		50
29059	NYC Streamliner Vista Dome Car, *99-00*		50
29060	NYC Streamliner Observation Car, *99-00*		45
29061	PRR Madison Passenger Car 4-pack, *99-00*		190
29062	PRR Indian Point Madison Baggage Car, *99-00*		50
29063	PRR Christopher Columbus Madison Coach, *99-00*		50
29064	PRR Andrew Jackson Madison Coach, *99-00*		50
29065	PRR Broussard Madison Observation Car, *99-00*		50
29066	CNJ Madison Passenger Car 4-pack, *99-00*		210
29067	CNJ Madison Baggage Car "420," *99-00*		50
29068	CNJ Beachcomber Madison Coach, *99-00*		50
29069	CNJ Echo Lake Madison Coach, *99-00*		50
29070	CNJ Madison Observation Car "1178," *99-00*		50
29071	NYC Baby Madison Car 4-pack, *00*		155
29072	NYC Baby Madison Baggage Car "1001," *00*		50
29073	NYC Baby Madison Coach "1005," *00*		50
29074	NYC Baby Madison Coach "1006," *00*		50
29075	NYC Detroit Baby Madison Observation Car "1019," *00*		40
29076	Southern Baby Madison Car 4-pack, *00*		155
29077	Southern Delaware Madison Baggage Car "702," *00*		30
29078	Southern North Carolina Madison Coach "800," *00*		50
29079	Southern Maryland Madison Coach "801," *00*		50
29080	Southern Madison Observation Car "1100," *00*		40
29081	ATSF Baby Madison Car 4-pack, *00*		160
29082	ATSF Baby Madison Baggage Car "1765," *00*		30

Exc Mint

		Exc	Mint
29083	ATSF Baby Madison Coach "3040," *00*		50____
29084	ATSF Baby Madison Coach "1535," *00*		50____
29085	ATSF Baby Madison Observation Car "10," *00*		45____
29086	Madison Car 3-pack, *99*		280____
29090	Lionel Liontech Madison Car "2656," *99*		75____
29091	Lawrence Cowen Lionel Legends Madison Coach "2657," *99-00*		75____
29105	PRR Trail Blazer Aluminum Passenger Car 4-pack, *04-05*		550____
29108	Searchlight Car, *00*		30____
29110	B&O Columbian Aluminum Passenger Car 4-pack, *04*		425____
29115	SP Daylight Aluminum Passenger Car 4-pack, *04-05*		550____
29122	Erie-Lack. F3 Diesel AB Passenger Set, *99*		840____
29123	Erie-Lack. Aluminum Coach/Baggage Car "203," *99*		100____
29124	Erie-Lack. Aluminum Coach/Diner "770," *99*		100____
29125	Erie-Lack. Eleanor Lord Aluminum Coach, *99*		100____
29126	Erie-Lack. Tavern Lounge Aluminum Observation Car "789," *99*		125____
29127	ACL Aluminum Baggage Car "152," *99*		NRS____
29128	ACL North Hampton Aluminum Coach, *99*		NRS____
29129	Texas Special Passenger Car 4-pack, *99*	650	700____
29130	Texas Special Edward Burleson Aluminum Coach "1200," *99*		115____
29131	Texas Special David G. Burnett Aluminum Coach "1201," *99*		115____
29132	Texas Special J. Pinckney Henderson Aluminum Coach "1202," *99*		115____
29133	Texas Special Stephen F. Austin Aluminum Observation Car "1203," *99*		100____
29135	California Zephyr Silver Poplar Aluminum Vista Dome Car, *99*		150____
29136	California Zephyr Silver Palm Aluminum Vista Dome Car, *99*		150____
29137	California Zephyr Silver Tavern Aluminum Vista Dome Car, *99*		150____
29138	California Zephyr Silver Planet Aluminum Vista Dome Car, *99*		150____
29139	Kughn Lionel Legends Madison Car "2655," *99*		113____
29140	NYC Castleton Bridge Aluminum Sleeper Car, *99*		120____
29141	NYC Martin Van Buren Aluminum Combination Car, *99*		120____
29142	CP Skyline Aluminum Vista Dome Car "596," *99*		125____
29143	CP Banff Park Aluminum Observation Car, *99*		125____
29144	Santa Fe El Capitan Aluminum Passenger Car 4-pack, *04*		400____
29149	CB&Q California Zephyr Aluminum Passenger Car 2-pack, *03*		300____
29152	Santa Fe Super Chief Aluminum Passenger Car 2-pack, *03*		190____
29155	D&H Aluminum Passenger Car 2-pack, *03*		190____
29158	Southern Aluminum Passenger Car 2-pack, *03*		205____
29165	Amtrak Superliner Passenger Car 2-pack, Phase IV, *04*		195____
29168	Amtrak Superliner Diner, StationSounds, Phase IV, *04*		200____
29169	Alaska Superliner Passenger Car 2-pack, *04*		200____
29172	Alaska Superliner Diner, StationSounds, *04*		200____

	Exc	Mint
29182 N&W Powhatan Arrow Aluminum Passenger Car 4-pack (std O), *05*		550
29187 N&W Powhatan Arrow Aluminum Passenger Car 2-pack (std O), *05*		290
29190 N&W Powhatan Arrow Aluminum Diner, StationSounds, *05*		290
29191 MILW Hiawatha Passenger Car 4-pack, *06*		370
29196 MILW Hiawatha Passenger Car 2-pack, *06*		190
29199 MILW Hiawatha Diner, StationSounds, *06*		190
29202 Santa Fe Map Boxcar "6464," *97 u*		53
29203 Maine Central Boxcar "6464-597," *97 u*		35
29205 Mickey Mouse Hi-Cube Boxcar "9555," *97*		70
29206 Vapor Records Boxcar #1, *97*		90
29209 Postwar "6464" Boxcar Series VII, 3 cars, *98*		95
29210 GN Boxcar "6464-450," *98*		33
29211 B&M Boxcar "6464-475," *98*		27
29212 Timken Boxcar "6464-500," *98*		28
29213 ATSF Grand Canyon Route 6464 Boxcar "6464-198," *98*		26
29214 Southern 6464 Boxcar "6464-298," *98*		27
29215 Canadian Pacific 6464 Boxcar "6464-398," *98*		26
29217 1997 Toy Fair Airex BoxCar, *97*		78
29218 Vapor Records Boxcar "6464-496," *97 u*		85
29220 Lionel Centennial Series Hi-Cube Boxcar Set, 4 cars, *97*		235
29221 Centennial Series Hi-Cube Boxcar "9697-1," *97*		65
29222 Centennial Series Hi-Cube Boxcar "9697-2," *97*		72
29223 Centennial Series Hi-Cube Boxcar "9697-3," *97*		65
29224 Centennial Series Hi-Cube Boxcar "9697-4," *97*		62
29225 H.O.R.D.E. Music Festival BoxCar, *97*	48	70
29229 Vapor Records Holiday Car, *98*		160
29231 Halloween Animated BoxCar, *98*		42
29233 Conrail PC Overstamped Boxcar "6464-598," *98*		38
29234 Conrail Erie Overstamped Boxcar "6464-698," *98*		32
29235 NYC Boxcar "6464-510," *99*		47
29236 MKT Boxcar "6464-515," *99*		40
29237 M&StL Boxcar "6464-525," *99*		25
29247 Mainline Classic Street Lamps, 3 pieces, *08-16, 18*		40
29250 Phoebe Snow Boxcar "6464-199," *99*		41
29251 BN Boxcar "6464-299," *99*		31
29252 CP Boxcar "6464-399," *99*		33
29253 B&M Boxcar "76032," *99*		50
29254 B&M Boxcar "76033," *99*		50
29255 B&M Boxcar "76034," *99*		50
29256 B&M Boxcar "76035," *99*		50
29257 Southern Boxcar "9464-199," *99*		38
29258 Reading Boxcar "9464-299," *99*		36
29259 NP Bicentennial Boxcar "9464-399," *99*		34
29265 Maine Central Boxcar "8661," *99*		36
29266 Frisco Boxcar "8722," *99*		36
29267 No. 6464 Boxcar 3-pack, Series VIII, *99*		85
29268 Rio Grande Boxcar "63067," *99*		40
29271 Lionel Cola Tractor and Trailer, *98*		12

		Exc	Mint
29279	Conrail Jersey Central Overstamped Boxcar "6464-28X," *99*		40 ___
29280	Conrail LV Overstamped Boxcar "6464-31X," *99*		41 ___
29281	Conrail Overstamped Boxcar 2-pack, *99*		70 ___
29282	Postwar "6464" BoxCar 3-pack, *99*		130 ___
29283	NYC BoxCar, *99*		55 ___
29284	GN BoxCar, *99*		40 ___
29285	Seaboard BoxCar, *99*		36 ___
29286	Overstamped Boxcar 2-pack, *99*		65 ___
29287	NH PC Overstamped Boxcar "6464-29X," *99*	18	34 ___
29288	Conrail Reading Overstamped Boxcar "6464-32X," *99*		38 ___
29289	Postwar "6464" Series IX, 3 cars, *99-00*		70 ___
29290	D&RGW Boxcar "6464-650," *00*		41 ___
29291	ATSF Boxcar "6464-700," *00*		38 ___
29292	NH Boxcar "6464-725," *00*		39 ___
29293	NH Boxcar "6464-425," *99*		95 ___
29294	Hellgate Bridge Boxcar "1900-2000," *99 u*		38 ___
29295	PRR "Don't Stand Me Still" Boxcar "24018," *99-00*		65 ___
29296	PRR "Merchandise" Boxcar "29296," *99-00*		65 ___
29297	PRR "No Damage" Boxcar "47158," *99-00*		65 ___
29298	Lionel Boxcar "6464-2000," *00*		46 ___
29300	50th Anniversary Clear Shell Aquarium Car, *10*		85 ___
29301	Postwar "3662" Transparent Milk Car with platform, *11, 13*		155 ___
29302	Christmas Music Reefer, *10*		75 ___
29303	North Pole Central Crane Car, *10-11*		65 ___
29305	UP Chisholm Trail Stock Car, Cattle Sounds, *11, 13*		200 ___
29306	PRR Hi-Cube Lighted Garland BoxCar, *10-11*		70 ___
29309	GN Pullman-Standard Diesel Freight Set, CC, *13*		830 ___
29310	Marine Science Deep Sea Exhibition Aquarium Car, *11*		75 ___
29311	Strasburg Derrick Car, *11*		45 ___
29312	Santa's Operating BoxCar, *11-12*		75 ___
29314	SP DD Boxcar "214051" (std O), *13-14*		75 ___
29317	CN DD Boxcar "214051" (std O), *13-14*		75 ___
29320	CNJ DD Boxcar "214051" (std O), *13-14*		75 ___
29321	Ice Skating Aquarium Car, *12*		80 ___
29322	Koi Aquarium Car, *13-14*		80 ___
29323	UP DD Boxcar "500019" (std O), *13-14*		75 ___
29324	Walking Zombie Brakeman Car, *12*		80 ___
29326	NP "Pig Palace" Operating Stock Car "84144," *12*		200 ___
29327	Bethlehem Steel Operating Hopper "2025," *12*		60 ___
29328	Beatles "Nothing is Real" Aquarium Car, *12-13*		85 ___
29329	Peanuts Halloween Aquarium Car, *12-13*		85 ___
29333	ATSF 89' Auto Carrier 2-pack (std O), *13-14, 16*		220 ___
29338	BN 89' Auto Carrier 2-pack (std O), *13-14*		220 ___
29344	C&NW DD Boxcar "57766" (std O), *13*		75 ___
29345	ATSF 89' Auto Carrier (std O), *13-14*		110 ___
29346	Soo Line 89' Auto Carrier 2-pack (std O), *13-16*		220 ___
29349	SP 89' Auto Carrier 2-pack (std O), *13-16*		220 ___
29364	NYC Water Level Steam Freight Set, CC, *12-13*		1600 ___
29365	N&W Pocahontas Steam Passenger Set, CC, *12*		1950 ___
29366	SP TankSet Diesel Set, CC, *12*		850 ___

		Exc	Mint
_____	**29372** BNSF 89' Auto Carrier "300267" (std O), *13*		110
_____	**29373** CN 89' Auto Carrier "710771" (std O), *13, 16*		110
_____	**29376** Conrail 89' Auto Carrier "964444" (std O), *13*		110
_____	**29377** CP 89' Auto Carrier 2-pack (std O), *13-14, 16*		220
_____	**29380** CSX 89' Auto Carrier "604544" (std O), *13*		110
_____	**29381** GTW 89' Auto Carrier "50450" (std O), *14-15*		110
_____	**29382** UP 89' Auto Carrier "604545" (std O), *13*		110
_____	**29384** DL&W USRA Double-sheathed Boxcar "44153" (std O), *13*		70
_____	**29385** ATSF USRA Double-sheathed Boxcar "39012" (std O), *13*		70
_____	**29386** PRR PS-4 Flatcar with stakes "469614" (std O), *13*		70
_____	**29387** GN PS-4 Flatcar with stakes "629387" (std O), *13*		70
_____	**29400** Bethlehem Steel Slag Car 3-pack (std O), *03*		185
_____	**29404** Bethlehem Steel Hot Metal Car 3-pack (std O), *03*		210
_____	**29408** PRR Coil Car, *01*		40
_____	**29411** Sherwin-Williams Vat Car, *02*		35
_____	**29412** Tabasco Brand Vat Car, *02*		36
_____	**29413** Airex Boat Loader Car "29413," *02*		42
_____	**29414** PRR Evans Auto Loader "480123," *01*		56
_____	**29415** WM Skeleton Log Car 3-pack #2 (std O), *02*		90
_____	**29419** West Side Lumber Skeleton Log Car 3-pack #2 (std O), *02*		90
_____	**29423** Wellspring Capital Management Happy Holidays Vat Car, *03 u*		255
_____	**29424** Meadow River Lumber Skeleton Log Car 3-pack (std O), *03*		90
_____	**29429** Campbell's Soup Vat Car "29429," *03*		38
_____	**29430** Meadow River Lumber Skeleton Log Car 3-pack #2 (std O), *03*		90
_____	**29434** Weyerhauser Skeleton Log Car 3-pack, *05*		100
_____	**29438** Trailer Train Flatcar with 2 UP trailers, *03*		60
_____	**29439** Postwar "6414," Evans Auto Loader, *02*		43
_____	**29441** UP FlatCar "53471" with grader, *02*		43
_____	**29442** CSX FlatCar "600513" with backhoe, *02*		43
_____	**29453** Elk River Lumber Skeleton Log Car 3-pack #2 (std O), *03*		90
_____	**29457** NS FlatCar "157590" with Caterpillar loader, *03*		42
_____	**29458** BNSF FlatCar "922268" with Caterpillar truck, *03*		44
_____	**29459** Water Barrel Car "1878," Archive Collection, *03*		40
_____	**29460** LL FlatCar "3460" with trailers, Archive Collection, *03*		39
_____	**29461** Postwar "6500" Flatcar with red-and-white airplane, *03*		32
_____	**29462** Postwar "6500" Flatcar with white-and-red airplane, *03*		31
_____	**29463** Postwar "6414" Evans Auto Loader, *03*		30
_____	**29464** U.S. Army Vat Car "29464," *04*		35
_____	**29465** U.S. Steel Slag Car 3-pack (std O), *04-05*		160
_____	**29469** U.S. Steel Hot Metal Car 3-pack (std O), *04-05*		190
_____	**29473** Youngstown Sheet & Tube Slag Car 3-pack (std O), *03*		150
_____	**29477** Youngstown Sheet & Tube Hot Metal Car 3-pack (std O), *03*		170
_____	**29481** Cass Scenic Railroad Skeleton Log Car 3-pack (std O), *03*		80

		Exc	Mint
29487	Boat-loader with 4 boats, *04*	65	____
29488	Cass Scenic Railroad Skeleton Log Car 3-pack #2 (std O), *04*	90	____
29492	Pickering Lumber Skeleton Log Car 3-pack #1 (std O), *04*	100	____
29496	Pickering Lumber Skeleton Log Car 3-pack #2 (std O), *04*	90	____
29602	Celanese Chemicals 1-D Tank Car, *05*	45	____
29603	Comet 1-D Tank Car, traditional, *05*	53	____
29604	Meadow Brook Molasses 1-D Tank Car, traditional, *05*	53	____
29606	Elvis Presley Gold Record Transport Car, *04*	120	____
29607	Las Vegas Mint Car, traditional, *05*	58	____
29609	Alien Suspension Car, *06*	60	____
29610	Dixie Honey 1-D Tank Car, *06*	60	____
29611	Sunoco 1-D Tank Car, *06*	60	____
29612	Las Vegas Poker Chip Car, *06*	40	____
29613	Postwar "6463" Rocket Fuel 2-D Tank Car, *06*	75	____
29617	Cities Service Tank Car, *06-07*	48	____
29618	Hooker Chemicals 3-D Tank Car, *07*	60	____
29619	Grave's Formaldehyde 1-D Tank Car, *07*	60	____
29622	Fort Knox Mint Car, lilac, Archive Collection, *07*	60	____
29624	Monopoly Mint Car with money, *08*	65	____
29626	"Case Closed" Mint Car with shredded documents, *08*	109	____
29628	Poinsettia Mint Car, *09*	70	____
29629	AEC Glow-in-the-Dark Tank Car, *09-10*	65	____
29633	Christmas Ornament Lighted Mint Car, *10*	70	____
29634	Federal Reserve Bailout Mint Car, *10*	70	____
29635	Monopoly "Go To Jail" Mint Car, *10*	70	____
29636	Vampire Transport Mint Car, *10-11*	70	____
29637	Candy Cane 2-D Tank Car, *10-11*	55	____
29640	Coca-Cola Tank Car, *10*	65	____
29642	Jolly Rancher 1-D Tank Car, *11*	55	____
29643	Hershey's Syrup 1-D Tank Car, *11*	58	____
29644	ATSF 1-D Tank Car, *11*	55	____
29645	Atlantic City Casino Mint Car, *11*	70	____
29646	Alaska Oil 2-D Tank Car, *11*	50	____
29647	Gingerbread Man Mint Car, *11*	70	____
29649	Lionel SP Smoke Pellets Mint Car, *12-13*	70	____
29650	Cleveland Federal Reserve Mint Car, *11*	70	____
29651	Richmond Federal Reserve Mint Car, *12*	70	____
29654	Boston Federal Reserve Mint Car, *13*	70	____
29655	PRR 16-wheel Flatcar with girders "469846," *12*	75	____
29656	ATSF 16-wheel Flatcar with transformer "90096," *12*	75	____
29671	Smoke Pellet Mint Car #2, *13-15*	70	____
29694	Hershey's Mint Car, *14*	90	____
29695	Trailer Set Maxi-Stack Pair "48," *13*	120	____
29697	Santa's Flatcar with submarine, *13*	70	____
29698	Tree Topper Star Transport Car, *13-14*	80	____
29699	Silver and Gold Christmas Mint Car, *13-14*	70	____
29703	PRR Porthole Caboose, *01*	45	____
29708	C&O Bay Window Caboose "8315," *04*	45	____

		Mint
____	**29709** Pennsylvania N5c Caboose "477938," *04*	40
____	**29711** Santa Fe Bay Window Caboose, *05*	60
____	**29712** Postwar "2420" Searchlight Caboose, *04*	50
____	**29718** N&W Work Caboose, *06*	48
____	**29719** Santa Fe Caboose "6427," Archive Collection, *06*	48
____	**29726** Virginian Caboose "6427," Archive Collection, *06-07*	50
____	**29727** "I Love U.S.A." Bay Window Caboose "1985," *06*	60
____	**29729** Bethlehem Steel Searchlight Caboose, *06*	90
____	**29732** PRR Caboose "477871," *08*	45
____	**29733** White Pass & Yukon Extended Vision Caboose, *09-10*	90
____	**29734** PRR NS Heritage CA-4 Caboose (std O), *10*	95
____	**29735** Conrail NS Heritage CA-4 Caboose (std O), *10*	95
____	**29737** ATSF Bay Window Caboose, traditional, *10-11*	70
____	**29739** B&M Transfer Caboose, *11*	50
____	**29765** TankSet Add-on 3-pack (std O), *12*	240
____	**29771** CN TankSet 2-pack (std O), *12*	160
____	**29774** GATX TankSet 2-pack (std O), *12*	160
____	**29777** Cibro TankSet 2-pack (std O), *12*	160
____	**29786** Bethlehem Steel PS-2 3-bay Hopper (std O), *13*	80
____	**29787** PRR PS-2 3-bay Hopper (std O), *13*	80
____	**29791** Wizard of Oz Anniversary BoxCar, *13-15*	70
____	**29792** Angela Trotta Thomas "Toyland Express" BoxCar, *13*	65
____	**29793** Where the Wild Things Are BoxCar, *13-15*	70
____	**29800** MOW Crane Car, TMCC, *04*	250
____	**29804** UP Crane Car "JPX 250," CC, *05*	320
____	**29805** Conrail Crane Car "50202," CC, *05*	320
____	**29806** Weyerhaeuser Log Dump Car, *05*	75
____	**29807** DM&IR Coal Dump Car, *05*	75
____	**29808** Candy Cane Dump Car, *05*	55
____	**29809** Dump Car with presents, *05*	60
____	**29810** Operating Egg Nog Car with platform, *05*	140
____	**29811** Merchant's Despatch Transit Hot Box Reefer "12425," *05*	85
____	**29811** LCCA Merchandise Dispatch Refrigerator Car w/Hot box, *2008u*	110
____	**29812** Santa Fe Hot Box Reefer "20699," *05*	90
____	**29813** Santa Fe Boom Car "19144," Crane Sounds, *05*	210
____	**29814** Pennsylvania Boom Car "491063," Crane Sounds, *05*	210
____	**29815** NYC Boom Car "X923," Crane Sounds, *05*	210
____	**29816** MOW Boom Car "X-816," Crane Sounds, *05*	210
____	**29817** UP Boom Car "909438," Crane Sounds, *05*	210
____	**29818** Conrail Boom Car, Crane Sounds, *05*	210
____	**29821** Postwar "2460" Lionel Lines Crane Car, gray cab, *05*	43
____	**29822** Postwar "773W" NYC Tender, whistle, *05*	48
____	**29823** Postwar "3484" Pennsylvania Operating BoxCar, *05*	38
____	**29827** Postwar "3419" Helicopter Launching Car, *06*	49
____	**29828** Postwar "3666" Minuteman Car with cannon, *06*	85
____	**29829** Postwar "6905" Radioactive Waste Car, *06*	85
____	**29830** PFE Hot Box Reefer "5890" (std O), *06*	105
____	**29831** Swift Hot Box Reefer "15342" (std O), *06*	150
____	**29832** Chessie System Crane Car "940504," CC, *06*	320
____	**29833** Chessie System Boom Car "940561," CC, *06*	210
____	**29834** LL Bay Window Caboose "834," TrainSounds (std O), *06-07*	110

		Exc	Mint
29835	SP Bay Window Caboose "4667," TrainSounds (std O), *06-07*	160	
29839	Cherry Picker Car, *06*	63	___
29849	Lionel Lines Crane Car, silver cab, *06*	60	___
29850	N&W J Class Tender, air whistle, *06-07*	70	___
29853	Postwar "6651" Big John Cannon Car, *08*	75	___
29854	Satellite Launching Car, *07*	70	___
29855	Lionel Lines Operating Milk Car with platform, *07*	140	___
29856	Monon Operating BoxCar, *06-07*	65	___
29857	Lionel Lines Boom Car, *06-07*	55	___
29858	CP Rail Crane Car "414475," CC, *07*	320	___
29859	CP Rail Boom Car "412567," CC, *07*	210	___
29865	Southern Operating Barrel Car, *07-08*	75	___
29866	Pirates Aquarium Car, *07*	75	___
29867	NYC Jet Snow Blower "X27207," *07*	120	___
29868	Alaska Jet Snow Blower, *07*	120	___
29869	Bethlehem Steel Crane Car, *06*	60	___
29870	MOW Jet Snow Blower "MWX-16," *07*	120	___
29874	Peanuts Halloween Aquarium Car, *12*	85	___
29877	Southern Crane Car "D76," CC, *08*	350	___
29882	Witches Operating Brew Car, *08*	150	___
29884	CNJ Twin Dump Car, *08*	85	___
29885	BN Crane Car "S-104," CC, *10*	340	___
29886	BN Boom Car "S-1040," CC, *10*	220	___
29888	Postwar "3494-625" Soo Lines Operating BoxCar, *08*	70	___
29893	PRR Operating Stock Car "129893," RailSounds, *09*	150	___
29894	Christmas Chase Gondola, *09*	65	___
29895	Christmas Operating Snow Globe Car, *10*	75	___
29897	CSX Chessie System Research Car "3440," *11*	65	___
29900	"I Love Wisconsin" BoxCar, *01*	35	___
29901	"I Love Kentucky" BoxCar, *01*	30	___
29902	"I Love Iowa" BoxCar, *01*	31	___
29903	"I Love Missouri" BoxCar, *01*	31	___
29904	2002 Toy Fair BoxCar, *02*	22	___
29906	"I Love Connecticut" BoxCar, *02*	33	___
29907	"I Love West Virginia" BoxCar, *02*	33	___
29908	"I Love Delaware" BoxCar, *02*	33	___
29909	"I Love Maryland" BoxCar, *02*	65	___
29910	Toy Fair Centennial BoxCar, *03*	40	___
29912	"I Love Alabama" BoxCar, *03*	30	___
29913	"I Love Mississippi" BoxCar, *03*	35	___
29914	"I Love Louisiana" BoxCar, *03*	35	___
29915	"I Love Arkansas" BoxCar, *03*	30	___
29918	2003 Toy Fair BoxCar, *03*	48	___
29919	2004 Toy Fair BoxCar, *04*	37	___
29920	"I Love North Dakota" BoxCar, *03*	35	___
29921	"I Love South Dakota" BoxCar, *03*	40	___
29922	"I Love Nebraska" BoxCar, *03*	30	___
29923	"I Love Kansas" BoxCar, *03*	30	___
29924	2004 Lionel Employee Christmas BoxCar, *2004u*	110	___
29925	Toy Fair Polar Express BoxCar, *05*	250	___
29927	"I Love Washington" BoxCar, *05*	45	___
29928	"I Love Oregon" BoxCar, *05*	40	___

		Exc	Mint
____	**29929** "I Love Idaho" BoxCar, *05*		45
____	**29930** "I Love Utah" BoxCar, *05*		45
____	**29932** "I Love Oklahoma" BoxCar, *06*		45
____	**29933** "I Love New Mexico" BoxCar, *06*		45
____	**29934** "I Love Hawaii" BoxCar, *06*		45
____	**29935** "I Love Alaska" BoxCar, *06*		45
____	**29936** "I Love Wyoming" BoxCar, *06*		45
____	**29937** 2006 Toy Fair BoxCar, *06*		38
____	**29942** Santa Fe Railroad Art BoxCar, *06*		50
____	**29943** Texas Special Railroad Art BoxCar, *06*		50
____	**29944** 1957 Lionel Art BoxCar, *06*		50
____	**29945** 1947 Lionel Art BoxCar, *06*		50
____	**29949** Weyerhaeuser Timber Skeleton Log Car 3-pack #2 (std O), *03*		90
____	**29949** 2007 Lionel Employee Christmas BoxCar, *2007u*		60
____	**29950** 1948 Lionel Art BoxCar, *08*		50
____	**29951** 1954 Lionel Art BoxCar, *08*		50
____	**29952** GN Art BoxCar, *08*		50
____	**29953** SP Art BoxCar, *08*		50
____	**29954** Dealer Christmas BoxCar, *07*		75
____	**29954** 2007 Lionel Dealer Appreciation BoxCar, *2007u*		30
____	**29955** Dealer BoxCar, *08*		75
____	**29955** 2008 Lionel Dealer Appreciation BoxCar, *2008u*		70
____	**29956** 2008 Lionel Employee Christmas BoxCar, *2008u*		60
____	**29958** Dealer BoxCar, *09*		50
____	**29958** 2009 Lionel Dealer Appreciation BoxCar, *2009u*		40
____	**29959** 1952 Lionel Art BoxCar, *09*		58
____	**29960** Rock Island Art BoxCar, *09-10*		58
____	**29961** Meet the Beatles Boxcar 2-pack, *10-14*		130
____	**29965** Lionel Art Boxcar 2-pack, *10-11*		116
____	**29968** Beatles "A Hard Day's Night" BoxCar, *11-14*		65
____	**29969** Beatles "Something New" BoxCar, *11-14*		65
____	**29973** NYC Pacemaker Boxcar "175005," *11*		60
____	**29974** SP Boxcar "128133," *11*		60
____	**29975** Holiday BoxCar, *11*		60
____	**29976** Holiday BoxCar, *12-13*		65
____	**29978** Railroad Museum of Pennsylvania BoxCar, *12*		65
____	**29979** Angela Trotta Thomas "Christmas Morning" BoxCar, *12-13*		60
____	**29980** Elvis Presley 35th Anniversary BoxCar, *12*		70
____	**29982** CV Milk Car "575" (std O), *16*		80
____	**29985** B&M Milk Car "1903" (std O), *16*		80
____	**29989** PFE Steel-sided Refrigerator Car 3-pack (std O), *14-15*		240
____	**29994** U.S. Army BoxCar, *13-15*		70
____	**29995** U.S. Navy BoxCar, *13-15*		70
____	**29996** U.S. Marines BoxCar, *13-15*		70
____	**29997** U.S. Air Force BoxCar, *13-15*		70
____	**29998** U.S. National Guard BoxCar, *13-16*		70
____	**29999** U.S. Coast Guard BoxCar, *13-16*		70
____	**30000** PRR Keystone Super Freight Steam Train, TMCC, *05*		450
____	**30001** Santa Fe El Capitan Passenger Set, TrainSounds, *05-10*		370
____	**30002** Neil Young's Greendale Diesel Freight Set, *04*		420

		Exc	Mint
30003	Pennsylvania Flyer Operating Freight Expansion Pack, *05*		99 ____
30004	Pennsylvania Flyer Passenger Expansion Pack, *05-08*		120 ____
30005	Disney Passenger Train, *05*		190 ____
30007	NYC Flyer Operating Freight Expansion Pack, *05*		99 ____
30008	NYC Flyer Passenger Expansion Pack, *05-08*		120 ____
30011	Holiday Expansion Pack, *05*		100 ____
30012	Thomas the Tank Engine Expansion Pack, *05-13, 16*		150 ____
30016	NYC Flyer Steam Freight Set, *06-08*		290 ____
30018	Pennsylvania Flyer Steam Freight Set, *06-07*		200 ____
30020	North Pole Central Christmas Steam Train, *06-07*		220 ____
30021	Cascade Range Steam Logging Train, *06-08*		190 ____
30022	Southwest Diesel Freight Set, TrainSounds, *06*		295 ____
30024	UP Fast Freight Steam Set, TrainSounds, *06-07*		340 ____
30025	Chesapeake Super Freight Steam Set, TMCC, *06-07*		475 ____
30026	CP Diesel Freight Set, TMCC, *06*		540 ____
30034	Great Western Train Set with Lincoln Logs, *07-09*		230 ____
30035	Sodor Freight Expansion Pack, *06-09*		120 ____
30036	Great Western Expansion Pack, *07-08*		120 ____
30037	Pennsylvania Flyer Operating Freight Expansion Pack, *06-08*		120 ____
30038	NYC Flyer Operating Freight Expansion Pack, *06-08*		120 ____
30039	North Pole Central Passenger Expansion Pack, *06-11*		110 ____
30040	North Pole Central Freight Expansion Pack, *06-11*		110 ____
30041	Southwest Diesel Freight Expansion Pack, *06*		110 ____
30042	Cascade Range Expansion Pack, *06*		110 ____
30044	NYC Empire Builder Steam Freight Set, TMCC, *06*		2800 ____
30045	Alaska Steam Work Train, *07-09*		270 ____
30046	Alaska Work Train Expansion Pack, *07-08*		110 ____
30047	Northwest Special Diesel Freight Set, TrainSounds, *07-08*		295 ____
30048	Northwest Special Freight Expansion Pack, *07-08*		110 ____
30049	D&RGW Fast Freight Set, TrainSounds, *08-09*		320 ____
30050	Pennsylvania Super Freight Set, CC, *08*		450 ____
30051	UP Diesel Freight Set, TMCC, *07*		500 ____
30056	Halloween Steam Freight Set, *07-10*		225 ____
30061	UPS Centennial Stream Freight Set, *07-08*		230 ____
30064	Pennsylvania Speeder Set, traditional, K-Line, *06*		75 ____
30066/67	C&O Empire Builder Steam Freight Set, CC, *07-09*		2700 ____
30065	Best Friend of Charleston Locomotive, *07*		425 ____
30068	North Pole Central Christmas Freight Set, *08*		220 ____
30069	Thomas & Friends Passenger Train, *08-12*		170 ____
30070	Lionel Lines 4-4-2 Steam Freight Set, *07*		300 ____
30076	Disney Christmas Train, *07*		400 ____
30081	UP Merger Special GP38 Freight Set, *08*		300 ____
30082	UP Heritage Freight Car 3-pack, *08*		100 ____
30084	British Great Western Shakespeare Express Passenger Train, *08*		300 ____
30085	MTA Metro-North M-7 Commuter Car Set, *07-08*		280 ____
30087	Alien Spaceship Recovery Freight Set, *08-09*		230 ____
30088	John Bull Passenger Train, *08*		430 ____
30089	Pennsylvania Flyer Freight Set, *08-10*		200 ____

		Exc	Mint
____	**30091** ATSF Steam Freight Set, *08-09*		270
____	**30094** Chicago & North Western Passenger Set, *08*		150
____	**30096** Pennsylvania Keystone Special Steam Freight Set, *09*		260
____	**30103** NYC 0-8-0 Steam Freight Set, *09-10*		300
____	**30108** American Fire and Rescue GP20 Freight Set, *09-10*		400
____	**30109** Nutcracker Route Christmas Train Set, *10-11*		270
____	**30111** Pullman Passenger Expansion Pack, *09-16*		155
____	**30112** Eastern Freight Expansion Pack, *09-17*		155
____	**30114** MTA LIRR M-7 Commuter Set, *09*		320
____	**30116** Lone Ranger Wild West Freight Set, *09-13*		400
____	**30118** A Christmas Story Steam Freight Set, *09-12*		330
____	**30120** Menards C&NW Steam Passenger Set, *09*		250
____	**30121** ATSF Baby Madison Car 3-pack, *10-11*		190
____	**30122** Wizard of Oz Steam Freight Set, *10-12*		310
____	**30123** Boy Scouts of America Steam Freight Set, *10*		310
____	**30124** Thunder Valley Quarry Steam Freight Set, *10-11*		300
____	**30125** Rio Grande Ski Train, TrainSounds, *10-11*		340
____	**30126** Pennsylvania Flyer Steam Freight Set, *10*		230
____	**30127** Scout Steam Freight Set, *10-12*		200
____	**30128** Western Freight Expansion Pack, *10-12*		138
____	**30131** Chessie System Merger Diesel Freight Set, *10*		300
____	**30133** Strasburg Steam Passenger Set, *10-13*		330
____	**30135** Scout Freight Expansion Pack, *11-15*		115
____	**30136** Thunder Valley Quarry Freight Car Add-on 2-pack, *10-11*		110
____	**30138** Chessie System Merger Freight Car Add-on 2-pack, *10-11*		120
____	**30139** Santa Fe Flyer Steam Freight Set, *10*		270
____	**30141** Sodor Tank and Wagon Expansion Pack, *10-16*		150
____	**30142** Texas Special Freight Set, TrainSounds, *10-11*		700
____	**30144** Operation Eagle Justice Diesel Freight Set, *10-11*		500
____	**30145** Maple Leaf Diesel Freight Set, *10-11*		550
____	**30146** Menards Soo Line Freight Set, *10*	175	275
____	**30147** MTA Long Island M-7 Commuter Set, *11*		320
____	**30153** CSX Diesel Freight Set, *11*		330
____	**30154** BNSF Diesel Freight Set, *11*		340
____	**30155** M&StL Diesel Freight Set, *11-12*		230
____	**30156** NYC Flyer Freight Set, TrainSounds, *11*		300
____	**30157** M&StL Flatcar and Erie-Lack. Gondola 2-pack, *11-15*		110
____	**30158** Norfolk Southern GP38 Diesel Freight Train Set, *11*		320
____	**30159** Wabash Blue Bird Passenger Set, *11-12*		360
____	**30161** Boy Scouts Steam Freight Set, *11-13*		320
____	**30162** Thomas & Friends Christmas Set, *13-15*		200
____	**30164** Santa's Flyer Steam Freight Set, *11-13*		250
____	**30165** Candy Cane Transit Commuter 2-pack, *11-13*		180
____	**30166** Coca-Cola 125th Anniversary Steam Set, *11-12*		350
____	**30167** SP Merger Steam Freight Train Set, *12*		400
____	**30168** Rio Grande General Set, TrainSounds, *11-12*		300
____	**30169** NJ Transit Train Set, *11*		350
____	**30170** Sodor Freight 3-pack, *11-13*		100
____	**30171** GG1 Electric Freight Train Set, *11-13*		550
____	**30173** Santa Fe Flyer Freight Set, *11-12*		270

	Exc	Mint
30174 Pennsylvania Flyer Freight Set, *11-13*		290____
30178 ATSF Super Chief Diesel Passenger Train Set, *12-13*		400____
30179 RI Rocket Diesel Freight Train Set, *12-13*		400____
30180 Horseshoe Curve Steam Freight Train Set, *12-13*		440____
30181 CP Diesel Passenger Set, RailSounds, *13, 15*		450____
30183 Scout Remote Steam Freight Set, *13, 15*		220____
30184 Polar Express Steam Freight Set, *13*		420____
30185 NJ Transit Diesel MOW Train Set, *12-13*		350____
30186 KCS Southern Belle Diesel Freight Train Set, *12-13*		350____
30187 Titanic Centennial Diesel Freight Train Set, *12-13*		450____
30188 UP Flyer Steam Freight Train Set, *12-13*		330____
30189 LIRR Diesel Passenger Train Set, *12-13*		330____
30190 Thomas & Friends Set, LionChief, *12-16*		200____
30191 Sodor Work Set 3-pack, *12-15*		100____
30193 Peanuts Christmas Steam Freight Set, *12-15*		370____
30194 North Pole Express Steam Freight Set, *12-13*		290____
30195 Grand Central Express Diesel Passenger Train Set, *12-14*		440____
30196 Hershey's Steam Freight Train Set, *12-13*		312____
30200 NYC Flyer Steam Freight Train Set, *12-13*		350____
30205 Silver Bells Christmas Steam Freight Set, *513-14*		240____
30206 Area 51 RS3 Diesel Freight Set, *13*		250____
30207 Santa Fe RS3 Diesel Freight Set, *13*		200____
30210 CP Rail Grain SetDiesel Freight Set, *13*		390____
30211 BNSF Maxi Stack Diesel Freight Set, *13*		440____
30213 Northeast NS Heritage Diesel Freight Set, *13*		410____
30214 Peanuts Halloween Steam Freight Set, *13, 15-16*		320____
30217 SP Black Widow Diesel Freight Set, *13, 15*		460____
30218 Polar Express Steam Passenger Set, *13-16*		400____
30218 Polar Express Steam Passenger Set w/Personalized Tender, LionChief, *18*		440____
30219 Gingerbread Junction Steam Freight Set, *13-14*		290____
30220 Polar Express 10th Anniversary Passenger Set, *13-14, 16*		500____
30221 Diesel Remote Control Set, *13-16*		200____
30222 Percy Remote Control Set, *13-15*		200____
30223 James Remote Control Set, *13-15*		200____
30224 Pennsylvania Limited Steam Passenger Set, *13*		340____
30225 Medal of Honor Train, *13*		430____
30226 NS Diesel Freight Set, RailSounds, *13*		410____
30228 Chattanooga Express Steam Passenger Set, *13*		250____
30233 Pennsylvania Flyer Remote Steam Freight Set, *13-17*		280____
31569 Western & Atlantic Passenger Car 2-pack, *08*		100____
31700 Postwar Girls Freight Set, *01*		570____
31701 Postwar Boys Freight Set, *02*		345____
31704 Alton Limited Steam Passenger Set, *02*		870____
31705 50th Anniversary Hudson Passenger Set, *02*		910____
31706 UP Burro Crane Set, *02*		210____
31707 C&O Diesel Freight Set, *03*		280____
31708 Postwar "1805" Marines Missile Launch Train, *03*		400____
31710 BN Diesel Coal Train, RailSounds, *03*		690____
31711 Postwar "1563W" Wabash Diesel Freight Set, RailSounds, *03*		570____
31712 UP Alco PA Diesel Passenger Set, RailSounds, *03*		1495____

		Exc	Mint
____	**31713** Southern Crescent Limited Steam Passenger Set, RailSounds, *03*		1195
____	**31714** Amtrak Acela Diesel Passenger Set, RailSounds, *04-05*		2000
____	**31715** Fire Rescue Steam Freight Set, *02*		300
____	**31716** Fire Rescue Steam Freight Set, *03*		280
____	**31717** CP Rail Snow Removal Train, *03*		255
____	**31718** SP "Oil Can" Tank Train Freight Set, *03*		1600
____	**31719** Western Maryland Fireball Diesel Freight Set, *04*		290
____	**31720** FEC Champion Diesel Passenger Set, RailSounds, *04*		900
____	**31721** Postwar "13138" Majestic Electric Freight Set, RailSounds, *04*		580
____	**31724** Nabisco 3-car Passenger Set, *03*		110
____	**31727** Postwar "2291W" Rio Grande Diesel Freight Set, RailSounds, *04*		640
____	**31728** Elvis "He Dared to Rock" Steam Freight Set, *04*		325
____	**31730** Norman Rockwell Boxcar 4-pack, *05*		95
____	**31733** Jones & Laughlin Steel Slag Train, *05*		250
____	**31734** Chessie Steam Special Passenger Set, TMCC, *05*		405
____	**31735** Chessie Diesel Freight Set, TMCC, *05-06*		670
____	**31736** CP Diesel Grain Train, TMCC, *05*		700
____	**31737** Napa Valley Wine Train, TMCC, *05*		900
____	**31739** Postwar "13150" Hudson Steam Freight Set, Super O, *05*		940
____	**31740** Postwar "2519W" Virginian Diesel Freight Set, TMCC, *05-07*		620
____	**31742** Postwar "2544W" Santa Fe Super Chief Diesel Passenger Set, *05*		700
____	**31746** GN Mountain Mover Steam Freight Set, *12-13*		430
____	**31747** Pennsylvania Electric Ballast Train, TMCC, *06*		550
____	**31748** Santa Fe U28CG Diesel Freight Set (std O), TMCC, *06-07*		770
____	**31749** Pennsylvania Diesel Coal Train, TMCC, *06*		770
____	**31750** NYC Hotbox Reefer Steam Freight Set, TMCC, *06-07*		530
____	**31751** New York City Transit Authority R27 Subway Train, CC, *07*		700
____	**31752** B&O Diesel Freight Set, TMCC, *06-07*		740
____	**31753** GN Diesel Freight Set, TMCC, *06-08*		740
____	**31754** Postwar "2545WS" N&W Space Freight Set, TMCC, *06-07*		960
____	**31755** Texas Special Diesel Passenger Set, CC, *07-08*		1280
____	**31757** Postwar "2289WS" Berkshire Freight Set, CC, *07*		750
____	**31758** Postwar "2270W" Jersey Central Diesel Passenger Car Set, CC, *08*		750
____	**31760** CSX SD40-2 Diesel Husky Stack Car Set, CC, *07-08*		770
____	**31765** Postwar "11268" C&O Diesel Freight Set, *08*		580
____	**31767** Bethlehem Steel Rolling Stock Set, K-Line, *06*		100
____	**31768** B&O Rolling Stock Set, K-Line, *06*		100
____	**31772** Conrail LionMaster Diesel Freight Set, CC, *08-09*		535
____	**31773** NS Dash 9 Diesel TankTrain Set, CC, *08*		785
____	**31774** AEC Burro Crane Set, traditional, *09-11*		260
____	**31775** "1562" Burlington GP Passenger Set, *08*		470
____	**31776** "2219W" Lackawanna Train Master Freight Set, *08*		415
____	**31777** "2124W" GG1 Passenger Set, *08*		470
____	**31778** "1484WS" Steam Passenger Set, *08*		610

		Exc	Mint
31779	Amtrak HHP-8 Amfleet Passenger Set, CC, *09*		500____
31782	ATSF Crane Car and Boom Car, CC (std O), *09-10*		560____
31783	BNSF Ice Cold Express Diesel Freight Set, CC, *10*		1000____
31784	No. 1593 UP Work Train Set, *09*		470____
31787	CN SD70M-2 Diesel Coal Train, CC, *09*		800____
31790	PRR GG1 Passenger Set, *10*		500____
31791	NYC LionMaster Diesel Freight Set, CC, *10*		700____
31793	White Pass & Yukon Freight Car Add-on 3-pack, *10-11, 13*		195 ____
31795	Pere Marquette Freight Car 3-pack (std O), *10-11*		210____
31796	Feather Route Freight Car 3-pack (std O), *10-11*		210____
31797	New York City Transit R16 Subway Set, CC, *10*		800____
31799	GN Empire Steam Freight Express Set, *10*		430____
31901	Christmas Steam Freight Set, *02*		145____
31902	PRR K4 Freight Set, *01-02*		580____
31904	C&O Steam Freight Set, RailSounds, *01*		400____
31905	NH Diesel Freight Set, CC, *01*		660____
31907	PRR Atlantic Freight Set, *01 u*		400____
31908	Reading Hobo Express Freight Set, *01 u*		365____
31909	Santa Fe Shell Tank Car Freight Set, *01 u*		320____
31910	Soo Line Diesel Freight Set, *01 u*		365____
31911	Snap-On Anniversary Steam Freight Set, *00 u*		615____
31913	PRR Flyer Steam Freight Set, *01*		145____
31914	NYC Flyer Steam Freight Set, RailSounds, *01-02*		170____
31915	Chessie GP38 Diesel Freight Set, *01-02*		155____
31916	Santa Fe Steam Freight Set, *01*		300____
31918	C&O Steam Freight Set, SignalSounds, *01*		315____
31919	T&P Steam Passenger Set, RailSounds, *01*		210____
31920	L.L. Bean Freight Set, *01 u*		270____
31922	Snap-On Tool Diesel Freight Set, *01 u*		360____
31923	PRR Flyer Freight Set, *01 u*		130____
31924	Union Pacific RS3 Diesel Freight Set, *02*		95____
31926	Area 51 FA Diesel Freight Set, *02*		160____
31928	Great Train Robbery Set, *02*		180____
31931	Ballyhoo Brothers Circus Train, *02*		190____
31932	NYC Limited Passenger Set, RailSounds, *02*		285____
31933	Santa Fe Steam Freight Set, RailSounds, *02*		320____
31934	Lionel 20th Century Express Steam Freight Set, *00 u*		285____
31936	Pennsylvania Flyer Steam Freight Set, *03-05*		190____
31938	Southern Diesel Freight Set, *03-04*		160____
31939	Great Train Robbery Steam Freight Set, *03*		185____
31940	NYC Flyer Steam Freight Set, RailSounds, *03*		225____
31941	Winter Wonderland Railroad Christmas Train, *03*		150____
31942	Norman Rockwell Christmas Train, *03*		330____
31944	NYC Limited Diesel Passenger Set, RailSounds, *03*		250____
31945	Santa Fe Steam Super Freight Set, RailSounds, *03*		350____
31946	Disney Christmas Steam Train, *04-05*		310____
31947	World of Disney Steam Freight Set, *03*		215____
31950	Kraft Holiday UP RS3 Diesel Freight Set, *02 u*		149____
31952	Great Northern Glacier Route Diesel Freight Set, *03-04*		110 ____
31953	"Riding the Rails" Hobo Train Set, *03-04*		225____
31956	Thomas the Tank Engine Set, *04-07*		195____
31958	Santa Fe Flyer Steam Freight Set, RailSounds, *04*		205____

		Exc	Mint
____	**31960** Polar Express Steam Passenger Set, *04-13*		420
____	**31961** Bloomingdale's Pennsylvania Flyer Steam Freight Set, *02 u*		160
____	**31962** Nickel Plate Road Super Freight Set, RailSounds, *04*		350
____	**31963** Southern Pacific Overnight Steam Freight Set, *04*		340
____	**31966** Holiday Tradition Steam Freight Set, *04-05*		210
____	**31969** NYC Flyer Steam Freight Set, RailSounds, *04*		205
____	**31976** Yukon Special Diesel Freight Set, *05*		225
____	**31977** New York Central Flyer Steam Freight Set, *05*		250
____	**31985** Santa Fe Steam Fast Freight Set, TrainSounds, *05*		320
____	**31987** Mickey's Holiday Express Train, *04*		280
____	**31989** UP Overland Freight Express Set, *04*		880
____	**31990** Copper Range Steam Freight Mine Set, *05*		175
____	**31993** NS Black Diamond Diesel Freight Set, TMCC, *05*		500
____	**32900** DC Billboard, *99*		24
____	**32902** Construction Zone Signs, set of 6, *99-18*		10
____	**32904** Hellgate Bridge, *99*	235	415
____	**32905** Irvington Factory, *99-00*		295
____	**32910** Rotary Coal Tipple with bathtub gondola, *02*		442
____	**32919** Animated Maiden Rescue, *99*		65
____	**32920** Animated Pylon with airplane, *99*		130
____	**32921** Electric Coaling Station, *99-01*		125
____	**32922** Highway Barrels, set of 6, *99-18*		10
____	**32923** Accessory Transformer, *99-03, 06-16*		46
____	**32929** Icing Station with Santa, *99*		90
____	**32930** Power Supply Setwith ZW controller and 2 power supplies, *99-02, 06-09*	240	425
____	**32933** Christmas Stocking Hanger Set, 4-piece, *99-00*		50
____	**32934** Stocking Hanger, gondola, *99-00*		15
____	**32935** Stocking Hanger, BoxCar, *99-00*		15
____	**32960** Hindenburger Cafe, *99*		195
____	**32961** Route 66 UFO Cafe, *99*		200
____	**32987** Hobo Campfire, *99-00*	25	45
____	**32988** Postwar "192" Railroad Control Tower, *99-00*		75
____	**32989** Postwar "464" Sawmill, *99-00*		75
____	**32990** Linex Oil Derrick, *99-00*		55
____	**32991** WLLC Radio Station, *99*		75
____	**32996** Postwar "362" Barrel Loader, *00*		125
____	**32997** Aluminum Rico Station, *00*		300
____	**32998** Hobby Shop, *99-00*		300
____	**32999** Hellgate Bridge, *99-00*		400
____	**33000** GP9 Diesel "3000" RailScope video camera system, *88-90*	125	170
____	**33002** RailScope Television Monitor, *88-90*	45	70
____	**34102** Amtrak Shelter, *04-08*		25
____	**34108** Lionelville Suburban House, *03*		20
____	**34109** Lionelville Large Suburban House, *03*		15
____	**34110** Lionelville Estate House, *03*		30
____	**34111** Lionelville Deluxe Fieldstone House, *03*		17
____	**34112** Lionelville Fieldstone House, *03*		17
____	**34113** Lionelville Large Suburban House, *03*		17
____	**34114** Late Illuminated Station and Terrace, red trim, *03*		475
____	**34117** Early Illuminated Station and Terrace, green trim, *03*		475
____	**34120** TMCC Direct Lockon, *04-16, 18*		54

		Exc	Mint
34121	Lionelville Bungalow, *04*	20	___
34122	Lionelville Bungalow with garage, *04*	20	___
34123	Lionelville Bungalow with addition, *04*	20	___
34124	Lionelville Anastasia's Bakery, *04*	20	___
34125	Lionelville Cotton's Candy, *04*	20	___
34126	Lionelville Market, *04*	20	___
34127	Lionelville O'Grady's Tavern, *04*	22	___
34128	Lionelville Pharmacy, *04*	15	___
34129	Lionelville Kiddie City Toy Store, *04*	20	___
34130	Lionelville Jim's 5&10, *04*	25	___
34131	Lionelville Al's Hardware, *04*	30	___
34144	Santa Fe Scrap Yard, *05-06*	80	___
34145	New Haven Scrap Yard, *06*	100	___
34149	Sly Fox and the Hunter, *05-07*	80	___
34150	Reading Room, *05-06*	70	___
34158	Ring Toss Midway Game, *05-06*	20	___
34159	Camel Race Midway Game, *05-06*	20	___
34162	Operating Oil Pump, *04-09*	53	___
34163	Speeder Shed, *04-06*	30	___
34164	Nutcracker Operating Gateman, *05-08*	80	___
34190	Carousel, *04-06*	165	___
34191	Hobo Depot, *04-05*	70	___
34192	Operating Lumberjacks, *04-06*	60	___
34193	UPS Animated Billboard, *04*	30	___
34194	UPS Package Station, *05*	120	___
34195	UPS People Pack, *06-09, 11*	27	___
34210	TMCC Direct Lockon, *09*	52	___
34359	2011 Lionel Dealer Appreciation BoxCar, *2011u*	40	___
34360	2012 Lionel Dealer Appreciation BoxCar, *2012u*	40	___
34500	Rio Grande FT Diesel "5484," traditional, *06*	245	___
34501	Southern FT Diesel "4102," traditional, *06*	400	___
34504	B&O F3 Diesel A Unit "2368," nonpowered, *06-07*	200	___
34505	B&O E7 Diesel AA Set, CC, *07*	700	___
34508	PRR E7 Diesel AA Set, CC, *07*	700	___
34509	PRR E7 Diesel B Unit, nonpowered (std O), *07*	170	___
34510	PRR E7 Diesel B Unit, powered, CC, *07*	300	___
34511	NYC F7 Diesel ABA Set, CC, *07-08*	900	___
34512	NYC F7 Diesel B Unit "2439," powered, CC, *07-08*	300	___
34513	WP F7 Diesel ABA Set, CC, *07-08*	900	___
34514	WP F7 Diesel B Unit "918C," powered, CC, *07-08*	300	___
34515	NYC F7 Diesel Breakdown B Unit "2440," RailSounds, *07*	270	___
34518	PRR E7 Diesel Breakdown B Unit, RailSounds, *07*	270	___
34519	NYC Sharknose RF-16 Diesel AA Set, CC, *07-08*	630	___
34520	NYC Sharknose Diesel B Unit "3818," nonpowered (std O), *07-08*	160	___
34521	Santa Fe F3 Diesel A Unit "17," traditional, *07*	265	___
34522	Santa Fe F3 Diesel B Unit "17," nonpowered (std O), *07*	150	___
34544	ATSF F3 Diesel B Unit, CC, *08*	270	___
34545	D&RGW F3 Diesel B Unit, CC, *08*	270	___
34546	Southern F3 Diesel B Unit, CC, *08*	270	___
34547	Texas Special F3 Diesel B Unit, CC, *08*	270	___
34559	Archive New Haven F3 Diesel AA Set, *10*	500	___

		Exc	Mint
____	**34564** SP Alco PA Diesel AA Set, CC, *10-11*		750
____	**34567** SP Alco PB B Unit, CC, *10-11*		400
____	**34568** ATSF Alco PA AA Diesel Set, CC, *11*		750
____	**34569** ATSF Alco PB Diesel, CC, *11*		400
____	**34570** B&O FA Diesel AA Set, CC, *10*		650
____	**34573** Postwar Scale ATSF F3 AA Diesel Set, CC, *11*		700
____	**34576** Postwar Scale NYC F3 AA Diesel Set, CC, *11*		700
____	**34579** Postwar Scale ATSF F3 B Unit, CC, *11*		380
____	**34580** Postwar Scale NYC F3 B Unit, CC, *11*		380
____	**34581** Postwar "2331" Virginian Train Master Diesel, CC, *10*		495
____	**34582** Postwar "2373" CP F3 Diesel AA Set, CC, *10*		700
____	**34585** Postwar "2375" CP F3 B Unit, CC, *10*		380
____	**34586** Postwar "2378" MILW F3 Diesel AB Set, CC, *10*		700
____	**34589** Postwar "2377" MILW F3 A, powered, CC, *10*		425
____	**34594** UP Alco PA AA Diesel Set, CC, *11*		750
____	**34597** UP Alco PB Diesel, CC, *11*		400
____	**34600** SP GP30 Diesel "5010," CC, *11*		500
____	**34601** SP GP30 Diesel "5012," CC, *11*		500
____	**34602** SP GP30 Diesel "5014," CC, *11*		380
____	**34603** SP GP30 Diesel "5017," nonpowered, *11*		240
____	**34604** Conrail GP30 Diesel "2178," CC, *11*		500
____	**34605** Conrail GP30 Diesel "2180," CC, *11*		500
____	**34606** Conrail GP30 Diesel "2182," *11*		380
____	**34607** Conrail GP30 Diesel "2185," nonpowered, *11*		240
____	**34608** Lionelville & Western GP30 Diesel "1100," CC, *11*		450
____	**34609** Lionelville & Western GP30 Diesel "1103," CC, *11*		450
____	**34610** Lionelville & Western GP30 Diesel "1107," *11*		330
____	**34611** Lionelville & Western GP30 Diesel "1112," nonpowered, *11*		190
____	**34612** NS SD70M-2 Diesel "2658," CC, *11*		550
____	**34613** NS SD70M-2 Diesel "2663," CC, *11*		550
____	**34614** CN SD70M-2 Diesel "8020," CC, *11*		550
____	**34615** CN SD70M-2 Diesel "8024," CC, *11*		550
____	**34616** FEC SD70M-2 Diesel "101," CC, *11*		550
____	**34617** FEC SD70M-2 Diesel "103," CC, *11*		550
____	**34618** George Bush SD70ACe Diesel "4141," CC, *11*		550
____	**34619** NH SD70ACe Diesel "8696," CC, *11*		550
____	**34620** NH SD70ACe Diesel "8699," CC, *11*		550
____	**34623** Texas Special SD70ACe Diesel "6340," CC, *11*		550
____	**34624** Texas Special SD70ACe Diesel "6344," CC, *11*		550
____	**34625** NP F3 AA Diesel Set, CC, *11*		700
____	**34628** NP F3 Diesel B Unit "6005C," CC, *11*		380
____	**34629** NP F3 Diesel B Unit "6006C," nonpowered, *11*		240
____	**34630** Frisco F3 AA Diesel Set, CC, *11*		700
____	**34633** Frisco F3 Diesel B Unit, CC, *11*		380
____	**34634** Frisco F3 Diesel B Unit, nonpowered, *11*		260
____	**34635** ATSF F3 AA Diesel Set, CC, *11*		700
____	**34638** ATSF F3 Diesel B Unit, CC, *11*		380
____	**34639** ATSF F3 Diesel B Unit, nonpowered, *11*		240
____	**34640** GTW F3 AA Diesel Set, CC, *11*		700
____	**34643** GTW F3 Diesel B Unit, CC, *11*		380
____	**34644** GTW F3 Diesel B Unit, nonpowered, *11*		260
____	**34645** CN F3 AA Diesel Set, CC, *11*		700
____	**34648** CN F3 Diesel B Unit, CC, *11*		380

	Exc	Mint
34649 CN F3 Diesel B Unit, nonpowered, *11*	260	___
34650 MILW DD35A Diesel "1535," CC, *11*	600	___
34651 MILW DD35A Diesel "1537," nonpowered, *11*	440	___
34662 RI GP9 Diesel "1331," CC, *12-13*	480	___
34663 RI GP9 Diesel "1327," CC, *12-13*	480	___
34664 GN GP9 Diesel "688," CC, *12-13*	480	___
34665 GN GP9 Diesel "695," CC, *12-13*	480	___
34666 L&N GP9 Diesel "504," CC, *12-13*	480	___
34667 L&N GP9 Diesel "525," CC, *12-13*	480	___
34668 CN GP90 Diesel "4463," CC, *12*	480	___
34669 CN GP90 Diesel "4455," CC, *12*	480	___
34670 C&O GP9 Diesel "6240," CC, *12-13*	480	___
34671 C&O GP9 Diesel "6243," CC, *12*	480	___
34672 PRR Baldwin Centipede Diesel AA, CC, *12-13*	2200	___
34673 UP Baldwin Centipede Diesel AA, CC, *12*	2200	___
34676 PRR Baldwin Centipede Diesel "5821," CC, *12-14*	1100	___
34677 Seaboard Baldwin Centipede Diesel "4503," CC, *12-14*	1100	___
34680 NdeM Baldwin Centipede Diesel "6402," CC, *12-14*	1100	___
34681 UP GP9 Diesel "256," CC, *12*	480	___
34682 UP GP9 Diesel "261," CC, *12*	480	___
34683 PRR Baldwin Centipede Diesel AA, CC, *12-13*	2200	___
34686 Baldwin Demonstrator Centipede AA, CC, *12*	2200	___
34689 WM F7 AA Diesel Set, CC, *12-13*	730	___
34692 WM F7 B Unit "410," CC, *12-13*	400	___
34693 WM F7 B Unit, *12-13*	250	___
34694 L&N F7 AA Diesel Set, CC, *12*	730	___
34697 L&N F7 B Unit "900," CC, *12-13*	400	___
34698 L&N F7 B Unit, *12-13*	250	___
34701 PRR Baldwin RF-16 Diesel AA Set, CC, *12-14*	730	___
34704 PRR Baldwin RF-16 Diesel B Unit, CC, *12-14*	400	___
34705 PRR Baldwin RF-16 Diesel B Unit, nonpowered, *12-14*	250	___
34731 NH Alco RS-11 Diesel "1413," nonpowered, *12*	240	___
34732 LV Alco RS-11 Diesel "7640," CC, *12*	480	___
34733 LV Alco RS-11 Diesel "7642," CC, *12*	480	___
34734 LV Alco RS-11 Diesel "7643," nonpowered, *12*	240	___
34735 ATSF GP9 Diesel "726," CC, *12*	480	___
34736 ATSF GP9 Diesel "741," CC, *12*	480	___
34737 NP GP9 Diesel "202," CC, *12*	480	___
34738 NP GP9 Diesel "317," CC, *12-13*	480	___
34739 RI GP9 Diesel "1325," nonpowered, *12*	240	___
34740 GN GP9 Diesel "668," nonpowered, *12*	240	___
34741 L&N GP9 Diesel "531," nonpowered, *12*	240	___
34742 CN GP90 Diesel "4527," nonpowered, *12*	240	___
34743 C&O GP9 Diesel "6249," nonpowered, *12*	240	___
34744 UP GP9 Diesel "268," nonpowered, *12*	240	___
34745 Monon Alco C-420 Diesel "509," CC, *12-13*	530	___
34746 Monon Alco C-420 Diesel "512," CC, *12-13*	530	___
34747 Monon Alco C-420 Diesel "514," nonpowered, *12-13*	260	___
34748 LV Alco C-420 Diesel "404," CC, *12*	530	___
34749 LV Alco C-420 Diesel "412," CC, *12*	530	___
34750 LV Alco C-420 Diesel "414," nonpowered, *12*	260	___
34754 Alaska Alco C-420 Diesel "1210," CC, *12*	530	___

		Exc/Mint
34755	Alaska Alco C-420 Diesel "1214," CC, *12*	530
34756	Alaska Alco C-420 Diesel "1217," nonpowered, *12*	260
34757	Seaboard Alco C-420 Diesel "127," CC, *12-13*	530
34758	Seaboard Alco C-420 Diesel "129," CC, *12-13*	530
34759	Seaboard Alco C-420 Diesel "134," nonpowered, *12-13*	260
34760	NKP Alco C-420 Diesel "578," CC, *12-13*	530
34761	NKP Alco C-420 Diesel "575," CC, *12-13*	530
34762	NKP Alco C-420 Diesel "572," nonpowered, *12-13*	260
34763	CNJ Scale NW2 Diesel Switcher "1060," CC, *12*	470
34764	CNJ Scale NW2 Diesel Switcher "1061," CC, *12*	470
34765	KCS Scale NW2 Diesel Switcher "1221," CC, *12*	470
34766	KCS Scale NW2 Diesel Switcher "1224," CC, *12*	470
34767	L&N Scale NW2 Diesel Switcher "2203," CC, *12*	470
34768	L&N Scale NW2 Diesel Switcher "2206," CC, *12*	470
34769	MKT Scale NW2 Diesel Switcher "8," CC, *12*	470
34770	MKT Scale NW2 Diesel Switcher "12," CC, *12*	470
34771	Reading Scale NW2 Diesel Switcher "102," CC, *12*	470
34772	Reading Scale NW2 Diesel Switcher "104," CC, *12*	470
34773	PRR Scale NW2 Diesel Switcher "9163," CC, *12*	470
34774	PRR Scale NW2 Diesel Switcher "9171," CC, *12*	470
34775	N&W SD40-2 Diesel "6106," nonpowered, *12-13*	240
34776	N&W SD40-2 Diesel "6121," CC, *12-13*	530
34777	N&W SD40-2 Diesel "6109," CC, *12-14*	530
34778	CSX SD40-2 Diesel "8023," nonpowered, *12-13*	240
34779	CSX SD40-2 Diesel "8028," CC, *12-13*	530
34780	CSX SD40-2 Diesel "8033," CC, *12-13*	530
34781	BN SD40-2 Diesel "7140," nonpowered, *12-13*	240
34782	BN SD40-2 Diesel "7153," CC, *12-13*	530
34783	BN SD40-2 Diesel "7162," CC, *12-13*	530
34784	Frisco SD40-2 Diesel "957," CC, *12-13*	530
34785	Frisco SD40-2 Diesel "950," nonpowered, *12-13*	240
34786	Frisco SD40-2 Diesel "952," CC, *12-13*	530
34787	C&NW SD40-2 Diesel "6816," nonpowered, *12-13*	240
34788	C&NW SD40-2 Diesel "6820," CC, *12-13*	530
34789	C&NW SD40-2 Diesel "6832," CC, *12-13*	530
34790	MKT SD40-2 Diesel "602," nonpowered, *12-13*	240
34791	MKT SD40-2 Diesel "609," CC, *12-13*	530
34792	MKT SD40-2 Diesel "620," CC, *12-13*	530
35100	NYC Vista Dome Car "7012," *07-09*	45
35101	NYC Baggage Car "5028," *07*	40
35102	Santa Fe El Capitan Streamliner Diner, *07*	65
35124	Alton Limited Madison Passenger Car 4-pack, *08-10*	240
35128	ATSF El Capitan Baggage Car "2103," *08*	70
35129	ATSF El Capitan Vista Dome Car "3153," *08*	70
35130	Polar Express Disappearing Hobo Car, *08-14, 16-17*	75
35133	MTA Metro-North M-7 Commuter Add-on 2-pack, *07-08*	85
35134	North Pole Central Vista Dome Car, *08*	45
35135	North Pole Central Diner, *08-10*	45
35167	PRR Diner "2044," *10*	52
35168	PRR Coach "4046," *09*	52
35173	North Pole Central Blitzen Coach, *09*	45
35174	MTA LIRR M-7 Add-on 2-pack, *09*	98

Exc Mint

		Exc	Mint
35184	Western & Atlantic Baggage Car, *09*		60 ____
35185	Great Western Passenger Car 2-pack, *09*		100 ____
35193	PRR Streamliner 4-pack, *10-11*		250 ____
35200	Strasburg Observation Car, *10*		60 ____
35205	D&RGW Pikes Peak Add-on Coach, *10-11*		70 ____
35211	Strasburg Passenger Car Add-on 2-pack, *10*		100 ____
35214	Rio Grande Winter Park Diner, *11*		70 ____
35219	Hallow's Eve Express Passenger Car 2-pack, *11*		120 ____
35229	Hogwarts Express Dementors Coach, *11-15*		60 ____
35239	NJ Transit 2-pack Passenger Car Add-on, *11-14*		100 ____
35247	Grand Central Express Passenger Car 2-pack, *12-13*		140 ____
35250	North Pole Coach 2-pack, *12-13*		120 ____
35256	Hallow's Eve Express Passenger Car 2-pack #2, *12*		120 ____
35257	ATSF Vista Dome, *12*		70 ____
35258	ATSF Baggage Car, *12-13*		70 ____
35259	LIRR Passenger Car 2-pack, *12-15*		110 ____
35281	ATSF Super Chief Diner "1495," *13*		70 ____
35282	LIRR Jamaica Coach, *13-15*		60 ____
35283	CP Baggage Car and Diner 2-pack, *13*		130 ____
35286	Peanuts Coach 3-pack, *13*		165 ____
35290	Polar Express Passenger Car Add-on 2-pack, *13-14, 16*		150 ____
35293	Angela Trotta Thomas "Toyland Express" BoxCar, *13*		45 ____
35294	Polar Express Snow Tower, *13-14*		28 ____
35295	Christmas Billboard Set, *13-14, 16*		13 ____
35403	NYC 20th Century Limited 18" Aluminum Passenger Car 4-pack (std O), *08*		625 ____
35408	NYC 20th Century Limited 18" Aluminum Passenger Car 2-pack (std O), *08*		325 ____
35411	NYC 20th Century Limited 18" Aluminum Diner, StationSounds (std O), *08*		325 ____
35412	Lenny Dean Passenger Coach, *08*		100 ____
35413	LL Streamliner Car 2-pack, *08*		270 ____
35415	UP 18" Streamliner Car 4-pack (std O), *08*		625 ____
35423	UP 18" Streamliner Car 2-pack (std O), *08*		325 ____
35430	Amtrak Coach		45 ____
35431	Amtrak Coach		45 ____
35432	Amtrak Coach		45 ____
35433	Amfleet Phase IVB Coach 2-pack (std O), *10*		140 ____
35445	SP Shasta Daylight 18" Passenger Car 4-pack (std O), *11*		640 ____
35446	SP Shasta Daylight 18" Passenger Car 2-pack (std O), *11*		320 ____
35454	Amfleet Cab Control End Car (std O), *10*		250 ____
35473	Amfleet Capstone Coach 3-pack (std O), *10*		180 ____
35481	NYC Add-on Passenger Car "M-498," *11*		120 ____
35490	Alaska Budd RDC Combination Car "702," nonpowered, *11*		130 ____
35497	RI Budd RDC Combination Car "751," nonpowered, *11*		130 ____
35498	RI Budd RDC Coach "750," nonpowered, *11*		130 ____
35499	Alaska Budd RDC Coach "712," nonpowered, *11*		130 ____
36000	Route 66 Flatcar with 2 red sedans, *98*		44 ____
36001	Route 66 Flatcar with 2 wagons, *98*		42 ____
36002	Pratt's Hollow Passenger Car 4-pack, *98*		445 ____

		Exc	Mint
_____ **36006** Uranium FlatCar "6508," _99_			60
_____ **36016** Flatcar with propellers, _98_			45
_____ **36020** FlatCar "TT-6424" with auto frames, _99_			32
_____ **36021** Alaska FlatCar "6424" with airplane, _99_			44
_____ **36024** J.B. Hunt FlatCar "64245" with trailer, _99_			44
_____ **36025** J.B. Hunt FlatCar "64246" with trailer, _99_			50
_____ **36026** Flatcar with J.B. Hunt trailers 2-pack, _99_			85
_____ **36027** Tredegar Iron Works Flatcar with cannon, _99_			45
_____ **36028** Heavy Artillery Flatcar with cannon, _99_			45
_____ **36029** SP Auto Carrier,"516712," _99_			44
_____ **36030** Troublesome Truck #1, _99_			35
_____ **36031** Troublesome Truck #2, _99_			35
_____ **36032** Christmas Gondola "6462" with presents, _99_			35
_____ **36036** C&O Gondola, _99_			20
_____ **36038** Construction Zone Gondola, _99 u_			NRS
_____ **36040** Bethlehem Flatcar with block (SSS), _99_			75
_____ **36041** Bethlehem Ore Car (SSS), _99_			40
_____ **36043** Custom Consist Flatcar with pickup truck, _99_			40
_____ **36044** Custom Consist Flatcar with dragster, _99_			40
_____ **36045** Flatcar with dragster, _04_			30
_____ **36046** Flatcar with custom truck, _04_			30
_____ **36047** Construction Zone Gondola, _99 u_			NRS
_____ **36048** Construction Zone Gondola, _99 u_			NRS
_____ **36054** Archaeological Expedition Gondola with eggs, _00 u_			55
_____ **36055** Flatcar with dragster, _01 u_			30
_____ **36056** Flatcar with roadster, _01 u_			30
_____ **36059** "Season's Greetings" Gondola, _99 u_			50
_____ **36062** NYC 6462 Gondola, _99-00_			22
_____ **36063** Conrail Gondola "604768," _99-00_			20
_____ **36064** Billboard FlatCar "6424," _00_			41
_____ **36065** Wabash FlatCar "25536" with trailer, _00_			35
_____ **36066** Christmas Gondola with presents, _00_			32
_____ **36067** King Auto Sales FlatCar "6424" with pink Cadillac, _00_			40
_____ **36068** Pine Peak Tree Transport Gondola, _00_			NRS
_____ **36079** Service Station Ltd. Flatcar with trailer, _00_			34
_____ **36082** Whirlpool Flatcar with trailer, _00 u_			NRS
_____ **36083** Santa Fe Gondola "168998," _01_			17
_____ **36084** Grand Trunk Western Coil Car, _00_			32
_____ **36085** FEC Coil Car, _00_			29
_____ **36086** SP Flatcar with trailer, _01_		34	35
_____ **36087** FlatCar "6424" with wooden whistle, _01_			25
_____ **36088** Allis Chalmers Condenser Car "6519," _00_			43
_____ **36089** Frisco Flatcar with airplane, _00_			35
_____ **36090** TT FlatCar "6424" with Pepsi truck, _01_			44
_____ **36091** Maersk FlatCar "250129" with die-cast tractors, _00_			55
_____ **36092** Maersk FlatCar "250130" with die-cast frames, _00_			55
_____ **36093** Soo TT Auto Carrier,"906760," _00_			49
_____ **36094** PC F9 Well Car "768122," _01_			41
_____ **36095** Christmas Chase Gondola, _01_			37
_____ **36098** PRR Gondola "385186," _01_			20
_____ **36099** NYC Flatcar with stakes and bulkheads, _01_			25
_____ **36104** Area 51 3-D Tank Car, _07_			60
_____ **36108** Candy Cane 1-D Tank Car, _07_			60

Exc Mint

		Exc	Mint
36112	NP 3-D Tank Car, *08*	35	____
36113	IC 1-D Tank Car, *08*	35	____
36114	ART Wood-sided Reefer, *08*	35	____
36117	Lionel Lines 2-D Tank Car, *08*	50	____
36118	NYC Pastel Stock Car "63561," *08-09*	55	____
36128	Texas & Pacific 3-D Tank Car, *09*	40	____
36129	British Columbia 1-D Tank Car, *09*	40	____
36131	Lackawanna Wood-sided Reefer "7000," *09-10*	40	____
36145	Philadelphia Quartz 3-D Tank Car "606," *10*	40	____
36146	Cities Service 1-D Tank Car "11800," *10*	40	____
36149	Strasburg Wood-sided Reefer "105," *10*	55	____
36151	Grave's Blood Bank Tank Car, *10*	50	____
36156	Pennsylvania Power & Light 1-D Tank Car, *10*	40	____
36162	Diamond Chemicals 3-D Tank Car, *11*	40	____
36163	Celanese 2-D Tank Car, *11-12*	40	____
36166	Polar Express Reefer, *11-12*	55	____
36169	Coca-Cola 3-D Tank Car, *11*	55	____
36170	Partridge in a Pear Tree Reefer, *11-13*	55	____
36172	Bubble Yum 1-D Tank Car, *11*	55	____
36173	Santa's Flyer Hot Cocoa 3-D Tank Car, *11*	40	____
36176	C&O 1-D Tank Car, *13*	43	____
36177	WP 3-D Tank Car, *12*	40	____
36178	Frisco 2-D Tank Car, *12-13*	40	____
36182	Eggnog Unibody 1-D Tank Car, *12*	70	____
36191	GN Waffle-sided BoxCar, *13*	43	____
36195	PRR Flatcar with patrol helicopter, *13*	60	____
36200	Quaker Life Cereal BoxCar, *00*	500	____
36203	Whirlpool BoxCar, *00 u*	150	____
36205	eBay BoxCar, *00*	275	____
36206	REA BoxCar, *01*	25	____
36207	Vapor Records Christmas BoxCar, *01*	80	____
36208	Father's Day BoxCar, *00*	35	____
36210	Burlington Hi-Cube Boxcar "19825," *01*	40	____
36211	NP Hi-Cube Boxcar "659999," *01*	33	____
36212	Lionel Employee Christmas BoxCar, *00 u*	410	____
36213	Vapor Records Christmas BoxCar, *00*	50	____
36215	Train Station 25th Anniversary BoxCar, *00 u*	48	____
36218	Snap-On BoxCar, *00 u*	150	____
36219	UP Boxcar "183518," *02*	78	____
36220	Pioneer Seed BoxCar, *00 u*	NRS	____
36221	PRR Boxcar "569356," *01*	20	____
36222	NYC Boxcar "162440," *01*	20	____
36223	Chessie System BoxCar, *01*	20	____
36224	Santa Fe Boxcar "16263," *01*	20	____
36225	C&O Boxcar "250549," *01*	20	____
36226	E-Hobbies BoxCar, *01 u*	200	____
36227	Monopoly Community Chest BoxCar, *00 u*	50	____
36228	Lionel Visitor Center BoxCar, *01 u*	34	____
36229	Island Trains 20th Anniversary BoxCar, *01 u*	29	____
36232	Farmall BoxCar, *01 u*	NRS	____
36236	TM Books "I Love Lionel" BoxCar "7474-1," *01 u*	43	____
36238	Snap-On Tool Team ASE Racing BoxCar, *01 u*	NRS	____
36239	L.L. Bean BoxCar, *01 u*	150	____

		Mint
_____ **36240**	Do It Best BoxCar, *01 u*	100
_____ **36242**	Erie-Lackawanna Boxcar "73113," *02*	24
_____ **36243**	Christmas Boxcar "2002," *02*	31
_____ **36244**	Teddy Bear Centennial BoxCar, *02*	36
_____ **36245**	Lionel 20th Century Boxcar "1900-1925," *00 u*	30
_____ **36246**	Lionel 20th Century Boxcar "1926-1950," *00 u*	30
_____ **36247**	Lionel 20th Century Boxcar "1951-1975," *00 u*	30
_____ **36248**	Lionel 20th Century Boxcar "1976-2000," *00 u*	30
_____ **36250**	NYC Early Bird BoxCar, *04*	20
_____ **36253**	Christmas Boxcar (O), *03*	32
_____ **36254**	Goofy Hi-Cube BoxCar, *03*	37
_____ **36255**	Donald Duck Hi-Cube BoxCar, *03*	40
_____ **36256**	GN Boxcar "6341," *03*	23
_____ **36261**	PRR BoxCar, *03-05*	15
_____ **36262**	Southern Central of Georgia BoxCar, *03 04*	20
_____ **36264**	Santa Fe Boxcar "600196, *02*	18
_____ **36265**	Angela Trotta Thomas "Window Wishing" BoxCar, *02*	38
_____ **36267**	Mickey Mouse Hi-Cube BoxCar, *03*	50
_____ **36270**	Angela Trotta Thomas "Home for the Holidays" BoxCar, *02-03*	30
_____ **36272**	New Haven Boxcar "6501," *04*	20
_____ **36273**	Railbox Hi-Cube Boxcar "15000," *04*	21
_____ **36275**	Christmas BoxCar, *04*	35
_____ **36276**	Angela Trotta Thomas,"Tis the Season" BoxCar, *04*	34
_____ **36277**	Pluto Hi-Cube BoxCar, *04-05*	50
_____ **36278**	Winnie the Pooh Hi-Cube BoxCar, *04-05*	50
_____ **36281**	B&O BoxCar, *04*	35
_____ **36291**	Simpsons BoxCar, *04-05*	44
_____ **36294**	UP Hi-Cube BoxCar, traditional, *05*	27
_____ **36295**	CN BoxCar, traditional, *05*	27
_____ **36296**	2005 Holiday BoxCar, *05*	48
_____ **36297**	Angela Trotta Thomas "Christmas Eve" BoxCar, *05*	48
_____ **36299**	Hammacher Schlemmer Music BoxCar, *04*	65
_____ **36305**	eBay BoxCar, *00 u*	120
_____ **36500**	Western Pacific Caboose "36500," *04*	23
_____ **36501**	D&RGW Caboose "36501," *04*	22
_____ **36502**	Reading Caboose "36502," *04*	25
_____ **36515**	North Pole Central Lines Caboose "36515," *04*	36
_____ **36519**	Lionel Lines Caboose, *04*	22
_____ **36520**	Santa Fe Caboose "36520," *04*	22
_____ **36525**	CSX Work Caboose, lighted, *05*	35
_____ **36526**	Pennsylvania Work Caboose, traditional, *05*	27
_____ **36527**	Santa Fe Work Caboose, traditional, *05*	28
_____ **36528**	Chesapeake & Ohio Work Caboose, traditional, *05*	40
_____ **36529**	North Pole Central Work Caboose with presents, traditional, *05*	38
_____ **36530**	Pennsylvania Caboose, traditional, *05*	33
_____ **36531**	Erie Caboose "C150," traditional, *05*	33
_____ **36532**	SP Caboose "1097," traditional, *05*	48
_____ **36533**	Reading Caboose "92803," traditional, *05*	33
_____ **36534**	NYC Center Cupola Caboose, traditional, *05*	40
_____ **36535**	LL Center Cupola Caboose, traditional, *05*	28
_____ **36536**	Southern Center Cupola Caboose, traditional, *05*	40
_____ **36544**	Alaska Caboose, *05*	35

		Exc	Mint
36547	Bethlehem Steel Transfer Caboose, traditional, *05*	40	____
36548	Transylvania RR Work Caboose, traditional, *05*	45	____
36550	Halloween Transfer Caboose, traditional, *06-07*	45	____
36551	Christmas Caboose, *06*	45	____
36552	U.S. Steel Work Caboose, traditional, *06-07*	45	____
36553	NYC Caboose, *08*	20	____
36554	SP Work Caboose, traditional, *06*	45	____
36555	Pennsylvania Transfer Caboose, *06*	45	____
36556	Lionel Lines Work Caboose, *06-07*	30	____
36557	Rio Grande Work Caboose, traditional, *06*	29	____
36558	Virginian Center Cupola Caboose "316," traditional, *06*	45	____
36559	WM Center Cupola Caboose "1863," traditional, *06*	45	____
36560	C&O Center Cupola Caboose "90876," traditional, *06*	45	____
36562	Army Transportation Work Caboose, traditional, *06*	45	____
36563	Reading Work Caboose, traditional, *06*	45	____
36565	UP SP-type Caboose, traditional, *06*	48	____
36566	NYC SP-type Caboose, traditional, *06*	48	____
36567	GN SP-type Caboose, traditional, *06*	48	____
36571	PRR Caboose, *08*	20	____
36580	B&O Center Cupola Caboose "C2047," traditional, *05*	40	____
36582	C&O Caboose, *05*	22	____
36583	Holiday Caboose, *07*	50	____
36587	SP Caboose "1121," *07-09*	40	____
36589	PRR Work Caboose, *07*	40	____
36590	UP Work Caboose, *07*	45	____
36591	Southern Caboose "X99," *08*	45	____
36592	Santa Fe Caboose "999471," *06*	48	____
36593	NYC Caboose, *06*	48	____
36601	UP Caboose, *06*	48	____
36602	UPS Centennial Caboose, *06*	45	____
36604	Pennsylvania Caboose, *06*	25	____
36607	K-Line Caboose, *06*	40	____
36611	Conrail Caboose "19674," *07*	40	____
36612	Alaska Caboose "1080," *07*	40	____
36613	NYC Caboose, *07*	30	____
36622	C&O Caboose "C-1838," *08-09*	40	____
36623	ATSF Caboose, *07-09*	40	____
36624	Lionel Lines Caboose, *08-09*	40	____
36625	B&M Caboose, *08*	50	____
36626	Erie Caboose "C101," *08-09*	45	____
36634	Holiday Porthole Caboose, green, *08*	50	____
36646	Monopoly Caboose, *10*	48	____
36647	Strasburg Caboose, *10*	48	____
36649	Pennsylvania Power & Light Work Caboose, *10*	45	____
36657	Western & Atlantic Caboose, *10-11*	48	____
36659	PRR Illuminated Porthole Caboose, *11*	35	____
36668	CSX Illuminated Square Window Caboose, *10*	35	____
36672	NS Caboose, *11*	25	____
36674	Polar Caboose, *11-12*	53	____
36701	Baldwin Locomotive Works Operating Welding Car "36701," *02*	60	____
36702	Bosco Operating Milk Car with platform, *02*	115	____
36703	Circus Horse Car with corral, *06*	150	____

		Exc	Mint
___	**36704** Animated Reindeer Stock Car and Corral, *02*		145
___	**36718** AEC Security Caboose, *02*		45
___	**36719** Lionel Lion Bobbing Head Car, *02*		20
___	**36720** Aladdin Aquarium Car, *03*		40
___	**36721** 101 Dalmatians Animated Gondola, *03*		45
___	**36722** Peter Pan Bobbing Head BoxCar, *03*		45
___	**36726** Santa Fe Searchlight Car "36726," *03*		50
___	**36727** Weyerhaeuser Moe & Joe FlatCar, *03*		65
___	**36728** SP Walking Brakeman Boxcar 163143," *03*		42
___	**36729** Lionel Lines Animated Caboose, *04-05*	6	68
___	**36730** U.S. Army Missile Launch Sound Car "44," *03*		175
___	**36731** Motorized Aquarium Car "3435," *03*		83
___	**36732** C&NW Jumping Hobo Car, *03*		41
___	**36733** Christmas Music BoxCar, *03*		45
___	**36734** Santa Fe Operating Searchlight Car "20611," *02*		25
___	**36735** WP Ice Car "7045," *02*		55
___	**36736** D&RGW Stock Car "39268," RailSounds, *04*		45
___	**36738** T&P Poultry Dispatch Car "36738," *02*		50
___	**36739** Postwar "3461" Lionel Lines Log Dump Car, *03*		50
___	**36740** Postwar "3469" Lionel Lines Coal Dump Car, *03*		49
___	**36743** Santa Claus Bobbing Head BoxCar, *03*		40
___	**36744** Little Mermaid Aquarium Car, *03*		55
___	**36745** Toy Story Animated Gondola, *03*		70
___	**36753** LFD Firecar with ladder, *02*		60
___	**36757** Southern Searchlight Car, *03-04*		NRS
___	**36758** Patriotic Lighted BoxCar, *02*		60
___	**36760** B&O Sentinel Operating Brakeman Boxcar "3424," Archive Collection, *02*		65
___	**36761** Wellspring Capital Management Lighted BoxCar, *02 u*		220
___	**36764** West Side Lumber Log Dump Car "36764," *03*		55
___	**36765** Alaska Coal Dump Car "401," *03*		50
___	**36766** Erie Chase Gondola, *03*		50
___	**36767** Santa's Radar Tracking Car, *03*		40
___	**36769** Fourth of July Lighted BoxCar, *03*		70
___	**36770** American Refrigerator Transit Ice Car "23701," *04*		42
___	**36771** CN Barrel Car "74208," *04*		48
___	**36772** Spokane, Portland & Seattle Log Dump Car "36772," *04*		46
___	**36773** Jersey Central Coal Dump Car "92926," *04*		45
___	**36774** PRR Moe & Joe Lumber FlatCar, *04*		50
___	**36775** Santa Fe Animated Caboose "999010," *05*		75
___	**36776** Santa Fe Walking Brakeman Car "19938," *04*		43
___	**36778** C&O Searchlight Car "216614," *04*		30
___	**36780** Sea-Monkeys Motorized Aquarium Car, *04*		45
___	**36781** Finding Nemo Aquarium Car, *04*		50
___	**36782** Goofy and Pete Jumping BoxCar, *05*		70
___	**36783** Disney Operating BoxCar, *04-05*		65
___	**36784** Monsters Inc. Bobbing Head BoxCar, *04*		40
___	**36786** Postwar "3494-150" MP Operating BoxCar, *03*		40
___	**36787** MOW Remote Control Searchlight Car, *04*		45
___	**36788** Lionel Lines Tender, TrainSounds, *04*		75
___	**36789** Railbox BoxCar, TrainSounds, *04-05*		105
___	**36790** Christmas Music BoxCar, *04*		70

		Exc	Mint
36793	Pennsylvania Derrick Car, *03*	22	___
36794	NYC Log Dump Car, *03*	25	___
36795	Southern Coal Dump Car, *03*	25	___
36796	GN Searchlight Car, *03*	24	___
36797	"Operation Iraqi Freedom" Minuteman Car, *03*	45	___
36803	Santa Animated Caboose, *06*	75	___
36804	Candy Cane Dump Car, *06*	80	___
36805	Reindeer Jumping BoxCar, *06*	70	___
36809	NYC Derrick Car, *07-08*	35	___
36810	PRR Searchlight Car, *07*	35	___
36811	UP Dump Coal Dump Car, *07*	35	___
36812	British Columbia Log Dump Car, *07-08*	35	___
36813	State of Maine Brakeman Car, *08*	80	___
36814	D&RGW Animated Caboose "01415," *07-09*	80	___
36815	Santa Fe Moe & Joe FlatCar, *07-08*	80	___
36816	Virginian Coal Dump Car, *08*	80	___
36818	U.S. Steel Searchlight Car, *07-08*	75	___
36821	"Naughty or Nice" Dump Car, *07*	80	___
36823	Halloween SpookySmoke BoxCar, *07*	115	___
36824	AlienSmoke BoxCar, *07*	110	___
36829	Alien Radioactive Car, *07*	70	___
36830	Trick or Treat Aquarium Car, *07*	75	___
36831	MOW Welding Car, *07-08*	75	___
36833	Christmas Music BoxCar, *07*	65	___
36834	Santa Fe Transparent Instruction Car, *07-08*	65	___
36838	Lionel Power Co. Voltmeter Car, K-Line, *06*	75	___
36839	Operating Milk Car with platform, K-Line, *06*	140	___
36841	Visitor Center 15th Anniversary Lighted BoxCar, *06*	70	___
36847	Polar Express Tender, TrainSounds, *08-14*	130	___
36848	Candy Cane Dump Car, *07*	80	___
36849	Tell-Tale Reindeer Car, *07*	53	___
36850	Santa and Snowman BoxCar, *07*	75	___
36851	Generator Car with Christmas tree, *07*	75	___
36853	U.S. Army Exploding BoxCar, *08*	60	___
36855	GW Horse Car and Corral, *08*	160	___
36856	W&ARR Sheriff and Outlaw Car, *08*	75	___
36857	Bobbing Ghost BoxCar, *08*	65	___
36859	Lionel Lines Aquarium Car, *08*	80	___
36861	PRR Poultry Dispatch Car, *08-09*	80	___
36863	Alien Security Car, *08*	80	___
36864	Bethlehem Steel Searchlight Car, *08*	40	___
36866	WP Coal Dump Car "52369," *08*	40	___
36868	NH Barrel Ramp Car, *08*	40	___
36869	Bobbing Santa BoxCar, *08*	65	___
36870	Postwar "6812" Track Maintenance Car, *08*	65	___
36874	PRR Searchlight Car, *09*	35	___
36875	Polar Express Coach, sound, *08-14, 16*	132	___
36878	NYC Track Cleaning Car, *08*	150	___
36879	REA Ice Car "1221," *08*	65	___
36880	Koi Fish Aquarium Car, *10*	75	___
36881	Christmas Music BoxCar, *08*	70	___
36887	Great Western Animated Gondola, *08-09*	65	___
36888	Casper Aquarium Car, *09-10*	90	___

		Exc	Mint
36889 PRR Barrel Ramp Car, *09-10*			46
36893 UP Transparent Instruction Car "195220," *09-10*			75
36896 Christmas Music BoxCar, *09*			80
36897 Pennsylvania Power & Light Coal Dump Car, *09-10*			46
36898 Wisconsin Central Log Dump Car, *09*			46
36900 Depressed Center Flatcar with backshop load, *99*			115
36913 Allied Chemical 1-D Tank Car 2-pack, *00*			150
36914 Allied Chemical 1-D Tank Car "68075," die-cast, white, *00*			90
36915 Allied Chemical 1-D Tank Car "68076," die-cast, white, *00*			90
36916 Allied Chemical 1-D Tank Car 2-pack, *00*			175
36917 Allied Chemical 1-D Tank Car "65124," die-cast, black, *00*			95
36918 Allied Chemical 1-D Tank Car "65125," die-cast, black, *00*			90
36927 B&O DC Hopper 6-pack, "435040-45," *01*			520
36935 Maersk Maxi-Stack Car 2-pack, "250131-32," *00*			135
36937 SP Maxi-Stack Car "513957," *02*			65
36998 Gingerbread Man Gateman, *12-13*			80
37001 No. 3444 Erie Animated Gondola, *09*			70
37002 Operating Plutonium Car 2-pack, *10-11*			140
37003 PRR Jet Snow Blower "491252," *09-10*			138
37004 Area 51 Searchlight Car, *09*			46
37006 Lionel Flatcar with operating LCD billboard, *09*			180
37009 Smoking Mount St. Helens BoxCar, *10-11*			125
37010 Pennsylvania Power & Light Searchlight Car, *10*			46
37011 B&M Operating Milk Car with platform, *10*			155
37012 GN Jumping Hobo BoxCar, *10*			75
37015 Jack-o-Lantern FlatCar, *11-13*			75
37016 Radioactive Plutonium FlatCar, *11*			70
37017 Plutonium Boom Car, *11*			70
37022 ATSF Blinking Billboard, *12*			25
37032 Postwar "3562" Operating Barrel Car, *11*			75
37033 Casper Animated Gondola, *11*			70
37035 Santa's Operating Snow Globe Car, *11*			75
37036 Halloween Operating Globe Car, *11*			78
37038 Halloween Searchlight Car, *12-13*			45
37039 Minuteman Searchlight Car, *11*			45
37040 UP Derrick Car, *11-12*			46
37041 Pennsylvania Power & Light Coal Dump Car, *11*			80
37042 IC Coal Dump Car, *11*			46
37043 Seaboard Log Dump Car, *11*			46
37044 CP Rail Log Dump Car, *11, 13*			80
37045 Beatles Yellow Submarine Aquarium Car, *11*			85
37047 Santa's Flyer Animated Gondola, *11*			55
37053 EL Derrick Car, *12*			45
37054 CSX Coal Dump Car, *12*			46
37055 SP Log Dump Car, *12*			46
37056 Zombie Aquarium Car, *12*			80
37057 Bethlehem Steel Culvert Car, *12*			65
37058 Ghost Globe Halloween Car, *12-15*			80
37059 Christmas Snow Globe Car, *12*			85
37060 LIRR Derrick Car, *13-14*			50

Exc Mint

		Exc	Mint
37061	UP Railroad Speeder, CC, *12-14*		150____
37062	NS Railroad Speeder, CC, *12-14*		150____
37063	PRR Railroad Speeder, CC, *12-14, 16*		150____
37064	CSX Railroad Speeder, CC, *12-14*		150____
37065	BNSF Railroad Speeder, CC, *12-14*		150____
37066	MOW Railroad Speeder, CC, *12-14*		150____
37067	NYC Railroad Speeder, CC, *12-14*		150____
37068	CN Railroad Speeder, CC, *12-14*		150____
37069	Strasburg RR Crane Car, *12*		65____
37070	Gingerbread Man and Santa Animated Gondola, *12*		55____
37071	MOW Searchlight Car, *12*		46____
37073	U.S. Marine Corps Cannon Car, *12*		75____
37075	Boy Scouts of America Crane Car, *13*		75____
37076	Bethlehem Steel Coal Dump Car, *13*		50____
37078	RI Searchlight Car, *13*		50____
37079	Santa Fe Derrick Car, *13*		50____
37081	Peanuts Pumpkin Jack-O-Lantern Car, *13*		85____
37082	Peanuts Animated Trick or Treat Chase Gondola, *14-16*		75 ____
37083	Strasburg Coal Dump Car, *13*		50____
37084	PRR Cop and Hobo Animated Gondola, *13*		65____
37085	BN Log Dump Car, *13*		50____
37086	Lionelville Aquarium Co. Aquarium Car, *13*		80____
37087	NH Walking Brakeman Car, *13-14*		75____
37089	Santa's List Snow Globe Car, *13*		90____
37090	Polar Express Searchlight Car, *13*		60____
37094	Wizard of Oz Aquarium Car, *13-15*		85____
37095	North Pole Sleigh Repair Welding Car, *13*		85____
37097	Where the Wild Things Are Aquarium Car, *13-15*		85____
37099	North Pole Central EV Caboose "2510" (std O), *13*		95____
37100	Barrel Loader Building, *12-14*		43____
37101	Smiley Water Tower, *12-14*		23____
37102	Watchman Shanty, *12-14*		30____
37103	O31 Curved Track (FasTrack), *13-14, 16, 18*		5____
37110	FasTrack Terminal, LionChief, *14-16, 18*		9____
37112	Helicopter 2-pack, *13-18*		35____
37115	Pedestrian Walkover, green, *16-18*		55____
37120	Railroad Crossing Signs, *13-18*		10____
37121	Christmas Station Platform, *13*		25____
37122	Santa Fe Blinking Billboard, *13*		25____
37123	Weyerhaeuser Timber Operating Sawmill, *12-13*		140____
37124	West Side Lumber Operating Sawmill, *12-13*		140____
37125	Legacy Writable Utility Mobile, *12-16*		20____
37127	Angela Trotta Thomas Gallery, *12*		75____
37129	Boy Scouts of America Girder Bridge, *13*		23____
37130	Boy Scouts of America Covered Bridge, *13*		60____
37139	Tis the Season Accessories, *12-13*		310____
37140	All Aboard Accessories, *12-13*		65____
37141	Rail Yard Accessories, *12-13*		277____
37142	Welcome Home Accessories, *12-13*		154____
37146	Legacy PowerMaster, *12-16, 18*		100____
37147	CAB-1L/Base-1L Command Set, *12-16, 18*		250____
37149	FasTrack Modular Layout Straight Section Kit, *13*		200____
37150	FasTrack Modular Layout Template, *13-16*		30____

		Exc	Mint
____	**37151** Christmas Classic Street Lamps, *14, 16-18*		40
____	**37152** Operating Coaling Station, *13-14*		180
	37153 FasTrack Modular Layout 45-Degree Reversible Corner Kit, *13*		225
____			
____	**37154** FasTrack Modular Layout 45-Degree Corner Kit, *13*		225
____	**37155** CAB-1L Remote Controller, *12-16*		150
____	**37156** Base-1L, *12-16*		125
____	**37158** Hershey's Water Tower, *13*		30
____	**37159** Peanuts Figure Pack, *13-15*		30
____	**37160** Strasburg Girder Bridge, *13*		21
____	**37161** Container 4-pack, *13*		40
____	**37162** Lionelville Water Tower, *13*		25
____	**37163** LIRR Girder Bridge, *13*		21
____	**37164** NS Girder Bridge, *13*		21
____	**37165** CP Water Tower, *13*		25
____	**37166** Crossing Shanty, *13-14, 16*		25
____	**37167** Freight Platform, *13*		30
____	**37169** Peanuts Psychiatric Booth, *13-16*		40
____	**37172** Gooseneck Lamp 2-pack, *13-18*		34
____	**37173** Globe Lamp 3-pack, *13-14, 16-18*		25
____	**37174** Classic Street Lamp 3-pack, black, *13-14, 16-18*		40
____	**37176** Santa Fe Shanty, *13*		25
	37183 Polar Express 10th Anniversary Pewter Snowman and Children Figure Pack, *13-14, 16-17*		37
____			
____	**37184** Christmas Half Covered Bridge, *13*		43
____	**37185** Christmas Railroad Signs, *13-14, 16-18*		10
____	**37187** Kris Kringle's Kloseout Shop, *13*		50
____	**37191** 36-watt Power Supply, LionChief, *14*		36
____	**37195** Grand Central Terminal 100th Anniversary, *13-15*		280
____	**37196** Christmas Extension Bridge, *13, 16-18*		15
____	**37197** North Pole Central Girder Bridge, *13-14, 16-17*		30
____	**37530** Santa Animated Caboose, *11*		80
____	**37807** Station Platform, *10-15*		23
____	**37808** Sunoco Spherical Oil Tank, *10-11*		100
____	**37810** Curved O Gauge Tunnel, *11-17*		65
____	**37813** Christmas Tractor and Trailer with trees, *10*		27
____	**37814** Christmas Crossing Shanty, *10-14*		30
____	**37816** Rockville Bridge, *11-12*		700
____	**37820** Lionel Auto Loader Cars 4-pack, *12-13, 16-17*		25
____	**37821** Smoke Fluid Loader, *11*		250
____	**37826** Classic Travel Billboard Set, *11-14*		13
____	**37827** Coca-Cola Covered Bridge, *11*		45
____	**37828** Vintage Boy Scouts Figure Pack, *11-14*		30
____	**37829** Polar Express Station Platform, *11-18*		40
____	**37831** NJ Transit Blinking Light Water Tower, *11-12*		30
____	**37834** Lionel Boat 4-pack, *11-18*		25
____	**37836** Monopoly Auto 4-pack, *12*		25
____	**37837** Polar Express Straight Tunnel, *12-14*		80
____	**37840** Santa Fe Diorama, *12-17*		15
____	**37841** Premium Smoke Fluid, *12-16*		7
____	**37842** CN Tractor with piggyback trailer, *12, 15*		90
____	**37846** PRR Tractor Trailer, *12*		90
____	**37847** SP Tractor Trailer, *12*		90
____	**37848** IC Tractor Trailer, *12*		90

		Exc	Mint
37849	ATSF Tractor Trailer, *12*	90	___
37850	REA Tractor Trailer, *12*	90	___
37851	Scale Telephone Poles, *12-18*	37	___
37852	Christmas People Pack, *12-14, 16-18*	20	___
37853	Alien Billboard, *13, 15*	13	___
37854	Classic Christmas Billboard, *12*	11	___
37855	Lionel Airplane 2-pack, *12-18*	37	___
37900	Silver Truss Bridge, *11*	70	___
37901	Lehigh Valley Tugboat, *10*	270	___
37902	Illuminated Barge, *10*	180	___
37903	Cell Tower, *10-16, 18*	70	___
37904	Boy Scouts Billboard Set, *10*	13	___
37907	Christmas Street Lamps with wreaths, *10-14*	30	___
37909	North Pole Central Jet Snowblower, *11-14*	138	___
37910	Operating Lighthouse, *10*	180	___
37911	D&RGW Blinking Light Water Tower, *10-11*	30	___
37912	Lighted Coaling Tower, *10-15*	180	___
37913	Hopper Shed, *10-15*	35	___
37914	Illuminated Work House, *10-18*	40	___
37916	Beige Brick Suburban House, *10*	80	___
37917	Red Brick Suburban House, *10*	80	___
37919	Operating Sawmill, *10*	130	___
37920	Bascule Bridge, *10*	350	___
37921	ZW-L Transformer, *11-16, 18*	900	___
37923	Coca-Cola Blinking Light Water Tower, *11*	28	___
37928	Passenger Station, sounds, *11*	90	___
37929	Coca-Cola Diner, *11, 13*	75	___
37930	Rotary Aircraft Beacon, *11-12*	81	___
37933	MG Switch Tower, *11-13*	300	___
37935	Operating Track Gang, *11*	100	___
37939	Scale Telephone Poles, *11-18*	43	___
37940	PRR Hobo Hotel, *12*	150	___
37941	House Under Construction, *11*	90	___
37942	Christmas Hobo Hotel, *12-13*	150	___
37944	Weathered 50,000-gallon Water Tank, *11-12*	170	___
37946	House Under Construction #2, *12-13*	90	___
37947	GW-180 180-watt Transformer, *12-18*	280	___
37948	Boy Scouts Flagpole with lights, *11*	30	___
37951	Postwar "342" Culvert Loader, *11*	165	___
37952	Postwar "345" Culvert Unloader, *11*	190	___
37953	Jacobs Pharmacy, *11*	50	___
37954	Halloween Station Platform, *11-13*	35	___
37955	Sodor Station Platform, *11-15*	35	___
37957	Deluxe Holiday House, *11*	85	___
37958	SP Scrap Yard, *11-14*	110	___
37959	Midway Basketball Shot Game, *11-13*	21	___
37960	Burning Switch Tower, *11-13*	100	___
37961	NYC Scrap Yard, *11-13*	110	___
37962	NJ Transit Station Platform, *11*	37	___
37964	Archive Operating Freight Terminal, *11-14*	150	___
37965	Christmas Operating Freight Terminal, *11-14, 16-17*	150	___
37966	Lionel Cylindrical Oil Tank, *11-17*	100	___
37967	Boy Scouts Troop Cabin, *12-13*	80	___

		Mint
____ **37971**	Bethlehem Steel Culvert Loader, *11*	165
____ **37972**	Bethlehem Steel Culvert Unloader, *11*	190
____ **37973**	Coca-Cola Station Platform, *12*	37
____ **37975**	PFE Operating Freight Terminal, *11-16*	150
____ **37977**	Hooker Tank Car Accident, *11-17*	130
____ **37978**	Deluxe Suburban House, *11-13*	80
____ **37979**	Rotary Coal Tipple, *12*	540
____ **37980**	Operating Coal Conveyor, *12*	90
____ **37984**	Santa's Repair Work House, *12-14*	40
____ **37985**	Operating Wind Turbine, *12-15*	75
____ **37986**	NJ Transit Blinking Billboard, *12-13*	28
____ **37989**	Sodor Train Shed, *12-16*	60
____ **37992**	Coca-Cola Blinking Light Billboard, *10-11*	28
____ **37993**	Snoopy and the Red Baron Animated Pylon, *12*	160
____ **37994**	Deluxe Holiday House #2, *12-14*	120
____ **37995**	Illuminated Scale Telephone Poles, *12-18*	50
____ **37996**	Postwar 192 Control Tower, *12*	70
____ **37997**	Christmas Lawn Figure Pack, *12-14, 16-18*	20
____ **37998**	Halloween Haunted Passenger Station, *12-13, 15*	75
____ **38004**	Virginian 4-6-0 10-wheel Locomotive "203," CC, *01-02*	570
____ **38005**	Long Island 4-6-0 10-wheel Locomotive "138," CC, *01-02*	510
____ **38007**	UP Auxiliary tender, black, CC, *01*	200
____ **38008**	UP Auxiliary tender, gray, CC, *01*	205
____ **38009**	D&RGW 4-6-6-4 Challenger Locomotive "3803," CC, *01*	1550
____ **38010**	Clinchfield 4-6-6-4 Challenger Locomotive "673," CC, *01*	1400
____ **38012**	Wheeling & Lake Erie 2-6-6-2 Locomotive "8005," CC, *01*	610
____ **38013**	D&H 4-6-6-4 Challenger Locomotive "1527," CC, *01*	720
____ **38014**	D&RGW 4-6-6-4 Challenger Locomotive "3800," CC, *01*	710
____ **38015**	NYC 4-6-4 Hudson Locomotive "773," CC, *01*	900
____ **38016**	Southern 0-8-0 Yard Goat Locomotive "6536," CC, *01-02, 05*	530
____ **38017**	CN 2-6-0 Mogul Locomotive "86," CC, *03, 05*	600
____ **38018**	Wabash 2-6-0 Mogul Locomotive "826," CC, *03*	485
____ **38019**	B&M 2-6-0 Mogul Locomotive "1455," CC, *03, 05*	600
____ **38020**	PRR 4-4-4-4 T1 Duplex Locomotive "5514," *02-03*	630
____ **38021**	WP 4-6-6-4 Challenger Locomotive "402," CC, *02*	650
____ **38022**	WM 4-6-6-4 Challenger Locomotive "1206," CC, *02*	690
____ **38023**	UP 4-6-6-4 Challenger Locomotive "3976," CC, *02*	620
____ **38024**	PRR 6-4-4-6 S-1 Duplex Locomotive "6100," TMCC, *03*	1000
____ **38025**	PRR 4-6-2 K4 Pacific Locomotive "1361," CC, *02*	950
____ **38026**	N&W 4-8-4 J Class Northern Locomotive "606," CC, *02*	1450
____ **38027**	Meadow River Lumber Heisler Geared Locomotive "6," CC, *03*	880
____ **38028**	PRR 6-8-6 S2 Steam Turbine Locomotive, *01*	650
____ **38029**	UP 4-12-2 Locomotive "9000," CC, *03*	570
____ **38030**	Santa Fe 2-8-8-2 Locomotive "1795," CC, *03*	920
____ **38031**	SP 2-8-8-4 AC-9 Locomotive "3809," CC, *04*	1100

		Exc	Mint
38032	Virginian 2-8-8-2 Locomotive "741," CC, *03*	928	___
38036	Long Island 2-8-0 Consolidation Locomotive, *01*	500	___
38037	PRR Reading Seashore 2-8-0 Consolidation Locomotive "6072," CC, *01*	495	___
38038	D&RGW Auxiliary Water Tender, *01*	230	___
38039	Clinchfield Auxiliary Water Tender, *01*	220	___
38040	LV 4-6-0 Camelback Locomotive, *01*	405	___
38042	C&NW 4-6-0 10-wheel Locomotive "361," CC, *02*	450	___
38043	Frisco 4-6-0 10-wheel Locomotive "719," CC, *02*	525	___
38044	PRR 4-6-2 K4 Pacific Locomotive "5385," CC, *02*	920	___
38045	NYC Hudson J-3a 4-6-4 Locomotive "5418," CC, *03*	495	___
38046	GN 0-8-0 Locomotive "815," CC, *02*	530	___
38047	N&W 0-8-0 Locomotive "266," CC, *02*	550	___
38048	NPR 0-8-0 Locomotive "303," CC, *02*	530	___
38049	N&W 2-6-6-4 Locomotive "1234," CC, *02*	690	___
38050	Nickel Plate 2-8-4 Berkshire Locomotive "779," CC, *03*	925	___
38051	Erie 2-8-4 Berkshire Locomotive "3315," CC, *03*	810	___
38052	Pere Marquette 2-8-4 Berkshire Locomotive "1225," CC, *03*	1000	___
38053	NYC 4-8-2 Mohawk L-2a Locomotive "2793," CC, *03*	915	___
38055	Santa Fe 4-8-4 Northern Locomotive "3751," CC, *04*	1100	___
38056	PRR 4-8-2 Mountain M1a Locomotive "6759," CC, *03*	850	___
38057	Weyerhaeuser Shay Locomotive, CC, *03*	1000	___
38058	C&O 2-8-8-2 H7 Locomotive "1580," CC, *04*	1200	___
38060	UP 2-8-8-2 H7 Locomotive "3590," CC, *04*	1200	___
38061	Cass Scenic Heisler Geared Locomotive "6," CC, *03*	940	___
38062	Lionel Lines 4-6-2 Pacific Locomotive "8062," CC, *02-03*	275	___
38065	UP 2-8-8-2 Mallet Locomotive "3672," CC, *02*	1002	___
38066	Elk River Shay Locomotive, CC, *03*	1000	___
38067	MILW 4-6-2 Pacific Locomotive "6316," CC, *03*	300	___
38068	WM 4-6-2 Pacific Locomotive "204," CC, *03*	300	___
38069	Erie Hudson Locomotive, whistle, *05*	150	___
38070	C&O 4-6-2 Pacific Locomotive "489," CC, *04*	300	___
38071	SP Cab Forward AC-12 Locomotive "4294," CC, *05*	1550	___
38075	UP 4-8-8-4 Big Boy Locomotive "4024," LionMaster, *03*	800	___
38076	C&O 2-8-4 Berkshire Locomotive "2699," CC, *04*	860	___
38077	Virginian 2-8-4 Berkshire Locomotive "508," CC, *04*	1000	___
38079	SP 4-8-4 Northern GS-2 Locomotive "4410," CC, *04*	980	___
38080	WP 4-8-4 Northern GS-64 Locomotive "485," CC, *04*	1000	___
38081	C&O 2-6-6-6 Allegheny Locomotive "1650," CC, *05-07*	1700	___
38082	Pennsylvania 2-8-8-2 Y3 Locomotive "374," CC, *04*	1000	___
38083	N&W 2-8-8-2 Y3 Locomotive "2009," CC, *04*	910	___
38085	NYC 4-6-4 Hudson J-3a Locomotive 5422," CC, *03*	495	___
38086	B&A 4-6-4 Hudson Locomotive "607," CC, *03*	495	___
38087	Nickel Plate 2-8-4 Berkshire Locomotive, RailSounds, *05*	190	___
38088	NYC 2-6-0 Mogul Locomotive "1924," CC, *03, 05*	600	___
38089	Pennsylvania 4-6-2 Pacific Locomotive "3678," CC, *04*	300	___

Item	Description	Exc	Mint
38090	Clinchfield 4-6-6-4 Challenger Locomotive "672," CC, 04		640
38091	NP 4-6-6-4 Challenger Locomotive "5121," CC, 04		660
38092	Pickering Lumber Heisler Locomotive "5," CC, 04		1000
38093	UP 4-6-6-4 Challenger Locomotive "3980," CC, 04		700
38094	MILW Hiawatha 4-4-2 Atlantic Locomotive, CC, 06		950
38095	N&W 4-8-4 J Class Locomotive "611," CC, 05-06		1250
38100	Texas Special F3 Diesel AB Set, 99	860	930
38103	Texas Special F3 Diesel "2245," 99	435	510
38114	ATSF FT Diesel B Unit, 99-00		170
38115	NYC FT Diesel B Unit "2403," nonpowered, 99-00		130
38116	B&O FT Diesel B Unit, 99-00		130
38144	C&O F3 Diesel AA Set,"7019, 7021," 00		700
38147	GN Alco FA2 AA Diesel Set, CC, 02		405
38150	Platinum Ghost,"2333," 99		495
38153	"Spirit of the Century" F3 Diesel AA Set, 99		800
38160	Pennsylvania Alco FB2 Diesel, 02		125
38161	MKT Alco FB2 Diesel, 02		125
38162	Burlington FT Diesel B Unit, 01		NRS
38167	Burlington FT Diesel AA Set, 01		225
38176	Pennsylvania Alco FA2 AA Diesel Set, CC, 02		405
38182	MKT Alco FA2 AA Diesel Set, CC, 02		360
38188	Southern F3 Diesel ABA Set, 00		557
38194	GN Alco FB2 Diesel, 02		125
38195	Santa Fe FT Diesel A Unit "170," 00		125
38196	Santa Fe FT Diesel A Unit "171," 00		175
38197	SP F3 Diesel ABA Set, 00		640
38202	Wild West HandCar, 10		75
38203	Holly Jolly Trolley 2-car Set, 10		160
38204	ATSF FT B Unit, nonpowered, 10		120
38210	PRR Alco Diesel AA Set, CC, 10		400
38214	Rio Grande Ski Train FT B Unit, nonpowered, 11		120
38215	ATSF FT Diesel "165," RailSounds, 10-11		280
38216	Rio Grande Ski Train FT A Unit, nonpowered, 11		120
38219	Texan FT B Unit Diesel, nonpowered, 11, 13-14		120
38221	CNJ Alco AA Diesel Set, 11		300
38224	Alaska Alco AA Diesel Set, 11		300
38234	Classic PRR GG1 Electric Locomotive "4866," 12		330
38235	Classic PC GG1 Electric Locomotive "4840," 12		330
38240	Elf Gang Car, 12		120
38241	MOW Gang Car, 12-13		120
38300	Postwar "2331" Virginian Train Master Diesel, 08	190	210
38303	Postwar "2340" GG1 Electric Locomotive, 08		280
38305	Postwar "2338" Milwaukee Road GP7 Diesel, 08		220
38308	Postwar 2146WS Berkshire Passenger Set, 12		460
38310	"2185W" NYC F3 Diesel Freight Set, 09		600
38311	"2276W" B&O RDC Commuter Set, 09		470
38312	"2343" Santa Fe F3 Diesel AA Set, 09		500
38313	B&O Budd RDC 2-pack, 09		350
38323	Postwar "2348" M&StL GP9 Diesel, CC, 10		390
38324	Postwar 2507W NH F3 Diesel Freight Set, 10		600
38328	Postwar 1623W NP GP9 Diesel Freight Set, 10		750
38329	Postwar 2261W Freight Hauler Set, 10		610
38334	Postwar 11288 Orbitor Diesel Freight Set, 10		500

MODERN ERA 1970-2019

Exc Mint

		Exc	Mint
38338	Postwar 2129WS Berkshire Freight Set, *12*	550	
38339	Postwar 2505W Virginian Rectifier Freight Set, *10*	470	
38340	Postwar 1587S Girl's Steam Freight Set, *10*	580	
38342	Postwar 1619W Santa Fe Freight Set, *10-11*	470	
38348	Postwar "2339" Transparent Wabash GP7 Diesel, *11*	290	
38349	Postwar 12885-500 C&O GP7 Freight Set, *11-12*	600	
38351	Postwar Archive UP GP7 Diesel, *11*	290	
38353	Postwar X-628 Promotional U.S. Navy Diesel Freight Set, *12-14*	600	
38354	Postwar 1464W UP Anniversary Alco Diesel Passenger Set, *12-14*	460	
38357	Postwar 221 U.S. Marine Corps Alco Diesel A Unit, *12-14*	300	
38358	Postwar 2239 IC F3 Freight Set, *12-14*	600	
38365	Archive ATSF Black Bonnet F3 AA Diesel Set, *12-14*	500	
38368	Archive NYC Red Lightning F3 AA Diesel Set, *12-14*	500	
38371	Postwar 2031 RI Alco Diesel AA Set, *12-13*	400	
38374	Postwar 221 U.S. Marine Corps Alco Diesel B Unit, *12-14*	120	
38377	Postwar 2363T F3 A Unit, nonpowered, *12-14*	170	
38379	Archive ATSF Black Bonnet F3 B Unit, *12-14*	170	
38380	Archive NYC Red Lightning F3 B Unit, *12-14*	170	
38386	Postwar "2367" Wabash F3 Diesel AB Units, *12-14*	500	
38388	Postwar "2367" Wabash F3 Diesel A Unit, nonpowered, *12-14*	170	
38389	Postwar "2362" UP F3 Diesel AA Set, *14*	460	
38392	Postwar "2362" F3 Diesel B Unit, nonpowered, *14*	170	
38393	PRR Round-roof Boxcar "76648" (std O), *14*	80	
38401	NYC M-497 Jet-Powered Rail Car, *10*	300	
38402	Amtrak HHP-8 Electric Locomotive, RailSounds, *10*	400	
38403	B&O CSX Heritage AC6000 Diesel "6607," CC, *11*	550	
38404	B&O CSX Heritage AC6000 Diesel "7812," CC, *11*	550	
38405	Chessie System CSX Heritage AC6000 Diesel, CC, *11-14*	550	
38406	Chessie System CSX Heritage AC6000 Diesel, CC, *11-14*	550	
38407	WM CSX Heritage AC6000 Diesel "2652," CC, *11*	550	
38408	WM CSX Heritage AC6000 Diesel "2659," CC, *11*	550	
38409	Clinchfield CSX Heritage AC6000 Diesel, CC, *11-13*	550	
38410	Clinchfield CSX Heritage AC6000 Diesel, CC, *11-14*	550	
38411	Family Lines CSX Heritage AC6000 Diesel "4825," CC, *11*	550	
38412	Family Lines CSX Heritage AC6000 Diesel "4837," CC, *11*	550	
38413	CSX Heritage AC6000 Diesel "607," CC, *11-13*	550	
38414	CSX Heritage AC6000 Diesel "654," CC, *11-13*	550	
38415	PRR U28C Diesel "6531," CC, *11-12*	530	
38416	PRR U28C Diesel "6534," CC, *11-12*	530	
38417	BN Bicentennial U30C Diesel "1776," CC, *11*	530	
38418	BN Bicentennial U30C Diesel "1777," CC, *11*	530	
38419	UP U30C Diesel "2918," CC, *11-12*	530	
38420	UP U30C Diesel "2897," CC, *11-12*	530	
38421	NP U33C Diesel "3305," CC, *11-12*	530	
38422	NP U33C Diesel "3307," CC, *11-12*	530	
38423	Southern U30C Diesel "3801," CC, *11-12*	530	

		Exc	Mint
38424	Southern U30C Diesel "3804," CC, *11-12*		530
38425	RI Budd RDC Jet Car, *11*		330
38428	Alaska Budd RDC Coach, *11*		300
38429	NYC Budd RDC M-497 Jet Car, *11*		330
38432	MKT H16-44 Diesel "1591," CC, *11*		500
38433	MKT H16-44 Diesel "1731," CC, *11*		500
38434	MKT H16-44 Diesel "1732," *11*		380
38435	MKT H16-44 Diesel "1733," nonpowered, *11*		240
38436	LIRR H-16-44 Diesel "1501," CC, *11*		500
38437	LIRR H-16-44 Diesel "1504," CC, *11*		500
38438	LIRR H-16-44 Diesel "1507," *11*		380
38439	LIRR H-16-44 Diesel "1509," nonpowered, *11*		240
38440	UP H-16-44 Diesel "1341," CC, *11*		500
38441	UP H-16-44 Diesel "1342," CC, *11*		500
38442	UP H-16-44 Diesel "1343," *11*		380
38443	UP H-16-44 Diesel "1344," nonpowered, *11*		240
38444	PRR H16-44 Diesel "8807," CC, *11*		500
38445	PRR H16-44 Diesel "8810," CC, *11*		500
38446	PRR H16-44 Diesel "8812," *11*		380
38447	PRR H16-44 Diesel "8815," nonpowered, *11*		240
38452	PC Alco RS-11 Diesel "7605," CC, *12*		480
38453	PC Alco RS-11 Diesel "7608," CC, *12*		480
38454	PRR Alco RS-11 Diesel "9622," CC, *12*		480
38455	PC Alco RS-11 Diesel "7625," nonpowered, *12*		240
38456	N&W Alco RS-11 Diesel "308," CC, *12-13*		480
38457	N&W Alco RS-11 Diesel "318," CC, *12*		480
38458	PRR Alco RS-11 Diesel "8631," CC, *12*		480
38459	N&W Alco RS-11 Diesel "330," nonpowered, *12*		240
38460	NKP Alco RS-11 Diesel "855," CC, *12*		480
38461	NKP Alco RS-11 Diesel "859," CC, *12*		480
38462	PRR Alco RS-11 Diesel "8639," nonpowered, *12*		240
38463	NKP Alco RS-11 Diesel "863," nonpowered, *12*		240
38464	Alaska Alco RS-11 Diesel "3602," CC, *12*		480
38465	Alaska Alco RS-11 Diesel "3604," CC, *12*		480
38466	NH Alco RS-11 Diesel "1403," CC, *12*		480
38467	Alaska Alco RS-11 Diesel "3607," nonpowered, *12*		240
38468	Seaboard Alco RS-11 Diesel "101," CC, *12-13*		480
38469	Seaboard Alco RS-11 Diesel "102," CC, *12*		480
38470	NH Alco RS-11 Diesel "1405," CC, *12*		480
38471	Seaboard Alco RS-11 Diesel "104," nonpowered, *12*		240
38472	C&O Alco S2 Diesel Switcher "5001," CC, *11*		470
38473	C&O Alco S2 Diesel Switcher "5505," CC, *11*		480
38474	C&O Alco S2 Diesel Switcher "5020," *11*		360
38475	C&O Alco S2 Diesel Switcher "5027," nonpowered, *11*		220
38476	CN Alco S2 Diesel Switcher "7946," CC, *11*		480
38477	CN Alco S2 Diesel Switcher "7949," CC, *11*		480
38478	CN Alco S2 Diesel Switcher "7951," *11*		360
38479	CN Alco S2 Diesel Switcher "7954," *11*		360
38480	NYC Alco S2 Diesel Switcher "8504," CC, *11*		480
38481	NYC Alco S2 Diesel Switcher "8507," CC, *11*		480
38482	NYC Alco S2 Diesel Switcher "8514," *11*		360
38483	NYC Alco S2 Diesel Switcher "8521," nonpowered, *11*		220

Exc Mint

		Exc	Mint
38484	Southern Alco S2 Diesel Switcher "2209," CC, 11	480	
38485	Southern Alco S2 Diesel Switcher "2211," CC, 11	480	
38486	Southern Alco S2 Diesel Switcher "2215," 11	360	
38487	Southern Alco S2 Diesel Switcher "2218," nonpowered, 11	220	
38488	Mopac Alco S2 Diesel Switcher "9108," CC, 11	480	
38489	Mopac Alco S2 Diesel Switcher "9113," CC, 11	480	
38490	Mopac Alco S2 Diesel Switcher "9116," 11	360	
38491	Mopac Alco S2 Diesel Switcher "9131," nonpowered, 11	220	
38493	ATSF Early Era Inspection Vehicle, CC, 12	150	
38494	CP DD35 Diesel "9864," CC, 12	600	
38495	CP DD35 Diesel "9868," nonpowered, 12	440	
38496	SP DD35A Diesel "9903," CC, 11	600	
38497	SP DD35A Diesel "9914," nonpowered, 11	440	
38498	PRR DD35A Diesel "2380," CC, 11	600	
38499	PRR DD35A Diesel "2383," nonpowered, 11	440	
38505	CSX GP-38 Diesel, 11	140	
38521	PRR GG1 Electric "4839," 11	330	
38522	Amtrak GG1 Electric "926," 11	330	
38524	NYC GP35 Diesel "6131," CC, 12	500	
38525	NYC GP35 Diesel "6138," CC, 12	500	
38526	NYC GP35 Diesel "6147," nonpowered, 12	260	
38527	UP GP35 Diesel "742," CC, 12	500	
38528	UP GP35 Diesel "753," CC, 12	500	
38529	UP GP35 Diesel "760," nonpowered, 12	260	
38530	SP GP35 Diesel "7465," CC, 12	500	
38531	SP GP35 Diesel "7474," CC, 12	500	
38532	SP GP35 Diesel "7481," nonpowered, 12	260	
38533	CP GP35 Diesel "5014," CC, 12	500	
38534	CP GP35 Diesel "5018," CC, 12	500	
38535	CP GP35 Diesel "5023," nonpowered, 12	260	
38536	PRR GP35 Diesel "2297," CC, 12	500	
38537	PRR GP35 Diesel "2302," CC, 12	500	
38538	PRR GP35 Diesel "2305," nonpowered, 12	260	
38539	N&W Alco RS-11 Diesel "308," CC, 12	480	
38539	Conrail GP35 Diesel "2297," CC, 12	500	
38540	Conrail GP35 Diesel "2302," CC, 12	500	
38541	Conrail GP35 Diesel "2305," nonpowered, 12	260	
38542	Milwaukee Road GP35 Diesel "361," CC, 12	500	
38543	Milwaukee Road GP35 Diesel "363," CC, 12	500	
38544	Milwaukee Road GP35 Diesel "366," nonpowered, 12	260	
38545	Pacific Harbor Line Genset Switcher "31," CC, 11	800	
38546	KCS Genset Switcher "1404," CC, 11-12	800	
38547	Santa Fe Genset Switcher "9910," CC, 11	800	
38548	EL GP35 Diesel "2555," CC, 12	500	
38549	EL GP35 Diesel "2558," CC, 12	500	
38550	EL GP35 Diesel "2561," nonpowered, 12	260	
38558	D&H Baldwin RF-16 Diesel AA Set, CC, 12	730	
38561	D&H Baldwin RF-16 Diesel B Unit, CC, 12	400	
38562	D&H Baldwin RF-16 Diesel B Unit, nonpowered, 12	250	
38563	B&O Baldwin RF-16 Diesel AA Set, CC, 12-14	730	
38566	B&O Baldwin RF-16 Diesel B Unit, CC, 12-14	400	

		Exc	Mint
____	**38567** B&O Baldwin RF-16 Diesel B Unit, nonpowered, *12-14*		250
____	**38568** NYC Baldwin RF-16 Diesel AA Set "3806-3808," CC, *12-14*		730
____	**38571** NYC Baldwin RF-16 Diesel B Unit, CC, *12-14*		400
____	**38572** NYC Baldwin RF-16 Diesel B Unit, nonpowered, *12-14*		250
____	**38573** SP Baldwin RF-16 Diesel AA Set, CC, *12-14*		730
____	**38576** SP Baldwin RF-16 Diesel B Unit, CC, *12-14*		400
____	**38577** SP Baldwin RF-16 Diesel B Unit, nonpowered, *12-14*		250
____	**38579** ATSF GP9 Diesel "744," nonpowered, *12*		240
____	**38580** NP GP9 Diesel "324," nonpowered, *12*		240
____	**38581** CSX SD80MAC Diesel "809," CC, *12-13*		530
____	**38582** CSX SD80MAC Diesel "812," CC, *12*		530
____	**38583** CSX SD80MAC Diesel "804," nonpowered, *12*		260
____	**38584** NS SD80MAC Diesel "7207," CC, *12*		530
____	**38585** NS SD80MAC Diesel "7203," CC, *12*		530
____	**38586** NS SD80MAC Diesel "7209," nonpowered, *12*		260
____	**38587** Conrail SD80MAC Diesel "4126," CC, *12*		530
____	**38588** Conrail SD80MAC Diesel "4129," CC, *12*		530
____	**38589** Conrail SD80MAC Diesel "4103," nonpowered, *12*		260
____	**38593** UP NW2 Diesel Switcher Locomotive "1028," CC, *12*		470
____	**38594** UP NW2 Diesel Switcher Locomotive "1043," CC, *12*		470
____	**38595** CB&Q Scale NW2 Diesel Switcher "9227," CC, *12*		470
____	**38596** CB&Q Scale NW2 Diesel Switcher "9245," CC, *12*		470
____	**38597** CB&Q F3 AA Diesel Set "9962A-9962C," CC, *12-13*		730
____	**38600** UP 0-6-0 Dockside Switcher "87," traditional, *07-09*		110
____	**38601** Lionel Lines 0-6-0 Dockside Switcher, traditional, *07-09*		110
____	**38605** PRR 0-4-0 Locomotive "94," traditional, *07*		170
____	**38606** SP 0-4-0 Locomotive "71," traditional, *07-08*		170
____	**38607** Southern 2-8-4 Berkshire Locomotive "2718," RailSounds, *07-08*		175
____	**38608** LL 2-8-2 Mikado Locomotive "57," RailSounds, *07*		260
____	**38609** NYC 2-8-2 Mikado Locomotive "1843," CC, *07*		370
____	**38610** NKP 2-8-4 Berkshire Locomotive "779," CC, *07-08*		370
____	**38619** Santa Fe 4-6-2 Pacific Locomotive "2037," traditional, K-Line, *06*		260
____	**38620** B&O Porter Locomotive "16," traditional, K-Line, *06*		100
____	**38621** 4-6-2 Pacific Locomotive, traditional, K-Line, *06*		260
____	**38626** Holiday 2-8-2 Mikado Locomotive "25," green, RailSounds, *08*		260
____	**38627** GN 4-4-2 Atlantic Locomotive "1702," traditional, *08-09*		110
____	**38630** U.S. Army 0-6-0 Dockside Switcher "486," traditional, *08-09*		110
____	**38634** NYC 4-6-4 Hudson Locomotive "5417," TrainSounds, *07*		200
____	**38635** C&O 4-6-4 Hudson Locomotive "309," TrainSounds, *08*		200
____	**38636** ATSF 4-6-4 Hudson Locomotive "3459," TrainSounds, *07*		200
____	**38637** LL 4-6-4 Hudson Locomotive "5242," TrainSounds, *08*		200
____	**38638** UP 4-6-2 Pacific Locomotive "2888," RailSounds, *08*		300

		Exc	Mint
38639	Erie 4-6-2 Pacific Locomotive "2939," RailSounds, *08*	300	___
38640	Southern 4-6-2 Pacific Locomotive "1317," RailSounds, *08*	300	___
38641	B&M 4-6-2 Pacific Locomotive "3713," RailSounds, *08*	300	___
38642	PRR 4-6-2 Pacific Locomotive "5385," RailSounds, *08*	300	___
38643	Alaska Mikado 2-8-2 Locomotive "701," CC, *08-09*	280	___
38644	T&P Mikado 2-8-2 Locomotive "810," CC, *08-09*	400	___
38649	Christmas 4-6-4 Hudson Locomotive, traditional, *08*	220	___
38651	Lionel Lines 0-8-0 Locomotive "100," traditional, *08-09*	120	___
38654	Bethlehem Steel 0-4-0 Locomotive, traditional, *08-09*	170	___
38657	Alton Limited Pacific 4-6-2 Locomotive "659," traditional, *08*	300	___
38658	W&ARR 4-4-0 General "1892," TrainSounds, *08-09*	165	___
38664	LL 4-4-2 Atlantic Locomotive "1058," traditional, *08-09*	110	___
38671	Santa Flyer 4-6-0 Locomotive, *09*	200	___
38677	Strasburg 0-6-0 Dockside Switcher "1252," *10*	130	___
38678	Monopoly Hudson Locomotive, TrainSounds, *10*	240	___
38679	ATSF 0-4-0 Switcher "1387," *10-11*	190	___
38684	Pennsylvania Power & Light Docksider Switcher, *10*	110	___
38687	Western & Atlantic 0-4-0 Locomotive "1897," *10-11*	190	___
38691	North Pole Central Santa Flyer "2," *10-11*	190	___
38692	Angela Trotta Thomas Signature Express, *10-11*	190	___
38700	CB&Q F3 B Unit "9962B," CC, *12-13*	400	___
38701	CB&Q F3 B Unit, *12-13*	250	___
38702	D&RGW F3 AA Diesel Set "5531-5533," CC, *12-14*	730	___
38705	D&RGW F3 B Unit "5532," CC, *12-14*	400	___
38706	D&RGW F3 B Unit, *12-14*	250	___
38707	WP F3 AB Diesel Set "803A-803B," CC, *12-14*	730	___
38710	WP F3 A Unit, nonpowered, *12-14*	380	___
38711	WP F3 B Unit "803C," CC, *12-14*	400	___
38712	Wabash F7 A Diesel Set "1102A-1102C," CC, *12-13*	730	___
38715	Wabash F7 B Unit "1102B," CC, *12-13*	400	___
38716	Wabash F7 B Unit, *12-13*	250	___
38717	Milwaukee Road F7 AA Diesel Set, CC, *12*	730	___
38720	Milwaukee Road F7 B Unit "109B," CC, *12*	400	___
38721	Milwaukee Road F7 B Unit, *12*	250	___
38722	Grand Trunk SD80MAC Diesel "9085," CC, *12*	530	___
38723	Grand Trunk SD80MAC Diesel "9088," CC, *12*	530	___
38724	Grand Trunk SD80MAC Diesel "9079," nonpowered, *12*	260	___
38725	CB&Q SD80MAC Diesel "9654," CC, *12*	530	___
38726	CB&Q SD80MAC Diesel "9651," CC, *12*	530	___
38727	CB&Q SD80MAC Diesel "9660," nonpowered, *12*	260	___
38728	PRR SD80MAC Diesel "9942," CC, *12*	530	___
38729	PRR SD80MAC Diesel "9945," CC, *12*	530	___
38730	PRR SD80MAC Diesel "9947," nonpowered, *12-13*	260	___
38731	Polar SD80MAC Diesel, CC, *12*	530	___
38732	CB&Q BNSF Heritage SD70ACe Diesel "1848," CC, *12-13*	530	___

		Exc	Mint
	38733 CB&Q BNSF Heritage SD70ACe Diesel "1852," CC, *12-13*		530
	38734 CB&Q BNSF Heritage SD70ACe Diesel "1856," nonpowered, *12-13*		260
	38735 ATSF BNSF Heritage SD70ACe Diesel "1996," CC, *12-13*		530
	38736 ATSF BNSF Heritage SD70ACe Diesel "1997," CC, *12-13*		530
	38737 ATSF BNSF Heritage SD70ACe Diesel "1999," nonpowered, *12-13*		260
	38738 Frisco BNSF Heritage SD70ACe Diesel "1876," CC, *12-13*		530
	38739 Frisco BNSF Heritage SD70ACe Diesel "1896," CC, *12-14*		530
	38740 Frisco BNSF Heritage SD70ACe Diesel "1916," nonpowered, *12-13*		260
	38741 BN BNSF Heritage SD70ACe Diesel "1970," CC, *12-13*		530
	38742 BN BNSF Heritage SD70ACe Diesel "1975," CC, *12-13*		530
	38743 BN BNSF Heritage SD70ACe Diesel "1980," nonpowered, *12-13*		260
	38744 GN BNSF Heritage SD70ACe Diesel "1889," CC, *12-13*		530
	38745 GN BNSF Heritage SD70ACe Diesel "1891," CC, *12-13*		530
	38746 GN BNSF Heritage SD70ACe Diesel "1893," nonpowered, *12-13*		260
	38747 NP BNSF Heritage SD70ACe Diesel "1870," CC, *12-13*		530
	38748 NP BNSF Heritage SD70ACe Diesel "1872," CC, *12-13*		530
	38749 NP BNSF Heritage SD70ACe Diesel "1875," nonpowered, *12-13*		260
	38750 EMD Demonstrator SD70ACe Diesel "2012," CC, *12-13*		530
	38751 CNJ F3 AA Diesel Set, CC, *13-14*		730
	38752 Vision Centipede AA Pilot Diesels, CC, *13*		2200
	38754 C&NW F7 AA Diesel Set, CC, *13-14*		730
	38757 SP F7 AA Diesel Set, CC, *13-14*		730
	38760 CNJ F3 B Unit, CC, *13-14*		400
	38761 CNJ F3 B Unit, *13-14*		250
	38762 C&NW F7 B Unit "410," CC, *13-14*		400
	38763 C&NW F7 B Unit, *13-14*		250
	38764 SP F7 B Unit "8219," CC, *13*		400
	38765 SP F7 B Unit, *13*		250
	38768 N&W GP35 Diesel "1306," CC, *13-14*		500
	38769 N&W GP35 Diesel "1308," nonpowered, *13-14*		260
	38770 RI GP35 Diesel "307," CC, *13-14*		500
	38771 RI GP35 Diesel "309," CC, *13-14*		500
	38772 RI GP35 Diesel "323," nonpowered, *13-14*		260
	38773 WP GP35 Diesel "3002," CC, *13-14*		500
	38774 WP GP35 Diesel "3009," CC, *13-14*		500
	38775 WP GP35 Diesel "3014," nonpowered, *13-14*		260
	38778 C&NW RS3 Diesel "1621," LionChief, *14-16*		330
	38779 NYC RS3 Diesel "8244," LionChief, *14-16*		330

Exc Mint

38782 C&BQ GP35 Diesel "990," CC, *13*	500	
38783 C&BQ GP35 Diesel "996," nonpowered, *13*	500	
38784 CN GP35 Diesel "4000," CC, *13*	500	
38785 CN GP35 Diesel "4005," CC, *13*	500	
38786 CN GP35 Diesel "4001," nonpowered, *13*	260	
38787 D&RGW GP35 Diesel "3031," CC, *13*	500	
38788 D&RGW GP35 Diesel "3034," CC, *13*	500	
38789 D&RGW GP35 Diesel "3038," nonpowered, *13*	260	
38790 DT&I GP35 Diesel "351," CC, *13*	500	
38791 DT&I GP35 Diesel "353," CC, *13*	500	
38792 DT&I GP35 Diesel "355," nonpowered, *13*	260	
38794 GN GP35 Diesel "3018," CC, *13-14*	500	
38795 GN GP35 Diesel "3036," nonpowered, *13-14*	260	
38796 Chessie System GP35 Diesel "1125," CC, *13*	500	
38797 Chessie System GP35 Diesel "1128," CC, *13*	500	
38798 Chessie System GP35 Diesel "1113," nonpowered, *13*	260	
38799 N&W GP35 Diesel "1302," CC, *13-14*	500	
38800 B&M Early Era Inspection Vehicle, CC, *12*	150	
38801 KCS Trackmobile, CC, *12-13*	300	
38802 North Pole Central Trackmobile, CC, *12*	300	
38803 MOW Trackmobile, CC, *12*	300	
38804 LIRR Trackmobile, CC, *12*	300	
38805 Conrail Trackmobile, CC, *12*	300	
38806 NS Trackmobile, CC, *12*	300	
38807 NP Trackmobile, CC, *12-13*	300	
38808 Chessie System Trackmobile, CC, *12*	300	
38809 CN Trackmobile, CC, *12*	300	
38810 PRR Early Era Inspection Vehicle, CC, *12*	150	
38811 D&RGW Early Era Inspection Vehicle, CC, *12*	150	
38812 SP Early Era Inspection Vehicle, CC, *12-13*	150	
38813 C&O Early Era Inspection Vehicle, CC, *12-13*	150	
38814 Milwaukee Road Early Era Inspection Vehicle, CC, *12*	150	
38815 Transylvania Early Era Inspection Vehicle, CC, *12*	150	
38816 PRR RS3 Diesel "5620," LionChief, *14-16*	330	
38819 D&RGW RS3 Diesel "5202," LionChief, *14-16*	330	
38821 AT&SF GP7 Diesel "2656," LionChief, *14-15*	330	
38824 NP GP7 Diesel "563," LionChief, *14-15*	330	
38825 UP GP7 Diesel "121," LionChief, *14-15*	330	
38827 CB&Q GP7 Diesel "1596," LionChief, *14-15*	330	
38848 Christmas Pioneer Zephyr Set, CC, *13-14*	1100	
38853 Santa and Mrs. Claus HandCar, *13*	90	
38855 GN GP35 Diesel "2519," CC, *13-14*	500	
38856 CB&Q Mark Twain Zephyr, CC, *13-14*	1100	
38860 CB&Q Pioneer Zephyr, CC, *13-14*	1100	
38864 Lionel Lines Zephyr, CC, *13-14*	1100	
38865 L&N GP35 Diesel "1105," CC, *13*	500	
38866 L&N GP35 Diesel "1109," CC, *13*	500	
38867 L&N GP35 Diesel "1114," nonpowered, *13*	260	
38868 C&BQ GP35 Diesel "978," CC, *13*	500	
38874 B&O GP9 Diesel "6448," CC, *13-14*	480	
38875 B&O GP9 Diesel "6456," CC, *13-14*	480	
38876 B&O GP9 Diesel "6461," nonpowered, *13-14*	240	
38877 B&M GP9 Diesel "1705," CC, *13*	480	

		Exc	Mint
___	**38878** B&M GP9 Diesel "1714," CC, *13*		480
___	**38879** B&M GP9 Diesel "1722," nonpowered, *13*		240
___	**38883** C&NW GP9 Diesel "701," CC, *13*		480
___	**38884** C&NW GP9 Diesel "704," CC, *13*		480
___	**38885** C&NW GP9 Diesel "712," nonpowered, *13*		240
___	**38886** Erie GP9 Diesel "1260," CC, *13*		480
___	**38887** Erie GP9 Diesel "1263," CC, *13*		480
___	**38888** Erie GP9 Diesel "1265," nonpowered, *13*		240
___	**38889** Nickel Plate Road GP9 Diesel "514," CC, *13*		480
___	**38890** Nickel Plate Road GP9 Diesel "452," CC, *13*		480
___	**38891** Nickel Plate Road GP9 Diesel "457," nonpowered, *13*		240
___	**38892** SP GP9 Diesel "3411," CC, *13*		480
___	**38893** SP GP9 Diesel "3415," CC, *13*		480
___	**38894** SP GP9 Diesel "3419," nonpowered, *13*		240
___	**38895** Wabash GP9 Diesel "484," CC, *13*		480
___	**38896** Wabash GP9 Diesel "488," CC, *13*		480
___	**38897** Wabash GP9 Diesel "491," nonpowered, *13*		240
___	**38918** Chessie System SD40-2 Diesel "7609," CC, *13*		530
___	**38919** Chessie System SD40-2 Diesel "7611," CC, *13*		530
___	**38920** Chessie System SD40-2 Diesel "7614," nonpowered, *13*		240
___	**38921** SP SD40T-2 Diesel Locomotive "8322," CC, *13*		530
___	**38922** SP SD40T-2 Diesel Locomotive "8326," CC, *13*		530
___	**38923** SP SD40T-2 Diesel, nonpowered, *13*		260
___	**38924** B&O SD40-2 Diesel "7602," CC, *13*		530
___	**38925** B&O SD40-2 Diesel "7607," CC, *13*		530
___	**38926** B&O SD40-2 Diesel "7611," nonpowered, *13*		240
___	**38933** Conrail SD40-2 Diesel "6424," CC, *13*		530
___	**38934** Conrail SD40-2 Diesel "6437," CC, *13*		530
___	**38935** Conrail SD40-2 Diesel "6468," nonpowered, *13*		240
___	**38936** UP SD40-2 Diesel "2929," CC, *13*		530
___	**38937** UP SD40-2 Diesel "2932," CC, *13*		530
___	**38938** UP SD40-2 Diesel "2947," nonpowered, *13*		240
___	**38939** NS SD40-2 Diesel "3355," CC, *13*		530
___	**38940** NS SD40-2 Diesel "3365," CC, *13*		530
___	**38941** NS SD40-2 Diesel "3379," nonpowered, *13*		240
___	**38942** Central of Georgia NS Heritage ES44AC Diesel, CC, *12*		550
___	**38943** Central of Georgia NS Heritage ES44AC Diesel, CC, *12*		550
___	**38944** Central of Georgia NS Heritage ES44AC Diesel, nonpowered, *12*		280
___	**38945** Conrail NS Heritage ES44AC Diesel, CC, *12*		550
___	**38946** Conrail NS Heritage ES44AC Diesel, CC, *12*		550
___	**38947** Conrail NS Heritage ES44AC Diesel, nonpowered, *12*		280
___	**38948** Interstate NS Heritage ES44AC Diesel Locomotive "8105," CC, *12*		550
___	**38949** Interstate NS Heritage ES44AC Diesel, CC, *12*		550
___	**38950** Interstate NS Heritage ES44AC Diesel, nonpowered, *12*		280
___	**38951** LV NS Heritage ES44AC Diesel, CC, *12*		550
___	**38952** LV NS Heritage ES44AC Diesel, CC, *12*		550
___	**38953** LV NS Heritage ES44AC Diesel, nonpowered, *12*		280

Exc Mint

Cat. No.	Description	Exc	Mint
38954	Nickel Plate Road NS Heritage ES44AC Diesel, CC, *12*		550
38955	Nickel Plate Road NS Heritage ES44AC Diesel, CC, *12*		550
38956	Nickel Plate Road NS Heritage ES44AC Diesel, nonpowered, *12*		280
38957	N&W NS Heritage ES44AC Diesel, CC, *12*		550
38958	N&W NS Heritage ES44AC Diesel, CC, *12*		550
38959	N&W NS Heritage ES44AC Diesel, nonpowered, *12*		280
38960	PRR NS Heritage ES44AC Diesel, CC, *12*		550
38961	PRR NS Heritage ES44AC Diesel, CC, *12*		550
38962	PRR NS Heritage ES44AC Diesel, nonpowered, *12*		280
38963	Southern NS Heritage ES44AC Diesel, CC, *12*		550
38964	Southern NS Heritage ES44AC Diesel, CC, *12*		550
38965	Southern NS Heritage ES44AC Diesel, nonpowered, *12*		280
38966	NS Heritage ES44AC Diesel, CC, *12*		550
38967	NS Heritage ES44AC Diesel, CC, *12*		550
38968	NS Heritage ES44AC Diesel, nonpowered, *12*		280
38969	North Pole Central GP35 Diesel "2525," CC, *13*		500
38970	North Pole Central GP35 Diesel "2512," CC, *13*		500
38971	North Pole Central GP35 Diesel "2513," nonpowered, *13*		260
38972	Reading GP35 Diesel "3625," CC, *13*		500
38973	Reading GP35 Diesel "3630," CC, *13*		500
38974	Reading GP35 Diesel "3633," nonpowered, *13*		260
38975	AT&SF GP35 Diesel "3312," CC, *13*		500
38976	AT&SF GP35 Diesel "3318," CC, *13*		500
38977	AT&SF GP35 Diesel "3329," nonpowered, *13*		260
38978	Alaska GP35 Diesel "2501," CC, *13*		500
38979	Alaska GP35 Diesel "2503," CC, *13*		500
38980	Alaska GP35 Diesel "2502," nonpowered, *13*		260
38981	B&O GP35 Diesel "2506," CC, *13-14*		500
38982	B&O GP35 Diesel "2511," CC, *13-14*		500
38983	B&O GP35 Diesel "2517," nonpowered, *13-14*		260
38984	C&O GP35 Diesel "3515," CC, *13-14*		500
38985	C&O GP35 Diesel "3521," CC, *13-14*		500
38986	C&O GP35 Diesel "3526," nonpowered, *13-14*		260
38987	MP GP35 Diesel "603," CC, *13*		500
38988	MP GP35 Diesel "607," CC, *13*		500
38989	MP GP35 Diesel "611," nonpowered, *13*		260
38990	GM&O GP35 Diesel "603," CC, *13-14*		500
38991	GM&O GP35 Diesel "607," CC, *13-14*		500
38992	GM&O GP35 Diesel "611," nonpowered, *13-14*		260
38993	WM GP35 Diesel "3576," CC, *13*		500
38994	WM GP35 Diesel "3578," CC, *13*		500
38995	WM GP35 Diesel "3580," nonpowered, *13*		260
38996	CSX GP35 Diesel "4355," CC, *13*		500
38997	CSX GP35 Diesel "4363," CC, *13*		500
38998	CSX GP35 Diesel "4390," nonpowered, *13*		260
38999	NS GP35 Diesel "2916," CC, *13*		500
39008	PRR Heavyweight Passenger Car 4-pack, *00*		225
39009	PRR Indian Rock Heavyweight Combination Car, *00*		50

		Mint
39010	PRR Andrew Carnegie Heavyweight Passenger Coach, *00*	60
39011	PRR Solomon P. Chase Heavyweight Passenger Coach, *00*	60
39012	PRR Skyline View Heavyweight Observation Car, *00*	50
39013	B&O Heavyweight Passenger Car 4-pack, *00*	400
39016	B&O Heavyweight Passenger Car 4-pack, *00*	200
39017	B&O Harper's Ferry Heavyweight Combination Car, *00*	50
39018	B&O Youngstown Heavyweight Passenger Coach, *00*	50
39019	B&O New Castle Heavyweight Passenger Coach, *00*	50
39020	B&O Chicago Heavyweight Observation Car, *00*	50
39028	LL Heavyweight Passenger Car 3-pack, *00*	195
39029	LL Irvington Heavyweight Coach "2625," *00*	60
39030	LL Madison Heavyweight Coach "2627," *00*	60
39031	LL Manhattan Heavyweight Coach "2628," *00*	60
39032	UP Madison Passenger Car 4-pack, *00*	275
39038	SP Madison Baggage Car "6015," *01*	NRS
39039	SP Madison Coach Car "1978," *01*	NRS
39040	SP Madison Coach "1975," *01*	NRS
39041	SP Madison Observation Car "2951," *01*	NRS
39042	N&W Heavyweight Passenger Car 4-pack, *00*	325
39047	B&O Heavyweight Passenger Car 2-pack, *01*	160
39050	PRR Heavyweight Passenger Car 2-pack, *01*	215
39053	Alaska Streamliner Car 2-pack, *01*	90
39056	NYC Streamliner Car 2-pack, *01*	75
39059	Santa Fe Streamliner Car 2-pack, *01*	100
39062	B&O Streamliner Car 2-pack, *01*	75
39065	PRR Streamliner Car 4-pack, *01*	165
39082	Blue Comet Heavyweight Passenger Car 2-pack, *02*	325
39085	"Freedom Train" Heavyweight Passenger Car 3-pack, *03*	260
39092	PRR Streamliner Car 2-pack, *01*	70
39099	Alton Limited Heavyweight Passenger Car 2-pack, *03*	230
39100	William Penn Congressional Coach, *00*	115
39101	Molly Pitcher Congressional Coach, *00*	100
39102	Betsy Ross Congressional Vista Dome Car, *00*	100
39103	Alexander Hamilton Congressional Observation Car, *00*	100
39104	Phoebe Snow Car, StationSounds, *99*	255
39105	Milwaukee Road Hiawatha Car, StationSounds, *99*	235
39106	CP Aluminum Passenger Car 2-pack, *00*	185
39107	CP Blair Manor Aluminum Passenger Coach "2553," *00*	115
39108	CP Craig Manor Aluminum Passenger Coach "2554," *00*	110
39109	"Spirit of the Century" Aluminum Passenger Car 4-pack, *99*	520
39110	"Spirit of the Century" Full Vista Dome Car, *99-00*	100
39111	"Spirit of the Century" Full Vista Dome Car, *99-00*	100
39112	"Spirit of the Century" Full Vista Dome Car, *99-00*	100
39113	"Spirit of the Century" Skytop Observation Car, *99-00*	100

		Exc	Mint
39118	Texas Special Garland Aluminum Passenger Coach "1203," StationSounds, *99-00*		220
39119	Southern Aluminum Passenger Car 4-pack, *00*		350
39120	Southern Grand Junction Aluminum Passenger/ Baggage Car, *00*		280
39121	Southern Charlottesville Aluminum Passenger Coach "812," *00*		90
39122	Southern Roanoke Aluminum Passenger Coach "814," *00*		250
39123	Southern Memphis Aluminum Observation Car "1152," *00*		90
39124	Amtrak Superliner Aluminum Passenger Car 4-pack, *02*		405
39129	Santa Fe Superliner Aluminum Passenger Car 4-pack, *02*		305
39141	RI Aluminum Passenger Car 4-pack, *01*		400
39146	UP Aluminum Passenger Car 4-pack, *01*		285
39151	CP Aluminum Passenger Car 2-pack, *01*		315
39154	PRR Congressional Aluminum Passenger Car 2-pack, *02*		195
39155	PRR Congressional Baggage Car, *02*		105
39156	PRR Robert Morris Congressional Coach, *02*		100
39157	Southern Aluminum Passenger Car 2-pack, *01*		290
39160	KCS Aluminum Passenger Car 2-pack, *01*	200	260
39163	Erie-Lack. Aluminum Passenger Car 2-pack, *01*		230
39166	Texas Special Aluminum Passenger Car 2-pack, *01*	300	430
39169	ACL Aluminum Passenger Car 4-pack, *01*		360
39179	NP Aluminum Passenger Car 2-pack, *02*		305
39182	WP Aluminum Passenger Car 2-pack, *02*		280
39185	Rio Grande Aluminum Passenger Car 2-pack, *02*		290
39194	UP Aluminum Passenger Car 2-pack, *02*		220
39197	CP Aluminum Passenger Coach, StationSounds, *02*		225
39198	PRR Aluminum Passenger Coach, StationSounds, *02*		210
39200	Hellgate Bridge Boxcar #2,"1900-2000," *00 u*		55
39202	Lionel Centennial Boxcar "1900-2000," *00*		46
39203	Postwar "6464" Series X, 3 cars, *01*		115
39204	New Haven Boxcar "6464-725," *01*		44
39205	Alaska Boxcar "6464-825," *01*		55
39206	NYC Boxcar "6464-900," *01*		40
39207	UP Boxcar "508500," red, *00*		50
39208	UP Boxcar "903658," silver, *00*		42
39209	UP Boxcar "500200," yellow, *00*		40
39210	6530 Fire Fighting Car, *00*		37
39211	Postwar "6464" BoxCar 3-pack #2, *00*		85
39212	Postwar "6464" SP&S BoxCar, *00*		NRS
39213	Postwar "6464" Wabash BoxCar, *00*		NRS
39214	Postwar "6464" Kansas, Oklahoma & Gulf BoxCar, *00*		NRS
39216	PRR DD Boxcar "47211," *01*		46
39220	B&LE Heavyweight Boxcar "82101," *01*		41
39221	L&N Heavyweight Boxcar "109829," *01*		41
39222	Conrail Heavyweight Boxcar "269198," *01*		44
39223	Postwar "6464" Archive Boxcar Set, 3-pack, *02*		125
39227	Postwar "6468" Automobile Boxcar 3-pack, *01*		95
39229	B&O DD BoxCar, *01*		40

		Exc	Mint
____	**39236** WP Boxcar "6464-250," *01*		55
____	**39238** Elvis BoxCar, *03*		36
____	**39239** P&LE Boxcar "22300, *02*		35
____	**39240** Pennsylvania Boxcar "118747," *02*		32
____	**39241** PC Boxcar "252455," *02*		28
____	**39242** Postwar "6464" BoxCar 3-pack #1, Archive Collection, *03-04*		80
____	**39243** Soo Line BoxCar, Archive Collection		35
____	**39247** NYC DD Boxcar "6468," *02*-03		32
____	**39248** Lackawanna DD Boxcar with hobo, *03*		45
____	**39250** Campbell's Kids Centennial BoxCar, *03-04*		40
____	**39252** Lenny Dean 60th Anniversary BoxCar, *04*		38
____	**39253** No. 6464 Boxcar 3-pack #2, Archive Collection, *04*		100
____	**39257** WP Boxcar "6464-100," boys set add-on, *03*		50
____	**39258** Elvis Presley "All Shook Up" BoxCar, *03-04*		40
____	**39259** Buick Centennial BoxCar, *03*		40
____	**39260** New Haven BoxCar, *04*		40
____	**39262** Elvis Presley "Elvis Has Left the Building" BoxCar, *04*		38
____	**39263** M&StL BoxCar, Postwar Celebration Series, *05*		35
____	**39267** No. 6464 Boxcar 3-pack #3, Archive Collection, *05*		100
____	**39271** State of Maine BoxCar, *04*		35
____	**39273** No. 6464 Boxcar 3-pack #4, Archive Collection, *06*		100
____	**39281** Florida State University BoxCar, *07*		48
____	**39282** Purdue University BoxCar, *08*		50
____	**39283** University of Virginia BoxCar, *08*		50
____	**39284** Penn State University BoxCar, *06-07*		45
____	**39285** U.S. Military Academy at West Point BoxCar, *08*		50
____	**39286** University of Illinois BoxCar, *06-07*		45
____	**39287** University of Alabama BoxCar, *06-07*		45
____	**39289** University of Oklahoma BoxCar, *06-08*		50
____	**39290** Postwar "6464" BoxCar 2-pack, rare variations, *08*		100
____	**39291** University of Michigan BoxCar, *06-07*		45
____	**39292** Monopoly Boxcar 3-pack, *08*		135
____	**39296** UPS Centennial Boxcar #3, *08-09*		55
____	**39297** Macy's Parade BoxCar, *07*		55
____	**39298** Monopoly Boxcar 3-pack #2, *08*		145
____	**39299** Lenny Dean Commemorative BoxCar, *08*		50
____	**39302** University of Maryland BoxCar, *08*		50
____	**39303** Villanova University BoxCar, *08*		50
____	**39304** Auburn University BoxCar, *08*		50
____	**39308** CP Rail "6565" Boxcar "58700," *08*-10		55
____	**39309** Macy's Parade BoxCar, *08*		50
____	**39310** Monopoly Boxcar 3-pack #3, *09-10*		170
____	**39316** New Haven Automobile BoxCar, *09-10*		60
____	**39317** Wizard of Oz Boxcar #1, *09-10*		60
____	**39318** Wizard of Oz Boxcar #2, *09-10*		60
____	**39319** Boy Scouts "Scout Law" Add-on BoxCar, *10*		60
____	**39321** Lionel Art Boxcar 2-pack, *10*		116
____	**39325** Macy's Parade BoxCar, *09*		45
____	**39326** UPS Centennial Boxcar #4, *10-11*		60
____	**39328** Monopoly Boxcar 3-pack #4, *10-11*		220
____	**39332** Holiday BoxCar, *10*		60
____	**39334** Coca-Cola Christmas BoxCar, *10*		70
____	**39335** Thomas Kinkade BoxCar, *10, 12*		60

		Exc	Mint
39336	Angela Trotta Thomas "My Turn Yet, Dad?" BoxCar, *10*	60	
39337	George Washington BoxCar, *11-12*	60	
39338	Abraham Lincoln BoxCar, *11-12*	60	
39339	Theodore Roosevelt BoxCar, *11-12*	60	
39340	Thomas Jefferson BoxCar, *11-12*	60	
39341	2010 Lionel Dealer Appreciation BoxCar, *2010u*	40	
39342	Strasburg BoxCar, *11*	55	
39343	New Jersey Central BoxCar, *10*	45	
39344	Monopoly Boxcar 3-pack #5, *11-12*	165	
39345	Monopoly Tennessee Avenue BoxCar, *11*	55	
39346	Monopoly Atlantic Avenue BoxCar, *11*	55	
39347	Monopoly Illinois Avenue BoxCar, *11*	55	
39348	Lionel NASCAR Collectables BoxCar, *11-12*	60	
39350	Thomas Kinkade "All Aboard for Christmas" BoxCar, *12-13*	60	
39351	Peanuts Thanksgiving BoxCar, *12*	70	
39354	Monopoly North Carolina Avenue BoxCar, *12*	70	
39358	Boy Scouts "Prepared For Life" BoxCar, *12*	60	
39359	Thanksgiving BoxCar, *12*	60	
39360	Boy Scouts Cub Scout BoxCar, *12-13*	60	
39361	Coca-Cola Polar Bear BoxCar, *14*	70	
39362	Thomas Kinkade "Emerald City" BoxCar, *12-15*	75	
39363	Peanuts Halloween BoxCar, *12*	65	
39364	Christmas BoxCar, *13*	60	
39376	Monopoly Boxcar 2-pack, States and Vermont Avenues, *13-15*	140	
39379	Monopoly Boxcar 2-pack, Mediterranean and St. James Avenues, *13-15*	140	
39383	Prewar "2719" BoxCar, *13*	65	
39385	U.S. Navy 1-D Tank Car, *13-15*	70	
39386	U.S. Marines 1-D Tank Car, *13-15*	70	
39387	U.S. Air Force 1-D Tank Car, *13-15*	70	
39388	U.S. National Guard 1-D Tank Car, *13-16*	70	
39389	U.S. Coast Guard 1-D Tank Car, *13-16*	70	
39391	U.S. Army FlatCar, *13-16*	70	
39392	U.S. Navy FlatCar, *13-16*	70	
39393	U.S. Marines FlatCar, *13-16*	70	
39394	U.S. Air Force FlatCar, *13-16*	70	
39395	U.S. National Guard FlatCar, *13-16*	70	
39396	U.S. Coast Guard FlatCar, *13-16*	70	
39398	Santa's Flyer Reefer, *13*	43	
39399	U.S. Army 1-D Tank Car, *13-15*	70	
39400	Republic Steel Slag Car 3-pack (std O), *04*	100	
39404	Republic Steel Hot Metal Car 3-pack (std O), *04*	130	
39411	Jones & Laughline Hot Metal Car 3-pack (std O), *05*	190	
39423	Postwar "3460" LL Flatcar with trailers, *05*	45	
39424	U.S. Steel 16-wheel Flatcar with girders, *05*	70	
39425	Hood's Flatcar with milk container, traditional, *05*	55	
39426	Nestle Nesquik Flatcar with milk container, traditional, *05*	55	
39428	Bethlehem Steel Slag Car #4 (std O), *05*	60	
39429	Bethlehem Steel Hot Metal Car #8 (std O), *05*	70	
39430	Youngstown Sheet & Tube Slag Car #7 (std O), *05*	60	

		Exc Mint
	39431 Youngstown Sheet & Tube Hot Metal Car #11 (std O), *05*	70
	39435 Postwar "6477" Flatcar with pipes, *06*	50
	39436 Postwar "6262" Wheel Car, *06*	50
	39437 Supplee Flatcar with milk container, *06*	60
	39439 6827 Flatcar with P&H power shovel, *04*	50
	39440 6828 Flatcar with P&H truck crane, *04*	50
	39443 U.S. Steel Slag Car 3-pack #2 (std O), *06*	170
	39447 Postwar "6561" LL Cable Reel Car, Archive Collection, *06-07*	55
	39450 Postwar "6414" Evans Auto Loader, Archive Collection, *06*	70
	39452 White Bros. Flatcar with milk container, *07*	60
	39457 Postwar "6175" Flatcar with rocket, *08*	55
	39458 Postwar "6844" Flatcar with missiles, *08*	55
	39463 Postwar "6430" Flatcar with trailers, *08*	55
	39468 Allis-Chalmers Car "52369," *08-09*	60
	39469 Christmas Egg Nog Barrel Car, *08*	50
	39470 UP Well Car "147128," *08*	65
	39471 Postwar "6264" FlatCar, *08*	60
	39472 ATSF Culvert Gondola, *08*	60
	39473 Play-Doh Vat Car, *08*	55
	39475 UPS Flatcar with trailer, *08*	65
	39476 Bethlehem Steel 16-wheel FlatCar, *08*	75
	39477 Christmas Flatcar with reindeer trailers, *08*	60
	39478 Postwar "6475" Pickles Vat Car, *08*	55
	39479 Postwar "6404" Flatcar with brown automobile, *08*	50
	39480 Western & Atlantic Cannon FlatCar, *09*	60
	39482 CSX WM Track Maintenance Car "6812," *11*	65
	39483 CSX P&LE Gondola "69812," *11*	65
	39484 Cocoa Marsh Vat Car, *10-12*	60
	39486 Deep Sea Challenger Submarine Car, *11*	60
	39488 Reese's Vat Car, *10*	60
	39490 Western & Atlantic Cannonball FlatCar, *10*	55
	39497 Christmas Reindeer Stock Car, *10-11*	60
	39498 CNJ Gondola with culvert pipes, *11*	55
	39499 Alaska Oil Barrel Ramp Car, *11*	50
	39502 Monongahela NS Heritage ES44AC Diesel, nonpowered, *13*	280
	39530 PRR 1955 Pickup Truck, CC, *13*	180
	39531 UP 1955 Pickup Truck, CC, *13*	180
	39532 ATSF 1955 Pickup Truck, CC, *13-14*	180
	39533 CP 1955 Pickup Truck, CC, *13-14*	180
	39534 D&RGW 1955 Pickup Truck, CC, *13*	180
	39535 GN 1955 Pickup Truck, CC, *13*	180
	39536 MKT 1955 Pickup Truck, CC, *13-14*	180
	39537 NYC 1955 Pickup Truck, CC, *13*	180
	39538 Nickel Plate Road 1955 Pickup Truck, CC, *13*	180
	39539 NP1955 Pickup Truck, CC, *13-14*	180
	39540 Southern 1955 Pickup Truck, CC, *13*	180
	39541 SP 1955 Pickup Truck, CC, *13-14*	180
	39542 Weyerhaeuser 1955 Pickup Truck, CC, *13-14*	180
	39543 Texas Special F3 B Unit, *13-14*	230
	39544 Texas Special F3 B Unit, CC, *13-14*	380

Exc Mint

	Exc	Mint
39547 PRR F3 B Unit, *13-14*	230	___
39548 PRR F3 B Unit, CC, *13-14*	380	___
39554 NS GP35 Diesel "3918," CC, *13*	500	___
39555 NS GP35 Diesel "2915," nonpowered, *13*	260	___
39556 CP GP35 Diesel "5004," CC, *13-14*	500	___
39557 CP GP35 Diesel "5007," CC, *13-14*	500	___
39558 CP GP35 Diesel "5009," nonpowered, *13-14*	260	___
39562 BN GP35 Diesel "2533," CC, *13-14*	500	___
39563 BN GP35 Diesel "2509," CC, *13-14*	500	___
39564 BN GP35 Diesel "2523," nonpowered, *13-14*	260	___
39565 ATSF Dash-9 Diesel "612," CC, *13*	530	___
39566 ATSF Dash-9 Diesel "623," CC, *13*	530	___
39567 ATSF Dash-9 Diesel "631," nonpowered, *13*	260	___
39568 BC Rail Dash-9 Diesel "4641," CC, *13*	530	___
39569 BC Rail Dash-9 Diesel "4647," CC, *13*	530	___
39570 BC Rail Dash-9 Diesel "4652," nonpowered, *13*	260	___
39571 BNSF Dash-9 Diesel "4023," CC, *13*	530	___
39572 BNSF Dash-9 Diesel "4037," CC, *13*	530	___
39573 BNSF Dash-9 Diesel "4046," nonpowered, *13*	260	___
39574 C&NW Dash-9 Diesel "8605," CC, *13*	530	___
39575 C&NW Dash-9 Diesel "8610," CC, *13*	530	___
39576 C&NW Dash-9 Diesel "8622," nonpowered, *13*	260	___
39577 SP Dash-9 Diesel "8112," CC, *13*	530	___
39578 SP Dash-9 Diesel "8123," CC, *13*	530	___
39579 SP Dash-9 Diesel "8129," nonpowered, *13*	260	___
39580 UP Dash-9 Diesel "9599," CC, *13*	530	___
39581 UP Dash-9 Diesel "9714," CC, *13*	530	___
39582 UP Dash-9 Diesel "9717," nonpowered, *13*	260	___
39583 CSX Dash-9 Diesel "9036," CC, *13*	530	___
39584 CSX Dash-9 Diesel "9048," CC, *13*	530	___
39585 CSX Dash-9 Diesel "9051," nonpowered, *13*	260	___
39586 NS Dash-9 Diesel "9310," CC, *13*	530	___
39587 NS Dash-9 Diesel "9322," CC, *13*	530	___
39588 NS Dash-9 Diesel "9334," nonpowered, *13*	260	___
39589 CN Dash-9 Diesel "2534," CC, *13*	530	___
39590 CN Dash-9 Diesel "2547," CC, *13*	530	___
39591 CN Dash-9 Diesel "2570," nonpowered, *13*	260	___
39592 CNJ NS Heritage SD70ACe Diesel "1071," CC, *13*	530	___
39593 CNJ NS Heritage SD70ACe Diesel "1831," CC, *13*	530	___
39594 CNJ NS Heritage SD70ACe Diesel "1834," nonpowered, *13*	260	___
39595 DL&W NS Heritage SD70ACe Diesel "1074," CC, *13*	530	___
39596 DL&W NS Heritage SD70ACe Diesel "1853," CC, *13*	530	___
39597 DL&W NS Heritage SD70ACe Diesel "1856," nonpowered, *13*	260	___
39598 Monongahela NS Heritage ES44AC Diesel "8025," CC, *12*	550	___
39599 Monongahela NS Heritage ES44AC Diesel "1901," CC, *12*	550	___
39600 PRR E8 AA Diesel Set, CC, *13*	930	___
39603 B&O E9 AA Diesel Set, CC, *13*	930	___
39606 FEC E9 AA Diesel Set, CC, *13*	930	___
39609 SP E9 AA Diesel Set, CC, *13*	930	___
39612 UP E9 AA Diesel Set, CC, *13*	930	___

		Exc	Mint
___	**39612** SP E9 AA Diesel Set, CC, *13*		930
___	**39615** CB&Q E9 AA Diesel Set, CC, *13*		930
___	**39618** MILW E9 AA Diesel Set, CC, *13*		930
___	**39621** KCS E9 AA Diesel Set, CC, *13*		930
___	**39624** Erie NS Heritage SD70ACe Diesel "1068," CC, *13*		530
___	**39625** Erie NS Heritage SD70ACe Diesel "1832," CC, *13*		530
___	**39626** Erie NS Heritage SD70ACe Diesel "1835," nonpowered, *13*		260
___	**39627** Illinois Terminal NS Heritage SD70ACe Diesel "1072," CC, *13*		530
___	**39628** Illinois Terminal NS Heritage SD70ACe Diesel "1896," CC, *13*		530
___	**39629** Illinois Terminal NS Heritage SD70ACe Diesel "1899," nonpowered, *13*		260
___	**39630** NYC NS Heritage SD70ACe Diesel "1066," CC, *13*		530
___	**39631** NYC NS Heritage SD70ACe Diesel "1831," CC, *13*		530
___	**39632** NYC NS Heritage SD70ACe Diesel "1834," nonpowered, *13*		260
___	**39633** Reading NS Heritage SD70ACe Diesel "1067," CC, *13*		530
___	**39634** Reading NS Heritage SD70ACe Diesel "1833," CC, *13*		530
___	**39635** Reading NS Heritage SD70ACe Diesel "1836," nonpowered, *13*		260
___	**39636** Savannah & Atlanta NS Heritage SD70ACe Diesel "1065," CC, *13*		530
___	**39637** Savannah & Atlanta NS Heritage SD70ACe Diesel "1915," CC, *13*		530
___	**39638** Savannah & Atlanta NS Heritage SD70ACe Diesel "1918," nonpowered, *13*		260
___	**39639** Virginian NS Heritage SD70ACe Diesel "1069," CC, *13*		530
___	**39640** Virginian NS Heritage SD70ACe Diesel "1907," CC, *13*		530
___	**39641** Virginian NS Heritage SD70ACe Diesel "1910," nonpowered, *13*		260
___	**39642** Wabash NS Heritage SD70ACe Diesel "1070," CC, *13*		530
___	**39643** Wabash NS Heritage SD70ACe Diesel "1877," CC, *13*		530
___	**39644** Wabash NS Heritage SD70ACe Diesel "1880," nonpowered, *13*		260
___	**39645** PC NS Heritage SD70ACe Diesel "1073," CC, *13*		530
___	**39646** PC NS Heritage SD70ACe Diesel "1968," CC, *13*		530
___	**39647** PC NS Heritage SD70ACe Diesel "1971," nonpowered, *13*		260
___	**51008** Burlington Pioneer Zephyr Diesel Passenger Set, RailSounds, *04*		875
___	**51009** Prewar "269E" Steam Freight Set, TrainSounds, *06*		630
___	**51010** Prewar "246E" Steam Passenger Set, TrainSounds, *07-08*		630
___	**51012** Christmas Tinplate Freight Set, *08*		675
___	**51014** Prewar "291W" Red Comet Passenger Car Set, *08*		675
___	**51220** NYC Imperial Castle Passenger Coach, *93 u*		500
___	**51221** NYC Niagara County Passenger Coach, *93 u*		500
___	**51222** NYC Cascade Glory Passenger Coach, *93 u*		500
___	**51223** NYC City of Detroit Passenger Coach, *93 u*		500

		Exc	Mint
51224	NYC Imperial Falls Passenger Coach, *93 u*		500___
51225	NYC Westchester County Passenger Coach, *93 u*		500___
51226	NYC Cascade Grotto Passenger Coach, *93 u*		500___
51227	NYC City of Indianapolis Passenger Coach, *93 u*		500___
51228	NYC Manhattan Island Observation Car, *93 u*		500___
51229	NYC Diner "680," *93 u*		500___
51230	NYC Baggage Car "5017," *93 u*		500___
51231	NYC Century Club Passenger Coach, *93 u*		500___
51232	NYC Thousand Islands Observation Car, *93 u*		500___
51233	NYC Diner "684," *93 u*		500___
51234	NYC Baggage Car "5020," *93 u*		500___
51235	NYC Century Tavern Passenger Coach, *93 u*		500___
51236	NYC City of Toledo Passenger Coach, *93 u*		500___
51237	NYC Imperial Mansion Passenger Coach, *93 u*		500___
51238	NYC Imperial Palace Passenger Coach, *93 u*		500___
51239	NYC Cascade Spirit Passenger Coach, *93 u*		500___
51240	NYC Diner "681," *93 u*		500___
51241	NYC City of Chicago Passenger Coach, *93 u*		500___
51242	NYC Imperial Garden Passenger Coach, *93 u*		500___
51243	NYC Imperial Fountain Passenger Coach, *93 u*		500___
51244	NYC Cascade Valley Passenger Coach, *93 u*		500___
51245	NYC Diner "685," *93 u*		500___
51300	Shell Semi-Scale 1-D Tank Car "8124," *91*	50	135___
51301	Lackawanna Semi-Scale Reefer "7000," *92*	119	161___
51401	PRR Semi-Scale Boxcar "100800," *91*	84	128___
51402	C&O Semi-Scale Stock Car "95250," *92*	98	138___
51501	B&O Semi-Scale Hopper "532000," *91*	78	108___
51502	LL Steel Die-cast Ore Car "6486-3" (SSS), *96*		80___
51503	LL Steel Die-cast Ore Car "6486-1" (SSS), *96*		80___
51504	LL Steel Die-cast Ore Car "6486-2" (SSS), *96*		70___
51600	NYC Depressed Center Flatcar with transformer "6418," *96*		105 ___
51701	NYC Semi-Scale Caboose "19400," *91*	84	123___
51702	PRR N-8 Caboose "478039," *91-92*	300	385___
52054	Carail BoxCar, *94 u*		300___
52066	Trainmaster Tractor and Trailer, *94 u*		120___
52069	Carail Tractor and Trailer, *94 u*		75___
52070	Knoebel's Boxcar #1, *95 u*		92___
52075	United Auto Workers BoxCar, *95 u*		90___
52082	Steamtown Lackawanna BoxCar, *95 u*		90___
52132	Knoebel's Boxcar #2, *99 u*		95___
52133	Knoebel's Boxcar #3, *98 u*		105___
52134	Knoebel's Boxcar #4, *00 u*		100___
52136A	Christmas Special Tractor and Trailer, *97*		NRS___
52136B	Frisco Special Tractor and Trailer, *98*		NRS___
52137	Red Wing Shoes Boot Oil Tank Car, *98*		65___
52141	Zep Manufacturing BoxCar, *96*		120___
52158	Monopoly Mint Car "M-0539," *98*		340___
52159	Monopoly Depressed Center Flatcar with transformer, *98*		95 ___
52160	Monopoly Water Works Tank Car, *98*		105___
52161	Monopoly SP-type Caboose "M-1006," *98*		55___
52168	Carail Flatcar with Trailer "17455," *99 u*		120___
52169	Zep Manufacturing Flatcar with trailer "62734," *99 u*		90___

		Exc	Mint
___	**52181** Monopoly Set #2, 4-pack, *99*		295
___	**52182** Monopoly Railroads Boxcar "M0636," *99 u*		78
___	**52183** Monopoly Jail Car "M-1131," *99*		75
___	**52184** Monopoly Free Parking Flatcar with 2 autos, *99*		60
___	**52185** Monopoly Chance Gondola "M-0893," *99*		50
___	**52187** Madison Hardware Flatcar with 2 trailers, *99*		98
___	**52188** Carail Aquarium with 2 autos, 25th Anniversary, *99*		95
___	**52189** Monopoly 4-6-4 Hudson Locomotive, *99*		550
___	**52200** TTOS SW SP Overnight Merchandise Service BoxCar, *2000u*		40
___	**52207** Lionel Lines SD40 Diesel, traditional, *00*		600
___	**52208** Lionel Lines Extended Vision Caboose, *00 u*		200
___	**52218** Monopoly 4-4-2 Steam Freight Set, *00 u*		388
___	**52219** Monopoly 4-6-4 Hudson Locomotive, bronze, *00 u*		530
___	**52224A** SP Flatcar with Navajo tractor and trailer, *01*		25
___	**52224B** SP Flatcar with Trailer Flatcar Service tractor and trailer, *01*		25
___	**52225** Monopoly 4-6-4 Hudson Locomotive, pewter, *01 u*		495
___	**52231** British Columbia 1-D Tank Car, *00 u*		65
___	**52249** Knoebel's Amusement Park 75th Anniversary BoxCar, *01 u*		95
___	**52262** Plasticville BoxCar, *01 u*		120
___	**52282** Western Pacific Feather BoxCar, red, *03*		365
___	**52315/20** PRR FM Diesel and Caboose, *04 u*		440
___	**52330** B&O Museum Fundraiser BoxCar, *03 u*		100
___	**52334** TTOS Smokey Bear 60th Anniversary 1-D Tank Car, *2004u*		80
___	**52335** TTOS Smokey Bear 60th Anniversary BoxCar, *2004u*		70
___	**52371** NYC Flatcar with tanker trailer, *05 u*		150
___	**52447** LCCA NH Alco Diesel and Passenger Cars, *2009u*		100
___	**52495** LCCA UP Water Tower, *2008u*		30
___	**58213** LCCA B&M GP7 Diesel, *2015u*		250
___	**58253** LCCA Lionel 115th Anniversary Trailer, *2015u*		25
___	**58255** LCCA Lionelville Transit Tractor, *2015u*		25
___	**58267** LCCA KCS Inspection Truck, *2016u*		125
___	**58269** LCCA Tacoma Pickup Truck, *17u*		75
___	**58270** LCCA NP Pickup Truck, *17u*		75
___	**58504** Lionel Flatcar w/Madison Hardware Trailer, *2015u*		120
___	**58513** LCCA Reading Blue Coal 2-bay Hopper w/ETD, *2012u*		75
___	**58515** LCCA NS Vulcan Switcher, *2012u*		50
___	**58517** NLOE LIRR Alco Diesels, *2013u*		300
___	**58527** LCCA Vulcan Switcher, *2013u*		80
___	**58528** LCCA Reading Vulcan Switcher, *2014u*		80
___	**58539** LCCA Texas Special B-W Caboose, *2013u*		95
___	**58545** LCCA Vulcan Switcher, Gold, *2012u*		75
___	**58550** LCCA Texas Special Unibody Tank Car, *2013u*		90
___	**58585** LCCA Wabash Auto Loader, *2014u*		125
___	**58586** LCCA South Shore Trolley, *2014u*		95
___	**58599** LCCA UP Cylindrical Hopper, *2011u*		150
___	**59002** LCCA TVRM BoxCar, *2013u*		150
___	**59015** LCCA Conway Scenic RR BoxCar, *2015u*		200
___	**62162** Postwar "262" Automatic Crossing Gate and Signal, *99-14*		60

		Exc Mint
62180	Railroad Signs, set of 14, *99-04, 08-18*	10___
62181	Telephone Pole Set, *99-04, 08-18*	10___
62283	Die-cast Illuminated Bumpers, *99-17*	27___
62709	Rico Station Kit, *99-00*	46___
62716	Short Extension Bridge, *99-03, 07-18*	15___
62900	Lockon, *99-13*	3___
62901	Ives Track Clips, 12 pieces (027), *99-10, 13-16*	5___
62905	Lockon with wires, *99-10, 13-14*	7___
62909	Smoke Fluid, *99-12*	7___
62927	Lubrication/Maintenance Set, *99-17*	25___
62985	The Lionel Train Book, *99-03*	12___
65014	Half Curved Track (027), *99-16*	1___
65019	Half Straight Track (027), *99-16*	1___
65020	90-degree Crossover (027), *99-16*	11___
65021	27" Manual Switch, left hand (027), *99-16*	17___
65022	27" Manual Switch, right hand (027), *99-16*	18___
65023	45-degree Crossover (027), *99-16*	11___
65024	35" Straight Track (027), *99-16*	5___
65033	27" Diameter Curved Track (027), *99-16*	2___
65038	9" Straight Track (027), *99-16*	2___
65041	Insulator Pins, dozen (027), *99-04, 06, 13-14*	3___
65042	Steel Pins, dozen (027), *99-04, 06-09, 13-14*	3___
65049	42" Diameter Curved Track (027), *99-16*	3___
65113	54" Diameter Curved Track (027), *99-16*	3___
65121	27" Path Remote Switch, left hand (027), *99-14*	43___
65122	27" Path Remote Switch, right hand (027), *99-14*	43___
65149	Uncoupling Track (027), *99-14*	12___
65165	72" Path Remote Switch, right hand (O), *99-14*	125___
65166	72" Path Remote Switch, left hand (O), *99-14*	125___
65167	42" Remote Switch, right hand (027), *99-14*	25___
65168	42" Remote Switch, left hand (027), *99-14*	25___
65500	10" Straight Track (O), *99-16*	2___
65501	31" Diameter Curved Track (O), *99-16*	2___
65504	Half Curved Track (O), *99-16*	2___
65505	Half Straight Track (O), *99-16*	2___
65514	Half Curved Track (027), *99-03*	3___
65523	40" Straight Track (O), *99-16*	7___
65530	Remote Control Track (O), *99-16*	38___
65540	90-degree Crossover (O), *99-14*	16___
65543	Insulator Pins, dozen (O), *99-16*	3___
65545	45-degree Crossover (O), *99-14*	27___
65551	Steel Pins, dozen (O), *99-16*	3___
65554	54" Diameter Curved Track (O), *99-16*	4___
65572	72" Diameter Curved Track (O), *99-16*	5___
65824	NLOE LIRR Hopper w/Coal load, *17u*	95___
71998	LCCA Amtrak Refrigerator Car (Std O), *2010u*	45___
81000	BNSF Waffle-sided Boxcar "496464," *14-15*	50___
81001	SP&S Flatcar with bulkheads, *14-16*	50___
81002	UP 3-D Tank Car, *14-15*	50___
81003	CP Bilevel Auto Carrier, *14-16*	50___
81004	B&O Depressed-Center Flatcar with transformer, *14-15*	50___
81005	Maine Central 2-bay Hopper "1005," *14-16*	50___
81006	PRR Hi-Cube Boxcar "31010," *14-16*	50___

		Mint
____	**81007** Seaboard Waffle-sided Boxcar "25335," *14-16*	50
____	**81008** Central of Georgia Boxcar "5818," *14-17*	50
____	**81009** Southern 2-D Tank Car "951005," *14-16*	50
____	**81010** FEC Gondola "6121" with reels, *14-16*	50
____	**81011** PFE Reefer "33280," *14-16*	50
____	**81012** T&P 1-D Tank Car, *14-16*	50
____	**81013** Frisco Boxcar "700117," *14-16*	50
____	**81014** D&RGW Ore Car "31101," *14-15*	50
____	**81015** B&M Reefer "1878," *14-16*	50
____	**81016** Coaling Station, *14, 16-18*	110
____	**81017** Barrel Loading Building, *14-18*	43
____	**81018** Shell Vat Car, *17*	80
____	**81019** Short Tunnel, *14-16-17*	45
____	**81021** B&M Paul Revere GP9 Diesel Freight Set, *14-15*	500
____	**81023** Jersey Central Yard Boss 0-4-0 Steam Freight Set, *14-15*	500
____	**81024** Christmas Train Set, *02-04*	150
____	**81025** Lackawanna Pocono Berkshire Steam Freight Set, *14-15*	480
____	**81027** Thomas the Tank Engine Set, *01-04*	120
____	**81028** Marquette GP38 Diesel Freight Set, *14-15*	430
____	**81029** C&NW Windy City GP38 Diesel Freight Set, *14-15*	400
____	**81030** UP Gold Coast Flyer Steam Freight Set, *14-15*	430
____	**81031** Dinosaur Diesel Freight Set, LionChief, *14-16*	175
____	**81038** MILW Heavy Mikado Locomotive "8693" CC, *15*	1300
____	**81063** Classic Automatic Gateman, *14-18*	95
____	**81064** Construction Zone Signs #2, *14-18*	10
____	**81066** Milwaukee Road Double-sheathed Boxcar "8775" (std O), *14*	80
____	**81067** Monopoly Aquarium Car, *14-15*	85
____	**81073** Monopoly Boxcar 2-pack, Ventnor and Indiana Avenues, *14-15*	135
____	**81076** Pennsylvania Salt 8,000-gallon 1-D Tank Car "4724" (std O), *14*	73
____	**81077** Pere Marquette 8,000-gallon 1-D Tank Car "71710" (std O), *14*	73
____	**81078** NYC 8,000-gallon 1-D Tank Car "107898" (std O), *14*	73
____	**81079** NKP 8,000-gallon 1-D Tank Car "50277" (std O), *14*	73
____	**81080** BN 8,000-gallon 1-D Tank Car "977100" (std O), *14*	73
____	**81081** Alaska Steel-sided Reefer "10806" (std O), *14*	80
____	**81090** NS Hi-Cube Boxcar 2-pack (std O), *14-15*	190
____	**81093** 2013 Lionel Dealer Appreciation BoxCar, *2013u*	40
____	**81094** Conrail "Big Blue" High-Cube Boxcar Diesel Freight Set, CC, *14*	970
____	**81095** Conrail Hi-Cube Boxcar 2-pack (std O), *14-16*	190
____	**81101** Polar Express 10th Anniversary Steam Passenger Set, LionChief, *14-15*	430
____	**81113** SP 50' DD Boxcar "214051" (std O), *14-15*	75
____	**81122** Christmas Inspection Truck, *15*	180
____	**81134** BN SD70MAC Diesel "9424," CC, *14*	550
____	**81135** BN SD70MAC Diesel "9431," CC, *14*	550
____	**81137** BNSF SD70MAC Diesel "9858," CC, *14*	550
____	**81138** BNSF SD70MAC Diesel "9860," CC, *14*	550
____	**81141** Conrail SD70MAC Diesel "4138," CC, *14*	550
____	**81142** PFE Steel-sided Reefers 3-pack (std O), *14*	300

		Exc	Mint
81144	CSX SD70MAC Diesel "781," CC, *14*	550	___
81147	KCS SD7CMAC Diesel "3950," CC, *14*	550	___
81148	KCS SD7CMAC Diesel "3953," CC, *14*	550	___
81151	Alaska SD7CMAC Diesel "4002," CC, *14*	550	___
81152	Alaska SD7CMAC Diesel "4005," CC, *14*	550	___
81153	CSX SD70MAC Diesel "778," CC, *14*	550	___
81154	UP ES44AC Diesel "7361," CC, *14*	550	___
81155	UP ES44AC Diesel "7388," CC, *14*	550	___
81160	CSX ES44AC Diesel "937," CC, *14*	550	___
81161	CSX ES44AC Diesel "944," CC, *14*	550	___
81169	Iowa Interstate ES44AC Diesel "504," CC, *14*	550	___
81170	Iowa Interstate ES44AC Diesel "507," CC, *14*	550	___
81171	Ferromex ES44AC Diesel "4617," CC, *14*	550	___
81172	Ferromex ES44AC Diesel "4626," CC, *14*	550	___
81176	CN ES44AC Diesel "2812," CC, *14*	550	___
81177	CN ES44AC Diesel "2818," CC, *14*	550	___
81179	2-8-2 Heavy Mikado Pilot Locomotive, CC, *14*	1300	___
81180	2-8-2 Heavy Mikado Locomotive, CC, *15*	1300	___
81181	Southern 2-8-2 Heavy Mikado Locomotive "4866," CC, *15*	1300	___
81182	L&N 2-8-2 Heavy Mikado Locomotive "1757," CC, *14*	1300	___
81183	MP 2-8-2 Heavy Mikado Locomotive "1496," CC, *14*	1300	___
81184	P&WV 2-8-2 Heavy Mikado Locomotive "1152," CC, *14*	1300	___
81185	CNJ 2-8-2 Heavy Mikado Locomotive "845," CC, *14*	1300	___
81186	Frisco 2-8-2 Heavy Mikado Locomotive "4126," CC, *14*	1300	___
81187	C&IM 2-8-2 Heavy Mikado Locomotive "551," CC, *14*	1300	___
81188	NYC 2-8-2 Heavy Mikado Locomotive "9506," CC, *14*	1300	___
81189	CB&Q 2-8-2 Heavy Mikado Locomotive "5509," CC, *15*	1300	___
81190	WP 2-8-2 Heavy Mikado Locomotive "334," CC, *15*	1300	___
81191	Erie 2-8-2 Heavy Mikado Locomotive "3207," CC, *15*	1300	___
81192	GN 2-8-2 Heavy Mikado Locomotive "3148," CC, *14*	1300	___
81193	Wheeling & Lake Erie 2-8-2 Heavy Mikado Locomotive "6012," CC, *15*	1300	___
81194	NKP 2-8-2 Heavy Mikado Locomotive "689," CC, *15*	1300	___
81195	PRR BoxCar, *14-15*	70	___
81196	Timken BoxCar, *14-15*	70	___
81197	Santa Fe BoxCar, *14-15*	70	___
81198	GN BoxCar, *14-15*	70	___
81199	PRR 1-D Tank Car, *14-15*	70	___
81200	Timken 1-D Tank Car, *14-16*	70	___
81201	GN 1-D Tank Car, *14-16*	70	___
81202	Santa Fe 1-D Tank Car, *14-15*	70	___
81203	PRR FlatCar, *14-15*	70	___
81204	Santa Fe FlatCar, *14-16*	70	___
81205	Timken FlatCar, *14-16*	70	___
81206	GN FlatCar, *14-16*	70	___
81207	CP H-24-66 Train Master Diesel "8900," CC, *14*	550	___
81208	CP H-24-66 Train Master Diesel "8903," CC, *14*	550	___
81209	CNJ H-24-66 Train Master Diesel "2401," CC, *14*	550	___

		Exc	Mint
____	**81210** CNJ H-24-66 Train Master Diesel "2406," CC, *14*		550
____	**81211** Reading H-24-66 Train Master Diesel "801," CC, *14*		550
____	**81212** Reading H-24-66 Train Master Diesel "804," CC, *14*		550
____	**81213** SP H-24-66 Train Master Diesel "4803," CC, *14*		550
____	**81214** SP H-24-66 Train Master Diesel "4809," CC, *14*		550
____	**81215** Southern H-24-66 Train Master Diesel "6300," CC, *14*		550
____	**81216** Southern H-24-66 Train Master Diesel "6303," CC, *14*		550
____	**81217** N&W H-24-66 Train Master Diesel "151," CC, *14*		550
____	**81218** N&W H-24-66 Train Master Diesel "164," CC, *14*		550
____	**81219** Santa Fe E8 Diesel AA Set "84/85," CC, *14*		930
____	**81222** PC E8 Diesel AA Set "4289/4325," CC, *14*		930
____	**81225** RI E8 Diesel AA Set "647/648," CC, *14*		930
____	**81228** C&O E8 Diesel AA Set "4027/4028," CC, *14*		930
____	**81231** Erie E8 Diesel AA Set "822/823," CC, *14*		930
____	**81234** MKT E8 Diesel AA Set "131/132," CC, *14*		930
____	**81237** SAL E8 Diesel AA Set "3051/3055," CC, *14*		930
____	**81240** Wabash E8 Diesel AA Set "1007/1011," CC, *14*		930
____	**81243** Pilot M1a 4-8-2 Locomotive, CC, *14*		1500
____	**81245** PRR M1a 4-8-2 Locomotive "6671," CC, *14*		1500
____	**81246** PRR M1a 4-8-2 Locomotive "6764," CC, *14*		1500
____	**81247** PRR M1a Coal Hauler Twin-hopper Steam Freight Set, CC, *14*		1800
____	**81248** 10" Girder Bridge Track, *14-18*		25
____	**81249** Christmas Girder Bridge Track, *14, 16-18*		25
____	**81250** FasTrack O-96 Curve, *14, 18*		7
____	**81251** FasTrack O-31 Manual Switch, right-hand, *14-16, 18*		50
____	**81252** FasTrack O-31 Manual Switch, left-hand, *14-16, 18*		50
____	**81253** FasTrack O-31 Remote Switch, right-hand, *14-16, 18*		110
____	**81254** FasTrack O-31 Remote Switch, left-hand, *14-16, 18*		110
____	**81256** Personalized Birthday Message BoxCar, *14-15*		85
____	**81257** Amtrak Water Tower, *14-18*		35
____	**81259** PRR Broadway Limited Steam Passenger Set, *14*		370
____	**81261** NYC Early Bird Special Steam Freight Set, *16-17*		380
____	**81262** UP Steam Freight Set, LionChief, *15*		400
____	**81263** CNJ Diesel Passenger Set, LionChief, *14-16*		390
____	**81264** Western Union Telegraph Steam Freight Set, *14-16*		390
____	**81266** Amtrak FT Diesel Passenger Set, LionChief, *14-15*		460
____	**81269** PRR Allegheny Hauler Steam Freight Set, *16-17*		420
____	**81270** Bethlehem Steel Steam Work Train, LionChief, *15*		340
____	**81279** Albert Hall European Steam Passenger Set, LionChief, *14-15*		430
____	**81280** Victorian Christmas Steam Passenger Set, *14*		400
____	**81284** Frosty the Snowman Steam Freight Set, LionChief, *14-16*		320
____	**81286** Lionel Junction "Little Steam" Freight Set, *14-15*		175
____	**81287** Lionel Junction UP Steam Freight Set, *14-15*		175
____	**81288** Pet Shop Diesel Freight Set, *14-16*		175
____	**81290** Thomas Kinkade Holiday Covered Bridge, *14*		70
____	**81292** Valley Central 1-D Tank Car "45003," *14-17*		45
____	**81294** LCS Sensor Track, *13-16, 18*		95
____	**81295** AT&SF 2-8-2 Locomotive "3158," LionChief, *14-16*		430

Exc Mint

		Exc	Mint
81296	GN 2-8-2 Locomotive "3123," LionChief, *14-15*	430	
81297	PRR 2-8-2 Locomotive "9633," LionChief, *14-15*	430	
81299	Chessie System 2-8-2 Locomotive "2103," LionChief, *14-15*	430	
81301	NYC 4-6-4 Locomotive "5421," LionChief, *14-15*	430	
81302	C&O 4-6-4 Locomotive "308," LionChief, *14-17*	430	
81303	UP 4-6-4 Locomotive "674," LionChief, *14-17*	430	
81304	CN 4-6-4 Locomotive "5702," LionChief, *14-17*	430	
81307	B&O 4-6-2 Locomotive "5307," LionChief, *14-17*	430	
81308	CP 4-6-2 Locomotive "2469," LionChief, *14-17*	430	
81309	SP 4-6-2 Locomotive "3106," LionChief, *14-17*	430	
81311	Alaska 4-6-2 Locomotive "652," LionChief, *14-17*	430	
81313	FasTrack Power Lockon, *15-18*	23	
81314	FasTrack Power Block Lockon, *15-18*	40	
81315	Coaling Station, *15-17*	160	
81316	Personalized Christmas Message BoxCar, *15*	80	
81317	FasTrack Accessory Activator Track Pack, *15-18*	24	
81325	LCS WiFi Module, *13-16, 18*	180	
81326	LCS Serial Converter #2, *14-16, 18*	50	
81331	Iron Arry Locomotive with Remote, LionChief, *14-15*	140	
81332	Iron Bert Locomotive with Remote, LionChief, *14-15*	140	
81373	Candy Cane Flatcar with bulkheads, *15*	60	
81395	Thomas Kinkade Christmas Passenger Set, LionChief, *14-15*	380	
81419	Alien Ooze 1-D Tank Car, *14-15*	65	
81420	PRR Truss-rod Gondola with tarp, *14-16*	65	
81422	NS Water Tower, *14*	31	
81423	Sodor Coal and Scrap Cars 2-pack, *14-16*	70	
81424	Sodor Crane Car and Work Caboose 2-pack, *14*	70	
81425	Frosty the Snowman Passenger Station, *14*	65	
81426	Frosty the Snowman Animated Gondola, *14*	75	
81427	Frosty the Snowman Aquarium Car, *14*	85	
81428	Frosty the Snowman BoxCar, *14*	65	
81430	Lionelville Shanty, *14*	22	
81432	PRR Girder Bridge, *14-15*	21	
81433	PRR Crossing Shanty, *14*	22	
81434	Pennsylvania Station Platform, *14-15*	23	
81435	N&W NS Heritage Quad Hopper with coal, *14-15*	60	
81436	Intermodal Container 4-pack, *14*	43	
81437	York Peppermint Patty Vat Car, *14-15*	70	
81439	Halloween Pumpkinheads HandCar, *14-16*	90	
81440	Western Union HandCar, *14-16*	100	
81441	North Pole Central Snowplow, CC, *16-18*	280	
81442	PRR Rotary Snowplow "1442," CC, *16, 18*	280	
81443	D&RGW Rotary Snowplow "443," CC, *16, 18*	280	
81444	PRR Tie-Jector, CC, *14-16*	200	
81445	MOW Tie-Jector, CC, *14-16*	200	
81446	Santa Fe Tie-Jector, CC, *14-16, 18*	200	
81447	NS Tie-Jector, CC, *14-16*	200	
81448	Amtrak Tie-Jector, CC, *14-16, 18*	200	
81449	Zombie Motorized Trolley, *14*	100	
81450	Polar Express Trolley, *14*	110	
81451	St. Louis Motorized Trolley, *14*	100	
81452	Neil Young Texas Special F3 AA Diesels, CC, *13-14*	650	

		Exc	Mint
____ 81453	Neil Young PRR F3 AA Diesels, CC, *13-14*		650
____ 81462	PRR Broadway Limited Add-on Baggage Car, *14-17*		70
____ 81463	CNJ Water Tower, *14-17*		31
____ 81464	CNJ Montclair Add-on Passenger Car, *14-16*		60
____ 81465	SP Flatcar with piggyback trailers, *14-16*		75
____ 81466	BN Maxi-Stack Pair, *14-16*		140
____ 81469	GN Bilevel Stock Car "65385," *14-17*		65
____ 81470	DC Comics Batman Phantom Train, *16-17*		400
____ 81475	DC Comics Batman M7 Subway Set, LionChief, *14-15*		370
____ 81479	Batman Add-on M7 Subway Car 2-pack, *14-15*		140
81480	John Deere RS-3 Diesel Freight Set, LionChief, *14-16*		320
____ 81486	NYC Patrol Flatcar with helicopter, *14-15*		65
____ 81487	Ronald Reagan Presidential BoxCar, *14-15*		70
____ 81488	Andrew Jackson Presidential BoxCar, *14-16, 18*		70
____ 81489	Warren G. Harding Presidential BoxCar, *14-16, 18*		70
____ 81490	Dwight D. Eisenhower Presidential BoxCar, *14-16*		70
____ 81491	Jersey Central Coal Dump Car, *14-15*		65
____ 81492	Strasburg RR Searchlight Car, *14*		50
____ 81493	U.S.A.F. Missile Carrying Car, *15-16*		65
____ 81494	Santa's Sleigh Rocket Fuel Tank Car, *16*		65
____ 81495	40-watt Power Supply, *15-18*		65
____ 81496	2014 Lionel Dealer Appreciation BoxCar, *2014u*		40
____ 81497	2015 Lionel Dealer Appreciation BoxCar, *2015u*		40
____ 81499	LCS Power Supply with DB9 cable, *13-16, 18*		37
____ 81500	LCS Sensor Track 1' Cable, *13-16, 18*		14
____ 81501	LCS Sensor Track 3' Cable, *13-16, 18*		15
____ 81502	LCS Sensor Track 10' Cable, *13-16, 18*		19
____ 81503	LCS Sensor Track 20' Cable, *13-16, 18*		19
____ 81504	Ann Arbor FA-2 Diesel AA Set "53/53A," CC, *14*		750
____ 81507	B&O FA-2 Diesel AA Set "817/827," CC, *14-15*		750
____ 81510	Erie FA-2 Diesel AA Set "736A/736D," CC, *14-15*		750
____ 81513	MKT FA-2 Diesel AA Set "331A/331C," CC, *14*		750
____ 81516	NYC FA-2 Diesel AA Set "1075/1078," CC, *14-15*		750
____ 81519	PRR FA-2 Diesel AA Set "9608/9609," CC, *14-15*		750
____ 81522	Ann Arbor FB2 Diesel "53B," CC, *14*		450
____ 81523	B&O FB2 Diesel "817B," CC, *14-15*		450
____ 81524	Erie FB2 Diesel "736B," CC, *14-15*		450
____ 81525	MKT FB2 Diesel "331B," CC, *14*		450
____ 81526	NYC FB2 Diesel "3327," CC, *14-15*		450
____ 81527	PRR FB2 Diesel "9608B," CC, *14*		450
____ 81528	Ann Arbor FB2 Diesel, nonpowered, *14*		350
____ 81529	B&O FB2 Diesel, nonpowered, *14-15*		350
____ 81530	Erie FB2 Diesel, nonpowered, *14-15*		350
____ 81531	MKT FB2 Diesel, nonpowered, *14*		350
____ 81532	NYC FB2 Diesel, nonpowered, *14-15*		350
____ 81533	PRR FB2 Diesel, nonpowered, *14-15*		350
____ 81534	Christmas Toys Stock Car, *14*		70
____ 81545	Operation Eagle Missile Launcher Car, CC, *15*		350
____ 81546	Operation Eagle Sound Car, CC, *15*		240
____ 81568	4th of July Parade BoxCar, *14-16*		80
____ 81596	Weathered UP 4-12-2 Locomotive "9000," CC, *13*		1400

MODERN ERA 1970-2019

Exc Mint

No.	Description	Exc	Mint
81597	Weathered B&O RF-16 Sharknose AA Diesels "855-857," CC, 13	830	___
81600	Weathered PRR RF-16 Sharknose AA Diesels "2020A-2021A," CC, 13	830	___
81603	72-watt Power Supply, LionChief, 14-18	55	___
81605	Santa Fe PS-1 Boxcar 5-pack (std O), 14	380	___
81615	UP 1-D Tank Car, 14	45	___
81617	Pet Shop 1-D Tank Car, 14-16	45	___
81619	Reading PS-1 Boxcar "109448" (std O), 14	80	___
81620	Zombie Figure Pack, 14-15	23	___
81621	John Deere Billboard Set, 15	25	___
81622	John Deere Water Tower, 15	40	___
81625	Amtrak Add-on Baggage Car, 14-16	85	___
81626	Barrel Shed, 14-16, 18	35	___
81627	Christmas Hopper Shed, 14, 16-17	45	___
81628	Grain Elevator, 15	80	___
81629	Lumber Shed Kit, 14-18	40	___
81635	Water Tower, 14	35	___
81639	LCS Accessory Switch Controller #2, 14-16, 18	120	___
81640	LCS Block Power Controller #2, 14-16, 18	120	___
81641	Layout Control System Accessory Motor Controller, 17-18	120	___
81644	Chessie System Baby Madison Passenger Car 3-pack, 14-16	270	___
81649	SP Baby Madison Passenger Car 3-pack, 14-16	270	___
81654	Philadelphia Energy Solutions 1-D Tank Car "0765," 15-18	60	___
81662	FasTrack O-31 Quarter Curved Track, 14, 16, 18	5	___
81668	Philadelphia Energy Solutions 1-D Tank Car "0771," 15-16, 18	60	___
81680	Dinosaur 1-D Tank Car, 14-16	45	___
81686	PRR GL-a 2-bay Hopper 3-pack (std O), 14	220	___
81687	LV GL-a 2-bay Hopper 2-pack (std O), 14-15	146	___
81688	CB&Q GL-a 2-bay Hopper 3-pack (std O), 14-16	220	___
81689	C&O GL-a 2-bay Hopper 3-pack (std O), 14-16	220	___
81693	Aerial Target Launcher, 15-16	90	___
81699	Polar Express Scale Twin Hopper, 15	80	___
81703	Santa Fe Hi-Cube Boxcar 2-pack (std O), 14-16	190	___
81704	Grand Trunk Hi-Cube Boxcar 2-pack (std O), 14-16	190	___
81705	Milwaukee Road Hi-Cube Boxcar 2-pack (std O), 14-16	190	___
81706	Frisco Hi-Cube Boxcar 2-pack (std O), 14-16	190	___
81707	NYC Hi-Cube Boxcar 2-pack (std O), 14-16	190	___
81708	Santa Fe Hi-Cube Boxcar "36715" (std O), 14-15	95	___
81710	Milwaukee Road Hi-Cube Boxcar "4980" (std O), 14-15	95	___
81711	Frisco Hi-Cube Boxcar "9125" (std O), 14-15	95	___
81712	NYC Hi-Cube Boxcar "67282" (std O), 14-15	95	___
81723	Postwar "3413" Mercury Capsule Launcher Car, 15	80	___
81725	UP Operating Merchandise Car, 14-15	80	___
81726	REA Operating Merchandise Car, 14-15	80	___
81729	Great Western Passenger Car Add-on 2-pack, 14	130	___
81733	Christmas BoxCar, 14	65	___
81734	FasTrack Oval Track and Power Pack, 14-17	200	___
81735	FasTrack Figure-8 Track and Power Pack, 14-17	250	___

____ **81736** Classic Lionel Catalogs Billboard Pack, *14-15*		13
____ **81737** Passenger Station, *14-15*		60
____ **81738** Lionel Auto Loader Cars 4-pack, *14-15, 17*		25
81739 Santa Fe Baby Madison Passenger Car 3-pack, *14-16*		270
____ **81744** CP Baby Madison Passenger Car 3-pack, *14-16*		270
____ **81749** Pullman Baby Madison Passenger Car 3-pack, *14-16*		270
____ **81754** NYC Baby Madison Passenger Car 3-pack, *14-16*		270
____ **81759** NYC Coach/Diner 2-pack, *14-16*		180
____ **81760** NYC Coach/Baggage Car 2-pack, *14-16*		180
____ **81763** Pullman Baby Madison Passenger Car 3-pack, *14-16*		180
____ **81764** Pullman Coach/Baggage Car 2-pack, *14, 16*		180
____ **81768** Chessie System Coach/Diner 2-pack, *14-16*		180
____ **81769** Chessie System Coach/Baggage Car 2-pack, *14-16*		180
____ **81773** SP Coach/Diner 2-pack, *14-16*		180
____ **81774** SP Coach/Baggage Car 2-pack, *14-16*		180
____ **81778** Santa Fe Coach/Diner 2-pack, *14-16*		180
____ **81779** Santa Fe Coach/Baggage Car 2-pack, *14-16*		180
____ **81783** CP Coach/Diner 2-pack, *14-16*		180
____ **81784** CP Coach/Baggage Car 2-pack, *14-16*		180
____ **81789** NH GL-a 2-bay Hopper 2-pack (std O), *14-16*		146
____ **81793** Berwind GL-a 2-bay Hopper 3-pack (std O), *14-15*		220
81800 Southern 18" Aluminum Observation/Coach Car, 2-pack (std O), *14*		320
81801 Southern 18" Aluminum Combination/Vista Dome Car, 2-pack (std O), *14*		320
____ **81806** PRR N5b Caboose "477814" (std O), *14*		95
____ **81807** Conrail N5b Caboose "22882" (std O), *14-15*		95
____ **81808** PC N5b Caboose "22802" (std O), *14-16*		95
____ **81809** LIRR N5b Caboose "2" (std O), *14-15*		95
____ **81810** Lionel Lines N5b Caboose "1402" (std O), *14-16*		95
____ **81811** Polar Express N5b Caboose, *16*		95
81812 RI 18" Aluminum Observation/Coach Car, 2-pack (std O), *14*		320
81813 RI 18" Aluminum Combination/Vista Dome Car, 2-pack (std O), *14*		320
81818 C&O 18" Aluminum Observation/Coach Car, 2-pack (std O), *14*		320
81819 C&O 18" Aluminum Combination/Vista Dome Car, 2-pack (std O), *14*		320
____ **81824** P&WV GL-a 2-bay Hopper 2-pack (std O), *14-16*		146
____ **81827** PC Round-roof Boxcar "100104" (std O), *14*		80
____ **81828** GN Round-roof Boxcar "5885" (std O), *14*		80
____ **81829** WP Round-roof Boxcar "10211" (std O), *14*		80
81830 MKT 18" Aluminum Observation/Coach Car, 2-pack (std O), *14*		320
81831 MKT 18" Aluminum Baggage/Diner Car, 2-pack (std O), *14*		320
____ **81836** Erie Double-sheathed Boxcar "71107" (std O), *14-15*		80
____ **81837** Frisco Double-sheathed Boxcar "128528" (std O), *14-15*		80
81838 CNJ Double-sheathed Boxcar "14014" (std O), *14-15*		80
____ **81839** Pacific Fright Express Steel-sided Reefer (std O), *14*		80
____ **81840** UP Ca-4 Caboose with smoke "3880" (std O), *14*		90

		Exc	Mint
81841	UP MOW Caboose "903224" (std 0), *14*		90____
81842	Wabash 18" Aluminum Dome-Observation/Coach Car, 2-pack (std 0), *14*		320 ____
81843	Wabash 18" Aluminum Combination/Vista Dome Car, 2-pack (std 0), *14*		320 ____
81858	PRR GL-a 2-bay Hopper 3-pack (std 0), *14*		220____
81862	FasTrack O-31 Curved Track 4-pack, *14, 16*		22____
81866	RI 18" Aluminum Baggage/Diner Car, 2-pack (std 0), *14*		320 ____
81869	C&O 18" Aluminum Baggage/Diner Car, 2-pack (std 0), *14*		320 ____
81871	Loggers Figure Pack, *16-18*		30____
81872	Wabash 18" Aluminum Baggage/Diner Car, 2-pack (std 0), *14*		320 ____
81875	MKT 18" Aluminum Combination/Vista Dome Car, 2-pack (std 0), *14*		320 ____
81878	Southern 18" Aluminum Baggage/Diner Car, 2-pack (std 0), *14*		320 ____
81881	SP Crane Car, CC, *14-16*		500____
81882	DT&I Crane Car, CC, *14-16*		500____
81883	CSX Crane Car, CC, *14-16*		500____
81884	Bethlehem Steel Crane Car, CC, *14*		500____
81885	MOW Crane Car, CC, *14-16*		500____
81886	SP Boom Car, RailSounds, CC, *14-16*		240____
81887	DT&I Boom Car, RailSounds, CC, *14-16*		240____
81888	CSX Boom Car, RailSounds, CC, *14-16*		240____
81889	MOW Boom Car, RailSounds, CC, *14-16*		240____
81890	Bethlehem Steel Boom Car, RailSounds, CC, *14*		240____
81891	BNSF 52' Gondola "523300" with 3-piece covers (std 0), *14*		80 ____
81892	Bethlehem Steel 52' Gondola "303022" with 3-piece covers (std 0), *14*		80 ____
81893	GTW 52' Gondola "145391" with 3-piece covers (std 0), *14*		80 ____
81894	CSX 52' Gondola "709190" with 3-piece covers (std 0), *14*		80 ____
81895	North Pole Central 52' Gondola "128925" with 3-piece covers (std 0), *14*		80 ____
81896	NYC PS-5 Flatcar "506266" with piggyback trailers (std 0), *14*		100 ____
81897	Milwaukee Road PS-5 Flatcar "64660" with piggyback trailers (std 0), *14*		100 ____
81898	Lionel PS-5 Flatcar with piggyback trailers (std 0), *14*		100 ____
81899	CP PS-5 Flatcar "301000" with piggyback trailers (std 0), *14*		100 ____
81900	UP PS-5 Flatcar "258255" with piggyback trailers (std 0), *14*		100 ____
81901	NYC Tractor and Piggyback Trailer, *14, 17*		90____
81902	Milwaukee Road Tractor and Piggyback Trailer, *14*		90____
81903	Lionel Tractor and Piggyback Trailer, *14*		90____
81904	CP Tractor and Piggyback Trailer, *14-15, 17*		90____
81905	UP Tractor and Piggyback Trailer, *14*		90____
81908	PFE Steel-sided Reefers 3-pack (std 0), *14*		240____
81912	New York Yankees BoxCar, *14*		70____
81913	St. Louis Cardinals BoxCar, *14*		70____

		Exc	Mint
____	**81914** Oakland Athletics BoxCar, *14*		70
____	**81915** San Francisco Giants BoxCar, *14*		70
____	**81916** Boston Red Sox BoxCar, *14*		70
____	**81917** Los Angeles Dodgers BoxCar, *14*		70
____	**81918** Cincinnati Reds BoxCar, *14*		70
____	**81919** San Diego Padres BoxCar, *14*		70
____	**81920** Detroit Tigers BoxCar, *14*		70
____	**81921** Atlanta Braves BoxCar, *14*		70
____	**81922** Baltimore Orioles BoxCar, *14*		70
____	**81923** Minnesota Twins BoxCar, *14*		70
____	**81924** Chicago White Sox BoxCar, *14*		70
____	**81925** Chicago Cubs BoxCar, *14*		70
____	**81926** Philadelphia Phillies BoxCar, *14*		70
____	**81927** Cleveland Indians BoxCar, *14*		70
____	**81928** New York Mets BoxCar, *14*		70
____	**81929** Toronto Blue Jays BoxCar, *14*		70
____	**81930** Miami Marlins BoxCar, *14*		70
____	**81931** Angels Baseball BoxCar, *14*		70
____	**81932** Pittsburgh Pirates BoxCar, *14*		70
____	**81933** Texas Rangers BoxCar, *14*		70
____	**81934** Milwaukee Brewers BoxCar, *14*		70
____	**81935** Houston Astros BoxCar, *14*		70
____	**81936** Colorado Rockies BoxCar, *14*		70
____	**81937** Tampa Bay Rays BoxCar, *14*		70
____	**81938** Seattle Mariners BoxCar, *14*		70
____	**81939** Washington Nationals BoxCar, *14*		70
____	**81940** Arizona Diamondbacks BoxCar, *14*		70
____	**81941** Kansas City Royals BoxCar, *14*		70
____	**81944** Rotary Beacon, yellow, *14-16, 18*		85
____	**81945** Polar Express Scale Coach, *14*		210
____	**81946** FasTrack O-36 Remote Switch, right-hand, *14-16, 18*		110
____	**81947** FasTrack O-36 Remote Switch, left-hand, *14-16, 18*		110
____	**81948** FasTrack O-48 Remote Switch, right-hand, *14-16, 18*		120
____	**81949** FasTrack O-48 Remote Switch, left-hand, *14-16*		120
____	**81950** FasTrack O-60 Remote Switch, right-hand, *14-16, 18*		120
____	**81951** FasTrack O-60 Remote Switch, left-hand, *14-16, 18*		120
____	**81952** FasTrack O-72 Remote Switch, right-hand, *14-16, 18*		120
____	**81953** FasTrack O-72 Remote Switch, left-hand, *14-16, 18*		120
____	**81954** FasTrack O-72 Remote Switch, wye, *14-16, 18*		120
____	**81968** Halloween Pacific Fright Express Caboose (std O), *14*		90
____	**81969** PRR 18" Aluminum Parlor/Coach Car, 2-pack (std O), *14-15*		320
____	**81972** B&O 18" Aluminum Baggage/Sleeper Car, 2-pack (std O), *14*		320
____	**81975** SP 18" Aluminum Sleeper/Coach Car, 2-pack (std O), *14-15*		320
____	**81978** UP 18" Aluminum Sleeper/Coach Car, 2-pack (std O), *14-15*		320
____	**81981** KCS 18" Aluminum Sleeper/Coach Car, 2-pack (std O), *14*		320
____	**81984** Postwar "1887" Christmas Flatcar with reindeer, *14*		70

Exc Mint

81985 Postwar "6428" Christmas Mail Car, *14*		60____
81986 Christmas Wish 1-D Tank Car, *14*		60____
81987 Angela Trotta Thomas "Santa's Letter" BoxCar, *14*		65____
81988 Angela Trotta Thomas Christmas Billboard Pack, *14*		15____
81990 Christmas Gondola with reindeer feed vats, *14*		65____
81992 Santa Claus Bobbing Head BoxCar, *14*		65____
81993 North Pole Central Santa Finder Searchlight Car, *14*		55____
81999 PRR Gondola with Christmas gifts and trees, *14*		65____
82000 PRR Christmas Crane Car, *14*		75____
82001 Merry & Bright Hot Cocoa Car, *14*		70____
82002 Old St. Nick Operating Billboard, *14, 16*		60____
82003 Christmas Blinking Water Tower, *14*		35____
82005 Christmas Wreath Clock Tower, *14, 16-17*		43____
82008 Bungalow House, *15-17*		80____
82009 Suburban House, *15-16*		80____
82010 Joe's Bait & Tackle Shop, *15-16*		65____
82011 Keystone Cafe, *15-16*		80____
82012 Single Floodlight Tower, *15-18*		75____
82013 Double Floodlight Tower, *15-18*		90____
82014 Postwar "192" Control Tower, *15-16*		100____
82015 Wind Turbine, *15-18*		80____
82016 Oil Pump, *15-18*		60____
82017 Lionel Art Operating Billboard, *15-18*		70____
82018 Track Gang, *15-16*		100____
82020 Burning Switch Tower, *15-17*		130____
82021 Bascule Bridge, *15*		450____
82022 Lionel Steel Gantry Crane, CC, *15-18*		400____
82023 Operating Sawmill, CC, *15-17*		350____
82024 Postwar "164" Log Loader, *15*		340____
82026 Postwar "497" Coaling Station, *15-17*		300____
82028 Postwar "352" Icing Station, *15-17*		150____
82029 Culvert Loader, CC, *15-18*		300____
82030 Culvert Unloader, CC, *15-18*		300____
82033 MOW Trackside Crane, CC, *16-17*		600____
82034 Loading Station, *16*		350____
82035 Work House, crane sounds, *16-18*		150____
82036 Luxury Diner, *15-17*		80____
82038 8" Female Pigtail Power Cable, *16-17*		10____
82039 36" Male Pigtail Power Cable, *16-18*		11____
82043 Plug-n-play Power Cable Extension, *16-18*		16____
82045 Plug-n-play Control Cable Extension, *16-18*		20____
82046 36" Power Tap Cable, *16-18*		16____
82047 Lionel Lines Log Dump Car, *15-16*		65____
82048 AT&SF Ice Car, *15-17*		75____
82049 Santa's Work Shoppe Log Dump Car, *16*		65____
82050 Santa's Work Shoppe Sawmill, *16-18*		240____
82051 North Pole Central Icing Station, *16-17*		150____
82052 PFE Ice Car, *15-17*		75____
82053 North Pole Central Icing Car, *16-17*		75____
82054 Weyerhaeuser Log Dump Car, *15-17*		65____
82055 Bethlehem Steel Trackside Crane, CC, *16-18*		600____
82056 Operating Freight Station, *18*		110____
82064 Halloween Operating Billboard, *15-18*		80____

		Exc Mint
____ **82066**	PRR Log Dump Car, *15*	65
____ **82067**	Lionel Lines Coal Dump Car, *15-17*	65
____ **82068**	NS Coal Dump Car, *15*	65
____ **82069**	Conrail Coal Dump Car, *15-17*	65
____ **82072**	Philadelphia Quartz Hopper "755," *15-18*	50
____ **82073**	CN Ore Car, *15-17*	50
____ **82074**	SP 1-D Tank Car, *15-17*	50
____ **82075**	NYC Waffle-sided BoxCar, *15-17*	50
____ **82076**	Chessie System Gondola with containers, *16-18*	50
____ **82077**	D&H Hi-Cube BoxCar, *16*	50
____ **82078**	NP 1-D Tank Car, *16*	50
____ **82079**	UP Wood-sided Reefer, *16*	50
____ **82080**	C&NW 3-D Tank Car, *16-18*	50
____ **82081**	CSX Auto Carrier, *16-18*	50
____ **82082**	NS Flatcar with pipes, *16-18*	50
____ **82083**	Central of Georgia Gondola with cable reels, *16*	50
____ **82084**	Virginian BoxCar, *16-18*	50
____ **82085**	AT&SF Waffle-sided BoxCar, *16-17*	50
____ **82086**	MKT Reefer, *16*	50
____ **82087**	WP Depressed Flatcar with generator, *16-18*	50
____ **82088**	Log Pack, *16-18*	10
____ **82091**	PRR Tie Work Car "82091," *14-16*	75
____ **82092**	MOW Tie Work Car "77," *14-16*	75
____ **82093**	AT&SF Tie Work Car "82093," *14-16*	75
____ **82094**	NS Tie Work Car "51," *14-16*	75
____ **82095**	Amtrak Tie Work Car "67," *14-16*	75
____ **82096**	Lionel Steel Culvert Gondola, *15-16*	65
____ **82097**	Bucyrus-Erie Gantry Crane, CC, *15-18*	400
____ **82098**	Bucyrus-Erie Culvert Gondola, *15*	65
____ **82099**	Zombie Apocalypse Survivors GP38 Diesel Freight Set, LionChief, *15*	440
____ **82100**	Polar Express Hero Boy's Home, *16-17*	90
____ **82101**	Postwar "6512" Mercury Capsule Astronaut Car, *15-16*	80
____ **82102**	Lumberjacks, *15-16*	65
____ **82103**	Playground Swing, *15-16*	75
____ **82104**	Playground Playtime, *15-16*	100
____ **82105**	Tire Swing, *15-16*	100
____ **82106**	Pony Ride, *15-17*	75
____ **82107**	Tug-of-War, *15-17*	65
____ **82108**	Hobo Campfire, *15*	100
____ **82110**	Extended Truss Bridge, *15-18*	300
____ **82111**	Lionel Industrial Coal 2-bay Hopper "28111," *15-17*	60
____ **82112**	B&M Alco S2 Diesel Switcher "1260," CC, *15*	650
____ **82113**	B&M Alco S2 Diesel Switcher "1263," CC, *15*	650
____ **82114**	CB&Q Alco S2 Diesel Switcher "9306," CC, *15*	650
____ **82115**	CB&Q Alco S2 Diesel Switcher "9308," CC, *15*	650
____ **82116**	CP Alco S2 Diesel Switcher "7020," CC, *15*	650
____ **82117**	CP Alco S2 Diesel Switcher "7024," CC, *15*	650
____ **82118**	GM&O Alco S2 Diesel Switcher "1001," CC, *15*	650
____ **82119**	GM&O Alco S2 Diesel Switcher "1007," CC, *15*	650
____ **82120**	GN Alco S2 Diesel Switcher "2," CC, *15*	650
____ **82121**	GN Alco S2 Diesel Switcher "5," CC, *15*	650
____ **82122**	PRR Alco S2 Diesel Switcher "5648," CC, *15*	650

	Exc	Mint
82123 PRR Alco S2 Diesel Switcher "5652," CC, *15*	650	
82124 South Buffalo Alco S2 Diesel Switcher "102," CC, *15*	650	
82125 South Buffalo Alco S2 Diesel Switcher "104," CC, *15*	650	
82126 UP Alco S2 Diesel Switcher "1111," CC, *15*	650	
82127 UP Alco S2 Diesel Switcher "1138," CC, *15*	650	
82128 C&O GP30 Diesel Locomotive "3011," CC, *15*	650	
82129 C&O GP30 Diesel Locomotive "3018," CC, *15*	650	
82130 EMD Demonstrator GP30 Diesel Locomotive "1962," CC, *15*	650	
82131 TP&W GP30 Diesel Locomotive "700," CC, *15*	650	
82132 PC GP30 Diesel Locomotive "2202," CC, *15*	650	
82133 PC GP30 Diesel Locomotive "2246," CC, *15*	650	
82134 GM&O GP30 Diesel Locomotive "501," CC, *15*	650	
82135 GM&O GP30 Diesel Locomotive "521," CC, *15*	650	
82136 N&W GP30 Diesel Locomotive "522," black, CC, *15*	650	
82137 N&W GP30 Diesel Locomotive "542," blue, CC, *15*	650	
82138 MILW GP30 Diesel Locomotive "344," CC, *15*	650	
82139 MILW GP30 Diesel Locomotive "350," CC, *15*	650	
82140 Southern GP30 Diesel Locomotive "2594," CC, *15*	650	
82141 Southern GP30 Diesel Locomotive "2601," CC, *15*	650	
82142 UP GP30 Diesel Locomotive "803" CC, *15*	650	
82143 UP GP30 Diesel Locomotive "830," CC, *15*	650	
82146 Soo Line PS-1 Boxcar "45025," *15*	80	
82147 N&W PS-1 Boxcar "44292," *15*	80	
82148 GB&W PS-1 Boxcar "777," *15*	80	
82150 Duluth, South Shore & Atlantic PS-1 Boxcar "15091," *15*	80	
82163 B&O NW2 Diesel Locomotive "9555," LionChief, *15-16*	300	
82164 BN NW2 Diesel Locomotive "546," LionChief, *15-16*	300	
82165 CB&Q NW2 Diesel Locomotive "9412A," LionChief, *15-16*	300	
82166 Southern NW2 Diesel Locomotive "2401A," LionChief, *15-16*	300	
82171 BNSF GP20 Diesel Locomotive "2050," LionChief, *15-17*	340	
82172 NYC GP20 Diesel Locomotive "2102," LionChief, *15-17*	340	
82173 NS GP20 Diesel Locomotive "10," LionChief, *15-17*	340	
82174 NYS&W GP20 Diesel Locomotive "1800," LionChief, *15-17*	340	
82175 Virginian Rectifier Locomotive "135," LionChief, *15-17*	340	
82176 N&W Rectifier Locomotive "235," LionChief, *15-17*	340	
82177 NH Rectifier Locomotive "306," LionChief, *15-17*	340	
82178 Conrail Rectifier Locomotive "4605," LionChief, *15-17*	340	
82179 PRR Rectifier Locomotive "4466," LionChief, *15-17*	340	
82184 PRR B6sb 0-4-0 Locomotive "1670," CC, *15*	700	
82185 D&RGW Bicentennial Gondola with canisters, *16*	50	
82186 Patriot Chemicals 1-D Tank Car "2015," *15, 18*	60	
82187 Bethlehem Steel Water Tower, *15*	35	
82188 Metro-North M7 Subway Set, LionChief, *15*	350	
82192 MTA LIRR M7 Set, LionChief, *18*	400	
82196 Metro-North Add-on 2-pack, *15*	130	

		Exc	Mint
____	**82199** MTA LIRR Add-on Passenger 2-pack, *18*		175
____	**82202** UP Big Boy Commemorative CA-4 Caboose, *15*		95
____	**82203** Remote Control Box, *15-18*		25
____	**82205** BNSF Golden Swoosh ES44AC Diesel Locomotive "7695," CC, *15*		650
____	**82206** N&W 2-6-6-4 Locomotive "1218," CC, *16*		1000
____	**82207** Iowa Interstate/Rock Island ES44AC Diesel Locomotive "513," CC, *15*		650
____	**82208** N&W 2-6-6-4 Locomotive "1212," CC, *16*		1000
____	**82209** NS ES44AC Diesel Locomotive "8056," CC, *15*		650
____	**82210** NS ES44AC Diesel Locomotive "8065," CC, *15*		650
____	**82213** KCS ES44AC Diesel Locomotive "4696," CC, *15*		650
____	**82214** KCS ES44AC Diesel Locomotive "4685," CC, *15*		650
____	**82215** AT&SF ES44AC Diesel Locomotive "440," CC, *15*		650
____	**82216** AT&SF ES44AC Diesel Locomotive "444," CC, *15*		650
____	**82218** FEC ES44AC Diesel Locomotive "802," CC, *15*		650
____	**82219** FEC ES44AC Diesel Locomotive "804," CC, *15*		650
____	**82220** SP Alco PA AA Diesel Locomotive Set "6006, 6015," CC, *15*		1000
____	**82223** D&RGW Alco PA AA Diesel Locomotive Set "6001, 6003," CC, *15*		1000
____	**82226** LV Alco PA AA Diesel Locomotive Set "601, 602," CC, *15*		1000
____	**82229** MP Alco PA AA Diesel Locomotive Set "8018, 8018," CC, *15*		1000
____	**82232** NKP Alco PA AA Diesel Locomotive Set "190, 189," CC, *15*		1000
____	**82235** PRR Alco PA AA Diesel Locomotive Set "5070A, 5071A," CC, *15*		1000
____	**82238** Southern Alco PA AA Diesel Locomotive Set "6900, 6901," CC, *15*		1000
____	**82241** Wabash Alco PA AA Diesel Locomotive Set "1020, 1020A," CC, *15*		1000
____	**82244** SP Alco PB Diesel Locomotive, CC, *15*		530
____	**82245** B&O 2-6-6-4 Locomotive "7620," CC, *16*		1000
____	**82246** D&RGW Alco PB Diesel Locomotive, CC, *15*		530
____	**82247** AT&SF 2-6-6-4 Locomotive "1798," CC, *16*		1000
____	**82248** LV Alco PB Diesel Locomotive, CC, *15*		530
____	**82249** Bethlehem Steel Boom Car, *15*		55
____	**82250** MP Alco PB Diesel Locomotive, CC, *15*		530
____	**82251** Zombie Animated Gondola, *15*		75
____	**82252** Nickel Plate Road Alco PB Diesel Locomotive, CC, *15*		530
____	**82253** John Deere 1-D Tank Car, *15*		65
____	**82254** PRR Alco PB Diesel Locomotive, CC, *15*		530
____	**82256** Southern Alco PB Diesel Locomotive, CC, *15*		530
____	**82258** Wabash Alco PB Diesel Locomotive, CC, *15*		530
____	**82260** PC 50' DD Boxcar "267210" (std O), *16-17*		80
____	**82261** Frisco 50' DD Boxcar "7002" (std O), *16-17*		80
____	**82263** PRR Scrapyard, *16-17*		130
____	**82265** MOW Welding Car, *15-16*		80
____	**82266** CN 4-6-0 Steam Locomotive "1158," CC, *15*		900
____	**82267** C&NW 4-6-0 Steam Locomotive "1385," CC, *15*		900
____	**82268** Frisco 4-6-0 Steam Locomotive "633," CC, *15*		900
____	**82269** NP 4-6-0 Steam Locomotive "1382," CC, *15*		900
____	**82270** SP 4-6-0 Steam Locomotive "2353," CC, *15*		900

		Exc	Mint
82271	NYC 4-6-0 Steam Locomotive "1258," CC, *15*		900___
82272	NH 4-6-0 Steam Locomotive "816," CC, *15*		900___
82273	ACL 4-6-0 Steam Locomotive "1031," CC, *15*		900___
82274	Chessie SD40 Diesel Locomotive "7500," CC, *15*		650___
82275	Chessie SD40 Diesel Locomotive "7593," CC, *15*		650___
82276	BN SD40 Diesel Locomotive "6314," CC, *15*		650___
82277	BN SD40 Diesel Locomotive "6320," CC, *15*		650___
82278	GT SD40 Diesel Locomotive "5922," CC, *15*		650___
82279	GT SD40 Diesel Locomotive "5927," CC, *15*		650___
82280	MP SD40 Diesel Locomotive "3007," CC, *15*		650___
82281	MP SD40 Diesel Locomotive "3014," CC, *15*		650___
82282	Conrail SD40 Diesel Locomotive "6308," CC, *15*		650___
82283	Conrail SD40 Diesel Locomotive "6350," CC, *15*		650___
82284	Conrail SD40 Diesel Locomotive "6300," CC, *15*		650___
82285	SP SD40 Diesel Locomotive "8402," CC, *15*		650___
82286	SP SD40 Diesel Locomotive "8451," CC, *15*		650___
82287	SP Daylight SD40 Diesel Locomotive "7342," CC, *15*		650___
82288	Clinchfield SD40 Diesel Locomotive "3000," CC, *15*		650___
82289	Clinchfield SD40 Diesel Locomotive "3006," CC, *15*		650___
82290	AT&SF FT AA Diesel Locomotive Set, LionChief, *15-17*		500___
82293	ACL FT AA Diesel Locomotive Set, LionChief, *15-17*		500___
82296	Erie FT AA Diesel Locomotive Set, LionChief, *15-17*		500___
82299	D&RGW FT AA Diesel Locomotive Set, LionChief, *15-17*		500___
82302	AT&SF FT B Unit, LionChief, *15-17*		280___
82303	ACL FT B Unit, LionChief, *15-17*		280___
82304	Erie FT B Unit, LionChief, *15-17*		280___
82305	D&RGW FT B Unit, LionChief, *15-17*		280___
82307	PRR B6sb 0-4-0 Locomotive "5244," CC, *15*		700___
82308	PRR B6sb 0-4-0 Locomotive "3233," CC, *15*		700___
82309	PRR-Reading Seashore Lines B6sb 0-4-0 Locomotive "6096," CC, *15*		700___
82310	LIRR B6sb 0-4-0 Locomotive "2015," CC, *15*		700___
82311	Polar RR B6sb 0-4-0 Locomotive "2515," CC, *15*		700___
82312	UP ACF 40-ton Stock Car "48133," *15*		80___
82313	GN ACF 40-ton Stock Car "55989," *15*		80___
82314	MILW ACF 40-ton Stock Car "104954," *15*		80___
82315	NP ACF 40-ton Stock Car "84161," *15*		80___
82316	NKP ACF 40-ton Stock Car "42040," *15*		80___
82324	Chessie Diesel Freight Set, LionChief, *15*		400___
82330	U.S.A.F. Minuteman Missile Launcher Car, CC, *15*		350___
82331	U.S.A.F. Missile Launch Sound Car, CC, *15*		240___
82333	Illuminated Hopper Shed, *15-18*		45___
82334	Ulysses S. Grant Presidential BoxCar, *15*		70___
82335	Franklin D. Roosevelt Presidential BoxCar, *15*		70___
82340	N&W Y6b 2-8-8-2 Steam Locomotive "2171," CC, *15*		2000___
82341	N&W Y6b 2-8-8-2 Steam Locomotive "2175," CC, *15*		2000___
82342	N&W Y6b 2-8-8-2 Steam Locomotive "2195," CC, *15*		2000___
82343	Lionel Steel Welding Car, *15*		80___
82344	WM Wood Chip Hopper "2945," *15-16*		65___
82349	Friday the 13th Jason Voorhees BoxCar, *16*		85___
82394	UP Auxiliary Water Tender "907853," CC, *15*		380___
82395	UP Auxiliary Water Tender "907856," CC, *15*		380___

		Exc	Mint
	82396 UP Commemorative Auxiliary Water Tender "809," CC, *15*		380
	82410 Virginian 2-bay Hopper "13168," *16-17*		60
	82411 N&W 2-bay Hopper "113733," *15-17*		60
	82412 Reading Birney Trolley, *15, 18*		100
	82413 Lionel Transit Birney Trolley, *15*		100
	82414 CNJ 4-6-0 Camelback Locomotive "777," LionChief, *15-16*		440
	82415 DL&W 4-6-0 Camelback Locomotive "1035," LionChief, *15-17*		440
	82416 LV 4-6-0 Camelback Locomotive "1602," LionChief, *15-17*		440
	82417 Philadelphia & Reading 4-6-0 Camelback Locomotive "675," LionChief, *15-17*		440
	82418 Erie 4-6-0 Camelback Locomotive "861," LionChief, *15-17*		440
	82419 UP 8-door Hi-Cube BoxCar, *16*		100
	82420 SP 8-door Hi-Cube BoxCar, *16*		100
	82421 B&O 8-door Hi-Cube BoxCar, *16*		100
	82422 PRR 8-door Hi-Cube BoxCar, *16*		100
	82423 C&NW 8-door Hi-Cube BoxCar, *16*		100
	82424 Chessie 8-door Hi-Cube BoxCar, *16*		100
	82425 PC 8-door Hi-Cube BoxCar, *16*		100
	82426 RI 8-door Hi-Cube BoxCar, *16*		100
	82427 Patriot U36B Diesel Freight Set, LionChief, *15-17*		360
	82436 Pennsylvania Keystone GP38 Diesel Freight Set, LionChief, *15*		450
	82442 Five-Star General Old-Time Steam Set, LionChief, *17-18*		400
	82447 Sheriff & Outlaw Car, *17*		80
	82453 Amtrak F40PH Diesel Phase II "200," CC, *16*		550
	82454 Amtrak F40PH Diesel Phase II "207," CC, *16*		550
	82455 Amtrak F40PH Diesel Phase III "364," CC, *16*		550
	82456 Amtrak F40PH Diesel Phase III "388," CC, *16*		550
	82460 CSX F40PH Diesel "9998," CC, *16*		550
	82461 CSX F40PH Diesel "9999," CC, *16*		550
	82473 N&W Early Era Inspection Vehicle, CC, *15*		200
	82474 BN Early Era Inspection Vehicle, CC, *15*		200
	82475 Bethlehem Steel Early Era Inspection Vehicle, CC, *15*		200
	82476 NH Early Era Inspection Vehicle, CC, *15*		200
	82477 Virginian Early Era Inspection Vehicle, CC, *15*		200
	82478 Reading Early Era Inspection Vehicle, CC, *15*		200
	82486 Weathered Virginian USRA Y-3 2-8-8-2 Locomotive "737," CC, *14*		1450
	82487 Weathered AT&SF USRA Y-3 2-8-8-2 Locomotive "1797," CC, *14*		1450
	82488 Weathered N&W USRA Y-3 2-8-8-2 Locomotive "2029," CC, *14*		1450
	82489 MILW 18" Aluminum Coach/Dining Car 2-pack, *14*		320
	82489 MILW Olympian 18" Aluminum Passenger Car 2-pack, *14-15*		320
	82494 Turbo Missile Launch FlatCar, *15*		60
	82495 D&RGW Scrapyard, *16-18*		130
	82498 Polar Express Mail Car, *16-17*		70
	82500 Polar Express Covered Bridge, *15*		70

		Exc	Mint
82501	Providence & Worcester 89' Auto Carrier "190091," *15-16*	110	
82502	C&NW 89' Auto Carrier "962255," *15-16*	110	
82503	Chessie 89' Auto Carrier "255798," *15-16*	110	
82504	TFM 89' Auto Carrier "987408," *15-16*	110	
82505	BNSF 89' Auto Carrier "212878," *15-16*	110	
82506	UP 89' Auto Carrier "992579," *15-16*	110	
82508	NYC Milk Car "6589" (std O), *16*	80	
82510	Polar Express Aquarium Car, *16*	85	
82512	Polar Express Work Caboose with presents, *15*	85	
82514	Polar Express Reindeer Stock Car, *15*	90	
82518	Moon Pie BoxCar, *15*	85	
82528	NYC Empire State Express Steam Passenger Set, CC, *15*	1950	
82534	NYC J3a 4-6-4 Hudson Locomotive "5429," tender, *15*	1500	
82535	NYC J3a 4-6-4 Hudson Locomotive "5426," tender, *15*	1500	
82536	NYC J3a 4-6-4 Hudson Locomotive "5429," tender, *15*	1500	
82537	NYC J3a 4-6-4 Hudson Locomotive "5426," tender, *15*	1500	
82543	Postwar "943" Exploding Ammunition Dump, *15-16, 18*	50	
82544	Missile Firing Range, *15-16*	65	
82545	Santa's Helper Steam Freight Set, *16-17*	340	
82550	Wabash 21" Streamlined Passenger Car 4-pack, *15*	600	
82555	Wabash 21" Streamlined Passenger Car 2-pack, *15*	300	
82558	Southern 21" Streamlined Passenger Car 4-pack, *15*	600	
82563	Southern 21" Streamlined Passenger Car 4-pack, *15*	300	
82566	RI 21" Streamlined Passenger Car 4-pack, *15*	600	
82571	RI 21" Streamlined Passenger Car 4-pack, *15*	300	
82574	Texas Special 21" Streamlined Passenger Car 4-pack, *15*	600	
82579	Texas Special 21" Streamlined Passenger Car 4-pack, *15*	300	
82582	C&O 21" Streamlined Passenger Car 4-pack, *15*	600	
82587	C&O 21" Streamlined Passenger Car 4-pack, *15*	300	
82590	Amtrak 21" Passenger Car 4-pack, *16*	600	
82595	Amtrak 21" Passenger Car 2-pack, *16*	300	
82598	NYC Empire State Passenger Car Add-on 2-pack, *15*	300	
82611	PRR GL-a 2-bay Hopper 3-pack, *15*	220	
82621	Buffalo Creek Flour PS-1 Boxcar "2366," *15*	80	
82622	U.S. Army PS-1 Boxcar "26875, *15*	80	
82623	West India Fruit & Steamship Co. PS-1 Boxcar "321," *15*	80	
82624	Linde Air Products PS-1 Boxcar "3019," *15*	80	
82625	Air Reduction Products PS-1 Boxcar "100," *15*	80	
82629	PRR N5b Caboose "478883," *15-16*	95	
82630	PRR N5b Caboose with trainphone antenna, *15-16*	95	
82631	B&M N5b Caboose "C-*16*," *15-16*	95	
82639	MILW Milk Car "370" (std O), *16*	80	
82640	UTLX 30,000-Gallon 1-D Tank Car 3-pack, *15*	250	
82644	Philadelphia Energy Solutions 1-D Tank Car 3-pack, *15*	250	

		Exc	Mint
____	**82648** Midwest Ethanol Transport 1-D Tank Car 3-pack, *15*		250
____	**82652** Global Ethanol Transport 1-D Tank Car 3-pack, *15*		250
____	**82656** Conrail 60' Boxcar "216010," *15-17*		90
____	**82657** WM 60' Boxcar "38020," *15-17*		90
____	**82658** BN 60' Boxcar "355145," *15-17*		90
____	**82659** RI 60' Boxcar "33825," *15-17*		90
____	**82660** N&W 60' Boxcar "600949," *15-17*		90
____	**82661** P&LE PS-5 Gondola and PS-4 FlatCar, *15-16*		175
____	**82664** B&LE PS-5 Gondola and PS-4 FlatCar, *15-16*		175
____	**82667** DT&I PS-5 Gondola and PS-4 FlatCar, *15-16*		175
____	**82670** Conrail PS-5 Gondola and PS-4 FlatCar, *15-16*		175
____	**82674** UP Bathtub Gondola 2-pack, *15*		140
____	**82677** Strasburg 3-D Tank Car, *16*		656
____	**82678** Angela Trotta Thomas Christmas BoxCar, *16*		85
____	**82683** Batman and Flash Justice League Boxcar 2-pack, *15-16*		170
____	**82684** Superman and Green Lantern Justice League Boxcar 2-pack, *15-16*		170
____	**82685** New York Giants Cooperstown BoxCar, *15*		85
____	**82686** Washington Senators Cooperstown BoxCar, *15*		85
____	**82687** Detroit Tigers Cooperstown BoxCar, *15*		85
____	**82688** Pittsburgh Pirates Cooperstown BoxCar, *15*		85
____	**82689** Operation Eagle Missile Carrying Car, *15-17*		65
____	**82690** Coca-Cola Anniversary Bottle BoxCar, *15*		90
____	**82691** Christmas BoxCar, *15*		75
____	**82693** Santa's Helper Crane, *15*		85
____	**82694** UP LionMaster 4-6-6-4 Challenger Locomotive "3985," CC, *15*		1000
____	**82695** UP LionMaster 4-6-6-4 Challenger Locomotive "3977," CC, *15*		1000
____	**82696** UP LionMaster 4-6-6-4 Challenger Locomotive "3989," CC, *15*		1000
____	**82697** D&RGW LionMaster 4-6-6-4 Challenger Locomotive "3803," CC, *15*		1000
____	**82698** WM LionMaster 4-6-6-4 Challenger Locomotive "1201," CC, *15*		1000
____	**82699** Angela Trotta Thomas Lionelville Christmas BoxCar, *15*		75
____	**82701** Escaping Snowmen HandCar, *15*		90
____	**82702** Ontario Northland PS-4 Flatcar with covered load, *15*		90
____	**82703** BN PS-4 Flatcar with covered load, *15*		90
____	**82704** D&RGW PS-4 Flatcar with covered load, *15*		90
____	**82705** Reading PS-4 Flatcar with covered load, *15*		90
____	**82706** Southern PS-4 Flatcar with covered load, *15*		90
____	**82708** Christmas Gingerbread Shanty, *16-18*		40
____	**82709** PRR Silver & Gold Ore Car 2-pack, *16-17*		130
____	**82710** PRR Ice Breaker Tunnel Car, *16-17*		65
____	**82711** Santa's Favorites Transparent Gift Car, *16*		85
____	**82713** Christmas Music BoxCar, *15*		80
____	**82716** Mickey's Holiday to Remember Freight Set, *16*		400
____	**82717** W. E. Disney Girder Bridge, *16-18*		33
____	**82718** Disney Villains Hi-Cube Boxcar 2-pack, *16-18*		160
____	**82721** Dumbo 75th Anniversary BoxCar, *16-17*		85
____	**82726** Postwar Alco FA Diesel Green Passenger Set, *17-18*		550
____	**82728** Layout Control System Switch Throw Monitor, *17-18*		100

		Exc	Mint
82734	New York Yankees Cooperstown BoxCar, *15*	85	___
82735	Polar Express Conductor Gateman, *18*	120	___
82736	North Pole Central Water Tower, *15*	40	___
82737	Coca-Cola Santa BoxCar, *15*	85	___
82739	North Pole Central BoxCar, *16-18*	80	___
82740	Winter Wonderland Aquarium Car, *15*	95	___
82741	Christmas Tinsel Vat Car, *16*	70	___
82742	Candy Mountain Christmas Quad Hopper, *16-17*	65	___
82743	Santa's Reindeer Station Platform, *15*	50	___
82744	Santa Claus Automatic Gateman, *16-17*	100	___
82745	Christmas Cocoa Barrel Shed, *15*	50	___
82746	Christmas Floodlight Tower, *16*	75	___
82747	Christmas Red Arch Under Bridge, *16*	30	___
82748	Silver Bell Casting Co. Hopper, *15*	70	___
82749	PRR GG1 Electric "4935," CC, *16*	1400	___
82751	PRR GG1 Electric "4913," CC, *16*	1400	___
82752	PRR GG1 Electric "4877," CC, *16*	1400	___
82754	PC GG1 Electric "4828," CC, *16*	1400	___
82755	Amtrak GG1 Electric "926," CC, *16*	1400	___
82757	CP SD90MAC Diesel "9116," CC, *16*	650	___
82758	CP SD90MAC Diesel "9130," CC, *16*	650	___
82759	NS SD90MAC Diesel "7230," CC, *16*	650	___
82760	NS SD90MAC Diesel "7245," CC, *16*	650	___
82761	UP SD90MAC Diesel "8130," CC, *16*	650	___
82762	UP SD90MAC Diesel "8133," CC, *16*	650	___
82763	UP SD90MAC Diesel "8025," CC, *16*	650	___
82764	UP SD90MAC Diesel "8055," CC, *16*	650	___
82765	Indiana SD90MAC Diesel "9003," CC, *16*	650	___
82766	Indiana SD90MAC Diesel "9006," CC, *16*	650	___
82767	C&O 2-6-6-6 Locomotive "1601," CC, *16*	2200	___
82768	C&O 2-6-6-6 Locomotive "1604," CC, *16*	2200	___
82769	C&O 2-6-6-6 Locomotive "1608," CC, *16*	2200	___
82770	Virginian 2-6-6-6 Locomotive "906," CC, *16*	2200	___
82825	CP GP38 Diesel Locomotive "3019," *16-17*	340	___
82826	CSX GP38 Diesel Locomotive "2145," *16-17*	340	___
82827	SP GP38 Diesel Locomotive "4846," *16-18*	340	___
82828	UP GP38 Diesel Locomotive "905," *16-17*	340	___
82840	AT&SF PS-4 Flatcar with trailer (std O), *16*	110	___
82841	E-L PS-4 Flatcar with trailer (std O), *16*	110	___
82842	GN PS-4 Flatcar with trailer (std O), *16*	110	___
82843	WM PS-4 Flatcar with trailer (std O), *16*	110	___
82844	PRR PS-4 Flatcar with trailer (std O), *16*	110	___
82845	B&O Truck with 40' trailer, *16*	90	___
82846	MILW Truck with 40' trailer, *16-17*	90	___
82847	MKT Truck with 40' trailer, *16-17*	90	___
82848	Logging Disconnect with load, *16*	65	___
82849	Logging Disconnect with load 2-pack, *16*	125	___
82850	MILW 40' Flatcar with lumber (std O), *16-17*	90	___
82851	NP 40' Flatcar with lumber (std O), *16-17*	90	___
82852	Meadow River 40' Flatcar with lumber (std O), *16-17*	90	___
82853	Pickering 40' Flatcar with lumber (std O), *16-17*	90	___
82854	PRR 40' Flatcar with lumber (std O), *16*	90	___
82855	ADM Unibody Tank Car "190516" (std O), *16*	75	___

		Mint
82856	GATX Unibody Tank Car "4415" (std O), *16*	75
82857	AFPX Unibody Tank Car "413303" (std O), *16*	75
82858	Shell Unibody Tank Car "82858" (std O), *16*	85
82859	Engelhard Unibody Tank Car "24586" (std O), *16*	75
82860	PC PS-5 Gondola "557065" (std O), *16*	90
82861	E-L PS-5 Gondola "14552" (std O), *16*	90
82862	Frisco PS-5 Gondola "61442" (std O), *16*	90
82863	CB&Q PS-5 Gondola "82050" (std O), *16*	90
82864	NYC PS-5 Gondola "712603" (std O), *16*	90
82865	PRR N5b Caboose "5017" (std O), *16*	90
82866	PRR N5b Caboose "477746" (std O), *16*	90
82867	PRR N5b Caboose "477625" (std O), *16*	90
82868	NH N5 Caboose "C-507" (std O), *16*	90
82869	IR Sensor Track O Gauge Tubular Compatible, *17-18*	95
82870	Loading Ramp, *16-18*	25
82872	Loader/Unloader Workers Figure Pack, *16-18*	30
82873	Loggers Cabin, sound, *16*	140
82874	Early Intermodal Work House, sound, *16-18*	130
82877	Thomas Kinkade Polar Express BoxCar, *16*	85
82878	Smithsonian BoxCar, *16*	85
82879	Coca-Cola Christmas BoxCar, *16-17*	85
82883	Legacy 360-watt PowerMaster, *16, 18*	220
82884	Wabash 21" Streamlined Dining Car, StationSounds, *15*	300
82885	Southern 21" Streamlined Dining Car, StationSounds, *15*	300
82886	RI 21" Streamlined Dining Car, StationSounds, *15*	300
82887	Texas Special 21" Streamlined Dining Car, StationSounds, *15*	300
82888	C&O 21" Streamlined Dining Car, StationSounds, *15*	300
82889	Amtrak 21" Diner, StationSounds, *16*	300
82890	NYC Empire State Express Diner, StationSounds, *15*	300
82906	Pluto Walking Brakeman Car, *16-18*	100
82908	Mickey's Christmas Shanty, *16-18*	50
82913	Winnie the Pooh BoxCar, *16-17*	85
82914	Disney Aquarium Car, *16-18*	85
82917	Disney Station Platform, *17-18*	55
82918	36" Power Cable Extension (3-pin, M/F), *17-18*	12
82921	Evil Queen Hi-Cube BoxCar, *17-18*	80
82922	Scar Hi-Cube BoxCar, *17-18*	80
82925	Scrooge McDuck Mint Car, *17-18*	80
82942	James Monroe Presidential BoxCar, *16, 18*	70
82943	John F. Kennedy Presidential BoxCar, *16*	70
82944	Herbert Hoover Presidential BoxCar, *16*	70
82945	James Madison Presidential BoxCar, *16*	70
82947	Wonder Woman/Green Arrow Boxcar 2-pack, *16*	170
82950	Aquaman/Martian Manhunter Boxcar 2-pack, *16*	170
82953	Joker/Lex Luthor Boxcar 2-pack, *16*	170
82954	Lionel Christmas BoxCar, *16*	65
82958	Christmas Floodlight, *17-18*	75
82960	NYC 2-8-2 Steam Locomotive "1548," *16-18*	430
82961	UP 2-8-2 Steam Locomotive "2537," *16-18*	430
82962	Southern 2-8-2 Steam Locomotive "4501," *16-18*	430
82963	Rio Grande 2-8-2 Steam Locomotive "1208," *16-18*	430

Exc Mint

		Exc	Mint
82964	MILW 4-6-4 Steam Locomotive "125," *16-18*	430	___
82965	AT&SF 4-6-4 Steam Locomotive "3450," *16-18*	430	___
82966	DL&W 4-6-4 Steam Locomotive "1151," *16-18*	430	___
82967	CB&Q 4-6-4 Steam Locomotive "3007," *16-18*	430	___
82968	LL 4-6-2 Steam Locomotive "462," *16-17*	430	___
82969	WM 4-6-2 Steam Locomotive "202," *16-18*	430	___
82970	Reading & Northern 4-6-2 Locomotive "425," *16-17*	450	___
82971	C&NW 4-6-2 Steam Locomotive "600," *16-18*	300	___
82972	Lionel Junction PRR Diesel Freight Set, *16-17*	175	___
82973	PRR A5 0-4-0 Locomotive "3891," *16-18*	450	___
82974	SP A5 0-4-0 Locomotive "1040," *16-18*	450	___
82975	B&O A5 0-4-0 Locomotive "317," *16-18*	450	___
82976	Bethlehem Steel A5 0-4-0 Locomotive "140," LionChief, *16-18*	450	___
82982	Christmas Express Steam Freight Set, LionChief, *17-18*	320	___
82984	NYC RS-3 Diesel Freight Set, *16-17*	260	___
82992	115th Anniversary BoxCar, *16*	90	___
83002	PRR Broadway Limited 21" Diner 2-pack, StationSounds, *16*	450	___
83003	PC 21" StationSounds Diner "4552," *16*	300	___
83006	UP 21" Excursion Diner, StationSounds, *16*	300	___
83007	PRR Broadway Limited 21" Passenger Car 2-pack, *16*	300	___
83010	PC 21" Passenger Car 2-pack, *16*	300	___
83019	UP 21" Excursion Passenger Car 2-pack, *16*	300	___
83022	PRR Broadway Limited 21" Passenger Car 4-pack, *16*	600	___
83027	PC 21" Passenger Car 4-pack, *16*	600	___
83042	UP 21" Excursion Passenger Car 4-pack, *16*	675	___
83063	AT&SF Super Chief Boxcar "143093," *16-18*	50	___
83071	Universal Remote, *16-18*	50	___
83072	PRR "Keystone Special" Steam Freight Set, LionChief, *17-18*	300	___
83080	Rio Grande 0-4-0 Switcher Freight Set, *16-17*	300	___
83092	Steel City Switcher Freight Set, CC, *16*	1300	___
83102	SP 21" Passenger Car 4-pack, *16*	600	___
83107	SP 21" Passenger Car 2-pack, *16*	300	___
83110	SP 21" Diner "290," StationSounds, *16*	300	___
83111	American Freedom Train 21" Passenger Car 4-pack, *16-17*	675	___
83116	American Freedom Train 21" Passenger Car 2-pack, *16-17*	300	___
83119	American Freedom Train 21" Crew Car, *16-17*	300	___
83120	CSX Office Car Special 21" Passenger Car 4-pack, *16-17*	600	___
83125	CSX Office Car Special 21" Passenger Car 2-pack, *16-17*	300	___
83128	CSX Office Car Special 21" Diner, StationSounds, *16-17*	300	___
83147	Lighted Yard Tower, *16*	60	___
83148	Christmas Express BoxCar, *16-17*	53	___
83157	Smithsonian Air & Space Boxcar 2-pack, *16*	170	___
83162	Nightmare on Elm Street BoxCar, *16*	85	___
83163	Thomas Kinkade Christmas BoxCar, *16-17*	85	___

		Exc	Mint
____	**83164** Frosty the Snowman 1-D Tank Car, *16-17*		60
____	**83165** PRR GG1 Electric "4899," CC, *16*		1400
____	**83166** PRR GG1 Electric "4800," CC, *16*		1400
____	**83167** Conrail Bicentennial GG1 Electric "4800," CC, *16*		1400
____	**83168** Iron Workers Figure Pack, *16, 18*		30
____	**83169** NYC Flatcar with piggyback trailers, *16-18*		75
____	**83170** Steel Mill Structure, sound, *16-18*		130
____	**83171** MOW Workers Figure Pack, *16-18*		30
____	**83172** MOW Work Structure, sound, *16-18*		130
____	**83173** Single Signal Bridge, *16-18*		80
____	**83174** Double Signal Bridge, *16-18*		100
____	**83175** Christmas Music BoxCar, *16*		80
____	**83176** Lionel Lines Christmas Caboose, *16-17*		75
____	**83177** Angela Trotta Thomas Caboose, *16-17*		80
____	**83178** Coca-Cola Caboose, *16*		75
____	**83179** Conrail Caboose "23878," *16-18*		75
____	**83180** PRR Caboose "477100," *16-17*		7
____	**83181** AT&SF Caboose "999316," *16-17*		75
____	**83182** ACL Caboose "0634," *16-18*		75
____	**83183** Erie Caboose "C226," *16-18*		75
____	**83184** UP Caboose "25214," *16-18*		75
____	**83185** Polar Express Elves Figure Set, *16-18*		33
____	**83186** NYC Caboose "21777," *16-18*		75
____	**83190** Moon Pie 1-D Tank Car, *16-17*		75
____	**83191** Lionel Christmas 1-D Tank Car, *16*		85
____	**83192** Smithsonian Dinosaur Aquarium Car, *16-17*		85
____	**83193** SP GS-4 4-8-4 Locomotive "4449," CC, *16*		1700
____	**83194** SP GS-4 4-8-4 Locomotive "4449," CC, *16*		1700
____	**83195** SP GS-4 4-8-4 Locomotive "4443," CC, *16*		1700
____	**83196** SP GS-4 4-8-4 Locomotive "4444," CC, *16*		1700
____	**83197** American Freedom Train GS-4 4-8-4 Locomotive, CC, *16*		1700
____	**83198** Reading T1 4-8-4 Locomotive "2100," CC, *16*		1700
____	**83199** Reading T1 4-8-4 Locomotive "2119," CC, *16*		1700
____	**83200** Reading T1 4-8-4 Locomotive "2102," CC, *16*		1700
____	**83201** Reading T1 4-8-4 Locomotive "2124," CC, *16*		1700
____	**83202** American Freedom Train T1 4-8-4 Locomotive, CC, *16*		1700
____	**83203** Chessie T1 4-8-4 Locomotive "2101," CC, *16*		1700
____	**83204** B&O 0-8-0 Locomotive "1695," CC, *16*		900
____	**83205** GTW 0-8-0 Locomotive "8380," CC, *16*		900
____	**83206** Indiana Harbor Belt 0-8-0 Locomotive "312," CC, *16*		900
____	**83208** Wabash 0-8-0 Locomotive "1526," CC, *16*		900
____	**83209** Terminal Railroad 0-8-0 Locomotive, CC, *16*		900
____	**83214** North Pole Central 4-6-2 Locomotive "1225," *16-17*		430
____	**83215** Transformer 2-pack, *16-18*		15
____	**83223** Steel I-Beam 12-pack, *16-18*		15
____	**83230** Amtrak Metal Girder Bridge, *16-18*		43
____	**83231** Polar Express Metal Girder Bridge, *16-17*		43
____	**83232** Bethlehem Steel Metal Girder Bridge, *16-18*		40
____	**83233** CSX Metal Girder Bridge, *16-18*		37
____	**83234** John Deere Plastic Girder Bridge, *16-18*		33
____	**83238** John Deere Flatcar with spreaders, *16-17*		80
____	**83239** Polar Express Bells Mint Car, *16-17*		80

Exc Mint

			Exc	Mint
83240	Shell Operating Oil Derrick, *16*		120	___
83241	Shell Oil Storage Tank with Light, *16*		85	___
83242	Shell 1-D Tank Car, *16*		75	___
83243	Shell 3-D Tank Car, *16-17*		75	___
83244	Shell Elevated Oil Tank, *17*		100	___
83246	Shell BoxCar, *16*		85	___
83247	Shell Billboard Pack, *16-17*		25	___
83248	"It's a Boy" BoxCar, *16*		90	___
83249	Polar Express Combination Car, *16-17*		70	___
83250	"It's a Girl" BoxCar, *16*		90	___
83251	Poultry Dispatch Sweep Car, *16-18*		120	___
83252	Gold Medal Milk Car with platform, *17-18*		180	___
83253	D&RGW Searchlight Car, *16-17*		63	___
83254	Western Union Animated Gondola, *16-18*		70	___
83256	GN Horse Transport, *16*		80	___
83257	Bobbing Werewolf BoxCar, *16-17*		75	___
83258	CP Boom Car, *16*		63	___
83266	Lionel Junction Santa Fe Steam Freight Set, *16*		175	___
83275	Sugar Cookie Scented Smoke Fluid, *17-18*		7	___
83276	Peppermint Scented Smoke Fluid, *17-18*		7	___
83277	Pine Scented Smoke Fluid, *17-18*		7	___
83278	Hot Chocolate Scented Smoke Fluid, *17-18*		7	___
83279	Wood Stove Scented Smoke Fluid, *17-18*		7	___
83280	Unscented Smoke Fluid, *17-18*		7	___
83284	Peekaboo Reindeer Operating BoxCar, *16-17*		75	___
83286	John Deere Steam Freight Set, *16-17*		400	___
83291	Christmas Half-covered Bridge, *16-18*		70	___
83292	Christmas Cookies & Candies Store, *16-17*		85	___
83304	North Pole Elves Work Shanty, *16*		40	___
83305	Illuminated Winter Covered Bridge, *16-18*		80	___
83308	North Pole Central Tank Car "122416," *16-17*		75	___
83311	Santa's Favorites Egg Nog Reefer, *16-18*		65	___
83312	Santa's Cookies Vat Car, *16-17*		70	___
83313	Reindeer Express Agency Flatcar with trailer, *16-17*		70	___
83315	Christmas Toys Stock Car, *16-18*		70	___
83316	Santa's Sleigh Aquarium Car, *16-18*		80	___
83317	BNSF 65' Mill Gondola "518357" (std 0), *17*		80	___
83318	C&NW 65' Mill Gondola "342036" (std 0), *17*		80	___
83319	CSX 65' Mill Gondola "491600" (std 0), *17*		80	___
83320	NS 65' Mill Gondola "195015" (std 0), *17*		80	___
83321	SP 65' Mill Gondola "365117" (std 0), *17*		80	___
83322	UP 65' Mill Gondola "96257" (std 0), *17*		80	___
83340	Boxcar Children BoxCar, *16*		85	___
83347	ACL USRA Double-sheathed BoxCar, *16*		85	___
83348	B&M USRA Double-sheathed BoxCar, *16*		85	___
83349	RI USRA Double-sheathed BoxCar, *16*		85	___
83350	Northwestern Pacific USRA Double-sheathed BoxCar, *16*		85	___
83351	Wabash USRA Double-sheathed BoxCar, *16*		85	___
83352	Polar Express USRA Double-sheathed BoxCar, *16*		95	___
83353	D&RGW Flatcar with snowplow (std 0), *16*		95	___
83354	NYC Flatcar with snowplow (std 0), *16*		95	___
83355	UP Flatcar with snowplow (std 0), *16*		95	___
83356	MOW Flatcar with Snowplow (std 0), *16*		95	___

		Exc	Mint
____	**83357** Reading NE-style Caboose "92882" (std O), *16*		90
____	**83358** Reading NE-style Caboose "92902" (std O), *16*		90
____	**83359** Reading & Northern NE-style Caboose "92884" (std O), *16*		90
____	**83360** C&O NE-style Caboose "90352" (std O), *16*		90
____	**83361** N&W NE-style Caboose "500830" (std O), *16*		90
____	**83362** WM NE-style Caboose "1887" (std O), *16*		90
____	**83368** EL SD45 Diesel Locomotive "3607," CC, *16*		650
____	**83369** EL SD45 Diesel Locomotive "3618," CC, *16*		650
____	**83370** EL Bicentennial SD45 Diesel Locomotive "3632," CC, *16*		650
____	**83371** GN "Hustle Muscle" SD45 Diesel Locomotive "400," CC, *16*		650
____	**83372** GN SD45 Diesel Locomotive "402," CC, *16*		650
____	**83373** GN SD45 Diesel Locomotive "407," CC, *16*		650
____	**83374** PC SD45 Diesel Locomotive "6235," CC, *16*		650
____	**83375** PC SD45 Diesel Locomotive "6237," CC, *16*		650
____	**83376** Southern SD45 Diesel Locomotive "3137," CC, *16*		650
____	**83377** Southern SD45 Diesel Locomotive "3156," CC, *16*		650
____	**83378** SP SD45 Diesel Locomotive "8801," CC, *16*		650
____	**83379** SP SD45 Diesel Locomotive "8820," CC, *16*		650
____	**83380** UP SD45 Diesel Locomotive "1," CC, *16*		650
____	**83381** UP SD45 Diesel Locomotive "21," CC, *16*		650
____	**83382** AT&SF NW2 Diesel Locomotive "2405," CC, *16*		500
____	**83383** B&M NW2 Diesel Locomotive "1200," CC, *16*		500
____	**83384** B&O NW2 Diesel Locomotive "9527," CC, *16*		500
____	**83385** CSX NW2 Diesel Locomotive "9565," CC, *16*		500
____	**83387** NYO&W NW2 Diesel Locomotive "116," CC, *16*		500
____	**83388** PRR NW2 Diesel Locomotive "9171," CC, *16*		500
____	**83389** Philadelphia, Bethlehem & New England NW2 Diesel Locomotive "27," CC, *16*		500
____	**83390** SP NW2 Diesel Locomotive "1423," CC, *16*		500
____	**83391** SP&S NW2 Diesel Locomotive "41," CC, *16*		500
____	**83392** Union NW2 Diesel Locomotive "555," CC, *16*		500
____	**83393** UP NW2 Diesel Locomotive "1011," CC, *16*		500
____	**83395** AC&Y H16-44 Diesel "201," CC, *16*		550
____	**83396** AC&Y H16-44 Diesel "202," CC, *16*		550
____	**83397** AT&SF H16-44 Diesel "2801," CC, *16*		550
____	**83398** AT&SF H16-44 Diesel "2807," CC, *16*		550
____	**83399** B&O H16-44 Diesel "6705," CC, *16*		550
____	**83400** B&O H16-44 Diesel "6708," CC, *16*		550
____	**83401** MILW H16-44 Diesel "402," CC, *16*		550
____	**83402** MILW H16-44 Diesel "404," CC, *16*		550
____	**83403** DL&W H16-44 Diesel "931," CC, *16*		550
____	**83404** DL&W H16-44 Diesel "934," CC, *16*		550
____	**83405** Southern H16-44 Diesel "6547," CC, *16*		550
____	**83406** Southern H16-44 Diesel "6550," CC, *16*		550
____	**83426** Johnstown Birney Trolley, *16*		100
____	**83434** Polar Express Passenger Station, *16-17*		90
____	**83435** World War II Pylon, *17*		160
____	**83437** Polar Express Conductor Announcement Car, *16-17*		110
____	**83438** Miller Coors Operating Billboard, *17*		80
____	**83440** Rico Station Kit, *16-18*		60
____	**83442** Large Suburban House, *17-18*		95

Exc Mint

		Exc	Mint
83443	Deluxe Bungalow House, *17-18*		95____
83444	Illuminated Station Platform, *16-17*		43____
83445	Smithsonian Old St. Nick BoxCar, *16-18*		85____
83455	Polar Express Operating Billboard, *16-17*		85____
83462	Bethlehem Steel Slag Car 3-pack, *16*		240____
83466	U.S. Steel Slag Car 3-pack (std O), *16*		240____
83470	Slag Car 3-pack (std O), *16*		240____
83474	Weathered Slag Car 3-pack (std O), *16*		240____
83478	Bethlehem Steel Hot Metal Car 2-pack, *16*		200____
83481	U.S. Steel Hot Metal Car 2-pack (std O), *16*		200____
83484	Hot Metal Car 2-pack (std O), *16*		200____
83487	Weathered Hot Metal Car 2-pack (std O), *16*		200____
83490	Lighted Coaling Tower, *16, 18*		180____
83491	Boston Red Sox Cooperstown BoxCar, *16*		85____
83492	St. Louis Cardinals Cooperstown BoxCar, *16*		85____
83493	Philadelphia Phillies Cooperstown BoxCar, *16*		85____
83494	Baltimore Orioles Cooperstown BoxCar, *16*		85____
83496	Station Platform, *16-18*		40____
83497	National Train Day BoxCar, *16-17*		85____
83503	Thomas with remote, *16*		120____
83504	Birthday Thomas with remote, *16-18*		120____
83510	Thomas Passenger Set, LionChief, *16-18*		200____
83512	Thomas & Friends Christmas Freight Set, *16-17*		200____
83518	PRR Boxcar "83518" (std O), *16*		100____
83519	REA SensorCar Steel Reefer "7844" (std O), *16*		130____
83520	North Pole Central Flatcar with snowplow, *16*		95____
83527	AT&SF PS-1 Boxcar "142501," sound (std O), *16*		130____
83528	BAR PS-1 Boxcar "5149," sound (std O), *16*		130____
83529	B&O PS-1 Boxcar "467931," sound (std O), *16*		130____
83530	BN PS-1 Boxcar "132909," sound (std O), *16*		130____
83531	C&NW PS-1 Boxcar "5," sound (std O), *16*		130____
83532	NYC PS-1 Boxcar "175001," sound (std O), *16*		130____
83533	PRR PS-1 Boxcar "47005," sound (std O), *16*		130____
83534	UP PS-1 Boxcar "196883," sound (std O), *16*		130____
83535	PRR GL-a 2-bay Hopper 3-pack #1 (std O), *16*		220____
83539	PRR GL-a 2-bay Hopper 3-pack #2 (std O), *16*		220____
83544	PRR N5b Caboose "477797" (std O), *16*		95____
83545	PFE Reefer 3-pack (std O), *16*		170____
83549	AT&SF Reefer 3-pack (std O), *16*		300____
83553	Heisler Log Train Set, CC, *16*		1450____
83555	Red Logging Disconnect Caboose "1" (std O), *16*		40____
83556	Brown Logging Disconnect Caboose "6" (std O), *16*		40____
83557	Logging Disconnect Boxcar (std O), *16*		40____
83558	Logging Disconnect Flatcar (std O), *16*		35____
83559	Logging Disconnect Gondola (std O), *16*		40____
83560	Logging Disconnect Tank Car (std O), *16*		40____
83561	ATSF Express 50' DD Boxcar "1342" (std O), *16-17*		80____
83562	CNJ PS-1 Express Boxcar "22487" (std O), *16-17*		80____
83563	C&EI PS-1 Express Boxcar "2" (std O), *16-17*		80____
83564	GN PS-1 Express Boxcar "2538" (std O), *16-17*		80____
83565	KCS PS-1 Express Boxcar "400" (std O), *16-17*		80____
83566	SP PS-1 Express Boxcar "5712" (std O), *16-17*		80____
83567	T&P PS-1 Express Boxcar "1721" (std O), *16-17*		80____

Exc Mint

		Exc Mint
____ 83568	C&S Grain-door PS-1 Boxcar "1650" (std O), *16-17*	80
____ 83569	CP Grain-door PS-1 Boxcar "260293" (std O), *16-17*	80
____ 83570	GN Grain-door PS-1 Boxcar "18119" (std O), *16-17*	80
____ 83571	CGW Grain-door PS-1 Boxcar "5450" (std O), *16-17*	80
____ 83572	IC Grain-door PS-1 Boxcar "19000" (std O), *16-17*	80
____ 83573	MKT Grain-door PS-1 Boxcar "92463" (std O), *16-17*	80
____ 83574	UP CA-4 Caboose "3824" (std O), *16*	90
____ 83575	UP CA-4 Caboose "25121" (std O), *16*	90
____ 83576	B&O Milk Car "847" (std O), *16-17*	80
____ 83577	Supplee Milk Car "7" (std O), *16-17*	80
____ 83579	Rutland Milk Car "351" (std O), *16-17*	80
____ 83580	BAR State of Maine 40' Trailer, 2-pack, *16-17*	65
____ 83581	C&NW 40' Trailer, 2-pack, *16-17*	65
____ 83582	PFE 40' Trailer, 2-pack, *16-17*	65
____ 83583	PC 40' Trailer, 2-pack, *16-17*	65
____ 83584	SP 40' Trailer, 2-pack, *16-17*	65
____ 83585	UP 40' Trailer, 2-pack, *16-17*	65
____ 83586	PRR Broadway Limited 21" Passenger Car 2-pack #2 (std O), *16*	300
____ 83587	Hood Milk Car "807" (std O), *16-17*	80
____ 83589	American Freedom Train Add-On 2-pack #2, *16-17*	300
____ 83592	American Freedom Train Add-On 2-pack #3, *16-17*	300
____ 83595	Conrail Office Car Special Diesel Passenger Set, CC, *17*	1250
____ 83601	Conrail Office Car Special Add-on 2-pack, *17*	310
____ 83604	Conrail Office Car Special 21" Dome Car "55," StationSounds, *17*	320
____ 83605	Presidents 2-8-2 Mikado Locomotive "1789," *16-17*	430
____ 83606	Halloween 2-8-2 Mikado Locomotive "1031," *16-17*	430
____ 83607	USRA2-8-2 Mikado Locomotive "4500," *16-18*	430
____ 83608	B&O 2-8-2 Mikado Locomotive "4500," *16-17*	430
____ 83609	C&O 2-8-2 Mikado Locomotive "1067," *16-17*	430
____ 83610	MKT 2-8-2 Mikado Locomotive "851," *16-17*	430
____ 83611	NYC Empire State Express 21" Coach 4-pack #2, *17*	620
____ 83616	NYC Empire State Express 21" Combine/Observation Car 2-pack #2, *17*	310
____ 83619	NYC Empire State Express 21" Diner #2, StationSounds, *17*	310
____ 83620	Hogwarts Express Passenger Set, *16-17*	400
____ 83624	UP Sherman Hill Scout RS-3 Freight Set, *16-17*	500
____ 83633	Alaska Gold Mint Car, *17*	70
____ 83634	Keystone Smoke Fluid Loader, *16-18*	350
____ 83635	North American Smoke Fluid Loader, *16-18*	350
____ 83637	Mets-Phillies Mascot Aquarium Car, *16*	85
____ 83644	Macy's Dry Goods BoxCar, *2015u*	100
____ 83645	Polar Express Boxcar 2-pack, *16-18*	170
____ 83648	New York Yankees Subway Set, *16*	390
____ 83653	21" Passenger Car Figure Pack, *16-18*	30
____ 83655	Hamm's Heritage Beer Wood-sided Reefer, *16-17*	80
____ 83656	Coors Heritage Beer Wood-sided Reefer, *16-17*	80
____ 83657	Miller Heritage Beer Wood-sided Reefer, *16-17*	80
____ 83658	Lionelville School Kit, *16-17*	60
____ 83659	PRR Keystone Special Steam Freight Set, *16-17*	280
____ 83688	Trackside Railroad Details Pack, *16, 18*	25

	Exc	Mint
83689 Angela Trotta Thomas Christmas Covered Bridge, *17-18*	70	____
83690 Company Row House, blue, *16-17*	60	____
83691 Company Row House, yellow, *16-17*	60	____
83692 Company Row House, white, *16-17*	60	____
83693 Company Row House, red, *16-17*	60	____
83694 Toymaker Limited Trolley Set, *18*	200	____
83696 NYC "Pacemaker" Lionel Junction Diesel Freight Set, *17*	175	____
83701 Alaska Gold Mine 0-4-0 Steam Freight Set, LionChief, *17*	320	____
83716 BNSF RS-3 Diesel Scout Freight Set, LionChief, *17*	280	____
83733 Lighted Aquarius Hi-Cube BoxCar, *17*	90	____
83734 Lighted Pegasus Hi-Cube BoxCar, *17*	90	____
83745 Lionelville Hospital Kit, *17-18*	80	____
83751 Yard Tower, *18*	65	____
83752 W&A Horse Car and Corral, *17-18*	180	____
83762 Personalized Christmas BoxCar, *16*	90	____
83763 Personalized Holiday BoxCar, *16*	90	____
83764 Happy Birthday BoxCar, *16*	90	____
83765 Anniversary BoxCar, *16-17*	90	____
83766 Personalized Polar Express Baggage Car, *16-18*	95	____
83779 Pearl Harbor 75th Anniversary BoxCar, *16-17*	85	____
83783 Rosie the Riveter BoxCar, *17*	85	____
83784 Heavies and Little Friends BoxCar, *17*	85	____
83785 Doolittle Raid BoxCar, *16-17*	85	____
83786 D-Day BoxCar, *17*	85	____
83788 Uncle Sam "Enlist Now" BoxCar, *16-17*	85	____
83790 Mickey Mouse Happy Holidays BoxCar, *17*	85	____
83791 Donald Duck Happy Holidays BoxCar, *17*	85	____
83792 Goofy Happy Holidays BoxCar, *17*	85	____
83794 75th Anniversary of Bambi BoxCar, *17*	80	____
83795 50th Anniversary of The Jungle Book BoxCar, *17*	80	____
83796 100th Anniversary Moon Pie BoxCar, *17*	85	____
83800 Happy Thanksgiving BoxCar, *17*	80	____
83801 Happy Hanukkah BoxCar, *17*	80	____
83802 Disney Happy Halloween BoxCar, *17*	85	____
83913 Personalized Halloween BoxCar, *17*	95	____
83918 Smithsonian BoxCar, John Bull, *17*	85	____
83923 Angela Trotta Thomas Santa's Cookies BoxCar, *17*	85	____
83924 Caddyshack BoxCar, *17*	80	____
83925 Frosty the Snowman BoxCar, *17*	85	____
83926 Personalized Polar Express BoxCar, *17-18*	95	____
83927 Lionel Smoke Fluid 1-D Tank Car, *17*	75	____
83928 Lionel Paint 1-D Tank Car, *17*	75	____
83929 Lionel Hydraulic Oil 1-D Tank Car, *17*	75	____
83938 Harry Potter Hogwarts House Gryffindor BoxCar, *17*	80	____
83939 Harry Potter Hogwarts House Ravenclaw BoxCar, *17*	80	____
83940 Harry Potter Hogwarts House Hufflepuff BoxCar, *17*	80	____
83941 Harry Potter Hogwarts House Slytherin BoxCar, *17*	80	____
83943 Polar Express BoxCar, *17-18*	85	____
83944 John Deere BoxCar, *17*	85	____
83945 Richard Nixon Presidential BoxCar, *17*	70	____
83946 Jimmy Carter Presidential BoxCar, *17*	70	____

		Exc	Mint
____	**83947** Woodrow Wilson Presidential BoxCar, *17*		70
____	**83948** William Howard Taft Presidential BoxCar, *17*		70
____	**83950** Personalized "It's A Boy" BoxCar, *17-18*		90
____	**83951** Personalized "It's A Girl" BoxCar, *17-18*		90
____	**83952** Minnie Mouse Happy Holidays BoxCar, *17*		85
____	**83959** Macy's Parade 90th Anniversary BoxCar, *2016u*		30
____	**83964** Mickey Mouse Christmas Express Steam Freight Set, LionChief, *17-18*		420
____	**83972** Harry Potter Hogwarts Steam Passenger Set, LionChief, *17-18*		420
____	**83974** CSX Diesel Intermodal Set, LionChief, *17-18*		460
____	**83979** Mickey & Friends B337Express Steam Freight Set, LionChief, *17*		370
____	**83984** Pennsylvania Flyer 0-8-0 Steam Freight Set, LionChief, *17*		300
____	**84000** DETX Rotary Gondola 4-pack (std O), *16-17*		280
____	**84005** CSX Rotary Gondola 4-pack (std O), *16-17*		280
____	**84010** UP Rotary Gondola 4-pack (std O), *16-17*		280
____	**84015** NS Rotary Gondola 4-pack (std O), *16-17*		280
____	**84020** PPLX Rotary Gondola 4-pack (std O), *16-17*		280
____	**84025** PPLX Rotary Gondola 2-pack (std O), *16-17*		140
____	**84028** BNSF Rotary Gondola 4-pack (std O), *16-17*		280
____	**84033** BNSF Rotary Gondola 2-pack (std O), *16-17*		140
____	**84045** BN 21" Passenger Car 4-pack, *17*		620
____	**84050** BN 21" Coach 2-pack, *17*		310
____	**84053** BN 21" Diner, StationSounds, *17*		310
____	**84063** Weathered N&W Y6B 2-8-8-2 Locomotive "2186," CC, *17*		2200
____	**84064** MILW 4-8-4 Northern Locomotive "261," CC, *17*		1700
____	**84065** MILW 4-8-4 Northern Locomotive "265," CC, *17*		1700
____	**84066** MILW 4-8-4 Northern Locomotive "262," CC, *17*		1700
____	**84067** MILW 4-8-4 Northern Locomotive "260 Hiawatha," CC, *17*		1700
____	**84068** DL&W 4-8-4 Northern Locomotive "1661," CC, *17*		1700
____	**84069** B&M 2-6-0 Mogul Locomotive "1397," CC, *16*		700
____	**84070** CV 2-6-0 Mogul Locomotive "397," CC, *16*		700
____	**84071** DL&W 2-6-0 Mogul Locomotive "565," CC, *16*		700
____	**84072** Everett 2-6-0 Mogul Locomotive "11," CC, *16*		700
____	**84073** GT 2-6-0 Mogul Locomotive "713," CC, *16*		700
____	**84074** Rutland 2-6-0 Mogul Locomotive "145," CC, *16*		700
____	**84075** ACL E8 Diesel AA Set "544, 545," CC, *17*		1000
____	**84078** BN E8 Diesel AA Set "9935, 9940," CC, *17*		1000
____	**84081** Conrail E8 Diesel AA Set "4020, 4021," CC, *17*		1000
____	**84084** EMD Demonstrator E8 Diesel A Unit "950," CC, *17*		650
____	**84085** L&N E8 Diesel AA Set "796, 797," CC, *17*		1000
____	**84088** NYC E8 Diesel AA Set "4036, 4037," CC, *17*		1000
____	**84091** PRR E8 Diesel AA Set "5763, 5764," CC, *17*		1000
____	**84094** Arkansas & Missouri SD70ACe Diesel Locomotive "70," CC, *16*		650
____	**84095** Arkansas & Missouri SD70ACe Diesel Locomotive "71," CC, *16*		650
____	**84096** BNSF SD70ACe Diesel Locomotive "9372," CC, *16*		650
____	**84097** BNSF SD70ACe Diesel Locomotive "9385," CC, *16*		650
____	**84098** CN SD70ACe Diesel Locomotive "8100," CC, *16*		650
____	**84099** CN SD70ACe Diesel Locomotive "8102," CC, *16*		650

	Exc	Mint
84100 CSX SD70ACe Diesel Locomotive "4837," CC, *16*		650____
84101 CSX SD70ACe Diesel Locomotive "4843," CC, *16*		650____
84102 EMDX SD70ACe Diesel Locomotive "72," CC, *16*		650____
84103 EMDX SD70ACe Diesel Locomotive "73," CC, *16*		650____
84104 Montana Rail Link SD70ACe Diesel Locomotive "4309," CC, *16*		650
84105 Montana Rail Link SD70ACe Diesel Locomotive "4312" CC, *16*		650 ____
84106 UP SD70ACe Diesel Locomotive "8360," CC, *16*		650____
84107 UP SD70ACe Diesel Locomotive "8415," CC, *16*		650____
84108 GN GP7 Diesel "601," *16-18*		330____
84109 L&N GP7 Diesel "405," *16-18*		330____
84110 Reading GP7 Diesel "619," *16-18*		330____
84111 WP GP7 Diesel "707," *16-18*		330____
84112 Cotton Belt 50' DD Boxcar "47509" (std 0), *16-17*		80____
84113 D&RGW 50' DD Boxcar "63689" (std 0), *16-17*		80____
84114 Seaboard 50' DD Boxcar "10090" (std 0), *16-17*		80____
84115 PRR K4s 4-6-2 Pacific Locomotive "5385," CC, *16*		1300____
84116 PRR K4s 4-6-2 Pacific Locomotive "5432," CC, *16*		1300____
84117 Burlington Refrigerator Express 40' Steel Reefer "76060" (std 0), *17*		85 ____
84118 BAR 40' Steel Reefer "7342" (std 0), *17*		85____
84119 BN 40' Steel Reefer "70609" (std 0), *17*		85____
84120 Eastern States ERDX 40' Steel Reefer "10060" (std 0), *17*		85 ____
84121 National Car Co. 40' Steel Reefer "2430" (std 0), *17*		85____
84122 FGE 40' Steel Reefer "41475" (std 0), *17*		85____
84123 B&M PS-2CD Covered Hopper "5717" (std 0), *17*		90____
84124 L&N PS-2CD Covered Hopper "37399" (std 0), *17*		90____
84125 MILW PS-2CD Covered Hopper "98333" (std 0), *17*		90____
84126 NP PS-2CD Covered Hopper "75675" (std 0), *17*		90____
84127 AT&SF PS-2CD Covered Hopper "304713" (std 0), *17*		90 ____
84128 TLDX Demonstrator PS-2CD Covered Hopper "91" (std 0), *17*		90 ____
84129 AT&SF Wide Vision Caboose "999705" (std 0), *17*		95 ____
84130 BN Freedom Train Wide Vision Caboose "12618" (std 0), *17*		95 ____
84131 BNSF Wide Vision Caboose "12584" (std 0), *17*		95____
84132 CSX Wide Vision Caboose "903180" (std 0), *17*		95____
84133 D&H Wide-Vision Caboose "35712," *18*		100____
84134 GN Wide-Vision Caboose "X-109," *18*		100____
84135 C&O Northeast Caboose "A918" (std 0), *17*		90____
84137 Conrail Northeast Caboose "18866" (std 0), *17*		90____
84138 Pere Marquette Northeast Caboose "A909" (std 0), *17*		90 ____
84139 WM Northeast Caboose circle herald "1874" (std 0), *17*		90 ____
84140 WM Northeast Caboose circus herald "1882" (std 0), *17*		90 ____
84141 WM USRA 2-bay Hopper 3-pack #1 (std 0), *17*		220____
84145 WM USRA 2-bay Hopper 3-pack #2 (std 0), *17*		220____
84149 Reading USRA 2-bay Hopper 3-pack (std 0), *17*		220____
84153 B&O 1905 2-bay Hopper 3-pack (std 0), *17*		220____

		Exc	Mint
84157	Bethlehem Steel 1905 2-bay Hopper 3-pack (std O), *17*		220
84161	Logging Disconnect Stock Car, *17*		40
84163	Logging Disconnect Christmas 4-pack (std O), *17*		160
84165	Logging Disconnect Dinner Train 4-pack (std O), *17*		160
84166	Logging Disconnect, 1-pair, brown (std O), *17*		65
84167	Logging Disconnect, 2-pair, brown (std O), *17*		125
84187	B&O 18" Heavyweight Coach 2-pack #1, *18*		400
84190	B&O 18" Heavyweight Coach 2-pack #2, *18*		400
84193	Reading, Blue Mountain & Northern 18" Heavyweight Coach 2-pack #1, *18*		400
84196	Reading, Blue Mountain & Northern 18" Heavyweight Coach 2-pack #2, *18*		400
84199	MILW 18" Heavyweight Coach 2-pack #1, *18*		400
84202	MILW 18" Heavyweight Coach 2-pack #2, *18*		400
84205	Nickel Plate Road 18" Heavyweight Coach 2-pack #1, *18*		400
84208	Nickel Plate Road 18" Heavyweight Coach 2-pack #2, *18*		400
84208	Smithsonian BoxCar, Southern "1401," *17*		85
84211	TH&B 18" Heavyweight Coach 2-pack #1, *18*		400
84214	TH&B 18" Heavyweight Coach 2-pack #1, *18*		400
84217	Wabash 18" Heavyweight Coach 2-pack #1, *18*		400
84220	Wabash 18" Heavyweight Coach 2-pack #2, *18*		400
84226	American Freedom Train Add-On 2-pack #4, *17*		300
84229	Conrail 21" Theater Inspection Car "9," *17*		340
84230	NS 21" Theater Inspection Car Buena Vista, *17*		340
84231	CSX 21" Theater Inspection Car Alabama, *17*		340
84232	UP 21" Theater Inspection Car Fox River, *17*		340
84237	Cass Scenic RR 3-Truck Shay Locomotive "6," CC, *17*		1500
84238	Elk River Lumber Co. 3-Truck Shay Locomotive "20," CC, *17*		1500
84239	WM 3-Truck Shay Locomotive "6," CC, *17*		1500
84240	West Side Lumber Co. 3-Truck Shay Locomotive "3," CC, *17*		1500
84248	SP AC-9 2-8-8-4 Locomotive "3800," CC, *17*		2000
84249	SP AC-9 2-8-8-4 Locomotive "3805," CC, *17*		2000
84250	SP AC-9 Daylight 2-8-8-4 Locomotive "3811," CC, *17*		2000
84251	AT&SF 2-8-4 Berkshire Locomotive "4103," *17-18*		450
84252	Nickel Plate Road 2-8-4 Berkshire Locomotive "767," *17-18*		450
84253	Pere Marquette 2-8-4 Berkshire Locomotive "1223," *17-18*		450
84254	IC 2-8-4 Berkshire Locomotive "8006," *17-18*		450
84255	Lionel Lines 2-8-4 Berkshire Locomotive "726," *17-18*		450
84256	AT&SF SD40 Diesel "5006," CC, *17*		650
84257	AT&SF SD40 Diesel "5018," CC, *17*		650
84258	UP SD40 Diesel "4057," CC, *17*		650
84259	UP SD40 Diesel "4062," CC, *17*		650
84260	CSX SD40 Diesel "4614," CC, *17*		650
84261	CSX SD40 Diesel "4621," CC, *17*		650
84262	PRR SD40 Diesel "6041," CC, *17*		650

	Exc	Mint
84263 PRR SD40 Diesel "6089," CC, *17*	650	
84264 Southern SD40 Diesel "3170," CC, *17*	650	
84265 Southern SD40 Diesel "3200," CC, *17*	650	
84267 SP SD40R Diesel "7372," CC, *17*	650	
84268 WM SD40 Diesel "7547," CC, *17*	650	
84269 WM SD40 Diesel "7549," CC, *17*	650	
84270 B&O EMD Torpedo GP9 Diesel "3414," CC, *18*	550	
84271 B&O EMD Torpedo GP9 Diesel "3419," CC, *18*	550	
84272 C&NW EMD Torpedo GP9 Diesel "1725," CC, *18*	550	
84273 C&NW EMD Torpedo GP9 Diesel "1730," CC, *18*	550	
84274 MILW EMD Torpedo GP9 Diesel "202," CC, *18*	550	
84275 MILW EMD Torpedo GP9 Diesel "208," CC, *18*	550	
84276 Nickel Plate Road EMD Torpedo GP9 Diesel "482," CC, *18*	550	
84277 Nickel Plate Road EMD Torpedo GP9 Diesel "484," CC, *18*	550	
84278 TH&B EMD Torpedo GP9 Diesel "402," CC, *18*	550	
84279 TH&B EMD Torpedo GP9 Diesel "403," CC, *18*	550	
84280 Wabash EMD Torpedo GP9 Diesel "484," CC, *18*	550	
84281 Wabash EMD Torpedo GP9 Diesel "486," CC, *18*	550	
84282 BN GE U33C Diesel "5716," CC, *18*	580	
84283 BN GE U33C Diesel "5723," CC, *18*	580	
84284 D&H GE U33C Diesel "757," CC, *18*	580	
84285 D&H GE U33C Diesel "762," CC, *18*	580	
84286 Guilford D&H GE U33C Diesel "650," CC, *18*	580	
84287 Guilford D&H GE U33C Diesel "654," CC, *18*	580	
84288 GN GE U33C Diesel "2530," CC, *18*	580	
84289 GN GE U33C Diesel "2541," CC, *18*	580	
84290 IC GE U33C Diesel "5052," CC, *18*	580	
84291 IC GE U33C Diesel "5054," CC, *18*	580	
84292 PC GE U33C Diesel "6547," CC, *18*	580	
84293 PC GE U33C Diesel "6561," CC, *18*	580	
84294 Sacramento Trolley, *17-18*	100	
84295 Connecticut Trolley, *17-18*	100	
84296 SP Salad Bowl Express Diesel Freight Set, CC, *17*	900	
84297 Logging Disconnect Steel Tank Car (std O), *17*	40	
84303 Bucking Feed and Tack, *17*	85	
84304 CB&Q Gondola with covers, *17*	55	
84306 Illuminated John Deere Flagpole, *17-18*	60	
84307 Illuminated Lionel Flagpole with flag, *17-18*	50	
84308 Gray Half-Covered Bridge, *17*	60	
84309 PRR Blinking Water Tower, *17-18*	45	
84310 Modular Train Car Repair Facility, *16-17*	110	
84312 Alaska RR Gondola with canisters, *17*	55	
84314 BNSF ACF Covered Hopper "405850," *18*	60	
84315 Branchline Water Tank Kit, *16-18*	40	
84317 Passenger Station, *17*	80	
84318 Illuminated Station Platform, *17-18*	43	
84327 Santa Fe Operating Billboard, *17*	70	
84328 Polar Express Steam Passenger Set, LionChief, *17-18*	420	
84330 Witches Brew 1-D Tank Car, *17-18*	70	
84332 Halloween BoxCar, SpookySounds, *17-18*	80	
84333 Strasburg RR Gondola with vats, *17*	65	

		Exc	Mint
____	**84334** Strasburg Half-covered Bridge, *17-18*		60
____	**84335** PRR Culvert Gondola "374200," *17*		65
____	**84336** UP Log Car, *17*		65
____	**84337** MKT Wood-chip Hopper, *17*		65
____	**84338** CSX Wood-chip Hopper, *17-18*		65
____	**84339** SP Jumping Hobo BoxCar, *17*		80
____	**84340** Santa and Snowman Operating BoxCar, *17-18*		90
____	**84341** Tell-Tale Reindeer Car, *17*		80
____	**84366** PRR Wood-chip Hopper, *17-18*		65
____	**84367** Christmas Pylon, *17*		160
____	**84369** NYC Welding Car "X939," *17*		80
____	**84369** L&N Hummingbird 21" Diner w/StationSounds, *18*		330
____	**84370** Polar Express Hopper with silver, *17-18*		70
____	**84371** Mickey's Holiday Hopper with presents, *17-18*		70
____	**84372** Christmas Station Platform, *17-18*		43
____	**84373** Special Trolley Announcement Track, *18*		50
____	**84374** Christmas Music BoxCar, *17*		80
____	**84375** Christmas BoxCar, *17*		65
____	**84376** Angela Trotta Thomas Signature Express Aquarium Car, *17-18*		85
____	**84377** Christmas Peppermint 1-D Tank Car, *17-18*		60
____	**84378** Santa's Choice Milk Car with platform, *17-18*		180
____	**84380** Reading & Northern Auxiliary Tender "425-A, CC, *18*		300
____	**84383** Elevated Oil Tank, *17-18*		95
____	**84388** Gray 10" Girder Bridge, *17-18*		25
____	**84400** BN "Pulling for Freedom" SD60M Diesel "1991," CC, *17*		650
	84401 BN SD60M Diesel "9200," CC, *17*		650
____	**84402** BN SD60M Diesel "9225," CC, *17*		650
____	**84403** Soo Line SD60M Diesel "6058," CC, *17*		650
____	**84404** Soo Line SD60M Diesel "6061," CC, *17*		650
____	**84405** Conrail SD60M Diesel "5504," CC, *17*		650
____	**84406** Conrail SD60M Diesel "5510," CC, *17*		650
____	**84407** CSX SD60M Diesel "8783," CC, *17*		650
____	**84408** CSX SD60M Diesel "8784," CC, *17*		650
____	**84409** NS SD60M Diesel "6808," CC, *17*		650
	84410 NS SD60M Diesel "6815," CC, *17*		650
____	**84411** UP SD60M Diesel "6165," CC, *17*		650
____	**84412** UP SD60M Diesel "6187," CC, *17*		650
____	**84413** B&O FA A-A Diesel Set, "814, 815," *17-18*		500
____	**84416** GN FA A-A Diesel Set, "278A, 278B," *17-18*		500
____	**84419** NH FA A-A Diesel Set, "417, 418," *17-18*		500
____	**84422** UP FA A-A Diesel Set, "1616, 1617," *17-18*		500
____	**84433** Polar Express 40' Scale Reefer "122517," *17*		90
____	**84434** NS 30,000-gallon 1-D Tank Car 3-pack (std O), *16*		250
____	**84438** NS 30,000-gallon 1-D Tank Car "362785" (std O), *16*		80
____	**84439** UTLX 30,000-gallon 1-D Tank Car 3-pack (std O), *16*		250
____	**84443** PESX 30,000-gallon 1-D Tank Car 3-pack (std O), *16*		250
____	**84447** TILX 30,000-gallon 1-D Tank Car 3-pack (std O), *16*		250
____	**84451** PRR Flatcar 6-pack, *17*		120
____	**84452** AT&SF Flatcar 6-pack, *17-18*		120
____	**84453** UP Flatcar 6-pack, *17-18*		120
____	**84454** Trailer Train Flatcar 6-pack, *17*		120
____	**84455** Assorted Flatcar 6-pack, *17-18*		120

Exc Mint

		Exc	Mint
84456	B&O Gondola 6-pack, *17-18*	120	___
84457	UP Gondola 6-pack, *17-18*	120	___
84458	East Assorted Gondola 6-pack, *17*	120	___
84459	Midwest Assorted Gondola 6-pack, *17*	120	___
84460	West Assorted Gondola 6-pack, *17-18*	120	___
84462	2-Rail Conversion Kit, 50-ton Scale Trucks, *16-18*	20	___
84463	2-Rail Conversion Kit, 70-ton Scale Trucks, *16-18*	20	___
84465	B&O 2-8-2 Light Mikado Locomotive "4500," CC, *17*	1300	___
84466	GTW 2-8-2 Light Mikado Locomotive "3734," CC, *17*	1300	___
84467	Maine Central 2-8-2 Light Mikado Locomotive "624," CC, *17*	1300	___
84468	NYC 2-8-2 Light Mikado Locomotive "5187," CC, *17*	1300	___
84469	PRR 2-8-2 Light Mikado Locomotive "9630," CC, *17*	1300	___
84470	Southern 2-8-2 Light Mikado Locomotive "4758," CC, *17*	1300	___
84471	UP 2-8-2 Light Mikado Locomotive "2537," CC, *17*	1300	___
84472	AT&SF 2-8-2 Mikado Locomotive, Brass Hybrid "3222," CC, *17*	1300	___
84480	John Deere Covered Bridge, *17-18*	70	___
84481	John Deere General Store, *17-18*	85	___
84482	John Deere Gondola with hay bales, *17-18*	75	___
84483	John Deere Grain Vat Car, *17*	75	___
84485	Disney Covered Bridge, *17-18*	70	___
84486	MILW NW2 Diesel Locomotive "1649," CC, *16*	500	___
84487	Donald Duck Holiday 1-D Tank Car, *17*	70	___
84489	Polar Express Covered Bridge, *17-18*	70	___
84490	NS First Responders Diesel Freight Set, LionChief, *17-18*	450	___
84496	Shell Service Station, *17*	150	___
84498	NS Fire Rescue Car, *17-18*	75	___
84499	Mickey Mouse & Friends Industrial Water Tower, *17-18*	100	___
84500	NS Unibody 1-D Tank Car "490112," *17-18*	75	___
84507	New York Central & Hudson River S2 Electric "3207," CC, *17*	800	___
84508	NYC S2 Electric "113," CC, *17*	800	___
84509	NYC S2 Electric "115," CC, *17*	800	___
84510	PC S2 Electric "4710," CC, *17*	800	___
84511	NYC "Lightning Stripe" S2 Electric "101," CC, *17*	800	___
84512	S2 Electric Scale Tinplate Freight Set, CC, *17*	1000	___
84525	Uptown Apartment Building, *17*	100	___
84526	Leuzure Marble Co. Warehouse, *17*	110	___
84529	NS Veterans Wide Vision Caboose "6920" (std O), *17-18*	95	___
84530	NS First Responders Wide Vision Caboose "9-1-1" (std O), *17-18*	95	___
84532	Nickel Plate Road 2-8-2 Light Mikado Locomotive "587," CC, *17*	1300	___
84538	NS 65' Mill Gondola "195029" (std O), *17*	80	___
84539	NS 65' Mill Gondola "195065" (std O), *17*	80	___
84553	Logging Disconnect Reindeer Train 4-pack A, *17*	160	___
84554	Logging Disconnect Reindeer Train 4-pack B, *17*	160	___
84555	Logging Disconnect Santa Claus Observation (std O), *17*	45	___

		Exc	Mint
____	84562 BN "Pulling for Freedom" SD60M Diesel "1991," LionChief, 17		500
____	84563 BN SD60M Diesel "9215," LionChief, 17		500
____	84564 Soo Line SD60M Diesel "6060," LionChief, 17		500
____	84565 Conrail SD60M Diesel "5509," LionChief, 17		500
____	84566 CSX SD60M Diesel "8757," LionChief, 17		500
____	84567 NS SD60M Diesel "6810," LionChief, 17		500
____	84568 UP SD60M Diesel "6170," LionChief, 17		500
____	84570 First Responders EMT BoxCar, 17-18		90
____	84571 First Responders Police BoxCar, 17-18		90
____	84572 First Responders Fire Fighter BoxCar, 17-18		90
____	84573 Happy Birthday BoxCar, 17		90
____	84574 Personalized 2017 Merry Christmas BoxCar, 17		90
____	84575 U.S. Army BoxCar, 17-18		90
____	84576 U.S. Marine BoxCar, 17-18		90
____	84577 U.S. Air Force BoxCar, 17-18		90
____	84578 U.S. Navy BoxCar, 17-18		90
____	84579 U.S. Coast Guard BoxCar, 17-18		90
____	84580 From The Home Front BoxCar, blue, 17-18		90
____	84581 From The Home Front BoxCar, green, -18		90
____	84582 BNSF 65' Mill Gondola "518375" (std O), 17		80
____	84583 BNSF 65' Mill Gondola "518392" (std O), 17		80
____	84584 C&NW 65' Mill Gondola "342045" (std O), 17		80
____	84585 C&NW 65' Mill Gondola "342049" (std O), 17		80
____	84586 CSX 65' Mill Gondola "491616" (std O), 17		80
____	84587 CSX 65' Mill Gondola "491638" (std O), 17		80
____	84590 SP 65' Mill Gondola "365136" (std O), 17		80
____	84591 SP 65' Mill Gondola "365142" (std O), 17		80
____	84592 UP 65' Mill Gondola "96267" (std O), 17		80
____	84593 UP 65' Mill Gondola "96281" (std O), 17		80
____	84599 Bucking Feed & Tack Building, 18		85
____	84600 Polar Express Combination Car, 18		75
____	84601 Polar Express Letters to Santa Mail Car, 18		75
____	84602 Polar Express Disappearing Hobo Car, 18		80
____	84603 Polar Express Hot Chocolate Car, 18		75
____	84604 Polar Express Diner, 18		75
____	84605 Polar Express Baggage Car, 18		75
____	84611 Lionel BlueTooth Radio Tower, 17		100
____	84616 Wonder Woman BoxCar, 17		80
____	84621 17 National Lionel Train Day BoxCar, 17		85
____	84622 D&RGW EMD SD40T-2 Diesel "5401," CC, 17		600
____	84623 D&RGW EMD SD40T-2 Diesel "5405," CC, 17		600
____	84624 KCS EMD SD40T-2 Diesel "6102," CC, 17		600
____	84625 KCS EMD SD40T-2 Diesel "6110," CC, 17		600
____	84626 Lancaster & Chester EMD SD40T-2 Diesel "6002," CC, 17		600
____	84627 GECX EMD SD40T-2 Diesel "8661," CC, 17		600
____	84628 GECX EMD SD40T-2 Diesel "8678," CC, 17		600
____	84629 Ohio Central EMD SD40T-2 Diesel "4026," CC, 17		600
____	84630 Ohio Central EMD SD40T-2 Diesel "4027," CC, 17		600
____	84631 RJ Corman EMD SD40T-2 Diesel "5361," CC, 17		600
____	84632 RJ Corman EMD SD40T-2 Diesel "5409," CC, 17		600
____	84633 SP EMD SD40T-2 Diesel "8532," CC, 17		600
____	84634 SP EMD SD40T-2 Diesel "8548," CC, 17		600

Exc Mint

		Exc	Mint
84635	UP EMD SD40T-2 Diesel "8593," CC, *17*	600	____
84636	UP EMD SD40T-2 Diesel "8715," CC, *17*	600	____
84637	Cotton Belt EMD SD40T-2 Diesel "9389," Bicentennial, CC, *17*	600	____
84638	ACL EMD E6 A-A Diesel Set "500-501," CC, *17*	1000	____
84641	AT&SF EMD E6 A-A Diesel Set "12-13," CC, *17*	1000	____
84644	C&NW EMD E6 A-A Diesel Set "5005A-5005B," CC, *17*	1000	____
84647	FEC EMD E3 A-A Diesel Set "1001-1002," CC, *17*	1000	____
84650	IC EMD E6 A-A Diesel Set "4003-4004," CC, *17*	1000	____
84653	KCS EMD E3 A-A Diesel Set "2-3," CC, *17*	1000	____
84656	L&N EMD E6 A-A Diesel Set "754-755," CC, *17*	1000	____
84659	MILW EMD E6 A-A Diesel Set "15A-15B," CC, *17*	1000	____
84662	UP EMD E6 A-A Diesel Set "996-*997*," CC, *17*	1000	____
84666	Battle for Guadalcanal, *17*	85	____
84667	Battle of the Bulge BoxCar, *17*	85	____
84668	Silent Service BoxCar, *17*	85	____
84669	Desert Storm BoxCar, *18*	90	____
84670	Korean War BoxCar, *18*	85	____
84671	Vietnam War BoxCar, *18*	85	____
84672	Memorial Day BoxCar, *18*	90	____
84674	AT&SF 2-8-2 Mikado Locomotive, Brass Hybrid, Painted, Unlettered, CC, *17*	1300	____
84675	AT&SF 2-8-2 Mikado Locomotive, Brass Hybrid, Unpainted, CC, *17*	1300	____
84676	Peanuts Hilltop BoxCar, *18*	90	____
84677	Peanuts Meadow BoxCar, *18*	90	____
84678	Peanuts Winter BoxCar, *18*	90	____
84679	AT&SF 4-6-2 Pacific Locomotive "1369," LionChief Plus, *17-18*	450	____
84680	CNJ 4-6-2 Pacific Locomotive "832," LionChief Plus, *17-18*	450	____
84681	Alton 4-6-2 Pacific Locomotive "5299," LionChief Plus, *17-18*	450	____
84682	Southern 4-6-2 Pacific Locomotive "1401," LionChief Plus, *17-18*	450	____
84683	MILW 4-6-2 Pacific Locomotive "810," LionChief Plus, *17-18*	450	____
84685	Polar Express Scale 2-8-4 Berkshire Locomotive "1225," CC, *17*	1500	____
84686	Nickel Plate Road 2-8-4 Berkshire Locomotive "759," CC, *17*	1500	____
84687	Nickel Plate Road 2-8-4 Berkshire Locomotive "765," CC, *17*	1500	____
84688	Nickel Plate Road 2-8-4 Berkshire Locomotive "767," CC, *17*	1500	____
84689	Southern 2-8-4 Berkshire Locomotive "2716," CC, *17*	1500	____
84690	W&LE 2-8-4 Berkshire Locomotive "6401," CC, *17*	1500	____
84691	American Railroads 2-8-4 Berkshire Locomotive "759," CC, *17*	1500	____
84692	RF&P 2-8-4 Berkshire Locomotive "752," CC, *17*	1500	____
84693	Pere Marquette 2-8-4 Berkshire Locomotive "1225," CC, *17*	1500	____
84694	Pere Marquette 2-8-4 Berkshire Locomotive "1223," CC, *17*	1500	____

		Exc	Mint
___ 84695	L&N 2-8-4 Berkshire Locomotive "1992," CC, *17*		1500
___ 84696	D&H Alco RS-3 Diesel "4121," LionChief Plus, *17-18*		350
___ 84697	AT&SF Alco RS-3 Diesel "2099," LionChief Plus, *17-18*		350
___ 84698	Peabody Coal Short Line Alco RS-3 Diesel "101," LionChief Plus, *17-18*		350
___ 84699	B&M Alco RS-3 Diesel "1536," LionChief Plus, *17-18*		350
___ 84700	Hot Wheels Diesel Freight Set, LionChief, *17-18*		400
___ 84705	Hot Wheels 50th Anniversary Auto Rack, *17-18*		85
___ 84706	Hot Wheels 50th Anniversary Auto Loader, *17-18*		90
___ 84707	Hot Wheels 50th Anniversary Flatcar w/Piggyback Trailers, *17-18*		85
___ 84708	Hot Wheels Auto Rack, *18*		85
___ 84709	NH RS-3 Diesel Freight Set, LionChief, *18*		300
84719	AT&SF Super Chief Diesel Passenger Set, LionChief, *18*		430
___ 84724	AT&SF Add-on Baggage Car "1386," *18*		90
___ 84725	AT&SF Add-on Vista Dome Car "500," *18*		95
84726	SP Rising Sun 0-8-0 Steam Freight Set, LionChief, *17-18*		320
___ 84732	BNSF Tier 4 Modern Freight Set, LionChief, *18*		400
84737	Construction Railroad Diesel Freight Set, LionChief, *18*		350
___ 84747	18 Christmas BoxCar, *18*		65
___ 84748	Christmas Music Boxcar #18, *18*		80
84754	Anheuser-Busch Clydesdale Old-Time Steam Freight Set, LionChief, *18*		420
___ 84760	Daisy Duck 1-D Tank Car, *18*		75
___ 84761	Chip 'n' Dale Chasing Gondola, *18*		80
___ 84762	SP Daylight 1-D Tank Car, *17-18*		60
___ 84763	Disney Villains Ursula BoxCar, *18*		80
___ 84764	Disney Villains Queen of Hearts BoxCar, *18*		80
___ 84765	Angela Trotta Thomas Christmas Passenger Car 2-pack, *18*		300
___ 84766	Gondola w/Construction Signs, *18*		65
___ 84767	Harry Potter Dementors Coach w/Sound, *18*		85
___ 84768	Moe & Joe Lumber FlatCar, *18*		90
___ 84769	Wile E. Coyote & Road Runner Ambush Shack, *18*		120
___ 84770	Peabody Coal Hopper 6-pack, *18*		150
___ 84771	PRR Hopper 6-pack, *18*		150
___ 84772	N&W Hopper 6-pack, *18*		150
___ 84773	UP Hopper 6-pack, *18*		150
___ 84774	NS Hopper 6-pack, *18*		150
___ 84775	DM&IR Ore Car 6-pack, *18*		150
___ 84776	C&NW Ore Car 6-pack, *18*		150
___ 84777	GN Ore Car 6-pack, *18*		150
___ 84778	MILW Ore Car 6-pack, *18*		150
___ 84779	B&LE Ore Car 6-pack, *18*		150
___ 84780	U.S. Caboose, *18*		75
___ 84781	ELX Halloween Caboose, *18*		75
___ 84782	Presidential Caboose, *18*		75
___ 84784	John Deere Harvest Dump Car, *18*		80
___ 84785	Naughty or Nice Ore Car 2-pack, *18*		80
___ 84786	Christmas Essentials Barrel Car, *18*		70
___ 84787	Santa Freight Lines Steam Set, LionChief, *18*		300

Exc Mint

		Exc	Mint
84792	House Under Construction, *18*	100	____
84794	Budweiser Bar & Grille, *18*	90	____
84795	Deluxe Christmas House, *18*	130	____
84797	Christmas Industrial Water Tower, *18*	85	____
84798	Hunting Rabbit Car, *18*	85	____
84799	Marvin the Martian Earth Stomper FlatCar, *18*	95	____
84801	Justice League BoxCar, *17*	85	____
84802	Gilbson Wine 1-D Tank Car "66719," *17*	75	____
84803	Tidewater 1-D Tank Car "1367," *17*	75	____
84804	A.E. Staley 1-D Tank Car "704," *17*	75	____
84805	Mid-Continent Petroleum 1-D Tank Car "1018," *17*	75	____
84806	Shell 1-D Tank Car "662," *17*	75	____
84807	John Deere 1-D Tank Car "236," *17*	75	____
84810	Polar Express 1-D Tank Car "122518," *17*	75	____
84811	Polar Express Scale Baggage Car, *17*	200	____
84812	Polar Express Scale Combine, *17*	200	____
84813	Polar Express Scale Coach, *17*	200	____
84814	Polar Express Scale Diner, *17*	200	____
84815	Polar Express Scale Observation, *17*	200	____
84816	PRR 1930 Broadway Limited Steam Passenger Set, CC, *17*	2000	____
84821	PRR Heavyweight Combine Liberty Hill, *17-18*	200	____
84822	PRR Heavyweight Sleeper Cent Fawn, *17-18*	200	____
84823	PRR Heavyweight Sleeper Central Park, *17-18*	200	____
84824	PRR Heavyweight Sleeper Lafayette Square, *17-18*	200	____
84825	PRR Heavyweight Diner "4498," *17-18*	200	____
84826	PRR Heavyweight Observation Colonel Lindbergh, *17-18*	200	____
84827	PRR Heavyweight Observation Washington Circle, *17-18*	200	____
84828	BNSF 66' Mill Gondola "518726," w/Graffiti, *17*	80	____
84829	BNSF 66' Mill Gondola "518770," *17*	80	____
84830	BNSF 66' Mill Gondola "518795," *17*	80	____
84831	GNTX Railgon 66' Mill Gondola "290146," w/Graffiti, *17*	80	____
84832	GNTX Railgon 66' Mill Gondola "290087," *17*	80	____
84833	GNTX Railgon 66' Mill Gondola "290102," *17*	80	____
84834	Atlantic & Western 66' Mill Gondola "400704," w/Graffiti, *17*	80	____
84835	Atlantic & Western 66' Mill Gondola "400664," *17*	80	____
84836	Atlantic & Western 66' Mill Gondola "400675," *17*	80	____
84837	Arkansas & Oklahoma 66' Mill Gondola "35018," w/Graffiti, *17*	80	____
84838	Arkansas & Oklahoma 66' Mill Gondola "35007," *17*	80	____
84839	Arkansas & Oklahoma 66' Mill Gondola "35055," *17*	80	____
84840	Steelton & Highspire 66' Mill Gondola "125," w/Graffiti, *17*	80	____
84841	Steelton & Highspire 66' Mill Gondola "117," *17*	80	____
84842	Steelton & Highspire 66' Mill Gondola "118," *17*	80	____
84843	Demonstrator GE AC6000 Diesel "6000," CC, *17*	650	____
84844	Demonstrator GE AC6000 Diesel "6001," CC, *17*	650	____
84845	Demonstrator GE AC6000 Diesel "6002," CC, *17*	650	____
84846	CSX GE AC6000 Diesel "691," CC, *17*	650	____
84847	CSX GE AC6000 Diesel "5014," CC, *17*	650	____
84848	CSX CSX GE AC6000 Diesel "Diversity 5000," CC, *17*	650	____

			Exc	Mint
___	**84849**	CSX CSX GE AC6000 Diesel "Diversity 5001," CC, *17*		650
___	**84850**	SP GE AC6000 Diesel "601," CC, *17*		650
___	**84851**	SP GE AC6000 Diesel "602," CC, *17*		650
___	**84852**	UP GE AC6000 Diesel "7566," CC, *17*		650
___	**84853**	UP GE AC6000 Diesel "7579," CC, *17*		650
	84854	TTX Husky Double-Stack Car "56210," w/Trailers, *17*		130
	84855	TTX Husky Double-Stack Car "56289," w/Trailers, *17*		130
	84856	TTX Husky Double-Stack Car "56368," w/Trailers, *17*		130
	84857	TTX Husky Double-Stack Car "56150," w/Trailers, *17*		130
	84858	TTX Husky Double-Stack Car "56168," w/Trailers, *17*		130
	84859	TTX Husky Double-Stack Car "56174," w/Trailers, *17*		130
___	**84860**	BNSF Husky Double-Stack Car "203003," w/Trailers, *17*		130
___	**84861**	BNSF Husky Double-Stack Car "203015," w/Trailers, *17*		130
___	**84862**	BNSF Husky Double-Stack Car "203032," w/Trailers, *17*		130
___	**84863**	ARZC Husky Double-Stack Car "100000," w/Trailers, *17*		130
___	**84864**	ARZC Husky Double-Stack Car "100002," w/Trailers, *17*		130
___	**84865**	ARZC Husky Double-Stack Car "100005," w/Trailers, *17*		130
___	**84866**	Southwind Husky Double-Stack Car "5003," w/Trailers, *17*		130
___	**84867**	Southwind Husky Double-Stack Car "5005," w/Trailers, *17*		130
___	**84868**	Southwind Husky Double-Stack Car "5008," w/Trailers, *17*		130
___	**84869**	Hot Wheels BoxCar, *18*		85
___	**84870**	NP 50' Flatcar "65110" w/NPT 40' Trailer, *17*		120
___	**84871**	NP 50' Flatcar "65126" w/NPT 40' Trailer, *17*		120
___	**84872**	PRR 50' Flatcar "469615" w/PRRZ 40' Trailer, *17*		120
___	**84873**	PRR 50' Flatcar "469675" w/PRRZ 40' Trailer, *17*		120
___	**84874**	Trailer Train 50' Flatcar "475227" w/SOUZ 40' Trailer, *17*		120
___	**84875**	Trailer Train 50' Flatcar "475274" w/SOUZ 40' Trailer, *17*		120
___	**84876**	UP 50' Flatcar "53017" w/UPZ 40' Trailer, *17*		120
___	**84877**	UP 50' Flatcar "53022" w/UPZ 40' Trailer, *17*		120
___	**84878**	Wabash 50' Flatcar "25535" w/WABZ 40' Trailer, *17*		120
___	**84879**	Wabash 50' Flatcar "25549" w/WABZ 40' Trailer, *17*		120
___	**84880**	D&RGW 50' Flatcar "21032" w/RGMW 40' Trailer, *17*		120
___	**84881**	D&RGW 50' Flatcar "21036" w/RGMW 40' Trailer, *17*		120
___	**84882**	C&O 40' Trailer 2-pack, *17*		65
___	**84883**	GM&O 40' Trailer 2-pack, *17*		65
___	**84884**	L&N 40' Trailer 2-pack, *17*		65
___	**84885**	SAL 40' Trailer 2-pack, *17*		65
___	**84886**	Frisco 40' Trailer 2-pack, *17*		65
___	**84887**	WP 40' Trailer 2-pack, *17*		65
___	**84888**	PRR X31 Boxcar "78401," w/Circle Keystone, *17*		120
___	**84889**	PRR X31 Boxcar "78498," w/Circle Keystone, *17*		80
___	**84890**	PRR X31 Boxcar "68408," w/Shadow Keystone, *17*		80
___	**84891**	PRR X31 Boxcar "77061," w/Shadow Keystone, *17*		80
___	**84892**	PRR X31 Boxcar "76803," w/Plain Keystone, *17*		80

Exc Mint

		Exc	Mint
84893	PRR X31 Boxcar "77734," w/Plain Keystone, 17	80	___
84894	PRR X31 Boxcar "497310," w/Stores, 17	80	___
84895	PRR X31 Boxcar "497329," w/Stores, 17	80	___
84896	N&W X31 Boxcar "46146," 17	80	___
84897	N&W X31 Boxcar "46340," 17	80	___
84898	Personalized Man's Best Friend BoxCar, 18	90	___
84899	Personalized World's Best Cat BoxCar, 18	90	___
84904	BNSF Scale Autorack, Orange "965375," 18	120	___
84905	BNSF Scale Autorack, Orange "965530," 18	120	___
84906	Ferromex Scale Autorack "705473," 18	120	___
84907	Ferromex Scale Autorack "953615," 18	120	___
84908	Southern Scale Autorack "159162," 18	120	___
84909	Southern Scale Autorack "159166," 18	120	___
84910	CSX Scale Autorack "156256," 18	120	___
84911	CSX Scale Autorack "973924," 18	120	___
84912	NS Scale Autorack "983818," 18	120	___
84913	NS Scale Autorack "992879," 18	120	___
84914	MKT Scale Autorack "254176," 18	120	___
84915	MKT Scale Autorack "942194," 18	120	___
84916	Union Tank Car Cylindrical Covered Hopper "44072," 18	90	___
84917	Union Tank Car Cylindrical Covered Hopper "44094," 18	90	___
84918	Davis Industries Cylindrical Covered Hopper "1002," 18	90	___
84919	Davis Industries Cylindrical Covered Hopper "1003," 18	90	___
84920	Conrail Cylindrical Covered Hopper "884244," 18	90	___
84921	Conrail Cylindrical Covered Hopper "884270," 18	90	___
84922	CSX Cylindrical Covered Hopper "225370," 18	90	___
84923	CSX Cylindrical Covered Hopper "225382," 18	90	___
84924	Wilkes-Barre Mining Cylindrical Covered Hopper "104," 18	90	___
84925	Wilkes-Barre Mining Cylindrical Covered Hopper "106," 18	90	___
84926	SP Cylindrical Covered Hopper "1002," 18	90	___
84927	SP Cylindrical Covered Hopper "1027," 18	90	___
84928	John Quincy Adams Presidential BoxCar, 18	70	___
84929	James K. Polk Presidential BoxCar, 18	70	___
84930	Benjamin Harrison Presidential BoxCar, 18	70	___
84934	NYC 4-6-4 Hudson Locomotive "5425," LionChief Plus, 17-18	450	___
84935	B&A 4-6-4 Hudson Locomotive "616," LionChief Plus, 17-18	450	___
84936	Nickel Plate Road 4-6-4 Hudson Locomotive "170," LionChief Plus, 17-18	450	___
84937	GN 4-6-4 Hudson Locomotive "171," LionChief Plus, 17-18	450	___
84938	AT&SF EMD GP38 Diesel "3441," LionChief Plus, 17-18	350	___
84939	NS First Responders EMD GP38 Diesel "5642," LionChief Plus, 17-18	350	___
84940	Seaboard System EMD GP38 Diesel "543," LionChief Plus, 17-18	350	___
84941	FEC EMD GP38 Diesel "506," LionChief Plus, 17-18	350	___
84942	PRR 4-4-2 Atlantic Locomotive "460," CC, 17	800	___

	Exc	Mint
___ **84943** PRR 4-4-2 Atlantic Locomotive "68," CC, *17*		800
___ **84944** PRR 4-4-2 Atlantic Locomotive "1163," CC, *17*		800
___ **84945** PRSL 4-4-2 Atlantic Locomotive "6009," CC, *17*		800
___ **84946** LIRR 4-4-2 Atlantic Locomotive "1611," CC, *17*		800
___ **84947** GN 4-4-2 Atlantic Locomotive "1707," CC, *17*		800
84948 PRR 2-8-0 Consolidation Locomotive "1288," CC, *18*		750
84949 PRSL 2-8-0 Consolidation Locomotive "8072," CC, *18*		750
___ **84950** LIRR 2-8-0 Consolidation Locomotive "109," CC, *18*		750
84951 Bellefonte Central 2-8-0 Consolidation Locomotive "21," CC, *18*		750
___ **84952** PRR 2-8-0 Consolidation Locomotive "3529," Weathered, CC, *18*		750
___ **84953** Pennsylvania Coal Hauler Steam Freight Set, CC, *18*		1100
84964 Angela Trotta Thomas 4-6-4 Hudson Locomotive, LionChief Plus, *18*		450
84965 Rio Grande A5 0-4-0 Locomotive "62," LionChief Plus, *18*		480
84966 NYC A5 0-4-0 Locomotive "1662," LionChief Plus, *18*		480
___ **84967** PRR A5 0-4-0 Locomotive "577," LionChief Plus, *18*		480
___ **84968** UP A5 0-4-0 Locomotive "218," LionChief Plus, *18*		480
___ **84985** LIRR B60 Baggage Car "7715," *17-18*		160
___ **84986** LIRR B60 Baggage Car "7724," *17-18*		160
___ **84987** PRR B60 Baggage Car, Clerestory "7918," *17-18*		160
___ **84988** PRR B60 Baggage Car, Clerestory "7941," *17-18*		160
___ **84989** PRR B60 Baggage Car, Round Roof "7919," *17-18*		160
___ **84990** PRR B60 Baggage Car, Round Roof "7938," *17-18*		160
___ **84991** PRR B60 Baggage Car, Round Roof, Messenger "9352," *17-18*		160
84992 PRR B60 Baggage Car, Round Roof, Messenger "9379," *17-18*		160
84993 PRR B60 Baggage Car, Round Roof, 1960s "9356," *17-18*		160
84994 PRR B60 Baggage Car, Round Roof, 1960s "9384," *17-18*		160
___ **84995** PRSL Baggage Car "5437," *17-18*		160
___ **84996** PRSL B60 Baggage Car "6403," *17-18*		160
___ **84997** LIRR 18" Heavyweight Passenger Coach 2-pack, #1, *17-18*		400
85000 LIRR 18" Heavyweight Passenger Coach 2-pack, #2, *17-18*		400
85003 PRSL 18" Heavyweight Passenger Coach 2-pack, #1, *17-18*		400
85006 PRSL 18" Heavyweight Passenger Coach 2-pack, #2, *17-18*		400
85009 PRR 18" Heavyweight Passenger Coach 2-pack, #1, *17-18*		400
85012 PRR 18" Heavyweight Passenger Coach 2-pack, #2, *17-18*		400
___ **85015** ACL/PRR Champion Passenger Car 4-pack, *17-18*		620
___ **85016** ACL/PRR Champion Passenger Car 2-pack, *17-18*		310
___ **85017** ACL Champion 21" Diner, w/StationSounds, *17-18*		310
___ **85018** ACL EMD SW7 Diesel "648," CC, *18*		500
___ **85019** BN EMD SW7 Diesel "111," CC, *18*		500

		Exc	Mint
85020	Conemaugh & Black Lick EMD SW7 Diesel "106," CC, *18*	500	
85021	Chessie System EMD SW7 Diesel "5224," CC, *18*	500	___
85022	LV EMD SW7 Diesel "222," CC, *18*	500	___
85023	MEC EMD SW7 Diesel "331," CC, *18*	500	___
85024	NYC EMD SW7 Diesel "8853," CC, *18*	500	___
85025	Frisco EMD SW7 Diesel "303," CC, *18*	500	___
85026	Southern EMD SW7 Diesel "1100," CC, *18*	500	___
85027	UP EMD SW7 Diesel "1808," CC, *18*	500	___
85028	AT&SF EMD SD45 Diesel "5305," CC, *18*	600	___
85029	AT&SF EMD SD45 Diesel "5319," CC, *18*	600	___
85030	B&P EMD SD45 Diesel "453," CC, *18*	600	___
85031	B&P EMD SD45 Diesel "455," CC, *18*	600	___
85032	C&NW EMD SD45 Diesel "6485," CC, *18*	600	___
85033	C&NW EMD SD45 Diesel "6568," CC, *18*	600	___
85034	Montana Rail Link EMD SD45 Diesel "320," CC, *18*	600	___
85035	Montana Rail Link EMD SD45 Diesel "331," CC, *18*	600	___
85036	MPI EMD SD45 Diesel "9009," CC, *18*	600	___
85037	MPI EMD SD45 Diesel "9011," CC, *18*	600	___
85038	N&W EMD SD45 Diesel "1776," CC, *18*	600	___
85039	N&W EMD SD45 Diesel "1790," CC, *18*	600	___
85040	NYS&W EMD SD45 Diesel "3612," CC, *18*	600	___
85041	NYS&W EMD SD45 Diesel "3614," CC, *18*	600	___
85042	WC EMD SD45 Diesel "6525," CC, *18*	600	___
85043	WC EMD SD45 Diesel "6580," CC, *18*	600	___
85046	BNSF EMD SD70ACe Diesel "9214," CC, *18*	600	___
85047	BNSF EMD SD70ACe Diesel "9287," CC, *18*	600	___
85048	CN EMD SD70ACe Diesel "8101," CC, *18*	600	___
85049	CN EMD SD70ACe Diesel "8103," CC, *18*	600	___
85050	CSX EMD SD70ACe Diesel "4849," CC, *18*	600	___
85051	Demonstrator EMD SD70ACe Diesel "1201," CC, *18*	600	___
85052	Demonstrator EMD SD70ACe Diesel "1202," CC, *18*	600	___
85053	KCS EMD SD70ACe Diesel "4156," CC, *18*	600	___
85054	KCS EMD SD70ACe Diesel "4164," CC, *18*	600	___
85055	NS EMD SD70ACe Diesel "1030," CC, *18*	600	___
85056	NS EMD SD70ACe Diesel "1111," CC, *18*	600	___
85057	UP EMD SD70ACe Diesel "8650," CC, *18*	600	___
85058	UP EMD SD70ACe Diesel "8665," CC, *18*	600	___
85059	MKT EMD NW2 Diesel "7," LionChief Plus, *18*	320	___
85060	PRR EMD NW2 Diesel "9172," LionChief Plus, *18*	320	___
85061	Nickel Plate Road EMD NW2 Diesel "13," LionChief Plus, *18*	320	
85062	UP EMD NW2 Diesel "1037," LionChief Plus, *18*	320	___
85063	MILW EMD NW2 Diesel "1649," LionChief Plus, *18*	320	___
85065	Hot Wheels 50th Anniversary BoxCar, *17-18*	85	___
85066	TTX Husky Double-Stack Car "56210," w/EOT Device, *17*	150	
85067	TTX Husky Double-Stack Car "56180," w/EOT Device, *17*	150	
85068	BNSF Husky Double-Stack Car "203054," w/EOT Device, *17*	150	
85069	ARZC Husky Double-Stack Car "100008," w/EOT Device, *17*	150	
85070	Southwind Husky Double-Stack Car "5009," w/EOT Device, *17*	150	

Exc Mint

		Exc	Mint
85071	AT&SF Wide-Vision Caboose w/Camera "999718," *18*		125
85072	BN Wide-Vision Caboose w/Camera "12345," *18*		125
85073	Chessie System Wide-Vision Caboose w/Camera "903118," *18*		125
85074	CSX Wide-Vision Caboose w/Camera "903282," *18*		125
85075	Reading Wide-Vision Caboose w/Camera "94116," *18*		125
85076	UP Wide-Vision Caboose w/Camera "13605," *18*		125
85077	NS Wide-Vision Caboose w/Camera "555059," *18*		125
85078	PRR Wide-Vision Caboose w/Camera "477900," *18*		125
85079	DODX Wide-Vision Caboose "902," *18*		100
85080	Montana Rail Link Wide-Vision Caboose "1005," *18*		100
85081	UTLX 30,000-Gallon 1-D Tank Car "212189" w/FreightSounds, *18*		150
85082	GATX 30,000-Gallon 1-D Tank Car "36323" w/FreightSounds, *18*		150
85083	Philadelphia Energy Solutions 30,000-Gallon 1-D Tank Car "0756" w/FreightSounds, *18*		150
85084	TILX 30,000-Gallon 1-D Tank Car "254088" w/FreightSounds, *18*		150
85085	ADM 30,000-Gallon 1-D Tank Car "29248" w/FreightSounds, *18*		150
85086	Cargill 30,000-Gallon 1-D Tank Car "7964" w/FreightSounds, *18*		150
85087	UTLX 30,000-Gallon 1-D Tank Car "212187" w/EOT Device, *18*		150
85088	GATX 30,000-Gallon 1-D Tank Car "36328" w/EOT Device, *18*		120
85089	ADM 30,000-Gallon 1-D Tank Car "29252" w/EOT Device, *18*		120
85090	Cargill 30,000-Gallon 1-D Tank Car "7968" w/EOT Device, *18*		120
85091	ACFX 30,000-Gallon 1-D Tank Car "89990" w/EOT Device, *18*		120
85092	Procor 30,000-Gallon 1-D Tank Car "43579" w/EOT Device, *18*		120
85093	American Potash PS-2 Covered Hopper "31259," *17*		75
85094	American Potash PS-2 Covered Hopper "31275," *17*		75
85095	Bucyrus Erie PS-2 Covered Hopper "1114," *17*		75
85096	Bucyrus Erie PS-2 Covered Hopper "1118," *17*		75
85097	Georgia Marble PS-2 Covered Hopper "31340," *17*		75
85098	Georgia Marble PS-2 Covered Hopper "31341," *17*		75
85099	Ready Mixed Concrete PS-2 Covered Hopper "331," *17*		75
85100	Ready Mixed Concrete PS-2 Covered Hopper "340," *17*		75
85101	Linde PS-2 Covered Hopper "209," *17*		75
85102	Linde PS-2 Covered Hopper "211," *17*		75
85103	U.S. Borax PS-2 Covered Hopper "31064," *17*		75
85104	U.S. Borax PS-2 Covered Hopper "31066," *17*		75
85105	Tank Train 2-Pack with EOT Device, #1, *17*		200
85108	Tank Train 2-Pack with EOT Device, #2, *17*		200
85111	Tank Train 2-Pack with EOT Device, #3, *17*		200
85114	GATX Tank Train 2-Pack with EOT Device, *17*		200
85117	CN Tank Train 2-Pack with EOT Device, *17*		200

Exc Mint

		Exc	Mint
85120	Cibro Tank Train 2-Pack with EOT Device, *17*	200	
85126	Tank Train Car #1, *17*	90	
85127	Tank Train Car #2, *17*	90	
85128	Tank Train Car #3, *17*	90	
85129	Tank Train Car #4, *17*	90	
85130	Tank Train Car #5, *17*	90	
85131	Tank Train Car #6, *17*	90	
85132	Tank Train Car #1, *17*	90	
85133	Tank Train Car #2, *17*	90	
85134	Tank Train Car #3, *17*	90	
85135	Tank Train Car #4, *17*	90	
85136	Tank Train Car #5, *17*	90	
85137	Tank Train Car #6, *17*	90	
85138	Tank Train Car #1, *17*	90	
85139	Tank Train Car #2, *17*	90	
85140	Tank Train Car #3, *17*	90	
85141	Tank Train Car #4, *17*	90	
85142	Tank Train Car #5, *17*	90	
85143	Tank Train Car #6, *17*	90	
85144	GATX Tank Train Car #1, *17*	90	
85145	GATX Tank Train Car #2, *17*	90	
85146	GATX Tank Train Car #3, *17*	90	
85147	GATX Tank Train Car #4, *17*	90	
85148	GATX Tank Train Car #5, *17*	90	
85149	GATX Tank Train Car #6, *17*	90	
85150	CN Tank Train Car #1, *17*	90	
85151	CN Tank Train Car #2, *17*	90	
85152	CN Tank Train Car #3, *17*	90	
85153	CN Tank Train Car #4, *17*	90	
85154	CN Tank Train Car #5, *17*	90	
85155	CN Tank Train Car #6, *17*	90	
85156	Cibro Tank Train Car #1, *17*	90	
85157	Cibro Tank Train Car #2, *17*	90	
85158	Cibro Tank Train Car #3, *17*	90	
85159	Cibro Tank Train Car #4, *17*	90	
85160	Cibro Tank Train Car #5, *17*	90	
85161	Cibro Tank Train Car #6, *17*	90	
85168	Tacoma Rail EMD SD70ACe Diesel "7001," CC, *18*	600	
85169	Tacoma Rail EMD SD70ACe Diesel "7002" CC, *18*	600	
85170	Atlanta & West Point USRA 4-6-2 Pacific Locomotive "290," CC, *18*	1400	
85171	B&O USRA 4-6-2 Pacific Locomotive "5300," CC, *18*	1400	
85172	Reading & Northern USRA 4-6-2 Pacific Locomotive "425," CC, *18*	1400	
85173	NP USRA 4-6-2 Pacific Locomotive "2256," CC, *18*	1400	
85174	Southern USRA 4-6-2 Pacific Locomotive "1372," CC, *18*	1400	
85175	Halloween USRA 4-6-2 Pacific Locomotive "1031," CC, *18*	1400	
85176	C&O USRA 2-6-6-2 Locomotive "1522," CC, *18*	1600	
85177	W&LE USRA 2-6-6-2 Locomotive "8007," CC, *18*	1600	
85178	B&O USRA 2-6-6-2 Locomotive "7555," CC, *18*	1600	
85179	Buffalo, Rochester & Pittsburgh USRA 2-6-6-2 Locomotive "755," CC, *18*	1600	

Exc Mint

		Exc	Mint
____	85180 GN USRA 2-6-6-2 Locomotive "1855," CC, 18		1600
____	85181 MEC USRA 2-6-6-2 Locomotive "1205," CC, 18		1600
____	85182 NYC USRA 2-6-6-2 Locomotive "1400," CC, 18		1600
____	85183 SP USRA 2-6-6-2 Locomotive "3932," CC, 18		1600
____	85184 WM USRA 2-6-6-2 Locomotive "960," CC, 18		1600
____	85185 Renz Hobby Shop, 17		300
____	85186 AT&SF EMD F3 A-A Diesel Set, CC, 17		850
____	85189 AT&SF Powered EMD F3 B Diesel, CC, 17		450
____	85190 At&SF SuperBass EMD F3 B Diesel, CC, 17		300
____	85191 GN EMD F3 A-A Diesel Set, CC, 17		850
____	85194 GN Powered EMD F3 B Diesel, CC, 17		450
____	85195 GN SuperBass EMD F3 B Diesel, CC, 17		300
____	85196 T&P EMD F7 A-A Diesel Set, CC, 17		850
____	85199 T&P Powered EMD F7 B Diesel, CC, 17		450
____	85200 T&P SuperBass EMD F3 B Diesel, CC, 17		300
____	85201 NYO&W EMD F3 A-A Diesel Set, CC, 17		850
____	85204 NYO&W Powered EMD F3 B Diesel, CC, 17		450
____	85205 NYO&W SuperBass EMD F3 B Diesel, CC, 17		300
____	85206 PRR EMD F7 A-A Diesel Set, CC, 17		850
____	85209 PRR Powered EMD F7 B Diesel, CC, 17		450
____	85210 PRR SuperBass EMD F7 B Diesel, CC, 17		300
____	85211 Reading EMD F3 A-A Diesel Set, CC, 17		850
____	85214 Reading Powered EMD F3 B Diesel, CC, 17		450
____	85215 ReadingSuperBass EMD F3 B Diesel, CC, 17		300
____	85216 Conrail EMD F7 A-A Diesel Set "1792-1730," CC, 17		850
____	85219 Conrail Powered EMD F7 B Diesel "3861," CC, 17		450
____	85220 Conrail SuperBass EMD F7 B Diesel "3872," CC, 17		300
____	85222 CSX Maxi-Stack "85222," 17		75
____	85223 BNSF Maxi-Stack "237342," 17-C55718		75
____	85227 GN Oriental Ltd Heavyweight Baggage/Coach, 17-18		400
____	85230 GN Oriental Ltd Heavyweight Sleeper/Coach, 17-18		400
____	85233 GN Oriental Ltd Heavyweight Sleeper/Diner, 17-18		400
____	85236 GN Oriental Ltd Heavyweight Sleeper/Observation, 17-18		400
____	85241 Mystery Machine FT Diesel Freight Set, Lionchief, 18		430
____	85246 Anheuser-Busch Vintage Refrigerator Car, 18		80
____	85247 Budweiser Clydesdale Vintage Refrigerator Car, 18		80
____	85248 Budweiser Vintage Refrigerator Car, 18		80
____	85253 End of the Line Express Diesel Freight Set, LionChief, 18		330
____	85258 AT&SF FT Ranger Diesel Freight Set, LionChief, 18		430
____	85263 Tomb of the Unknown Soldier Walking Brakeman Car, 18		100
____	85264 Harry Potter Hogwarts Add-on Coach, 18		75
____	85269 Scooby Doo Sam Witches Cafe, 18		100
____	85270 Hot Wheels Checkered Flagpole, 18		60
____	85271 Polar Express Flagpole, 18		60
____	85274 PRR Gla Hopper 3-pack #1, 18		225
____	85278 PRR Gla Hopper 3-pack #2, 18		225
____	85282 PRR Coal Goes To War Gla Hopper 3-pack #3, 18		225
____	85286 Berwind Gla Hopper 3-pack, 18		225
____	85290 PRR MOW PRR Gla Hopper 3-pack #4, 18		225
____	85294 Lionelville Hobby Shop, 18		300
____	85295 Layout Control System CSM2, 18		110
____	85296 Layout Control System IRV2, 18		100

		Exc	Mint
85297	PRR N5 Caboose "477819," *18*	100	
85298	PRR N5 Caboose "478884," *18*	100	
85299	Reading & Northern N5 Caboose "477514," *18*	100	
85300	PRSL N5 Caboose "202," *18*	100	
85301	RJ Corman N5 Caboose, *18*	100	
85309	Flight Night Halloween Pylon, *18*	150	
85310	Witches Brew Storage Tank, *18*	85	
85315	UP EMD SD70ACe Diesel "1943," CC, *18*	600	
85316	UP Wide-Vision Caboose, Spirit of Union Pacific "1943," *18*	100	
85317	UP Spirit of the Union Pacific BoxCar, *18*	85	
85318	Personalized Happy Birthday BoxCar, *18*	90	
85319	Personalized 18 Merry Christmas BoxCar, *18*	90	
85320	Personalized Happy Anniversary BoxCar, *18*	90	
85321	John Deere Flatcar w/Tractor Load, *18*	80	
85322	Personalized 18 Halloween BoxCar, *18*	90	
85323	Scooby Doo BoxCar, *18*	85	
85324	Thomas & Friends Christmas Freight Set, LionChief, *18*	200	
85326	NYC Vision Baggage Car "9152," *18*	330	
85327	NYC Baggage Car 2-pack #1, *18*	350	
85330	NYC Baggage Car 2-pack #2, *18*	350	
85333	NYC Baggage/Combine 2-pack, *18*	400	
85336	NYC 18" Heavyweight Baggage Car 2-pack, *18*	350	
85339	SP Scale RPO Passenger Car "5124," *18*	160	
85340	L&N Scale RPO Passenger Car "1099," *18*	160	
85341	LIRR Scale RPO Passenger Car "737," *18*	160	
85342	MILW Scale RPO Passenger Car "2105," *18*	160	
85343	NYC Scale RPO Passenger Car "4819," *18*	160	
85344	PRR Scale RPO Passenger Car "5265," *18*	160	
85345	PRR Scale RPO Passenger Car "5269," *18*	160	
85346	PC Scale RPO Passenger Car "5267," *18*	160	
85347	UP Scale RPO Passenger Car "2060," *18*	160	
85348	MILW 18" Columbian Passenger Car 2-pack #A, *18*	400	
85351	MILW 18" Columbian Passenger Car 2-pack #B, *18*	400	
85354	MILW 18" Columbian Passenger Car 2-pack #C, *18*	400	
85357	MILW 18" Columbian Passenger Car 2-pack #D, *18*	400	
85360	UP Challenger 21" Passenger Car 4-pack, *18*	700	
85361	UP Challenger 21" Passenger Car 2-pack, *18*	350	
85362	UP Challenger 21" Diner w/StationSounds, *18*	330	
85367	L&N Hummingbird 21" Passenger Car 4-pack, *18*	700	
85368	L&N Hummingbird 21" Passenger Car 2-pack, *18*	350	
85370	Reading & Northern 18" Excursion and Business Car 2-pack #A, *18*	400	
85373	Reading & Northern 18" Excursion and Business Car 2-pack #B, *18*	400	
85376	Reading & Northern 21" Dome Car w/StationSounds, *18*	350	
85377	MOW Disconnect Work Car 4-pack, *18*	160	
85378	PRR Disconnect Work Car 4-pack, *18*	160	
85379	AT&SF Disconnect Work Car 4-pack, *18*	160	
85380	UP Disconnect Work Car 4-pack, *18*	160	
85381	NYC Disconnect Work Car 4-pack, *18*	160	
85382	D&RGW Disconnect Work Car 4-pack, *18*	160	

		Exc	Mint
___ 85383	Layout Control System IRV2 Sensor Add-on, *18*		30
___ 85384	Orange 10" Straight FasTrack 4-pack, *18*		25
85386	Pennsylvania Lines 2-8-0 Consolidation Locomotive "7109," CC, *18*		750
___			
85387	Western Allegheny 2-8-0 Consolidation Locomotive "85," CC, *18*		750
___			
___ 85389	White 10" Straight FasTrack 4-pack, *18*		25
___ 85390	White O-36 Curve Fastrack 4-pack, *18*		25
___ 85391	White PEP Activation Track, *18*		25
___ 85392	White 10" Terminal FasTrack, *18*		10
___ 85401	UP LED Flag BoxCar, Yellow and Gray "1862," *18*		120
___ 85402	UP LED Flag BoxCar, C&NW Heritage "1995," *18*		120
___ 85403	UP LED Flag BoxCar, MKT Heritage "1988," *18*		120
___ 85404	UP LED Flag BoxCar, MP Heritage "1982," *18*		120
___ 85405	UP LED Flag BoxCar, D&RGW Heritage "1989," *18*		120
___ 85406	UP LED Flag BoxCar, SP Heritage "1996," *18*		120
___ 85407	UP LED Flag BoxCar, WP Heritage "1983," *18*		120
85408	UP LED Flag BoxCar, Spirit of Union Pacific "1943," *18*		120
___			
___ 85409	UP LED Flag BoxCar, Steam Program "4-8-8-4," *18*		120
___ 85410	Polar Express Hero Boy's Home, *18*		90
___ 85411	Pylon with World War II Planes, *18*		145
___ 85412	Santa's Sleigh Pylon, *18*		135
___ 99000	Keebler Elf Express Steam Freight Set, *99 u*		1175
___ 99001	Mickey's Holiday Express Freight Set, *99 u*		180
___ 99002	Looney Tunes Square Window Caboose, *99 u*		NRS
___ 99006	Keebler Bulkhead FlatCar, *99 u*		NRS
___ 99007	Smuckers Fudge 1-D Tank Car, *99 u*		90
___ 99008	Mickey's Merry Christmas BoxCar, *99 u*		NRS
99009	Mickey's Holiday Express Square Window Caboose, *99 u*		NRS
___			
___ 99013	Case Cutlery Tank Car "1889," *00 u*		NRS
___ 99014	Case Cutlery Gondola "1889," *00 u*		NRS
___ 99015	Case Cutlery Boxcar "1889," *00 u*		NRS
___ 99018	Case Cutlery Rolling Stock 3-pack, *00 u*		210
___ 79C95204C	Sears Santa Fe Diesel Freight Set, *71 u*	150	165
___ 79C9715C	Sears 4-unit Diesel Freight Set, *75 u*	50	65
___ 79C9717C	Sears 7-unit Steam Freight Set, *75 u*	150	165
___ 79N95223C	Sears 6-unit Diesel Freight Set, *74 u*	150	165
___ 79N9552C	Sears 6-unit Steam Freight Set, *72 u*	150	165
___ 79N9553C	Sears 6-unit Diesel Freight Set, *72 u*	150	165
___ 79N96178C	Sears 4-unit Steam Freight Set, *74 u*	50	65
___ 79N97082C	Sears Steam Freight Set, *70 u*		NRS
___ 79N97101C	Sears 5-unit Steam Freight Set, *72 u*	150	165
___ 79N98765C	Sears Logging Empire Set, *78 u*	100	115
T1428RRODTS	Tony Stewart NASCAR Steam Freight Set, *12-14*		300
___			
T1828RRMMKB	Kyle Busch NASCAR Steam Freight Set, *12-14*		300
___			
T2428RRDUJG			300
___	Jeff Gordon NASCAR Steam Freight Set, *12-14*		
T4828RRLOJJ	Jimmy Johnson NASCAR Steam Freight Set, *12-14*		300
___			
T4828RRLOJJ	Dale Earnhardt Jr. NASCAR Steam Freight Set, *12-14*		300
___			

TX328RRGMDE Dale Earnhardt NASCAR Steam Freight Set,   300
12-14   ___
6446- N&W Covered Quad Hopper, *70 u*   203 290
25   ___
UCS   Remote Control Track (O), *70*   4   7___

Unnumbered Items   ___
   Amtrak Passenger Car Set, *89, 89 u*   640 770___
   B&A Hudson and Standard O Car Set, *86 u*   1500 1700___
   Baltimore & Ohio Set, *94, 96*   NRS___
   Black Cave Flyer Playmat, *82*   8___
   Blue Comet Set, *78-80, 87 u*   560 620___
   Burlington Texas Zephyr Set, *80, 80 u*   980 1150___
   C&NW Passenger Car Set, *93*   385 460___
   Cannonball Freight Playmat, *81-82*   8___
   Chesapeake & Ohio Set, *95-96*   NRS___
   Chessie System Special Set, *80, 86 u*   560 620___
   Chicago & Alton Limited Set, *81, 86 u*   560 620___
   Commando Assault Train Playmat, *83-84*   8___
   D&RGW California Zephyr Set, *92, 93*   900___
   Erie Set (FF 7), *93*   385 460___
   Erie-Lackawanna Passenger Car Set, *93, 94*   940 980___
   Favorite Food Freight Set, *81-82*   250 350___
   Frisco Set (FF 5), *91*   405 425___
   GN Empire Builder Set, *92, 93*   620 730___
   Great Northern Set (FARR 3), *81, 81 u*   620 690___
   IC City of New Orleans Set, *85, 87, 93*   885 1045___
   Illinois Central Set, *91-92, 95*   255 285___
   Jersey Central Set, *86*   345 370___
   Joshua Lionel Cowen Set, *80, 80 u, 82*   540 580___
   L.A.S.E.R. Playmat, *81-82*   8___
   Lionel Lines Madison Car Set, *91, 93*   560 620___
   Lionel Lines Set, *82-84 u, 86, 86-87 u, 94-95*   530 620___
   Mickey Mouse Express Set, *77-78, 78 u*   1050 1800___
   Milwaukee Road Set (FF 2), *87, 90 u*   380 405___
   Mint Set, *79 u, 80-83, 84 u, 86 u, 87, 91 u, 93*   940 1073___
   Missouri Pacific Set, *95*   390___
   N&W Powhatan Arrow Passenger Car Set, *95*   370 445___
   N&W Powhatan Arrow Set, *81, 81 u, 82 u, 91 u*   1450 1700___
   New Haven Set, *94-95*   400___
   New York Central Set, *89, 91*   240 270___
   Nickel Plate Road Set (FF 6), *92*   385 460___
   Northern Pacific Set, *90-92*   190 250___
   NYC 20th Century Limited Set, *83, 83 u, 95*   1000 1200___
   Pennsylvania Set (FARR 5), *84-85, 89 u*   600 660___
   Pennsylvania Set, *79-80, 79-80 u, 81 u, 83 u*   1200 1350___
   Pennsylvania Set, *87-90, 95*   240 270___
   Pere Marquette Set, *93*   720 770___
   Rock Island & Peoria Set, *80-82*   240 315___
   Rocky Mountain Platform, *83-84*   8___
   Santa Fe Set (FARR 1), *79, 79 u*   460 580___
   Santa Fe Super Chief Set, *91, 91 u, 92 u, 93, 95* 1400 1700

   Southern Crescent Limited Set, *77-78, 87 u*   540 650___

	Exc	Mint
Southern Pacific Daylight Diesel Set, *82-83, 82-83 u, 90 u*	2150	2300
Southern Set (FARR 4), *83, 83 u*	620	690
SP Daylight Steam Set, *90, 92, 93*	790	940
Spirit of "76 Set, *74-76*	600	720
Station Platform, *83-84*		8
The General Set, *77-80*	240	285
Toys "R" Us Thunderball Freight Set, *75 u*		NRS
Union Pacific Set (FARR 2), *80, 80 u*	540	580
Union Pacific Set, *94*	430	500
UP Overland Route Set, *84, 92 u*	770	840
Wabash Set (FF 1), *86, 87*	755	905
Western Maryland Set (FF 4), *89*	345	405

		Retail
10-1027	No. 236 B Leipzig Station (German)	1200 ____
11-1001	No. 400E Locomotive, black, brass trim (std)	900 ____
11-1002	No. 400E Locomotive, gray, nickel trim (std)	900 ____
11-1003	No. 400E Locomotive, gray, brass trim (std)	900 ____
11-1005	No. 390 Locomotive, green	600 ____
11-1006	No. 400E Locomotive, crackele black, brass trim	900 ____
11-1008	No. 400E Lionel Lines Locomotive	900 ____
11-1009	No. 400E Locomotive, blue, brass trim	900 ____
11-1010	No. 385E Locomotive (std)	700 ____
11-1012	No. 1835E Locomotive, black, nickel trim	700 ____
11-1013	AF No. 4694 Warrior Passenger Set	1400 ____
11-1014	AF No. 4694 Iron Monarch Passenger Set	1250 ____
11-1015	No. 392E Locomotive, black, brass trim	800 ____
11-1016	No. 392E Locomotive, gray, nickel trim	800 ____
11-1017	No. 400E Locomotive, blue, nickel trim (std)	900 ____
11-1018	No. 7 Lionel Locomotive (std)	900 ____
11-1019	No. 6 Pennsylvania Locomotive (std)	900 ____
11-1020	American Flyer No. 4696 Locomotive	1000 ____
11-1021	No. 400E Presidential Locomotive (std)	1000 ____
11-1022	No. 400E Red Comet Locomotive (std)	1000 ____
11-1023	No. 400E Locomotive, blue, brass trim (std)	900 ____
11-1024	No. 400E Locomotive, black, brass trim (std)	900 ____
11-1025	No. 400E Lionel Lines Locomotive (std)	900 ____
11-1026	No. 400E Locomotive, pink (std)	1000 ____
11-1027	No. 400E Locomotive, state green (std)	1000 ____
11-1028	No. 400E Locomotive, black, brass trim (std)	1000 ____
11-1029	No. 6 NYC Locomotive (std)	900 ____
11-1030	No. 6 General Locomotive (std)	900 ____
11-1031	No. 6 Texas Locomotive (std)	950 ____
11-1038	No. 6 B&O Locomotive (std)	900 ____
11-1039	No. 6 Long Island Locomotive (std)	900 ____
11-1040	No. 6 Strasburg Locomotive (std)	900 ____
11-1041	No. 6 PRR Locomotive (std)	900 ____
11-1042	Great Northern Steam Locomotive (std)	1000 ____
11-1043	Lehigh Valley Steam Locomotive (std)	1000 ____
11-1044	NYC Steam Locomotive (std)	1000 ____
11-1045	PRR Steam Locomotive (std)	1000 ____
11-1046	No. 392E LL Locomotive, blue, nickel trim (std)	650 ____
11-1047	No. 392E LL Locomotive, blue, brass trim (std)	650 ____
11-1048	No. 390 LL Locomotive, black, brass trim (std)	650 ____
11-1049	No. 390 LL Locomotive, green, brass trim (std)	650 ____
11-1050	No. 390 LL Locomotive, gray, nickel trim (std)	650 ____
11-1051	No. 400E LL Locomotive, blue, nickel trim (std)	1000 ____
11-1052	No. 400E Locomotive, blue, brass trim (std)	1000 ____

____ 11-1053	No. 400E Locomotive, black, brass trim (std)	1000
____ 11-1054	No. 400E LL Locomotive, gray, nickel trim (std)	1000
____ 11-1055	No. 400E UP Locomotive, yellow (std)	1000
____ 11-1056	No. 400E NW Locomotive (std)	1000
____ 11-1057	No. 392E LL Locomotive, black, brass trim (std)	900
____ 11-1058	No. 392E Lionel Lines Locomotive (std)	900
____ 11-1059	No. 392E LL Locomotive, gray, nickel trim (std)	900
____ 11-1060	No. 392E PRR Locomotive (std)	900
____ 11-1061	No. 392E Lehigh Valley Locomotive (std)	900
11-1062 ____	No. 390E LL Gauge Steam Engine, black, brass trim (std)	650
____ 11-2003	No. 8E Electric Locomotive, olive green (std)	500
____ 11-2004	No. 8E Electric Locomotive, dark olive green (std)	500
____ 11-2005	No. 8E Electric Locomotive, orange (std)	500
____ 11-2006	No. 8E Electric Locomotive, red/cream (std)	500
____ 11-2007	American Flyer Presidential Passenger Set (std)	1800
____ 11-2008	AF No. 4689 Presidential Locomotive, blue (std)	800
____ 11-2009	Big Brute Electric Engine, zinc chromate	1500
____ 11-2010	Big Brute Electric Engine, green	1500
____ 11-2015	Super 381 Electric Engine, state green (std)	1300
____ 11-2016	Super 381 MILW Electric Engine (std)	1300
____ 11-2017	No. 408E Electric Locomotive (std)	900
____ 11-2018	No. 408E Electric Locomotive, Mojave	900
____ 11-2019	No. 408E Electric Locomotive, pink	900
____ 11-2020	No. 9 Electric Locomotive, green	600
____ 11-2021	No. 9 Electric Locomotive, orange	600
____ 11-2022	No. 9 Electric Locomotive, gray, nickel trim	600
____ 11-2023	No. 9 Electric Locomotive, dark green	600
____ 11-2024	No. 8 Trolley (std)	530
____ 11-2025	No. 9 Trolley (std)	650
____ 11-2026	No. 8 Christmas Trolley (std)	570
____ 11-2027	No. 381E Electric Locomotive, blue (std)	900
____ 11-2028	No. 381E Electric Locomotive, brown (std)	900
____ 11-2029	No. 381E Great Northern Electric Locomotive (std)	900
____ 11-2031	No. 4689 President's Locomotive, red (std)	900
____ 11-2033	Big Brute Electric Locomotive, brown (std)	1600
____ 11-2034	Big Brute Electric Locomotive, orange (std)	1600
____ 11-2038	Super 381 MILW Electric Locomotive (std)	1300
____ 11-2039	Super 381 PRR Electric Locomotive (std)	1300
____ 11-2040	Super 381 Electric Locomotive, two-tone brown (std)	1300
____ 11-2041	Super 381 New Haven Electric Locomotive (std)	1300
____ 11-2042	No. 408E LL Electric Locomotive, dark green (std)	950
____ 11-2043	No. 408E LL Electric Locomotive, apple green (std)	950
____ 11-2044	No. 408E LL Electric Locomotive, blue (std)	950
____ 11-2045	No. 408E MILW Electric Locomotive (std)	950
____ 11-2046	No. 408E GN Electric Locomotive (std)	950

LIONEL CORPORATION TINPLATE

Retail

11-2047	No. 318E LL Electric Locomotive, black (std)	500
11-2048	No. 318E LL Electric Locomotive, green (std)	500 ____
11-2049	No. 318E LL Electric Locomotive, gray (std)	500 ____
11-2050	No. 318E LL Electric Locomotive, brown (std)	500 ____
11-2051	No. 318E MILW Electric Locomotive (std)	500 ____
11-2052	No. 318E New Haven Electric Locomotive (std)	500 ____
11-5001	No. 384 Locomotive Passenger Set, black, brass trim	600 ____
11-5002	No. 384 Locomotive Christmas Freight Set (std)	600 ____
11-5003	No. 384 Locomotive LV Passenger Set (std)	600 ____
11-5004	No. 384 Locomotive NYC Freight Set	600 ____
11-5006	No. 384E Locomotive Girl's Passenger Set	600 ____
11-5007	No. 386 Freight Set (std)	600 ____
11-5008	No. 340E Coal Freight Set (std)	600 ____
11-5009	No. 342E Baby State Passenger Set (std)	600 ____
11-5010	No. 384E Blue Comet Passenger Set (std)	600 ____
11-5011	No. 386 Christmas Freight Set (std)	600 ____
11-5012	No. 342E Passenger Set (std)	600 ____
11-5013	No. 318E Christmas Freight Set (std)	600 ____
11-5014	No. 384E PRR Steam Passenger Set (std)	600 ____
11-5501	No. 263E Steam Christmas Freight Set	600 ____
11-5502	No. 263E Steam B&O Freight Set	600 ____
11-5505	No. 249E Christmas Steam Passenger Set	500 ____
11-5506	No. 299 Freight Set	450 ____
11-5507	No. 269E Distant Control Freight Set	500 ____
11-5508	Celebration Passenger Set	480 ____
11-5509	No. 269E Christmas Distant Control Freight Set	500 ____
11-5510	No. 269E Distant Control Freight Set	500 ____
11-6001	No. 263E Locomotive, black, brass trim	430 ____
11-6002	No. 263E Locomotive, blue	430 ____
11-6003	No. 277W Remote Control Work Train	680 ____
11-6004	Blue Comet Distant Control Passenger Set	650 ____
11-6005	No. 275W Distant Control Freight Set	600 ____
11-6006	UP Streamliner Passenger Set, silver	800 ____
11-6007	UP Streamliner Passenger Set, yellow	800 ____
11-6008	No. 249E Steam Passenger Set, black, brass trim	600 ____
11-6009	No. 249E Steam Passenger Set, blue	600 ____
11-6010	No. 249E Steam Passenger Set, gray, nickel trim	600 ____
11-6012	No. 260E Locomotive, black, brass trim	430 ____
11-6013	No. 255E Locomotive, gray, nickel trim	430 ____
11-6014	No. 255E Lionel Lines Locomotive	430 ____
11-6015	No. 279E Distant Control Passenger Set	750 ____
11-6016	No. 295E Distant Control Passenger Set	750 ____
11-6017	Hiawatha Distance Control Streamliner Set	900 ____
11-6018	Hiawatha Passenger Train Set	900 ____
11-6019	Hiawatha Distance Control Freight Set	900 ____
11-6020	UP City of Denver Passenger Set, green	590 ____
11-6021	UP City of Denver Passenger Set, yellow/brown	700 ____

____ **11-6022**	No. 262E Locomotive, black, brass trim	300
____ **11-6023**	No. 262E Locomotive, black, nickel trim	300
____ **11-6024**	No. 260E Locomotive, black, brass trim	450
____ **11-6025**	No. 214 Armored Motor Car Set	400
____ **11-6028**	No. 256 Electric Locomotive, orange	450
____ **11-6029**	No. 214 Armored Motor Car Set	400
____ **11-6030**	No. 295E Distant Control Passenger Set	750
____ **11-6031**	No. 279E NYC Distance Control Passenger Set	700
____ **11-6033**	No. 265E Commodore Vanderbilt Locomotive	430
____ **11-6036**	No. 263E Baby Blue Comet Locomotive	460
____ **11-6037**	Girls Freight Set	830
____ **11-6038**	No. 284E Distant Control Freight Set	700
____ **11-6039**	No. 616 Flying Yankee Passenger Set, black/chrome	590
____ **11-6040**	No. 616 Flying Yankee Passenger Set, red/chrome	590
____ **11-6041**	No. 616 Flying Yankee Passenger Set, green/chrome	590
____ **11-6046**	No. 279E Distant Control Passenger Set	700
____ **11-6047**	No. 264 Red Comet Locomotive	460
____ **11-6048**	No. 263E Baby Blue Comet Locomotive, brass trim	500
____ **11-6050**	No. 256 New Haven Electric Locomotive	500
____ **11-6051**	No. 256 Great Northern Electric Locomotive	500
____ **11-6052**	No. 263E Locomotive, black, nickel trim	500
____ **11-6053**	No. 263E Chessie Locomotive	500
____ **11-6054**	No. 263E Southern Locomotive	500
____ **11-6055**	Boys Freight Set	900
____ **11-6056**	No. 261E LL Locomotive and Tender	350
____ **11-6057**	No. 216E Locomotive and Tender	350
____ **11-6061**	No. 256 MILW Electric Locomotive	500
____ **11-6062**	No. 256 PRR Electric Locomotive	500
____ **11-6063**	No. 263E Lionel Lines Locomotive, orange/blue	500
____ **11-6064**	No. 263E Lionel Lines Locomotive, black, brass trim	500
____ **11-6065**	No. 263E Lionel Lines Locomotive, gray, nickel trim	500
____ **11-6066**	No. 263E Norfolk & Western Locomotive	500
____ **11-6067**	No. 263E UP Locomotive, yellow	500
____ **11-6068**	No. 214 Armored Motor Car Set, gray	400
____ **11-6069**	No. 214 Armored Motor Car Set, tan	400
____ **11-6070**	No. 263E Lionel Lines Locomotive, blue, brass trim	500
____ **11-6071**	No. 263E Lionel Lines Locomotive, blue, nickel trim	500
____ **11-30004**	No. 213 Cattle Car, cream/maroon (std)	130
____ **11-30005**	No. 213 Cattle Car, terra-cotta/green (std)	130
____ **11-30006**	No. 214 Boxcar, cream/orange (std)	130
____ **11-30007**	No. 214 Boxcar, yellow/brown (std)	130
____ **11-30008**	No. 214R Refrigerator Car, white/blue (std)	130
____ **11-30009**	No. 215 Tank Car, silver, nickel trim (std)	130
____ **11-30010**	No. 215 Tank Car, green, brass trim (std)	130
____ **11-30011**	No. 215 Tank Car, white (std)	130
____ **11-30012**	No. 216 Hopper Car, red (std)	130
____ **11-30013**	No. 217 Caboose, orange/maroon (std)	140
____ **11-30014**	No. 217 Caboose, red (std)	160

LIONEL CORPORATION TINPLATE

Retail

11-30015	No. 513 Cattle Car, green/orange, brass trim (std)	100 ____
11-30016	No. 514 Boxcar, cream/orange (std)	120 ____
11-30017	No. 514R Refrigerator Car, ivory/peacock, brass trim (std)	120 ____
11-30018	No. 515 Tank Car, terra-cotta, brass trim (std)	100 ____
11-30019	No. 516 Hopper Car, red, brass trim (std)	120 ____
11-30020	No. 517 Caboose, pea green/red (std)	120 ____
11-30021	No. 212 Gondola, maroon (std)	110 ____
11-30022	No. 212 Gondola, pea green (std)	110 ____
11-30023	No. 513 Cattle Car, cream/maroon, nickel trim (std)	100 ____
11-30024	No. 514R Refrigerator Car, white/blue, nickel trim (std)	120 ____
11-30025	No. 515 Tank Car, silver, nickel trim (std)	100 ____
11-30026	No. 516 Hopper Car, red, nickel trim (std)	100 ____
11-30027	No. 517 Caboose, red, nickel trim (std)	120 ____
11-30028	No. 520 Floodlight Car, green, nickel trim (std)	130 ____
11-30029	No. 520 Floodlight Car, terra-cotta, brass trim (std)	130 ____
11-30030	No. 514R Christmas Refrigerator Car, (std)	100 ____
11-30031	No. 514 Christmas Boxcar (std)	100 ____
11-30032	No. 515 MTH/Lionel Tank Car (std)	100 ____
11-30033	No. 211 Flatcar, black, brass trim, with wood (std)	120 ____
11-30034	No. 211 Flatcar, black, nickel trim, with wood (std)	120 ____
11-30035	No. 218 Dump Car, Mojave, nickel trim (std)	140 ____
11-30036	No. 218 Dump Car, Mojave, brass trim (std)	140 ____
11-30037	No. 219 Crane Car, white (std)	200 ____
11-30038	No. 219 Crane Car, yellow, nickel trim (std)	200 ____
11-30039	No. 219 Crane Car, yellow (std)	380 ____
11-30042	No. 514 Boxcar, red/black (std)	100 ____
11-30043	No. 512 Gondola, peacock, brass trim (std)	80 ____
11-30044	No. 512 Gondola, green, nickel trim (std)	80 ____
11-30045	No. 514 Boxcar, yellow/brown (std)	120 ____
11-30046	No. 511 Flatcar, black, brass trim, with wood (std)	100 ____
11-30047	No. 511 Flatcar, black, nickel trim, with wood (std)	100 ____
11-30048	No. 216 Hopper Car, dark green (std)	130 ____
11-30050	No. 219 Crane Car, white, brass trim (std)	380 ____
11-30051	No. 514R NYC Refrigerator Car (std)	100 ____
11-30055	No. 212 Gondola, gray (std)	110 ____
11-30056	No. 213 Cattle Car, Mojave/maroon (std)	130 ____
11-30057	No. 213 Cattle Car, terra-cotta/maroon (std)	130 ____
11-30058	No. 214 Boxcar, terra-cotta/black, brass trim (std)	130 ____
11-30059	No. 214R Refrigerator Car, white/peacock, brass trim (std)	130 ____
11-30060	No. 214R Refrigerator Car, ivory/peacock, brass trim (std)	130 ____
11-30061	No. 215 Tank Car, silver, brass trim (std)	130 ____
11-30062	No. 215 Tank Car, silver, nickel trim (std)	130 ____
11-30063	No. 217 Caboose, olive green (std)	140 ____
11-30064	No. 217 Lionel Lines Caboose (std)	140 ____
11-30065	No. 217 Caboose, pea green/red (std)	140 ____

____ **11-30066**	No. 217 Caboose, red/peacock (std)	160
____ **11-30067**	No. 218 Dump Car, gray (std)	140
____ **11-30068**	No. 218 Dump Car, pea green (std)	140
____ **11-30069**	No. 218 Dump Car, peacock (std)	140
____ **11-30070**	No. 219 Crane Car, peacock/dark green (std)	200
____ **11-30071**	No. 219 Lionel Lines Crane Car (std)	380
____ **11-30072**	No. 220 Floodlight Car, green, nickel trim (std)	140
____ **11-30073**	No. 220 Floodlight Car, terra-cotta, brass trim (std)	140
____ **11-30074**	No. 513 Cattle Car, orange/pea green (std)	100
____ **11-30075**	No. 514 Christmas Boxcar (std)	100
____ **11-30076**	No. 514R Refrigerator Car, ivory/blue (std)	100
____ **11-30077**	No. 515 Tank Car, cream (std)	100
____ **11-30078**	No. 515 Tank Car, ivory (std)	100
____ **11-30079**	No. 515 Tank Car, orange (std)	100
____ **11-30080**	No. 516 Christmas Hopper Car (std)	120
____ **11-30081**	No. 516 Hopper Car, red (std)	120
____ **11-30082**	No. 517 Caboose, red/black (std)	120
____ **11-30083**	No. 520 Floodlight Car, green, nickel trim (std)	130
____ **11-30087**	No. 516 Hopper Car, red, brass trim (std)	100
____ **11-30088**	AF 4018 Automobile Car, white/blue	150
____ **11-30089**	AF 4020 Stock Car, blue	150
____ **11-30090**	AF 4006 Hopper Car, red	150
____ **11-30091**	AF 4017 Sand Car, green	150
____ **11-30092**	AF 4010 Tank Car, cream/blue	150
____ **11-30093**	AF 4022 Machine Car, orange	110
____ **11-30094**	AF 4021 Caboose, red	160
____ **11-30095**	AF 4018 Automobile Car, orange/maroon	130
____ **11-30096**	AF 4022 Machine Car, blue	110
____ **11-30097**	AF 4022 Machine Car, orange/green	110
____ **11-30098**	AF 4010 Tank Car, blue	130
____ **11-30099**	AF 4017 Sand Car, maroon	130
____ **11-30100**	AF 4006 Hopper Car, green	130
____ **11-30101**	AF 4020 Stock Car, cream/maroon	130
____ **11-30102**	AF 4021 Caboose, red/maroon	140
____ **11-30103**	AF 4021 Caboose, cream/red	140
____ **11-30104**	No. 215 Tank Car (std)	130
____ **11-30105**	No. 214R Refrigerator Car (std)	130
____ **11-30107**	No. 214R Altoona 36 Lager Refrigerator Car (std)	130
____ **11-30108**	No. 214R Budweiser Refrigerator Car (std)	140
____ **11-30109**	No. 214R Burp-oh Beer Refrigerator Car (std)	130
____ **11-30110**	No. 214R Hood's Dairy Refrigerator Car (std)	130
____ **11-30111**	No. 214R Old Reading Refrigerator Car (std)	130
____ **11-30112**	No. 214R Palisades Park Refrigerator Car (std)	130
____ **11-30113**	No. 214 Circus Boxcar (std)	130
____ **11-30114**	No. 214 M&M's Christmas Boxcar (std)	140
____ **11-30115**	No. 215 Budweiser Tank Car (std)	140
____ **11-30116**	No. 215 Freedomland Tank Car (std)	130
____ **11-30117**	No. 215 Gulf Tank Car (std)	130

Retail

11-30118	No. 215 Tropicana Tank Car (std)	130 _____
11-30119	No. 513 UP Cattle Car (std)	100 _____
11-30120	No. 513 WM Cattle Car (std)	100 _____
11-30121	No. 514 B&O Boxcar (std)	100 _____
11-30122	No. 514 State of Maine Boxcar (std)	120 _____
11-30123	No. 514R PFE Refrigerator Car (std)	100 _____
11-30124	No. 514R Tropicana Refrigerator Car (std)	120 _____
11-30125	No. 515 Anheuser Busch Tank Car (std)	110 _____
11-30126	No. 515 Hooker Chemicals Tank Car (std)	100 _____
11-30127	No. 516 Blue Coal Hopper Car (std)	100 _____
11-30128	No. 516 Waddell Coal Hopper Car (std)	120 _____
11-30129	No. 517 Pennsylvania Caboose (std)	120 _____
11-30130	No. 517 Santa Fe Caboose (std)	140 _____
11-30131	No. 215 Lionel Lines Tank Car (std)	130 _____
11-30134	No. 515 Christmas Tank Car (std)	100 _____
11-30136	No. 214 Christmas Boxcar (std)	150 _____
11-30137	No. 214 UP Boxcar (std)	150 _____
11-30138	No. 214R Horlacher's Brewing Refrigerator Car (std)	150 _____
11-30139	No. 214R Coors Refrigerator Car (std)	140 _____
11-30140	No. 215 Keystone Gasoline Tank Car (std)	150 _____
11-30141	No. 215 Texaco Tank Car (std)	150 _____
11-30142	No. 216 Peabody Hopper Car (std)	130 _____
11-30143	No. 216 Pennsylvania Power & Light Hopper Car (std)	130 _____
11-30144	No. 213 Cattle Car (std)	130 _____
11-30146	No. 217 Jersey Central Caboose (std)	140 _____
11-30147	No. 214 Jersey Central Boxcar (std)	130 _____
11-30148	No. 214 U.S. Army Boxcar (std)	130 _____
11-30149	No. 215 MTH/Lionel Tank Car	130 _____
11-30150	No. 212 Lionel Lines Gondola (std)	130 _____
11-30151	No. 212 Circus Gondola (std)	130 _____
11-30152	No. 212 NYC Gondola (std)	130 _____
11-30153	No. 214 MKT Boxcar (std)	150 _____
11-30154	No. 214 NYC Boxcar (std)	150 _____
11-30155	No. 215 C&O Tank Car (std)	150 _____
11-30156	No. 215 Shell Tank Car (std)	150 _____
11-30157	No. 216 Hopper Car, red, brass trim (std)	150 _____
11-30158	No. 216 LV Hopper Car (std)	150 _____
11-30159	No. 217 Pennsylvania Caboose (std)	160 _____
11-30160	No. 219 B&O Crane Car (std)	220 _____
11-30161	No. 219 Crane Car, ivory/red (std)	400 _____
11-30162	No. 219 Lionel Lines Crane Car (std)	220 _____
11-30163	No. 219 Crane Car, red/silver (std)	400 _____
11-30164	No. 514R Christmas Refrigerator Car (std)	120 _____
11-30168	No. 515 PRR Tank Car (std)	120 _____
11-30169	No. 515 Texaco Tank Car (std)	120 _____
11-30170	No. 515 Esso Tank Car (std)	120 _____
11-30180	No. 219 Crane Car, black/cream (std)	220 _____
11-30182	No. 217 NYC Illuminated Caboose (std)	160 _____

LIONEL CORPORATION TINPLATE

Retail

____ 11-30185	No. 212 Gondola, pea green (std)	150
____ 11-30193	No. 514R Altoona Brewing Refrigerator Car (std)	120
____ 11-30194	No. 514R PFE Refrigerator Car (std)	120
____ 11-30195	No. 514R REA Refrigerator Car (std)	120
____ 11-30196	No. 514R Robin Hood Beer Refrigerator Car (std)	120
____ 11-30197	No. 514 UP Boxcar (std)	120
____ 11-30198	No. 514 Santa Fe Boxcar (std)	120
____ 11-30199	No. 514 PRR Boxcar (std)	120
____ 11-30200	No. 514 B&O Boxcar (std)	120
____ 11-30201	No. 215-3 Shell 3-D Tank Car (std)	150
____ 11-30202	No. 215-3 Mazda Lamps 3-D Tank Car (std)	150
____ 11-30203	No. 215-3 Celanese Chemicals 3-D Tank Car (std)	150
____ 11-30204	No. 215-3 Clark Oil 3-D Tank Car (std)	150
____ 11-30205	No. 215-2 Sterling Fuels 2-D Tank Car (std)	150
____ 11-30206	No. 215-2 Philadelphia Quartz 2-D Tank Car (std)	150
____ 11-30207	No. 215-2 Cook's Paints 2-D Tank Car (std)	150
____ 11-30208	No. 215-2 Hercules 2-D Tank Car (std)	150
____ 11-30209	No. 216-1 PRR Covered Hopper (std)	150
____ 11-30210	No. 216-1 P&LE Covered Hopper (std)	150
____ 11-30211	No. 216-1 Jack Frost Covered Hopper (std)	150
____ 11-30212	No. 216-1 GE Lamps Covered Hopper (std)	150
____ 11-30213	No. 212-1 PRR Covered Gondola Car (std)	150
____ 11-30214	No. 212-1 Covered Gondola Car (std)	150
____ 11-30215	No. 212-1 NYC Covered Gondola Car (std)	150
____ 11-30216	No. 212-1 GN Covered Gondola Car (std)	150
____ 11-30217	No. 211 Flatcar with wheel load (std)	150
____ 11-30218	No. 211 Altoona Shops Flatcar with wheel load (std)	150
____ 11-30219	No. 211 Baldwin Flatcar with wheel load (std)	150
____ 11-30220	No. 211 Lima Flatcar with wheel load (std)	150
____ 11-30221	No. 217-1 Chessie Bay Window Caboose (std)	160
____ 11-30222	No. 217-1 UP Bay Window Caboose (std)	160
____ 11-30223	No. 217-1 NYC Bay Window Caboose (std)	160
____ 11-30224	No. 217-1 Long Island Bay Window Caboose (std)	160
____ 11-30225	PRR Automobile Car (std)	150
____ 11-30226	NYC Automobile Car (std)	150
____ 11-30227	Shell Tank Car (std)	150
____ 11-30228	Gulf Tank Car (std)	150
____ 11-30229	Blue Coal Hopper (std)	150
____ 11-30230	Waddell Coal Hopper (std)	150
____ 11-30231	NYC Caboose (std)	160
____ 11-30232	PRR Caboose (std)	160
____ 11-30234	No. 514 Boxcar (std)	120
____ 11-30235	No. 514R Refrigerator Car (std)	120
11-30237	No. 217 LL Illuminated Caboose, orange (std)	160
11-30238	No. 217 Lionel Illuminated Caboose, pea green (std)	160
11-30239	No. 217 LL Illuminated Caboose, olive green (std)	160
11-30240	No. 214R Refrigerator Car, white/blue (std)	150
11-30241	No. 214R Refrigerator Car, ivory/peacock (std)	150

LIONEL CORPORATION TINPLATE

Retail

Item	Description	Retail
11-30242	No. 514 Boxcar, 1923 catalog cover (std)	150 ____
11-30243	No. 514 Boxcar, 1924 catalog cover (std)	150 ____
11-30244	No. 514 Boxcar, 1925 catalog cover (std)	150 ____
11-30245	No. 514 Boxcar, 1926 catalog cover (std)	150 ____
11-30246	No. 212-1 UP Covered Gondola Car (std)	150 ____
11-30247	No. 212-1 Reading Covered Gondola Car (std)	150 ____
11-40001	Presidential Passenger Set, blue (std)	1200 ____
11-40002	No. 339 Pullman Car, green (std)	150 ____
11-40003	No. 332 Mail/Baggage Car, green (std)	150 ____
11-40004	No. 332 LV Ithaca Baggage Car	150 ____
11-40005	No. 339 LV Easton Passenger Coach	150 ____
11-40007	300 Series 3-Car Passenger Set, blue/silver (std)	400 ____
11-40009	3-Car State Passenger Set, green (std)	1200 ____
11-40010	Pennsylvania State Baggage Car, green (std)	400 ____
11-40011	Illinois State Coach, green (std)	400 ____
11-40012	Solarium State Car, green (std)	400 ____
11-40013	MILW 3-Car State Passenger Set (std)	1200 ____
11-40014	MILW State Baggage Car (std)	400 ____
11-40015	MILW State Passenger Coach (std)	400 ____
11-40016	MILW Solarium State Car (std)	400 ____
11-40017	3-Car Showroom Passenger Set, green (std)	1500 ____
11-40018	Showroom Passenger Coach, green (std)	500 ____
11-40019	3-Car Showroom Passenger Set, zinc chromate (std)	1500 ____
11-40020	Showroom Passenger Coach, zinc chromate (std)	500 ____
11-40021	3-Car Blue Comet Passenger Set (std)	1100 ____
11-40022	No. 432 Olbers Blue Comet Baggage Car (std)	380 ____
11-40023	No. 419 Tuttle Blue Comet Passenger Coach (std)	380 ____
11-40024	No. 4343 Diner Car	180 ____
11-40025	339 Series Passenger Car, pink	130 ____
11-40026	332 Series Baggage Car, pink	130 ____
11-40027	309 Series 3-Car State Passenger Set, brown (std)	1200 ____
11-40028	Pennsylvania State Baggage Car, brown (std)	400 ____
11-40029	Illinois State Passenger Coach, brown (std)	400 ____
11-40030	Solarium State Car, brown (std)	400 ____
11-40031	State 3-Car Passenger Set, blue (std)	1200 ____
11-40032	Pennsylvania State Baggage Car, blue (std)	400 ____
11-40033	Illinois State Passenger Coach, blue (std)	400 ____
11-40034	Solarium State Car, blue (std)	400 ____
11-40035	309 Series 3-Car Passenger Set, blue (std)	400 ____
11-40036	309 Series 3-Car Passenger Set, green (std)	400 ____
11-40037	309 Series 3-Car Passenger Set, red (std)	400 ____
11-40038	No. 309 Passenger Coach (std)	140 ____
11-40039	No. 310 Baggage Car (std)	140 ____
11-40040	3-Car Blue Comet Passenger Set, nickel trim (std)	1100 ____
11-40041	No. 432 Blue Comet Baggage Car, nickel trim (std)	380 ____
11-40042	No. 423 Blue Comet Passenger Coach, nickel trim (std)	380 ____
11-40043	3-Car Stephen Girard Set, brass trim	600 ____
11-40044	No. 4427 Stephen Girard Baggage Car, brass trim	200 ____

____ **11-40045**	No. 427 Stephen Girard Passenger Coach, brass trim	200
____ **11-40046**	3-Car Stephen Girard Set, nickel trim	600
____ **11-40047**	No. 4427 Stephen Girard Baggage Car, nickel trim	200
____ **11-40048**	No. 427 Stephen Girard Passenger Coach, nickel trim	200
____ **11-40049**	No. 418 3-Car Passenger Set, green, brass trim (std)	600
____ **11-40050**	No. 418 Diner, green, brass trim (std)	200
____ **11-40051**	No. 418 3-Car Passenger Set, orange, brass trim (std)	600
____ **11-40052**	No. 418 Diner, orange brass trim (std)	200
____ **11-40053**	No. 418 3-Car Passenger Set, Mojave, brass trim (std)	600
____ **11-40054**	No. 418 Diner, Mojave, brass trim (std)	200
____ **11-40055**	No. 418 3-Car Passenger Set, pink, brass trim (std)	600
____ **11-40056**	No. 418 Diner, pink, brass trim (std)	200
____ **11-40057**	Lionel 3-Car Pullman Passenger Set (std)	700
____ **11-40058**	Pennsylvania 3-Car Pullman Passenger Set (std)	700
____ **11-40059**	No. 332 Baggage Car (std)	140
____ **11-40060**	No. 339 Passenger Coach (std)	140
____ **11-40061**	Great Northern State 3-Car Passenger Set (std)	1200
____ **11-40062**	Great Northern State Baggage Car (std)	430
____ **11-40063**	Great Northern State Passenger Coach (std)	430
____ **11-40064**	Great Northern State Solarium Car (std)	430
____ **11-40065**	Presidential 3-Car Passenger Set (std)	1200
____ **11-40066**	Presidential Baggage Car (std)	430
____ **11-40067**	Presidential Passenger Coach (std)	430
____ **11-40068**	Red Comet 3-Car Passenger Set (std)	1140
____ **11-40069**	Red Comet Baggage Car (std)	400
____ **11-40070**	Red Comet Passenger Coach (std)	400
____ **11-40072**	President's Passenger Set, red (std)	1300
____ **11-40073**	No. 310 Baggage Car (std)	140
____ **11-40074**	No. 309 Passenger Coach (std)	140
____ **11-40076**	Green Comet 3-Car Passenger Set (std)	1140
____ **11-40077**	NYC 3-Car Passenger Set, brown (std)	700
____ **11-40078**	General 3-Car Pullman Passenger Set (std)	700
____ **11-40079**	Green Comet Baggage Car (std)	400
____ **11-40080**	Green Comet Passenger Coach (std)	400
____ **11-40081**	Showroom 3-Car Passenger Set, brown (std)	1600
____ **11-40082**	Showroom Passenger Coach, brown (std)	540
____ **11-40083**	Showroom 3-Car Passenger Set, orange (std)	1600
____ **11-40084**	Showroom Passenger Coach, orange (std)	540
____ **11-40095**	3-car B&O Pullman Passenger Set (std)	700
____ **11-40096**	3-car Long Island Pullman Passenger Set (std)	700
____ **11-40097**	3-car Strasburg Pullman Passenger Set (std)	700
____ **11-40098**	3-car PRR Pullman Passenger Set (std)	700
____ **11-40099**	3-car MILW State Passenger Set (std)	1200
____ **11-40100**	MILW State Solarium Car (std)	400
____ **11-40101**	MILW State Passenger Coach (std)	400
____ **11-40102**	MILW State Baggage Car (std)	400
____ **11-40103**	3-car PRR State Passenger Set (std)	1200
____ **11-40104**	PRR State Solarium Car (std)	400

11-40105	PRR State Passenger Coach (std)	400 ___
11-40106	PRR State Baggage Car (std)	400 ___
11-40107	3-car State Passenger Set, two-tone brown (std)	1200 ___
11-40108	State Solarium Car, two-tone brown (std)	400 ___
11-40109	State Passenger Coach, two-tone brown (std)	400 ___
11-40110	State Baggage Car, two-tone brown (std)	400 ___
11-40111	3-car Great Northern Presidential Set (std)	1200 ___
11-40112	Great Northern Presidential Diner (std)	400 ___
11-40113	3-car Lehigh Valley Presidential Set (std)	1200 ___
11-40114	Lehigh Valley Presidential Diner (std)	400 ___
11-40115	3-car New Haven State Passenger Set (std)	1200 ___
11-40116	New Haven State Solarium Car (std)	400 ___
11-40117	New Haven State Passenger Coach (std)	400 ___
11-40118	New Haven State Baggage Car (std)	400 ___
11-60033	No. 607 Christmas Coach Passenger	90 ___
11-70002	No. 2814 Boxcar, cream/orange	80 ___
11-70003	No. 2814R Refrigerator Car, white/brown	80 ___
11-70004	No. 2814R Christmas Refrigerator Car	80 ___
11-70005	No. 2814R Refrigerator Car, Ivory/peacock	80 ___
11-70006	No. 2815 Tank Car, silver	90 ___
11-70007	No. 2815 Tank Car, orange, nickel trim	80 ___
11-70008	No. 2817 Caboose, red/green	90 ___
11-70009	No. 2815 Christmas Tank Car	80 ___
11-70010	No. 2813 Cattle Car, cream/maroon	80 ___
11-70011	No. 2812 Gondola, apple green	80 ___
11-70012	No. 2811 Flatcar, silver	70 ___
11-70013	No. 2816 Hopper Car, red	90 ___
11-70014	No. 2816 Hopper Car, olive green	80 ___
11-70015	No. 2820 Floodlight Car, terra-cotta	90 ___
11-70016	No. 2815 Sunoco Tank Car	80 ___
11-70017	No. 2810 Crane Car, terra-cotta/maroon	180 ___
11-70018	No. 2811 Flatcar, maroon	70 ___
11-70019	No. 2814R MTH/Lionel Refrigerator Car	90 ___
11-70024	No. 2814 Christmas Boxcar	80 ___
11-70025	No. 2814 Boxcar, cream/orange	80 ___
11-70026	No. 2814 Boxcar, orange/brown	80 ___
11-70027	No. 2814 Boxcar, white brown	80 ___
11-70028	No. 2816 Christmas Hopper Car	80 ___
11-70029	No. 2817 Caboose, red/brown	90 ___
11-70030	No. 2812 Gondola, dark orange	70 ___
11-70031	No. 813 Cattle Car, brown	80 ___
11-70032	No. 2816 Hopper Car, black	80 ___
11-70033	No. 2820 Floodlight Car, light green	90 ___
11-70034	No. 2814R Refrigerator Car, white/brown	80 ___
11-70035	No. 2651 Flatcar, green	60 ___
11-70036	No. 2652 Gondola, red	60 ___
11-70037	No. 2653 Hopper Car, black	60 ___
11-70038	No. 2654 Shell Tank Car, yellow	60 ___

____ 11-70039	No. 2655 Boxcar, yellow/brown	60
____ 11-70040	No. 2656 Cattle Car, red/brown	60
____ 11-70041	No. 2657 Caboose, red/maroon	60
____ 11-70042	No. 659 Dump Car, green	60
____ 11-70043	No. 659 Dump Car, orange	60
____ 11-70045	No. 2814 Boxcar, yellow/brown	90
____ 11-70046	No. 2817 Caboose, red	100
____ 11-70047	No. 2814 Christmas Boxcar	80
____ 11-70048	No. 2815 Christmas Tank Car	90
____ 11-70049	No. 2814R Refrigerator Car, silver frame	90
____ 11-70050	No. 2814R Refrigerator Car, black frame	80
____ 11-70051	No. 2817 Caboose, red/maroon	90
____ 11-70052	No. 2654 Shell Tank Car, gray	60
____ 11-70053	No. 2654 Shell Tank Car, black	60
____ 11-70054	No. 2653 Hopper Car, green	60
____ 11-70055	No. 2653 Hopper Car, red	60
____ 11-70056	No. 2655 Boxcar, yellow/maroon	60
____ 11-70057	No. 2655 Boxcar, yellow/brown	60
____ 11-70058	No. 2656 Cattle Car, gray/red	60
____ 11-70059	No. 2656 Cattle Car, burnt orange	60
____ 11-70060	No. 659 Dump Car, blue	60
____ 11-70061	No. 900 Ammunition Car, gray	60
____ 11-70064	No. 2814R Hoods Dairy Refrigerator Car	80
____ 11-70065	No. 2814R Isaly's Refrigerator Car	80
____ 11-70066	No. 2814R Sheffield Farms Refrigerator Car	90
____ 11-70067	No. 2814R Palisades Park Refrigerator Car	80
____ 11-70068	No. 2654 UP Tank Car, yellow	60
____ 11-70069	No. 2654 M&M's Tank Car	70
____ 11-70070	No. 2654 Baker's Chocolate Tank Car	60
____ 11-70071	No. 2654 Budweiser Tank Car	70
____ 11-70072	No. 2655 Delaware & Hudson Boxcar	60
____ 11-70073	No. 2655 Railbox Boxcar	60
____ 11-70074	M&M's Christmas Boxcar	70
____ 11-70076	No. 2654 LL Tank Car, orange/blue	70
____ 11-70078	No. 900 Ammunition Car, green	60
____ 11-70079	No. 2820 LL Floodlight Car, black/orange	120
____ 11-70080	No. 2820 U.S. Army Air Corps Floodlight Car	120
____ 11-70081	No. 2810 Crane Car, yellow/red	180
____ 11-70082	No. 2810 Crane Car, white/red	180
____ 11-70083	No. 2660 Crane Car, cream/red	100
____ 11-70084	No. 2660 Crane Car, terra-cotta/maroon	100
____ 11-70085	No. 2660 Crane Car, yellow/red	100
____ 11-70086	No. 2660 Crane Car, peacock/dark green	100
____ 11-70087	No. 2813 LL Cattle Car, cream/tuscan	90
____ 11-70088	No. 2813 LL Cattle Car, terra cotta/pea green	90
____ 11-70089	No. 2810 B&O Crane Car	180
____ 11-70091	No. 2815 LL Tank Car, cream, orange/blue	80
____ 11-70092	No. 2810 Crane Car, blue	180

LIONEL CORPORATION TINPLATE

		Retail
11-70095	No. 2820 LL Floodlight Car, black/peacock	120 _____
11-70096	No. 2814 Southern Boxcar	90 _____
11-70097	No. 2814 Chessie Boxcar	90 _____
11-70098	No. 2814 Blue Comet Boxcar, nickel trim	90 _____
11-70099	No. 2814 Blue Comet Boxcar, brass trim	90 _____
11-70102	No. 2654 Mobilgas Tank Car	70 _____
11-70103	No. 2654 Esso Tank Car	70 _____
11-70104	No. 2653 Blue Coal Hopper	70 _____
11-70105	No. 2653 Peabody Hopper	70 _____
11-70106	No. 2655 Altoona Brewing Boxcar	70 _____
11-70107	No. 2655 Hood's Grade A Milk Boxcar	70 _____
11-70108	No. 2655 LL Boxcar	70 _____
11-70109	No. 2657 LL Caboose, green/red	70 _____
11-70110	No. 2657 LL Caboose, orange/red	70 _____
11-70113	No. 2814 PRR Boxcar	90 _____
11-70114	No. 2814 ATSF Grand Canyon Boxcar	90 _____
11-70115	No. 2814 Long Island Boxcar	90 _____
11-70116	No. 2814 Alaska Boxcar	90 _____
11-70117	No. 2814R M. K. Goetz Brewing Refrigerator Car	90 _____
11-70118	No. 2814R Gerber Refrigerator Car	90 _____
11-70119	No. 2814R Roberts & Oake Meats Refrigerator Car	90 _____
11-70120	No. 2814R Sullivan's Packing Refrigerator Car	90 _____
11-70121	No. 2816 Western Maryland Coal Car	90 _____
11-70122	No. 2816 P&LE Coal Car	90 _____
11-70123	No. 2816 Waddell Mining Coal Car	90 _____
11-70124	No. 2816 Blue Coal Car	90 _____
11-70125	No. 2815 Clark Oil Tank Car	90 _____
11-70126	No. 2815 Celanese Chemicals Tank Car	90 _____
11-70127	No. 2815 Shell Tank Car	90 _____
11-70128	No. 2815 Cook's Paints Tank Car	90 _____
11-70129	No. 2817 C&O Caboose	100 _____
11-70130	No. 2817 Long Island Caboose	100 _____
11-70131	No. 2817 Southern Caboose	100 _____
11-70132	No. 2817 Jersey Central Caboose	100 _____
11-70133	No. 2814R Gerber Refrigerator Car	90 _____
11-70144	No. 2815 Shell Tank Car	90 _____
11-70154	No. 2814 ATSF Grand Canyon Boxcar	90 _____
11-70156	No. 2814R LL Refrigerator Car, orange/blue	90 _____
11-70157	No. 2814R LL Blue Comet Refrigerator Car	90 _____
11-70158	No. 2817 Lionel Lines Caboose, orange/blue	100 _____
11-70159	No. 2817 Lionel Lines Caboose, red/brown	100 _____
11-70160	No. 2817 NYC Caboose	100 _____
11-70161	No. 2817 Jersey Central Blue Comet Caboose	100 _____
11-70164	No. 2814R LL Refrigerator Car, red/brown	90 _____
11-80001	2600 Series 4-Car Blue Comet Passenger Set	430 _____
11-80002	UP Articulated Baggage Car, silver	150 _____
11-80003	UP Articulated Baggage Car, yellow	150 _____
11-80004	UP Articulated Coach, silver	150 _____

___ **11-80005**	UP Articulated Coach, yellow	150
___ **11-80006**	No. 2613 Series Pullman Coach, blue	110
___ **11-80007**	2600 Series 3-Car Passenger Set, red	300
___ **11-80008**	2600 Series 3-Car Passenger Set, green	300
___ **11-80009**	Milwaukee Road Articulated Baggage Car	150
___ **11-80010**	Milwaukee Road Articulated Coach	150
___ **11-80011**	Articulated Streamliner Baggage Car	150
___ **11-80012**	Articulated Streamliner Coach	150
___ **11-80013**	No. 2613 Series Pullman Coach, red	100
___ **11-80014**	No. 2613 Series Pullman Coach, green	100
___ **11-80015**	No. 605 Christmas Baggage Car	90
___ **11-80016**	710 Series 3-Car Passenger Set, blue	350
___ **11-80017**	No. 710 Series Baggage Car, blue	120
___ **11-80018**	No. 710 Series Passenger Coach, blue	120
___ **11-80019**	710 Series 3-Car Passenger Set, orange	350
___ **11-80020**	No. 710 Series Baggage Car, orange	120
___ **11-80021**	No. 710 Series Passenger Coach, orange	120
___ **11-80022**	710 Series 3-Car Passenger Set, red	350
___ **11-80023**	No. 710 Series Baggage Car, red	120
___ **11-80024**	No. 710 Series Passenger Coach, red	120
___ **11-80025**	No. 1695 3-Car Passenger Set, blue/silver	350
___ **11-80026**	No. 1685 Passenger Car, blue/silver	120
___ **11-80027**	1695 Series 3-Car Passenger Set, red/maroon	380
___ **11-80028**	No. 1695 Passenger Coach, red/maroon	130
___ **11-80029**	City of Denver Coach, yellow/green	110
___ **11-80030**	City of Denver Coach, green	110
___ **11-80031**	No. 605 Baggage Car	90
___ **11-80032**	No. 607 Passenger Coach	90
___ **11-80034**	No. 2613 NYC Pullman Car, LCCA 2012 Convention	100
___ **11-80036**	No. 605 Red Comet Baggage Car	90
___ **11-80039**	600 Series 3-Car Red Comet Passenger Set	270
11-80040	2600 Series 4-Car Blue Comet Passenger Set, brass trim	430
___ **11-80041**	No. 2613 Pullman Coach, brass trim	110
___ **11-80042**	Flying Yankee Chrome Coach	110
___ **11-80047**	710 Series 3-Car NH Passenger Set	400
___ **11-80048**	710 Series 3-Car GN Passenger Set	400
___ **11-80049**	2600 Series 4-Car Chessie Passenger Set	430
___ **11-80050**	2600 Series 4-Car Southern Passenger Set	430
___ **11-80051**	No. 2613 Chessie Pullman Coach	110
___ **11-80052**	No. 2613 Southern Pullman Coach	110
___ **11-80053**	No. 710 NH Baggage Car	140
___ **11-80054**	No. 710 NH Passenger Coach	140
___ **11-80055**	No. 710 GN Baggage Car	140
___ **11-80056**	No. 710 GN Passenger Coach	140
___ **11-80059**	710 Series 3-car MILW Passenger Set	400
___ **11-80060**	No. 713 MILW Baggage Car	140
___ **11-80061**	No. 710 MILW Passenger Coach	140

LIONEL CORPORATION TINPLATE

Retail

11-80062	710 Series 3-car PRR Passenger Set	400 ____
11-80063	No. 713 PRR Baggage Car	140 ____
11-80064	No. 710 PRR Passenger Coach	140 ____
11-80065	2600 Series 4-car LL Passenger Set, blue, nickel trim	430 ____
11-80066	2600 Series 4-car LL Passenger Set, blue, brass trim	430 ____
11-80067	2600 Series 4-car LL Passenger Set, orange/blue	430 ____
11-80068	2600 Series 4-car NW Passenger Set	430 ____
11-80069	2600 Series 4-car UP Passenger Set, yellow	430 ____
11-90001	No. 300 Hellgate Bridge, green/cream	500 ____
11-90002	No. 300 Hellgate Bridge, silver/white	500 ____
11-90003	No. 092 Signal Tower, cream/red	70 ____
11-90006	No. 437 Switch Tower	280 ____
11-90007	No. 155 Freight Shed	330 ____
11-90008	No. 116 Passenger Station	400 ____
11-90009	No. 438 Signal Tower	150 ____
11-90010	No. 192 Villa Set	200 ____
11-90011	No. 191 Villa	70 ____
11-90012	No. 54 Street Lamp Set, green	45 ____
11-90013	No. 54 Street Lamp Set, red	45 ____
11-90014	No. 56 Gas Lamp Set, green	35 ____
11-90015	No. 56 Gas Lamp Set, maroon	35 ____
11-90016	No. 57 Corner Lamp Set, black	40 ____
11-90017	No. 57 Corner Lamp Set, red	35 ____
11-90018	No. 58 Lamp Set, single arc, cream	35 ____
11-90019	No. 58 Lamp Set, single arc, dark green	35 ____
11-90020	No. 59 Gooseneck Lamp Set, black	40 ____
11-90021	No. 59 Gooseneck Lamp Set, maroon	40 ____
11-90022	No. 1184 Bungalow (std)	200 ____
11-90023	No. 1184 Bungalow (std)	200 ____
11-90024	No. 1189 Villa (std)	300 ____
11-90025	No. 1191 Villa (std)	300 ____
11-90026	No.165 Magnetic Crane	300 ____
11-90027	No. 441 Weighing Station (std)	380 ____
11-90028	No. 69 Operating Warning Bell	50 ____
11-90029	No. 78 Automatic Control Signal (std)	70 ____
11-90030	No. 79 Flashing Railroad Signal	70 ____
11-90031	No. 80 Operating Semaphore	70 ____
11-90032	No. 63 Lamp Post Set, aluminum	50 ____
11-90033	No. 87 Railroad Crossing Signal	50 ____
11-90034	No. 92 Floodlight Tower Set	160 ____
11-90035	No. 94 High Tension Tower Set	150 ____
11-90036	No. Automatic Block Signal (std)	70 ____
11-90037	No. 163 Freight Accessory Set, green cart	100 ____
11-90038	No. 163 Freight Accessory Set, orange cart	100 ____
11-90039	No. 208 Tools and Chest, dark gray	80 ____
11-90040	No. 208 Tools and Chest, silver	80 ____
11-90041	No. 550 Miniature Figures	100 ____
11-90042	No. 64 Lamp Post Set, light green	30 ____

____	**11-90043**	No. 85 Race Car Set	700
____	**11-90044**	Straight Race Car Track Section	20
____	**11-90045**	Inside Curve Race Car Track Section	20
____	**11-90046**	Outside Curve Race Car Track Section	20
____	**11-90047**	No. 55 Airplane & No. 49 Airport Set with mat	800
____	**11-90048**	No. 49 Airport Mat	60
____	**11-90049**	No. 90 Flagpole	50
____	**11-90050**	No. 205 Merchandise Containers, 3 pieces (std)	130
____	**11-90052**	No. 442 Diner	160
____	**11-90053**	No. 43 Runabout Boat, red/white	450
____	**11-90054**	No. 44 Speed Boat	450
____	**11-90055**	No. 71 Telegraph Post Set, gray/red	80
____	**11-90056**	Teardrop Lamp Set, pea green	20
____	**11-90057**	No. 46 Crossing Gate	40
____	**11-90058**	Small Oil Drum Set	20
____	**11-90060**	No. 115 Passenger Station, beige/pea green	300
____	**11-90061**	No. 115 Passenger Station, cream, orange/blue	300
____	**11-90062**	No. 134 Lionel City Station with stop	330
____	**11-90063**	No. 444 Roundhouse Section	500
____	**11-90064**	No. 200 Turntable, red/black	200
____	**11-90065**	No. 89 Flagpole, blue base (std)	50
____	**11-90066**	No. 89 Flagpole, white base (std)	50
____	**11-90067**	No. 89 American Flag Pole, white base (std)	50
____	**11-90068**	Operating Industrial Crane	350
____	**11-90069**	Operating Industrial Crane, TCA 2010 Convention	350
____	**11-90070**	No. 552 Diner, orange/blue	200
____	**11-90071**	No. 552 Diner, white/blue	200
____	**11-90072**	No. 911 Country Estate, cream/red	140
____	**11-90073**	No. 911 Country Estate, red/green	140
____	**11-90074**	No. 912 Suburban Home, ivory/peacock	140
____	**11-90075**	No. 912 Suburban Home, mustard/green	140
____	**11-90076**	No. 913 Landscaped Bungalow, white/maroon	110
____	**11-90077**	No. 913 Landscaped Bungalow, light green/peacock	110
____	**11-90078**	AF No. 2050 Old Glory Flag Pole	100
____	**11-90079**	No. 43 Runabout Boat, orange/blue	400
____	**11-90084**	No. 57 Lamp Post Set, Lionel & American Flyer Aves.	40
____	**11-90085**	No. 57 Lamp Post Set, orange, 21st St. & Fifth Ave.	40
____	**11-90086**	AF No. 2013 Corner Lamp Set, yellow	40
	11-90087	No. 440 Signal Bridge and Control Panel, silver	300
	11-90088	No. 440 Signal Bridge and Control Panel, gray	300
____	**11-90089**	No. 436 Power Station, cream	150
____	**11-90090**	No. 436 Power Station, terra-cotta	150
____	**11-90094**	No. 438 Signal Tower	160
____	**11-90095**	No. 116 Passenger Station	400
____	**11-90096**	No. 1184 Bungalow, gray/green	200
____	**11-90097**	No. 1184 Bungalow, white/maroon	200
____	**11-90098**	No. 1189 Villa (std)	300
____	**11-90099**	No. 1191 Villa (std)	300

LIONEL CORPORATION TINPLATE

Retail

11-90100	No. 442 Diner	160 _____
11-90101	No. 54 Lamp Post Set, pea green	45 _____
11-90102	No. 54 Lamp Post Set, state brown	45 _____
11-90103	No. 58 Lamp Post Set, peacock	35 _____
11-90104	No. 58 Lamp Post Set, orange	35 _____
11-90105	No. 59 Lamp Post Set, dark green	40 _____
11-90106	No. 59 Lamp Post Set, light green	40 _____
11-90107	No. 92 Floodlight Tower Set	170 _____
11-90108	No. 79 Flashing Signal	70 _____
11-90109	No. 69 Warning Signal	50 _____
11-90110	No. 94 High Tension Tower Set	170 _____
11-90111	No. 57 Corner Lamp Set, orange, Lionel	40 _____
11-90112	No. 57 Corner Lamp Set, blue, Lionel	40 _____
11-90113	No. 57 Corner Lamp Set, blue/yellow	40 _____
11-90114	No. 152 Operating Crossing Gate	50 _____
11-90115	No. 153 Operating Block Signal	50 _____
11-90116	No. 154 Highway Flashing Signal	50 _____
11-90117	No. 437 Switch Signal Tower, cream/orange	300 _____
11-90118	No. 437 Switch Signal Tower, terra-cotta/green	300 _____
11-90119	AF No. 4230 Roadside Flashing Signal	100 _____
11-90120	No. 200 Turntable, gray/green	200 _____
11-90121	No. 200 Turntable, orange/blue	200 _____
11-90122	No. 437 Switch Tower	280 _____
11-90123	No. 98 Coal Bunker	180 _____
11-90124	No. 550 Railroad Figure Set	100 _____
11-90125	No. 550 Railroad Figure Set	100 _____
11-90126	No. 205 3-piece Container Set, green (std)	130 _____
11-90127	No. 205 3-piece Container Set, black (std)	130 _____
11-90128	No. 205 3-piece Container Set, yellow (std)	130 _____
11-90129	No. 163 Freight Accessory Set, green/yellow	100 _____
11-90130	No. 163 Freight Accessory Set, peacock/orange	100 _____
11-99006	No. 20 90-degree Crossover (std)	50 _____
11-99030	No. 25 Illuminated Track Bumpers (std)	60 _____
11-99044	42" Diameter Gauge Switch, right hand, green base (std)	110 _____
11-99045	42" Diameter Gauge Switch, left hand, green base (std)	110 _____
11-99046	42" Diameter Gauge Switch, right hand, black base (std)	110 _____
11-99047	42" Diameter Gauge Switch, left hand, black base (std)	110 _____
11-99074	72" Wide Radius Gauge Switch, right hand, green base (std)	120 _____
11-99075	72" Wide Radius Gauge Switch, left hand, green base (std)	120 _____
11-99076	72" Wide Radius Gauge Switch, right hand, black base (std)	120 _____
11-99077	72" Wide Radius Gauge Switch, left hand, black base (std)	120 _____

Exc Mint

Artrain

		Exc	Mint
___ 9486	GTW "I Love Michigan" Boxcar, *87*	155	305
___ 17885	1-D Tank Car, *90*	35	65
___ 17891	GTW 20th Anniversary Boxcar, *91*	40	75
___ 19425	CSX Flatcar with "Art in Celebration" trailer, *96*	40	80
___ 52013	Norfolk Southern Flatcar with trailer, *92*	115	230
___ 52024	Conrail Auto Carrier, *93*	45	90
___ 52049	BN Gondola with coil covers, *94*	30	55
___ 52097	Chessie System Reefer, *95*	20	35
___ 52140	Union Pacific Bunk Car, *97*	20	35
___ 52165	SP Caboose "6256," *98*	30	60
___ 52197	Santa Fe GP38 Diesel, *99*	125	245
___ 52227	"Artistry in Space" Boxcar, *00*	40	75
___ 52255	30th Anniversary Flatcar with billboard, *01*	50	100
___ 52283	Paint Vat Car, *02*	30	60
___ 52331	Flatcar with "America's Railways" trailer, *03*	75	150
___ 52349	Hometown Art Museum Hopper, purple, *04*	20	35
___ 52350	"Native Views" 3-bay Hopper, *04*	35	65
___ 52411	"35 Years" 1-D Tank Car, *06*	20	35

Carnegie Science Center

		Exc	Mint
___ 25085	Miniature Railroad & Village Boxcar, *09*	25	50
___ 26750	Great Miniature Railroad & Village Boxcar, *99*	40	80
___ 36202	Great Miniature Railroad 80th Anniversary Boxcar, *00*	55	110
___ 36234	Great Miniature Railroad & Village Boxcar, *01*	25	50
___ 52277	Carnegie Science Center 10th Anniversary Boxcar, *02*	30	60
___ 52332	Miniature Railroad & Village Boxcar, *03*	30	60
___ 52362	Miniature Railroad & Village 50th Anniversary Boxcar, *04*	25	50
___ 52399	MRR&V Express Boxcar, *05*	25	50
___ 52432	Miniature Railroad & Village Boxcar, *06*	25	50
___ 52510	Miniature Railroad & Village Caboose, *08*	25	50

Chicagoland Railroad Club

		Exc	Mint
___ 52081	C&NW Boxcar "6464-555," *96*	35	70
___ 52101	BN Maxi-Stack Flatcar "64287" with containers, *97*	40	80
___ 52102	SF Extended Vision Caboose, red roof, *96*	40	75
___ 52103	SF Extended Vision Caboose, black roof, *96*	40	75

CLUB CARS AND SPECIAL PRODUCTION

		Exc	Mint	
52120	Shedd Aquarium Car "3435-557," 98	50	100	____
52148	REA/Santa Fe Operating Boxcar, 99	35	70	____
52170	SP Operating Boxcar "52170-561," 99	35	65	____
52171	UP Operating Boxcar "52171-561," 99	35	65	____
52178	Burlington Operating Boxcar "52178-559," 00	35	70	____
52179	ACL Operating Boxcar "52179-560," 00	40	75	____
52215	C&NW 3-bay Cylindrical Hopper, 01	30	60	____
52216	C&NW Cylindrical Hopper, 02	30	60	____
52223	REA/Santa Fe Centennial Operating Boxcar, 00	35	65	____
52251	PRR Express Car, green, 01	35	65	____
52259	MP GP20 Diesel, traditional, 01	125	250	____
52292	PRR Express Car, tuscan red, 02	25	50	____
52327	City of Los Angeles Express Car, 04	35	65	____
52328	City of New Haven Express Car, 04	30	55	____
52363	City of New Orleans Express Car, 04	30	55	____
52364	City of New York Express Car, 04	35	65	____
52388	Great Northern Tool Car, 06	25	50	____
52389	Great Northern Crew Car, 06	25	50	____
52390	Great Northern Welding Caboose, 06	40	80	____
52391	Great Northern Racing Crew Car, 06	25	50	____
52426	City of San Francisco Express Car, 07	30	55	____
52427	Rock Island Rocket Express Car, 07	30	55	____
52475	Western Pacific UP Heritage Boxcar, 07	30	60	____

Classic Toy Trains

52126	MILW Boxcar "21027" with CTT Logo, 97	25	50	____

Dept. 56

16270	Heritage Village Boxcar "9796," 96	30	55	____
52096	Snow Village Boxcar "9756," 95	45	85	____
52139	Square Window Caboose "6256," 97	35	70	____
52157	Holly Brothers 3-D Tank Car, 98	45	85	____
52175	4-6-4 Hudson Locomotive, CC, 99	175	350	____
52199	4-bay Hopper "6756," 00	30	55	____
52254	"Happy Holidays" Gondola, 01	20	35	____

Eastwood Automobilia

16275	Radio Flyer Boxcar "16275," 96	25	50	____
16757	Johnny Lightning Auto Carrier "3435," 96	45	90	____
16985	Flatcar with 2 Ford vans, 97	25	50	____
52044	Vat Car, 95	15	30	____
52083	PRR Flatcar "21697" with tanker, 95	20	40	____
52130	Flatcar with Hot Wheels tanker, 97	30	60	____

Gadsden-Pacific Division
Toy Train Operating Museum

			Exc	Mint
___	17872	Anaconda Ore Car, *88*	35	70
___	17878	Magma Ore Car, *89*	30	55
___	17881	Phelps Dodge Ore Car, *90*	20	40
___	17886	Cyprus Ore Car, *91*	15	30
___	19961	Inspiration Consolidated Copper Ore Car, *92*	15	30
___	52011	Tucson, Cornelia & Gila Bend Ore Car, *93*	15	30
___	52027	Pinto Valley Mine Ore Car, *94*	15	30
___	52071	Copper Basin Railway Ore Car, *95*	15	30
___	52089	SMARRCO Ore Car, *96*	10	25
___	52124	El Paso & Southwestern Ore Car, *97*	20	40
___	52164	SP Ore Car, *98*	20	35
___	52177	Arizona Southern Ore Car, *99*	20	35
___	52213	BHP Copper Ore Car, *00*	15	30
___	52248	Tombstone & Western Ore Car, *01*	20	40
___	52279	Dragoon & Northern Ore Car, *02*	25	50
___	52307	Twin Buttes Ore Car, *03*	20	35
___	52358	AJO & Southwestern Ore Car, *04*	25	45
___	52386	Ray & Gila Bend Ore Car, *05*	24	45
___	52421	Calabasas, Tuscon & Northwestern Ore Car, *06*	25	45
___	52473	Mascot & Western Ore Car, *07*	45	90
___	52524	Tucson, Globe & Northern Ore Car, *08*	20	40
___	52558	Port of Tucson Ore Car, *09*	25	45
___	52579	Rosemont Copper Ore Car, *10*	20	40
___	52588	ASARCO Ore Car, *11*	20	40
___	58234	ASARCO Haden Smelter Ore Car, *15*		45
___	58262	Union Pacific Ore Car, *16*		45
___	58513	Freeport-McMoRan Ore Car, *12*	20	40
___	58557	San Pedro & Southwestern Ore Car, *13*	20	40
___	58583	Arizona Eastern Ore Car, *14*	20	40

Houston Tinplate Operators Society

			Exc	Mint
___	8900	Sam Houston Mint Car, *00*	60	120
___	8901	Miracle Petroleum 1-D Tank Car, *01*	50	100
___	8902	USS Houston Submarine Car, *02*	50	100
___	8903	Railway Express Boxcar, *03*	50	100
___	8904	Lone Star Bay Window Caboose, *04*	50	100
___	8999	Lone Star Aquarium Car, mermaid or trout, *99*	50	100

Inland Empire Train Collectors Association

		Exc	Mint	
1979	Boxcar, 79	5	15	____
1980	SP-type Caboose, 80	5	15	____
1981	Quad Hopper, 81	5	15	____
1982	3-D Tank Car, 82	5	15	____
1983	Reefer, 83	5	15	____
1986	Bunk Car, 86	5	15	____
7518	Carson City Mint Car, 84	25	45	____

Lionel Central Operating Lines

		Exc	Mint	
1981	Boxcar, 81	10	25	____
1986	Work Caboose, shell only, 86	5	15	____
5724	Pennsylvania Bunk Car, 84	20	40	____
6508	Canadian Pacific Crane Car, 83	20	40	____
6907	NYC Wood-sided Caboose, 97	25	50	____
9184	Erie Bay Window Caboose, 82	10	20	____
9475	D&H "I Love NY" Boxcar, 85	20	35	____
16342	CSX Gondola with coil covers, 92	10	20	____
17221	NYC Boxcar, 95	15	30	____

Lionel Collectors Association of Canada

		Exc	Mint	
5710	Canadian Pacific Reefer, 83	110	215	____
5714	Michigan Central Reefer, 85	75	150	____
6100	Ontario Northland Covered Quad Hopper, 82	125	250	____
8103	Toronto, Hamilton & Buffalo Boxcar, 81	75	150	____
8204	Algoma Central Boxcar, 82	75	150	____
8507/08	Canadian National F3 Diesel AA, shells only, 85	200	400	____
8912	Canada Southern Operating Hopper, 89	50	95	____
9413	Napierville Junction Boxcar, 80	5	10	____
9718	Canadian National Boxcar, 79	10	20	____
17893	BAOC 1-D Tank Car "914," 91	60	120	____
52004	Algoma Central Gondola "9215" with coil covers, 92	45	90	____
52005	Canadian National F3 Diesel B Unit "9517," 93	15	30	____
52006	Canadian Pacific Boxcar "930016" (std O), 93	55	110	____
52115	Wabash Lake Railway 2-tier Auto Carrier "9519," 98		100	____
52125	TH&B Gondola 2-pack, 99	45	90	____
86009	Canadian National Bunk Car, 86	60	115	____
87010	Canadian National Express Reefer, 87	60	115	____
88011	Canadian National Caboose (std O), 88	250	500	____
830005	Canadian National Boxcar, 83	150	300	____
840006	Canadian Wheat Board Covered Quad Hopper, 84		165	____
900013	Canadian National Flatcar with trailers, 90	115	225	____

Lionel Collectors Club of America

LCCA National Convention Cars

		Exc	Mint
___ 6112	Commonwealth Edison Quad Hopper with coal, *83*	40	80
___ 6323	Virginia Chemicals 1-D Tank Car, *86*	35	65
___ 6567	Illinois Central Gulf Crane Car "100408," *85*	35	65
___ 7403	LNAC Boxcar, *84*	10	25
___ 9118	Corning Covered Quad Hopper, *74*	45	90
___ 9155	Monsanto 1-D Tank Car, *75*	25	45
___ 9159UP	UP Reefer, *10*	50	100
___ 9212	Seaboard Coast Line Flatcar with trailers, *76*	15	30
___ 9259	Southern Bay Window Caboose, *77*	15	40
___ 9358	"Sands of Iowa" Covered Quad Hopper, *80*	20	35
___ 9435	Central of Georgia Boxcar, *81*	15	30
___ 9460	D&TS Automobile Boxcar, *82*	20	35
___ 9701	Baltimore & Ohio Automobile Boxcar, *72*	85	170
___ 9727	TA&G Boxcar, *73*	70	135
___ 9728	Union Pacific Stock Car, *78*	10	25
___ 9733	Airco Boxcar with tank car body, *79*	25	50
___ 17870	East Camden & Highland Boxcar (std O), *87*	20	35
___ 17873	Ashland Oil 3-D Tank Car, *88*	35	70
___ 17876	Columbia, Newberry & Laurens Boxcar (std O), *89*	20	40
___ 17880	D&RGW Wood-sided Caboose (std O), *90*	30	55
___ 17887	Conrail Flatcar with Armstrong Tile trailer (std O), *91*	25	50
___ 17888	Conrail Flatcar with Ford trailer (std O), *91*	40	80
___ 17892	Conrail Flatcar with Armstrong and Ford Trailers (std O), *91*	70	140
___ 17899	NASA Tank Car "190" (std O), *92*	25	50
___ 27019	Imco PS-2 Covered Hopper, *09*	25	50
___ 52023	D&TS 2-bay ACF Hopper "2601" (std O), *93*	20	40
___ 52038	Southern Hopper "360794" with coal (std O), *94*	25	45
___ 52074	Iowa Beef Packers Reefer "197095" (std O), *95*	15	30
___ 52090	Pere Marquette DD Boxcar "71996" (std O), *96*	25	50
___ 52110	CStPM&O Boxcar "71997" (std O), *97*	25	50
___ 52151	Amtrak Baggage Boxcar "71998" (std O), *98*	35	65
___ 52176	Fort Worth & Denver Boxcar "8277" (std O), *99*	30	55
___ 52195	Double-stack Car with 2 containers, *00*	50	100
___ 52244	Louisville & Nashville Horse Car "2001," *01*	25	50
___ 52266	PRR "Coal Goes To War" Hopper "707025," *02*	45	85
___ 52267	PRR "Coal Goes To War" Hopper "707026," *02*	45	90
___ 52299	Las Vegas Mint Car, *03*	40	80
___ 52343	MILW Milk Car, orange, *04*	80	160
___ 52344	MILW Milk Car, blue, *04*	105	205
___ 52393	MKT Speeder, yellow, nonpowered, *05*	10	20
___ 52394	Frisco Speeder, red, powered, *05*	10	25

CLUB CARS AND SPECIAL PRODUCTION

		Exc	Mint
52395	Frisco Flatcar, silver, *05*	10	25 ____
52396	Frisco Flatcar with 2 speeders, *05*	65	125 ____
52412	UP Auxiliary Power Car, *06*	30	55 ____
52455	C&NW/UP Tank Car, *07*	55	110 ____
52491	PS-2 Covered Hopper 2-pack, *08*	70	140 ____
52507	NYC Water Tower, *08*	45	85 ____
52514	ATSF Mint Car with Gold, *09*	140	275 ____
52543	BNSF Mechanical Reefer, *09*	70	140 ____
52559	UP Cylindrical Hopper, *10*	50	100 ____
52562	D&RGW Uranium Transport Mint Car, *10*	115	230 ____
58254	Providence & Worcester Flatcar, *15*	50	130 ____
58271	MP Maxi-Stack Container Car with containers, *16*		100 ____
58509	Norfolk Southern Camouflage PS-1 Boxcar, *12*	50	95 ____
58560	Southern Tennessean Boxcar, *13*	45	90 ____
58576	Monon Operating Boxcar, *14*	65	125 ____
72511	Alamo Mint Car, *11*	75	150 ____
75511	Federal Reserve Mint Car, *11*	100	200 ____

LCCA Meet Specials

1130	Tender, *76*	5	15 ____
6014-900	Frisco Boxcar (O27), *75*	15	30 ____
6483	Jersey Central SP-type Caboose, *82*	15	30 ____
9016	Chessie System Hopper (O27), *79*	10	20 ____
9036	Mobilgas 1-D Tank Car (O27), *78*	10	20 ____
9142	Republic Steel Gondola, green or blue, with canisters, *77*	10	25 ____

Other LCCA Production

4001	RJ Corman Boxcar, *99*	40	80 ____
4002	RJ Corman Boxcar, *99*	20	40 ____
6464-2002	Maddox Retirement Boxcar, *02*	50	100 ____
8068	Rock Island GP20 Diesel, *80*	60	120 ____
9739	D&RGW Boxcar, *78*	10	25 ____
9771	Norfolk & Western Boxcar, *77*	15	30 ____
14154	Water Tower with LCCA plaque, *04*	45	90 ____
17174	Great Northern 3-bay Hopper, *03*	10	25 ____
17234	Port Huron & Detroit Boxcar, *00*	25	45 ____
17377	American Railway Express Reefer "302," *06*	25	50 ____
17412	Gondola, blue, *02*	15	30 ____
17895	LCCA Tractor, *91*	10	20 ____
17896	Lancaster Lines Tractor, *91*	15	30 ____
18090	D&RGW 4-6-2 Locomotive and Tender, *90*	155	305 ____
18483	C&O Ballast Tamper, *07*	40	75 ____
18490	UP Ballast Tamper, yellow, *06*	65	125 ____
19998	"Seasons Greetings" Boxcar, *03*	20	40 ____
26023	Flatcar with bulldozer, *04*	30	55 ____
26024	Flatcar with scraper, *04*	35	65 ____

CLUB CARS AND SPECIAL PRODUCTION

		Exc	Mint
26049	Speedboat Willie Flatcar with boat, *05*	25	45
26132	UP 1-D Tank Car, *06*	15	30
26780	Operating Giraffe Car, green or pink, *05*	35	70
26791	UP Chase Gondola, red, *03*	15	30
26791	Rio Grande Chase Gondola, black, *06*	15	30
26795	Mrs. O'Leary's Dairy Farm Stock Car, *07*	50	100
26834	"La Cosa Nostra Railway" Operating Ice Car, *07*	40	75
29232	Lenny the Lion Hi-Cube, signed by Lenny Dean, *98*	35	65
52025	Madison Hardware Tractor and Trailer, *93*	10	20
52039	"Track 29" Bumper, *94*	10	25
52055	SOVEX Tractor and Trailer, *94*	10	20
52056	Southern Tractor and Trailer, *94*	15	25
52091	Lenox Tractor and Trailer, *95*	5	15
52092	Iowa Interstate Tractor and Trailer, *95*	10	20
52100	Grand Rapids Station Platform, *98*	10	25
52107	On-track Pickup, orange, *96*	25	50
52108	On-track Van, blue, *96*	20	35
52131	Beechcraft Airplane, blue, *97*	10	25
52138	Beechcraft Airplane, orange, *97*	10	25
52152	Ben Franklin and Liberty Bell Reefer, *98*	60	120
52153	6414 Auto Set, 4-pack, *98*	35	70
52206	SD40 Diesel and Extended Vision Caboose, *00*	325	650
52257	"Season's Greetings" Gondola, *01*	20	35
52273	Flatcar with submarine, *02*	110	220
52300	Halloween General Train, *04*	180	360
52348	Halloween General Sheriff and Outlaw Car, *04*	60	115
52405	Halloween General Add-on Cars, *06*	80	160
52406	Halloween General Cannon, *08*	70	135
52423	New Haven Alco Diesel Passenger Set, *09*	255	510
52468	Postwar "2434" Passenger Coach, *09*	40	75
52469	Postwar "2432" Passenger Coach, *09*	40	75
52528	Burlington Alco Diesel Passenger Set, *09*	150	340
52540	Passenger Shelter, *09*	10	25
52581	Texas Special Milk Car, *10*	55	110
52582	Gondola with dinosaurs, *12*	25	45
58217	B&M Smoking Caboose, *15*		105
58224	Walking Brakeman Car, *15*		100
58249	Holiday Boxcar, *15*	20	80
58251	Maine Central Flatcar with trailers, *15*		100
58272	MKT Maxi-Stack Container Car with containers, *16*		100
58526	Texas Special Cow and Calf SW9 Switchers, *14*		375
58532	Lou Caponi Blue Coal Train, *14*	100	200
58549	Texas Special Diamonds Mint Car, *14*	40	75
58561	Southern Pelican Boxcar, *13*	35	70
58584	45th Anniversary Auto Rack Loader, *14*	60	120

Lionel Operating Train Society

LOTS National Convention Cars

		Exc	Mint	
303	Stauffer Chemical 1-D Tank Car, *85*	105	210	___
3764	Kahn's Brine Tank Reefer, *81*	45	85	___
6111	L&N Covered Quad Hopper, *83*	20	40	___
6211	C&O Gondola with canisters, *86*	45	90	___
9414	Cotton Belt Boxcar, *80*	30	55	___
16812	Grand Trunk 2-bay ACF Hopper (std O), *96*	30	60	___
16813	Pennsylvania Power & Light Hopper (std O), *97*	40	80	___
17874	Milwaukee Road Log Dump Car "59629," *88*	75	150	___
17875	Port Huron & Detroit Boxcar "1289," *89*	25	50	___
17882	B&O DD Boxcar "298011" with ETD, *90*	35	65	___
17890	CSX Auto Carrier "151161," *91*	40	80	___
18890	Union Pacific RS3 Diesel "8805," *89*	75	145	___
19960	Western Pacific Boxcar "1952" (std O), *92*	35	65	___
38356	Dow Chemical 3-D Tank Car, *87*	65	125	___
52014	BN TTUX Flatcar Set with N&W trailers, *93*	105	205	___
52041	BN TTUX Flatcar Set with Conrail trailers, *94*	45	85	___
52067	Burlington Operating Ice Car "50240," *95*	30	60	___
52135	ATSF Reefer "22739," *98*	30	55	___
52162	Gulf Mobile & Ohio DD Boxcar "24580," *99*	35	65	___
52196	CP Maxi-Stack Flatcar "524115" with 2 containers, *00*	50	95	___
52234	WM Well Car with transformer, *01*	30	60	___
52261	Schlitz Beer Reefer "92132," *02*	30	60	___
52281	PRR Operating Boxcar, *03*	30	55	___
52342	Southern Stock Car, sound, *04*	30	55	___
52346	D&H PS-2 Cement Hopper, *06*	35	65	___
52347	SF SD80 MAC Diesel, TMCC, *04*	175	350	___
52380/81	Virginian Coal Hopper, *05*	25	50	___
52382	SF Extended View Caboose, *05*	165	325	___
52425	SP&S Boxcar (std O), *07*	45	90	___
52474	NYC Evans Auto Loader with 4 Studebakers, *08*	40	80	___
52550	NC&StL Dixieland Boxcar, *09*	40	75	___
52566	NH State of Maine Boxcar, *10*	30	60	___
52580	Robin Hood Beer Double-sheathed Boxcar, *11*	40	80	___
58223	Chicago Great Western Flatcar with Edelweiss Beer Trailers, *15*		75	___
58508	Genesee Beer & Ale Double-sheathed Boxcar, *11*	35	70	___
58553	UP Maxi-Stack Car with WP feather containers, *13*	40	75	___
58575	H. J. Heinz Double-sheathed Boxcar, *14*	35	70	___
80948	Michigan Central Boxcar, *82*	115	230	___
83862	Cradle of Liberty Boxcar, *16*		75	___
83863	Santa Fe Warbonnet Tank Car, *16*		75	___
83872/3	D&RGW 2-car Ore Car Set, *17*		110	___
121315	Pennsylvania Hi-Cube Boxcar, *84*	175	345	___

CLUB CARS AND SPECIAL PRODUCTION

Exc Mint

LOTS Meet Specials

			Exc	Mint
____	52413	Saratoga Brewery Reefer, 06	30	60
____	52456	Alpenrose Dairy Milk Car, 07	50	95
____	52506	Studebaker Automobile Parts Boxcar, 08	40	75
____	52552	Radioactive Waste Removal Car, 09	45	85
____	58236	Tucker Automobile Parts Boxcar, 15		75

Other LOTS Production

			Exc	Mint
____	1223	Seattle & North Coast Hi-Cube Boxcar, 86	100	200
____	52042	BN TTUX Flatcar "637500C" with CN trailer, 94	30	60
____	52048	Canadian National Tractor and Trailer "197993," 94	20	35
____	52129	Lighted Billboard with Angela Trotta Thomas art, 97	15	30
____	52217	LOTS/LCCA 2000 Convention Billboard, 00	5	10
____	52260	National Aquarium in Baltimore Car, 01	55	110
____	52280	"More Precious than Gold" Mint Car, 02	45	90
____	52309	Patriotic Tank Car, 03	35	70
____	52359	Silver Anniversary Ore Car "1979," 04	20	40
____	52360	Silver Anniversary Ore Car "2004," 04	20	40
____	52419	Touring Layout Aquarium Car, 05	45	90
____	52477	Santa Fe Warbonnet Boxcar, 07	40	75
____	52523	Santa Fe Flatcar with trailer and tractor, 08	45	90
____	52553	Tennessee Aquarium Car, 09	35	65
____	52567	Santa Fe ACF 2-bay Hopper, 10	30	60
____	52590	Santa Fe Warbonnet Mint Car, 11	40	75
____	58228	Burlington Zephyr Double-sheathed Boxcar, 15		75
____	58535	Santa Fe ACF Transparent Boxcar, 12	40	75
____	58566	Virginia & Truckee Carson City Mint Car, 13	35	70
____	58593	Porter Locomotive Parts Boxcar, 14		70
____	58594/5	Santa Fe Crane and Work Caboose, 14		135

Lionel Century Club

			Exc	Mint
____	14532	PRR Sharknose Diesel AA Set, LCC II, 00	350	690
____	18053	2-8-4 Berkshire Locomotive "726," 97	360	705
____	18057	6-8-6PRR S2 Steam Turbine Locomotive "671," 98	290	570
____	18058	4-6-4 Hudson Locomotive "773," 97	375	735
____	18068	Tender for PRR Steam Turbine Locomotive "773," 99	105	210
____	18135	NYC F3 Diesel AA Set, 99	325	650
____	18178	NYC F3 Diesel B Unit, 99	115	230
____	18314	PRR GG1 Electric "2332," 97	280	560
____	18340	FM Train Master Set, LCC II, 00	450	900
____	24510	PRR Sharknose Diesel B Unit, LCC II, 00	100	200

CLUB CARS AND SPECIAL PRODUCTION

		Exc	Mint
28069	NYC 4-8-6 Niagara Locomotive "6024," CC, LCC II, *00*	460	920 ____
29173	Empire State Express Passenger Car 4-pack, LCC II, *02*	175	350 ____
29178	Empire State Express Passenger Car 2-pack, LCC II, *02*	90	175 ____
29181	Empire State Express Diner, LCC II, *02*	95	190 ____
29204	Boxcar "1900-2000," *96*	165	330 ____
29226	Berkshire Boxcar, *97*	75	145 ____
29227	GG1 Boxcar, *98*	30	55 ____
29228	PRR Turbine Boxcar "671," *99*	30	60 ____
29248	F3 Boxcar "2333," *99*	35	65 ____
31716	Niagara Milk Train Set, LCC II, *00*	150	300 ____
31726	PRR Sharknose Coal Train Set, LCC II, *00*	90	180 ____
31731	Train Master Freight Train Set, LCC II, *00*	90	180 ____
38000	NYC 4-6-4 Hudson Empire State Locomotive, LCC II, *02*	495	990 ____
39201	Hudson Boxcar "773," *00*	30	60 ____
39215	Niagara Boxcar, LCC II, *01*	25	50 ____
39217	Boxcar, LCC II, *00*	30	60 ____
39218	Gold Boxcar, LCC II, *00*	45	85 ____
39237	M-10000 Boxcar, LCC II, *00*	35	70 ____
39246	PRR Sharknose Boxcar, LCC II, *00*	30	55 ____
39265	Fairbanks-Morse Train Master Boxcar, LCC II, *00*	30	60 ____
39266	Empire State Boxcar, LCC II, *00*	20	40 ____
51007	UP M-10000 4-car Passenger Set, LCC II, *00*	485	970 ____
51249	UP Overland Route Sleeper Car, LCC II, *02*	60	120 ____

Lionel Railroader Club

780	Boxcar, *82*	35	65 ____
781	Flatcar with trailers, *83*	25	50 ____
782	1-D Tank Car, *85*	25	45 ____
784	Covered Quad Hopper, *84*	30	60 ____
11183	Lincoln Funeral Train	400	800 ____
11319	PRR Tuscan K4 Locomotive, CC	450	900 ____
11320	PRR Tuscan K4 Locomotive	375	750 ____
12875	Tractor and Trailer, *94*	10	20 ____
12921	Illuminated Station Platform, *95*	10	20 ____
14274	Water Tower, *07*	10	20 ____
15034	50th Anniversary Mail Car, *10*	25	50 ____
15035	Holiday Boxcar, *10*	25	50 ____
16800	Ore Car, yellow, *86*	35	70 ____
16801	Bunk Car, blue, *88*	20	35 ____
16802	Tool Car, *89*	25	35 ____
16803	Searchlight Car, *90*	10	25 ____
16804	Bay Window Caboose, *91*	15	30 ____

CLUB CARS AND SPECIAL PRODUCTION

			Exc	Mint
____	**16839**	Covered Bridge, *11*	25	50
____	**18680**	4-6-4 Hudson Locomotive, *00*	150	300
____	**18684**	4-6-2 Pacific Locomotive, *99*	110	220
____	**18818**	GP38-2 Diesel, *92*	100	115
____	**19399**	Christmas Boxcar, *13*	30	60
____	**19437**	Flatcar with trailer, *97*	30	55
____	**19473**	Operating Log Dump Car "3351," *99*	20	40
____	**19685**	Western Union Dining Car, *02*	20	40
____	**19695**	Western Union 1-D Tank Car, *03*	10	20
____	**19774**	Porthole Caboose, *99*	25	50
____	**19775**	Stock Car, *99*	25	50
____	**19924**	Boxcar, *93*	10	20
____	**19930**	Quad Hopper with coal, *94*	10	20
____	**19935**	1-D Tank Car, *95*	10	25
____	**19940**	Vat Car, *96*	15	30
____	**19953**	6464 Boxcar, *97*	20	35
____	**19965**	Aquarium Car "3435," *99*	30	55
____	**19966**	Gondola "9820" (std O), *98*	15	30
____	**19978**	Gold Membership Boxcar, *99*	25	45
____	**19991**	Gold Membership Boxcar, *00*	35	65
____	**19992**	Western Union Tool Car "3550," *00*	25	50
____	**19993**	Gold Membership Boxcar, *01*	35	65
____	**19994**	Western Union Passenger Car "1307," *01*	30	60
____	**19995**	25th Anniversary Boxcar (std O), *01*	25	50
____	**24217**	Animated Billboard, *08*	15	30
____	**25073**	Holiday Boxcar, *09*	20	50
____	**25631**	Lincoln Train Passenger Car 2-pack	150	300
____	**25635**	Red Passenger Car 3-pack, *12*	210	420
____	**25635**	Red Arrow Diner, *12*	70	140
____	**26089**	Western Union Gondola with handcar, *05*	35	65
____	**26165**	Western Union Reefer, *04*	15	30
____	**26382**	Flatcar with tractor and tanker, *08*	30	60
____	**26413**	Commemorative 4-bay Hopper, *08*	35	70
____	**26636**	"6830" 50th Anniversary Flatcar with submarine, *11*	30	55
____	**26637**	"6640" 50th Anniversary USMC Missile Launching Car, *11*	35	65
____	**27940**	"6469" Liquified Gas Tank Car, *13*	25	50
____	**27943**	"6416" Boat Loader, *13*	25	50
____	**27944**	"3413" Mercury Capsule Launch Car, *13*	30	60
____	**27945**	"6460-60" LV Covered Quad Hopper, *13*	30	55
____	**28062**	4-6-4 Hudson Locomotive, *00*	575	1150
____	**28571**	GP9 Diesel, CC, *07*	125	250
____	**28665**	Western Union 2-8-4 Berkshire Locomotive "665," *05*	90	175
____	**29200**	Lionel Boxcar "9700," *96*	20	40

CLUB CARS AND SPECIAL PRODUCTION

		Exc	Mint
29313	"3409" 50th Anniversary Helicopter Car, 11	35	70 ____
29657	"6413" 50th Anniversary Mercury Capsule Car, 12	30	55 ____
29658	"6465" 50th Anniversary Cities Service 2-D Car, 12	25	50 ____
29931	Holiday Boxcar, 05	10	25 ____
29939	30th Anniversary Boxcar, 06	25	50 ____
29941	Holiday Boxcar, 06	10	25 ____
29946	Holiday Boxcar, 07	20	35 ____
29947	Commemorative Boxcar, 07	15	30 ____
29957	Holiday Boxcar, 08	25	50 ____
29977	Holiday Boxcar, 11	30	60 ____
36521	Western Union Searchlight Caboose, 05	15	30 ____
36769	4th of July Lighted Boxcar, 03	35	70 ____
37968	Clock Tower with wreath, 11	25	45 ____
39249	Holiday Boxcar, 03	15	30 ____
39264	Holiday Boxcar, 04	25	50 ____
39352	"6445" 50th Anniversary Fort Knox Mint Car, 12	35	70 ____
39353	50th Anniversary Santa Fe Boxcar, 11	30	55 ____
39496	"6475" 50th Anniversary Vat Car, 10	30	60 ____
58613	Holiday Boxcar, 14	30	90 ____
58632	1955 Maintenance of Way Truck, 13	85	165 ____
81116	Polar Express Operating Billboard, 14	30	60 ____
81117	Polar Express Flatcar with silver bell, 14	25	45 ____

Lionel Railroad Club Milwaukee

		Exc	Mint
52116	MILW Flatcar "194797," black, with tractor and trailer, 97	40	75 ____
52163	CMStP&P "Hiawatha" DD Automobile Boxcar, 98	30	60 ____
52180	MILW Flatcar "194799," tuscan, with trailer, 99	40	75 ____
52228	CMStP&P 1-D Water Tank Car "908309," 00	25	50 ____
52229	MILW 1-D Diesel Fuel Tank Car "907797," 00	25	50 ____
52230	1-D Tank Car 2-pack, 00	70	140 ____
52246	CMStP&P "Olympian" Boxcar "194701," 01	35	65 ____
52265	MILW/Zoological Society Aquarium Car "4701," orange, 02	30	55 ____
52278	MILW/Zoological Society Aquarium Car "4702," blue, 03	50	95 ____
52297	MILW Reefer "194703," yellow, 03	35	65 ____
52298	MILW Flatcar "194704" with orange trailer, 04	60	115 ____
52337	MILW/Zoological Society Motorized Aquarium Car, 04	45	90 ____
52368	MILW Flatcar "472004," black, 05	35	65 ____
52369	MILW Trailer Train Auto Carrier "194705," 05	45	85 ____
52370	CMStP&P Milk Car "364," tan, 05	40	80 ____
52387	CMStP&P Flatcar "194706," gray, 06	25	50 ____
52400	MILW PS-2 2-bay Hopper "99607," orange, 06	45	85 ____

CLUB CARS AND SPECIAL PRODUCTION

			Exc	Mint
___	52401	MILW PS-2 2-bay Hopper "98809," yellow, 06	35	65
___	52402	CMStP&P URTX Operating Ice Car "4706," 06	45	85
	52428	CMStP&P 0-4-0 Switcher and Caboose Set, 60th Anniversary, 06	140	275
___	52429	CMStP&P 0-4-0 Switcher, 06	100	200
___	52430	CMStP&P Offset Cupola Caboose, 06	35	70
___	52458	MILW Stock Car "102721" (std O), 07	35	65
___	52466	CMStP&P Stock Car "105254" (std O), 07	35	65
___	52551	MILW "Big M" DD Boxcar "200947," yellow, 09	30	60
___	52572	MILW Reiman Aquarium Car, 11	40	75
___	52599	MILW 2-bay ACF Hopper, 12	30	60
___	58263	Breast Cancer Awareness Boxcar, 16		80
___	58563	CMStP&P Round-Roof Boxcar, 13	35	70
___	58591	MILW Flatcar with auto frames, 14	30	60

Long Island Toy Train Locomotive Engineers

___	58520	Entenmann's Vat Car, 12	35	65
___	58556	Flatcar with U.S. Navy airplane, 13	35	70
	58562	Entenmann's Quad Hopper, 14	40	75

Nassau Lionel Operating Engineers

___	8389	Long Island Boxcar, 89	50	100
___	8390	Long Island Covered Quad Hopper, 90	50	100
___	8391A	Long Island Bunk Car, 91	45	90
___	8391B	Long Island Tool Car, 91	45	90
___	8392	Long Island 1-D Tank Car, 92	55	105
___	52007	Long Island RS3 Diesel "1552," 93	125	250
___	52019	Long Island Boxcar, 93	35	65
___	52020	Long Island Bay Window Caboose, 93	50	95
	52026	Long Island Flatcar "8394" with Grumman trailer, 94	235	465
	52061	Long Island Stern's Pickle Products Vat Car "8395," 95	100	200
___	52072	Grumman Tractor, 94	40	75
___	52076	Long Island Observation Car "8396," 96	175	350
	52112	Long Island Ronkonkoma Vista Dome Car "9783," 97	150	300
___	52122	Meenan Oil 1-D Tank Car "8397" (std O), 97	30	60
___	52123	Long Island Hicksville Diner Car "9883," 98	150	300
___	52144	Long Island Flatcar with Grumman van, 99	50	95
___	52145	Long Island Jamaica Passenger Coach, 99	150	300
___	52145	Long Island Penn Station Passenger Coach, 99	150	300
	52166	Long Island Flatcar "8398" with Grumman trailer, 98	40	75
___	52174	REA Baggage Car "0083," 00		400
___	52186	Grucci Fireworks Boxcar, 00	35	70

CLUB CARS AND SPECIAL PRODUCTION

		Exc	Mint
52209	World's Fair Sleeper/Roomette Car "0183," 01		170 ___
52232	Central RR of Long Island Boxcar, 01	30	60 ___
52235	World's Fair Vista Dome Car "0283," 02		NRS ___
52256	New York & Atlantic Boxcar "8302," 02	30	60 ___
52263	World's Fair Combination Car "0383," 02		NRS ___
52296	Long Island Flatcar with Republic tanker, 03	40	80 ___
52329	New York & Atlantic Caboose, 04	40	80 ___
52341	Long Island Flatcar with Pan Am trailer, 05	45	85 ___
52365	Long Island Flatcar with Lilco transformer, 04	70	135 ___
52420	Long Island 80th Anniversary Boxcar, 06	25	45 ___
52480	Long Island Flatcar with pipes, 08	25	50 ___
52489	Long Island Flatcar with P.C. Richard & Son trailer, 07	35	65 ___
52555	Martha Clara Vineyards Vat Car, 09	30	60 ___
52568	Flatcar with NY Islanders refrigerated trailer, 10	30	60 ___
52586	Flatcar with Cradle of Aviation Museum trailer, 11	25	50 ___
52592	Petland Discounts Aquarium Car, 11	35	70 ___
58212	Cross Harbor Round-roof Boxcar, 15		65 ___
58240	LIRR GLa Hopper, black, 16		80 ___
58240	LIRR GLa Hopper, tuscan, 16		80 ___
58266	Nathan's 100th Anniversary Reefer, 16		65 ___
58500	Nassau County Firefighters Museum Tank Car, 12	30	55 ___
58567	Nathan's Famous Reefer "83131," 13	40	75 ___
58568	Nathan's Famous Reefer "83132," 13	40	75 ___
58573	Long Island PS1 Boxcar "8312," 14		80 ___
58581	Long Island Double-sheathed Boxcar, 14		65 ___
	LIRR PS-2CD Scale Hopper, 17		70 ___

Railroad Museum of Long Island

		Exc	Mint
52416	RMLI 15th Anniversary LIRR Boxcar, 05	85	170 ___
52433	Atlantis Marine World Aquarium Car, 06	75	145 ___
52453	North Fork Bank Mint Car, 07	45	90 ___
52497	LIRR Flatcar with Entenmann's trailer and tractor, 08	55	110 ___
52498	Boeing Fairchild Container Car, 10	40	75 ___
52548	RMLI "Celebrating 175 Years of Railroading" Boxcar, 09	45	90 ___
52557	Entenmann's Operating Boxcar, 10	45	90 ___
52570	Riverhead Building Supply Boxcar, 11	30	60 ___
52571	Riverhead Visitor's Center Boxcar, 11	30	60 ___
52577	King Kullen Boxcar, 11	30	60 ___
52595	J. P. Holland Submarine Car, 12	30	60 ___
58227	World's Fair Crew Car, 15		75 ___
58259	Steam Up LIRR 39 Boxcar, 16		85 ___
58521	Wonder Bread PS-2 Covered Hopper, 12	30	60 ___

		Exc	Mint
___ 58551	Flatcar with White Castle refrigerated trailer, *13*	30	60
___ 58554	RCA Operating Radar Car, *13*	30	60
___ 58555	Flatcar with produce trailers, *15*		75
___ 58579	World's Fair Exhibit Car, *14*		80
___ 58580	World's Fair Tool Car, *15*		60

St. Louis Lionel Railroad Club

		Exc	Mint
___ 52099	MP Flatcar with St. Louis trailer, *96*	35	65
___ 52104	St. Louis tractor and trailer, *96*	10	20
___ 52117	Wabash Flatcar with REA tractor and trailer, *97*	35	65
___ 52136A	Christmas Tractor and Trailer, *97*		NRS
___ 52136B	Frisco Tractor and Trailer, *98*		NRS
___ 52147	Frisco Campbell TOFC Flatcar, *98*	40	75
___ 52150	Frisco Campbell TOFC Flatcar, *98*	65	130
___ 52167	ATSF Flatcar "831999" with Navajo trailer, *99*	40	75
___ 52190	IC Flatcar with trailers, *00*	40	80
___ 52222	Cotton Belt Flatcar with SP tractor and trailer, *01*	25	50
___ 52224A	SP Flatcar with Navajo tractor and trailer, *01*	10	25
___ 52224B	SP Flatcar with service tractor and trailer, *01*	10	25
___ 52258	UP Flatcar with UP tractor and trailer, *02*	30	55
___ 52290	UP Flatcar with tractor trailer, *03*	40	75
___ 52336	U.S. Army Flatcar with tanker truck, *04*	65	125
___ 52371	NYC Flatcar with Fire Company tanker truck, *05*	70	145
___ 52392	PRR Flatcar with Hood's Milk tanker truck, *06*	50	100
___ 52440	U.S.M.C. Flatcar with tractor and trailer, *07*	70	135
___ 52490	Silver Special Flatcar with USA tractor and trailer, *08*	50	100
___ 52513	Frisco Flatcar with U.S.A.F. trailer, *09*	60	120

Train Collectors Association

TCA National Convention Cars

		Exc	Mint
___ 511	St. Louis Baggage Car, *81*	20	40
___ 2671-1968	TCA Tender, shell only, *68*	30	55
___ 5734	REA Reefer, *85*	25	50
___ 6315	Pittsburgh 1-D Tank Car, *72*	30	60
___ 6436-1969	Open Quad Hopper, red, *69*	35	65
___ 6464-1965	Pittsburgh Boxcar, blue, *65*	125	210
___ 6464-1970	Chicago Boxcar, *70*	45	85
___ 6464-1971	Disneyland Boxcar, *71*	210	240
___ 6517-1966	Bay Window Caboose, *66*	150	250
___ 6926	New Orleans Extended Vision Caboose, *86*	20	40
___ 7205	Denver Combination Car, *82*	25	50
___ 7206	Louisville Passenger Car, *83*	30	55
___ 7212	Pittsburgh Passenger Car, *84*	25	50

CLUB CARS AND SPECIAL PRODUCTION

		Exc	Mint	
7812	Houston Stock Car, 77	10	25	___
8476	4-6-4 Locomotive "5484," 85	155	310	___
9123	Dearborn 3-tier Auto Carrier, 73	20	35	___
9319	"Silver Jubilee" Mint Car, 79	65	130	___
9544	Chicago Observation Car, 80	25	50	___
9611	Boston Hi-Cube Boxcar, 78	10	25	___
9774	Orlando "Southern Belle" Boxcar, 75	15	35	___
9779	Philadelphia Boxcar "9700-1976," 76	20	35	___
9864	Seattle Reefer, 74	25	50	___
11737	TCA 40th Anniversary F3 Diesel ABA Set, 93	265	530	___
17879	Valley Forge Dining Car, 89	30	60	___
17883	New Georgia Passenger Car, 90	35	65	___
17898	Wabash Reefer "21596," 92	25	45	___
19211	Vermont Railway Flatcars (2) with 4 trailers, 08	80	160	___
52008	Bucyrus Erie Crane Car, 93	25	50	___
52035	Yorkrail GP9 Diesel "1750," shell only, 94	30	55	___
52036	TCA 40th Anniversary Bay Window Caboose, 94	20	40	___
52037	Yorkrail GP9 Diesel "1754," 94	75	150	___
52062	Skytop Observation Car, 95	180	360	___
52085	Full Vista Dome Car, 96	60	115	___
52106	City of Phoenix Diner, 97	50	100	___
52142	Massachusetts Central Maxi-Stack Flatcar "5100-01," 98	60	120	___
52143	City of Providence Passenger Car, 98	70	140	___
52146	Ocean Spray Reefer, 98	120	235	___
52155	City of San Francisco Baggage Car, 99	70	140	___
52191	City of Grand Rapids Aluminum Passenger Car, 00	70	135	___
52210	Rico Station, 00	15	30	___
52220	City of Chattanooga Vista Dome Car, 01	70	140	___
52221	Norfolk Southern Boxcar, 01	25	50	___
52274	City of Los Angeles Railway Post Office Car, 03	35	80	
52237	Lionel Gondola, yellow, 01	55	110	___
52238	Lionel Gondola, red, 01	55	110	___
52239	Lionel Gondola, silver, 01	55	110	___
52240	Lionel Gondola 3-pack, 01	55	110	___
52241	Lionel Gondola, black, 02	5	15	___
52242	Lionel Gondola, blue, 02	20	35	___
52250	City of Chicago Combination Car, 02	65	130	___
52272	Lionel Gondola, gold, 02	40	80	___
52276	California Gold Mint Car, 03	35	65	___
52333	Harmony Dairy Milk Car, 04	45	90	___
52338	Lionel 50th Anniversary Mint Car, 04	40	75	___
52339	50th Anniversary Convention Banquet Car with coin, 04	180	360	___
52340	Train Order Building, 04	45	90	___
52373	Montana Rail Link 2-car Set, 05	45	90	___

CLUB CARS AND SPECIAL PRODUCTION

			Exc	Mint
___	52374	Montana Rail Link 2-bay Hopper, *05*	25	50
___	52375	Montana Rail Link Flatcar with pulp-wood logs, *05*	25	50
___	52376	GN Reefer, *05*	30	60
___	52403	T&P Stock Car (std O), *06*	40	75
___	52414	Flatcar with 3 snowmobiles, *07*	40	80
___	52481	Ben & Jerry's Reefer, *08*	50	95
___	52500	ATSF Grand Canyon Reefer, *09*	30	60
___	52508	Celebrate America Mint Car, *09*	50	95
___	58216	NYC Merchants Despatch Reefer, *15*		90
___	58258	Made in the USA Boxcar, *16*		80
___	58544	St. Louis Reefer, *13*	45	85
___	58547	Cotton Belt Blue Streak Merchandise Boxcar, *13*	35	75
___	58571	Bethlehem Steel PS-1 Boxcar, *14*	40	80
___	58572	Reading Philadelphia Mint Car, *14*	40	80

TCA Museum-Related and Other Cars

			Exc	Mint
___	1018-1979	Mortgage Burning Hi-Cube Boxcar, *79*	20	35
___	5731	L&N Reefer, *90*	50	95
___	7780	TCA Museum Boxcar, *80*	10	25
___	7781	Hafner Boxcar, *81*	10	25
___	7782	Carlisle & Finch Boxcar, *82*	10	25
___	7783	Ives Boxcar, *83*	10	25
___	7784	Voltamp Boxcar, *84*	10	25
___	7785	Hoge Boxcar, *85*	10	25
___	9771	Norfolk & Western Boxcar, *77*	15	30
___	16811	Rutland Boxcar "5477096," *96*	20	35
___	52045	Pennsylvania Dutch Milk Car "61052," *94*	45	90
___	52051	Baltimore & Ohio Sentinel Boxcar "6464095," *95*	20	40
___	52052	TCA 40th Anniversary Boxcar, *94*	45	90
___	52063	NYC Pacemaker Boxcar "6464125," *95*	175	345
___	52064	Missouri Pacific Boxcar "6464150," *95*	185	370
___	52065	Pennsylvania Dutch Grain Operating Boxcar "9208," *96*	50	100
___	52118	Rio Grande Boxcar "5477097," *97*	30	55
___	52119	TCA Museum 20th Anniversary Boxcar, *97*	35	70
___	52128	Pennsylvania Dutch Pretzels Boxcar, *99*	40	80
___	52172	L&N "Share the Freedom" Boxcar "5477099," *99*	25	55
___	52198	Frisco Boxcar "5477000," *00*	25	45
___	52215	Museum Work Train Gondola with pipes, *03*	30	55
___	52226	Angela Trotta Thomas Boxcar "2000," *01*	50	100
___	52243	Museum Work Train 1-D Tank Car, *01*	25	50
___	52271	Museum Work Train Flatcar with wheel load, *02*	10	20
___	52289	National Toy Train Museum 25th Anniversary Bullion Car, *02*	40	75
___	52295	National Toy Train Museum Gondola with pipes, *03*	5	15

CLUB CARS AND SPECIAL PRODUCTION

		Exc	Mint
52310	Museum Work Train Boxcar, *04*	30	55 ____
52311	50th Anniversary Golden Express Freight Set, *04*	200	450 ____
52321	SP Trainmaster Locomotive, *04*	175	345 ____
52372	Museum Work Train Baggage Car, *05*	35	70 ____
52408	N&W Caboose, *06*	30	55 ____
52409	Museum Work Train Idler Caboose, *06*	35	70 ____
52437	Museum Work Train Crane Car, *07*	40	80 ____

TCA Bicentennial Special Set

		Exc	Mint
1973	Bicentennial Observation Car, *76*	25	50 ____
1974	Bicentennial Passenger Car, *76*	25	50 ____
1975	Bicentennial Passenger Car, *76*	25	50 ____
1976	Bicentennial U36B Diesel, *76*	85	165 ____

Atlantic Division

		Exc	Mint
1980	Atlantic Division Flatcar with trailers, *80*	20	35 ____
6101	Burlington Northern Covered Quad Hopper, *82*	20	35 ____
9186	Conrail N5c Caboose, *79*	15	30 ____
9193	Budweiser Vat Car, *84*	55	110 ____
9466	Wanamaker Boxcar, *83*	70	135 ____
9788	Lehigh Valley Boxcar, *78*	10	25 ____
58598	Philly Pretzel Factory Boxcar, *14*		40 ____
	Wawa Hoagiefest Boxcar, *17*		70 ____

Desert Division

		Exc	Mint
52088	Desert Division 25th Anniversary On-track Step Van, *96*	60	120 ____
52105	Superstition Mountain Operating Gondola "61997," *97*	40	80 ____
52442	Verde Canyon Boxcar, *07*	30	55 ____
52443	Grand Canyon Boxcar, *07*	30	55 ____
58222	Los Alamos Mint Car, *16*		80 ____
58226	Cumbres & Toltec Boxcar, *16*		80 ____
	Fred Harvey Boxcar, *17*		80 ____

Dixie Division

		Exc	Mint
27007/87	Dixie Division 20th Anniversary PS-1 Boxcar, *06*	40	80 ____
52127	Dixie Division 10th Anniversary Southern 3-bay Hopper, *98*	35	70 ____

Eastern Division

		Exc	Mint
52059	Clinchfield Quad Hopper "16413" with coal, *94*	55	110 ____

CLUB CARS AND SPECIAL PRODUCTION Exc Mint

Eastern Division: Washington, Baltimore & Annapolis Chapter

		Exc	Mint
____ 9412	Richmond, Fredericksburg & Potomac Boxcar, *79*	10	25
____ 9740	Chessie System Boxcar, *76*	10	25
____ 9771	Norfolk & Western Boxcar, *78*	15	30
____ 9783	B&O Time-Saver Boxcar, *77*	15	30

Fort Pitt Division

____ 1984-30X	Heinz Ketchup Boxcar, *84*	250	500

Great Lakes Division

____ 1983	Churchill Downs Boxcar, *83*	100	200
____ 1983	Churchill Downs Reefer, *83*	125	250
____ 9740	Chessie System Boxcar, *76*	10	25

Great Lakes Division: Detroit-Toledo Chapter

____ 8957	Burlington Northern GP20 Diesel, *80*	115	230
____ 8958	Burlington Northern GP20 Diesel Dummy Unit, *80*	75	150
____ 9119	Detroit & Mackinac Covered Quad Hopper, *77*	10	20
____ 9272	New Haven Bay Window Caboose, *79*	10	20
____ 9401	Great Northern Boxcar, *78*	10	25
____ 9730	CP Rail Boxcar, *76*	10	25
____ 52000	Detroit-Toledo Division Flatcar with trailer, *92*	45	85

Great Lakes Division: Three Rivers Chapter

____ 9113	Norfolk & Western Quad Hopper, *76*	15	30

Great Lakes Division: Western Michigan Chapter

____ 9730	CP Rail Boxcar, *74*	10	25

Lake & Pines Division

____ 52018	3-M Boxcar, *93*	225	450

Lone Star Division

____ 7522	New Orleans Mint Car with coin, *86*	210	420
____ 52093	Lone Star Division Boxcar "6464696," *96*	15	30
____ 52585	Texas Special Mint Car, *11*	35	65
____ 58512	SP Daylight Mint Car, *12*	35	65
____ 58552	Texas Special Mint Car with silver bars, *12*	35	65

Lone Star Division: North Texas Chapter

____ 9739	D&RGW Boxcar, *76*	10	20

CLUB CARS AND SPECIAL PRODUCTION

Exc Mint

METCA

		Exc	Mint
10	Jersey Central F3 A Unit, shell only, *71*	10	25 ____
9272	New Haven Bay Window Caboose, *79*	10	25 ____
9754	New York Central Pacemaker Boxcar, *76*	15	30 ____
52485	New York Central Mint Car with copper load, *08*	60	120 ____
52486	Pennsylvania Mint Car, green, *09*	65	125 ____
52487	Pennsylvania Mint Car, tuscan, *09*	65	125 ____
52488	NYC Lightning Stripe Mint Car, *10*	30	60 ____
52574	Fort Knox 50th Anniversary Mint Car, *11*	50	100 ____
52583	B&O Capitol Dome Mint Car, *11*	50	100 ____
52596	LIRR Mint Car, *12*	50	100 ____
58033	Jersey Central Boxcar, *16*		80 ____
58174	Lehigh Valley Map Boxcar, *16*		80 ____
58280	REA Christmas Boxcar, *16*		80 ____
58523	Blue Comet Mint Car, *13*	35	70 ____
58243	Entenmann's Gondola with load, *15*		70 ____
58285	Brookside Milk Reefer, *17*		85 ____
58286	Riverside Milk Reefer, *17*		85 ____
58534	Jersey Central Mint Car, *13*	35	70 ____
58569	Erie Lackawanna Mint Car, *14*	35	70 ____

Midwest Division

		Exc	Mint
4	C&NW F3 Diesel A Unit, shell only, *77*	40	80 ____
5	Midwest Division Covered Quad Hopper, *78*	25	45 ____
1287	C&NW Reefer, *84*		NRS ____
7600	Frisco "Spirit of '76" N5c Caboose "00003," *76*	20	40 ____
9872	PFE Reefer "00006," *79*	205	410 ____

Midwest Division: Museum Express

		Exc	Mint
9264	ICG Covered Quad Hopper, *78*	10	25 ____
9289	C&NW N5c Caboose, *80*	25	45 ____
9785	Conrail Boxcar, *77*	20	35 ____
9786	C&NW Boxcar, *79*	10	20 ____

NETCA

		Exc	Mint
1203	Boston & Maine NW2 Diesel, shell only, *72*	35	65 ____
5710	Canadian Pacific Reefer, *82*	25	45 ____
5716	Vermont Central Reefer, *83*	15	30 ____
6124	Delaware & Hudson Covered Quad Hopper, *84*	15	30 ____
8051	Hood's Milk Boxcar, *86*	40	75 ____
9181	Boston & Maine N5c Caboose, *77*	20	35 ____
9400	Conrail Boxcar, tuscan or blue, *78*	10	25 ____
9415	Providence & Worcester Boxcar, *79*	20	35 ____
9423	NYNH&H Boxcar, *80*	15	30 ____
9445	Vermont Northern Boxcar, *81*	20	40 ____
9753	Maine Central Boxcar, *75*	20	35 ____

CLUB CARS AND SPECIAL PRODUCTION

		Exc	Mint
_____ 9768	Boston & Maine Boxcar, 76	20	40
_____ 9785	Conrail Boxcar, 78	10	25
_____ 16911	B&M Flatcar with trailer, 95	75	150
_____ 22677	B&M Baked Beans Boxcar, 10	25	45
_____ 52001	B&M Quad Hopper with coal, 92	40	75
_____ 52016	B&M Gondola with coil covers, 93	35	65
_____ 52043	L.L. Bean Boxcar, 94	105	210
_____ 52080	B&M Flatcar "91095" with trailer, 95	110	215
_____ 52111	Ben & Jerry's Flatcar with trailer, 96	160	315
_____ 52212	Berkshire Brewing Reefer, 00	80	155
_____ 52236	Moxie Boxcar, 01	80	160
_____ 52270	Jenney Manufacturing Tank Car, 02	75	150
_____ 52306	NH Flatcar with New England Transportation trailer, 03	75	150
_____ 52352	Poland Spring Boxcar, 04	65	130
_____ 52379	CP Rail with W.B. Mason trailer, 05	40	75
_____ 52383	Fisk Tire Boxcar, 05	55	110
_____ 52397	D&H Flatcar with Vermont Railway trailer, 06	45	90
_____ 52418	Indian Motocycle Boxcar, 06	95	190
_____ 52434	New England Central Flatcar with Cabot's trailer, 07	50	95
_____ 52448	Oilzum Tanker 2-car Set, 08	55	105
_____ 52457	Cape Cod Potato Chip Boxcar, 07	50	95
_____ 52484A	Cabot's Reefer, 08	125	250
_____ 52484B	Bay State Beer Reefer, 09	45	90
_____ 52589	B&M Flatcar with Howard Johnson trailer, 11	50	100
_____ 58221	G. Fox & Co. Boxcar, 15		60
_____ 58522	Grafton & Upton Flatcar with Spag's trailer, 12	45	90
_____	Warwick Ice Cream Reefer, 17		100

Ozark Division: Gateway Chapter

		Exc	Mint
_____ 5700	Oppenheimer Reefer, 81	55	110
_____ 9068	Reading Bobber Caboose, 76	10	20
_____ 9601	Illinois Central Gulf Hi-Cube Boxcar, 77	10	20
_____ 9767	Railbox Boxcar, 78	10	20
_____ 52003	"Meet Me In St. Louis" Flatcar with trailer, 92	260	520

Pacific Northwest Division

		Exc	Mint
_____ 52077	Great Northern Hi-Cube Boxcar "9695," 95	230	460

Rocky Mountain Division

		Exc	Mint
_____ 1971-1976	Rocky Mountain Division Reefer, 76	40	75

CLUB CARS AND SPECIAL PRODUCTION

Exc Mint

Sacramento Sierra Chapter

		Exc	Mint
6401	Virginian Bay Window Caboose, *84*	20	35 ___
9301	U.S. Mail Operating Boxcar, *76*	20	40 ___
9414	Cotton Belt Boxcar, *80*	20	35 ___
9427	Bay Line Boxcar, *81*	15	30 ___
9444	Louisiana Midland Boxcar, *82*	20	35 ___
9452	Western Pacific Boxcar, *83*	20	35 ___
9705	D&RGW Boxcar, *75*	20	40 ___
9723	Western Pacific Boxcar, *73*	15	30 ___
9726	Erie-Lackawanna Boxcar, *79*	10	25 ___
9730	CP Rail Boxcar, *77*	15	30 ___
9785	Conrail Boxcar, *78*	10	20 ___

Southern Division

1976	FEC F3 Diesel ABA, shells only, *76*	140	275 ___
1986	Southern Division Bunk Car, *86*	15	30 ___
6111	L&N Covered Quad Hopper, *83*	10	20 ___
9287	Southern N5c Caboose, *77*	10	20 ___
9352	Trailer Train Flatcar with circus trailers, *80*	30	55 ___
9403	Seaboard Coast Line Boxcar, *78*	10	20 ___
9405	Chattahoochie Boxcar, *79*	10	20 ___
9443	Florida East Coast Boxcar, *81*	10	25 ___
9471	ACL Boxcar, *84*	10	25 ___
9482	Norfolk & Southern Boxcar, *85*	10	25 ___
16606	Southern Searchlight Car, *88*	10	25 ___
19942	Southern Division 30th Anniversary Boxcar, *96*	10	20 ___

Western Division

52275	Western Pacific Boxcar, *03*	55	105 ___

Toy Train Operating Society

TTOS National Convention Cars

1984	Sacramento Northern Boxcar, *84*	45	85 ___
1985	Snowbird Covered Quad Hopper, *85*	30	55 ___
6017	SP-type Caboose, blue, *68*	125	210 ___
6017	SP-type Caboose, brown, *69*	200	300 ___
6057	SP-type Caboose, orange, *69*	125	210 ___
6076	Santa Fe Hopper (O27), *70*	45	85 ___
6167-1967	Hopper, olive drab with gold lettering, *67*	45	85 ___
6257	SP-type Caboose, red, *69*	125	210 ___
6476-1	LV Hopper, gray, *69*	40	75 ___
6582	Portland Flatcar with wood, *86*	30	55 ___
9326	Burlington Northern Bay Window Caboose, *82*	10	25 ___
9347	Niagara Falls 3-D Tank Car, *79*	25	45 ___

CLUB CARS AND SPECIAL PRODUCTION

			Exc	Mint
____	**9355**	Delaware & Hudson Bay Window Caboose, *82*	25	50
____	**9361**	C&NW Bay Window Caboose, *82*	30	55
____	**9382**	Florida East Coast Bay Window Caboose, *82*	35	70
____	**9512**	Summerdale Junction Passenger Car, *74*	30	55
____	**9520**	Phoenix Combination Car, *75*	20	35
____	**9526**	Snowbird Observation Car, *76*	25	50
____	**9535**	Columbus Baggage Car, *77*	35	50
____	**9678**	Hollywood Hi-Cube Boxcar, *78*	15	30
____	**9868**	Oklahoma City Reefer, *80*	25	45
____	**9883**	Phoenix Reefer, *83*	25	50
____	**17871**	NYC Flatcar "81487" with Kodak and Xerox trailers, *87*	110	215
____	**17877**	MKT 1-D Tank Car "3739469," *89*	35	70
____	**17884**	Columbus & Dayton Terminal Boxcar (std O), *90*	20	40
____	**17889**	SP Flatcar "15791" (std O) with trailer, *91*	35	65
____	**19963**	Union Equity 3-bay ACF Hopper "86892" (std O), *92*	20	40
____	**52010**	Weyerhaeuser DD Boxcar "838593" (std O), *93*	20	40
____	**52029**	Ford 1-D Tank Car "12" (O27), *94*	20	40
____	**52030**	Ford Gondola "4023," *94*	15	30
____	**52031**	Ford Hopper "1458" (O27), *94*	20	35
____	**52057**	Western Pacific Boxcar "64641995," *95*	25	50
____	**52087**	New Mexico Central Boxcar "64641996," *96*	30	55
____	**52114**	NYC Flatcar with Gleason and SASIB trailers, *97*	30	60
____	**52149**	Conrail Flatcar with Blum coal shovel, *98*	30	60
____	**52192**	SP Crane and Gondola Set, *00*	40	75
____	**52193**	SP Gondola "6060," *00*	25	50
____	**52194**	SP Crane Car "7111," *00*	20	35
____	**52231**	British Columbia 1-D Tank Car, *01*	10	25
____	**52253**	San Pedro Boxcar, *02*	20	35
____	**52288**	D&RGW Cookie Boxcar, *03*	10	20
____	**52293**	D&RGW 1-D Tank Car, *03*	20	40
____	**52351**	BNSF Icicle Reefer with ETD, *04*	30	60
____	**52378**	Las Vegas & Tonopah Boxcar, *05*	35	70
____	**52410**	SP Flatcar with 2 trailers, *06*	35	70
____	**52441**	Pennsylvania Operating Hopper, *07*	30	60
____	**52445**	Pennsylvania Boxcar, *07*	35	70
____	**52545**	Erie "6464" Boxcar, *09*	25	50
____	**58257**	50th Anniversary Mint Car, *16*		65
____	**58333**	Sierra Railroad Sierra Beer Boxcar, *13*	35	70
____	**58535**	Smokey Bear Gondola, *15*		55

CLUB CARS AND SPECIAL PRODUCTION

Exc Mint

TTOS Division Cars

		Exc	Mint	
52009	Sacramento Valley Division WP Boxcar, *93*	25	45	____
52040	Wolverine Division GTW Flatcar with tractor and trailer, *94*	25	50	____
52058	Central California Division Santa Fe Boxcar, *95*	20	40	____
52086	Canadian Division Pacific Great Eastern Boxcar, *96*	25	50	____
52113	Northeastern Division Genesee & Wyoming 3-bay Hopper, *97*	20	35	____
52264	New Mexico Division Durango & Silverton Operating Hopper, *02*	30	55	____

Other TTOS Production

		Exc	Mint	
1983	Phoenix 3-D Tank Car, *83*	50	100	____
17894	Southern Pacific Tractor, *91*	10	20	____
27148	BNSF "4427" PS2 Hopper, *06*	25	50	____
52021	Weyerhaeuser Tractor and Trailer, *93*	15	30	____
52022	Union Pacific Boxcar, *93*	200	400	____
52032	Ford 1-D Tank Car (O27) with Kughn inscription, *94*	50	95	____
52046	ACL Boxcar "16247," *94*	55	110	____
52053	Carail Boxcar, *94*	30	55	____
52068	Toy Train Parade Contadina Boxcar "16245," *94*	30	55	____
52078	Southern Pacific SD9 Diesel "5366," *96*	120	235	____
52079	Southern Pacific Bay Window Caboose, *96*	30	55	____
52084	Union Pacific I-Beam Flatcar "16380" with load, *95*	80	155	____
52384	Transparent Damage Control Boxcar, *03*	35	70	____
52451	Pennsylvania "X2454" Boxcar, *07*	90	175	____
52505	Forest Service/Smokey Bear Flatcar with airplane, *08*	25	45	____
52525	SP "X6454" Boxcar, *08*	25	50	____
52526	SP "X6454" Boxcar, *08*	45	90	____
52547	C&NW Reefer, *09*	30	50	____

TTOS Southwestern Division

		Exc	Mint	
19962	Southern Pacific 3-bay ACF Hopper "496035" (std O), *92*	35	65	____
52047	Cotton Belt Wood-sided Caboose (std O), smoke, *93–94*	35	70	____
52073	Pacific Fruit Express Reefer "459402" (std O), *95*	30	65	____
52098	National Bureau of Standards Boxcar (std O), *96*	20	45	____
52121	Mobilgas Tank Car "238" (std O), *97*	40	75	____
52154	Pacific Fruit Express Reefer "459403" (std O), *98*	25	55	____
52205	SP Overnight Merchandise Service Boxcar 5-pack, *00*	95	185	____
52287	Operating MX Missile Car, *02*	30	55	____

CLUB CARS AND SPECIAL PRODUCTION

			Exc	Mint
____	**52385**	Ward Kimball Boxcar, *05*	30	55
____	**52431**	Operating MX Missile Car, *06*	30	60
____	**52476**	Life Savers Tank Car, *07*	45	85
____	**52515**	Life Savers Wild Cherry Tank Car, *08*	40	75
____	**52565**	Life Savers Pep O Mint Tank Car, *09*	30	60
____	**52569**	Life Savers Butter Rum Tank Car, *10*	30	60
____	**52591**	Life Savers Wint O Green Tank Car, *11*	30	60
____	**58208**	Life Savers Peppermint Tank Car, *14*	30	60
____	**58548**	Life Savers Bay Window Caboose, *13*	40	80

Virginia Train Collectors

____	**7679**	Boxcar, *79*	5	15
____	**7681**	N5c Caboose, *81*	10	25
____	**7682**	Covered Quad Hopper, *82*	10	25
____	**7683**	Virginia Fruit Express Reefer, *83*	10	25
____	**7684**	Vitraco 3-D Tank Car, *84*	10	25
____	**7685**	Boxcar, *85*	10	25
____	**7686**	GP7 Diesel, *86*	50	100
____	**7692-1**	Baggage Car (027), *92*	25	45
____	**7692-2**	Combination Car (027), *92*	25	45
____	**7692-3**	Dining Car (027), *92*	25	45
____	**7692-4**	Passenger Car (027), *92*	25	45
____	**7692-5**	Vista Dome Car (027), *92*	25	45
____	**7692-6**	Passenger Car (027), *92*	25	45
____	**7692-7**	Observation Car (027), *92*	25	45
____	**7696**	20th Anniversary Station, *96*	35	65
____	**52060**	Tender "7694" with whistle, *94*	35	70

For more information on determining the condition of a box and a description of box types, see pages 8 and 9.

		Good (P-5)	Exc (P-7)
022	Switch Controller	2	7____
020	"O" 90 Degree Crossover	7	14____
020X	"O" 45 Degree Crossover	8	16____
022	Remote Control Switches, pair (with both inserts)	7	21____
022	Remote Control Switches, pair (yellow, with both inserts)	8	25____
022A	Remote Control Switches, pair (with both inserts)	12	33____
25	Bumper	3	10____
26	Bumper	2	8____
30	Water Tower	17	46____
35	Boulevard Lamp	5	16____
36	Operating Car Remote Control Set	5	14____
37	Uncoupling Track Set	4	8____
38	Operating Water Tower	24	100____
40	Hookup Wire, 8 reels (dealer box)	33	118____
41	U.S. Army Switcher	13	54____
42	Manual Switches	4	15____
42	Picatinny Arsenal Switcher	25	80____
44	U.S. Army Mobile Launcher	29	89____
44	U.S. Army Mobile Launcher (with orange sleeve)	30	123____
45	U.S. Marines Mobile Launcher	45	110____
45/45N	Automatic Gateman	6	23____
48	Super O Insulated Straight Track, 6 pieces (dealer box)	15	48____
49	Super O Insulated Curved Track, 6 pieces (dealer box)	15	43____
50	Section Gang Car (early classic)	11	45____
50	Section Gang Car (brown corrugated)	5	18____
50	Section Gang Car (orange picture)	15	41____
51	Navy Yard Switcher	25	87____
52	Fire Car	37	83____
53	Rio Grande Snowplow	40	100____
54	Ballast Tamper	19	42____
55	PRR Tie-Jector Car	15	44____
56	Lamp Post	5	17____
56	M&StL Mine Transport	38	140____
57	AEC Switcher	77	281____
58	Lamp Post	10	24____
58	Great Northern Rotary Snow Blower	78	236____
59	Minuteman Switcher	80	280____

BOXES		Good (P-5)	Exc (P-7)
_____ 60	Lionelville Rapid Transit Trolley (classic)	12	39
60	Lionelville Rapid Transit Trolley (brown corrugated)	13	40
_____			
_____ 64	Highway Lamp Post	9	30
_____ 65	Handcar	13	87
_____ 68	Executive Inspection Car	19	87
_____ 69	Maintenance Car	18	92
_____ 70	Yard Light	5	17
_____ 71	Lamp Post	5	10
_____ 75	Goose Neck Lamps	3	15
_____ 76	Boulevard Street Lamps	5	30
_____ 76	Boulevard Street Lamps (Hillside Checkerboard)	10	70
_____ 89	Flagpole	6	26
_____ 91	Circuit Breaker	15	40
_____ 93	Water Tower	14	36
_____ 97	Coal Elevator	14	65
_____ 108	Trestle Set (overstamped)	10	40
_____ 110	Graduated Trestle Set	1	6
_____ 111	Elevated Trestle Set	5	24
_____ 112	Remote Control Switches, pair (Super O)	10	25
_____ 112LH	Remote Control Super O Switch, left-hand	8	26
_____ 112RH	Remote Control Super O Switch, right-hand	7	26
_____ 114	Newsstand with horn	9	33
115	Passenger Station (113-1, Star Corp. stamped on box)	41	140
_____			
_____ 118	Newsstand with whistle	9	37
_____ 122	Lamp Assortment	23	100
_____ 123	Lamp Assortment	10	100
_____ 125	Whistle Shack	5	19
_____ 128	Animated Newsstand	14	39
_____ 130	60-degree Crossing (Super O)	3	10
_____ 132	Passenger Station	16	32
_____ 133	Passenger Station	10	25
_____ 138	Water Tower	16	39
_____ 140	Automatic Banjo Signal (classic)	4	13
_____ 142	Manual Switches, pair (Super O)	5	15
_____ 145	Automatic Gateman (brown corrugated)	8	21
_____ 145	Automatic Gateman (cellophane), *66*	12	59
_____ 148	Dwarf Trackside Signal	5	22
_____ 150	Telegraph Pole Set	5	18
_____ 151	Automatic Semaphore	4	10
151	Automatic Semaphore (narrower box, earlier postwar)	16	37
_____			
_____ 151	Automatic Semaphore (blister pack enclosure)	20	75
_____ 152	Automatic Crossing Gate	3	13
_____ 153	Automatic Block Control Signal	5	17

BOXES

		Good (P-5)	Exc (P-7)
154	Automatic Highway Signal (cellophane)	5	23____
154	Automatic Highway Signal (all other boxes)	3	10____
155	Blinking Light Signal	9	43____
156	Station Platform	19	56____
157	Station Platform	9	27____
160	Unloading Bin	21	110____
161	Mail Pickup Set (with liner)	13	43____
163	Single Target Block Signal (white box)	20	65____
164	Log Loader	23	70____
167	Whistle Controller	4	10____
175	Rocket Launcher	22	66____
175-50	Rocket, separate sale	75	190____
175-50	Dealer Display Box, 6 rockets	75	468____
182	Magnetic Crane	23	73____
192	Operating Control Tower	35	143____
193	Industrial Water Tower	14	51____
195	Floodlight Tower	6	25____
195	Floodlight Tower (cellophane)	5	30____
195-75	Floodlight Extension, 8-bulb (classic)	6	47____
195-75	Floodlight Extension, 8-bulb (white box)	6	55____
197	Rotating Radar Antenna	9	40____
197-15	Separate Sale Radar Head	33	115____
199	Microwave Relay Tower	7	62____
202	UP Alco Diesel A Unit	11	50____
204	Santa Fe Alco AA Set (master carton)	89	215____
204	Santa Fe Alco AA Set (P and T boxes)	20	124____
204P	Santa Fe A Unit	18	48____
204T	Santa Fe Diesel Dummy A Unit	19	42____
208	Santa Fe Alco AA Set (master carton)	49	254____
208	Santa Fe Alco AA Set (P and T boxes)	21	100____
208P	Santa Fe Alco A Unit	18	78____
208T	Santa Fe Alco Dummy A Unit	45	76____
209	New Haven Alco AA Set (master carton)	104	369____
209	New Haven Alco AA Set (P and T boxes)	111	298____
209P	New Haven Alco A Unit	20	95____
209T	New Haven Diesel Dummy A Unit	45	135____
210	Texas Special Alco AA Set (P and T boxes)	12	92____
210P	Texas Special Alco A Unit	9	25____
210T	Texas Special Alco Dummy A Unit	19	40____
211	Texas Special Alco AA Set (P and T boxes)	29	132____
211P	Texas Special Alco A Unit (brown corrugated)	20	60____
212	Santa Fe AA Master Carton		170____
212P	USMC Alco Diesel A Unit	42	80____
212T	USMC Diesel Dummy A Unit	136	509____
214	Plate Girder Bridge (classic)	3	10____
214	Plate Girder Bridge (Hillside orange picture)	9	28____

BOXES

		Good (P-5)	Exc (P-7)
_____ 216	Burlington Alco Diesel A Unit	15	93
_____ 217	B&M Alco AB Set (C and P boxes)	32	148
_____ 217C	B&M Alco B Unit	15	50
_____ 217P	B&M Alco A Unit	18	54
_____ 217-16	Sleeve for 217 and 218 outer boxes	38	85
_____ 218	Santa Fe Alco AA Set (master carton)	19	110
_____ 218C	Santa Fe Alco Diesel B Unit	20	54
_____ 218P	Santa Fe Alco Diesel A Unit	18	58
_____ 218T	Santa Fe Diesel Dummy A Unit	18	60
_____ 220	Santa Fe Alco AA Set (P and T boxes)	17	93
_____ 220T	Santa Fe Alco Dummy A Unit	20	115
_____ 221	2-6-4 Locomotive	15	60
_____ 221T	Tender	10	27
_____ 221W	Whistling Tender	12	39
_____ 223P	Santa Fe Alco A Unit	15	86
_____ 224	2-6-2 Locomotive	17	46
_____ 224	U.S. Navy Alco AB Set (C and P boxes)	26	128
_____ 224C	U.S. Navy B Unit	45	102
_____ 224P	U.S. Navy Alco A unit	45	210
_____ 225	C & O Alco Diesel A Unit	12	64
_____ 226	B&M Alco Diesel AB Set (C and P boxes)	24	100
_____ 226P	B&M Alco Diesel A Unit	9	44
_____ 228P	CN Alco Diesel A Unit	20	66
_____ 229C	M&StL Alco B Unit	11	39
_____ 229P	M&StL Alco A Unit (brown corrugated)	8	40
_____ 230P	C&O Alco A Unit	14	64
_____ 231P	Rock Island Alco A Unit	12	49
_____ 233	2-4-2 Scout Locomotive	10	35
_____ 234W	Whistle Tender	18	40
_____ 235	2-4-2 Scout Locomotive	26	89
_____ 236	2-4-2 Scout Locomotive	10	45
_____ 237	2-4-2 Scout Locomotive	10	39
_____ 243	2-4-2 Scout Locomotive	10	33
_____ 243W	Tender	5	20
_____ 244T	Tender (overstamped 1625T box)	23	79
_____ 245	2-4-2 Scout Locomotive	15	60
_____ 246	2-4-2 Scout Locomotive	13	39
_____ 247	2-4-2 Scout Locomotive	13	35
_____ 247T	Tender	5	37
_____ 248	2-4-2 Scout Locomotive	9	45
_____ 249	2-4-2 Scout Locomotive	18	48
_____ 250	2-4-2 Scout Locomotive	10	30
_____ 250T	Tender	8	27
_____ 252	Crossing Gate	3	10
_____ 253	Block Control Signal	5	14
_____ 256	Illuminated Freight Station	11	35

BOXES		Good (P-5)	Exc (P-7)
257	Freight Station with diesel horn	9	35____
260	Bumper (Hagerstown checkerboard)	5	21____
260	Bumper (all other boxes)	2	4____
262	Highway Crossing Gate	4	58____
264	Operating Forklift Platform	24	62____
282	Portal Gantry Crane	25	113____
299	Code Transmitter Beacon Set	10	68____
308	Railroad Sign Set	2	11____
309	Yard Sign Set	3	13____
310	Billboard Set	1	7____
313	Bascule Bridge	35	133____
314	Scale Model Girder Bridge	3	11____
315	Illuminated Trestle Bridge	24	88____
316	Trestle Bridge	5	15____
317	Trestle Bridge	8	25____
321	Trestle Bridge	5	14____
321-100	Trestle Bridge	7	20____
332	Arch-Under Trestle Bridge	5	17____
334	Operating Dispatching Board	10	57____
342	Culvert Loader	21	58____
345	Culvert Unloader	25	75____
350	Engine Transfer Table	13	59____
350-50	Transfer Table Extension	15	57____
352	Ice Depot	19	73____
353	Trackside Control Signal	3	14____
356	Operating Freight Station	8	37____
356-35	Baggage Trucks Set	10	46____
362	Barrel Loader	5	26____
362-78	Wooden Barrels	1	8____
364	Conveyor Lumber Loader	10	24____
365	Dispatching Station	15	38____
375	Turntable	26	77____
394	Rotary Beacon	7	28____
394-37	Rotating Beacon Cap	2	8____
395	Floodlight Tower	10	34____
397	Operating Coal Loader	11	39____
397	Operating Coal Loader (separate label on box)	10	40____
400	B&O Passenger Rail Diesel Car	28	57____
404	B&O Baggage-Mail Rail Diesel Car	32	93____
410	Billboard Blinker	3	10____
413	Countdown Control Panel	6	20____
415	Diesel Fueling Station	15	34____
419	Heliport Control Tower	22	142____
443	Missile Launching Platform	12	29____
445	Switch Tower	10	24____
448	Missile Firing Range Set	15	50____

BOXES

		Good (P-5)	Exc (P-7)
____ 450	Operating Signal Bridge	4	20
____ 452	Overhead Gantry Signal	11	51
____ 455	Operating Oil Derrick	21	70
____ 456	Coal Ramp	18	49
____ 460	Piggyback Transportation Set	16	40
____ 460-150	Two Trailers	71	224
____ 461	Platform with truck and trailer	10	45
____ 462	Derrick Platform Set	50	172
____ 464	Lumber Mill	9	43
____ 465	Sound Dispatching Station	13	38
____ 470	Missile Launching Platform	5	33
____ 494	Rotary Beacon (classic)	5	25
____ 497	Coaling Station	29	57
____ 600	MKT NW2 Switcher	19	87
____ 601	Seaboard NW2 Switcher	23	84
____ 602	Seaboard NW2 Switcher	29	78
____ 610	Erie NW2 Switcher	15	140
____ 611	Jersey Central NW2 Switcher (overstamped 621 box)	50	124
____ 613	UP NW2 Switcher	26	105
____ 614	Alaska NW2 Switcher	36	137
____ 616	Santa Fe NW2 Switcher	23	165
____ 617	Santa Fe NW2 Switcher	30	150
____ 621	Jersey Central NW2 Switcher	27	67
____ 622	Santa Fe NW2 Switcher	44	187
____ 623	Santa Fe NW2 Switcher	19	63
____ 624	C&O NW2 Switcher	29	64
____ 625	LV GE 44-ton Switcher	100	450
____ 626	B&O GE 44-ton Switcher	42	175
____ 628	Northern Pacific GE 44-ton Switcher	20	76
____ 629	Burlington GE 44-ton Switcher	32	176
____ 634	Santa Fe NW2 Switcher	26	113
____ 637	2-6-4 Locomotive	14	55
____ 637LTS	2-6-4 Locomotive and Tender (master carton)	40	194
____ 646	4-6-4 Locomotive	29	58
____ 665	4-6-4 Locomotive	19	55
____ 665LTS	4-6-4 Locomotive and Tender (master carton)	45	280
____ 671	6-8-6 Steam Turbine Locomotive	41	99
____ 671R	6-8-6 Steam Turbine Locomotive	36	137
____ 671W	Whistle Tender	14	93
____ 671-75	Smoke Lamp, 12 volt	2	10
____ 675	2-6-2 Locomotive (classic), *47-49*	24	66
____ 675	2-6-2 Locomotive (brown corrugated), *52*	37	72
____ 681	6-8-6 Steam Turbine Locomotive	28	134
____ 681LTS	6-8-6 Steam Turbine Locomotive and Tender (master carton)	150	500

BOXES

		Good (P-5)	Exc (P-7)
682	6-8-6 Steam Turbine Locomotive	52	158 ____
682LTS	6-8-6 Steam Turbine Locomotive and Tender (master carton)	400	850 ____
685	4-6-4 Hudson Locomotive	28	66 ____
685LTS	4-6-4 Hudson Locomotive and Tender (master carton)	185	450 ____
726	2-8-4 Berkshire Locomotive, *46*	63	184 ____
726	2-8-4 Berkshire Locomotive (after 1946)	44	134 ____
726RR	2-8-4 Berkshire Locomotive	23	63 ____
736	2-8-4 Berkshire Locomotive, *50*	39	101 ____
736	2-8-4 Berkshire Locomotive	30	67 ____
736X	2-8-4 Berkshire Locomotive	33	118 ____
736LTS	2-8-4 Berkshire Locomotive and Tender (master carton)	63	231 ____
736W	Pennsylvania Tender	17	69 ____
746	N&W 4-8-4 Locomotive	57	159 ____
746LTS	N&W 4-8-4 Locomotive and Tender (master carton)	170	420 ____
746W	N&W Whistle Tender	30	158 ____
746WX	N&W Whistle Tender, long stripe	50	188 ____
760	Curved Track	9	29 ____
773	4-6-4 Hudson Locomotive, *50*	102	334 ____
773	4-6-4 Hudson Locomotive, *64-66*	80	151 ____
773LTS	4-6-4 Hudson Locomotive and Tender (master carton), *50*	100	542 ____
773LTS	4-6-4 Hudson and Whistle Tender (master carton), *64-66*	65	342 ____
773W	NYC Tender	19	89 ____
810	Milwaukee Road Freight Set	75	450 ____
920-2	Tunnel Portals	7	20 ____
920	Scenic Display Set	15	43 ____
927	Lubricating Kit	2	9 ____
928	Maintenance and Lubricating Kit	5	25 ____
943	Ammo Dump	3	10 ____
951	Farm Set	14	45 ____
952	Figure Set	13	35 ____
953	Figure Set	13	50 ____
957	Figure Set	20	55 ____
959	Barn Set	18	52 ____
960	Barnyard Set	10	35 ____
961	School Set	30	182 ____
963	Frontier Set	15	75 ____
965	Farm Set	15	55 ____
966	Firehouse Set	15	55 ____
969	Construction Set	8	45 ____
970	Ticket Booth	7	40 ____
972	Landscape Tree Assortment	10	35 ____

BOXES		Good (P-5)	Exc (P-7)
____ 981	Freight Yard Set	12	37
____ 983	Farm Set	15	46
____ 984	Railroad Set	10	75
____ 986	Farm Set	18	115
____ 1000W	Steam Freight Set	49	95
____ 1001	Diesel Freight Set	20	65
____ 1001	2-4-2 Scout Locomotive	8	40
____ 1001T	Tender	6	12
____ 1002	Gondola	4	10
____ X1004	PRR Baby Ruth Boxcar	4	10
____ 1005	Sunoco 1-D Tank Car	4	10
____ 1007	LL SP-type Caboose	4	10
____ 1009	Manumatic Track Section	10	35
____ 1019	Remote Control Track Set (027)	10	20
____ 1024	Manual Switches for 027 Track Set	6	15
____ 1025	Illuminated Bumper (027)	3	8
____ 1032	Transformer, 75 watts	2	7
____ 1033	Transformer, 90 watts	4	11
____ 1034	Transformer, 75 watts	2	8
____ 1041	Transformer, 50 watts	3	11
____ 1041	Transformer, 60 watts	6	17
____ 1043	Transformer, 50 watts	5	15
____ 1043-500	Transformer, 50 watts, ivory	15	71
____ 1044	Transformer, 90 watts	5	13
____ 1045	Operating Watchman	6	26
____ 1047	Operating Switchman	31	93
____ 1060	2-4-2 Locomotive (brown corrugated)	23	102
____ 1107	Steam Freight Set	20	45
____ 1109	Steam Freight Set	15	40
____ 1110	2-4-2 Locomotive	5	24
____ 1112	Scout Set	8	25
____ 1113	Scout Set	15	45
____ 1119	Scout Set	15	40
____ 1120	2-4-2 Scout Locomotive	5	18
____ 1121	027 Remote Control Switches, pair	3	12
____ 1121LH	027 Remote Control Switch, left-hand	4	14
____ 1121RH	027 Remote Control Switch, right-hand	4	19
____ 1122	027 Remote Control Switches, pair	4	16
____ 1130	2-4-2 Locomotive	10	29
____ 1130T	Tender (classic)	5	22
____ 1130T	Tender (orange perforated)	17	41
____ 1130T-500	Tender, pink, from Girls Set	53	180
____ 1232	Transformer, 75 watts, made for export	4	14
____ 1407B	Steam Switcher Work Set	45	310
____ 1417WS	Steam Work Train Set	40	145
____ 1423W	Steam Freight Set	28	124

BOXES

		Good (P-5)	Exc (P-7)
1425B	Steam Switcher Freight Set	70	212____
1427WS	Steam Freight Set	10	35____
1429WS	Steam Freight Set	47	150____
1431	Steam Freight Set	15	75____
1432W	027 Steam Passenger Set	80	242____
1435WS	Steam Freight Set	10	35____
1447WS	Turbine Locomotive Set	33	150____
1451WS	027 Steam Freight Set	37	110____
1453WS	027 Steam Freight Set	28	83____
1455WS	Steam Freight Set	30	92____
1457B	Santa Fe Freight Set (marked "1457"), *49*	73	193____
1457B	Santa Fe Freight Set, *50*	62	198____
1459WS	Steam Freight Set	44	95____
1463WS	Steam Freight Set	45	105____
1464W	Union Pacific Diesel Passenger Set	196	425____
1465	Steam Freight Set	32	76____
1467W	Union Pacific Freight Set	50	135____
1469WS	Steam Freight Set	25	73____
1471	Steam Freight Set	25	70____
1471WS	Steam Freight Set	20	53____
1473WS	Steam Freight Set	20	80____
1475WS	Steam Freight Set	15	145____
1479WS	Steam Freight Set	16	54____
1481WS	Steam Freight Set	28	80____
1483WS	Steam Freight Set	35	113____
1485WS	Steam Freight Set	29	65____
1500	Steam Freight Set	15	68____
1502WS	Steam Freight Set	238	558____
11480	Diesel Freight Set	70	225____
1503WS	Steam Freight Set	30	109____
1505WS	Steam Freight Set	33	93____
1507WS	Steam Freight Set	34	114____
1511S	Steam Freight Set	23	65____
1513S	Steam Freight Set	35	108____
1515WS	Steam Freight Set	39	119____
1517W	Texas Special Freight Set	35	191____
1519WS	Steam Freight Set	50	170____
1520W	Texas Special Passenger Set	170	658____
1521WS	Steam Work Train Set	77	268____
1523	Diesel Freight Set	55	155____
1525	Diesel Freight Set	35	80____
1527	027 Steam Work Train Set	57	175____
1529	Pennsylvania Diesel Freight Set	92	250____
1531W	Diesel Freight Set	28	125____
1533WS	Steam Freight Set	28	65____
1534W	Burlington Diesel Passenger Set	169	466____

BOXES		Good (P-5)	Exc (P-7)
____ 1535W	Diesel Freight Set	105	300
____ 1536W	Diesel Passenger Set	75	343
____ 1537WS	Steam Freight Set	25	50
____ 1538WS	Hudson Passenger Set	155	775
____ 1539W	Santa Fe Diesel Freight Set	88	250
____ 1541WS	Steam Freight Set	50	157
____ 1542	Electric Freight Set	10	47
____ 1543	Lehigh Valley Freight Set	13	41
____ 1547S	Steam Freight Set	20	50
____ 1549	Steam Work Train Set	38	95
____ 1551W	Diesel Freight Set	10	58
____ 1552W	Diesel Passenger Set	70	300
____ 1553W	Diesel Freight Set	28	60
____ 1555WS	027 Steam Freight Set	30	71
____ 1557	Diesel Freight Set	30	88
____ 1559W	MILW Diesel Freight Set	35	90
____ 1561WS	Steam Freight Set	23	55
____ 1562W	Burlington GP7 Diesel Passenger Set	30	200
____ 1569	UP Diesel Freight Set	28	73
____ 1571	LV Diesel Freight Set	30	68
____ 1573	Steam Freight Set	33	75
____ 1575	Diesel Freight Set	30	73
____ 1577S	Steam Freight Set	32	75
____ 1578S	Steam Passenger Set	200	397
____ 1579S	Steam Freight Set	28	70
____ 1581	Jersey Central Mixed Set	40	79
____ 1583WS	Steam Freight Set	35	70
____ 1585W	Diesel Freight Set	30	75
____ 1586	Diesel Passenger Set	30	90
____ 1587S	Girls Train Set	430	1154
____ 1589WS	027 Steam Freight Set	45	180
____ 1590	Steam Freight Set	33	60
____ 1591	USMC Military Set	77	617
____ 1593	UP Diesel Work Train Set	35	90
____ 1599W	Texas Special Freight Set	39	106
____ 1600	Diesel Passenger Set	180	590
____ 1601W	Wabash GP7 Diesel Set	52	310
____ 1603WS	Steam Freight Set	45	110
____ 1605W	Santa Fe Diesel Freight Set	50	145
____ 1607WS	Steam Work Train Set	18	45
____ 1608W	New Haven Passenger Set	76	485
____ 1609W	Steam Freight Set	40	85
____ 1611	027 Alaska Diesel Freight Set	78	220
____ 1612	027 General Set	40	140
____ 1613S	Steam Freight Set	35	110
____ 1615	B&M Diesel Freight Set	20	50

BOXES

		Good (P-5)	Exc (P-7)
1615	0-4-0 Locomotive	21	53____
1615LTS	0-4-0 Locomotive and Tender (master carton)	29	119____
1615T	Tender	10	68____
1619W	Santa Fe Diesel Freight Set	45	125____
1621WS	O27 Steam Freight Set (brown corrugated)	95	275____
1621WS	O27 Steam Freight Set (suitcase)	40	125____
1623W	NP Diesel Freight Set	50	165____
1625	0-4-0 Locomotive	23	100____
1625T	Tender	18	107____
1625WS	Steam Freight Set	41	171____
1626W	Santa Fe Diesel Passenger Set	89	159____
1629WS	C&O Diesel Freight Set	20	115____
1631WS	O27 Steam Freight Set	29	82____
1633	U.S. Navy Diesel Freight Set	110	372____
1635WS	Steam Freight Set	41	135____
1637	Santa Fe Diesel Freight Set	20	50____
1640-100	Presidential Kit	19	56____
1643	C&O Diesel Freight Set	20	55____
1645	Diesel Freight Set	36	95____
1647	U.S. Marines Military Set	40	90____
1648	Steam Freight Set	8	23____
1649	Santa Fe Diesel Freight Set	20	60____
1650	Steam Military Set	43	86____
1651	Passenger Train Set	39	149____
1654	2-4-2 Locomotive	5	28____
1655	2-4-2 Locomotive	10	40____
1656	0-4-0 Locomotive	26	133____
1656LTS	4-4-0 Locomotive and Tender (master carton)	50	225____
1665	0-4-0 Locomotive	30	173____
1666	2-6-2 Locomotive	15	45____
1682T	Tender	5	22____
1800	General Gift Pack	20	115____
1805	Marine Land Sea and Air Gift Pack	813	1596____
1809	Western Gift Pack	8	60____
1862	4-4-0 Civil War General Locomotive	25	88____
1862T	Tender	15	65____
1865	Western & Atlantic Coach	10	46____
1866	Western & Atlantic Mail-Baggage Car	10	45____
1872	4-4-0 Civil War General Locomotive	35	100____
1872LTS	4-4-0 Locomotive and Tender (master carton)	115	400____
1872T	Tender	18	58____
1875	Western & Atlantic Coach	38	183____
1875W	Western & Atlantic Coach, whistle	15	91____
1876	Western & Atlantic Baggage Car	13	73____
1877	Flatcar with fence and horses	8	40____
2001	Track Make-up Kit (O27)	800	2000____

BOXES

		Good (P-5)	Exc (P-7)
_____ 2002	Track Make-up Kit (027)	700	1400
_____ 2016	2-6-4 Locomotive	7	30
_____ 2018	2-6-4 Locomotive	14	30
_____ 2020	6-8-6 Steam Turbine Locomotive	22	73
_____ 2020W	Tender	11	72
_____ 2023	Union Pacific Alco AA Set (master carton), *50*	40	103
_____ 2023	Union Pacific Alco AA Set (master carton), *51*	30	105
_____ 2025	2-6-2 or 2-6-4 Locomotive	13	50
_____ 2026	2-6-2 or 2-6-4 Locomotive	10	95
_____ 2028	Pennsylvania GP7 Diesel	25	93
_____ 2029	2-6-4 Locomotive	12	47
_____ 2031	Rock Island Alco AA Set (master carton), *52*	61	144
_____ 2032	Erie Alco AA Set (master carton)	36	85
_____ 2033	Uinion Pacific Alco AA Set (master carton)	36	92
_____ 2034	2-4-2 Scout Locomotive	6	53
_____ 2035	2-6-4 Locomotive	17	75
_____ 2036	2-6-4 Locomotive	9	58
_____ 2036LTS	2-6-4 Locomotive and Tender (master carton)	450	1397
_____ 2037	2-6-4 Locomotive (brown corrugated)	12	33
_____ 2037-500	2-6-4 Locomotive, pink, from Girls Set	54	250
_____ 2046	4-6-4 Locomotive	34	77
_____ 2046LTS	4-6-4 Locomotive and Tender (master carton)	90	302
_____ 2046T	Lionel Lines Tender, for export	23	77
_____ 2046W	Lionel Lines Tender (early classic, with liner)	19	82
_____ 2046W	Lionel Lines Tender (marked "2046")	16	72
_____ 2046W	Pennsylvania Tender	30	130
_____ 2046W-50	Pennsylvania Tender	10	55
_____ 2055	4-6-4 Locomotive	22	74
_____ 2055LTS	4-6-4 Locomotive and Tender (master carton)	50	253
_____ 2056	4-6-4 Locomotive	22	58
_____ 2065	4-6-4 Locomotive	23	51
_____ 2103W	Steam Freight Set	25	90
_____ 2105WS	Steam Freight Set	65	130
_____ 2113WS	Steam Freight Set	28	213
_____ 2121WS	Steam Freight Set	45	255
_____ 2124W	GG1 Passenger Set	144	1457
_____ 2125WS	Steam Freight Set	58	110
_____ 2126WS	Steam Turbine Passenger Set	60	871
_____ 2136WS	Steam Passenger Set	40	108
_____ 2139W	GG1 Freight Set	331	919
_____ 2140WS	Steam Turbine Passenger Set	60	816
_____ 2141WS	Steam Turbine Freight Set	40	232
_____ 2145WS	Steam Freight Set	80	283
_____ 2146W	Berkshire Passenger Set	75	448
_____ 2148WS	Hudson Passenger Set	232	1694
_____ 2149	Santa Fe Diesel Freight Set	105	435

BOXES

		Good (P-5)	Exc (P-7)	
2151W	F3 Freight Set	113	280	____
2153WS	Steam Freight Set	60	175	____
2155WS	Berkshire Freight Set	25	162	____
2159W	GG1 Freight Set	134	715	____
2161W	Santa Fe Twin Diesel Freight Set	42	150	____
2163WS	Steam Freight Set	45	160	____
2165WS	Steam Freight Set	50	125	____
2167WS	Steam Freight Set	36	162	____
2171W	NYC Diesel Freight Set	30	90	____
2173WS	Steam Freight Set	85	185	____
2175W	Santa Fe Diesel Freight Set	49	183	____
2177WS	Steam Freight Set	15	84	____
2179WS	Steam Freight Set	20	75	____
2183WS	Steam Freight Set	43	90	____
2185W	NYC Diesel Freight Set	55	100	____
2187WS	Steam Freight Set	25	60	____
2190W	Santa Fe Diesel Passenger Set	30	103	____
2191W	Santa Fe Diesel Freight Set	43	172	____
2193W	NYC Diesel Freight Set	47	93	____
2201WS	Steam Freight Set	43	102	____
2203WS	Steam Freight Set	92	235	____
2205WS	Steam Freight Set	30	75	____
2207W	Santa Fe Diesel Freight Set	38	152	____
2209W	NYC Diesel Freight Set	41	105	____
2211WS	Steam Freight Set	30	87	____
2213WS	Steam Freight Set	33	70	____
2217WS	Steam Turbine Freight Set	71	167	____
2219W	Diesel Freight Set	112	352	____
2221WS	Steam Freight Set	36	132	____
2222WS	Hudson Passenger Set	109	786	____
2223W	Lackawanna FM Freight Set	122	493	____
2225T	Tender	20	100	____
2225WS	Steam Freight Set	30	170	____
2226W	Tender	40	115	____
2226WX	Lionel Lines Tender	50	130	____
2227W	Santa Fe Diesel Freight Set	88	234	____
2231W	Southern Diesel Freight Set	65	280	____
2234W	Santa Fe Passenger Set	67	365	____
2235W	Milwaukee Road Diesel Freight Set	60	148	____
2237WS	Steam Freight Set	60	170	____
2239W	Illinois Central Freight Set	130	654	____
2240	Wabash F3 AB Set (C and P boxes)	56	310	____
2240	Wabash F3 AB Set (master carton)	107	775	____
2240C	Wabash F3 B Unit	40	120	____
2240P	Wabash F3 A Unit	39	106	____
2241WS	Steam Freight Set	20	60	____

BOXES

		Good (P-5)	Exc (P-7)
____ 2242	New Haven F3 AB Set (C and P boxes)	73	600
____ 2242	New Haven F3 AB Set (master carton)	300	1025
____ 2242C	New Haven F3 B Unit	105	420
____ 2242P	New Haven F3 A Unit	163	338
____ 2243	Santa Fe F3 AB Set (C and P boxes)	24	102
____ 2243	Santa Fe F3 AB Set (master carton)	38	143
____ 2243C	Santa Fe F3 B Unit	25	60
____ 2243P	Santa Fe F3 A Unit	35	110
____ 2243W	Diesel Freight Set	30	85
____ 2244W	Wabash Passenger Set	223	899
____ 2245	Texas Special F3 AB Set (C and P boxes)	54	255
____ 2245	Texas Special F3 AB Set (master carton)	300	800
____ 2245C	Texas Special F3 B Unit	35	113
____ 2245P	Texas Special F3 A Unit	26	92
____ 2247W	Wabash F3 Diesel Freight Set	80	280
____ 2251W	Diesel Freight Set	35	170
____ 2254W	Pennsylvania GG1 Passenger Set, *55*	249	1283
____ 2255W	Diesel Work Train Set	34	169
____ 2257	SP-type Caboose	4	16
____ 2257WS	Steam Freight Set	28	131
____ 2259W	New Haven Electric Freight Set	38	171
____ 2261WS	Steam Freight Set	30	90
____ 2263W	New Haven Freight Set	40	305
____ 2265WS	Steam Freight Set	27	117
____ 2267W	Diesel Freight Set	57	250
____ 2269W	B&O Diesel Freight Set	120	731
____ 2270W	Jersey Central Passenger Set	167	1130
____ 2271W	Pennsylvania GG1 Freight Set	23	385
____ 2273W	Milwaukee Road Diesel Freight Set	93	685
____ 2274W	Pennsylvania Passenger Set	230	779
____ 2275W	Wabash GP7 Freight Set	70	130
____ 2276W	Budd Passenger Set	25	318
____ 2277WS	Work Train Set	20	170
____ 2285W	Diesel Freight Set	87	229
____ 2283W	Steam Freight Set	20	125
____ 2289WS	Berkshire Super O Freight Set	46	206
____ 2291W	Rio Grande Diesel Freight Set	147	486
____ 2292WS	Steam Passenger Set	109	979
____ 2293W	Pennsylvania GG1 Freight Set	156	897
____ 2295WS	N&W Steam Freight Set	154	869
____ 2296W	Canadian Pacific Passenger Set	258	1253
____ 2297WS	N&W Steam Freight Set	99	602
____ 2321	Lackawanna FM Train Master Diesel	62	130
____ 2322	Virginian FM Train Master Diesel	30	102
____ 2328	Burlington GP7 Diesel	33	101
____ 2329	Virginian Electric Locomotive	53	248

BOXES

		Good (P-5)	Exc (P-7)
2330	Pennsylvania GG1 Electric Locomotive	69	290 ___
2331	Virginian FM Train Master Diesel	33	117 ___
2332	Pennsylvania GG1 Electric Locomotive	42	129 ___
2332-275	Pennsylvania GG1 Electric Locomotive	73	227 ___
2333	NYC F3 AA Set (master carton)	45	136 ___
2333	NYC F3 AA Set (P and T boxes)	38	203 ___
2333P	NYC F3 A Unit (brown corrugated)	25	85 ___
2333	Santa Fe F3 AA Set (master carton)	73	159 ___
2333	Santa Fe F3 AA Set (P and T boxes)	35	121 ___
2333T	Santa Fe F3 Dummy A Unit	25	105 ___
2333P	Santa Fe F3 A Unit	17	70 ___
2337	Wabash GP7 Diesel, *58*	28	232 ___
2338	MILW GP7 Diesel (classic)	35	132 ___
2338	MILW GP7 Diesel (brown corrugated)	10	77 ___
2338X	MILW GP7 Diesel (brown corrugated marked "2338X")	32	122 ___
2339	Wabash GP7 Diesel, *57*	34	114 ___
2340-10	Pennsylvania GG1 Electric, tuscan	83	205 ___
2340-25	Pennsylvania GG1 Electric, green, gold stripes	41	169 ___
2341	Jersey Central FM Train Master Diesel	169	791 ___
2343	Santa Fe F3 AA Set (master carton)	45	125 ___
2343	Santa Fe F3 AA Set (P and T boxes)	40	147 ___
2343C	Santa Fe F3 B Unit	28	92 ___
2343P	Santa Fe F3 A Unit	23	52 ___
2343T	Santa Fe F3 Dummy Unit	23	82 ___
2344	NYC F3 AA Set (master carton)	83	218 ___
2344	NYC F3 AA Set (P and T boxes)	60	210 ___
2344C	NYC F3 B Unit	41	79 ___
2344P	NYC F3 A Unit	58	164 ___
2344T	NYC F3 Dummy Unit	33	166 ___
2345	Western Pacific F3 AA Set (master carton)	175	513 ___
2345	Western Pacific F3 AA Set (P and T boxes, brown corrugated)	50	352 ___
2345P	Western Pacific F3 A Unit	40	160 ___
2345T	Western Pacific F3 Dummy A Unit	92	255 ___
2346	B&M GP9 Diesel	29	132 ___
2347	C&O GP9 Diesel	450	1300 ___
2348	M&StL GP9 Diesel	37	173 ___
2349	Northern Pacific GP9 Diesel	88	198 ___
2349-12	Sleeve for 2349 and 2359 outer boxes	17	101 ___
2350	New Haven EP-5 Electric Locomotive	40	105 ___
2351	Milwaukee Road EP-5 Electric Locomotive	34	127 ___
2352	Pennsylvania EP-5 Electric Locomotive	50	195 ___
2353	Santa Fe F3 AA Set (master carton)	88	237 ___
2353	Santa Fe F3 AA Set (P and T boxes)	40	144 ___
2353P	Santa Fe F3 A Unit (brown corrugated)	29	60 ___

BOXES

			Good (P-5)	Exc (P-7)
____	2353T	Santa Fe F3 Dummy Unit	33	120
____	2354	NYC F3 AA Set (master carton)	31	295
____	2354P	NYC F3 A Unit (brown corrugated)	58	136
____	2354T	NYC F3 Dummy Unit	38	134
____	2355	Western Pacific F3 AA Set (master carton)	97	355
____	2355	Western Pacific F3 AA Set (P and T boxes)	60	349
____	2355P	Western Pacific F3 A Unit	50	166
____	2355T	Western Pacific F3 Dummy A Unit	40	151
____	2356	Southern F3 AA Set (master carton)	84	422
____	2356C	Southern F3 B Unit	41	244
____	2356P	Southern F3 A Unit	44	119
____	2356T	Southern F3 Dummy Unit	71	265
____	2357	SP-type Caboose	6	18
____	2358	Great Northern EP-5 Electric Locomotive	72	204
____	2358-12	Outer Box Sleeve	48	119
____	2359	Boston & Maine GP9 Diesel	27	104
____	2360-10	Pennsylvania GG1 Electric Locomotive, tuscan	108	227
____	2360-25	Pennsylvania GG1 Electric Locomotive, green	39	207
____	2363	Illinois Central F3 AB Set (master carton)	183	671
____	2363	Illinois Central F3 AB Set (C and P boxes)	94	409
____	2363C	Illinois Central F3 B Unit	90	243
____	2363P	Illinois Central F3 A Unit	28	132
____	2365	C&O GP7 Diesel	15	81
____	2367C	Wabash F3 B Unit	24	317
____	2367P	Wabash F3 A Unit	38	130
____	2368	B&O F3 AB Set (master carton)	200	884
____	2368C	B&O F3 B Unit	71	262
____	2368P	B&O F3 A Unit	28	195
____	2373	CP F3 AA Set (P and T boxes)	168	495
____	2373P	CP F3 A Unit	55	209
____	2373T	CP F3 Dummy A Unit	55	209
____	2378	Milwaukee Road F3 AB Set (master carton)	169	884
____	2378C	Milwaukee Road F3 B Unit	85	270
____	2378P	Milwaukee Road F3 A Unit	64	200
____	2379	Denver and Rio Grande F3 AB Set (master carton)	179	706
____	2379C	Rio Grande F3 B Unit	48	263
____	2379P	Rio Grande F3 A Unit	60	157
____	2383	Santa Fe F3 AA Units (master carton)	55	222
____	2383P	Santa Fe F3 A Unit	17	109
____	2383T	Santa Fe F3 Dummy Unit	32	80
____	2400	Maplewood Pullman Car	19	104
____	2401	Hillside Observation Car	18	88
____	2402	Chatham Pullman Car	18	84
____	2403B	Tender with bell	18	102
____	2404	Santa Fe Vista Dome Car	18	54

BOXES

		Good (P-5)	Exc (P-7)
2405	Santa Fe Pullman Car	17	52____
2406	Santa Fe Observation Car	16	46____
2408	Santa Fe Vista Dome Car	15	48____
2409	Santa Fe Pullman Car	15	55____
2410	Santa Fe Observation Car	14	56____
2411	Lionel Lines Flatcar	10	37____
2412	Santa Fe Vista Dome Car	19	61____
2414	Santa Fe Pullman Car	17	53____
2416	Santa Fe Observation Car (orange perforated)	15	69____
2416	Santa Fe Observation Car (orange picture)	15	53____
2419	DL&W Work Caboose	14	43____
2420	DL&W Work Caboose with searchlight	25	57____
2421	Maplewood Pullman Car	13	45____
2422	Chatham Pullman Car	15	43____
2423	Hillside Observation Car	13	43____
2426W	Hudson Tender (early classic)	76	248____
2426W	Hudson Tender (middle classic)	78	209____
2429	Livingston Pullman Car	19	69____
2430	Pullman Car, blue	12	36____
2431	Observation Car, blue	12	39____
2432	Clifton Vista Dome Car	16	43____
2434	Newark Pullman Car	15	39____
2435	Elizabeth Pullman Car	21	53____
2436	Mooseheart Observation Car	16	37____
2436	Mooseheart Observation Car (classic)	9	33____
2440	Pullman Car, green	8	30____
2441	Observation Car, green	8	30____
2442	Pullman Car, brown	8	30____
2442	Clifton Vista Dome Car	19	59____
2443	Observation Car, brown	9	30____
2444	Newark Pullman Car	15	50____
2445	Elizabeth Pullman Car	25	104____
2446	Summit Observation Car	15	46____
2452	Pennsylvania Gondola	11	28____
2452X	Pennsylvania Gondola	5	15____
X2454	Pennsylvania Boxcar (marked "Box Car")	16	65____
X2454	Pennsylvania Boxcar (marked "Merchandise Car")	20	66 ____
2456	Lehigh Valley Hopper	6	47____
2457	Pennsylvania N5-type Caboose	7	35____
2458	Pennsylvania Automobile Boxcar	12	37____
2460	Bucyrus Erie Crane Car (box with toy logo)	12	49____
2460	Bucyrus Erie Crane Car (box without toy logo)	23	106____
2461	Transformer Car	20	50____
2465	Sunoco 2-D Tank Car	3	15____
2466T	Tender	5	26____

BOXES

		Good (P-5)	Exc (P-7)
_____ 2466W	Tender	14	39
_____ 2466WX	Tender	15	42
_____ 2472	PRR N5-type Caboose	3	12
_____ 2481	Plainfield Pullman Car	35	180
_____ 2482	Westfield Pullman Car	37	179
_____ 2483	Livingston Observation Car	37	196
_____ 2501W	M&StL Diesel Freight Set	24	277
_____ 2503WS	Super O Steam Freight Set	30	70
_____ 2505W	Super O Electric Freight Set	60	317
_____ 2507W	New Haven Diesel Freight Set	44	524
_____ 2509WS	Super O Steam Freight Set	72	224
_____ 2511W	Pennsylvania Electric Work Set	49	248
_____ 2513W	Virginian Rectifier Set	88	399
_____ 2515WS	Super O Steam Freight Set	165	565
_____ 2517W	Rio Grande Diesel Freight Set	85	185
_____ 2518W	Pennsylvania Electric Passenger Set	72	882
_____ 2519W	Virginian Train Master Super O Freight Set	32	523
_____ 2521	President McKinley Observation Car	22	77
_____ 2521WS	Super O Steam Freight Set	25	110
_____ 2522	President Harrison Vista Dome Car	35	113
_____ 2523	President Garfield Pullman Car	27	76
_____ 2523W	Santa Fe Super O Freight Set	30	319
_____ 2525WS	Super O Steam Work Train Set	213	562
_____ 2526W	Santa Fe Passenger Set	33	565
_____ 2527	Missile Launcher Set, yellow	29	101
_____ 2528WS	Super O General Set	35	167
_____ 2530	REA Baggage Car	21	113
_____ 2530	REA Baggage Car (orange perforated)	118	411
_____ 2531	Silver Dawn Observation Car	21	57
_____ 2531WS	Super O Steam Freight Set	55	140
_____ 2532	Silver Range Vista Dome Car	19	57
_____ 2533	Silver Cloud Pullman Car	25	62
_____ 2533W	Super O GN Electric Freight Set	120	540
_____ 2534	Silver Bluff Pullman Car	20	50
_____ 2535WS	Steam Freight Set	45	192
_____ 2537W	New Haven Freight Set	39	352
_____ 2541	Alexander Hamilton Observation Car	28	66
_____ 2541W	Santa Fe Super O Freight Set	149	650
_____ 2542	Betsy Ross Vista Dome Car	23	73
_____ 2543	William Penn Pullman Car	22	78
_____ 2543WS	Berkshire Freight Set	113	478
_____ 2544	Molly Pitcher Pullman Car	25	78
_____ 2544W	Santa Fe Passenger Set	104	1050
_____ 2545WS	Super O Military Set	110	1000
_____ 2547WS	Super O Steam Freight Set	25	82
_____ 2549W	Super O Military Set	23	118

BOXES

		Good (P-5)	Exc (P-7)
2550	B&O Baggage-Mail Rail Diesel Car	45	185____
2551	Banff Park Observation Car	28	103____
2551W	GN Electric Set	120	624____
2552	Skyline 500 Vista Dome Car	33	106____
2553	Blair Manor Pullman Car	62	167____
2553WS	Berkshire Freight Set	65	289____
2554	Craig Manor Pullman Car	69	163____
2555	Sunoco 1-D Tank Car	10	46____
2555	Sunoco 1-D Tank Car (overstamped 2755 box)	22	87____
2559	B&O Passenger Rail Diesel Car	49	135____
2560	Lionel Lines Crane Car	33	103____
2561	Vista Valley Observation Car	38	125____
2561	Vista Valley Observation Car (orange perforated)	88	173____
2562	Regal Pass Observation Car	33	125____
2562	Regal Pass Observation Car (orange perforated)	68	173____
2563	Indian Falls Pullman Car	39	128____
2570	Super O Santa Fe Work Train Set	46	240____
2572	Boston & Maine Military Set	39	155____
2574	Santa Fe Military Set	85	305____
2625	Irvington Pullman Car	40	150____
2627	Madison Pullman Car	24	108____
2628	Manhattan Pullman Car	27	104____
2671T	Pennsylvania Tender, for export	17	63____
2671W	Pennsylvania Tender	26	78____
2671WX	Lionel Lines Tender	23	59____
2755	Sunoco 1-D Tank Car	17	96____
2758	PRR Automobile Boxcar	8	32____
2855	Sunoco 1-D Tank Car	29	148____
3330	Flatcar with submarine kit	17	68____
3330-100	Operating Submarine Kit, separate sale	47	194____
3349	Turbo Missile Launch Car	7	30____
3356	Operating Horse Car and Corral Set (classic)	23	62____
3356	Operating Horse Car and Corral Set (orange picture)	23	88
3356-2	Horse Car	71	476____
3356-100	Black Horses (classic)	4	15____
3356-100	Black Horses (white box)	8	23____
3356-150	Horse Car Corral	65	785____
3357	Hydraulic Maintenance Car	11	36____
3357-27	Trestle Components for Cop and Hobo Car	10	29____
3359	Lionel Lines Twin-bin Coal Dump Car	14	53____
3360	Operating Burro Crane	19	79____
3361	Operating Log Dump Car	5	23____
3361X	Operating Log Dump Car	5	28____
3362	Helium Tank Unloading Car	19	42____

BOXES

		Good (P-5)	Exc (P-7)
3362/3364	Operating Unloading Car (Hagerstown checkerboard)	20	50
3364	Log Unloading Car	9	33
3366	Circus Car Corral Set	42	152
3366-100	White Horses	8	38
3370	W&A Outlaw Car	9	42
3376	Bronx Zoo Car	15	54
3376-160	Bronx Zoo Car, green	14	53
3410	Helicopter Car	18	80
3413	Mercury Capsule Car	13	82
3419	Helicopter Car	15	44
3424	Wabash Operating Boxcar	27	62
3424-75	Low Bridge Signal (marked "3424-75" or overstamped on 3424-100 box)	103	288
3424-100	Low Bridge Signal	4	14
3428	U.S. Mail Operating Boxcar	12	67
3434	Poultry Dispatch Car	30	72
3435	Traveling Aquarium Car	40	111
3444	Erie Operating Gondola	11	28
3451	Operating Log Dump Car	9	40
3454	PRR Operating Merchandise Car	33	122
3456	N&W Operating Hopper	19	58
3459	LL Operating Coal Dump Car (no toymaker's logo)	29	111
3459	LL Operating Coal Dump Car (toymaker's logo)	29	100
3461	LL Operating Log Car	10	25
3461X	Automatic Lumber Car	28	63
3461X-25	Lionel Lines Operating Log Car, green	10	38
3462	Automatic Milk Car	13	50
3464	NYC Operating Boxcar	4	17
3469	LL Operating Coal Dump Car	18	47
3469X	LL Operating Coal Dump Car	8	23
3470	Target Launching Car	16	41
3472	Automatic Milk Car	17	43
3474	Western Pacific Operating Boxcar	10	64
3482	Automatic Milk Car	18	46
3484	Pennsylvania Operating Boxcar	11	30
3484-25	ATSF Operating Boxcar	7	40
3494	NYC Operating Boxcar	17	43
3494-150	Missouri Pacific Operating Boxcar	13	52
3494-275	State of Maine Operating Boxcar	16	48
3494-550	Monon Operating Boxcar	46	194
3494-625	Soo Operating Boxcar	54	189
3509	Satellite Launching Car	15	76
3512	Fireman and Ladder Car	17	79
3519	Satellite Launching Car	16	39

BOXES

		Good (P-5)	Exc (P-7)
3520	Searchlight Car	13	36 ____
3530	GM Generator Car	15	56 ____
3530-50	Searchlight with pole and base, separate sale	46	93 ____
3535	Security Car with searchlight	14	72 ____
3540	Operating Radar Car	27	74 ____
3545	Operating TV Monitor Car	21	98 ____
3559	Operating Coal Dump Car	17	43 ____
3562-1	ATSF Operating Barrel Car	29	136 ____
3562-25	ATSF Operating Barrel Car, gray	18	65 ____
3562-50	ATSF Operating Barrel Car, yellow	19	55 ____
3562-75	ATSF Operating Barrel Car, orange	27	55 ____
3619	Helicopter Reconnaissance Car	13	57 ____
3620	Searchlight Car with insert	11	65 ____
3650	Extension Searchlight Car	11	34 ____
3656	Operating Cattle Car	13	57 ____
3656	Stockyard with cattle (set box with car box)	16	76 ____
3656-9	Cattle (marked "3656" on 4 sides, unnumbered tuck flaps)	8	19 ____
3656-9	Cattle (marked "3656" on 4 sides, "3656-44" on 1 tuck flap)	3	12 ____
3656-9	Cattle (marked "3656-34" on 4 sides, "3656-44" on 1 tuck flap)	3	10 ____
3656-9	Cattle (marked "3656" on 4 sides, "3656-44" on 1 tuck flap, OPS markings)	10	25 ____
3656-9	Cattle (unnumbered sides, marked "3656-44" on 1 tuck flap)	10	25 ____
3656-9	Cattle (unnumbered sides, marked "3656-34" on 1 tuck flap)	13	35 ____
3656-150	Corral Platform, separate sale	161	767 ____
3662	Automatic Milk Car (classic), *55*	19	45 ____
3662	Automatic Milk Car (orange picture), *64*	16	88 ____
3662	Automatic Milk Car (white box), *66*	20	80 ____
3665	Minuteman Operating Car	23	50 ____
3672	Bosco Operating Milk Car	62	171 ____
3820	USMC Operating Submarine Car	20	50 ____
3830	Operating Submarine Car	20	49 ____
3854	Automatic Merchandise Car	73	450 ____
3927	Lionel Lines Track Cleaning Car	10	32 ____
4109WS	Electronic Control Set	90	485 ____
4357	SP-type Caboose, electronic	25	107 ____
4452	PRR Gondola, electronic	29	98 ____
4454	Baby Ruth PRR Boxcar, electronic	20	123 ____
4457	PRR N5-type Caboose, tintype, electronic	20	79 ____
4671W	Tender	27	148 ____
5160	Viewing Stand	10	60 ____
5459	LL Coal Dump Car, electronic	18	183 ____
6001T	Tender	2	10 ____

BOXES

		Good (P-5)	Exc (P-7)
____ 6002	NYC Gondola	2	7
____ 6004	Baby Ruth PRR Boxcar	3	12
____ 6007	Lionel Lines SP-type Caboose	2	9
____ 6009	Remote Control Uncoupling Track	3	20
____ 6012	Gondola	4	12
____ 6014	Boxcar	3	14
____ 6014-60	Frisco Boxcar, white (middle classic)	12	20
____ 6014-60	Frisco Boxcar, white	6	21
____ 6014-85	Bosco or Frisco Boxcar, orange (classic)	8	33
____ 6014-100	Airex Boxcar, red	8	22
____ 6014-100	Airex Boxcar, red (orange perforated)	15	45
____ 6014-150	Wix Boxcar	30	201
____ 6014-335	Frisco Boxcar	6	26
____ 6014-410	Frisco Boxcar	16	76
____ 6015	Sunoco 1-D Tank Car	4	16
____ 6017	Lionel Lines SP-type Caboose	2	9
____ 6017-1	Caboose	10	28
____ 6017-50	U.S. Marine Corps SP-type Caboose (box marked "6017-60")	17	82
____ 6017-85	Lionel Lines SP-type Caboose, gray	8	29
____ 6017-100	B&M SP-type Caboose	16	58
____ 6017-185	ATSF SP-type Caboose	3	22
____ 6017-200	U.S. Navy SP-type Caboose	22	139
____ 6017-235	ATSF SP-type Caboose	8	29
____ 6019	Remote Control Track	2	6
____ 6020W	Tender	8	38
____ 6024	Nabisco Shredded Wheat Boxcar	5	21
____ 6024-60	RCA Whirlpool Boxcar	15	68
____ 6025	Gulf 1-D Tank Car (classic)	7	19
____ 6025-60	Gulf 1-D Tank Car	4	29
____ 6025-60	Gulf 1-D Tank Car (classic, overstamped 6024 box)	7	45
____ 6025-85	Gulf 1-D Tank Car (classic)	6	43
____ 6026T	Lionel Lines Tender	8	23
____ 6026W	Lionel Lines Tender (classic or picture)	13	35
____ 6027	Alaska SP-type Caboose	50	274
____ 6029	Remote Control Uncoupling Track (classic)	5	24
____ 6029	Remote Control Uncoupling Track (orange picture)	7	41
____ 6032	Short Gondola	3	15
____ X6034	Baby Ruth PRR Boxcar	2	13
____ 6035	Sunoco 1-D Tank Car	4	16
____ 6037	Lionel Lines SP-type Caboose	2	8
____ 6050	Lionel Savings Bank Boxcar	7	32
____ 6050-110	Swift Boxcar	7	28
____ 6057	Lionel Lines SP-type Caboose	7	76

BOXES

		Good (P-5)	Exc (P-7)
6059	M&StL SP-type Caboose	9	24 ___
6059-50	M&StL SP-type Caboose (Hagerstown checkerboard)	8	20 ___
6062	NYC Gondola	6	23 ___
6066T	Tender	7	20
6110	2-4-2 Locomotive	4	20
6111-75	Flatcar with logs	12	78 ___
6111-110	Flatcar	18	68 ___
6112-1	Canister Car	10	45 ___
6112-25	Canister Set	8	27 ___
6112-85	Short Gondola (marked "Canister Car")	4	26 ___
6112-110	Gondola Car with Canisters	6	29 ___
6112-135	Short Gondola (marked "Canister Car")	5	38 ___
6119	DL&W Work Caboose, red	5	22 ___
6119-25	DL&W Work Caboose, orange	7	38 ___
6119-50	DL&W Work Caboose, brown	10	29 ___
6119-75	DL&W Work Caboose	10	41 ___
6119-100	DL&W Work Caboose (classic)	8	37 ___
6119-100	DL&W Work Caboose (picture, perforated, or window)	9	94 ___
6121	Flatcar with pipes	13	49 ___
6121-60	Flatcar with pipes	14	82 ___
6121-85	Flatcar with pipes (classic)	15	72 ___
6130	ATSF Work Caboose (cellophane)	10	42 ___
6130	ATSF Work Caboose (Hagerstown checkerboard)	11	40 ___
6130	ATSF Work Caboose (all other boxes)	5	28 ___
6149	Remote Control Uncoupling Track, *64-69*	7	11 ___
6151	Flatcar with patrol truck	12	45 ___
6162-60	Alaska Gondola	34	199 ___
6162-110	NYC Gondola, blue (orange picture)	10	42 ___
6162-110	NYC Gondola, red, separate sale (orange picture with label)	21	83 ___
6167-85	Union Pacific SP-type Caboose	22	82 ___
6175	Flatcar with rocket	9	39 ___
6220	Santa Fe NW2 Switcher	23	92 ___
6250	Seaboard NW2 Switcher	31	129 ___
6257	SP-type Caboose	4	10 ___
6257X	SP-type Caboose	13	37 ___
6257-25	SP-type Caboose	2	9 ___
6257-50	SP-type Caboose	6	13 ___
6262	Flatcar with wheel load	6	35 ___
6264	Flatcar with lumber, separate sale	33	142 ___
6311	Flatcar with pipes	11	76 ___
6315	Gulf 1-D Chemical Tank Car (classic)	16	41 ___
6315	Gulf 1-D Chemical Tank Car (Hagerstown checkerboard)	24	48 ___
6315-60	Gulf 1-D Chemical Tank Car (orange picture)	6	32 ___

BOXES

		Good (P-5)	Exc (P-7)
___ 6342	NYC Gondola	22	144
___ 6343	Barrel Ramp Car	11	41
___ 6346	Alcoa Quad Hopper	12	37
___ 6356	NYC Stock Car	7	27
___ 6357	SP-type Caboose (classic)	8	24
6357	SP-type Caboose (orange perforated, overstamped)	18	84
___ 6357-50	ATSF SP-type Caboose	122	442
___ 6361	Timber Transport Car	14	43
6361	Timber Transport Car (Hagerstown checkerboard)	24	82
___ 6362	Truck Car	10	52
___ 6376	LL Circus Stock Car	10	51
___ 6401	Flatcar, gray	25	105
___ 6403B	Tender with bell	22	63
___ 6405	Flatcar with piggyback van	6	37
___ 6407	Flatcar with rocket	118	337
___ 6411	Flatcar with logs	5	26
___ 6413	Mercury Capsule Carrying Car	21	61
___ 6414	Evans Auto Loader (classic)	25	59
___ 6414	Evans Auto Loader (orange picture)	29	101
6414	Evans Auto Loader (orange picture, overstamped 6416 box)	30	152
___ 6414	Evans Auto Loader (orange perforated), *59*	18	102
6414	Evans Auto Loader (cellophane), *66*	24	104
___ 6414-25	Four Automobiles, separate sale	155	608
___ 6414-85	Evans Auto Loader (orange picture)	165	489
___ 6415	Sunoco 3-D Tank Car (classic)	7	22
___ 6415	Sunoco 3-D Tank Car (orange picture)	15	38
___ 6415	Sunoco 3-D Tank Car (cellophane)	24	76
___ 6415	Sunoco 3-D Tank Car (Hillside checkerboard)	21	42
___ 6415	Sunoco 3-D Tank Car (orange picture with label)	45	109
___ 6416	Boat Transport Car	25	117
___ 6417	PRR N5c Porthole Caboose	4	18
6417-1	PRR N5c Porthole Caboose, without "New York Zone"	9	38
___ 6417-25	Lionel Lines N5c Porthole Caboose	7	29
___ 6417-50	Lehigh Valley N5c Porthole Caboose	22	103
___ 6418	Machinery Car	24	64
___ 6419	DL&W Work Caboose	12	41
___ 6419-25	DL&W Work Caboose	7	27
___ 6419-50	DL&W Work Caboose	9	40
___ 6419-100	N&W Work Caboose	32	66
___ 6420	DL&W Work Caboose with searchlight	11	41
___ 6424	Twin Auto Flatcar	17	47
___ 6424-60	Twin Auto Flatcar	10	42
___ 6424-85	Twin Auto Flatcar	10	74

BOXES

		Good (P-5)	Exc (P-7)
6424-110	Twin Auto Flatcar	25	85 ___
6425	Gulf 3-D Tank Car	10	30 ___
6427	Lionel Lines N5c Porthole Caboose	9	24 ___
6427-1	Caboose	10	24 ___
6427-60	Virginian N5c Porthole Caboose	80	211 ___
6427-500	PRR N5c Porthole Caboose, sky blue, from Girls Set	32	84 ___
6428	U.S. Mail Boxcar	13	48 ___
6429	DL&W Work Caboose	36	173 ___
6430	Flatcar with trailers	12	45 ___
6431	Flatcar with vans and tractor (cellophane), *66*	40	168 ___
6434	Poultry Dispatch Stock Car	13	47 ___
6436	Lehigh Valley Open Quad Hopper, black	9	30 ___
6436-25	Lehigh Valley Open Quad Hopper, maroon	8	31 ___
6436-110	Lehigh Valley Open Quad Hopper, red	9	30 ___
6436-500	Lehigh Valley Open Quad Hopper, lilac, from Girls Set	34	112 ___
6436-1969	TCA Hopper (Hagerstown checkered)	14	48 ___
6437	PRR N5c Porthole Caboose	5	20 ___
6440	Flatcar with vans	13	40 ___
6440	Green Pullman Car	9	37 ___
6441	Green Observation Car	9	36 ___
6442	Brown Pullman Car	9	39 ___
6443	Brown Observation Car	9	36 ___
6445	Fort Knox Gold Reserve Car	19	48 ___
6446	N&W Covered Quad Hopper	10	27 ___
6446	N&W Covered Quad Hopper (orange picture)	15	68 ___
6446-25	N&W Covered Quad Hopper	11	33 ___
6446-60	Lehigh Valley Covered Quad Hopper	86	384 ___
6447	PRR N5c Porthole Caboose	42	267 ___
6448	Exploding Target Range Boxcar	9	29 ___
6452	Pennsylvania Gondola	3	18 ___
X6454	Santa Fe, NYC, or Baby Ruth Boxcar	5	23 ___
X6454	PRR Boxcar	7	29 ___
X6454	PRR Boxcar (classic, overstamped 3464 box)	7	34 ___
X6454	SP Boxcar	6	25 ___
X6454	Erie Boxcar	7	31 ___
6456	Lehigh Valley Short Hopper	6	19 ___
6456-25	LV Short Hopper ("25" rubber-stamped on end flaps)	8	36 ___
6456-75	Lehigh Valley Short Hopper	27	146 ___
6457	SP-type Caboose	7	19 ___
6460	Bucyrus Erie Crane Car	18	42 ___
6460-25	Bucyrus Erie Crane Car, red cab	13	49 ___
6461	Transformer Car	7	29 ___
6462	NYC Gondola, black	4	14 ___

BOXES

			Good (P-5)	Exc (P-7)
____	6462-25	NYC Gondola, green	6	20
____	6462-75	NYC Gondola, red	4	19
____	6462-125	NYC Gondola, red plastic	5	18
____	6462-500	NYC Gondola, pink, from Girls Set	43	122
____	6463	Rocket Fuel 2-D Tank Car	11	36
____	6464-1	Western Pacific Boxcar	11	48
____	6464-25	Great Northern Boxcar	19	49
____	6464-50	M&StL Boxcar	15	41
____	6464-50	M&StL Boxcar (overstamped with "S" and "Silver")	15	55
____	6464-75	Rock Island Boxcar	18	52
____	6464-100	Western Pacific Boxcar	25	89
____	6464-125	NYC Pacemaker Boxcar	27	118
____	6464-150	Missouri Pacific Boxcar	26	62
____	6464-175	Rock Island Boxcar	11	73
____	6464-175	Rock Island Boxcar (overstamped with "S" and "Silver")	15	75
____	6464-200	Pennsylvania Boxcar	10	94
____	6464-200	Pennsylvania Boxcar (Hagerstown checkerboard)	15	40
____	6464-225	SP Boxcar	13	43
____	6464-250	Western Pacific Boxcar (orange picture with label)	38	138
____	6464-250	Western Pacific Blue Feather Boxcar (classic for 6464-100), *54*	93	463
____	6464-250	Western Pacific Boxcar (cellophane)	23	92
____	6464-275	State of Maine Boxcar	22	67
____	6464-300	Rutland Boxcar, *55*	25	96
____	6464-325	B&O Sentinel Boxcar	64	199
____	6464-350	MKT Boxcar	28	146
____	6464-375	Central of Georgia Boxcar	17	48
____	6464-400	B&O Time-Saver Boxcar	13	37
____	6464-425	New Haven Boxcar (classic)	10	46
____	6464-425	New Haven Boxcar (Hagerstown)	17	43
____	6464-450	Great Northern Boxcar	13	43
____	6464-450	Great Northern Boxcar (cellophane)	19	64
____	6464-475	B&M Boxcar (classic)	11	39
____	6464-475	B&M Boxcar (orange picture)	23	113
____	6464-500	Timken Boxcar	15	77
____	6464-510	NYC Pacemaker Boxcar	70	306
____	6464-515	MKT Boxcar	75	245
____	6464-525	M&StL Boxcar	10	56
____	6464-650	D&RGW Boxcar (cellophane)	15	44
____	6464-700	Santa Fe Boxcar	19	58
____	6464-725	New Haven Boxcar (orange picture, "735" on box)	10	31
____	6464-725	New Haven Boxcar (Hagerstown checkerboard)	20	68
____	6464-825	Alaska Boxcar	45	189

BOXES

		Good (P-5)	Exc (P-7)
6464-900	NYC Boxcar	8	43____
6464-960	TCA Boxcar, 1965	47	95____
6465	Gulf 2-D Tank Car, black (classic)	5	17____
6465	Sunoco 2-D Tank Car (classic, overstamped 2465 box)	3	18 ____
6465	Sunoco 2-D Tank Car (classic, overstamped 6555 box)	6	16 ____
6465	Sunoco 2-D Tank Car (orange picture, 6464-900 label)	9	64 ____
6465-60	Gulf 2-D Tank Car (classic)	5	23____
6465-60	Sunoco 2-D Tank Car (classic)	3	16____
6465-85	Lionel Lines 2-D Tank Car (orange perforated)	29	84____
6465-110	Cities Service 2-D Tank Car (orange perforated)	16	55____
6465-160	Lionel Lines Tank Car (orange picture)	46	153____
6466T	Lionel Lines Tender	7	17____
6466W	Lionel Lines Tender (with liner)	13	37____
6466WX	Lionel Lines Tender (with liner)	19	40____
6467	Miscellaneous Car	12	43____
6468	B&O Auto Boxcar, tuscan (marked "X")	41	121____
6468	B&O Auto Boxcar, blue	9	33____
6468-25	NH Auto Boxcar	17	38____
6469	Liquified Gas Tank Car	23	124____
6470	Explosives Boxcar	12	34____
6472	Refrigerator Car	7	32____
6473	Horse Transport Car	11	36____
6473	Horse Transport Car (end flaps half white, half orange)	30	104 ____
6475	Pickles Vat Car (orange picture)	22	74____
6476	Lehigh Valley Short Hopper	6	22____
6476	Lehigh Valley Short Hopper (orange perforated)	14	44____
6476-85	Lehigh Valley Short Hopper	15	58____
6476-135	Lehigh Valley Short Hopper	8	26____
6476-160	Lehigh Valley Short Hopper (Hagerstown checkerboard)	9	28 ____
6477	Miscellaneous Car with pipes	10	49____
6482	Refrigerator Car	7	39____
6500	Flatcar with Bonanza airplane	100	236____
6501	Flatcar with jet boat	27	65____
6511	Flatcar with pipes	10	32____
6512	Cherry Picker Car	12	38____
6517	Lionel Lines Bay Window Caboose	14	37____
6517-60	Bay Window Caboose (TCA)	30	106____
6517-75	Erie Bay Window Caboose	56	239____
6518	Transformer Car	17	55____
6519	Allis-Chalmers Flatcar (classic)	25	99____
6519	Allis-Chalmers Flatcar (orange perforated)	27	133____
6520	Searchlight Car	14	48____

BOXES		Good (P-5)	Exc (P-7)
____ 6520	(A) Searchlight Car 2 City	14	57
____ 6520	(B) Searchlight Car 3 City	19	124
____ 6530	Firefighting Instruction Car	11	71
____ 6536	M&StL Open Quad Hopper	19	73
____ 6544	Missile Firing Car	22	78
____ 6555	Sunoco 1-D Tank Car	12	23
____ 6556	MKT Stock Car	52	191
____ 6557	SP-type Smoking Caboose	27	101
____ 6560	Bucyrus Erie Crane Car (Hagerstown checkerboard)	17	79
____ 6560	Bucyrus Erie Crane Car (all other boxes)	13	45
____ 6560-25	Bucyrus Erie Crane Car, 8-wheel (with liner)	18	91
____ 6561	Cable Car, 2 reels	9	33
____ 6562-1	NYC Gondola, gray	6	21
____ 6562-25	NYC Gondola, red	5	20
____ 6562-50	NYC Gondola, black	6	21
____ 6572	REA Reefer (classic)	18	60
____ 6572	REA Reefer (orange picture)	17	48
____ 6636	Alaska Open Quad Hopper	17	49
____ 6646	Lionel Lines Stock Car	6	26
____ 6650	IRBM Rocket Launcher	12	36
____ 6654W	Whistle Tender	10	20
____ 6656	Stock Car	10	36
____ 6657	Rio Grande SP-type Caboose	31	93
____ 6660	Boom Car	8	51
____ 6670	Derrick Car	15	53
____ 6672	Santa Fe Refrigerator Car	10	41
____ 6736	Detroit & Mackinac Open Quad Hopper	15	68
____ 6800	Flatcar with airplane (classic)	16	65
____ 6800	Flatcar with airplane (orange perforated)	17	81
____ 6800-60	Airplane, separate sale	93	192
____ 6801	Flatcar with brown and white boat	7	39
____ 6801-50	Flatcar with yellow and white boat	10	47
____ 6801-60	Boat, separate sale	30	92
____ 6801-75	Flatcar with blue and white boat	11	53
____ 6802	Flatcar with girders (late classic)	9	36
____ 6802	Flatcar with girders (orange perforated)	25	55
____ 6803	Flatcar with USMC tank and sound truck	35	109
____ 6804	Flatcar with USMC trucks	19	79
____ 6805	Atomic Energy Disposal Flatcar	20	97
____ 6806	Flatcar with USMC trucks	31	82
____ 6807	Flatcar with boat	15	88
____ 6808	Flatcar with military units	18	62
____ 6809	Flatcar with USMC trucks	26	92
____ 6810	Flatcar with trailer	7	35
____ 6812	Track Maintenance Car	15	64

BOXES

		Good (P-5)	Exc (P-7)
6814	Rescue Caboose	20	64____
6816	Flatcar with Allis-Chalmers bulldozer	42	152____
6816-100	Allis-Chalmers bulldozer	125	415____
6817	Flatcar with Allis-Chalmers motor scraper	47	185____
6818	Flatcar with transformer	8	30____
6819	Flatcar with helicopter	7	72____
6820	Aerial Missile Transport Car with helicopter	71	257____
6821	Flatcar with crates	6	38____
6822	Searchlight Car	13	32____
6823	Flatcar with IRBM missiles	15	75____
6825	Flatcar with arch trestle bridge	7	26____
6826	Flatcar with Christmas trees	19	59____
6827	Flatcar with Harnischfeger power shovel	28	80____
6827-100	Harnischfeger Power Shovel	32	80____
6828	Flatcar with Harnischfeger crane (cellophane, no crane kit box)	30	87 ____
6828	Flatcar with Harnischfeger crane (orange picture, no crane kit box)	16	66 ____
6828	Harnischfeger Crane Kit, used with flatcar	12	90____
6828-100	Harnischfeger Crane, separate sale	41	153____
6830	Flatcar with submarine	23	49____
6844	Missile Carrying Car	18	122____
11001	Steam Freight Set (advance catalog 1962)	7	23____
11011	Diesel Freight Set	30	85____
11201	Steam Freight Set	20	65____
11212	Diesel Freight Set	60	110____
11222	027 Steam Freight Set	25	70____
11232	NH Diesel Freight Set	20	65____
11242	Steam Freight Set	30	70____
11252	Diesel Space Set	28	68____
11268	Military Set	38	105____
11278	Steam Freight Set	25	55____
11288	Steam Freight Set	43	100____
11331	Steam Freight Set	15	40____
11375	027 Steam Freight Set	15	55____
11415	Steam Freight Set (advance catalog 1963)	14	49____
11420	Steam Freight Set	10	30____
11440	Diesel Freight Set	15	70____
11450	Steam Freight Set	30	65____
11460	Steam Freight Set	15	30____
11490	Santa Fe Passenger Set	48	100____
11500	Steam Freight Set	50	110____
11520	Steam Freight Set	45	95____
11530	Diesel Freight Set	35	70____
11550	Steam Freight Set	20	55____
11560	Texas Special Set	15	42____

BOXES

		Good (P-5)	Exc (P-7)
11590	Santa Fe Passenger Set	30	88
11710	Steam Freight Set	45	95
11750	Steam Freight Set	22	54
12710	Steam Freight Set	32	119
12730	Santa Fe Diesel Freight Set	75	193
12760	Berkshire Freight Set	175	400
12780	Santa Fe Passenger Set	230	594
12800	B&M Diesel Freight Set	25	75
12800X	B&M Diesel Freight Set	75	190
12820	Virginian Train Master Freight Set	88	348
12840	Steam Freight Set	40	250
12850	Diesel Freight Set	40	160
13008	Super O Introductory Set	20	66
13018	Santa Fe Space-age Military Set	349	959
13028	Super O Space Set	160	300
13048	Super O Steam Freight Set	65	140
13058	Santa Fe Space-age Military Set	150	400
13088	Santa Fe Passenger Set	424	1053
13098	Steam Freight Set	120	275
13118	Berkshire Freight Set	75	330
13128	Santa Fe Space-age Military Set	250	650
13150	Hudson Freight Set	335	900
A	Transformer, 90 watts	10	20
CO-1	Track Clips, 100	5	15
ECU-1	Electronic Control Unit	15	139
KW	Transformer, 190 watts	6	22
KW	Transformer, 190 watts (yellow)	5	23
LW	Transformer, 125 watts	7	20
R	Transformer, 110 watts	8	15
RCS	Remote Control Track	6	17
RW	Transformer, 110 watts	6	17
S	Transformer, 80 watts	3	10
SW	Transformer, 130 watts	7	17
TW	Transformer, 175 watts	3	15
UCS	Remote Control Track (O)	3	9
UTC	Lockon	10	18
VW	Transformer, 150 watts	5	15
ZW	Transformer, 275 watts (classic)	13	50
ZW	Transformer, 275 watts (orange, with inserts)	12	49
ZW	Transformer, 275 watts (yellow, with inserts)	13	57

Exc

		Exc
463W	Steam Freight Set, *45* (224, 2466W, 2458, 2452, 2555, 2457)	615 ____
1000W	O27 Steam Freight Set, *55* (2016, 6026W, 6014, 6012, 6017)	320 ____
1001	O27 Diesel Freight Set, *55* (610, 6012, 6014, 6017)	250 ____
1111	O27 Scout Freight Set, *48* (1001, 1001T, 1002, 1005, 1007)	225 ____
1112	O27 Scout Freight Set, *48* (1001 or 1101, 1001T, 1002, 1004, 1005, 1007)	250 ____
1113	O27 Scout Freight Set, *50* (1120, 1001T, 1002, 1005, 1007)	115 ____
1115	O27 Scout Freight Set, *49* (1110, 1001T, 1002, 1005, 1007)	190 ____
1117	O27 Scout Freight Set, *49* (1110, 1001T, 1002, 1005, 1004, 1007)	150 ____
1119	O27 Freight Scout Set, *51–52* (1110, 1001T, 1002, 1004, 1007)	160 ____
1400	O27 Steam Passenger Set, *46* (221, 221T, two 2430, 2431)	600 ____
1400W	O27 Steam Passenger Set, *46* (221, 221W, two 2430 2431)	720 ____
1401	O27 Steam Freight Set, *46* (1654, 1654T, 2452X, 2465, 2472)	120 ____
1401W	O27 Steam Freight Set, *46* (1654, 1654W, 2452X, 2465, 2472)	220 ____
1402	O27 Steam Passenger Set, *46* (1666, 2466T, two 2440, 2441)	550 ____
1402W	O27 Steam Passenger Set, *46* (1666, 2466W, two 2440, 2441)	550 ____
1403	O27 Steam Freight Set, *46* (221, 221T, 2411, 2465, 2472)	400 ____
1403W	O27 Steam Freight Set, *46* (221, 221W, 2411, 2465, 2472)	500 ____
1405	O27 Steam Freight Set, *46* (1666, 2466T, 2452X, 2465, 2472)	145 ____
1405W	O27 Steam Freight Set, *46* (1666, 2466W, 2452X, 2465, 2472)	280 ____
1407B	O27 Steam Switcher Set, *46* (1665, 2403B, 2560, 2452X, 2419)	1370 ____
1409	O27 Steam Freight Set, *46* (1666, 2466T, 3559, 2465, 3454, 2472)	425 ____
1409W	O27 Steam Freight Set, *46* (1666, 2466W, 3559, 2465, 3454, 2472)	435 ____
1411W	O27 Steam Freight Set, *46* (1666, 2466WX, 2452X, 2465, 2454, 2472)	250 ____
1413WS	O27 Steam Freight Set, *46* (2020, 2466WX, 2452X, 2465, 2454, 2472)	350 ____
1415WS	O27 Steam Freight Set, *46* (2020, 2020W, 3459, 3454, 2465, 2472)	530 ____
1417WS	O27 Steam Work Train Set, *46* (2020, 2020W, 2465, 3451, 2560, 2419)	720 ____

SETS

Exc

			Exc
1419WS	027 Steam Freight Set, *46* (2020, 2020W, 3459, 2452X, 2560, 2419, 97)		880
1421WS	027 Steam Freight Set, *46* (2020, 2020W, 3451, 2465, 3454, 2472, 164)		1100
1423W	027 Steam Freight Set, *48–49* (1655, 6654W, 6452, 6465, 6257)		220
1425B	027 Steam Switcher Freight Set, *48* (1656, 2403B, 6456, 6465, 6257X)		825
1425B	027 Steam Switcher Freight Set, *49* (1656, 6403B, 6456, 6465, 6257)		825
1426WS	027 Steam Passenger Set, *48–49* (2026, 6466WX, two 6440, 6441)		560
1427WS	027 Steam Freight Set, *48* (2026, 6466WX, 6454, 6465, 6257)		275
1429WS	027 Steam Freight Set, *48* (2026, 6466WX, 3451, 6454, 6465, 6257)		225
1430WS	027 Steam Passenger Set, *48–49* (2025, 6466WX, 2400, 2401, 2402)		800
1431	027 Steam Freight Set, *47* (1654, 1654T, 2452X, 2465, 2472)		220
1431W	027 Steam Freight Set, *47* (1654, 1654W, 2452X, 2465, 2472)		160
1432	027 Steam Passenger Set, *47* (221, 221T, two 2430, 2431)		850
1432W	027 Steam Passenger Set, *47* (221, 221W, two 2430 2431)		795
1433	027 Steam Freight Set, *47* (221, 221T, 2411, 2465, 2457)		560
1433W	027 Steam Freight Set, *47* (221, 221 W, 2411, 2465, 2457)		375
1434WS	027 Steam Passenger Set, *47* (2025, 2466WX, two 2440, 2441)		555
1435WS	027 Steam Freight Set, *47* (2025, 2466WX, 2452X, 2454, 2457)		240
1437WS	027 Steam Freight Set, *47* (2025, 2466WX, 2452X, 2465, 2454, 2472)		590
1439WS	027 Steam Freight Set, *47* (2025, 2466WX, 3559, 2465, 3454, 2457)		470
1441WS	027 Steam Work Train Set, *47* (2020, 2020W, 2560, 2461, 3451, 2419)		1225
1443WS	027 Steam Freight Set, *47* (2020, 2020W, 3459, 3462, 2465, 2457)		400
1445WS	027 Steam Freight Set, *48* (2025, 6466WX, 6454, 3559, 6465, 6357)		325
1447WS	027 Steam Work Train Set, *48* (2020, 6020W, 3451, 2461, 2460, 6419)		460
1447WS	027 Steam Work Train Set, *49* (2020, 6020W, 6461, 3461, 2460, 6419)		475
1449WS	027 Steam Freight Set, *48* (2020, 6020W, 3462, 3459, 6411, 6465, 6357)		430
1451WS	027 Steam Freight Set, *49* (2026, 6466WX, 6462, 3464, 6257)		230
1453WS	027 Steam Freight Set, *49* (2026, 6466WX, 3464, 6465, 3461, 6357)		325
1455WS	027 Steam Freight Set, *49* (2025, 6466WX, 6462, 6465, 3472, 6357)		335

		Exc	
SETS			
1457B	027 Diesel Freight Set, *49–50* (6220, 3464, 6462, 6520, 6419)	540	___
1459WS	027 Steam Freight Set, *49* (2020, 6020W, 6411, 3656, 6465, 3469, 6357)	1090	___
1461S	027 Steam Freight Set, *50* (6110, 6001T, 6002, 6004, 6007)	175	___
1463W	027 Steam Freight Set, *50* (2036, 6466W, 6462, 6465, 6257)	230	___
1463WS	027 Freight Set, *51* (2026, 6466W, 6462, 6465, 6257)	175	___
1464W	027 UP Diesel Passenger Set, *50* (2023 AA, 2481, 2482, 2483)	985	___
1464W	027 UP Passenger Set, *51* (2023 AA, 2421, 2422, 2423)	865	___
1464W	027 UP Passenger Set, *52–53* (2033 AA, 2421, 2422, 2423)	830	___
1465	027 Steam Freight Set, *52* (2034, 6066T, 6032, 6035, 6037)	180	___
1467W	027 UP Diesel Freight Set, *50–51* (2023 AA, 6656, 6465, 6456, 6357)	585	___
1467W	027 Erie Diesel Freight Set, *52–53* (2032 AA, 6656, 6456, 6465, 6357)	760	___
1469WS	027 Steam Freight Set, *50–51* (2035, 6466W, 6462, 6465, 6456, 6257)	270	___
1471WS	027 Steam Freight Set, *50–51* (2035, 6466W, 3469, 6465, 6454, 3461, 6357)	415	___
1473WS	027 Steam Freight Set, *50* (2046, 2046W, 3464, 6465, 6520, 6357)	560	___
1475WS	027 Steam Freight Set, *50* (2046, 2046W, 3656, 3461, 6472, 3469, 6419)	615	___
1477S	027 Steam Freight Set, *51–52* (2026, 6466T, 6012, 6014, 6017)	210	___
1479WS	027 Steam Freight Set, *52* (2056, 2046W, 6462, 6465, 6456, 6257)	375	___
1481WS	027 Steam Freight Set, *51* (2035, 6466W, 3464, 3472, 6465, 6462, 6357)	510	___
1483WS	027 Steam Freight Set, *52* (2056, 2046W, 3472, 6462, 6465, 3474, 6357)	1010	___
1484WS	027 Steam Passenger Set, *52* (2056, 2046W, 2421, 2422, 2423, 2429)	1270	___
1485WS	027 Steam Freight Set, *52* (2025, 6466W, 6462, 6465, 6257)	235	___
1500	027 Steam Freight Set, *53* (1130, 6066T, 6032, 6034, 6037)	170	___
1500	027 Steam Freight Set, *54* (1130, 1130T, 6032, 6034, 6037)	125	___
1501S	027 Steam Freight Set, *53* (2026, 6066T, 6032, 6035, 6037)	250	___
1502WS	027 Steam Passenger Set, *53* (2055, 2046W, 2421, 2422, 2423)	750	___
1503WS	027 Steam Freight Set, *53–54* (2055, 6026W, 6462, 6465, 6456, 6257)	390	___
1505WS	027 Steam Freight Set, *53* (2046, 2046W, 6462, 6464-1, 6415, 6357)	595	___
1507WS	027 Steam Freight Set, *53* (2046, 2046W, 6415, 6462, 3472, 6468, 6357)	450	___

SETS   Exc

1509WS	027 Steam Freight Set, *53* (2046, 2046W, 6456, 3520, 3469, 6460, 6419)	500
1511S	027 Steam Freight Set, *53* (2037, 6066T, 6032, 3474, 6035, 6037)	250
1513S	027 Steam Freight Set, *54–55* (2037, 6026T, 6012, 6014, 6015, 6017)	260
1515WS	027 Steam Freight Set, *54* (2065, 2046W, 6462, 6415, 6464-25, 6456-25, 6357)	340
1516WS	027 Passenger Set, *54* (2065, 2046W, 2434, 2432, 2436)	650
1517W	027 Diesel Freight Set, *54* (2245P/C AB, 6464-225, 6561, 6462-25, 6427)	1250
1519WS	027 Steam Freight Set, *54* (2065, 6026W, 6356, 6462-75, 3482, 3461-25, 6427)	450
1520W	027 Texas Special Passenger Set, *54* (2245P/C AB, 2432, 2435, 2436)	1700
1521WS	027 Steam Work Train Set, *54* (2065, 2046W, 3620, 6561, 6460, 3562, 6419)	690
1523	027 Diesel Work Train Set, *54* (6250, 6511, 6456-25, 6460-25, 6419-25)	615
1525	027 Diesel Freight Set, *55* (600, 6111, 6014, 6017)	165
1527	027 Steam Work Train Set, *55* (1615, 1615T, 6462-125, 6560, 6119)	500
1529	027 PRR Diesel Freight Set, *55* (2028, 6311, 6436, 6257)	650
1531W	027 Diesel Freight Set, *55* (2328, 6462-125, 6465, 6456 or 6456-25, 6257)	575
1533WS	027 Steam Freight Set, *55* (2055, 6026W, 3562-50, 6436, 6465, 6357)	465
1534W	027 Diesel Passenger Set, *55* (2328, 2432, 2434, 2436)	1000
1535W	027 Diesel Freight Set, *55* (2243P/2243C AB, 6462-125, 6436, 6464-50 or 6468X, 6257)	1650
1536W	027 Texas Special Passenger Set, *55* (2245P/C AB, two 2432, 2436)	1800
1537WS	027 Steam Freight Set, *55* (2065, 6026W, 3469, 6464-275, 3562-50, 6357)	500
1538WS	027 Steam Passenger Set, *55* (2065, 2046W, 2432, 2434, 2435, 2436)	900
1539W	027 Santa Fe Diesel Freight Set, *55* (2243P/C AB, 3620, 6446, 6561, 6560, 6419)	850
1541WS	027 Steam Freight Set, *55* (2065, 2046W, 3482, 6415, 3461-25, 3494-1, 6427)	600
1542	027 Electric Freight Set, *56* (520, 6014, 6012, 6017)	215
1543	027 Diesel Freight Set, *56* (627, 6121, 6112, 6017)	285
1545	027 Diesel Freight Set, *56* (628, 6424, 6014, 6025, 6257)	265
1547S	027 Steam Freight Set, *56* (2018, 6026T, 6121, 6112, 6014, 6257)	155
1549S	027 Steam Work Train Set, *56* (1615, 1615T, 6262, 6560, 6119-25)	980
1551W	027 Diesel Freight Set, *56* (621, 6362, 6425, 6562-25, 6257)	545

SETS

		Exc
1552	027 Diesel Passenger Set, *56* (629, 2432, 2434, 2436)	840 ___
1553W	027 MILW Diesel Freight Set, *56* (2338, 6430, 6462-125, 6464-425, 6346, 6257)	565 ___
1555WS	027 Steam Freight Set, *56* (2018, 6026W, 3361, 6464-400, 6462-125, 6257)	280 ___
1557W	027 Diesel Work Train Set, *56* (621, 6436, 6511, 3620, 6560, 6119-25)	455 ___
1559W	027 MILW Diesel Freight Set, *56* (2338, 6414, 3562-50, 6362, 3494-275, 6357)	800 ___
1561WS	027 Steam Freight Set, *56* (2065, 6026W, 3424, 6262, 6562-25, 6430, 6257)	730 ___
1562W	027 Diesel Passenger Set, *56* (2328, two 2442, 2444, 2446)	2000 ___
1563W	027 Wabash Diesel Freight Set, *56* (2240P/C AB, 6467, 3562-50, 6414, 3620, 6357)	1570 ___
1565WS	027 Steam Freight Set, *56* (2065, 6026W, 3662, 3650, 6414, 6346, 6357)	535 ___
1567W	027 Santa Fe Diesel Freight Set, *56* (2243P/C AB, 3356, 3424, 6430, 6672, 6357)	1200 ___
1569	027 UP Diesel Freight Set, *57* (202, 6014, 6111, 6112, 6017)	220 ___
1571	027 LV Diesel Freight Set, *57* (625, 6424, 6476, 6121, 6112, 6017)	400 ___
1573	027 Steam Freight Set, *57* (250, 250T, 6112, 6025, 6476, 6464-425, 6017)	195 ___
1575	027 MP Diesel Freight Set, *57* (205P/T AA, 6121, 6112, 6111, 6560-25, 6119-100)	320 ___
1577S	027 Steam Freight Set, *57* (2018, 1130T, 6014, 6121, 6464-475, 6111, 6112, 6017)	235 ___
1578S	027 Steam Passenger Set, *57* (2018, 1130T, 2432, 2434, 2436)	500 ___
1579S	027 Steam Freight Set, *57* (2037, 1130T, 6476, 6121, 6468-25, 6111, 6112, 6025, 6017)	260 ___
1581	027 Jersey Central Diesel Freight Set, *57* (611, 6464-650, 6424, 6024, 6025, 6476, 6560-25, 6119-100)	495 ___
1583WS	027 Steam Freight Set, *57* (2037, 6026W, 6482, 6112, 6646, 6121, 6476, 6017)	260 ___
1585W	027 Seaboard Diesel Freight Set, *57* (602, 6014, 6111, 6464-525, 6025, 6121, 6112, 6476, 6024, 6017)	455 ___
1586	027 Santa Fe Diesel Passenger Set, *57* (204P/T AA, two 2432, 2436)	670 ___
1587S	027 Steam Freight Set (Girls Set), *57–58* (2037-500, 1130T-500, 6462-500, 6464-515, 6436-500, 6464-510, 6427-500)	3145 ___
1589WS	027 Steam Freight Set, *57* (2037, 6026W, 6424, 6464-450, 6025, 6024, 6111, 6112, 6017)	500 ___
1590	027 Steam Freight Set, *58* (249, 250T, 6014, 6151, 6112, 6017)	390 ___
1591	027 Military Set, *58* (212, 6803, 6809, 6807, 6017-50)	970 ___
1593	027 UP Diesel Work Set, *58* (613, 6476, 6818, 6660, 6112, 6119-100)	590 ___

SETS		Exc
1595	027 Military Set, *58* (1625, 1625T, 6804, 6806, 6808, 6017-85)	2050
1597S	027 Steam Freight Set, *58* (2018, 1130T, 6014, 6818, 6476, 6025, 6112, 6017)	355
1599	027 Texas Special Freight Set, *58* (210P/T AA, 6801, 6014, 6424, 6112, 6465, 6017)	430
1600	027 Burlington Diesel Passenger Set, *58* (216, 6572, 2432, 2436)	750
1601W	027 Wabash Diesel Freight Set, *58* 2337, 6800, 6464-425, 6801, 6810, 6017)	745
1603WS	027 Steam Freight Set, *58* (2037, 6026W, 6424, 6014, 6112, 6017)	340
1605W	027 Santa Fe Diesel Freight Set, *58* (208P/T AA, 6800, 6464-425, 6801, 6477, 6802, 6017)	900
1607WS	027 Steam Work Train Set, *58* (2037, 6026W, 6465, 6818, 6464-425, 6660, 6112, 6119-100)	450
1608W	027 NH Diesel Passenger Set, *58* (209P/T AA, two 2432, 2434, 2436)	1865
1609	027 Steam Freight Set, *59–60* (246, 1130T, 6162-25, 6476, 6057)	145
1611	027 Alaska Diesel Freight Set, *59* (614, 6825, 6162-60, 6465, 6027)	520
1612	027 General Set, *59–60* (1862, 1862T, 1866, 1865)	300
1613S	027 B&O Steam Freight Set, *59* (247, 247T, 6826, 6819, 6821, 6017)	345
1615	027 B&M Diesel Freight Set, *59* (217P/C AB, 6800, 6464-475, 6812, 6825, 6017-100)	520
1617S	027 Steam Work Train Set, *59* (2018, 1130T, 6816, 6536, 6812, 6670, 6119-100)	800
1619W	027 Santa Fe Diesel Freight Set, *59* (218P/T AA, 6819, 6802, 6801, 6519, 6017-185)	450
1621WS	027 Steam Freight Set, *59* (2037, 6026W, 6825, 6519, 6062, 6464-475, 6017)	340
1623W	027 NP Diesel Freight Set, *59* (2349, 3512, 3435, 6424, 6062, 6017)	1600
1625WS	027 Steam Freight Set, *59* (2037, 6026W, 6636, 3512, 6470, 6650, 6017)	400
1626W	027 Santa Fe Diesel Passenger Set, *59* (208P/T AA, 3428, two 2412, 2416)	875
1627S	027 Steam Freight Set, *60* (244, 244T, 6062, 6825, 6017)	185
1629	027 C&O Diesel Freight Set, *60* (225, 6650, 6470, 6819, 6219)	305
1631WS	027 Steam Freight Set, *60* (243, 243W, 6519, 6812, 6465, 6017)	275
1633	027 U.S. Navy Diesel Freight Set, *60* (224P/C AB, 6544, 6830, 6820, 6017-200)	1185
1635WS	027 Steam Freight Set, *60* (2037, 6026W or 243W, 6361, 6826, 6636, 6821, 6017)	400
1637W	027 Santa Fe Diesel Freight Set, *60* (218P/T AA, 6475, 6175, 6464-475, 6801 or 6424-110, 6017-185)	610

SETS

		Exc	
1639WS	027 Steam Freight Set, *60* (2037, 6026W or 243W, 6816, 6817, 6812, 6530, 6560, 6119-100)	1250	___
1640W	027 Santa Fe Diesel Passenger Set, *60* (218P/T AA, 3428, two 2412, 2416, 1640-100)	750	___
1641	027 Steam Freight Set, *61* (246, 244T, 3362, 6162, 6057)	150	___
1642	027 Steam Freight Set, *61* (244, 1130T, 3376, 6405, 6119)	225	___
1643	027 C&O Diesel Freight Set, *61* (230, 3509, 6050, 6175, 6058)	395	___
1644	027 General Set, *61* (1862, 1862T, 3370, 1866, 1865)	425	___
1645	027 Diesel Freight Set, *61* (229, 3410, 6465-110, 6825, 6059)	250	___
1646	027 Steam Freight Set, *61* (233, 233W, 6162, 6343, 6476, 6017)	325	___
1647	027 U.S. Marines Military Set, *61* (45, 3665, 3519, 6830, 6448, 6814)	1055	___
1648	027 Steam Freight Set, *61* (2037, 233W, 6062, 6465-110, 6519, 6476, 6017)	335	___
1649	027 Santa Fe Diesel Freight Set, *61* (218P/C AB, 6343, 6445, 6475, 6405, 6017)	460	___
1650	027 Steam Military Set, *61* (2037, 233W, 6544, 6470, 3330, 3419, 6017)	500	___
1651	027 Santa Fe Diesel Passenger Set, *61* (218P/T or 220T AA, two 2412, 2414, 2416)	675	___
1800	General Gift Pack, *59–60* (1862, 1862T, 1865, 1866, 1877, storybook)	385	___
1805	027 Military Set (Land-Sea and Air Gift Pack), *60* (45, 3429, 3820, 6640, 6824)	1600	___
1809	Western Gift Pack, *61* (244, 1130T, 3370, 3376, 1877, 6017)	300	___
1810	Space Age Gift Pack, *61* (231, 3665, 3519, 3820, 6017)	1165	___
2100	Steam Passenger Set, *46* (224, 2466T, two 2442, 2443)	550	___
2100W	Steam Passenger Set, *46* (224, 2466W, two 2442, 2443)	640	___
2101	Steam Freight Set, *46* (224, 2466T, 2555, 2452, 2457)	350	___
2101W	Steam Freight Set, *46* (224, 2466W, 2555, 2452, 2457)	395	___
2103W	Steam Freight Set, *46* (224, 2466W, 2458, 3559, 2555, 2457)	375	___
2105WS	Steam Freight Set, *46* (671, 2466W, 2555, 2454, 2457)	445	___
2110WS	Steam Passenger Set, *46* (671, 2466W, three 2625)	1875	___
2111WS	Steam Freight Set, *46* (671, 2466W, 3459, 2411, 2460, 2420)	895	___
2113WS	Steam Freight Set, *46* (726, 2426W, 2855, 3854, 2857)	1900	___
2114WS	Steam Passenger Set, *46* (726, 2426W, three 2625)	2500	___
2115WS	Steam Work Train Set, *46* (726, 2426W, 2458, 3451, 2460, 2420)	1325	___

		Exc
SETS		
2120S	Steam Passenger Set, *47* (675, 2466T, two 2442, 2443)	500
2120WS	Steam Passenger Set, *47* (675, 2466WX, two 2442, 2443)	500
2121S	Steam Freight Set, *47* (675, 2466T, 2555, 2452, 2457)	400
2121WS	Steam Freight Set, *47* (675, 2466WX, 2555, 2452, 2457)	405
2123WS	Steam Freight Set, *47* (675, 2466WX, 2458, 3559, 2555, 2457)	450
2124W	PRR Electric Passenger Set, *47* (2332 GG-1 green, 2625 Irvington, 2625 Madison, 2625 Manhattan)	3200
2125WS	Steam Freight Set, *47* (671, 671W, 2411, 2454, 2452, 2457)	550
2126WS	Steam Passenger Set, *47* (671, 671W, 2625 Irvington, 2625 Madison, 2625 Manhattan)	1950
2127WS	Steam Work Train Set, *47* (671, 671W, 3459, 2461, 2460, 2420)	705
2129WS	Steam Freight Set, *47* (726, 2426W, 3854, 2411, 2855, 2457)	2250
2131WS	Steam Work Train Set, *47* (726, 2426W, 3462, 3451, 2460, 2420)	1200
2133W	Diesel Freight Set, *48* (2333P/T AA, 2458, 3459, 2555, 2357)	1350
2135WS	Steam Freight Set, *48* (675, 2466WX, 2456, 2411, 2357)	350
2135WS	Steam Freight Set, *49* (675, 6466WX, 6456, 6411, 6457)	345
2136WS	Steam Passenger Set, *48* (675, 2466WX, two 2442, 2443)	620
2136WS	Steam Passenger Set, *49* (675, 6466WX, two 6442, 6443)	640
2137WS	Steam Freight Set, *48* (675, 2466WX, 2458, 3459, 2456, 2357)	720
2139W	PRR Electric Freight Set, *49* (2332, 6456, 3464, 3461, 6457)	1360
2139W	PRR Electric Freight Set, *48* (2332, 2458, 3451, 2456, 2357)	1425
2140WS	Steam Passenger Set, *48–49* (671, 2671W, 2400, 2401, 2402)	1270
2141WS	Steam Freight Set, *48* (671, 2671W, 3451, 3462, 2456, 2357)	375
2143WS	Steam Work Train Set, *48* (671, 2671W, 3459, 2461, 2460, 2420)	795
2144W	PRR Electric Passenger Set, *48–49* (2332, 2625, 2627, 2628)	2065
2145WS	Steam Freight Set, *48* (726, 2426W, 3462, 2411, 2460, 2357)	815
2146WS	Steam Passenger Set, *48–49* (726, 2426W, 2625, 2627, 2628)	2000
2147WS	Steam Freight Set, *49* (675, 6466WX, 3472, 6465, 3469, 6457)	400
2148WS	Hudson Passenger Set, *50* (773, 2426W, 2625, 2627, 2628)	5550
2149B	Diesel Work Train Set, *49* (622, 6520, 3469, 2460, 6419)	690

SETS

		Exc	
2150WS	Steam Passenger Set, *50* (681, 2671W, 2421, 2422, 2423)	1000	___
2151W	Diesel Freight Set, *49* (2333P/T AA, 3464, 6555, 3469, 6520, 6457)	850	___
2153WS	Steam Work Train Set, *49* (671, 2671W, 3469, 6520, 2460, 6419)	620	___
2155WS	Steam Freight Set, *49* (726, 2426W, 6411, 3656, 2460, 6457)	795	___
2159W	Electric Freight Set, *50* (2330, 3464, 6462, 3461, 6456, 6457)	3000	___
2161W	Santa Fe Diesel Freight Set, *50* (2343P/T AA, 3469, 3464, 3461, 6520, 6457)	1520	___
2163WS	Steam Freight Set, *50* (736, 2671WX, 6472, 6462, 6555, 6457)	550	___
2163WS	Steam Freight Set, *51* (736, 2671WX, 6472, 6462, 6465, 6457)	600	___
2165WS	Steam Freight Set, *50* (736, 2671WX, 3472, 6456, 3461, 6457)	690	___
2167WS	Steam Freight Set, *50–51* (681, 2671W, 6462, 3464, 6457)	475	___
2169WS	Hudson Freight Set, *50* (773, 2426W, 3656, 6456, 3469, 6411, 6457)	2810	___
2171W	NYC Diesel Freight Set, *50* (2344P/T AA, 3469, 3464, 3461, 6520, 6457)	1100	___
2173WS	Steam Freight Set, *50* (681, 2671W, 3472, 6555, 3469, 6457)	595	___
2173WS	Steam Freight Set, *51* (681, 2671W, 3472, 6465, 3469, 6457)	515	___
2175W	Santa Fe Diesel Freight Set, *50* (2343P/T AA, 6456, 3464, 6555, 6462, 6457)	925	___
2175W	Santa Fe Diesel Freight Set, *51* (2343 AA, 6456, 3464, 6465, 6462, 6457)	935	___
2177WS	Steam Freight Set, *52* (675, 2046W, 6462, 6465, 6457)	235	___
2179WS	Steam Freight Set, *52* (671, 2046WX, 3464, 6465, 6462, 6457)	330	___
2183WS	Steam Freight Set, *52* (726, 2046W, 3464, 6462, 6465, 6457)	900	___
2185W	NYC Diesel Freight Set, *50* (2344P/T AA, 6456, 3464, 6555, 6462, 6457)	960	___
2185W	NYC Diesel Freight Set, *51* (2344 AA, 6456, 3464, 6465, 6462, 6457)	1050	___
2187WS	Steam Freight Set, *52* (671, 2046WX, 6462, 3472, 3469, 6456, 6457)	650	___
2189WS	Steam Freight Set, *52* (726, 2046W, 3520, 3656, 6462, 3461, 6457)	630	___
2190W	Santa Fe Diesel Passenger Set, *52* (2343P/T AA, 2531, 2532, 2533, 2534)	1900	___
2190W	Santa Fe Diesel Passenger Set, *53* (2353P/T AA, 2531, 2533, 2532, 2534)	1900	___
2191W	Santa Fe Diesel Freight Set, *52* (2343P/C/T ABA, 6462, 6656, 6456, 6457)	1350	___
2193W	NYC Diesel Freight Set, *52* (2344P/C/T ABA, 6462, 6656, 6456, 6457)	1040	___
2201WS	Steam Freight Set, *53* (685, 6026W, 6462, 6464-50, 6465, 6357)	365	___

SETS

			Exc
	2203WS	Steam Freight Set, *53* (681, 2046WX, 6415, 3520, 6464-25, 6417)	665
	2205WS	Steam Freight Set, *53* (736, 2046W, 3484, 6415, 6468, 6456, 6417)	575
	2207W	Santa Fe Diesel Freight Set, *53* (2353P/C/T ABA, 6462, 3484, 6415, 6417)	965
	2209W	NYC Diesel Freight Set, *53* (2354P/C/T ABA, 6462, 3484, 6415, 6417)	1200
	2211WS	Steam Freight Set, *53* (681, 2046WX, 3656, 6464-75, 3461, 6417)	740
	2213WS	Steam Freight Set, *53* (736, 2046W, 3461, 3520, 3469, 6460, 6419)	650
	2217WS	Steam Freight Set, *54* (682, 2046WX, 6464-175, 3562-25, 6356, 6417)	1000
	2219W	Diesel Freight Set, *54* (2321, 6456-25, 6464-50, 6462-25, 6415, 6417)	1535
	2221WS	Steam Freight Set, *54* (646, 2046W, 6468, 3620, 3469, 6456-25, 6417-25)	500
	2222WS	Steam Passenger Set, *54* (646, 2046W, 2530, 2531, 2532)	1800
	2223W	Diesel Freight Set, *54* (2321, 6464-100, 3461-25, 3482, 6462-125, 6417-50)	2085
	2225WS	Steam Work Train Set, *54* (736, 2046W, 3461-25, 3562 or 3562-25, 3620, 6460, 6419)	1020
	2227W	Santa Fe Diesel Freight Set, *54* (2353P/T AA, 3562-25, 6356, 6456-75, 6468, 6417-25)	1725
	2229W	NYC Freight Set, *54* (2354P/T AA, 3562-25, 6356, 6456-75, 6468, 6417-25)	1300
	2231W	Southern Diesel Freight Set, *54* (2356P/C/T ABA, 6511, 6561, 3482, 6415, 6417-25)	2610
	2234W	Santa Fe Diesel Passenger Set, *54* (2353P/T AA, 2530, 2531, 2532, 2533)	1045
	2235W	MILW Diesel Freight Set, *55* (2338, 6436-25, 6362, 6560, 6419)	575
	2237WS	Steam Freight Set, *55* (665, 6026W, 3562-50, 6464-275, 6415, 6417)	380
	2239W	Illinois Central Diesel Freight Set, *55* (2363P/C AB, 6672, 6464-125, 6414, 6517)	1700
	2241WS	Steam Freight Set, *55* (646, 2046W, 3359, 6446, 3620, 6417)	535
	2243W	Diesel Freight Set, *55* (2321, 3662, 6511, 6462-125, 6464-300, 6417)	1400
	2244W	Wabash Diesel Passenger Set, *55* (2367P/C AB, 2530, 2531, 2533)	3650
	2245WS	Steam Freight Set, *55* (682, 2046WX, 3562-25, 6436-25, 6561, 6560, 6419)	1150
	2247W	Wabash Diesel Freight Set, *55* (2367P/C AB, 6462-125, 3662, 6464-150, 3361, 6517)	2200
	2249WS	Steam Freight Set, *55* (736, 2046W, 6464-275, 6414, 3359, 3562-50, 6517)	1000

SETS

		Exc	
2251W	Diesel Freight Set, *55*		
	(2331, 6464-275, 3562-50, 6414, 3359, 6517)	2000	___
2253W	PRR Electric Freight Set, *55*		
	(2340-25, 3361, 6464-300, 3620, 6414, 6417)	2700	___
2254W	PRR Electric Passenger Set, *55*		
	(2340, 2541, 2542, 2543, 2544)	5500	___
2255W	Diesel Work Train Set, *56*		
	(601, 3424, 6362, 6560, 6119-25)	725	___
2257WS	Steam Freight Set, *56*		
	(665, 2046W, 3361, 6346, 6467, 6462-125, 6427)	500	___
2259W	NH Electric Freight Set, *56*		
	(2350, 6464-425, 6430, 3650, 6511, 6427)	775	___
2261WS	Steam Freight Set, *56*		
	(646, 2046W, 3562-50, 6414, 6436-25, 6376, 6417)	570	___
2263W	NH Electric Freight Set, *56*		
	(2350, 3359, 6468-25, 6414, 3662, 6517)	1000	___
2265WS	Steam Freight Set, *56*		
	(736, 2046W, 3620, 3424, 6430, 6467, 6517)	675	___
2267W	Diesel Freight Set, *56*		
	(2331, 3562-50, 3359, 3361, 6560, 6419-50)	1700	___
2269W	B&O Diesel Freight Set, *56*		
	(2368P/C AB, 3356, 6518, 6315, 3361, 6517)	3200	___
2270W	Jersey Central Diesel Passenger Set, *56*		
	(2341, 2531, 2532, 2533)	5000	___
2271W	PRR Electric Freight Set, *56*		
	(2360-25, 3424, 3662, 6414, 6418, 6417)	2200	___
2273W	MILW Diesel Freight Set, *56*		
	(2378P/C AB, 342, 6342, 3562-50, 3662, 3359, 6517)	3500	___
2274W	PRR Electric Passenger Set, *56*		
	(2360, 2541, 2542, 2543, 2544)	2650	___
2275W	Wabash Diesel Freight Set, *57*		
	(2339, 3444, 6464-475, 6425, 6427)	790	___
2276W	Budd RDC Set, *57*		
	(404, two 2559)	2035	___
2277WS	Steam Work Train Set, *57*		
	(665, 2046W, 6446-25, 3650, 6560-25, 6119-75)	585	___
2279W	NH Electric Freight Set, *57*		
	(2350, 3424, 6464-425, 6424, 6477, 6427)	730	___
2281W	Santa Fe Diesel Freight Set, *57*		
	(2243P/C AB, 6464-150, 3361, 3562-75, 6560-25, 6119-75)	1050	___
2283WS	Steam Freight Set, *57*		
	(646, 2046W, 3424, 3361, 6464-525, 6562-50, 6357)	750	___
2285W	Diesel Freight Set, *57*		
	(2331, 6418, 6414, 6425, 3662, 6517)	2000	___
2287W	MILW Electric Freight Set, *57*		
	(2351, 342, 6342, 6464-500, 3650, 6315, 6427)	2000	___
2289WS	Super O Steam Freight Set, *57*		
	(736, 2046W, 3359, 3494-275, 3361, 6430, 6427)	1105	___
2291W	Super O Rio Grande Diesel Freight Set, *57*		
	(2379P/C AB, 3562-75, 3530, 3444, 6464-525, 6657)	1965	___
2292WS	Super O Steam Passenger Set, *57*		
	(646, 2046W, 2530, 2531, 2532, 2533)	2000	___
2293W	Super O PRR Electric Freight Set, *57*		
	(2360, 3662, 3650, 6414, 6518, 6417)	2400	___

SETS

2295WS	Super O Steam Freight Set, *57* (746, 746W, 342, 6342, 3530, 3361, 6560-25, 6419-100)	2290
2296W	Super O CP Diesel Passenger Set, *57* (2373P/T AA, 2551, 2552, 2553, 2554)	4670
2297WS	Super O Steam Freight Set, *57* (746, 746W, 264, 6264, 3356, 3662, 345, 6342, 6517)	2300
2501W	Super O Diesel Work Train Set, *58* (2348, 6464-525, 6802, 6560-25, 6119-100)	680
2502W	Super O Budd RDC Set, *58* (400, 2550, 2559)	2000
2503WS	Super O Steam Freight Set, *58* (665, 2046W, 3361, 6434, 6801, 6536, 6357)	525
2505W	Super O Electric Freight Set, *58* (2329, 6805, 6519, 6800, 6464-500, 6357)	1400
2507W	Super O Diesel Freight Set, *58* (2242P/C AB, 3444, 6464-425, 6424, 6468-25, 6357)	2000
2509WS	Super O Steam Freight Set, *58* (665, 2046W, 6414, 3650, 6464-475, 6805, 6357)	800
2511W	Super O Electric Work Set, *58* (2352, 3562-75, 3424, 3361, 6560-25, 6119-100)	1100
2513W	Super O Electric Freight Set, *58* (2329, 6556, 6425, 6414, 6434, 3359, 6427-60)	3000
2515WS	Super O Steam Freight Set, *58* (646, 2046W, 3662, 6424, 3444, 6800, 6427)	785
2517W	Super O Rio Grande Diesel Freight Set, *58* (2379P/C AB, 6519, 6805, 6434, 6800, 6657)	2550
2518W	Super O PRR Electric Passenger Set, *58* (2352, 2531, 2533, 2534)	1850
2519W	Super O Diesel Freight Set, *58* (2331, 6434, 3530, 6801, 6414, 6464-275, 6557)	1900
2521WS	Super O Steam Freight Set, *58* (746, 746W, 6805, 3361, 6430, 3356, 6424, 6557)	2000
2523W	Super O Santa Fe Diesel Freight Set, *58* (2383P/T AA, 264, 6264, 6434, 6800, 3662, 6517)	1300
2525WS	Super O Steam Work Train Set, *58* (746, 746W, 342, 345, 6519, 6518, 6560-25, 6419-100)	2300
2526W	Super O Santa Fe Diesel Passenger Set, *58* (2383P/T AA, 2530, 2531, two 2532)	1775
2527	Super O Missile Launcher Set, *59–60* (44, 3419, 6844, 6823, 6814, 943)	755
2528WS	Super O General Set, *59–61* (1872, 1872T, 1877, 1876, 1875W)	845
2529W	Super Electric Work Train Set, *59* (2329, 3512, 6819, 6812, 6560, 6119-25 or 6119-100)	1300
2531WS	Super O Steam Freight Set, *59* (637, 2046W, 3435, 6817, 6636, 6825, 6119-100)	1300
2533W	Super O GN Electric Freight Set, *59* (2358, 6650, 6414, 3444, 6470, 6357)	1910
2535WS	Super O Steam Freight Set, *59* (665, 2046W, 3434, 6823, 3672, 6812, 6357)	840
2537W	Super O NH Diesel Freight Set, *59* (2242P/C AB, 3435, 3650, 6464-275, 6819, 6427)	2500

		Exc	
2539WS	Super O Steam Freight Set, *59* (665, 2046W, 3361, 6464-825, 3512, 6812, 6357, 464)	1015	___
2541W	Super O Santa Fe Diesel Freight Set, *59* (2383P/T AA, 3356, 3512, 6519, 6816, 6427)	2400	___
2543WS	Super O Steam Freight Set, *59* (736, 2046W, 264, 6264, 3435, 6823, 6434, 6812, 6557)	1590	___
2544W	Super O Santa Fe Diesel Passenger Set, *59–60* (2383P/T AA, 2530, 2561, 2562, 2563)	1860	___
2545WS	Super O Military Set, *59* (746, 746W, 175, 6175, 6470, 3419, 6650, 3540, 6517)	3000	___
2547WS	Super O Steam Freight Set, *60* (637, 2046W, 3330, 6475, 6361, 6357)	675	___
2549W	Super O Military Set, *60* (2349, 3540, 6470, 6819, 6650, 3535)	1160	___
2551W	Super O GN Electric Freight Set, *60* (2358, 6828, 3512, 6827, 6736, 6812, 6427)	2300	___
2553WS	Super O Steam Freight Set, *60* (736, 2046W, 3830, 3435, 3419, 3672, 6357)	1615	___
2555W	Super O Santa Fe Freight Set with matching HO Set, *60* (2383P/T AA, 3434, 3366, 6414, 6464-900, 6357-50)	10000	___
2570	Super O Santa Fe Work Train Set, *61* (616, 6822, 6828, 6812, 6736, 6130)	800	___
2571	Super O Steam Freight Set, *61* (637, 736W, 3419, 6445, 6361, 6119-100)	550	___
2572	Super O B&M Diesel Freight Set, *61* (2359, 6544, 3830, 6448, 3519, 3535)	800	___
2573	Super O Steam Freight Set, *61* (736, 736W, 3545, 6416, 6475, 6440, 6357)	1400	___
2574	Super O Santa Fe Diesel Freight Set, *61* (2383P/T AA, 3665, 3419, 3830, 448, 6448, 6437)	1500	___
2575	Super O PRR Electric Freight Set, *61* (2360, 6530, 6828, 6464-900, 6827, 6736, 6560, 6437)	2500	___
2576	Super O Santa Fe Diesel Passenger Set, *61* (2383P/T AA, 2561, two 2562, 2563)	3030	___
4109WS	Electronic Control Set, *46* (671R, 4424W, 4452, 4454, 5459, 4457)	1085	___
4110WS	Electronic Control Set, *48–49* (671R, 4671W, 4452, 4454, 5459, 4357, 151, 97)	2500	___
11201	027 Steam Freight Set, *62* (242, 1060T, 6042-75, 6502, 6047)	125	___
11011	027Diesel Freight Set, *62* (222, 3510, 6076, 6120)	145	___
11212	027 Santa Fe Diesel Freight Set, *62* (633, 3349, 6825, 6057)	375	___
11222	027 Steam Freight Set, *62* (236, 1050T, 3357, 6343, 6119-100)	195	___
11232	027 NH Diesel Freight Set, *62* (232, 3410, 6062, 6413, 6057-50)	450	___
11242	027 Steam Freight Set, *62* (233, 233W, 6465-100, 6476, 6162, 6017)	175	___
11252	027 Texas Special Space Set, *62* 211P/T AA, 3509, 6448, 3349, 6463, 6057)	500	___

	SETS	Exc

11268 027 C&O Diesel Freight Set, *62*
(2365, 3619, 3470, 3349, 6501, 6017)   1425

11278 027 Steam Freight Set, *62*
(2037, 233W, 6473, 6162, 6050-110, 6825, 6017)   260

11288 027 Space Set, *62*
(229P/C AB, 3413, 6512, 6413, 6463, 6059)   1215

11298 027 Steam Freight Set, *62*
(2037, 233W, 6544, 3419, 6448, 3330, 6017)   500

11308 027 Santa Fe Diesel Passenger Set, *62*
(218P/T AA, two 2412, 2414, 2416)   730

11311 027 Steam Freight Set, *63*
(1062, 1061T, 6409-25, 6076-100, 6167-25)   100

11321 027 Rio Grande Diesel Freight Set, *63*
(221, 3309, 6076-75, 6042-75, 6167-50)   300

11331 027 Steam Freight Set, *63*
(242, 1060T, 6473, 6476-25, 6142, 6059-50)   100

11341 027 Santa Fe Diesel Freight Set, *63*
(634, 3410, 6407, 6014-325, 6463, 6059-50)   950

11351 027 Steam Freight Set, *63*
(237, 1060T, 6050-100, 6465-150, 6408, 6162,
6119-110)   190

11361 027 Texas Special Space Set, *63*
(211P/T AA, 3665-100, 3413-150, 6470, 6413,
6257-100)   750

11375 027 Steam Freight Set, *63*
(238, 234W, 6822-50, 6465-150, 6414-150,
6476-75, 6162, 6257-100)   700

11385 027 Santa Fe Space Set, *63*
(223P/218C AB, 3619-100, 3470-100, 3349-100,
3830-75, 6407, 6257-100 or 6017-235)   2000

11395 027 Steam Freight Set, *63*
(2037, 233W or 234W, 6464-725, 6469-50, 6536,
6440-50, 6560-50, 6119-100)   600

11405 027 Santa Fe Diesel Passenger Set, *63*
(218P/T AA, two 2412, 2414, 2416)   750

11420 027 Steam Freight Set, *64*
(1061, 1061T, 6042-250, 6167-25)   200

11430 027 Steam Freight, *64*
(1062, 1061T, 6176, 6142, 6167-125)   135

11440 027 Rio Grande Diesel Freight Set, *64*
(221, 3309, 6176-50, 6142-125, 6167-100)   285

11450 027 Steam Freight Set, *64*
(242, 1060T, 6473, 6142-75, 6176-50, 6059-50)   195

11460 027 Steam Freight Set, *64*
(238, 234W, 6014-335, 6465-150, 6142-100,
6176-75, 6119-100)   150

11470 027 Steam Freight Set, *64*
(237, 1060T, 6014-335, 6465-150, 6142-100,
6176-75, 6119-100)   150

11480 027 Diesel Freight Set, *64*
(213P/T AA, 6473, 6176-50, 6142-150, 6014-335,
6257-100 or 6059)   560

11490 027 Diesel Passenger Set, *64–65*
(212P/T AA, 2404, 2405, 2406)   360

11500 027 Steam Freight Set, *64*
(2029, 234W, 6465-150, 6402-50, 6176-75,
6014-335, 6257-100 or 6059)   275

SETS		Exc
11500	027 Steam Freight Set, *65* (2029, 234W, 6465-150, 6402-50, 6076, 6014-335, 6257-100 or 6059)	275 ____
11500	027 Steam Freight Set, *66* (2029, 234W, 6465-150, 6402-50, 6176-75, 6014-335, 6059)	275 ____
11510	027 Steam Freight Set, *64* (2029, 1060T, 6465-150, 6402-50, 6176-75, 6014-335, 6257-100 or 6059)	300 ____
11520	027 Steam Freight Set, *65–66* (242, 1062T, 6176, 3362/64, 6142, 6059)	165 ____
11530	027 Santa Fe Diesel Freight, *65–66* (634, 6014, 6142, 6402, 6130)	155 ____
11540	027 Steam Freight Set, *65–66* (239, 242T, 6473, 6465, 6176, 6119-100)	155 ____
11550	027 Steam Freight Set, *65–66* (239, 234W, 6473, 6465, 6176, 6119)	225 ____
11560	027 Texas Special Freight Set, *65–66* (211P/T AA, 6473, 6076, 6142, 6465, 6059)	210 ____
11590	027 Santa Fe Diesel Passenger Set, *66* (212P/T AA, 2408, 2409, 2410)	640 ____
11600	027 Steam Freight Set, *68* (2029, 234W, 6014, 6476, 6315, 6560, 6130)	1280 ____
11710	027 Steam Freight Set, *69* (1061, 1061T or 1062T, 6402, 6142, 6059)	170 ____
11720	Diesel Freight Set, *69* (2024, 6142, 6402, 6176, 6057)	240 ____
11730	027 UP Diesel Freight Set, *69* (645, 6402, 6014-85, 6176, 6142, 6167-85)	800 ____
11740	027 RI Diesel Freight Set, *69* (2041P/T AA, 6315, 6142, 6014-410, 6476, 6057)	310 ____
11750	027 Steam Freight Set, *69* (2029, 234T, 6014-85, 6476, 6473, 6315, 6130)	360 ____
11760	027 Steam Freight Set, *69* (2029, 234W, 6014-410, 6315, 6476, 3376, 6119)	355 ____
12502	Prairie-Rider Gift Pack, *62* (1862, 1862T, 3376, 1877 or 6473, 1866, 1865)	600 ____
12512	Enforcer Gift Pack, *62* (45, 3413, 3619, 3470, 3349, 6017)	1100 ____
12700	Steam Freight Set, *64* (736, 736W, 6464-725, 6162-100, 6414-75, 6476-125, 6437, no transformer)	1000 ____
12710	Steam Freight Set, *64–66* (736, 736W, 6464-725, 6162-100, 6414-75, 6476-125, 6437, LW transformer)	1150 ____
12720	Santa Fe Diesel Freight Set, *64* (2383P/T AA, 6464-725, 6162-100, 6414-75, 6476-125, 6437, no transformer)	1500 ____
12730	Santa Fe Diesel Freight Set, *64–66* (2383P/T AA, 6464-725, 6162-100, 6414-75, 6476-125, 6437, LW transformer)	895 ____
12740	Santa Fe Diesel Freight Set, *64* (2383P/T AA, 3662, 6361, 6436-110, 6315-60, 6464-525, 6822, 6437)	1500 ____
12760	Steam Freight Set, *64* (736, 736W, 3662, 6361, 6436-110, 6315-60, 6464-525, 6822, 6437)	1100 ____

SETS

Exc

12780	Santa Fe Diesel Passenger, *64–66* (2383P/T AA, 2521, 2522, two 2523)	1855
12800	B&M Diesel Freight Set, *65–66* (2346, 6428, 6436, 6464-475, 6415, 6017-100)	510
12820	Diesel Freight Set, *65* (2322, 3662, 6822, 6361, 6464-725, 6436, 6315, 6437)	1525
12840	Steam Freight Set, *66* (665, 736W, 6464-375, 6464-450, 6431, 6415, 6437)	925
12850	Diesel Freight Set, *66* (2322, 3662, 6822, 6361, 6464-725, 6436, 6315, 6437)	1700
13008	Super O Steam Freight Set, *62* (637, 736W, 3349, 6448, 6501, 6119-100)	500
13018	Super O Santa Fe Diesel Freight Set, *62* (616, 6500, 6650, 3519, 6448, 6017-235)	1200
13028	Super O Space Set, *62* (2359, 3665, 3349, 3820, 3470, 6017-100)	1000
13036	Super O General Set, *62* (1872, 1872T, 6445, 3370, 1876, 1875W)	980
13048	Super O Steam Freight Set, *62* (736, 736W, 6822, 6414, 3362, 6440, 6437)	720
13058	Super O Space Set, *62* (2383P/T AA, 3619, 3413, 6512, 470, 6470, 6437)	1600
13068	Super O PRR Electric Freight Set, *62* (2360, 6464-725, 6828, 6416, 6827, 6530, 6475, 6437)	3200
13078	Super O PRR Electric Passenger Set, *62* (2360, 2521, two 2522, 2523)	3500
13088	Super O Santa Fe Diesel Passenger Set, *62* (2383P/T AA, 2521, two 2522, 2523)	2500
13098	Super O Steam Freight Set, *63* (637, 736W, 6469, 6464-900, 6414, 6446, 6447)	2000
13108	Super O Santa Fe Space Set, *63* (617, 3665, 3419, 6448, 3830, 3470, 6119-100)	1000
13118	Super O Steam Freight Set, *63* (736, 736W, 6446-60, 6827, 3362, 6315-60, 6560, 6429)	1500
13128	Super O Santa Fe Space Set, *63* (2383P/T AA, 3619, 3413, 6512, 448, 6448, 64337)	1750
13138	Super O PRR Electric Freight Set, *63* (2360, 6464-725, 6828, 6416, 6827, 6315-60, 6436-110, 6437)	3800
13148	Super O Santa Fe Diesel Passenger Set, *63* (2383P/T AA, 2521, 2522, two 2523)	2500
13150	Super O Hudson Steam Freight Set, *64* (773, 736W or 773W, 3434, 6361, 3662, 6415, 3356, 6436-110, 6437)	2500

ABBREVIATIONS

Descriptions

AAR	Association of American Railroads (truck type)
AEC	Atomic Energy Commission
AF	American Flyer
CC	Command Control
DD	Double-door
EMD	Electro-Motive Division
ETD	End-of-train device
FARR	Famous American Railroad Series
FF	Fallen Flag Series
FM	Fairbanks-Morse
GE	General Electric
LL	Lionel Lines
MOW	Maintenance-of-way
MU	Multiple unit (commuter cars)
O	Lionel gauge (1¼" between outside rails)
OO	Lionel gauge (¾" between outside rails)
PFE	Pacific Fruit Express
REA	Railway Express Agency
SSS	Service Station Special
std	Standard gauge (2⅛" between outside rails)
std O	Standard O (scale length and dimension)
TMCC	TrainMaster Command Control
USMC	United States Marine Corps
1-D	One dome
2-D	Two dome
3-D	Three dome

ABBREVIATIONS

Railroad names

ACL	Atlantic Coast Line
ATSF	Atchison, Topeka & Santa Fe
B&A	Boston & Albany
BAR	Bangor & Aroostook
B&LE	Bessemer & Lake Erie
B&M	Boston & Maine
BN	Burlington Northern
BNSF	Burlington Northern Santa Fe
B&O	Baltimore & Ohio
C&IM	Chicago & Illinois Midland
C&EI	Chicago & Eastern Illinois
CB&Q	Chicago, Burlington & Quincy
CMStP&P	Chicago, Milwaukee, St. Paul & Pacific
CN	Canadian National
CNJ	Central of New Jersey
C&IM	Chicago & Illinois Midland
C&NW	Chicago & North Western
C&O	Chesapeake & Ohio
CP	Canadian Pacific
D&H	Delaware & Hudson
DL&W	Delaware, Lackawanna & Western
DM&IR	Duluth, Missabe & Iron Range
D&RGW	Denver & Rio Grande Western
D&TS	Detroit & Toledo Shore Line
DT&I	Detroit, Toledo & Ironton
EJ&E	Elgin, Joliet & Eastern
Erie-Lack.	Erie-Lackawanna
FEC	Florida East Coast
GM&O	Gulf, Mobile & Ohio
GN	Great Northern
GTW	Grand Trunk Western
IC	Illinois Central
ICG	Illinois Central Gulf
KCS	Kansas City Southern
L&N	Louisville & Nashville
LIRR	Long Island Railroad
LNAC	Louisville, New Albany & Corydon

Railroad names

LV	Lehigh Valley
MD&W	Minnesota, Dakota & Western
MKT	Missouri-Kansas-Texas
MN&S	Minneapolis, Northfield & Southern
MP	Missouri Pacific
MPA	Maryland & Pennsylvania
MILW	Milwaukee Road
M&StL	Minneapolis & St. Louis
NC&StL	Nashville, Chattanooga & St. Louis
NdeM	Nacionales de Mexico Railway
NH	New Haven
NKP	Nickel Plate Road
NP	Northern Pacific
NS	Norfolk Southern
N&W	Norfolk & Western
NYC	New York Central
NYNH&H	New York, New Haven & Hartford
NYO&W	New York, Ontario & Western
PC	Penn Central
P&E	Peoria & Eastern
P&LE	Pittsburgh & Lake Erie
PRR	Pennsylvania Railroad
RF&P	Richmond, Fredericksburg & Potomac
RI	Rock Island
SMARRCO	San Manuel Arizona Railroad Company
SP	Southern Pacific
SP&S	Spokane, Portland & Seattle
TA&G	Tennessee, Alabama & Georgia
TH&B	Toronto, Hamilton & Buffalo
T&P	Texas & Pacific
TP&W	Toledo, Peoria & Western
UP	Union Pacific
V&TRR	Virginia & Truckee Railroad
W&ARR	Western & Atlantic Railroad
WM	Western Maryland
WP	Western Pacific

Build Your Toy Train Library

Collectible Lionel Classics

In his new book, *Collectible Lionel Classics*, toy train expert, Roger Carp, provides detailed information on 100 popular postwar Lionel locomotives (steam, diesel, and electric), motorized units, rolling stock, and accessories. Whether you're an experienced collector or new to the hobby, this invaluable guide will be your go-to resource for historical information, product features, and buying tips. The book includes 100 color photos and an in-depth introduction of each product category.

10-8806 • $25.99

American Flyer Pocket Price Guide 1946–2019

This essential pocket-sized guide provides accurate current market values for American Flyer S gauge trains and accessories manufactured by A.C. Gilbert and Lionel. It also contains ready-to-run S gauge trains from contemporary manufacturers like American Models and MTH. This functional, easy-to-read volume is published every other year and is a valuable and reliable source for pricing information.

10-8619 • $15.99

Buy now from your local hobby shop!
Shop at KalmbachHobbyStore.com